Comparative Peace Processes
in Latin America

COMPARATIVE PEACE
PROCESSES
IN LATIN AMERICA

Edited by Cynthia J. Arnson

Woodrow Wilson Center Press
Washington, D.C.

Stanford University Press
Stanford, California

EDITORIAL OFFICES

The Woodrow Wilson Center Press
One Woodrow Wilson Plaza
1300 Pennsylvania Avenue, N.W.
Washington, D.C. 20523
Telephone 202-691-4029
wwics.si.edu

ORDER FROM

Stanford University Press
CUP Distribution Center
110 Midland Avenue
Port Chester, N.Y. 10573-4930
Telephone 1-800-872-7423

2 4 6 8 9 7 5 3 1

Library of Congress Cataloging-in-Publication Data

Comparative peace processes in Latin America / edited by Cynthia J.
Arnson.
    p.   cm.
   Includes bibliographical references and index.
   ISBN 0-8047-3588-3 (cloth : alk. paper). — ISBN 0-8047-3589-1
(pbk. : alk. paper)
   1. Latin America—Politics and government—1980- 2. Conflict
management—Latin America—History—20th century.
3. Reconciliation. 4. Guerrillas—Latin America—History—20th
century. 5. Civil-military relations—Latin America—History—20th
century.   I. Arnson, Cynthia.
F1414.2.C573   1999
980.03′3—dc21   99-17745
                                               CIP

Contents

Preface

Since 1995, the Project on Comparative Peace Processes has examined six cases of internal armed conflict in Latin America, in an effort to identify variables that facilitate or impede negotiated settlements to guerrilla wars, as well as the key tasks of the postconflict period. The goals have been to contribute to the knowledge about the resolution of civil conflict through a carefully structured comparative analysis, and, through dialogue and exchange, to build confidence in the peace process in individual countries among diverse actors. In pursuit of both these ends, the Project has sponsored conferences and seminars throughout Latin America and in Washington, D.C., enlisting the participation of those most directly involved in peace processes and facilitating contact between practitioners from different countries. Respect for the uniqueness of each case has been coupled with the belief that lessons drawn from one experience can enrich and inform the understanding of others, and that scholars and practitioners throughout the region can gain valuable insights from adopting the broadest possible comparative framework.

In its ongoing work, the Project has benefited from the talents of a core group of researchers from Latin America and the United States, including country experts and specialists on particular themes. Many of their contributions are reflected in this book. One contribution painfully absent is that of Joaquín Tacsan of the Costa Rican-based Arias Foundation, who participated in our first organizational efforts and died tragically in a plane crash in late 1996.

With minor exceptions, the chapters and commentaries in this book were first commissioned for a March 1997 conference in Washington sponsored by the Woodrow Wilson Center, the Peruvian-based Instituto de Defensa Legal, and the Friedrich Ebert Foundation, Washington office. Revisions and updating continued well into the summer and early fall of 1998. The chapters covering Central America, however, were completed before Hurricane Mitch unleashed its fury on the region, altering the economic, social, and political landscape for decades to come. Thus, while every effort has been made to stay current, it goes without saying that the stories told within these covers continue to unfold.

Acknowledgments

I have incurred many debts, and owe thanks and appreciation, to many people who helped make this book possible.

First and foremost, I am grateful to Carlos Basombrío of the Instituto de Defensa Legal, a former Fellow of the Woodrow Wilson Center, and founding co-director of the Project on Comparative Peace Processes. Carlos's intellectual contribution and generosity of spirit have enriched the Project in all of its phases; this book reflects his sustained interest and steadfast support.

Several institutions also provided generous financial backing. The Friedrich Ebert Foundation, Washington office, and the Swedish International Development and Cooperation Agency provided funding for the March 1997 Washington conference. Additional support for the book came from the Woodrow Wilson Center's Division of Historical, Cultural, and Literary Studies and from the Ford Foundation. I am grateful to the latter, and to the United States Institute of Peace, for their generous support of other activities of the Project.

A vast array of additional friends and colleagues have provided the necessary doses of insight, humor, and prodding at critical moments.

Joseph Tulchin, director of the Woodrow Wilson Center's Latin American Program, has offered indispensable guidance and created the "space" in which the Project has flourished. Thanks also to my colleagues Allison Garland, Ralph Espach, Kathy Morse, and Javier Icaza, for their helpfulness and congeniality in this and other endeavors of the Latin American Program.

Dinorah Azpuru, Teresa Whitfield, Rachel McCleary, and Cynthia McClintock provided expertise, unflagging support, and friendship during the long process of editing.

Carol Walker, Joseph Brinley, and Alex Breckon of the Woodrow Wilson Center Press gave generously of their time and professionalism in ably walking a cumbersome manuscript through all stages of production.

Elisabeth Wood and Johanna Mendelson Forman provided pointed critique and helpful advice regarding the entire manuscript.

George Bowen, Rositta Hickman, David Moore, Michelle Granson, and Francis Parks provided computer support with patience and skill, curing viruses and the resultant meltdowns of equipment and persons.

Amelia Brown of Wellesley College assisted with fact-checking and additional research, providing the benefit of her high standards, commitment, and precision.

I am also grateful to Renee Williams, whose shared passion for baseball includes (occasionally) opening her heart to the Cleveland Indians.

Credit and desserts are to be shared, blame never. I alone bear responsibility for any errors that might have survived the many filters erected to prevent such mishaps.

Finally, my husband, Gerry Serotta, and children Zack, Jeanne, and Micah, provide the grounding and inspiration that make this work possible. It is to them that I dedicate this book, in the hope for a world less diminished by violence.

Cynthia J. Arnson

1

Introduction

CYNTHIA J. ARNSON

This is a book about ending guerrilla conflict in Latin America through political means. It is a book about peace processes, defined as processes of dialogue over time between representatives of contesting forces, with or without an intermediary, aimed at securing an end to hostilities in the context of agreements over issues that transcend a strictly military nature; that is, peace processes involve an effort to end armed confrontation by reaching agreements that touch on at least some of the principal political, economic, social, and ethnic imbalances that led to conflict in the first place. There is no presumption that peace processes will succeed in addressing all political, institutional, social, and economic roots of the conflict; it is presumed, rather, that root causes will form the core of the negotiating agenda, linking the end of fighting to the key issue of reforms.

Peace processes as defined here are thus distinct from cease-fires and demobilizations, which, even if they contain provisions aimed at the political and economic reintegration of insurgent forces, do so largely within existing political and economic structures and absent a broader scope of institutional and structural change.

To pose a definition of peace processes that includes some attempt to address root causes is to posit both that armed insurgencies arise from

The author wishes to thank Carlos Basombrío, Raúl Benítez Manaut, Patricia Weiss Fagen, Rachel McCleary, Cynthia McClintock, Carlo Nasi, Teresa Whitfield, and Elisabeth Wood for their insightful and valuable comments on an earlier draft.

1

grievances that had not or could not be addressed in the existing political system[1] and that it is possible to address such grievances through political action.[2] If, as Karl von Clauswitz stated, war is the continuation of politics by other means, then a central objective of peace processes is to restore conflict to the political, rather than the military, arena, albeit under revised rules of the game. There is no presumption that negotiations are possible or appropriate in all cases involving insurgency—to have legitimate grievances is not to say that guerrilla violence per se is legitimate. But a belief expressed throughout this book is that military effort divorced from political action, even if successful in defeating or containing an insurgency, produces an inherently unstable peace. That is, successful counterinsurgency devoid of measures aimed at addressing root causes of conflict invites further cycles of violence.

The countries explored in this book—Colombia, El Salvador, Guatemala, Mexico, Nicaragua, and Peru—have widely divergent political, economic, and social histories, and insurgent groups differ (or differed) in their origins, objectives, and degrees of popular support and legitimacy. But the six countries share many common characteristics. All have experienced guerrilla warfare that outlasted the end of the Cold War, although as the chapters on Nicaragua, El Salvador, and Guatemala indicate, those conflicts most deeply penetrated by the politics of the Cold War were easiest to resolve when the Berlin Wall fell. Another common characteristic is that all six governments are nominally democratic, in that their leaders were openly elected in contests generally judged as fair. At the same time, qualitative aspects of a democratic regime, including such factors as the rule of law, civilian control of the armed forces, and a vibrant civil society in which citizens enjoy broad rights of association, expression, and participation, have been deeply compromised by the continuation of guerrilla warfare; indeed, deficits in these areas most often contributed to the outbreak of insurgent conflict.[3] In addition, all but Peru have attempted or concluded political negotiations with the leaders of guerrilla insurgencies aimed, at a minimum, at securing the participation in the political system of those formerly in violent opposition to it and, more expansively, at reordering the political and social landscape to address sources of dysfunction.

These characteristics suggest that there is an overlapping and symbiotic relationship between conflict resolution in Latin America and the processes of democratic transition and consolidation.[4] If the two fields have not always overlapped, it is an assumption of this comparative study that both areas of inquiry can generate useful insights to explain how and why peace processes are possible, and how and why the nature of the political system is altered by the process of making peace.[5] If assumption can lead to hope, it is also the intention of this book to explore how the experience of resolving past conflicts might contribute to an understanding of how to settle those that continue. To that end, and because, in the real world, theory and practice are never far apart, this book includes the perspectives of actual participants in peace negotiations and in postconflict efforts to consolidate peace as well as the work of scholars and analysts of individual countries in Latin America.

Consider the following examples explored in Part I of this book:

• In Nicaragua, members of the U.S.-backed Nicaraguan Resistance (the so-called contra rebels) laid down their weapons following the 1990 election of Violeta Barrios de Chamorro and in exchange for promises of land, credit, and participation in local security forces. Chamorro defeated the Sandinista National Liberation Front, the political party of guerrilla rebels who had overthrown a military dictatorship in 1979. As Chapter 2 indicates, the election, and the equation of that election with democracy, provided the context in which the demobilization took place, but the weakness of political institutions, the devastating economic effects of the war, and unkept promises to former combatants on both sides of the conflict led to additional cycles of polarization and violence. In his Reflections, Alejandro Bendaña, meanwhile, discusses the need for "bottom-up," grass-roots mechanisms for conflict resolution, particularly in the absence of preexisting structures for the integration and absorption of ex-combatants and their families. The continuance of violence and poverty, and the absence of justice, he argues, provide an important counterweight to the achievement of procedural democracy.

• In El Salvador, the government of President Alfredo Cristiani and guerillas of the Farabundo Martí National Liberation Front (FMLN) signed a peace accord in January 1992, ending a seemingly intractable military conflict in the context of profound political and institutional reform. The peace talks were mediated by the United Nations, representing the first time in U.N. history that the international body became involved in negotiations to end an internal rather than interstate conflict. In another first, the United Nations deployed an observer mission to verify human rights conditions in El Salvador prior to a cease-fire and later expanded the mission to oversee implementation of all key aspects of the accord. As Antonio Cañas and Héctor Dada argue in Chapter 3, the period of measuring formal compliance with the accord ended with the holding of national elections in 1994. But the transformation of democratic institutions mandated in the peace accords has fallen short in many important respects, compromising the country's overall political direction.

• In Guatemala, thirty-six years of guerilla war came to an end on December 29, 1996, when remnants of a once-powerful insurgent army signed a peace accord with the government of President Álvaro Arzú Irigoyen. The accord, covering indigenous, human rights, socioeconomic, electoral, and military issues, laid out an ambitious blueprint for the transformation of Guatemalan society. The breadth of the negotiating agenda was striking given that, by the time direct talks between the Guatemalan government and the Unidad Revolucionaria Nacional Guatemalteca (Guatemalan National Revolutionary Unity, or URNG) got under way in mid-1991, the guerrillas had been largely defeated as a military force. As in El Salvador, the United Nations played a key role in the peace talks and in verifying its implementation.

Chapter 4 explores how a process of democratic transition and liberalization in Guatemala predated the peace talks but could only be deepened with their successful conclusion. In addition, Chapter 11 examines how the peace process became a vehicle for the articulation of indigenous rights and identity in Guatemala, where indigenous peoples, who constitute the majority of the population, had borne the brunt of the war and had suffered centuries of discrimination and neglect. Finally, in his Reflections, former Minister of Defense Julio Balconi discusses the secret talks between the army and the guerrillas, through which former enemies on the battlefield overcame deep distrust and came to view each other as partners in the search for peace.

• In Colombia, a peace process begun in 1982 and spanning four presidential administrations brought about the demobilization of several major as well as smaller guerrilla organizations. But the two largest groups, the Fuerzas Armadas Revolucionarias de Colombia (Revolutionary Armed Forces of Colombia, FARC) and the Ejército de Liberación Nacíonal (National Liberation Army, ELN), continued fighting and by 1998 constituted a significant military challenge to the government. Attempts to revive the peace process during the administration of President Ernesto Samper stalled amid a political scandal linking his presidential campaign to the Cali drug-trafficking cartel. President Andrés Pastrana, who took office in August 1998, met with senior guerrilla leaders and pledged to revive the peace process.

As Chapter 6 details, however, the scenario for making peace in Colombia is complicated—but not obliterated—by the proliferation of violent actors such as right-wing paramilitary groups and narcotraffickers, and a peace process with the guerrillas is unlikely to eradicate other forms of human rights abuse and criminal violence. The guerrillas themselves, while advancing proposals for peace, have systematically augmented their military capabilities and actions since the late 1980s. They are demanding major structural reforms and concessions as the price for peace, though many still question their commitment to the process. In his Reflections, former peace advisor Jesús Antonio Bejarano, meanwhile, suggests that shifts in elite perceptions of the economic toll of the war may make conditions for a settlement more favorable, even if the government and guerrillas remain deeply divided over what is to be negotiated at the peace table;

• In Peru, the pitiless war waged by Sendero Luminoso (Shining Path) attenuated following the 1992 capture of its principal leader, Abimael Guzmán Reynoso. But unlike the other countries examined in this book, Peru defeated the guerrilla movement largely through military means. While there is still debate in Peru as to whether the police, the intelligence apparatus, the armed forces, or the Peruvian population itself can claim credit for the "strategic defeat" of Sendero Luminoso, there is little question that the defeat has been achieved absent an agenda of reforms that addresses root causes of the conflict. Chapters 7 and 8, and the comments of anthropologist Carlos Iván Degregori, reflect on the methods and meaning of Sendero's defeat, the costs to Peruvian democracy, and the reasons that no organized sector of opinion in Peru or abroad has called for political negotiations with the remnants of insurgent groups.

• In Mexico, a January 1994 uprising by the Ejército Zapatista de Liberación Nacional, Zapatista National Liberation Army (EZLN) in Chiapas took Mexican and international public opinion by surprise, just as the North American Free Trade Agreement (NAFTA) went into effect. Concerned about its international image and investor confidence, the Mexican government entered into peace talks with the EZLN within days of the uprising. Although the period of open military conflict was on the scale of weeks rather than months or years, the EZLN succeeded initially in galvanizing a broad swath of Mexican civil society fed up with official corruption and in favor of democratic reform, only to see that support fade following elections in 1997 in which the opposition to the ruling party made unprecedented gains.

Peace talks yielded an accord on indigenous rights in February 1996, but the negotiations fell apart after the government failed to introduce the necessary legislative measures to see the accord implemented. The Chiapas crisis faded into the background of national concerns, only to return to center stage when paramilitary groups sympathetic to the ruling party massacred dozens of unarmed peasants in December 1997.

Chapter 5 shows how the absence of incentives and of elite or international pressure has impeded an overall peace settlement in Mexico. Chapter 10 explores how the Chiapas uprising became a catalyst for the resurgence and redefinition of indigenous identity in Mexico, even if the government was intent on limiting the scope of the peace talks to indigenous, rather than national issues. Michael Conroy's Reflections, meanwhile, explore the close connection between Mexico's economic crisis and the Chiapas conflict, showing how the reactions of Mexican and international financial elites constrained the response of the Mexican government to both crises and undermined prospects for reform.

Unique circumstances generated and sustained conflict in Colombia, El Salvador, Guatemala, Mexico, Nicaragua, and Peru. And unique circumstances defined the prospects for a peace process in El Salvador and Guatemala, a demobilization in Nicaragua, and an attempt at both in Colombia. Yet several generalizations emerge having to do with the conditions in which peace processes flourish. One must caution against drawing "lessons" that imply a static model of transference from one case to another. Rather, what stand out are common themes that arise within the specific domestic and international circumstances of each country.

First, there is a causal and mutually reinforcing relationship between processes of democratic transition and peace: Negotiations are made possible by a prior process of democratic opening, however shallow, and the peace process furthers that transition. Thus guerrilla wars, in whose name governments seek to justify harshly antidemocratic practices and widespread repression, can themselves become forces for democratization. This is true when democratic openings are initiated at the state level to provide a political response to the insurgency and when ending the war provides the opportunity to renegotiate dysfunctional elements of the political and economic system. Elections and constitutional reform undertaken during a war—democracy in its most formalistic mode—provide a common legal framework and infrastructure that allow both the left and the right to fight over democracy's more substantive and institutional aspects at the peace table.

Second, the literature on democratic transitions in Latin America, which focuses primarily on the move from military dictatorship to civilian rule in the Southern Cone, does not adequately address democratic transitions related to peace processes. The transition from war to peace involves multiple issues not present in the move from authoritarianism to democracy.

The demobilization and reintegration of combatants from both sides, attending to the needs of refugees and the displaced, and the reconstruction of war-devastated economies, for example, pose enormous technical and financial burdens on governments whose poverty, weak institutional capacity, and lack of responsiveness to social demands contributed to the outbreak of conflict. In addition, and unlike many countries in the Southern Cone, postwar societies face the task of *constructing*, not reconstructing, democratic institutions such as electoral regimes and judicial systems, which if they functioned at all, served as factors of exclusion.[6] In general, civil society tends to be weaker, its atrophy also a cause and consequence of war. Thus, while postwar transitions and transitions from bureaucratic authoritarianism share many common elements, among them the issues of subordinating the armed forces to civilian control and demilitarizing internal security functions, the absence of prior institutional development and the multiplicity of postwar tasks makes postwar transitions more fragile and difficult to consolidate.

Third, successful negotiations can be carried forward only when government leaders, and presidents in particular, are viewed as legitimate by the politically active population and the insurgents. The legitimacy of governments is important not only to overcome potential resistance to the peace process of key political actors such as the military or landed elite but also because the guerrillas themselves seek an interlocutor with the capacity to deliver on agreements signed at the table. The politically conservative president Alfredo Cristiani won presidential elections in El Salvador in 1989 with 54 percent of the vote and without a runoff. The center-right president Álvaro Arzú in Guatemala won elections in 1995 with only a slim majority, but his party also gained control of the legislature, and the naming of center-left intellectuals to key government posts contributed to Arzú's credibility. Both presidents made the peace process a priority immediately upon (and in the case of Arzú before) taking office, when their administrations possessed maximum flexibility and support. By contrast, Colombian president Ernesto Samper entered office in 1994 with a strong commitment to the peace process, but his legitimacy was undermined by the scandal linking his presidential campaign to the Cali drug-trafficking cartel. Despite several attempts by Samper to jump-start the peace talks, the guerrillas ruled out serious discussions with his government.

The legitimacy of guerrilla negotiators must be such that they can command the loyalty of the rank-and-file and "sell" difficult compromises to their supporters at the grass-roots level. The legitimacy of guerrilla forces vis-a-vis the rest of the population must be sufficient that their place at the table is broadly accorded, but it is less essential as long as what is agreed to at the bargaining table satisfies the demands of broad sectors of society.

Fourth, the scope of the reform agenda is not solely a product of the military correlation of forces or, more specifically, a function of guerrilla military strength but also a product of political will at the elite level. If it is true that El Salvador's FMLN fought the armed forces to a bloody stalemate, reflected most dramatically in a November 1989 offensive, it is also true that the Guatemalan government sat down and negotiated broad-reaching reforms with an essentially defeated Guatemalan National Revolutionary Unity (URNG).

The FMLN's ability to negotiate sweeping changes in the structure of the security apparatus, for example, was a function not only of military strength but also of the army's disrepute in the wake of its murder of six Jesuit priests and two women, a human rights case with profound international repercussions. In that context, El Salvador's civilian leaders, along with the FMLN, used the peace process to reform the armed forces and diminish the preeminent political and internal security role it had played in the past. Similarly, an exaggerated focus on the role of military force in negotiations might have predicted a negotiated surrender for the URNG based on its military weakness. In fact, however, elites, both in the civilian government apparatus and the armed forces, used the negotiating process in an attempt to modernize key institutions of the state. Seen in this light, a peace process becomes a vehicle for addressing structural issues that previously had not or could not be addressed within the existing political system.

Fifth, conflict resolution theory has long held that the "ripest" moments for negotiation involved a "mutually hurting stalemate," defined as "mutually blocking vetoes" over outcomes in which escalation of the conflict provided no prospect of escape and parties were thus open to the consideration of other options.[7] The implication that such a stalemate was predominantly an objective condition rooted in military balance has given way to the "softer notion of a perceived stalemate as a no-win situation for both sides" in the absence of power equality between the contending forces.[8] This study of peace processes suggests that perceptions, with or without a hurting stalemate, are indeed the key to a ripe moment, and help explain why peace was possible in El Salvador and in Guatemala under radically different military conditions. Similarly, the escalation of military conflict by insurgents or government forces in order to approach the condition of stalemate may lead away from, rather than toward, the peace table, as in Colombia.

In other words, the "realist" worldview that has equated power with military force does not adequately take into account the fact that governments also want "other things," among them international legitimacy or the chance to compete in a new globalized economy, goals that cannot be achieved—and indeed often are blocked—by military supremacy alone. Altered perceptions of interest may themselves be rooted in changes in actual conditions or circumstance, but the human elements of perception and choice cannot be separated from the external realities on which they are based.

Thus, as Jean Arnault, the U.N. negotiator for Guatemala explains in his Reflections, a peace process can provide more than an escape from a painful military condition; the armed confrontation in Guatemala was a peripheral element in setting the national agenda. What allowed the negotiations to succeed was their eventual conversion into the core of the national agenda, around which diverse groups with a variety of different goals and interests coalesced.

Sixth, if peace accords represent new pacts at the elite level, the incorporation of civil society during the period of negotiations expands the representativity of the agreements and creates new stakeholders in the postaccord outcome. If the El Salvador accords were criticized precisely because the mechanisms for including others than the warring parties were weak, the Guatemalan peace process represented a conscious effort to enlist the contribution of civil society via the Civil Society Assembly (Asamblea de la Sociedad Civil, or ASC). Many of the proposals arrived at by consensus within the ASC made their way into the formal accords, and the process of consultation served to move nongovernmental organizations with a tradition of street protest into a more collaborative effort with the government. Similarly, when governments and insurgents find it difficult to meet each other face to face, groups in civil society can play a bridging role that eventually enhances the prospects for formal talks.

Seventh, the role of the international community, through such institutions as the United Nations and the Organization of American States, and also through the actions of individual governments, has been essential to the conclusion of peace agreements.[9] As Chapter 9 points out, the U.N. role involved both mediation and on-the-ground verification of the peace accords, and a distinct learning curve from the experience in El Salvador informed U.N. involvement in Guatemala. The internal conditions under which peace was forged in each country differed dramatically, but as a result of perceived shortcomings in El Salvador, the United Nations made a greater effort in Guatemala to coordinate during the negotiations with the international donor community, and worked more intensively from the start to bolster domestic institutions whose adequate functioning was critical to the construction of the postwar order.

But as Chapter 9 implies, ultimately the central ingredient for international involvement has been, and will be even more so in the future, the commitment of both sides to a negotiated settlement. The hope that the United Nations or other third party will become involved in a peace process in order to rescue a nation from itself is ever more remote in an era of shrinking U.N. budgets and the reluctance of national governments to become involved in conflict absent a clear-cut "exit strategy." A body such as the United Nations can facilitate agreement, and the skills of an individual mediator can play a definitive role. External actors, however, cannot substitute for the will of the parties.

Although this book is concerned primarily with the factors that make peace negotiations possible, peace processes do not end with the signing of a final accord. The periods of implementation and consolidation, in which aspects of a formal accord are put into practice and, if specified in the accord, verified by national or international bodies, represent periods of intense uncertainty and struggle over the pace and scope of prescribed change. While a full discussion of postconflict peace building is beyond the scope of this inquiry,[10] several issues stand out for the dilemmas they pose. These issues are explored in Part II.

First is the question of justice. Rhetoric of governments aside, and despite the best efforts of the international community to establish legal regimes governing the behavior of warring parties, the practice of counterinsurgency and insurgent war is never clean. In the name of combatting guerrillas, governments in Latin America and elsewhere have carried out torture and "disappearance," murder and massacre, blurring the distinction between civilian and combatant, ostensibly in the pursuit of state survival. While repression and human rights abuse may have predated armed conflict and in many ways contributed to its outbreak, there is no doubt that wars perpetuate and intensify abuse, as all opposition activity gets subsumed under the subversive label, and the distinction between the guerrillas and those who might sympathize with them is observed in the breach.

At the same time, insurgents themselves violate state law and international humanitarian law by murdering civilians, carrying out indiscriminate attacks, kidnapping, and extorting, activities rationalized in the name of building a financial war chest, denying the state authority in areas the insurgents deem their zones of influence, or simply eliminating suspected informers or those who do not share their revolutionary agenda.

Peace is thus declared over the ashes of many victims. The issue of what to do with perpetrators, both in the name of justice for victims and the consolidation of the rule of law, becomes a critical one in the construction of the postwar order. As Chapters 12 and 13 and the Reflections by Alvaro de Soto indicate, what is desirable on a moral level and what is possible politically often conflict. Most sobering in this regard is de Soto's identification of a "peacemaker's dilemma," involving trade-offs and pressures to sacrifice longer-term goals of peace building for the short-term goal of separating combatants and ending the fighting. The approach taken by each country reflects unique configurations of residual power held by the military, prior institutional development, and the attitudes and commitments of political leaders and civil society as a whole.

A second dilemma involves the reform of the security apparatus. To solve a crisis that fueled the conflict, peace accords have sought to purge the military and police of corrupt and abusive elements, subordinate the military to civilian authority, and separate the functions of internal and external security, assigning the former to police bodies and the latter to the military. Yet the demand for rapid transformation of military and police structures runs headlong into the need to maintain security in the postwar environment, a setting that has witnessed spectacular rises in common crime, the use of weapons of war to commit crime, and the penetration of drug-trafficking and other organized syndicates into a fluid and disorganized setting. Chapter 14 explores the complex and at times contradictory tasks of maintaining order and pursuing reform, while Francisco Thoumi's Reflections discuss the challenges to governmental authority of social and criminal violence in Colombia. In almost every case, the weakness of the judiciary compounds police inefficiency and vice versa.

The needs of postwar reconstruction pose a third set of dilemmas. Even if a peace accord does not expressly reorder a country's socioeconomic landscape, it poses both long- and short-term tasks. In the immediate postwar environment, addressing the needs of ex-combatants is a political imperative linked to demobilization. Over the medium and long term, addressing grievances arising from economic deprivation and marginalization—of both civilian supporters of the guerrillas and the majority of the population who are poor—can affect the success and viability of a peace process.

As Chapter 15 points out, however, postwar economic policies emphasizing trade liberalization as the key to rapid growth do not by themselves address issues of human and social capital development, which are critical to reduce or eliminate inequalities. If the poor are to benefit from growth, the government must efficiently direct policies as well as resources to such areas as education, affordable transportation, and health care. As James Boyce argues in his Reflections, however, the need to increase social spending at the end of a war may conflict with the international financial community's prescription for fiscal discipline as a condition of aid. Meanwhile, the role of the international donor community, explored by both Boyce and by German ambassador Gerhard Henze in his Reflections, can only partially offset the need for domestic revenues to finance social goals. The generation of these revenues often depends on reform of the tributary system, producing the potential for future conflict.

The next section attempts to concretize observations about the making and consolidation of peace by providing an overview of peace agreements in Nicaragua, El Salvador, and Guatemala and identifying the changing international and internal contexts that made them possible. While each case is the product of unique circumstances, none is so divorced from a Latin American context that it is devoid of implications for other countries in the region. Indeed, the peace settlements in Central America have been closely studied by governments, insurgents, and policymakers in Latin America for the precise purpose of determining how and why a negotiated solution was achieved.

The Shifting International Context

It has become a commonplace to view the settlement of armed conflict in Central America as a post–Cold War phenomenon, made possible by the collapse of the Soviet Union and the removal of the East-West ideological and security dimension of internal struggles. This, while accurate, tells only part of the story. Equally essential, and in the case of Nicaragua, predating the end of the Cold War, was the erosion of U.S. domestic consensus over Central America policy, and the resulting imperative for the executive branch to craft a policy aimed at something less than achieving military victory.

The breakdown of consensus was reflected in increased congressional activism involving the termination or reduction of aid to sustain the region's wars. It was prompted by the Iran-contra affair of 1986–1987 and by the murder of six Jesuit priests and two women in El Salvador in 1989. The shift in U.S. policy away from military confrontation toward a graceful exit from the region's wars facilitated the emergence of other actors in the Central American drama, whose actions in turn further shaped the political process in the United States.[11]

In Nicaragua, the Reagan administration policy of funding paramilitary war to oust the Sandinista government was never backed by a stable majority in Congress. Funding for the contra war was banned outright in 1984 and approved in 1985 and 1986 by slim margins, more because legislators feared the domestic consequences of appearing "soft on communism" than they did the Sandinista threat. The majority in favor of aid dissipated when Justice Department officials revealed in November 1986 that the Reagan administration had sold arms to the Khomeini regime in Iran and had used some of the profits to provide military aid to the contras in violation of the law.

The resulting months of congressional hearings, which culminated in a scathing report by a joint House-Senate Iran-contra committee, spelled the end of U.S. funding for the contra war. Following the scandal, Congress provided limited amounts of nonlethal, so-called humanitarian aid to the contras, but it refused to provide military aid for an ongoing war effort.

The Central American peace plan known as Esquipulas II was launched during this period of U.S. disarray and retrenchment. Initially put forward by the Costa Rican president Oscar Arias in February 1987 and formally launched at a meeting of Central American presidents in August 1987, the peace plan called for the end of outside support to Central American insurgencies, cease-fires, internal democratization and elections, and dialogue and reconciliation with unarmed opponents.[12]

The plan was essential in laying the groundwork for subsequent peace settlements. It served as a rallying point in Congress for those seeking an alternative to Reagan administration policy in Nicaragua, providing one more peg in the coffin of contra aid. At the same time, the plan committed the Sandinistas to political liberalization, dialogue, and early elections. In El Salvador, exiled political leaders, at considerable personal risk, returned home to test and widen the political space for opposition activity.[13] In Guatemala, although the government refused to meet directly with the URNG, the Arias plan provided the impetus for the formation of a National Reconciliation Commission that ultimately brokered a dialogue between armed combatants and numerous groups in civil society, including the private sector, church, and popular organizations.

While none of these steps alone could have produced a settlement of armed conflict in Central America, together they contributed to political openings in all three countries at war and posited dialogue, not fighting, as the means to resolve conflict.

Nicaragua

The erosion of domestic support for Nicaragua policy and advances under the auspices of the Arias plan influenced the approach taken by George Bush, elected president in November 1988. Before and in the weeks immediately after taking office in January 1989, Bush and Secretary of State James A. Baker III sought a bipartisan accord with Congress that would end the rancor over Nicaragua policy and seek a graceful exit for the United States. The focus of U.S. policy shifted from an effort to overthrow the Sandinistas militarily to that of seeking their defeat in upcoming elections.

The Arias plan set in motion a series of events in the region that continued to spin out of the U.S. administration's control. Efforts to disband the contras as a fighting force took a step forward in February 1989, when the Central American presidents called for the "voluntary demobilization, repatriation or relocation" of the rebel forces.[14] At the same time, and because they were included as full partners in the search for peace,[15] the Sandinistas made concessions they would never have contemplated in the face of contra military pressure alone, reiterating their commitment to democratic practices and opening the country to unprecedented scrutiny of the upcoming 1990 elections.

To the shock of the Sandinistas, opposition candidate Violeta Barrios de Chamorro won the February 1990 elections. To ensure a peaceful transition of power and remove any pretext by which the Sandinistas would attempt to remain in office, the Bush administration put concerted pressure on the contras to lay down their arms and return to Nicaragua. "Strike your tents, shut this thing down" was the way a senior U.S. official involved in the contra program described the U.S. message.[16] The pressure on contra forces to demobilize reflected the administration's desire to extricate the United States from the contra war as well as the long-standing, if questionable, equation of elections with democracy.

Unable to continue their war without foreign military and political backing, some 22,500 rebels and their logistical supporters demobilized during 1990 under the watchful eye of the United Nations and Organization of American States.[17] The combatants were offered land and subsistence aid and the opportunity to form police forces in zones of concentration known as development poles. But the close linkage between the elections and the contras' demobilization, as well as their dependence on outside forces, meant that broader contra political demands, such as an end to Sandinista control of the army and police, were never considered in the context of their demobilization.

In the postwar period, ex-combatants complained of violence directed at them by state agents and Sandinista supporters. This insecurity, and the difficulty the government had of making good on promises of land, sparked substantial political violence in 1990–1991.[18] Frustrated by Sandinista dominance of key institutions and denouncing the government for failing to provide security or an economic livelihood, hundreds of demobilized rebels took up arms again in 1991, forming bands known as re-contras. Originally with a political agenda (and at times staging joint actions with disgruntled former army troops known as recompas, most of the groups remaining after a series of demobilization efforts have been engaged in criminal pursuits, serving as a destabilizing force in significant areas of the northern countryside.

El Salvador

The conditions—both international and internal—that led to the signing of a comprehensive peace agreement in El Salvador differed dramatically from those of Nicaragua, even if the end of the Cold War and the subsequent "space" afforded international actors other than the United States provided a common backdrop. Most observers agree that the punishing FMLN military offensive in November 1989 had a decisive outcome on the shape of the negotiated settlement, in which, unlike Nicaragua, the FMLN's demobilization was linked to major institutional reform. Less acknowledged in the outcome, however, is the evolution in the political positions of both sides and how elites came to view as unacceptable the costs of continuing the war. These changes at the political and perceptual level were essential preconditions to successful negotiations.

The year 1989 witnessed two important shifts in the internal political context in El Salvador. In January the FMLN offered to participate in upcoming presidential, legislative, and municipal elections, modifying a longstanding position that there were no conditions for free and fair elections as long as the repressive apparatus of the state remained intact. Two considerations appear to have influenced that decision. The first was the staggering economic toll of the contra war in Nicaragua and the knowledge that even if a revolutionary government were to take power, it could expect implacable hostility from the United States. The second was the burgeoning economic crisis of the Soviet Union and its Eastern Bloc allies and, as a consequence, Cuba, which meant that Eastern Bloc aid to a postrevolutionary government would be reduced, if available at all, and that command economies offered a poor model of organization and development. Guerrilla leaders undertook diplomatic tours of Latin American and European capitals in 1988 and received an unequivocal message: There was no support for a continuation of the war.[19]

Attitudes within the government camp were also changing. President Alfredo Cristiani represented a business-oriented, technocratic wing of the ultra-conservative Alianza Republicana Nacionalista (ARENA) party that viewed the war as an ever-greater drain on the country's resources, with no possibilities of military victory in sight.[20] Cristiani asked a close confidant to draft his 1989 inaugural speech in a way that would couple a call for peace with a concrete offer of dialogue.[21] Cristiani's speech addressed the FMLN by name rather than using the vernacular of "delinquent terrorists." He defined as the country's "basic challenge" as the search "for a solution to the armed conflict," and called for a dialogue commission to contact the FMLN.[22]

The FMLN and Salvadoran negotiators met twice in September and October 1989, in Mexico City and San José, respectively, but the positions of the two sides remained widely apart.[23] The talks fell apart when right-wing terrorists, possibly linked to the government, placed a bomb at the headquarters of a major leftist labor federation, killing or wounding dozens of people. Another bomb exploded at the headquarters of COMADRES, a human rights group identified with the left, wounding four.[24]

The FMLN responded in November 1989 by launching its largest military offensive ever and massively infiltrating the capital for the first time during the war. In the midst of that offensive, and facing the prospect that it might lose control of the capital, the military high command ordered a crime with immense domestic and international repercussions. It dispatched an elite, U.S.-trained counterinsurgency unit to the campus of the Jesuit-run Central American University (UCA), with the mission to kill UCA rector Father Ignacio Ellacuría. Ellacuría was a longtime government critic and one of El Salvador's leading intellectuals and proponents of a negotiated solution. In the eyes of the armed forces, however, he was one of the intellectual authors of the rebellion.[25] When the army unit was finished, it had murdered six Jesuit priests, their housekeeper, and her teenage daughter, a crime that sent shock waves around the world, isolated the Salvadoran government and especially the armed focus, and ultimately contributed to the constellation of factors that allowed for a negotiated settlement.[26]

The offensive itself had several major effects. First, it demonstrated to the FMLN the lack of popular support for their call for general insurrection; in the words of FMLN commander Salvador Samayoa, "military means could not alter the correlation of forces as much as had been predicted."[27] Second, it demonstrated that, contrary to official claims and predictions, massive numbers of FMLN troops could enter and leave the capital at will.[28] The offensive thus served to shift basic perceptions that both sides held about their own capabilities and that of the enemy.

Another shift also occurred at the level of perceptions. While many analysts have described the offensive as the manifestation par excellence of a military stalemate,[29] equally or perhaps more important was the perception of the *costs* imposed by war. "It's absurd to think that a military victory wasn't possible," said General Mauricio Vargas, military representative to the negotiating team.

"But," he continued, "a rational person looks for the least-cost solution. We in the military saw death every day for ten years. We lived the structural factors, the poverty, the lack of health care, electricity, and drinking water. We didn't discover these things in the *Washington Post,* but rather, in the most remote corners of the country."[30]

Or, in the words of former guerrilla commander Ana Guadalupe Martínez, "what obliged us to sit down at the table was the stalemate. But what obliges one to negotiate is something different. We saw the attrition of our forces, and the rejection by society of military forms of struggle."[31]

A final consequence of the offensive, one rich in Salvadoran and international implications, was the battered prestige of the armed forces as a result of the Jesuit murders. Almost immediately, testimony from an eyewitness and circumstantial evidence implicated the military, despite ham-handed efforts by the U.S. and Salvadoran governments to pin the murders on the FMLN. When President Cristiani publicly announced in January 1990 the names of nine suspects, including an army colonel and seven members of the elite counterinsurgency Atlacatl battalion,[32] the only question remaining was whether responsibility for the crime lay solely with those arrested or reached higher into the senior ranks of the army.

Contributing further to a pillorying of the armed forces was the work of a U.S. House task force established to look into the Jesuit killings. Appointed by the Speaker of the House and chaired by Representative John Joseph Moakley (D-MA), the task force and its staff conducted a virtually unprecedented congressional investigation on the soil of a foreign country, developing sources within the Salvadoran armed forces itself. In a series of scathing reports between April 1990 and November 1991, the task force lambasted the army high command for its cover-up of the murders. It ultimately implicated the army chief of staff and other top officers in the decision to kill the priests.[33]

The work of the task force led Congress to adopt an unprecedented 50 percent cut in aid to the Salvadoran army in 1990. If, during the Cold War, Congress was willing to overlook major human rights abuses for the sake of combatting communist insurgents, no such imperative held U.S. policy together following the Cold War's end. Aid cuts furthered the political isolation of the Salvadoran military. By signaling the breakdown of consensus over El Salvador policy, the aid cuts also pressured the Bush administration to support a negotiated settlement.

In late 1989, following the FMLN's offensive and the Jesuit murders, both the Salvadoran government and the guerrillas made separate requests to the United Nations to participate in the search for peace.[34] The direct requests of both parties, and the explicit support of the Central American presidents for a U.N. role, led the United Nations to take the unprecedented step of agreeing to mediate an internal, as opposed to international, dispute.[35]

The two sides met under U.N. auspices in Geneva in April 1990, agreeing that the contours of the negotiations would consist of both direct meetings and "intermediation" by the United Nations.[36] Later they agreed to a two-stage process by which the reincorporation of the FMLN into Salvadoran society would come as a result of prior political agreements leading to a cease-fire. These political agreements were to cover the armed forces, human rights, the judicial system, electoral system, constitutional reform, economic and social issues, and verification by the United Nations (in that order).[37]

Thus, the Salvadoran negotiations helped establish the precedent that discussions regarding the end of military hostilities would come *after* the conclusion of agreements on substantive issues, reversing the preference usually expressed by governments that the fighting stop before talks begin. In addition, agreement on an agenda for the talks assured that both sides concurred on the issues to be addressed, if not on the actual outcome of those discussions.

The first real fruit of the negotiating process was a July 1990 human rights accord, reflecting in many ways the centrality of human rights issues in the Salvadoran crisis. While critics dismissed the accord at the time as providing little more than a reiteration of existing commitments by both sides, the agreement did provide for a U.N. mission to verify the human rights practices of both sides following a cease-fire.

However, at the parties' request, the mission, known by its acronym ONUSAL, formally opened its offices in July 1991, well before the cessation of armed conflict. Its "dissuasive" presence contributed to an improvement in the observance of human rights in El Salvador.[38] In retrospect, the human rights mission served as a confidence-building measure on the path to a wider accord, although there was nothing at the time to indicate that agreement on human rights issues would lead to a comprehensive peace.

Throughout the course of the negotiations, the parties struggled with the issue of the reform of the armed forces. For the FMLN, the restructuring and purging, if not dissolution, of the armed forces was seen as paramount to resolve one of the underlying structural factors that had given rise to the war and, as a more practical matter, to permit the guerrillas to demobilize without simply being massacred. By the end of the talks, the government and guerrillas had agreed to reduce the size of the military and create an Ad Hoc Commission to purge it of corrupt and abusive members, dissolve the National Guard and the Treasury Police, create a new National Civilian Police open to the FMLN as well as to members of the existing National Police, dissolve all rapid-reaction army counterinsurgency battalions implicated in some of the worst human rights abuses of the war, and establish a truth commission whose mandate did not preclude the naming of names of those responsible for abuses.[39]

That such sweeping reforms were possible owed to factors beyond the military stalemate. They included: (1) the priority attached by the FMLN to reform of the armed forces; (2) the position of the FMLN as well U.N. officials that ending the war meant addressing its root causes; (3) pressure on the military by the United States, particularly in late 1991, to accept a negotiated settlement[40]; and (4) acceptance on the part of the Salvadoran negotiating team that such changes were appropriate and necessary.

This latter point deserves elaboration, as it represented a break in the historical alliance between the military and the economic elite. As described by government negotiator Oscar Santamaría, "the army had taken control of the security forces for a purely warlike end; they had lost their internal security function, devised in the last century, and the crisis in human rights was attributable to them. . . . This represented a distortion of the function of an army. These were institutions that needed to change."[41]

Two additional and highly idiosyncratic issues explain how it was possible to reach a final accord. First was the pressure of an absolute deadline. Pérez de Cuéllar's term as U.N. secretary-general expired on December 31, 1991, and it was not clear to what extent his successor would make peace in El Salvador a priority. Second and related, the priority attached by the FMLN to political/military issues left little time for a detailed discussion of the socioeconomic agenda; moreover, the ARENA government had made it clear that such change was not up for negotiation.

In the end, the FMLN was forced to accept that it could not negotiate changes in both the military and economic arenas without risking the entire accord.[42] "We hadn't won militarily, so we couldn't ask for everything," explained an FMLN official involved in the negotiations, describing the rationalization that allowed the FMLN to concede these parts of the negotiating agenda.[43] The FMLN team concluded that the bulk of socioeconomic demands related to land reform, agricultural credits, and the like (most of which had been rejected outright by the government side) would become part of what would be contested subsequently in the electoral arena.[44] The signing of the final accord on December 31, 1991, reflected the decision of both parties to conclude a less-than-perfect agreement that nonetheless was the only one possible at that moment.[45] The accord brought a cruel war to an end, even if the very lack of specificity on socioeconomic issues generated substantial conflict in the postwar era.

Guatemala

On December 29, 1996, almost five years to the day after the signing of the El Salvadoran peace accord, the Guatemalan government and the URNG signed a comprehensive peace accord. There were profound differences in the circumstances that led to peace in Guatemala. But the two cases share a recognition by key elites on both sides that the costs of continuing the war were greater than the possibilities that might be realized through negotiation.

The differences between El Salvador and Guatemala raise the question of why a peace process was possible at all. Unlike in El Salvador, where the war was felt throughout the country, in Guatemala the war had not been a significant factor affecting the population since the dramatic and bloody scorched-earth campaigns by the Guatemalan army in the early 1980s.[46] There was thus no "hurting stalemate" in which the mutual capacity to inflict pain impelled both sides to the bargaining table, and the talks themselves went much further than the military correlation of forces would have dictated.[47] However, as the guerrillas were not defeated altogether, they constituted an obstacle to democratic development as well as to the modernization and professionalization of the army.

Second, the isolation of Guatemala internationally due to its disastrous human rights record meant that the armed forces were less susceptible to international pressure. In contrast to the Salvadoran army's dependency on U.S. military aid during the course of the war, for example, the Guatemalan army prided itself on having "gone it alone" during the most intense period of fighting, following the termination of U.S. military aid during the Carter administration.[48] International actors such as the United Nations, the Central American presidents, and the Group of Friends of the Guatemalan peace process played decisive roles in the outcome of the peace talks, but not through strong-arm tactics aimed at the military or other sectors of Guatemalan society.

Why, then, and in the absence of a military imperative, was a settlement possible? Internally, several changes at the perceptual level appear to have influenced the way key Guatemalan actors viewed their future with or without peace.

First was a recognition by certain governmental elites in the late 1980s and early 1990s that the process of transition to civilian rule, reflected in the 1985 election of Christian Democrat Vinicio Cerezo and in the subsequent approval of a new constitution, would be incomplete, if not impossible to consolidate, without an end to the war.[49] Guatemala's limited transition to democracy—at first, little more than a decision by the armed forces to cede the office of the president to a civilian—was characterized by growing, if tenuous, efforts by civilian authorities to maximize their power vis-à-vis the armed forces. In the view of these civilians, the war's persistence constituted an obstacle in the ongoing process of transition.[50]

Second, one must not underestimate the cost imposed on Guatemala by international isolation, a direct product of the army's flagrant abuse of human rights. Campaigns by international human rights and trade union organizations conveyed pariah status on the military as well as on civilian political leaders, who were viewed as unwilling to or incapable of curbing military abuses. The consequences, in prestige, aid, and investment, were substantial; more important, as the decade of the 1980s wore on, they were *perceived* as substantial by military, civilian, and private sector elites alike. As wars subsided in Nicaragua and El Salvador, the war in Guatemala was viewed more and more as an anachronism; the peace process was seen as a way for Guatemala to overcome its "horrendous international image" and restore its legitimacy and standing within the international community.[51]

Third was the explicit recognition that involving Guatemala in the "process of economic and political globalization" necessitated internal changes.[52] More liberal-minded commercial sector leaders understood the positive correlation between levels of underdevelopment in different areas of the country and the intensity of the war, and feared being looked over in the competition for international resources if human capital and infrastructure needs went unaddressed.[53] Hence, as in El Salvador, Guatemalan civilians saw that it was not enough simply to end the armed conflict; rather, it was essential to address the multitude of imbalances that had led to conflict in the first place.[54]

This view appears to have dovetailed with a growing belief held by some in the military that it was in the interest of the armed forces to promote a measure of social justice in Guatemala, as they had borne the cost of preserving the status quo in the 1970s and early 1980s. The pattern in Guatemala was thus the reverse of that in El Salvador: Whereas in El Salvador political elites representing the private sector had come to see the military as part of the problem, not the solution, in Guatemala, it was just the reverse.

Fourth, negotiations would not have been possible if the URNG had not also recognized that, with military victory an impossibility, the negotiating table could become the arena for new political struggles to change Guatemalan society.[55] Indeed, important political changes had already taken place in the country. These included the wholesale rejection by Guatemalan society of the attempted self-coup by President Jorge Elías Serrano in 1993 and the appointment of former human rights ombudsman Ramiro de León Carpio as president following the failed coup. Renewed activism by nongovernmental organizations, reflected in the convening of the Asamblea de la Sociedad Civil (Civil Society Assembly) to provide input into the talks, and the participation of a grass-roots, leftist coalition, the Frente Democrático Nuevo Guatemala (FDNG) in the 1995 elections, also demonstrated that the political spaces for opposition activity were widening, with or without the URNG.

Fifth, the international community maintained an active presence in the talks. In 1987, and at the urging of the Central American presidents, then-President Vinicio Cerezo convened the National Reconciliation Commission (CNR), which provided the first internal mechanism for dialogue among the URNG, sectors of Guatemalan society, and eventually, the government itself. U.N. involvement came about as a result of the 1990 "Oslo Accord" (Acuerdo Básico), which called on the U.N. secretary-general to appoint an observer to the peace process. The U.N. role expanded following the initiation of direct talks between the URNG and the government, when a 1994 "Framework Accord" called for the naming of a moderator, not simply an observer.[56] As in El Salvador, the United Nations established an on-the-ground presence in Guatemala to monitor human rights prior to a cease-fire, opening the doors of the verification mission, MINUGUA, in November 1994.

Nonetheless, the heightened U.N. role was insufficient to overcome a stalling of the peace talks in late 1995. Attempts to generate discipline via agreement on a schedule for concluding the talks, as well as confidence-building measures such as the deployment of the human rights mission before a cease-fire, could not overcome the URNG's fear that a final accord negotiated with the caretaker government of Ramiro de León Carpio would not have binding force.[57]

It took the election in 1995 of President Álvaro Arzú Irigoyen to overcome the remaining obstacles to a final accord.[58] In an important symbolic gesture, prior to his inauguration Arzú met with the URNG as well as with returning Guatemalan refugees. With the support of "institutionalists" in the military, he carried out a purge of the army and police, including virtually the entire high command, and moved into senior posts those officers with a long history of involvement in and support for the peace talks. His choice to head the governmental peace commission COPAZ was himself a former member of a guerrilla organization. Through these steps, Arzú established himself as a credible interlocutor with an interest in reaching and delivering on agreements at the bargaining table. The peace talks progressed rapidly throughout 1996, reaching their conclusion at the end of the year.

The purpose of this discussion has been to show how the demobilization in Nicaragua and peace processes in El Salvador and Guatemala differ, how military stalemates do or do not determine the outcome of negotiations, how perceptions influence the prospects for a settlement, and how the role of external actors facilitates but does not guarantee a successful outcome. At the same time, the discussion should serve to indicate how conditions of the moment, created by unique and unrepeatable circumstances, generate the unique environment in which peace is negotiated. The search for recurring patterns is thus tempered by an awareness that templates cannot simply be transferred from one country to another. Respect for the balance between that which is peculiar and that which can be imitated provides the right frame of mind for considering the remainder of this book.

Notes

1. As defined by I. William Zartman, internal conflicts "begin with the breakdown of normal politics." I. William Zartman, *Elusive Peace: Negotiating an End to Civil Wars* (Washington, D.C.: The Brookings Institution, 1995), 5.

2. Theories of social movements and their relationship to insurgency have made important contributions to the field of conflict resolution. See Louis Kriesberg, "The Development of the Conflict Resolution Field," in I. William Zartman and J. Lewis Rasmussen, eds., *Peacemaking in International Conflict: Methods and Techniques* (Washington, D.C.: United States Institute of Peace, 1997), 59. The distinction between a political logic and a military one is amply developed in Carlos Basombrío Iglesias, *La Paz: Valor y Precio* (Lima: Instituto de Defensa Legal, 1996), a detailed comparative study of violence and peace processes in El Salvador, Guatemala, Colombia, and Peru.

3. The distinction between the "form" (the procedural aspects of electoral democracy) and the "content" of a consolidated democratic regime has long been made in the literature on democratic transitions. See Juan J. Linz and Alfred Stepan, *Problems of Democratic Transition and Consolidation: Southern Europe, South America, and Post-Communist Europe* (Baltimore, Md.: The Johns Hopkins University Press, 1996); Terry Karl, "Dilemmas of Democratization in Latin America," *Comparative Politics* 23, No. 1 (Oct. 1990): 1–20; Jorge I. Domínguez and Abraham Lowenthal, eds., *Constructing Democratic Governance: Mexico, Central America, and the Caribbean in the 1990s* (Baltimore, Md.: The Johns Hopkins University Press, 1996); and Mitchell A. Seligson and John A. Booth, *Elections and Democracy in Central America: Revisited* (Chapel Hill: University of North Carolina Press, 1995), 1–21. For the way that the U.S. political system has digested the issue, see Thomas Carothers, *In the Name of Democracy: U.S. Policy Toward Latin America in the Reagan Years* (Berkeley: University of California Press, 1991); and Abraham F. Lowenthal, ed., *Exporting Democracy: The United States and Latin America* (Baltimore, Md.: The Johns Hopkins University Press, 1991), vols. 1 and 2.

4. Linz and Stepan point out that it is not entirely clear when a process of transition is over and considered complete. However, they define behavioral, attitudinal, and constitutional aspects of a consolidated democracy in which, in Guiseppe di Palma's phrase, democracy has become "the only game in town." See *Problems of Democratic Transition and Consolidation*, 4–15.

5. Among the principal works on democratic transitions, see: Elizabeth Jelin and Eric Hershberg, *Constructing Democracy: Human Rights, Citizenship, and Society in Latin America* (Boulder, Colo.: Westview Press, 1996); Scott Mainwaring, Guillermo O'Donnell, and J. Samuel Valenzuela, *Issues in Democratic Consolidation: The New South American Democracies in Comparative Perspective* (Notre Dame, Ind.: University of Notre Dame Press, 1992); Guillermo O'Donnell and Philippe C. Schmitter, *Transitions from Authoritarian Rule: Tentative Conclusions about Uncertain Democracies* (Baltimore, Md.: The Johns Hopkins University Press, 1986); Guillermo O'Donnell, Philippe C. Schmitter, and Laurence Whitehead, eds., *Transitions from Authoritarian Rule: Latin America* (Baltimore, Md.: The Johns Hopkins University Press, 1986).

Important works in the field of conflict resolution include: Fen Osler Hampson, *Nurturing Peace: Why Peace Settlements Succeed or Fail* (Washington, D.C.: United States Institute of Peace, 1996); Louis Kriesberg, Terrell A. Northrup, and Stuart J. Thorson, eds., *Intractable Conflicts and Their Transformation* (Syracuse, N.Y.: Syracuse University Press, 1989); I. William Zartman, "Ripening Conflict, Ripe Moment, Formula, and Mediation," in Diane B. Bendahmane and John W. McDonald, Jr., eds., *Perspectives on Negotiation: Four Case Studies and Interpretations* (Washington, D.C.: Center for the Study of Foreign Affairs, Foreign Service Institute, 1986), 205–27; and the more recent works Zartman, *Elusive Peace,* and Zartman and Rasmussen, eds., *Peacemaking in International Conflict.*

6. One should not exaggerate this distinction, as postwar societies face simultaneous tasks of construction and reconstruction. The key factor in distinguishing between the two, it would seem, involves the level of pretransition institutional development. Central America and countries of the Southern Cone differ profoundly in this regard.

7. See Zartman, "Ripening Conflict," 216–20. For a critique of the concept, see Hampson, *Nurturing Peace,* 13–16.

8. Zartman, *Elusive Peace,* 18.

9. On the role of third-party mediation, see Sadia Touval and I. William Zartman, *Interna-*

tional Mediation in Theory and Practice (Boulder, Colo.: Westview Press, 1985); Jacob Bercovitch, "Mediation in International Conflict: An Overview of Theory, A Review of Practice," in Zartman and Rasmussen, eds., *Peacemaking in International Conflict,* 125–53.

10. For discussions of the postconflict period, see Nicole Ball with Tammy Halevy, *Making Peace Work: The Role of the International Development Community* (Washington, D.C.: Overseas Development Council, 1996); and the collection of papers presented at the conference, "After the War Is Over . . . What Comes Next? Promoting Democracy, Human Rights, and Reintegration in Post-conflict Societies," (sponsored by the U.S. Agency for International Development, Center for Development Information and Evaluation, October 30–31, 1997, Washington, D.C.)

11. The following discussion of U.S. policy in Central America draws heavily on the author's *Crossroads: Congress, the President, and Central America* (University Park, Pa.: Penn State Press, 1993), 218–64; and Cynthia J. Arnson and Johanna Mendelson Forman, "United States Policy in Central America," *Current History* 90, No. 554 (March 1991): 97–100, 136–37.

12. Secretaría de Relaciones Públicas, Presidencia de la República, "Procedimiento Para Establecer la Paz Firme y Duradera en Centro América," Guatemala City, August 6–7, 1987, 8–13. See also Jack Child, *The Central American Peace Process, 1983–1991: Sheathing Swords, Building Confidence* (Boulder, Colo.: Lynne Rienner, 1992).

13. Those returning included, most notably, Rubén Zamora and Guillermo Ungo, leaders of the Frente Democrático Revolucionario, Revolutionary Democratic Front (FDR), allied with the FMLN.

14. Presidential elections in Nicaragua also were moved up to February 1990. Nina M. Serafino, "Central American Peace Prospects: U.S. Interests and Response" (Congressional Research Service, Library of Congress, Washington, D.C., September 1, 1989), 6–8.

15. See William Goodfellow and James Morrell, "Esquipulas: Politicians in Command," in L. Goodman, W. Leogrande, and J. Mendelson Forman, eds., *Political Parties and Democracy in Central America* (Boulder, Colo.: Westview Press, 1992), 267–85.

16. Senior U.S. official who requested anonymity, interview with author, Washington, D.C., March 31, 1994. Senior U.S. officials visited contra base camps in Honduras, and a host of U.S. officials in Washington, including the president, vice president, and secretary of state, made open declarations that the war was over.

17. Santiago Murray, interview with author, Managua, November 6, 1990. Murray was director of the OAS Commission for Verification and Support (CIAV).

18. Americas Watch, *Fitful Peace: Human Rights and Reconciliation Under the Chamorro Government* (New York: Americas Watch, July 1991). A tripartite commission established to investigate political violence subsequently determined that not all violence against ex-rebels was directed by Sandinistas.

19. Ana Guadalupe Martínez, interview with author, San Salvador, February 23, 1995; Tom Gibb and Frank Smyth, *El Salvador: Is Peace Possible? A Report on the Prospects for Negotiations and U.S. Policy* (Washington, D.C.: Washington Office on Latin America, April 1990); Douglas Farah, "Salvadoran Rebels Shift Stance, Offer to Take Part in Vote, *Washington Post,* January 24, 1989:A15, A18, Col 1.

20. Oscar Santamaría, interview with author, Washington, D.C., March 22, 1996. Santamaría was a member of Salvadoran government negotiating team. See also Tommie Sue Montgomery, *Revolution in El Salvador,* 2d ed. (Boulder, Colo.: Westview Press, 1995).

21. David Escobar Galindo, interview with author, San Salvador, February 25, 1995.

22. San Salvador Domestic Service, "Alfredo Cristiani Delivers Inaugural Speech," *Foreign Broadcast Information Service,* Latin America, June 2, 1989, 17.

23. The government continued to call, for example, for an immediate cease-fire and the FMLN's dissolution. See Lindsey Gruson, "Salvador Foes at Peace Talks Say No to Each Other's Ideas," *New York Times,* October 18, 1989: A8.

24. See Comisión de la Verdad para El Salvador, *De la locura a la esperanza: La guerra de 12 años en El Salvador* (San Salvador and New York: United Nations, March 1993), 96–99. The re-

port, released in New York on March 15, 1993, was subsequently published as U.N. Doc. S/25500, April 1, 1993.

25. For details of the operation, see ibid., 47.

26. For a moving account of the murder of the Jesuits, their role in the intellectual life of El Salvador, and the ways the murder investigation became entwined with the negotiations and with U.S. policy, see: Teresa Whitfield, _Paying the Price: Ignacio Ellacuría and the Murdered Jesuits of El Salvador_ (Philadelphia: Temple University Press, 1994). See also Martha Doggett, _Death Foretold: The Jesuit Murders in El Salvador_ (Washington, D.C.: Georgetown University Press, 1993).

27. Salvador Samayoa, interview with author, San Salvador, February 27, 1995.

28. Among the excellent journalistic accounts of the offensive and its aftermath, see Mark A. Uhlig, "Lesson from San Salvador: Rebels Come and Go at Will," _New York Times_, November 24, 1989:A10.

29. For a full discussion of the negotiations process, see Ricardo Córdova Macias, _El Salvador: las negociaciones de paz y los retos de la postguerra_ (San Salvador: IDELA, 1993). See also Terry Lynn Karl, "El Salvador's Negotiated Revolution," _Foreign Affairs 71, No. 2 (1992): 147–64; William Leogrande, "After the Battle of San Salvador,"_ World Policy Journal 7, No. 2 (Spring 1990): 331–56; and George Vickers, "The Political Reality After Eleven Years of War," in Joseph S. Tulchin with Gary Bland, eds., _Is There a Transition to Democracy in El Salvador?_ (Boulder, Colo.: Lynne Rienner, 1992), 25–57.

30. General (ret.) Mauricio Vargas, interview with author, San Salvador, February 24, 1995.

31. Martínez interview.

32. Lawyers Committee for Human Rights, "The Jesuit Case a Year Later: An Interim Report," November 15, 1990, 28–29.

33. Speaker's Task Force on El Salvador, _Interim Report_, Washington, D.C., April 30, 1990; Jim McGovern and Bill Woodward, Memorandum to Honorable Joe Moakley, Chairman, Speaker's Task Force on El Salvador, Washington, D.C., October 18, 1990; Statement of Representative Joe Moakley, Chairman of the Speaker's Task Force on El Salvador, Washington, D.C., January 16, 1991; Statement of Representative Joe Moakley, Chairman of the Speaker's Task Force on El Salvador, Washington, D.C., November 18, 1991.

34. Alvaro de Soto, "The Negotiations Following the New York Agreement," in Tulchin with Bland, eds., _Is There a Transition to Democracy_ 139–40.

35. The United Nations was involved in other firsts as a result of the Central American peace process. It oversaw the Nicaraguan electoral process in 1989–1990, the first time it had overseen elections in a sovereign state and the first major U.N. operation in the Western hemisphere. The United Nations Observer Group in Central American (ONUCA), which began as a military observer force, expanded to monitor the cease-fire between the contras and the Sandinista government and to oversee the demobilization and disarmament of the contra forces. This was the first time the United Nations had received weapons from an insurgent group. See Americas Watch, "Peace and Human Rights: Successes and Shortcomings of the United Nations Observer Mission in El Salvador (ONUSAL)," New York: September 2, 1992, 5–6.

36. De Soto, "Negotiations Following the New York Agreement," 140.

37. United Nations, "General Agenda and Schedule for Comprehensive Negotiation Process Between Government of El Salvador and FMLN" (press release, CA/24, May 21, 1990).

38. See Americas Watch, "Peace and Human Rights," 7–25. See also Lawyers Committee for Human Rights, _Improving History: A Critical Evaluation of the United Nations Observer Mission in El Salvador_ (New York: Lawyers Committee for Human Rights, 1995).

39. Many of these reforms were negotiated in September 1991 in New York, following a personal invitation to the parties by Secretary-General Pérez de Cuéllar. See "Acuerdo de Nueva York," mimeograph, September 25, 1991, 1–7; and United Nations, "Secretary-General Announces 'Break in Deadlock' in El Salvador Talks," U.N. Doc SG/SM/4624, (September 25, 1991).

40. See, for example, Joseph G. Sullivan, "How Peace Came to El Salvador," _Orbis_ 38 (Win-

ter 1994): p 83–98. Sullivan served as deputy assistant secretary of state for Inter-American Affairs, 1989 to 1992.

41. Santamaría interview, Washington, D.C., March 22, 1996.

42. Martínez interview. "This was a difficult decision," she said. "We were more poor than when we began. Leaving the economic part for another moment was not easy, and created conflict with our social base."

43. Salvador Sanabria, interview with the author, Washington, D.C., November 24, 1992.

44. Martínez and Samayoa interviews.

45. For elaboration of that point, see presentation by Ricardo Córdova Macias in ASIES and Woodrow Wilson Center, *Memoria de la Conferencia Procesos de Paz Comparados* (Guatemala City: 1996), 65–89.

46. David Holiday, "Guatemala's Long Road to Peace," *Current History* 96, No. 607 (February 1997): 68–74. For accounts of the early 1980s, see: Susanne Jonas, *The Battle for Guatemala: Rebels, Death Squads, and U.S. Power* (Boulder, Colo.: Westview Press, 1991); Americas Watch, *Human Rights in Guatemala: No Neutrals Allowed* (New York: Americas Watch, 1982); and Amnesty International, *Guatemala: A Government Program of Political Murder* (London: Amnesty International, 1981).

47. See Zartman, "Ripening Conflict;" John Hamilton, U.S. Department of State, interview with author, Washington, D.C. December 23, 1996.

48. Guatemala rejected U.S. aid following U.S. criticism of its human rights record in 1977. Israel and Taiwan were among the international suppliers that stepped in. Small amounts of assistance were resumed during the Reagan administration. On the extent of U.S. training and equipment to Guatemala in the Cold War period, see Michael McClintock, *The American Connection: State Terror and Popular Resistance in Guatemala* (London: Zed Books, 1985), 76–122.

49. One must use the term "democratic transition" with extreme care with respect to Guatemala, as the parameters of civilian authority were extremely limited and repression remained a central feature of Guatemala's political landscape. See Jonas, *Battle for Guatemala*, 161–94; Robert Trudeau and Lars Schoultz, "Guatemala," in Morris Blachman, William Leogrande, and Kenneth Sharpe, eds., *Confronting Revolution* (New York: Pantheon, 1986), 23–49; and Linz and Stepan, *Problems of Democratic Transition and Consolidation*, 4.

50. For an overview of Guatemala's political opening, see Rachel McCleary, "Guatemala's Postwar Prospects," *Journal of Democracy* 8, No. 2 (April 1997) 129–43. See also presentation by Guatemalan Vice-minister of Foreign Relations Gabriel Aguilera in Woodrow Wilson Center, Fundación Friedrich Ebert de Colombia (FESCOL), and Centro de Estudios Internacionales, Universidad de los Andes, *Procesos de Paz y Negociación en Colombia* (Washington, D.C.: Woodrow Wilson Center, 1996), 16–20; and "La Negociación a las Puertas de la Paz," in FLACSO-Guatemala, *Procesos de Negociación Comparados en África y América Latina* (Guatemala City: FLACSO-Guatemala, 1994), 141–48.

51. Address by Eduardo Stein, Guatemalan Foreign Minister, Georgetown University School of Foreign Service, Washington, D.C., April 24, 1996; presentation by head of the Peace Commission (COPAZ) Gustavo Porras, in ASIES and Woodrow Wilson Center, *Memoria de la Conferencia*, 169.

A "white paper" prepared by the Guatemalan government in 1995 admitted that "elements of the Guatemalan Army engaged in human rights abuses in the course of the internal armed confrontation." It stated, however, that "these abuses were committed in the context of chronic guerrilla warfare and terrorism." Government of Guatemala, "Guatemala Today and Tomorrow" (June 5, 1995, mimeographed), 4.

52. Stein address at Georgetown University.

53. See presentation by Víctor Suárez of CEPAZ, the Peace Commission of the powerful business group CACIF, in ASIES and Woodrow Wilson Center, *Memoria de la Conferencia*, 179–87.

54. Héctor Rosada of COPAZ, interview with author, Guatemala City, February 28, 1995.

55. One might indeed question whether the URNG had a choice in this matter, as its virtual

military defeat left little alternative than to wait for political conditions in Guatemala to change to favor a negotiated settlement.

56. The Framework Accord also called for the formation of a Group of Friends (Colombia, Mexico, Norway, Spain, the United States, and Venezuela) to lend diplomatic support to the peace talks.

The augmented U.N. role reinvigorated the peace talks, resulting in the signing of four intermediate accords between March 1994 and March 1995. These were: the global accord on human rights (March 1994); the accord on the resettlement of uprooted populations (June 1994); the accord to establish a "historical clarification" commission to report on past human rights abuses (June 1994); and the accord on the rights and identities of indigenous peoples (March 1995). See Cynthia Arnson, "Negotiating Peace: A Guatemala Conference Report" (Woodrow Wilson Center, Washington, D.C., June 1996; mimeographed); presentation of former COPAZ member Ernesto Viteri in ASIES and Woodrow Wilson Center, *Memoria de la Conferencia,* 9–11; and Rachel Mc-Cleary, *Guatemala: Negotiating Peace to Foster Democracy, 1994,* (Washington, D.C.: Democracy Projects, School of International Service, American University, 1994), 21–23.

57. Officials of the Guatemalan government, United Nations, and non-governmental organizations, interviews with the author, Guatemala City, February 28–March 3, 1995; letter, United Nations Under-Secretary-General Marrack Goulding to His Excellency Mr. Ramiro de León Carpio, February 17, 1995, 1–7; speech by Jean Arnault (Woodrow Wilson Center, Washington, D.C., December 6, 1995), summarized in Latin American Program, *Noticias* (Winter 1995–96): 1–2.

58. The 1995 elections also saw the URNG-supported FDNG capture six congressional seats as well as a number of municipalities.

Part I

Case Studies and Issues

2

From Low-Intensity War to Low-Intensity Peace: The Nicaraguan Peace Process

Introduction

President Violeta Barrios de Chamorro's greatest accomplishment, according to an April 1996 Nicaraguan opinion poll, was bringing peace to her wartorn country.[1] When Chamorro was elected in 1990, Nicaraguans had lived through over a decade of war. The Frente Sandinista de Liberación Nacional (FSLN, or Sandinista)–led insurrection (1978–1979) against the regime of Anastasio Somoza, which cost 50,000 lives (roughly 2 percent of the population), was followed closely by the "contra" war against the Sandinista regime (1980–1989), which left another 31,000 dead.[2] The Chamorro government took on the formidable task of ending the war and pursuing national reconciliation. Although by 1996 the Nicaraguan population viewed the outgoing Chamorro government unfavorably in most respects, its performance in advancing the cause of peace was generally viewed as a success.

I want to thank Jack Spence, Cynthia Arnson, Craig Auchter, Alejandro Bendaña, and Cynthia McClintock for their helpful comments on an earlier version of this chapter. I also wish to thank Raúl Rosende for his assistance in organizing visits to meet with participants in several CIAV-sponsored Comisiones de Paz, and Leigh Payne and Judy Butler for their useful fieldwork suggestions.

Assessments of peace-building processes, however, involve complicated calculations; much depends on how the task of peace-building is defined. Although the Chamorro government deserves recognition for concluding the war, Nicaraguan political elites remain quite polarized, and violence erupts all too easily. One reason for the brittle character of Nicaragua's peace was the absence of a full-fledged peace process. Peace negotiations were subsumed under the processes of regime transition, which stunted the construction of a peace dialogue. Instead of attending to the complex work of building peace, both domestic and international actors rushed to an electoral transition and a paper conclusion of the war. In the Nicaraguan case, peace negotiations were all too readily equated with simple troop demobilization. A host of related issues, including the social reinsertion of demobilized troops, opening political space for these marginalized sectors of former combatants, the creation of mechanisms for local-level reconciliation, and the reconstruction of the wartorn economy, were not addressed adequately. As a result, violent conflict continued to flicker and flare in postwar Nicaragua.

Low-intensity conflicts such as the contra war can be particularly difficult to resolve. Because they are not designed to generate decisive engagements and absolute military victories, low-intensity wars can simmer for long periods, continuing to exact a toll that the participants regard as "tolerable." Unless the parties to the conflict come to reappraise the cumulative costs of the war, and unless some viable alternatives emerge, low-intensity warfare may settle in as a permanent or recurring feature in the society. Peace, if it comes, may itself be "low intensity," tipping back easily into scattered violence and confrontation. In the Nicaraguan case, "low-intensity war" has been followed by "low-intensity peace," a condition in which former combatants are not well integrated into civil society; enmities remain sharply held in a polarized and conflict-riddled society; the government is unable to carry out basic responsibilities, such as maintaining order and ensuring the physical security of the citizens; and, as a result, the regime suffers from a low level of legitimacy in the eyes of a substantial portion of the population.

In Nicaragua, the initial negotiation process led to a formal end to the contra war in 1990, but the first phase of the demobilization process collapsed quickly and combatants returned to arms in 1991. The laborious second phase of the peace process, running between 1992 and 1997, produced a fuller demobilization but left behind a pattern of conflict that continued to pose challenges to peace and democracy. Fuller consolidation of peace in Nicaragua would require an expansion of political space for organizations of former combatants; a competent and responsive government with enough capacity and resources to address major problems; a minimum consensus about national objectives shared by leaders and citizens; the growth of civic organizations that are actively engaged in the promotion of peace values; a meaningful role for international actors supporting local peace efforts; and sustained international assistance for economic reconstruction.

Moving to Negotiation: Actors and Motives

In Nicaragua, there were four main sets of actors involved in making the contra war. Two were internal—the Sandinista government and the Resistencia Nicaragüense (RN), or contras,[3]—and two were external—the U.S. government and the other Central American governments. In the late 1980s these four groups came, at different paces and to varying degrees, to accept some form of peace negotiation.

First, the heads of the Central American governments launched the Esquipulas Peace Process in 1987.[4] Fearful that local conflicts could flare into uncontainable regional war, Central American leaders began to look harder for an exit. Led by Costa Rican President Oscar Arias and building on the early initiatives of the Contadora Group,* the Esquipulas process outlined a concrete set of steps that could lead to regionwide cease-fires and eventual demobilization. By accepting the legitimacy of the Sandinista government and validating its responses to Esquipulas recommendations, the other Central American presidents created a mechanism whereby the FSLN could be admitted into the international peace dialogue. Its inclusion was a prerequisite for any advance toward peace.

The Esquipulas process, in turn, affected the U.S. government's position on the war. By setting up an international process that Reagan administration critics could endorse, the Arias plan pulled key sectors of the U.S. government away from the contra war. The divisions in the U.S. Congress over the war had led, when a shallow pool of representatives shifted positions, either to increases in or to shutoffs of military aid to the contras.[5] As the Reagan administration dipped into starkly illegal actions

---

*In January 1983, the foreign ministers of Mexico, Venezuela, Panama, and Colombia met on the island of Contadora, off the Panamanian coast, and drafted a peace proposal for Central America based on dialogue and negotiation [ed.].

leading to the Iran-contra scandal, and as its second term waned, the availability of a peaceful alternative that was locally constructed and backed by a range of Latin American allies proved attractive to swing voters in Congress. Faced with a more firmly resistant Congress and bolstered by its own view of the contra war as a political liability, the succeeding Bush administration began in 1989 advancing an electoral approach to the Nicaraguan conflict that was, at least superficially, consistent with the Esquipulas process.[6]

As external actors began to shift out of entrenched positions, so did internal forces. The Sandinista government, which had rejected negotiations with anyone except the United States (in its view, the "puppeteer"), abruptly changed tactics in 1988 and accepted the idea of direct negotiations with the contra leadership. This decision was a critical, and difficult, one for the FSLN. Military command of the core of the contra force, the Fuerza Democrática Nicaragüense (FDN), was in the hands of former National Guard officers, and Sandinista hostility to this residue of *somocismo* (the network of forces loyal to the Somoza regime) was deep and intense.[7] Furthermore, although the contra war proved very costly to the FSLN—much more costly than the Sandinistas realized at the time—it also tended to heroicize the regime domestically and abroad by accentuating the FSLN's anti-imperial character. This aspect of the war strengthened the FSLN's support base in key domestic and international sectors, making continued conflict attractive in some ways.

Nonetheless, by the late 1980s, key Sandinista leader were reappraising both the nature and the costs of this conflict. Unlike El Salvador, where military stalemate propelled opponents into negotiations, the military threat presented by the contras was modest. Although the contra army's capacity rose and fell at different points, the FDN proved incapable of seizing and holding territory or staging attacks on urban areas. Nonetheless, evidence mounted of the war's growing economic and political costs. By 1988 the conflict was increasingly perceived as having elements of a "mutually hurting stalemate," in which steady losses were suffered on both sides.[8] Unlike the Mexican case described by Neil Harvey in Chapter 5, in which government incentives to negotiate with rebels were low, or the Peruvian case where, as Cynthia McClintock notes in Chapter 8, the mass repudiation of Sendero and its "strategic defeat" made negotiation a moot point, the FSLN leaders did have forceful reasons for pursuing negotiation.

For one, the contra army continued to expand through the 1980s. FSLN mythology about the contras began to tatter as the contra army grew and evidence mounted that the military opposition was not simply a residue of Somoza-era National Guardsmen and mercenaries, as Sandinista rhetoric had suggested.[9] Vote tallies from the 1984 elections showed relatively weak support for the FSLN in many of the interior's rural areas. This electoral assessment, plus the difficulty of carrying out the military draft in these zones, led to a growing debate within the FSLN about the nature of the contra army. Some Sandinista activists and leaders became persuaded that elements of the contra force represented a genuine domestic opposition, although this perspective was a distinctly minority view prior to the Sandinistas' 1990 electoral defeat.[10] When policy adjustments in the later 1980s, such as allowing the peoples of the Atlantic Coast to return to their villages, eliminating the restrictions on intraregional marketing of basic grains, and slowing the pace of land expropriations, failed to dissipate rural opposition, part of the Sandinista leadership began to push the idea of negotiation with the Resistance.

This decision to open discussions was reinforced by calculations about the cumulative economic costs of the war, which already had topped $1.2 billion by 1985.[11] Unable to modernize production or infrastructure, or even to maintain historical levels of output, Nicaragua experienced dizzying economic decline; production in the mid-1980s hovered around levels not seen since 1960.[12] By 1987 defense spending had soared to 62 percent of the government's budget.[13] These heavy demands were covered by inorganic emissions from the central bank and triggered inflation levels that topped a staggering 33,000 percent in 1988.[14] Although it was never seriously threatened with military defeat by the contra army, the Sandinista leadership soon saw that low-intensity war would destroy the revolution's ability to develop the country and raise the population's standard of living.

In 1987–1988 FSLN leaders moved to back peace negotiations, naming longtime critic Cardinal Miguel Obando y Bravo to head the National Reconciliation Commission and unilaterally adopting a slew of Esquipulas recommendations. In part, the FSLN's acceptance of the Esquipulas process was a tactic designed to leverage Latin American opposition to the Reagan war. Unable, by itself, to have an impact on the contra aid policy of the U.S. government, the Sandinista government hoped to build "one of the broadest anti-interventionist international fronts in modern times"[15] and more effectively challenge the Reagan administration's policy. But this decision was not simply tactical; at least in part, the Sandinistas' commitment to the peace process reflected an incipient recognition of their own failed policies and a desire to mend internal fences. It did not, at that time, appear to be a process that would threaten their revolution.

The Resistencia Nicaragüense (Nicaraguan Resistance, or RN) was slower to come to the table. Of the four sets of actors involved in the conflict, the Resistance was arguably the least inclined to support a negotiated settlement. Although the contras' political leadership was less steadfast and key members defected from hardline politics,[16] the contras' core military leadership was uncompromising. The RN military chiefs wanted to wipe the revolution out. In the words of one RN leader, "We wanted to cut off Sandinism at the roots, like the Sandinistas did with Somoza."[17]

In the end, however, they were pushed to accept a cease-fire and demobilization process by their external allies. The decision in the U.S. Congress to end military support and continue only "humanitarian" assistance in early 1988 did not reduce the contras' fighting capacity immediately. The concept of humanitarian aid, after all, was elastic, and large stockpiles of supplies had been accumulated.[18] The cutoff of military aid did have an impact, however, on Resistance morale and resolve. Without clear assurances that their fight would be sustained financially by the U.S. government, important contra leaders began to lose leverage over their followers, and public infighting erupted.

The 1989 Tela Accord, in which Central American leaders agreed to deny territorial access to irregular forces and to set up internationally sponsored demobilization procedures, pulled the rug out from under contra forces that had operated freely in Honduras and Costa Rica. With the prospect of sanctuary being denied and with external military support drying up, war became much more difficult to sustain. The January 1990 internal uprising against contra military commander Enrique Bermúdez and his replacement by base-level commander Israel Galeano (Comandante "Franklin") reflected the deepening turmoil within the contra camp. In a matter of months, the contra army went from being a significant force, with substantial military and political resources, to disintegration.

The contras long claimed that their central goal was "democracy." The simplicity of this demand made it possible for the Bush administration—once it was persuaded to modify its purely military approach—to repackage the conflict in electoral terms. Lacking any coherent political organization of its own, the Resistance was encouraged by the Bush administration to build a strong rhetorical alliance with the Unión Nacional Opositora (UNO), a fourteen-party coalition designed to defeat the FSLN at the polls. Elements of the contra movement, recognizing that there was now no alternative, agreed to support the Chamorro government and present the electoral outcome as their shared victory. Once the FSLN lost soundly to UNO candidates in February 1990, the contras lost all possibilities for maintaining themselves as an opposition military force and conducting a systematic peace negotiation. Unlike the irregular forces entering negotiations with the governments of El Salvador and Guatemala with the understanding that they were dealing with an adversary, the contras entered negotiations with a government that they perceived as an alliance partner, albeit one that they did not know well.

The blurring of the boundaries between regime transition and peace negotiations, as the country moved from a revolutionary to a postrevolutionary government, created special problems for postwar Nicaragua. Peace building is not an inevitable extension of regime transition, and it should not be subsumed under an electoral process. Peace processes have a separate dynamic and need to confront a series of special problems. These processes should, for example, allow combatants to raise the issues that brought the society to war. The construction of peace requires careful attention to the development of new organizational forms and responses to a previously submerged set of demands. Opposing sides should be given the opportunity to prioritize their objectives and calculate carefully the costs of proposed concessions. A schedule for implementation of agreements should be designed and penalties for noncompliance should be agreed upon. An extended negotiation dialogue should give opposing sides the opportunity to demonstrate credibility and good-faith commitment. Careful consultation by top negotiators with the rank-and-file should strengthen the political linkages that connect former combatants to their national leaders.

In the Nicaraguan case, however, where the war simply collapsed, negotiations were defined as simple scripts for disarming and demobilization. The truncated character of this process meant that most issues separating the opposing forces were not clearly articulated or advanced. A price was to be paid for this abrupt transition. Festering resentment soon led to remobilizations and a climate of instability that endured for years.

Truncated Negotiation and the Limits to Peace (1990–1991)

By the end of July 1990, virtually all of the contra troops had demobilized and the contra war had ended. The first phase of the Nicaraguan peace process was, however, beset by three major problems: The contra army was highly fractured and could not congeal around a peace agenda; the alliance between the Chamorro government and the contra force proved illusory and ephemeral; and the international organization charged with overseeing peace negotiations lacked the political and organizational characteristics needed for the job.

The political and military leadership of the Resistance had been forged largely by the U.S. security apparatus, conspicuously including National Security Council staffer Lieutenant Colonel Oliver North and operatives from the Central Intelligence Agency. Divisions within and among sectors of the contra force were papered over with U.S. financing. As this financing became more precarious, tensions within the organization surged, exposing large fissures and rivalries. When the Bush administration decided to shift tactics in 1989 and throw its support to an electoral opposition, the contra command structure fell apart. Acute divisions within the RN sped its disintegration and made negotiations problematic. Highly fractured political identities and crisscrossing loyalties meant agreements that were satisfactory to one sector of the RN were not always tolerable to another. Any differences in the agreements or in their implementation were the source of further factionalism in this diffuse network of rebels.

In addition, the Chamorro government had little real connection to the Resistance. The contras' allies within the UNO coalition (Vice-President Virgilio Godoy; and former RN National Directorate members Alfredo César, former Sandinista Central Bank president and Southern Front leader, and Azucena Ferrey, both of whom became prominent members of the National Assembly after 1990) soon spun off into splinter-prone opposition movements, weakening whatever frail bridge the contras had to the government. Both in terms of their social class extraction (elites vs. medium-to-poor peasants) and regional base (Pacific coast vs. interior), Chamorro government officials had few links with the contra base. In the absence of effective liaisons, the government consistently regarded the Resistance as a force to be diffused rather than a constituency to be represented.

Finally, the international organizations charged with the task of overseeing the end of the war were ill-prepared to play a forceful mediation role. In part this was due to inexperience; in part it was due to politicization. The Organization of American States (OAS) was given prime responsibility for overseeing the conclusion of the Nicaraguan war. In the early 1990s this organization had little prior experience with peace negotiations and was not well equipped for this delicate task. In addition, the mandate given to it was both biased in favor of the Resistance and oriented to the short term. These features distorted the peace process and, in some ways, may even have exacerbated the tendency toward polarization.

Formally, Nicaragua's internal peace process began with the historic

March 1988 meeting between FSLN and RN political and military leaders in the Nicaraguan border town of Sapoá. This meeting, which took place only weeks after the February 1988 military aid cutoff by Congress, brought face to face some of the war's military commanders. It included a new lineup of contra representatives, among them Alfredo César and four contra officers drawn from the regional level of the contra command structure.[19] Their agreement with Humberto Ortega, brother of Sandinista President Daniel Ortega and long-term chief of the Sandinista military, produced a sixty-day cease-fire to be monitored by Cardinal Obando and OAS Secretary General João Clemente Baena Soares. A rudimentary discussion was launched at the Sapoá meeting about political reform and a demobilization process.[20]

The dialogue initiated at this meeting collapsed quickly, however, as César tried to up the ante on political reform in subsequent rounds, adding stipulations that would force the resignation of the Supreme Court, allow the contras to open offices in Managua, and permit draftees to drop out of the army.[21] This apparent agreement and then escalation of demands hinted at some of the divisions and internal maneuvering within the RN camp and at the mixed messages different contra leaders were extracting from the U.S. congressional debate.

Divisions within the contra force had been palpable throughout the war. Papered over in 1987, when the various contra armies formed a new umbrella organization and took the name Resistencia Nicaragüense, the contras had long been divided into three major groups: the northern-based, National Guard–led FDN, which was the most significant militarily; the indigenous forces under YATAMA (Yapti Tasba Masraka nanih Aslatakanka, or the Organization of the Nations of the Motherland) on the Atlantic Coast; and the ARDE (the Alianza Revolucionaria Democrática) forces operating out of Costa Rica, initially under the leadership of former Sandinista Edén Pastora. Within each of these groups there were deep divisions and long-held animosities among rival claimants to leadership. These tensions had led to a tangled web of ousters, coups, plots, and even alleged assassinations.[22]

Each of the major groups wound up negotiating a separate peace with the Chamorro government. On March 23, 1990, a month before Chamorro was inaugurated, the RN leadership, now represented by Comandante "Rubén,"[23] signed the Acuerdos de Toncontín with government representative Antonio Lacayo. This first, very general accord offered mutual recognition and government pledges to help secure resources for the RN; on the eve of Chamorro's inauguration, it was supplemented by an annex (signed on April 18) in which disarmament by June 10 was scheduled in return for government pledges to remove the Nicaraguan military from designated security zones. A separate accord was signed at the same time with YATAMA forces. The third and last accord, signed with the RN Southern Front, was not completed until May 18, almost a month after Chamorro became president.

Disgruntled over Chamorro's decision to retain Sandinista leader Humberto Ortega as army chief (following his hasty resignation from the FSLN) and the vagueness of the government's commitments to assistance, many contra troops failed to disarm as scheduled. At the end of May 1990 a second round of accords was produced, this one containing more extensive pledges of resources.[24] The government promised to construct a series of twenty-three development poles in which demobilized contra forces would receive land, housing, credit, and a full range of social services. Contra troops would be integrated into municipal governments and a new local police force that would patrol the development poles. Confiscated properties of demobilized contras would be returned, and war victims would receive pensions and indemnizations. Representatives of demobilized Resistance fighters would be named to key ministries, including Health, Agrarian Reform, and Labor. A new government agency, the Instituto Nicaragüense de Repatriación, was set up to oversee these accords. Responding to this clearer material commitment from the government, Resistance leaders pledged to demobilize one hundred troops a day per zone.[25]

International agencies set up in 1989 by the United Nations and the OAS as part of the Esquipulas process were charged with overseeing this demobilization and disarmament. Responsibilities of ONUCA—the U.N. Observer Group in Central America—centered on halting border-crossing violations and demobilizing the handful of troops who remained in Honduras after the massive August to October 1989 exodus; the OAS wing of the Comisión Internacional de Apoyo y Verificación (CIAV) was given responsibility for disarmament in Nicaragua and oversight of the reinsertion of former contras back into society. A total of 22,413 troops were reportedly demobilized by CIAV-OAS between May and July 1990.[26]

The government's extensive commitments to the contras went largely unfulfilled. Meant to pacify potentially unruly and disruptive sectors, these pledges would have required a massive infusion of resources. These resources were obviously not available; the government was already contracting many of its activities in its effort to reduce the fiscal deficit. Evidence from a government study, the "Documento de Evaluación de los

Acuerdos RN-GOB," indicated that one year after the second round of accords (June 16, 1991) the government had not implemented these agreements fully in any area.[27] Only 53 percent of the demobilized contras were found to have obtained access to land; those who did get land grants had received only certificates ("constancias"), not full title, and were ineligible for bank credit. One-third of the contra troops claimed to have had resources expropriated by the Sandinista government; these resources were returned to fewer than one-third of this group. Functionaries at government ministries in charge of providing social services were found to be unaware of the commitments made in the accords. Their compliance, inevitably, was low.

Perhaps the agreements made to end the war would have been more realistic, and compliance would have been better, if there had been more effective international oversight of the process. We know, from cases such as El Salvador, where a peace process unfolded more smoothly, that forceful and relatively neutral international mediation can play a constructive role in forging sucessful negotiations. Tasks that international organizations may take on include:

- Pressuring opponents to incorporate the main issues triggering the conflict into the agenda for discussion. This reduces the chance that agreements fail to address the controversies that are central to the conflict and that agreements end almost immediately in a renewal of hostilities.
- Pushing adversaries to make commitments that are reasonably consistent with actual possibilities, to devise a planning process, to set up a schedule for implementation, and to prioritize activities.
- Encouraging signatories to the agreement to consult broadly with those they represent in order to secure generalized acceptance of and cooperation with the accords. Leaders of ex-combatants should be pushed to inform their followers about the proposed accords and invite them for consultations; the government should be pressured to inform affected government agencies about its commitments and to coordinate their compliance.
- Verifying the level of implementation of the accords, and connecting implementation with the mobilization of international financial and material resources to support economic recovery.

By carefully calibrating moments of closed discussion and public disclosure, and by linking the flow of international support to the successful implementation of accords, international mediators can play a supporting role in a peace process that conflicting local actors find difficult to replicate.

In Nicaragua, however, the international programs involved in the early peacemaking process were rudimentary and, at least in the case of CIAV-OAS, not designed to be politically neutral. The work of the United Nations was concluded quickly and its operations closed down in 1991, long before peace was consolidated; the OAS, overseeing contra reinsertion, maintained its CIAV program through multiple extensions but, for the first few years, under a strictly partisan mandate. Designed initially when the Sandinistas were still in power, CIAV gave special attention to protecting the contras from retaliation and abuse; even after the FSLN defeat, the CIAV mandate continued for several years to focus on human rights abuses directed against the former Resistance forces to the exclusion of other groups. Funded almost entirely by U.S. contributions, CIAV was sometimes perceived at home and abroad as an extension of U.S. contra aid policy.[28]

CIAV called attention to Sandinista security violations and problems of military impunity, issues that were important elements of the conflict in Nicaragua. It was energetic and inventive in positioning itself as a highly visible, engaged operation, and repeatedly stepped in during moments of crisis.[29] But it also exacerbated conflicts at times by failing to provide neutral mediation between adversaries, and in its early years it did little to promote the development of local institutions for conflict resolution. Gradually recognizing the limitations of its contribution, in its later years, the mission did come to push for greater neutrality and, as a participant in the Tripartite Commission formed in 1992, to investigate human rights abuses suffered by Sandinista activists. After 1994 CIAV also began to develop a network of local-level peace commissions that could step in to address community conflicts. But its initial role during the crucial transition period was less constructive. Problems of this sort have led some analysts to argue that regional organizations such as the OAS may not be not the appropriate international vehicles for peace-building processes.[30]

The Nicaraguan case, coming first in a series of Latin American peace settlements, suggests some of the limitations of a home-grown peace process loosely overseen by a regional organization saddled with a partisan agenda. In subsequent Central American peace processes, the United Nations was given primary responsibility for international mediation. For example, the U.N. role in El Salvador and Guatemala involved designing a broader agenda and verification process. In El Salvador the United Nations helped the parties to the conflict to bring all the major issues to the table, including discussion of the military's mission, reconfiguration of the police force, the creation of a Truth Commission, and access to land for demobilized fighters; it also supported the careful calibration and scheduling of the accords.[31] The Salvadoran peace process is widely regarded as a more successful experience than the Nicaraguan, in large part because military violence did not flare again in Salvador in the postwar era.[32]

Mobilization Redux

Under the best of circumstances, peace would have been slow to develop in Nicaragua. The country's depressed economy and persistent ideological polarization complicated the reinsertion and reconstruction processes that mark the real passing of war. The character of the negotiations, however, made peace even more elusive. Within weeks after the accords were signed, rebels concentrated in the pre-designated development poles began to drift away and return to their places of origin. There they found themselves without land, resources, or training. As this self-styled reinsertion process failed, thousands began to reorganize in military formation. By 1991 a significant part of the contra army had remobilized.

Warning signs appeared early. Foot-dragging over actual demobilization suggested the contra troops' lack of confidence in the process; feuds and threats of expulsions between top leaders revealed suspicions about co-optation and betrayal. Conflicts erupted quickly between the RN's most prominent military commanders, "Rubén" and "Franklin," over leadership selection when the Asociación Cívica de la Resistencia Nicaragüense (ACRN) was formed in July 1990.[33] Charges by ACRN President "Rubén" that "Franklin" had sold out to the government indicated the deepening complexity in the contras' relationship with the Chamorro administration. Conflicts over the removal of a Frente Sur leader as police chief of Yolaina in the Nueva Guinea development pole escalated into a major crisis in November 1990; ex-Resistance fighters joined forces with UNO mayors and Vice President Virgilio Godoy to challenge the Chamorro government's policy of reconciliation/collaboration with the FSLN.[34] Encouraged by hardline allies, contra troops returned to arms.

By 1992 official estimates were that 22,835 irregular troops had remobilized.[35] Not all of these rearmed troops were former contras (the "recontras"); roughly one-third were "recompas" ("recompañeros"), or discharged soldiers and officers from the Sandinista army, police, or security agents.[36] Just as several thousand former contras decided to rearm and return to military struggle, so too did several thousand discharged soldiers and military officers.

These figures may overstate the severity of the military threat by including some people who were only marginally involved and others who saw remobilization more as a political statement than as a military one. Statistics on the size and capacity of irregular armies must be assessed with some caution. It is clear, however, that in the Nicaraguan case, there was a major crash in the peace process.

The process of constructing peace became in some ways even more complex as a host of decentralized paramilitary forces sprang up to challenge the state. As Nicaraguan sociologist Orlando Núñez suggests, ". . . the society passed from being a polarized society to being a society that was conflictively divided, parcelized and anarchized."[37] Within both the recontra and recompa forces, no one process gave rise to remobilization, and these bands were not united by a clear set of goals.

A United Nations Development Program–financed study of the Nicaraguan peace process identified three basic types of rearmed groups: those acting for highly political and ideological reasons; those using remobilization as a tool to press for government compliance with past agreements; and those that sank into banditry and criminality.[38] The first group contained recontra leaders who were militantly opposed to the Sandinistas and closely aligned with anti-Sandinista politicians of the dissident UNO line. For them the key issues were the continued power of the FSLN in postrevolutionary Nicaragua, particularly in the Ejército Popular Sandinista (EPS), and the Chamorro government's negotiations with the FSLN. Much of the discourse of more visible and better-publicized recontra leaders centered on these themes.

The second group of recontras focused more on the government's failure to deliver the material resources pledged in the disarmament accords; for them, remobilization was a tool to press for fuller compliance. Nicaragua had developed a strong tendency toward "shove politics," characterized by stark confrontation and brinkmanship. There was a widespread belief that political leaders responded only to those who employed the greatest force. The battle for state resources became harsher as those resources shrank.[39] Under these circumstances, demobilized troops concluded that they must take drastic measures to force state representatives to attend to their needs, for conventional appeals and legal claims would have no impact.

A third group was unable to adjust to the constraints of civilian life and turned instead to criminal activities. Describing the contras' reinsertion and remobilization problems, a former FDN head of intelligence suggested several relevant themes. "We could not," he noted, "exercise any selection over those who volunteered. We took those who came, the good and the bad."[40] Without screening and selection processes, contra forces contained a series of uncontrolled elements who resisted the confines of a legal order and functioned as a law unto themselves. Once released from formal service, they continued to use terror to dominate the population. In areas where recontras operated, it was common to hear people identify specific recontra chiefs as "sick from the war," referring to psychological damage that made them hunger after violence and seek authority based on terror.[41]

Full explanation of the recontra phenomenon requires discussion of at least two other elements: fierce antistate sentiments that have prevailed historically in parts of the Nicaraguan interior and the generalized economic collapse of the country. It is not coincidental that several prominent contra and recontra leaders hailed from the area surrounding Quilalí.[42] This area, also the main military base for Augusto César Sandino's troops who fought the U.S. Marines in the 1930s and a fertile area of FSLN recruitment in the 1970s, had a long tradition of bristling localism, familism, and hostility to the state.[43] Its distinctive culture of rebellion has produced generations of fighters who have challenged the often weak arm of the central government. In his effort to explain the regional patterns of peasant participation in guerrilla struggles in Latin America from the 1950s to the 1980s, sociologist Timothy Wickham-Crowley notes the existence of several rebel-prone zones in countries where guerrilla struggles occurred, such as the Oriente Province in Cuba, Falcón State in Venezuela, and Tolima and Santander in Colombia.[44] The Quilalí region and several parts of the rugged mountainous terrain in central Nicaragua fit with this general pattern of localized rebelliousness. For these regions, state efforts to impose order may lead only to the spread of resistance and a deepening of antistate conflict.

Finally, the special problems of the ex-combatants soon blended with the problem of generalized economic distress to fuel the remobilization process. Unemployment, the virtual elimination of credit for small and medium-size agricultural producers, and malnutrition plagued the whole country, especially the rural areas.[45] Under these circumstances, many ex-combatants were unable to attend to their most basic needs. Over two-thirds (67 percent) of the demobilized Resistance troops claimed, in a 1990 CIAV-OAS demobilization census, to be landless. Their educational levels were abysmally low, even by Nicaraguan standards; 84 percent of this population had completed only one to three grades of school.[46] Neoliberal transition offered this group little possibility of economic reinsertion.

Postwar malaise reinforced the identities that contra troops had assumed during the war. With few opportunities to return to the workforce or rejoin a vibrant civil society, many of these troops were unable to move on to a postwar phase of life. Some turned to military confrontation to squeeze resources out of the state; others turned to banditry to squeeze resources out of the local population, particularly those who were more prosperous or were political adversaries. As Angel Saldomando, a scholar of Nicaragua's postwar period concludes, ". . . pacification is a medium-term process linked increasingly to the fortunes of the countryside and the ability to manage structural tensions that characterize the general context of the nation."[47] It is difficult to address the problem of remobilization in Nicaragua without addressing the general problems of poverty and despair.

In some ways the forces behind the recompa phenomenon were similar. The rapid contraction of the formal military, which began even before the 1990 election, displaced 71,500 troops between 1989 and the end of 1993.[48] For draftees, who were the first to go, the release from conscription was often a source of jubilation. For an estimated 20,000 professional soldiers and 10,760 officers, however, the dismissals that took place between 1990 and 1992 were traumatic.[49] As Sergio Ortega, president of the Association of Retired Military Personnel (AMIR), describes it, "We were thrown in the street by the military commanders, abandoned by our party, and forced to confront the government's neoliberal economic policy all at once."[50] This free fall in their political and economic status and generalized sense of abandonment propelled thousands of ex-military into the streets.

Just as recontras employed a series of tactics pursuing a range of priorities, so the recompas varied in their approaches. Some viewed the government as an ideological foe; others, as a bank vault to be sprung. Some, such as the Fuerzas Punitivas de la Izquierda (Punitive Forces of the Left) turned to assassination and targeted opponents, including Arges Sequeira, president of the Association of Confiscated Propertyholders, for execution. Others used conventional forms of political pressure that sporadically tipped into violence.[51]

The problem of rearmed forces, both recontras and recompas, was deepened by the widespread availability of weapons in postwar Nicaragua. According to Saldomando, between the weapons delivered to the contras and the weapons dispersed among Sandinista supporters after the electoral defeat, an estimated 300,000 arms were held in the country at the time of Chamorro's inauguration. Roughly one-third were turned in during the 1990 disarmament process, leaving two-thirds still in private hands or in arms caches scattered in the countryside.[52] Remobilization was an all-too-simple procedure. Returning to arms offered Nicaragua's rural poor one of the few means of influence available to ordinary citizens. For a displaced population with few skills, little formal education, and no established social role, remobilization provided a host of social goods, including a sense of identity, comaraderie, and social projection, in addition to concrete resources such as political leverage, access to land and money, and international visibility. With few alternatives and with so much to gain, thousands of demobilized troops returned to arms.

Peace Redux (1992–1996)

The Chamorro government used three tactics to try again to restore order: periodic general amnesties, weapons-buying campaigns, and new accords with specific groups. General amnesties were offered three times between 1990 and 1993, in spite of disgruntlement by human rights organizations complaining about problems of impunity. A total of forty-one new accords were signed with rearmed groups in the one-year period between October 1991 and October 1992.[53] This frenzy of peacemaking activity reflected the sharp fragmentation of the remobilized groups and the government's penchant for a divide-and-rule strategy. The results were painfully slow and flawed.

The government promoted the arms-buying programs as an efficient way to sop up the weapons that were so readily available in the Nicaraguan countryside. Premiums offered by the government proved somewhat attractive; in 1992–1993 the Special Disarmament Brigades reportedly collected 46,325 arms plus thousands of explosives, grenades, and projectiles.[54] Either through an arms-buying transaction or as part of a formal accord signed with a specific band of rearmed troops, by the end of 1993 the government reportedly acquired perhaps a quarter of the arms that remained in circulation after the 1990 demobilization process.[55]

In addition to disarmament provisions, new accords specified a wide range of resources that the government offered in exchange for a second demobilization. In some cases the agreements offered more land or legal titles for resettled troops; in others the commitment was to payments of cash and vehicles for contra leaders.[56] In a completely ad hoc and uneven fashion, out of sight from the media or legislative authorities, the government made widely varying arrangements with a range of contra bands.

There was strong debate in Nicaragua about whether these accords contributed to pacification or actually accelerated remobilization, and policy on this issue shifted back and forth in the period from 1993 to 1996. Supporters of the new concessions argued that these postwar accords provided the only means to ensure the permanent reinsertion of combatants into civilian life or to force the government to comply with its commitments. Critics, on the other hand, alleged that this policy actually made weapons ownership even more attractive and contributed to the wide dispersal of arms. Some rearmed troops reportedly went through repeated demobilizations, securing hefty payments for their chiefs and a steady income for themselves in 1992–1993. Faced with increased criticism and a tighter budget, the government began adjusting its tactics in 1993. Instead of negotiations, it moved to deny the legitimacy of the remaining forces and began responding militarily.

Between the buyoffs and increased military pressure, the size of the paramilitary forces did decline. From a peak of 22,835 in 1992, official estimates of the number of irregular troops participating in armed actions fell to 960 in 1993. Following the final negotiation with recontra leader "Chacal" (the Jackal) in 1994,[57] the number of rearmed troops declined further, dropping to 300 to 600 in mid-1996.[58] But while the numbers were down from their 1992 peak, these irregular forces had not fully dissolved seven years after the "end" of the war. In pockets of the Nicaraguan interior, locally based recontra forces continued to move about fairly easily. The 1996 ambush of leading presidential candidate Arnoldo Alemán by recontra chief "El Lobo," and the June 1996 kidnappings of scores of electoral officials by bands under "Pajarillo" and "El Licenciado," suggested the dangers that these groups still posed to the public order.

The overall impact of renewed mobilization on peace building was mixed. These actions succeeded in getting more ex-contra troops added into the police force and Special Disarmament Brigades in areas where recontras operated. They pushed an anemic government with a different agenda to increase resources for this economically disenfranchised population. They also may have played a role in the Chamorro government's 1994 decision to remove military chief Humberto Ortega from his position and push through the new Military Code (Código Militar de Organización, Jurisdicción y Previsión Social Militar), which placed the military under firmer civilian control. But these mobilizations prolonged instability and turmoil in the Nicaraguan interior, and they upped the ante in the country's "shove-politics" game. Just as violence in Colombia became socially entrenched and fed recurring guerrilla wars for thirty years, so the contra war left a lingering legacy of rebellion and lawlessness that threatens to become an endemic feature in parts of the Nicaraguan countryside.

Alternatives to Violence: Constructing Peace and Democracy in Postrevolutionary Nicaragua

A peace process must not only end war; it must construct alternatives to violence. In order to move from low-intensity peace, in which encrusted conflicts resist resolution and political violence flickers on, to a well-consolidated peace, in which problems are addressed using consensual methods and violence ends, a peace process would need to introduce a series of changes into the society. Four areas of change are particularly important in the Nicaraguan case. These changes should be seen as intermediate steps that focus specifically on the problem of peace building, not as a full list of measures needed to resolve the economic and political problems that confront the nation.

First, the peace process should encourage ex-combatants to organize effectively. If the demobilized populations can advance their demands through a democratic process, their need to use force will diminish. Second, peace negotiations should push the government to develop its institutional capacity and moral commitment to respond to the damage left behind by war. Third, a peace process should call on the citizenry to embrace peace as a pivotal norm and to cultivate the skills that serve it. This goal suggests the importance of developing a new sector of civil society that focuses its energies on conflict mediation and transformation. Finally, peace processes should help identify ways in which the international community can contribute constructively to the consolidation of peace through the coordination of technical and material resources and effective support for the implementation of agreements.

Political Space for Ex-Combatants

The construction of adequate political space for former combatants has been complicated in Nicaragua. In spite of the large numbers of people involved in the contra demobilization and repatriation effort[59] and the general political openness of the society, the contras' civic organizations never flourished. Unlike better-organized and more politically sophisticated guerrilla armies in, for example, El Salvador, that gave more attention to political and ideological development, the RN came out of the war with little programmatic coherence or organizational capacity. The contra army had developed in the 1980s in several waves responding to shifts in government policy and a wide range of social, ethnic, and subregional concerns. Access to U.S. funds and logistical support drew many types of groups into the fray. In its attempt to demonstrate widespread opposition to the Sandinista government, the United States imposed little ideological unity or political cohesion on the contra army. The RN ended the war with a large but motley base that was afflicted by internal tensions and leadership competition.

Several second-tier contra leaders did belatedly establish a political party, the Partido de la Resistencia Nicaragüense (PRN), in 1993, but this was well after the contra force had fragmented and declined. The 1996 takeover of the PRN nominating convention by a group of outsiders, and the party's weak performance in the 1996 election,[60] highlighted the institutional weaknesses of this organization.

Without a clear agenda of its own, the contra force easily scattered into other movements. Three top ex-Resistance leaders, "Rubén," Boanerges Matus, and "Franklin," for example, accepted second-level positions in the Chamoro government (in the Repatriation Institute, the Ministry of Agrarian Reform, and the Ministry of the Interior, respectively) early in 1991.[61] Most contra fighters, however, threw their weight to harder-line forces. In a highly decentralized fashion, former contras added amply to Arnoldo Alemán's 1996 margin of victory in the country's interior. Tagging along, however, without extracting clear guarantees or concessions from their erstwhile allies, contra activists found it difficult to push any particular agenda very forcefully. A sector of the contra force even aligned with the FSLN in the final weeks of the 1996 electoral campaign, lured by the promise of three cabinet-level positions and a sympathetic ear.[62] Weakly organized and under leaders who were quick to cut deals, by 1993 the contra force had lost much of its capacity to project itself politically.

Analysis of RN organizational dynamics suggests a counterintuitive conclusion: Peace may be better promoted by strengthening organizations of demobilized soldiers than by speeding along their dissolution. Although it might seem preferable that former combatants flow quickly out of associations constructed during wartime and into civilian components of civil society, the rapid disintegration of military-era organizations actually may flood the society with unorganized, alienated forces that move quickly to violence or angry disengagement. To advance toward postwar democracy, former combatants on both sides need to be able to construct coherent and effective organizations that can negotiate on their behalf and hold leaders accountable for their commitments. Ironically, the cause of peace may be better served when steps are taken to bolster the organization and performance of associations forged by war.

Adequate State Capacity

The ability of civil society, including organizations of ex-combatants, to negotiate effectively on behalf of citizens presumes, of course, that the government will be reasonably receptive to popular pressures and capable of implementing programs in response to these demands. The weakness of the state in postwar Nicaragua placed these issues into question. Nicaragua's overwhelming foreign debt ($11 billion in 1994 in a $1.8 billion economy)[63] gave international financial institutions enormous influence over economic policy and the national budget; some critics accused the Chamorro government of simply following the dictates of the International Monetary Fund.[64] Civilian leaders also faced the challenge of exercising control over a bureaucratic apparatus characterized by weak institutional coherence and inadequate resources. Particularly challenging for postwar governments is the task of controlling the military[65] and constructing a functioning justice system.

There is ample evidence to suggest that the postwar Nicaraguan government had difficulty maintaining basic functions. This is seen not only in the political impasses that frequently characterized executive-legislative relations and led repeatedly to governmental paralysis[66] but also in the day-to-day functioning of key government operations.

From the standpoint of peace building, the weakness of the criminal justice system is particularly noteworthy. There is some reason to think that the contra war was less terminated than transformed and that the era of military conflict fed the rise of more routine violence and crime. Although the political violence of war and the social violence of crime are analytically distinct concepts, in postwar contexts the connections between them may be quite strong. Certainly the crime rate in Nicaragua rose precipitously in the postwar period. According to Fernando Caldera, director of the National Police, the number of violent crimes reported to the police in 1990 was 8,056; this soared to 18,037 for 1995, an increase of 112 percent.[67] In an April 1996 CID-Gallup poll, almost one-fifth of the respondents (19 percent) stated that they or someone in their household had been the victim of a robbery or assault in the previous four months.[68] The widespread availability of arms, the intense preparation for their use, the difficulties of reinsertion into civilian life, and the lingering problems of polarization and frustration all primed society for increased violence.

At the same time, the government's stringent belt-tightening meant that few resources were available for the already overburdened police force. In 1996 police chief Caldera reported that there were only sixteen police officers for every 10,000 inhabitants in Nicaragua.[69] Those few who remained in the police force were badly equipped for the job. The scarcity of resources for an overburdened police force plus the general weakness of the court system meant that arrests were low and convictions were rare. This gap between victimization and conviction fostered vigilante actions and a privatization of the justice system, particularly in the interior parts of the country where state penetration was weak. The result was a spiral of violence that the state had difficulty controlling and that threatened the country's already fragile peace.

Culture of Peace

The development of effective and coherent political processes through which to rechannel the conflicts of war is obviously an important first step in moving toward peace. But it is not enough. To consolidate a peace process, the nonviolent settlement of disputes and use of political means to seek change must be broadly accepted. Strong social norms against the use of violence must be pervasive, and significant social organizations must push a peace agenda. New forms of conflict mediation are needed in order to build a "culture of peace."[70]

Developing this set of norms is challenging, especially in a context of lingering polarization and resentment. Hard tensions remain in Nicaragua. In addition to the 40,000 people receiving government pensions for war disabilities and losses in 1990[71] (and thousands in the Resistance who were not insured), CIAV-OEA estimates that 650,000 Nicaraguans (over 15 percent of the population) were demobilized, repatriated, or internally displaced.[72] Bitterness over war losses and dislocations dissipated after 1990, but it did not disappear. Tolerance for antithetical views and respect for opponents are difficult to achieve under these circumstances, especially for those who have occupied opposing ends of the political spectrum.

A host of organizations and programs in Nicaragua emerged in the postwar period to promote the development and broad dissemination of conflict mediation skills. These programs come out of a range of political movements and were based on different principles. In general, however, sponsoring organizations are exploring ways both to encourage civic expression and to disseminate information about the principles of cooperation.

The Consejo de Iglesias Evangélicas Pro-Alianza Denominacional (CEPAD, formerly the Comité Evangélico Pro Ayuda al Desarrollo),[73] the Centro de Estudios Internacionales (CEI),[74] and CIAV-OEA[75] all have been actively building local mediation capacity.[76] Working with small groups in conflict-ridden communities, these organizations focus on bolstering civil society in order to fill the gaps created by a missing or rejected state. They train mediators in techniques to promote dialogue and reinforce their peace work in parts of the country where conflict remains high and government intervention fails.

The problems these organizations face are substantial. For example, although all of these groups have become more inclusive over time, generalized perceptions about their partisan origins sometimes have made it difficult for foes and competitors to ascribe legitimacy to their actions or perceive them as bona fide conciliators. With limited ability to call opponents to dialogue or enforce the agreements that they broker, these organizations offer a weak substitute for a functioning justice system. Questions also may be raised about how much the funding priorities of their international donors determine the activities of these groups and whether their programs will survive when funders withdraw.

Nonetheless, the development of these programs is a positive sign, as group after group begins to put together activities that include participants from diverse positions on the political spectrum. In hundreds of communities in which tensions have been high and the state has proved unable to remove the threat of violence, these civil organizations have been actively supporting a social climate that impedes a return to violence and promotes the use of political methods for seeking change.[77] This initiative should be strengthened through the construction of a cooperative network among these organizations and their strategic cosponsorship of local conciliation projects. In the end, these organizations will need to cooperate not just with each other but also with the government to promote a stronger justice system and improved social services.

International Support

The promotion of peace in a context of scarcity and misery is particularly difficult. The Nicaraguan case suggests the importance of a coordinated effort on the part of mediators and donors to attend to the legacy of war and support economic recovery.

The call for greater international involvement in a peace process is, of course, subject to challenge. International actors, particularly the United States, were critical forces in supporting the war. International mediators such as CIAV-OAS, at least initially, played at best a mixed role in peace-building work. Pressure from international financial institutions such as the International Monetary Fund to cut the fiscal deficit may have reduced state capacity to respond to the economic dislocations produced by war. Given this actual experience with international actors, there are reasons to argue against extensive external participation in the construction of a peace process.[78]

Nonetheless, the international community can play an important role in supporting the consolidation of a peace process, particularly in cases like Nicaragua, where peace arrived in the wake of profound economic devastation. Unlike Colombia, El Salvador, and Guatemala, where the economy continued to grow even as war was waged, the Nicaraguan economy had been devastated by the war. The combination of the insurrection against Somoza and the contra war had reduced Nicaraguan economic activity to levels not seen for decades. The neoliberal restructuring undertaken by the Chamorro administration came with its own set of costs as Nicaragua suddenly was pushed to compete with its much better prepared Central American neighbors. Low levels of growth and high levels of unemployment in the early 1990s prevented the successful economic reinsertion of tens of thousands of demobilized troops. This set the stage for remobilizations and political unrest born of social and economic frustration.

When war produces major economic damage, as in the Nicaraguan case, the construction of a durable peace requires a concerted effort to rebuild the nation's infrastructure and restart production. Nicaragua provides a powerful lesson about the problems that develop when peace negotiators and international financial institutions do not cooperate in their efforts to support peace and democracy in wartorn countries. Most postwar societies can, of course, reasonably claim to need financial support for reconstruction. Because of the severity of Nicaragua's economic problems, however, peace building there requires much more in the way of international financial support, targeted specifically toward economic recovery, than is required in the other cases. Moreover, distribution of this aid should be conditioned on the government's performance in building postwar peace. Special attention should be given to the construction of a functioning justice system and the equitable extension of government services throughout the country. The stabilization and adjustment agendas favored by the international financial institutions should be tempered with a commitment to economic recovery and the incorporation of marginal sectors into the development process.[79] These approaches to international aid serve the cause of lasting peace.

Conclusions

A number of developments in the 1990s suggest that the Nicaraguan peace process has progressed substantially. First, the end of the Cold War defused the Nicaraguan conflict by removing external assistance to warring parties. Although the United States has continued to play an active role in Nicaraguan politics, particularly on issues of property disputes and the military, it generally has accepted the legitimacy of all the key actors in Nicaragua, including the FSLN. This stance has helped to shift conflict into political channels and to promote peace.

Second, new regional norms have developed that militate against renewed violence. Not only are other Central American nations unlikely to harbor insurgents actively attacking a neighboring country, but now they are working cooperatively on economic, political, and even military projects.[80]

Third, people in Nicaragua are weary of war. On both sides of the spectrum, there is a strong realization that war, revolution, and coups no longer represent viable strategies for social change. The climate in Nicaragua, even in the turbulent interior, now runs against physical confrontation and destruction of infrastructure as methods for promoting change. This perspective is more fully developed in the southern part of the interior than the northern for a series of complex reasons, but it is deepening in both.[81]

Fourth, major progress has been made in demobilizing combatants. Recontra forces now number only a few hundred, and some are linked only superficially to the former contra armies. Increasingly their members are teenagers with no prior military experience whose activities are more criminal than political. Although Nicaragua has moved toward peace on an unsteady course, there is a tremendous difference between the level of military conflict in 1990 and that of 1997.

Fifth, the level of ideological rancor and polarization in the society has generally diminished. Although the heat of the 1996 electoral campaign raised these tensions once again, many former foes recognize that they must find a way to work together. There is some reason to believe that the polarization of the political elite may be more acute than that which prevails in the general society.[82]

Finally, one of the most fertile areas for organization in Nicaragua in recent years has been in peace work. Growing networks of peace activists are emerging, forming teams to mediate conflicts and propose alternatives, not simply to denounce abuses. This new emphasis on local level activism helps to resolve conflicts before they escalate into violent confrontations and to decelerate them once they have.

At the same time, the peace process has faced a series of special challenges in Nicaragua. Peace negotiation in this case was defined essentially as a demobilization process without careful discussion of the issues that divided the society. Peace accords were drafted within a matter of weeks after the Sandinistas' electoral defeat. Neither side had time to prepare for a new era or build toward serious dialogue. Both Sandinistas and contras entered peacetime with deep suspicions about their adversaries and little real commitment to living side by side. Pushed quickly to "reconcile," without a chance to air their grievances, clarify abuses, and call to account, combatants on both sides were hostile and unreceptive. Without the support of an international mission capable of helping all sides define a meaningful agenda and supporting compliance, Nicaragua tipped quickly back into demiwar.

Nicaragua's political institutions are neither strong nor democratic enough to handle these postwar problems easily. Elected officials still are pushing for more effective oversight of the military; the branches of government still are struggling over a power-sharing formula; the police and court system function only minimally and lack national reach; and the general level of approval of the political system is quite low.[83] The October 1996 election of Arnoldo Alemán did little to resolve these problems. Although Alemán received 51 percent of the vote and won the presidency on the first round of balloting, and turnout has been estimated at a strong 86 percent of eligible voters, the electorate was still highly divided and social consensus on basic issues remained elusive.[84] Alemán's proposal for further contraction of the state sector, while perhaps inevitable given the financial forces at play, is unlikely to address the major sources of division in Nicaragua. Low-intensity peace is likely to endure but not deepen.

It will not be easy for Nicaraguan democracy to consolidate under these circumstances, in part because of the strong polarization of visions that prevails in the society. Nicaraguans still have not forged a basic consensus about the social and economic rules under which they wish to be governed.[85] Without agreement on fundamental questions about how the state should function, sharp conflicts and tensions are likely to persist. To address these issues, the political leadership will need to construct a minimum national consensus about the social and economic framework of the country. Further strengthening of both civil society and government institutions, so that citizens can demand effectively and the government can respond, are prerequisites for the construction of an enduring peace in Nicaragua.

Notes

1. Thirty-three percent of respondents identified this as the Chamorro government's main achievement; another 31 percent chose a related item, the ending of the draft. See Borge y Asociados, *Encuesta de Opinión Pública: Frecuencias Simples,* April 1996, n.p.

2. Thomas W. Walker, "Introduction," in Thomas W. Walker, ed., *Revolution and Counterrevolution in Nicaragua* (Boulder, Colo.: Westview Press, 1991), 8; Peter Kornbluh, "The U.S. Role in the Counterrevolution," in ibid., 344.

3. Because the names of the military forces opposed to the FSLN government changed frequently in the 1980s following periodic divisions and reshufflings, I use the term "contras" here as a generic reference to all those groups that used military means to challenge the Sandinistas. "Resistencia Nicaragüense" (Nicaraguan Resistance) refers to the formal organization that most contra troops, to a greater or lesser extent, were affiliated with at the time of the 1990 election.

4. See Jack Child, *The Central American Peace Process, 1983–1991: Sheathing Swords, Building Confidence* (Boulder, Colo.: Lynne Rienner Publishers, 1992).

5. Kornbluh identifies sixty undecided "moderates" in the House of Representatives who held the balance in the final military cutoff vote in February 1988. The margin of victory in that decision was eight votes. Kornbluh, "U.S. Role in the Counterrevolution," 382. See also Cynthia Arnson, *Crossroads: Congress, the President, and Central America, 1976–1983* (University Park, Pa: Pennsylvania State University Press, 1993), and Cynthia Arnson and Philip Brenner, "The Limits of Lobbying: Interest Groups, Congress, and Aid to the Contras," in Richard Sobel, ed., *Public Opinion in U.S. Foreign Policy: The Controversy over Contra Aid* (Lanham, Md.: Rowman and Littlefield, 1993).

6. According to Wiarda, James Baker, President Reagan's Secretary of the Treasury and White House chief of staff who later became George Bush's campaign manager and then Secretary of State, determined that the Central America conflict represented a high-cost, no-win situation and that a Bush administration would need to extract itself from the region in order to focus on higher priorities. See Howard J. Wiarda, "From Reagan to Bush: Continuity and Change in U.S. Latin American Policy," in John D. Martz, *United States Policy in Latin America* (Lincoln: University of Nebraska Press, 1995), 32–37.

7. Although there were changes over time and some obfuscation on this point, Brody found that forty-six of the forty-eight officers in the FDN Command Structure in 1985 were former National Guard officers. See Reed Brody, *Contra Terror in Nicaragua* (Boston: South End Press, 1985), 136. This military apparatus was led by Enrique Bermúdez, an ex–National Guard colonel and the Somoza government's defense attache in Washington at the time of its overthrow. In its response to these allegations, the U.S. State Department contended that only 27 percent of senior FDN military personnel were former members of the National Guard. See U.S. Department of State, "Documents on the Nicaraguan Resistance: Leaders, Military Personnel, and Program," *Special Report,* No. 142 (March 1986): 11–12. This response reduced the percentage by including FDN officers involved in support services like medical care in the pool. But even this report acknowledged that six of the seven members of the FDN Strategic Command were former National Guard officers.

8. See Chapters 1 and 9 in this book for discussion of this concept and for an introduction to I. William Zartman's notion of "ripening" moments for negotiation.

9. See, for example, Humberto Ortega, "The People Are Going to Defeat and Annihilate the Mercenary Forces," in Bruce Marcus, ed., *Nicaragua: The Sandinista People's Revolution, Speeches by Sandinista Leaders* (New York: Pathfinder Press, 1985), 300–8.

10. This view was embraced publicly by prominent Sandinista intellectuals after 1990. See Alejandro Bendaña, compiler, *Una Tragedia Campesina: Testimonios de la Resistencia* (Managua: Editora de Arte, S.A. y Centro de Estudios Internacionales, 1991), and Orlando Núñez, ed., *La Guerra en Nicaragua* (Managua: Centro para la Investigación, la Promoción y el Desarrollo Rural y Social, 1991).

11. E. V. K. FitzGerald, "An Evaluation of the Economic Costs to Nicaragua of U.S. Aggression: 1980–1984," in Rose J. Spalding, ed., *The Political Economy of Revolutionary Nicaragua* (Boston: Allen & Unwin, 1987), 213. In its claim against the U.S. government before the International Court of Justice at the Hague, the Sandinista government estimated the total economic costs of the war from 1980 to 1988 at $17 billion. See Jaime Wheelock Román, *La Reforma Agraria Sandinista* (Managua: Editorial Vanguardia, 1990), 126.

12. Bill Gibson, "A Structural Overview of the Nicaraguan Economy," in Spalding, ed., *Political Economy*, 24.

13. Michael E. Conroy, "The Political Economy of the 1990 Nicaraguan Elections," *International Journal of Political Economy* 20, no. 3 (Fall 1990): 5–33.

14. Comisión Económica para América Latina y el Caribe, "Balance preliminar de la economía de América Latina y el Caribe 1992)," *Notas sobre la economía y el desarrollo*, nos. 537/538 (December 1992): 45.

15. Alejandro Bendaña, as cited in Hazel Smith, *Nicaragua: Self-Determination and Survival* (London: Pluto Press, 1993), 281.

16. Two moderates who served for a time in the political directorship of the FDN, Edgar Chamorro and Arturo Cruz, subsequently removed themselves from it. Chamorro denounced this organization as a front and became a prominent critic. See Edgar Chamorro, *Packaging the Contras: A Case of CIA Disinformation* (New York: Institute for Media Analysis, 1987).

17. Edgar Molinares, interview by author, Managua, June 27, 1996.

18. William I. Robinson, *A Faustian Bargain: U.S. Intervention in the Nicaraguan Elections and American Foreign Policy in the Post–Cold War Era* (Boulder, Colo: Westview Press, 1992), 134–36.

19. The four contra officers named to the Cease-Fire Commission and signatories to the Sapoá agreement were Walter Calderón López (commander of the Tactical Operations Command and former National Guard lieutenant), Osorno Coleman (military commander of the Atlantic Front of the YATAMA Resistance), Diógenes Hernández Membreño (commander of the Jorge Salazar III Regional Command), and Arturo Salazar Barbarena (former Sandinista and Southern Regional Commander). See U.S. Department of State, "Nicaragua: Negotiating Documents of the Sapoa [sic] Truce," *Central America Regional Brief* (July 1988), 3; and U.S. Department of State, *Nicaraguan Biographies: A Resource Book*, Special Report No. 174 (January 1988), revised edition, 40, 46, 50, 55–56.

20. See Child, *Central American Peace Process*, 54–55.

21. William Goodfellow and James Morrell, "From Contadora to Esquipulas to Sapoá and Beyond," in T. Walker, ed., *Revolution and Counterrevolution*, 383–84.

22. Pastora, for example, was ousted in 1985 by a cluster of rivals who complained about his military leadership style and his hostility to an alliance with the FDN. Divisions between coastal indigenous leaders Steadman Fagoth and Brooklyn Rivera were fierce and ultimately led these two Miskitu leaders into opposing contra camps. Allegations of executions and expulsions within the upper ranks of the FDN were rampant. See, for example, Dieter Eich and Carlos Rincón, *The Contras: Interviews with Anti-Sandinistas* (San Francisco: Synthesis Publications, 1985), 190–91, on

"El Suicido's" murder; Molinares interview; Roger Herman, interview by author, Managua, June 18, 1996.

23. "Rubén" was Oscar Sobalvarro, a former Sandinista soldier and one of the first non-Guard commanders to rise to leadership in the Northern Front.

24. These accords included the "Protocolo de Managua" (May 30, 1990); the "Establecimiento de Polos" (May 30, 1990); and the "Acuerdo de cese al fuego efectivo y definitivo entre el Gobierno de Nicaragua y el Frente Sur de la Resistencia" (June 12, 1990). See discussion in Angel Saldomando, *Documento de análisis: Proceso de pacificación en Nicaragua 1990–1994* (Managua: Gobierno de Nicaragua-Ministerio de la Presidencia-Programa de las Naciones Unidas de Desarrollo, 1995), 42–43.

25. Saldomando, *Documento de análisis,* 42–43; Carlos García Agurto, Danilo Silva Sandovál, Martha L. Cerna Méndez, and Félix Medina Beltrán, "From War to Demobilization in Nicaragua," in Centro de Estudios Internacionales (CEI), *Demobilized Soldiers Speak* (Managua: CEI, 1996), 12–13; Zoilamérica Ortega, *Desmovilizados de guerra en la construcción de la paz en Nicaragua* (Managua: CEI, 1996), 6–10.

26. Comisión Internacional de Apoyo y Verificación-Organización de los Estados Americanos (CIAV-OEA), "Cuadros Estadísticos del Proceso de Desmovilización y Repatrición en Nicaragua," internal report, Managua, July 1991, 1.

27. See Saldomando, *Documento de análisis,* 44–45; see also Genaro Pérez Merlo, "The Reintegration Process of the Nicaraguan Resistencia," in CEI, *Demobilized Soldiers Speak,* 17–23.

28. United States Agency for International Development (USAID) provided 97 percent ($42.1 million of $43.5 million) of CIAV-OAS's total budget for April 1990 to June 1993. See CIAV-OEA, "La Misión," internal report, Managua, March 1994, 4. Also problematic was the high profile of Argentines in the mission, because of the popular (mis)association between CIAV and Argentine military trainers who had helped organize the original contra force in 1980–1981. See Child, *Central American Peace Process,* 86.

29. See interview with CIAV director Sergio Caramagna, "Vine a apagar incendios . . ." *Juntos* 1, No. 1 (1996): 17–19. See also Jennie K. Lincoln, "Resettling the Contras: The OAS in Nicaragua," paper presented at the North-South Center Conference on peace-making and democratization in the hemisphere: multilateral approaches," Miami, Fl., April 11–13, 1996.

30. Laurence Whitehead, "Pacification and Reconstruction in Central America: The International Components," paper presented at the International Meeting of the Latin American Studies Association, Washington, D.C., Sept. 28–30, 1995, 22.

31. See Chapter 9; see also Ian Johnstone, *Rights and Reconciliation: UN Strategies in El Salvador* (Boulder, Colo.: Lynne Rienner Publishers, 1995).

32. For a comparative analysis of the two cases, see Michael Dodson and Laura O'Shaughnessy, "Foundational Pacts, Political Transition, and Democratic Consolidation in El Salvador and Nicaragua," paper presented at International Meeting of the Latin American Studies Association Meeting, Washington, D.C., Sept. 28–30, 1995.

33. Oscar-René Vargas, *Adónde va Nicaragua* (Managua: Ediciones Nicarao, 1991), 275. See also the interview of Oscar Sobalvarro by Isabel Rodríguez, "La Resistencia Nicaragüense Sigue en Armas," *Pensamiento Propio* 9, No. 76 (November-December 1990): 32–34.

34. Núñez, *Guerra en Nicaragua,* 490.

35. Saldomando, *Documento de análisis,* 12. Though labeled "rearmed" ("los rearmados"), technically many of these troops had not disarmed but had turned in only one of several weapons to which they had access.

36. Drawing on data from the Brigada Especial de Desarme, a special joint army-contra brigade set up to oversee the second demobilization process, Saldomando calculates that 62 percent (13,868 of 22,393 in 1992) of these rearmed troops were "recontras"; the remainder were "recompas." See Saldomando, *Documento de análisis,* 20. Some remobilized forces subsequently combined elements of both and were colloquially labeled "revueltos," or scrambled.

60 *Rose J. Spalding*

37. Núñez, *Guerra en Nicaragua*, 475.

38. Saldomando, *Documento de Análisis*, 17–18.

39. This issue became complicated because the government sometimes contended that it had complied, at least to the extent possible, while disgruntled ex-combatants, interpreting the accords "from the optic of their needs," (ibid., 11) claimed to be shortchanged.

40. Rodolfo Ampié, interview by author, Managua, June 19, 1996.

41. Ampié continued: "In regular armies, soldiers serve for a time on the front lines, then they are moved to the rear and have a period of retraining before they return to the front. For us, we had troops who spent years on the front line. This affected them mentally, and some have not recovered."

42. According to Salvador Talavera, executive director of the Centro de Estudios Estratégicos de Nicaragua and younger brother of José Angel Talavera ("Chacal"), eight of the top one hundred commanders of the FDN and one-fifth of the FDN fighting forces were from the general Quilalí area. Interview by author, Managua, June 18, 1996.

43. On the political culture of the mountainous region of the Segovias during the 1920s and 1930s, see Richard Grossman, "'La Patria es Nuestra Madre:' Género, Patriarcado y Nacionalismo Dentro del Movimiento Sandinista, 1927–1934," paper presented at the III Congreso Centroamericano de Historia, San José, Costa Rica, July 15–18, 1996.

44. Timothy P. Wickham-Crowley, *Guerrillas and Revolution in Latin America* (Princeton, N.J.: Princeton University Press, 1992), 131–37.

45. The 1993 World Bank poverty study concluded that 50.3 percent of the population lived in poverty and 19.4 percent lived in extreme poverty, that is, had incomes below the level needed to cover daily minimum caloric requirements. World Bank, "Nicaraguan Country Economic Memorandum," Report 12066-NI, February 2, 1994, 8.

46. CIAV-OEA, "Cuadros Estadísticos," 4–5.

47. Saldomando, *Documento de Análisis*, summary, n.p.

48. Comandancia General/Estado Mayor General, "Naturaleza, funciones, organización, estructura y despliegue operativo del Ejército de Nicaragua," in Oscar-René Vargas, compiler/ed., *Nicaragua: Gobernabilidad democrática y reconversión militar* (Managua: Centro de Estudios Estratégicos de Nicaragua y Instituto Nacional Demócrata para Asuntos Internacionales, 1996), 197.

49. Officers were dismissed in three waves with benefit packages offering between six months and three years of salary and urban lots, arable land, or access to government enterprises undergoing privatization. See García et al., "From War to Demobilization," 14.

50. Sergio Ortega, interview by author, Managua, June 25, 1996.

51. Recounting the response of his organization between 1990 and 1992, AMIR president Sergio Ortega summarized: "We had three demonstrations at the Ministry of Finance, ten at the Presidency, one at the army chiefs of staff command post, and three at the mayor's office. We were so desperate that we even planted a pipe bomb at the presidency. And that was just in Managua." Ibid.

52. Saldomando, *Documento de Análisis*, 68.

53. Ibid., 45–57.

54. Ibid., 67. As a general model, officers in these brigades were to be drawn in equal proportion from the EPS and the police, while the troops were to be divided equally between recontras and recompas. This gave the former contras a substantial presence at the troop level but less in the officer corps.

55. Ibid., 68.

56. In one accord with "Indomable" and his group, the government agreed to provide, among other things, eight passports and eight airline tickets. See the description of the Matagalpa accord, January 29, 1992, in Saldomando, *Documento de Análisis*, 48.

57. By 1994 the most important group still operating was that led by José Angel Talavera

("Chacal"). When the government escalated the military pressure on this group in mid-1993, "Chacal" stunned the nation by seizing an official delegation, including members of the National Assembly, and demanding the resignation of military chief Humberto Ortega along with Antonio Lacayo, minister of the presidency and Chamorro's son-in-law, in August of that year. Retaliation by a recompa group, which then seized several right-wing political leaders in Managua, showed how brittle the Nicaraguan peace was. In the months that followed, the Chamorro government signed another accord, offering to the forces of "Chacal" a generous package of resources (land, credit, etc.) in return for their demobilization.

58. Raúl Rosende, director, Programa Apoyo Institucional, CIAV, interview by author, Managua, June 17, 1996; Alejandro Bendaña, director, Centro de Estudios Internacionales, interview by author, Managua, June 18, 1996. Consejo Supremo Electoral sources and army spokesperson Coronel José García both estimated the number of rearmed troops at 400 in mid-1996. See Carter Center, *Report on the Pre-Electoral Mission to Nicaragua of the Council of Freely Elected Heads of Government, June 7–11, 1996* (Atlanta: The Carter Center of Emory University, 1996), 4, and the interview with Coronel José García, "Una Necesidad para Reconciliación y Reinserción," *Juntos* 1, No. 1 (1996): 15.

59. According to CIAV-OEA, in addition to 22,500 demobilized combatants, the organization also attended to around 100,000 repatriated Nicaraguans and other family members for a total of approximately 120,000 people. See CIAV-OEA, "La Misión," 1–2.

60. During the national convention to choose the party's presidential candidate, the PRN president, Favio Gadea, was passed over in favor of Enrique Quiñones, a newcomer who had mobilized a large group of followers to attend this open meeting. The dispute about the propriety of this electoral coup raged for months and triggered a host of speculations about who Quiñones represented and his authenticity as a member of the Resistance. Gadea's sudden appearance as the top-slated candidate for the Central American Parliament under Arnoldo Alemán's Liberal Alliance created further divisions within the PRN. The party succeeded in winning only 0.33 percent of the valid presidential vote and one out of ninety-three seats in the National Assembly in 1996. See electoral results reported in Carter Center, *The Observation of the 1996 Nicaraguan Elections* (Atlanta, Georgia: The Carter Center, 1997), 59–60.

61. Núñez, *Guerra en Nicaragua*, 491. The quick resignation of "Rubén" and the death of "Franklin" in a traffic accident meant that even this tenuous link to political power was soon lost.

62. Sandinista sources optimistically claimed that the FSLN's contra allies in October 1996 represented roughly a quarter of the total contra force. See "Laying the Basis for Peace," *Barricada Internacional*, No. 401 (October 1996): 4–5.

63. World Bank, *World Development Report* (Oxford: Oxford University Press, 1996), 210, 220.

64. See comments by Nicaraguan business leaders Ramiro Gurdián and Gilberto Cuadra as cited in Rose J. Spalding, "Economic Elite," in Thomas W. Walker, ed., *Nicaragua Without Illusions: Regime Transition and Structural Adjustment in the 1990s* (Wilmington, Del.: Scholarly Resources, 1997), 258. For another interpretation emphasizing the hegemonic role of the U.S. government, see William I. Robinson, "Nicaragua and the World: A Globalization Perspective," in ibid., 23–42.

65. The National Democratic Institute for International Affairs (NDI) has been particularly interested in this question. Between 1992 and 1996, it hosted a series of seminars and conferences on the topic in Nicaragua and commissioned a series of reports. According to the NDI, the problem was not simply that civilian authorities did not exercise close scrutiny over the military but that there were too few civilians with the background and training needed to monitor the military's activities effectively, even if they and the military were so inclined. See NDI, *Relaciones civiles-militares en Nicaragua* (Washington, D.C.: NDI, June 1995). If the civilians were to push for fuller control, the military might reasonably resist turning decisions about its operations over to government officials who were not only antagonistic but technically unprepared. The task of developing

effective oversight, therefore, depends not only on securing military cooperation, which seems increasingly assured, but on developing an intricate dialogue in which both military professionalism and civilian supremacy are respected.

66. Polarization and acrimony within the legislature was extreme, leading FSLN deputies to walk out for three months in 1991 and for four in 1992; a substantial sector of the UNO bloc walked out for the whole legislative session in 1993. Efforts by the assembly to change the constitution and reduce presidential power led to a six-month standoff between the executive and legislature in 1995 that paralyzed the government. Rose J. Spalding, "Nicaragua: Politics, Poverty and Polarization," in Jorge I. Domínquez and Abraham F. Lowenthal, eds., *Constructing Democratic Governance in Latin America: Mexico, Central America, and the Caribbean in the 1990s* (Baltimore: The Johns Hopkins University Press, 1996), 12–13.

67. Violent crimes are defined as "assassinations, homicides, kidnappings, rape and other forms of sexual assault, battery, and armed robbery." See Comandante de Brigada Fernando Caldera Azmitia, "Policía y seguridad ciudadana," in CEEN y NDI, *Justicia militar: Una visión comparada, Ponencias de invitados especiales curso-Seminario relaciones civiles-militares, enero de 1996, Managua, Nicaragua* (Managua: CEEN and NDI, 1997), 34.

68. CID-Gallup, *Opinión Pública #17: Nicaragua* (April 1996): 31.

69. Caldera, "Policía," 33.

70. For a brief history of the development of this idea in UNESCO's work, see Carlos Tünnermann Bernheim, "Cultura de paz: Un nuevo paradigma en Centroamérica," *Cultura de Paz 2*, No. 9 (July–September 1996):37–55.

71. Judy Butler, "Nicaragua's Lessons in the Four R's: Reconciliation, Reconstruction, Reinsertion and Rehabilitation," paper presented at the International Meeting of the Latin American Studies Association, Washington, D.C., Sept. 28–30, 1995, 2.

72. CIAV-OEA, *Nicaragua: La frontera del conflicto* (Managua: CIAV-OEA, 1995), 2. According to a Hemisphere Initiatives report, at the end of the war there were 72,000 repatriated refugees; 41,000 RN combatants and family members; 72,000 discharged armed forces personnel; over 5,000 discharged from the Ministry of Government; and 354,000 internally displaced people. David Dye et al, *Contesting Everything, Winning Nothing: The Search for Consensus in Nicaragua, 1990–1995* (Cambridge, Mass.: Hemisphere Initiatives, 1995), 34–35.

73. CEPAD was one of the first organizations to work on mediating disputes in Nicaragua's conflict zones. This group drew on over a decade of experience with local-level peace commissions, some of which first emerged during the final years of the contra war following CEPAD director Gustavo Parajón's appointment to the Esquipulas-mandated Verification Commission in 1987. Gustavo Parajón, interview with LASA group, Managua, June 27, 1996. Many evangelical pastors and parishioners represented by CEPAD received deferments from the draft for religious reasons during the war. This allowed them to project themselves into a relatively neutral space in a highly polarized postwar setting and to take on mediation roles with some credibility in the eyes of community members.

74. CEI was founded after the FSLN's defeat by Alejandro Bendaña, former secretary general of the Nicaraguan Foreign Ministry under the Sandinista government. CEI worked closely with a new organization of former combatants, the Fundación de Ex-Combatientes por la Paz, la Reconciliación y el Desarrollo, which brought together a carefully balanced group of former contras, discharged soldiers, and discharged police. CEI worked with the foundation and other veterans' groups to compose mediation teams that included representatives of both sides, to promote dialogue between opposing forces, and to offer assistance in "conflict transformation" to communities. Alejandro Bendaña, interview by author, Managua, June 18, 1996. See also Zoilamérica Ortega, *Desmovilizados*, 59–68; Carlos García [interview], "Persisten grupos armados en Nicaragua," *Juntos 1*, No. 1 (1996): 8.

75. The most recent addition to this group, CIAV-OEA began to promote the creation of a network of Peace Commissions in conflict zones in 1994. Recognizing that its time in Nicaragua

was rapidly coming to an end, and hoping to construct a permanent peace keeping operation to leave behind in the areas of greatest conflict, CIAV moved to promote the development of local peace commissions through much of the interior of the country. Raúl Rosende, Responsable Nacional, Programa de Apoyo Institucional, CIAV-OEA, interview by author, Managua, June 17, 1996. See also Rosende, "Peacekeeping in Nicaragua: Human Rights Verification and Civil Society's Strengthening," unpublished paper, September 1996. CIAV-OEA attempted to develop its peace commissions in cooperation with local churches, arguing that churches represented the strongest element of civil society in Nicaragua.

76. Other institutional initiatives to mediate conflict and promote dialogue include activities of organizations such as UNESCO, the Mediation Center of the Universidad Nacional Autónoma de Nicaragua (UNAN) School of Law, the Martin Luther King Institute, the Women's Coalition and the Minimum Agenda effort, the Center for Education for Democracy, and Grupo FUNDEMOS.

77. In mid-1996 CEPAD administered ninety-five peace commissions in the southern part of Nicaragua plus a growing number in the east and north. CIAV supported the operations of peace commissions in fifty-six towns or hamlets. CEI reported a presence in thirty towns in 1995. Parajón interview with LASA group,; Raúl Rosende, interview with author, Managua, June 17, 1996; and CEI, *Memoria 1995* (Managua: Editora de Arte, S.A., 1996), 14.

78. See, for example, comments by Alejandro Bendaña at the Woodrow Wilson International Center for Scholars, Instituto de Defensa Legal, Lima, Peru, and Friedrich Ebert Foundation, Washington Office conference on comparative peace processes in Latin America, Washington, D.C., March 13–14, 1997.

79. Shifts in United States Agency for International Development (USAID) funding priorities after 1995 represent a belated move to target a larger portion of U.S. bilateral aid to marginal sectors. See Lisa Haugaard, "Development Aid: Some Small Steps Forward," *NACLA Report on the Americas* 31, No. 2 (September/October 1997): 29–33.

80. See the statement on peace and social development issued jointly by Generals Julio Balconi Turcios (Guatemala), Mario Raúl Hung Pacheco (Honduras), Joaquín Cuadra Lacayo (Nicaragua) and Jaime Guzmán Morales (El Salvador) at the June 1996 UNESCO-sponsored meeting analyzing the role of the armed forces in Central America reprinted in "Armed Forces as Peacemakers?" *Envío* 15, No. 182 (September 1996): 20–21.

81. See Judy Butler, "Violence and Reconciliation in Nicaragua: The Situation of the Uprooted Populations," unpublished Consultant's Report for the Project Counselling Service for Latin American Refugees, December 1993, 38. Butler cites the following explanation for this difference: "[The south] does not have the north's long history of polarization and violence; the Southern Front was made up of people from the area and had no National Guard members or leadership; the early and extensive provision of land to demobilizing RN [in the south] siphoned off some of the frustration felt in Region I [in the north-central part of Nicaragua] . . . and, finally, [there is] the role played by the local peace commissions."

82. Barnes argues, based on poll data from 1990 and 1996, that perhaps half of the Nicaraguan electorate is located in what he calls the "mixed middle" of the political spectrum and is mobilized to support candidates in the opposing extremes only during the heat of electoral campaigns. See William A. Barnes, "Elections in Incomplete Democracies: The Myth and Reality of Polarization, and the Puzzle of Voter Turnout, in Nicaragua and El Salvador," Paper presented at the International Meeting of the Latin American Studies Association, Guadalajara, Mexico, April 17–19, 1997, 17–19.

83. According to a study of political culture in urban Nicaragua at the end of 1995, only 43 percent agreed with the statement that "one ought to support the political system of Nicaragua." See Mitchell A. Seligson, "Political Culture in Nicaragua: Transitions, 1991–1995," Ms., January 1996, 19–20.

84. FSLN candidate Daniel Ortega received a still-impressive 38 percent of the vote. Data from the Consejo Supremo Electoral on voter participation suggests only a 77 percent turnout rate, with

the difference due to vote tallies annulled by the CSE because of voting irregularities. See Universidad Centroamericana (UCA)-Nitlapán-Envío Team, "How Nicaraguans Voted," *Envío* 15, No. 185–186 (December 1996–January 1997): 38–39.

85. An April 1996 poll by CID-Gallup, for example, found that 37 percent of respondents wanted "unrestricted" protection of private property while a full 50 percent felt that the state should expropriate the property of the wealthy if it was necessary for the "good of the people." CID-Gallup, *Opinión,* 19.

Reflections

ALEJANDRO BENDAÑA

Peace is not simply a matter of laying down weapons. It is also a matter of increasing salaries. That is the way the issue has been explained to us in great wisdom by a lot of Nicaraguans who fought the war. Peace is about justice.

I would like to suggest that demobilization is in many ways a bad idea. What is needed and what has occurred in Nicaragua is a kind of *remobilization*. Remobilization is a negative component if it is linked to violence. But we should speak of a civic remobilization; thus, as the Guatemalan Unidad Revolucionaria Nacional Guatemalteca (URNG) has said, our soldiers do not demobilize but continue to be mobilized peacefully on behalf of justice and social transformation. This points to the need for an engaged civil society and of demobilized soldiers as part of civil society in turning a cease-fire into a process of transformation.

In both Nicaragua and Colombia, veterans of guerrilla groups have become independent actors through military remobilization. In Nicaragua, for example, the total number of contrás who were formally demobilized in 1990 is smaller than the number of people who have given up their weapons in subsequent cease-fires over the last seven years. When members of the Resistance who remobilized or simply had never demobilized were asked why they had done so, they replied that "the promises that were made to us were not kept." The first element always cited is the question of physical security.

Remobilizing in a civic sense means using civic weapons to demand reintegration. Here we run into a problem of vocabulary. We speak of *re*integration, *re*settlement, *re*conciliation, *re*insertion, as if there were something to go back to, if there were something positive in the way people were inserted, conciliated, and settled, or in the way the economy and the society worked before.

Had such conditions existed, then perhaps there would not have been a war in the first place. The vocabulary does not allow us to capture the essence of transformation envisioned by the veterans themselves, to think of peace as a possible space for transformation, for redefining the terms of insertion. Such transformation means, in essence, redefining the terms of an entire society, not simply to guarantee physical security—although that is a prerequisite—but also to redesign the economic setting, the system of land tenure, and so on. It is thus somewhat of a contradiction to speak of a negotiated revolution. If a broad-based consensus includes some of those sectors that were part of the oppressive or repressive structure, then other sectors might have little to gain by way of peace.

Simply making liberalism a reality in Central America is revolutionary, and Marxists have contributed more to that than liberals themselves. But keep in mind that the political spaces peace processes open up are just that—spaces. How those spaces are used is an entirely different question, and they can be used against the Frente Farabundo Martí para la Liberación Nacional (FMLN), the Sandinistas, or the URNG. Some argue that the demobilization of some Colombian guerrilla groups has served to legitimize the system, that having a few ex-guerrillas here and there in government posts as window dressing allows the system to perpetuate itself. This is *reencaucha,* the retreading of old tires, not social renovation.

It is not *reencaucha,* however, when demobilized veterans engage in a civic struggle that uses new spaces to create linkages with other sectors of civil society. The issue for a peace process is to create multilevel, multilayered, long-term possibilities for national-local dialogues in which different sectors, including veterans, can participate.

The process of reintegration cannot be divorced from the rest of civil society or from a process of transformation. It must be a national process that avoids the temptation of using external mediators who can inhibit veterans and other groups from establishing linkages to other sectors of civil society. Seven years after the Nicaraguan cease-fire, the CIAV-OAS mission was still operating in Nicaragua.* This mission should have ended much earlier and its tasks been assumed by Nicaraguans themselves. Did the CIAV remain because Nicaraguans did not want to take over its roles, or did its very presence prevent Nicaraguans from assuming the process and making it sustainable? There is an additional question of the linkage between reintegration and foreign funding. External funding can create a privileged class of demobilized soldiers, which feeds intracommunity divi-

---

*The CIAV ended operations in July 1997 [ed.].

sions. The task is to conceive of reintegration by engaging veterans as coalition builders who have both short-term demands and a long-term view around which different sectors can coalesce.

There is a tendency among some international agencies and nongovernmental organizations to work with people on the basis of what they would like them to think or what they would like them to be instead of working with them on the basis of what their reality is. One cannot say, for example, that one wants to help organize civil society in a remote corner of northern Nicaragua and then argue that because the Sandinistas and the contras are too conflictive, one has to work with somebody else. There is no one else.

The demobilized have an identity, and both sides hold on to it as a salvation. That must be taken into consideration, and people must not be treated simply as refugees or the unemployed. Questions of identity have enormous consequences.

Postwar does not mean postconflict. Many ex-soldiers, as well as most Nicaraguans, find it very amusing to learn that they live in postconflict Nicaragua. The primary reason that the country is not postwar is that it is not postviolence; in fact, there has been a dramatic increase in violence.

Moreover, there is a difference between microdisarmament, on the one hand, and the building of peace structures that are embedded in the community, on the other. President Violeta Chamorro came in and negotiated microdisarmament agreements with groups of twenty-five or thirty fighters, offering such things as a visa to the United States, a four-wheel-drive pickup, $10,000 in cash, and a few acres of land. This policy succeeds in buying off the heads of the local movements, but the remainder continue fighting. And once those privileged have spent what they received, they go and rearm.

What is needed is to examine ways that civil society, at the community level and particularly in areas of conflict, can work to reduce levels of violence and do so with a recognition that structural problems exist. International agencies typically have tried to strengthen the judiciary and the police, and doing so is valid. But these are long-term solutions, and herein lies the problem. What can be done in the short term? And what can be done by civil society, or is the process in the hands of the international agencies themselves? Sometimes the agencies believe that they have to intervene, and if there's another problem, they will intervene even more. At that point the conduct of the peace process and of postwar reconstruction no longer occurs in one's own capital but in Washington.

The problem is different in Guatemala, for example, where an international verification presence serves to counterbalance a political right wing that still carries considerable weight. But in the long term, there is a price to be paid for making external actors part of a permanent internal political and peace process. Such external intervention, after all, is what the history of Central America has been all about.

3

Political Transition and Institutionalization in El Salvador

ANTONIO CAÑAS AND HÉCTOR DADA

Introduction

This chapter represents an evaluation of the achievements, prospects, and challenges facing El Salvador in the first five years since the signing of the peace accords in 1992. Several institutions and organizations have undertaken this assessment, including the United Nations itself, which mediated the peace talks between the Salvadoran government and the Farabundo Martí National Liberation Front (Frente Farabundo Martí para la Liberación Nacional, or FMLN) and then spent several years verifying the implementation of the peace accords.[1] In summing up the period between 1992 and 1997, the United Nations found that

> El Salvador has largely been demilitarized: the armed structure of [the] FMLN has disappeared and its combatants have been reintegrated into civilian life; and the armed forces have been reduced and have respected the profound changes in their nature and role called for by the peace accords. But the most notable development has been that the peace process has also allowed for the opening up of space for democratic participation. A climate of tolerance prevails today, unlike any the country has known before. Since the signing of the peace agreements, no national sector has taken refuge in or supported violence as a form of political action.[2]

69

Our chapter divides the democratic transition in El Salvador into two phases. The first—from the January 1992 signing of the peace agreement until the March 1994 presidential, legislative, and municipal elections—constituted the *transición pactada* (literally, the "pacted transition), in which the basic elements of the transition as well as a timetable for implementation were derived from the peace accords themselves. Although much still remained to be done to implement the letter and spirit of the accords, following the elections El Salvador's transition entered a second phase, one in which democratic norms, institutions, and practices were to take root and prevail. During this period the extralegal supervisory functions, such as those of the United Nations Observer Mission in El Salvador (ONUSAL), the countries organized into Groups of Friends, and direct negotiations between the government and the FMLN over issues of implementation were to be transferred to the state apparatus. This, in fact, had been the essence of the peace accords: to re-create state institutions so as to legitimize and confer credibility on democracy and its rules; in other words, to establish a true rule of law.

In examining the second phase of this transition, in which the nature of the political regime is being defined and consolidated, this chapter focuses on the degree of institutionalization of the electoral system, analyzed by looking at the 1994 and 1997 elections, the first to take place in peacetime; and the degree of credibility of two institutions created by the peace accords to ensure public security and respect for human rights: the National Civilian Police (Policía Nacional Civil, or PNC), and the Office of the Human Rights Ombudsman (Procuraduría para la Defensa de los Derechos Humanos). Although the sustainability and irreversibility of the peace process depend on the proper implementation of the accords by the entire institutional apparatus of the state, we focus on elections, public security, and human rights precisely because it was electoral fraud, repressive security forces, and systematic violations of human rights that activated the latent social conflict in El Salvador and contributed to the outbreak and continuation of the war.

The emphasis on the degree of institutionalization within which state entities function is not fortuitous. In a society such as El Salvador's, where historically power, influence, and efficiency were pseudoinstitutional or wholly outside an institutional framework, the recognition that institutions provide a more trustworthy and just framework for governance is, in and of itself, a major advance. Stated in negative terms, the more inefficient and/or arbitrary the new institutions, the greater the temptation to revert to old patterns of conduct, and the greater the possibility that society, in its collective conscience, will accept as normal first a state of anarchy and, ultimately, authoritarianism.

The question that this chapter addresses is: Has the behavior of the new institutions created by the peace accords sent a clear message to the population that the new rules of the game require fair play, or is the message that the democratic game is played with loaded dice? The record to date is not encouraging. Numerous crucial events illustrate that, within the forces and authorities charged with leading state institutions, interests and powers persist that have found it more beneficial to operate by the old system of unwritten, undemocratic rules of the game than to cultivate respect for and adherence to the rule of law.

Overview of the Peace Accords

A brief summary of the content and objectives of the peace accords themselves is essential to evaluate the changes that have and have not taken place in El Salvador. As noted by United Nations Secretary-General Boutros Boutros-Ghali during the January 1992 signing of the accords at Chapultepec Castle in Mexico City:

> It is no exaggeration to say that, taken together, and given their breadth and scope, these agreements constitute a prescription for a revolution achieved by negotiation. The armed forces are to be given a role, clearly subordinated to the civilian authorities, commensurate with their responsibilities as redefined in the new Constitution. The armed forces will be streamlined, reformed and restructured accordingly. The judiciary is to be reformed and strengthened and its independence bolstered, including provision for a percentage of the national budget to be automatically assigned to it. Persons without party affiliations are to participate in the Electoral Tribunal, and the system will be overhauled so as to render it more reliable than in the past.
>
> Principles and guidelines have been agreed regarding contentious economic and social questions, including those related to land, and mechanisms have been established for following up on these matters. Furthermore, the parties have agreed to the creation of the Commission on Truth . . . charged with the task, which is essential to reconciliation, of bringing the truth to light concerning the more infamous acts of violence of the past decade.[3]

Certainly it is debatable whether the accords achieved a revolution "by negotiation," in the true sense of the word. To the degree that the accords addressed social and economic issues, the provisions had more to do with needs to dismantle the military forces on both sides of the conflict than with addressing structural economic problems or widespread social poverty. (See Chapters 1 and 9.)[4]

Nonetheless, the agreements represented an important transformation of Salvadoran reality. To have changed the role of the armed forces in national political life by purging it, reducing it in size, and redefining its central mission is undoubtedly a significant achievement, as was the drawing of a distinction between internal security and national defense.[5] At the same time, systematically dismantling the contours of the exclusionary political regime opened the possibility that all political forces would participate, something that had not been possible in the sixty years prior to the accords. Giving greater independence to the judiciary and requiring that members of the Supreme Court be elected by a two-thirds majority of the legislature created better conditions for judicial autonomy, a positive, albeit insufficient, step for reducing the opportunities for impunity. The creation of the Office of the Human Rights Ombudsman provided an additional instrument of protection for the citizenry.

What cannot be overemphasized, however, is the limitations of the accords in the economic and social spheres. The agreements made reference to constitutional provisions restricting the size of landholdings, distributed land to ex-combatants and supporters, and created a Foro de Concertación Económico Social (Forum for Socioeconomic Consensus). These provisions were obviously more limited than those related to the military forces or the constitutional changes aimed at establishing a more participatory political system. They did not attack—nor could they—the causes of social and economic exclusion. Nor was the model of market economy in place at that point up for discussion.[6] The decision to distribute parcels of land to ex-combatants was oriented more to reincorporating them into civilian life than to guaranteeing social justice, and the reference to land ownership in excess of the legal limit did nothing more than reiterate the constitutional provision written as part of counterinsurgency policy. The Forum for Socioeconomic Consensus was an entity that should have created dialogue between workers and owners, and ultimately a debate on economic policy, but it never achieved its potential.[7]

The impossibility of the conflict ending in a military victory by one of the parties, the disappearance of the ideological context in which the war was generated, and the prospects for greater stability if peace were achieved caused the government and its internal and external allies to accept incorporating the enemy into the political system, converting it to a mere adversary within that system. If, for the FMLN, the latter stages of the conflict had as an objective "peace with democracy," and if the reason for taking up arms had been "social injustice," then the rationale for accepting the accords was that the FMLN could join the political struggle to obtain political and economic democracy. This rationale explains the urgency and diligence with which the parties discussed institutional reforms aimed at guaranteeing relatively equitable electoral competition as well as the dismantling of the authoritarian system.

The record of compliance with the peace accords in the five years after they were signed is, at best, mixed. One notable aspect is that the cease-fire between the government and the FMLN was never broken. It is also important to emphasize that cases of political assassination have been surprisingly few in number, even considering the violent nature of El Salvador's political history and the extensive role that political assassination played during the war. The armed forces markedly reduced their number of troops, despite resistance at times from civilian as well as military sectors, and went through a process of purging based on the recommendations of the so-called Ad Hoc Commission (Comisión Ad Hoc), composed of three civilians who reviewed the records of senior officers. The three infamous security forces—the National Police (Policía Nacional), Treasury Police (Policía de Hacienda), and National Guard (Guardia Nacional)—were disbanded and a new National Civilian Police created. Although plagued by shortcomings since its inception, the very conception and creation of the PNC represents a major change in the national reality.

There also have been notorious deficiencies. Prolonged delays in the transfer of land to ex-combatants demonstrated the scant political will to act in conformity with the spirit of the accords. The Truth Commission (Comisión de la Verdad), established to investigate grave acts of violence during the war, made an invaluable contribution to a systematic and documented account of much of the cruel conflict that the country lived through. But, regrettably, shortly after the commission issued its report in March 1993, the government of President Alfredo Cristiani decreed a general amnesty, attempting to cover with a false mantle of forgetfulness the events that, in one way or another, had touched most Salvadorans. That amnesty constituted an attack on true reconciliation. (See Chapter 13.)

Nevertheless, we are far from calling the limited compliance with the peace accords a failure: Although the record is mixed, qualitative factors must prevail over quantitative ones. In addition, any judgment of the effectiveness of the accords must start from an understanding of their central objective: to guarantee that political democracy—especially its electoral aspects—would function and that the incorporation of the FMLN into the political system and civilian life would take place in a secure climate. Despite the grandiloquent pronouncements of those who signed the agreement at Chapultepec, the stroke of a pen could not guarantee the radical transformation of a society in which authoritarianism was so deeply rooted. Indeed, the political manifestations of that authoritarianism are but one element of a much more complex reality.

The Elections of 1994 and 1997

Difficulties and Deficiencies

Free elections are a necessary yet not sufficient condition for democratic governance. This universally accepted truth has a heightened significance in El Salvador, not only because past electoral fraud, coupled with deepening repression, is widely regarded as having set off the conflict, but also because the elections that took place during the war were clearly part of the counterinsurgency effort designed to legitimize government authority, while isolating and obtaining the unconditional surrender of the FMLN. The wartime elections were plainly a significant improvement over those of the 1970s; although they were conducted under war conditions and the left was politically excluded, centrist parties were permitted to campaign and win office, and the military respected the balloting results. Indeed, to play their intended legitimizing role, the elections had to respect the popular will in the eyes of national and international public opinion.

In spite of the improvements in the electoral system during the conflict, various obstacles to the clear and free expression of the popular will have carried on into the present. Problems experienced in 1994 reappeared in 1997, despite efforts to clean up the voter registry and to improve the administration of the electoral process. Difficulties in transporting voters to the polls persisted in 1997; during the balloting itself there were still no procedures in place to register citizens who could not vote because of prior defects in the registry. There are no exact statistics on the percentage of the population that was unable to vote because of problems of this nature. However, according to a poll conducted in February 1997 by the University Institute of Public Opinion (IUDOP) of the Central American University (UCA), 5 percent of those questioned stated that they did not have an electoral registration card.[8] These shortcomings are beginning to show the signs of frustrating "incorrigibility."

Disorder and disorganization on election day in 1997 caused many important polling places, such as those in the populous municipalities of San Salvador, to be unable to open until about noon, after almost half the election day was over; this led voters to give up. These factors discredited the electoral system in 1994 and in 1997, producing voter abstentions and widespread apathy regarding the electoral process. The need for reform had been underscored by U.N. Secretary-General Boutros Boutros-Ghali in his speech at Chapultepec when the peace accords were signed. Five years later the fact that problems still had not been corrected indicated a lack of political will.

It might seem that shortcomings in the electoral system affect all of the parties in the contest equally and that even though they may induce the desertion of voters and greater abstentionism (which are themselves antidemocratic), they do not alter the overall results or the distribution of power. If this were true, then defective or not, the system would represent a positive step forward compared to the previous era of fraudulent elections, when the police and military forces and the ruling political party manipulated and altered the results so as to favor a particular candidate. However, given the intent of the peace accords, the existing system does not measure up. Persistent shortcomings still tilt the balance and have a detrimental and harmful effect mostly on the smaller parties, which have fewer logistical and organizational capabilities. The majority parties, meanwhile, have a permanent elite force of voters—what policy institutes call the "hardcore vote"—who will go to the ballot boxes even under the most adverse conditions.[9]

The disparities in the organizational, logistical, and financial power of the various parties translate into advantages in the field, at the polling place, and in centers where votes are tallied. These advantages take various forms. One is the massive presence at the polls of armies of "poll watchers" wearing party identification, who influence and even coerce undecided voters. Moreover, the higher social position and attributes of "authority" of the party representatives at a polling place or on the municipal and departmental electoral boards can be decisive in determining the fate of a disputed ballot, or in making the final decision on a contested act, whether or not that decision is valid.

Perhaps these gaps in the law, or in the electoral system as such, would not be significant in a context other than El Salvador's. But the prevailing political and cultural climate is still one in which the average person has shaky knowledge of and commitment to the electoral legislation, and the social status of a party representative or election official continues to carry weight. Under these circumstances, shortcomings become determining factors.

Pending Reforms and the Lessons from the Elections

Numerous efforts were made to overcome the persistent deficiencies in the 1994 and 1997 elections. One of the most promising long-range projects—and one that has backing from the international community—has been the training of citizens and grass-roots activists in all the parties in electoral legislation and organization. However, true modernization and the guarantee of impartiality in elections awaits the implementation of "structural" reforms in the electoral system. Above all, still pending is the removal of representatives of political parties from the Supreme Electoral Tribunal (Tribunal Supremo Electoral, or TSE), so that it may, in Boutros-Ghali's words, be a tribunal led by "persons without party affiliations."[10] Equally important is the setting up a system that would make it possible for citizens to vote near their homes, eliminating the need for transportation. Perhaps even more important is the implementation of the new Registro Nacional de Personas Naturales (National Register of Persons), which will replace the obsolete and incomplete voter rolls still in use.

Prolonged and unjustifiable delays in the implementation of these reforms, which were backed by all of the political parties in 1995, reflect the politically motivated resistance that belies a professed faith in the new institutional arrangements. Although the government resorted to budgetary excuses for not implementing the national register, the continual offers of technical and financial support from the international community reveal instead a lack of political will primarily on the part of the ruling party. The official excuse has changed as the 1999 elections approach and the debate over the electoral system once again revives; this time the argument is that there is insufficient time to implement reforms.

Notwithstanding the problems of 1994 that were repeated in the elections of 1997, there were also notable differences, not only in their outcomes but in their intrinsic credibility.

The general disdain for politicians and politics is widespread in Salvadoran society and is reflected in reduced voter turnout. From 1994 to 1997 in El Salvador there was a downward trend in voting, to the point that only 40 percent of the duly registered and documented electorate voted.[11] This is an alarming figure, considering that the trend has occurred in the context of a fundamentally new institutional arrangement, with expanded opportunities for participation and facing the difficult task of consolidating democracy.

It is also true that in El Salvador, as elsewhere, the economic model in place has tended to reduce the scope of what is considered to be the public domain. In the feverish reduction of the state dictated by neoliberal "modernization," a smaller portion of what is in the public interest is submitted to the popular will, as many services and policies that were public are transferred to the private sector. It is hard to say whether the decrease in electoral participation is a clear reflection of a social awareness of the diminution in economic power and the capacity for political decision making that is at stake in the elections. For the time being, it is clear that this loss of interest and lack of political participation in the election of state authorities has not been offset or replaced by alternative activities that sufficiently maintain and foster citizen responsibility and participation in the functioning of public institutions.

Whatever the precise reason for the poor electoral participation, it is clear that the perceptions and attitudes of everyday citizens about politics are markedly negative. A 1991 pre-election opinion poll carried out by IUDOP revealed that 70 percent of the population believed that during that year's campaign, the parties were not telling people the truth and that their only purpose was to take power. It is unlikely that this perception has improved in recent years. Various surveys carried out in 1996 and 1997 by the public opinion institutes of the private universities,[12] as well as those by firms that have been taking polls since the 1980s reveal the scant credibility of state authorities and various state institutions. The level of credibility and popular participation in the elections is much lower than the minimum acceptable for contributing to democratic consolidation.[13]

A New Political Correlation

Problems aside, the 1994 elections created better conditions of governance and opened up new spaces of negotiation. Most legislative decisions required only a simple majority of deputies, and the combination of the votes of the Alianza Republicana Nacionalista (ARENA) and Partido de Conciliación Nacional (PCN) parties gave the government a kind of automatic control. But those that required the approval of a two-thirds majority of the representatives necessitated cutting deals with other opposition parties. Additionally, the parliamentary coexistence of parties that supported the counterinsurgency war and the legislative group of former

FMLN rebels generated and shaped new forms of political behavior relatively unprecedented in El Salvador.

The legislative and municipal elections of 1997 witnessed a rapid evolution of relations in the party system, as the representative force of the FMLN increased dramatically. The ruling ARENA party lost the largest municipalities in the country as well as control over those decisions in the National Assembly that required a simple majority. What occurred was nothing less than the breakup of the political hegemony held by ARENA for almost a decade. ARENA's spectacular defeat in the elections was caused largely by the desertion of its traditional members and leadership cadres at the national, local, and sectoral levels, and was the result of deep divisions and infighting that took place in 1996 over the control and direction of the party.[14]

The eight years of ARENA government that began in 1989 produced an inevitable decline in its political strength. The serious economic crisis felt especially by the poor also caused attrition, especially at a time when the government's macroeconomic figures were claiming impressive growth statistics.[15] But its loss of prestige and leadership in the eyes of the citizenry; its growing internal divisions; its many scandals of corruption in the government, the municipalities, businesses, and within the party, as well as its patent irresponsibility in the discussion or framing of important laws are not simply attributable to the voter attrition that comes from a long stay in power. These are, rather, symptoms of the perversion that the stay in power induced in ARENA.

In terms of social and economic power, it is still premature to make predictions on ARENA's future.[16] It is clear that the current government economic policy continues to be the cause of displeasure among groups in power that before had given their unconditional support. Still one cannot anticipate the kind of turnabout that might come from an important and decisive capital sector; this still-undefined sector is undergoing the same experience of disillusionment and drifting that the midlevel and lower sectors have experienced since the early 1990s or are still experiencing.

The Institutional Framework Called into Question

The most significant and worrisome qualitative difference between the 1994 and 1997 elections was the repeated modifications to and attacks on the electoral law in the 1997 elections. The hurried reforms enacted during the campaign—the last of them made less than a month before the elections—were approved by the ARENA-dominated parliamentary majority with the connivance of the Supreme Electoral Tribunal;[17] they were aimed at impeding the opposition parties' alliances and at enhancing the possibility that ARENA might maintain parliamentary control by issuing decrees that improved the chances of those minority parties within the ARENA sphere of interest.[18]

This illegal and antidemocratic conduct not only illustrated that the ARENA leadership was aware of its diminished electoral possibilities but also that it was determined to manipulate the rules of the game to improve its prospects, using the instruments of governmental power under its control.[19] However, the electoral results were relatively unaffected by this manipulation. Indeed, it is probable that the hasty political maneuvers ended up hurting their own authors because they sent an implicit message of desperation— a prelude to the party's defeat—especially to the undecided voters.

Thus it can be concluded that in 1997, the transparency of the elections, the guarantee of the outcome, and, consequently, the credibility of the democratic system were not anchored in an institutional framework reflecting an adherence to electoral law; on the contrary, that framework was manipulated repeatedly for convenience. Only the very presence and logistical organization of both ARENA and the FMLN effectively guaranteed the equilibrium and moderation observed at most polling places on election day.[20]

This was substantially different from previous circumstances in which ARENA had come into the elections. This time the governing party was deprived of its electoral machinery that, because of its size and conduct at the polling centers, was always tinged with coercion.[21] The FMLN, on the other hand, was able to improve the organization of its electoral logistical apparatus. The other parties again showed weakness and an inability to exercise oversight at the national level in order to guarantee a fair and transparent process, a role that is assigned to them by law.

In any event, it is clear that in 1997 one of the two central pillars supporting the peace process and democratization in El Salvador, the elections, proved to be fragile and vulnerable. A careful consideration of the national and international efforts in this regard could keep the 1999 presidential elections from furthering the dangerous deterioration and loss of trust that affected the system that year.

The Election Results: A Verdict Against the Economic Policy or a Threat to Democratic Stability?

Public opinion polls are a well-known means of examining the aspirations or the disenchantment of a country's population regarding various aspects of its national situation. The polls also are recognized as loudspeakers for the citizenry's message requiring the serious attention of those who compete for popular support and access to power. Thus it should be asked whether the results of the last elections represent a simple yet blunt rejection of government policy, or whether they should be interpreted as a warning that the stability and consolidation of the democratic system are being threatened. It was noted earlier that the low level of participation observed in the 1997 elections speaks poorly for the credibility that the renewed institutional arrangement should be enjoying as a peaceful and democratic means of transforming a situation of grave and widespread deterioration in the popular economy.

The few and most recent statistics available on the socioeconomic indexes of the country reveal an alarming social crisis as well as exhaustion of the current economic model, evident in a slowdown of growth and an incapacity to stimulate the productive sectors. Opinion polls suggest widespread discouragement regarding the possibilities for improvement. According to the 1997 *World Development Indicator,* the population below the poverty line in El Salvador reached 48.3 percent: 55.7 percent in rural areas, and 43.1 percent in the cities. For 1996, according to the official figures released by the Ministry of Economy's Information Bureau, 22 percent of Salvadoran households are in extreme poverty, and 30 percent in poverty.[22]

The overall deterioration of the national economy from 1992 to 1997 is felt more sharply by family economies than is reflected in these figures. In El Salvador, according to a prominent analyst, "techniques are used to manipulate the index of the volume of economic activity (IVAE) and the wholesale price index, and especially the real rate of inflation or cost of the basic basket of goods." The same source states that since the year before the 1994 elections, and even more since 1996, "various research institutions and business associations have warned of [this] inconsistency . . . which in the final analysis results in a loss of public credibility." Similarly, with the official "traffic in accounting data," the authorities fruitlessly attempt to hide "our structural weaknesses, economic disintegration, growth with unemployment, the bias of bank loans to unproductive sectors, the truth about the cost of living, and the skyrocketing of poverty and unemployment," all of which make it difficult to devise "the best national responses to tackle these serious problems in a concerted way.[23]

Unfortunately, as was the case with the peace accords, the initiatives that most take into account the need to abandon the attitude that leads to the "loss of public credibility" comes from abroad. The World Bank has been making (curiously confidential) calls for a transparent and consensus-based approach to the problem. On February 19, 1997, the office of the president of the World Bank forwarded a strategic assistance plan to the Salvadoran government. One of its objectives is "to achieve a sustainable peace" over the coming two-year period; to that end, the bank made a call for negotiation and consensus-building: "Implementation of the Government's development agenda will require a significant degree of social consensus, without which political and social pressures could severely test the Government's resolve."[24] In this context, it is worth underscoring that poverty is growing more rapidly in the rural areas and that it is precisely the countryside that has been most abandoned and hard hit by the economic policies implemented since 1989. This issue has opened the largest fissure among economically dominant sectors in ARENA.[25]

Popular perceptions, revealed through the survey carried out by the IUDOP in February 1997, remain relatively unchanged: 22 percent of the population sees poverty and unemployment as the country's principal problem; 35.5 percent identify it as the economy and inflation. Combining these two categories, 55.5 percent of the population perceives the economic crisis and its effects as the most serious national problem. This is followed by 33.3 percent of the population that pointed to crime as the most serious problem. In 1996 and 1997 these issues, with minor variations, created the most concern among Salvadorans.[26]

If the ARENA party is responding with so little honesty to this degree of national awareness of the country's problems, as appears to be the case, its electoral failure is not surprising. Yet in a context in which institutional credibility continues to be so low, what is most serious is not that a party loses an election but that the hope for a better future, promised by the peace accords, might end in disillusionment and indifference due to the consolidation of a process that throws great masses of population into poverty.

Public Security and Respect for Human Rights

Institutionality Misunderstood

Just as elections are indispensable for good governance, a climate of public security is essential for peaceful coexistence and establishing harmonious relations and trust among individuals, communities, groups, and institutions. In the absence of such a climate, it is unlikely that peace, reconciliation, and concern for the common good and the economy will prosper or that the citizenry will accept and trust in the law and the authorities; hence the crucial importance of the roles played by the consolidation of the institutional trilogy made up of the National Civilian Police, the Office of the Human Rights Ombudsman, and the judiciary. The first two are creations of the accords; the latter, which already existed, was called upon to reform itself.

It is not easy to make the transition from an atmosphere of war, rights violations, insecurity, and confrontation to one in which humanist values predominate or are reborn. As a result, it is not easy to put the written word into practice, to infuse the essence and spirit of the peace accords into daily life. Setting aside the dead-weight throwback legacies of an authoritarian society, and the legacy of the language and confrontational attitudes that characterize a society in conflict, practical realities above and beyond the greater or lesser political will of the individuals vested with authority impede the full implementation of the peace accords.

The lack of a criminal justice policy to concentrate police and judicial efforts already has restricted coordination and cooperation among these institutions. In addition, the lack of harmonious functioning and coordination between a new National Civilian Police and the traditional judiciary, which should have self-reform as its main mission, is another source of friction that impairs spontaneous and tacit mutual understanding. One could say that there is a "generation gap" between these state entities. It is also understandable that the unprecedented experience of being subjected to the scrutiny of the new Office of the Human Rights Ombudsman has been strongly resisted by the heads of state institutions accustomed to making incontestable decisions concerning citizens' rights and complaints. It is only logical to suppose that some time must pass before the old institution stops producing antibodies to this new organ. Finally, although this is by no means the last word on the subject, successfully implementing an idea and a program that exist on paper requires capable people entirely given over to this service in all of the key posts in the process of building this new institutional order. This requires exceptional human qualities and virtues which, to put it kindly, are not in abundance.

However, among these and other objective difficulties, the largest problem has been the lack of awareness on the part of the government authorities, in particular those in charge of public security, regarding their serious responsibility for attaining the goals of the peace accords, even conceding that they may have done their utmost to ensure the optimal functioning of all of the institutions under their charge. On too many occasions this scant understanding of their historical mission has engendered false and absurd confrontations over the objectives and the specific roles of one institution vis-à-vis the others, provoking skepticism and a serious deterioration of public trust in the country's institutional framework. If there is a failure to achieve this trust and promote general adherence to the new rule of law, reviewing figures, evaluating institutions, and declaring compliance with the formalities of the accords will be useless.

Public security is undoubtedly the first place on which to construct a direct and daily sense of security, where citizens' problems can be confidently submitted to state authorities. This is why a severe blow has been dealt to the cultivation of public trust, because the top-ranking authorities in the new National Civilian Police, and in particular the minister of public security,[27] created a climate of skepticism and distrust with respect to the guarantees that were to be expected from the new institutional arrangement. On repeated occasions this minister accused the judicial system of fostering crime, and he has expressed indignation over judicial decisions that allowed individuals detained by the PNC to go free.[28] The most serious aspect of his accusations was that they were always generic, with concrete cases mentioned only by way of example or illustration. The minister never used legal channels to lodge a complaint against a judge, who, in his view, had hindered police work or the effectiveness of crime control.

It is difficult to gauge the effect on the collective conscience of seeing that even the minister of public security was so little inclined to use the resources that the institutional setup offered him, which revealed their scant credibility as useful and effective instruments for accomplishing their lofty goals. His spontaneous recourse to and the apparent effectiveness of public confrontation was a strategy more fitted to psychological warfare.

This analysis, however, is less concerned with the motives of authorities and individuals and more interested in fleshing out their objective effects on the construction of democracy and respect for democratic means. The negative impact on the public of these events in the upper echelons of politics cannot be measured. There are two equally worrisome readings here. First, if the population is not interested, if it does not feel directly affected by these disputes among the presumed guarantors of their security, it would have to be conceded that the peace process has put down only superficial roots in Salvadoran life. Second, it can be deduced that the same attitude and sentiment expressed by the minister with respect to the judicial system and its authorities has been assimilated and is shared by his subordinates in performing their functions. This has poisoned (not irreparably, it is hoped) the environment of mutual respect and cooperation that both institutions need on the ground to achieve their ultimate purposes, which are the prevention and prosecution of crime and ending of impunity.

It would be extremely difficult to identify precisely all of the effects and reactions that this confrontational environment produces in the different social sectors,[29] and in particular in the police corps. Yet it was in this context that summary executions and "social cleansing" proliferated in the eastern zone beginning in late 1994 and extended to other areas of the country throughout 1995.[30]

The minister's accusations did not go unanswered. One of the Supreme Court justices, among others who deplored his attitude,[31] lamented the lack of training in public safety and the ignorance of police procedure displayed by the highest responsible police authorities. For a long time the same minister also showed a heightened hostility toward the present human rights ombudsman, Victoria de Avilés, discrediting her decisions and actions as politically motivated, especially when her statements pointed to the alleged involvement of police agents in criminal acts.[32] If the strategic and operational objectives of those in charge of implementing the essential aspects of the accords had included inculcating and consolidating confidence in the new institutional framework, in the light of the alarming crime rate,[33] this confrontation would never have taken place.

The ombudsman repeatedly has stated in various national and international fora that her role is not understood by government officials whose decisions and actions are the subject of investigations by her office. But more dangerous to the office of the ombudsman than the lack of understanding is the silent veto imposed on her office by the central government through a progressive budgetary asphyxiation. In 1997, when the institution was still expanding and consolidating, the government allocated it a budget 10 percent lower than it had received the previous year. This is equivalent to condemning to ineffectiveness and institutional dwarfism one of the offices created by the Chapultepec accords for no less a task than changing and democratizing how power is used in state institutions.

The problem for the ombudsman's office is not minor, nor a mere rationalization of fiscal policy, as the government claims. This new institutional entity is essential for the growth of peace and democracy, as outlined in the accords. Indeed, it is so important that a disabled and hobbled ombudsman's office would be the truest reflection of the failure to implement the peace accords. It appears that the government leadership has not adequately understood or accepted their higher commitment to a new rule of law, which does not include mere self-assured and empty declarations that the accords have been carried out.

Fighting Impunity: The First Opportunity Missed

To prosecute crime, fight impunity, and cultivate collective recognition of and adherence to a well-constructed police institution with a solid foundation, when it has been so manipulated and distorted, is a complex and difficult task. The same can be said for the judicial system and the other institutions that participate in the administration of justice. As important as daily and conscientious practice, deeds of symbolic importance also are needed to stir the social conscience and modify the understandable attitude of skepticism, indifference, or rejection with which the public responded to the pantomime of democracy that prevailed almost up to the signing of the peace accords.[34]

The most promising recommendations of the truth commission, aimed at punishing the worst violations of human rights and eradicating impunity, were simply ignored or even opposed by the government authorities responsible for their implementation. One week after the commission released its report, clarifying the reality of the crimes and violations that had shaken Salvadoran society and the international community, the government and its parliamentary majority approved a hasty amnesty, one that only the general population should and could have conceded. Nine months after this decree, amid the series of assassinations of former FMLN commanders that appeared politically motivated, the Joint Group to Investigate Politically Motivated Illegal Armed Groups (Grupo Conjunto para la Investigación de los Grupos Armados Ilegales con Motivación Política) was formed, at the urging of the secretary-general of the United Nations.[35] The investigation into such criminal structures, and the warning about their possible resurgence, was one of the most important recommendations of the commission;[36] the recommendation was ignored and resisted by President Cristiani, until the impact and gravity of the incidents forced him to accept it.

The investigation was the responsibility of representatives of the United Nations Observer Mission in El Salvador (ONUSAL) and the Office of the Human Rights Ombudsman, as well as two independent lawyers designated by the government. The results of their report were

released in July 1994, by which time Armando Calderón Sol had assumed the presidency. Its principal recommendations met the same fate
as those of the Truth Commission: They either were ignored or were implemented more formally than effectively.[37] The investigation into the
most important cases, which was delivered to President Calderón and the
Office of the Attorney General in the form of confidential appendixes,
was never reopened by the Salvadoran authorities, as originally agreed.
Moreover, the sporadic allusions to it made by members of the government, especially the attorney general, criticized the "insufficiency" of the
evidence obtained through the investigation. A year after the report was
scorned and forgotten, the practice of kidnapping returned.[38] In 1996
history repeated itself when police agents assassinated citizens for political reasons. In effect, members of the Criminal Investigations Division
(División de Investigaciones Criminales, or DIC) killed former FMLN
commander Francisco Manzanares in the city of San Miguel. In October
1997 the judge determined that the assassination had all the hallmarks of
a politically motivated killing.[39]

It would be an exaggeration to claim that if the government had paid serious attention to the recommendations of the Truth Commission and the
Joint Group, criminal acts such these and many others would not have occurred. Yet the public revelation and prosecution of organized crime structures, the return of which was feared by the commission and some of which
were identified by the joint group, surely would have neutralized some of
these powerful groups and prevented the rise of others. It is even less understandable that the findings and recommendations were ignored when,
at the outset of the Calderón administration, the then vice minister of public security admitted the existence of "organized crime, even in state institutions." And President Calderón himself, during his first days in office,
could not deny that "there could be a tie between organized crime, death
squads, and common crime."[40]

Coinciding with the president's statements, the Joint Group's investigation characterized the composition and operation of organized crime
in the following terms: "These structures show a high degree of organization, in both urban and rural areas. An analysis of these structures leads
to the conclusion that they have sufficient capacity to remain in a latent
state and to activate themselves when they consider circumstances to be
appropriate, using violent means to attain political goals." Further on it
concludes that "the Joint Group believes that the conditions necessary
for the survival of politically-motivated illegal armed groups and orga-

nized crime structures are complementary, as the objectives can easily be transferred from one field of action to the other." Moreover, it noted that

> even if the Joint Group has not found evidence to affirm that the existence of these groups is due to state policy, this does not mean that they are totally detached from the state apparatus, for evidence has been gathered to indicate that active-duty members of the armed forces and National Police as well as persons who hold public office have been identified as members of these clandestine structures. In addition, it can be affirmed that some of these illegal activities were directed, supported, covered up, or tolerated by members of the armed forces, police, judiciary, or municipal authorities.[41]

It is useless to lament the squandering of so much effort to investigate, anticipate, and prevent crime. Nor does one get anywhere by pausing to identify the cause of this strange and defensive government attitude with respect to the observations and recommendations of such highly credible entities. What is needed now, and in the long run, is an effective and credible police and judiciary. To this end, it is essential that there be fostered at all levels a robust culture of absolute respect for rules and procedures, whose spirit was molded in the Chapultepec Accords. Operating exclusively by institutional channels is the only effective means of detecting and eradicating the corrupt elements and practices found by the Joint Working Group in some state institutions, and practices that have so often since then displayed their ability to survive and even reproduce.

The National Civilian Police: Institutionality Postponed

Unfortunately, it is not only police and judicial effectiveness that has been called into question in light of crime statistics; members of these very institutions themselves have behaved in ways that confirm the force and pertinence of the joint group's observations.

Even worse, policies that distort or nullify the institutional consolidation of the PNC also have been detected.[42] The long-standing problems and the inefficient and disoriented institutionalization has hindered the development and professionalization of the PNC;[43] meanwhile the minister responsible for security matters continues inappropriately as the operational commander of the institution. Regulations governing access to the courses needed for promotion at the National Academy for Public Security have yet to be approved, and the lack of such regulation, which precludes a transparent and objective selection of the most-qualified candidates, sparked a crisis in the first round of promotions in September 1997.[44] The institution and the motivation of its personnel are seriously damaged if promotion processes remain subjectively and arbitrarily tied to the officers in charge and ultimately the minister. In such a situation, servility and personal loyalty, not loyalty to the institution, easily can become the means of getting ahead. It does not require great insight to imagine how police agents and commanders could interpret and apply this arbitrary decision-making mode to essential aspects of the institution.

The directors of the National Academy for Public Security and the National Civilian Police were also the protagonists in a public quarrel in August and September 1997, which intensified as a result of a rash of crimes involving police corporals, sergeants, and detectives. The director of the academy noted and warned that none of the PNC corporals or sergeants had taken the necessary courses to qualify for the responsible exercise of their authority.[45] He was right to fear the lack of formal training of the midlevel police commanders; most of them did not have more than a ninth-grade education, the minimum level necessary to enter basic training at the police academy.

The police director responded by praising the instruction that was given to the detectives and members of specialized police units by the PNC, at the same time putting down the programs and the quality of the specialized courses offered by the academy. He then referred to the practical limitations that make it difficult to do without personnel if they are sent off to prolonged training and promotion courses.

This visible dispute had a pernicious effect on public opinion, especially among graduates of the academy and midlevel police commanders and their subordinates. It also has extremely serious institutional consequences. First, it is unacceptable for police commanders to continue to exercise authority indefinitely without having to take tests to guarantee their proficiency, for the good of both the citizenry and the police. Second, the certification of agents' and detectives' training should be handled in a rigorous, academic way. The short courses and practical training that may be provided by generous and well-intentioned international cooperation agencies cannot replace a well-structured and academically recognized process of professionalizing the police. It also should be borne in mind that the lack of coordination and cooperation that prevails between the PNC and the academy strains and squanders the assistance given by the various cooperation agencies.

Apart from the lack of or deficiencies in the statutes and regulations that should govern the PNC, the minister of security has shown a decided inclination to use parallel structures, independent of the line of police command, to investigate and solve some of the potentially most politically sensitive cases.[46] New information recently came to light about the participation of a "Detective Zacarías"—the former head of a nonofficial investigative unit directly under the command of the minister and outside the regular structure of the PNC—in the investigation of such serious cases as the kidnapping of the son of the advisor to former President Cristiani. The same "Detective Zacarías" who had commanded the unofficial unit was entrusted with the investigation of the alleged involvement of seven police agents, including the chief of a police post, in the assassination of a youth in 1995. Two years later the minister had to admit that he had authorized these *intervenciones "extrapoliciales"* (actions outside of normal police structures), arguing that in the latter case, the participation of a person from outside the institution provided greater guarantees of impartiality, given the likely "solidarity" with the allegedly criminal agents of their colleagues at the same institution. Since the minister has primary responsibility for fostering public confidence in the PNC's internal control mechanisms and conveying to the community absolute certainty that possible police cover-ups and complicities are subject to institutional controls, his evident distrust of the professionalism and credibility of the police's internal control units is demoralizing.

Furthermore, in assigning important cases to "private persons,"[47] the minister is downplaying the role that the specialized units of the police are called on to play in the institution. This does not foster the self-esteem and the professional growth of the Criminal Investigations Division (DIC). If the minister himself cannot set an example and follow police directives in fighting common and organized crime, there is simply no room to shape and cultivate an esprit de corps, which is especially important in the start-up phase, when attitudes and practices are being shaped and taking root in the personnel.

The above-mentioned issues and problems affecting the institutional structure of public security do not cover all of the condemnable acts and policies carried out in this sector, nor have they been set forth in all of their complexity. The marked deficiencies of the police internal control mechanisms, and the scant capacity and creativity of the inspector general to perform his oversight functions merit lengthy examination. Yet the ground covered here suffices to illustrate the dangerously arbitrary way in which this sector has been handled during the crucial stage of consolidating the new police force. With more than enough justification, the unofficial report of July 1996, submitted by the secretary-general to the United Nations Security Council, deplored the difficulties hampering consolidation of the sector, making special reference to

> the different conceptions of public security held by the policy makers within the sector. Accordingly there remains the risk, first identified by MINUSAL in its September 1995 evaluation of the public security sector which was conducted at the request of President Calderón Sol, that the PNC might lose its identity as an institution at the service of the community and become, instead, a new instrument of power, unaccountable to the public and prone to authoritarianism, of which there are increasing signs.[48]

Conclusion

Five years is a very short time for taking stock of historic changes. It is also very little time for a movement to renew the institutional framework of a country to have given the first jolt to the last and most conservative caboose in the social structure. Yet the fact that the very hallmark institutions of the peace accords have such pronounced delays and deviations in their formation and regulation demands attention.

As we noted at the outset, the Chapultepec Accords trusted that the renewal and institutional democratization of the country would become sufficiently dynamic to drive the economic and social transformation of El Salvador. The force of change needs to be bolstered if it is to reach this goal, without exhausting its energies in an endless fight for proper institutionalization. Encouraging signs are now coming from the socioeconomic arena, and from the right of the ideological spectrum, that converge regarding the need to strengthen the institutional framework and transparency in the management of the national economy.[49] If political and economic initiatives converge to bring about the real institutionalization of the country, it will no doubt prove the peace negotiators historically correct in declining to discuss the economic model, trusting the future to democratic forces. Nevertheless, it must be realized that before becoming the new society envisaged in the accords, a whole generation must cross the desert of doubts with regard to the future and place itself above the temptations to return to the system of deeply rooted authoritarianism and imposition.

Notes

1. Much has been written about the periods of negotiation and implementation of the accords. Among the many sources are: Ricardo Córdova Macias, *El Salvador: Las negociaciones de paz y los retos de la postguerra* (San Salvador: Instituto de Estudios de América Latina, 1993); Gino Costa, *La transformación de la seguridad pública: Resistencias, dificultades, y Desafíos* (San Salvador: Universidad Centroamericana José Simeón Cañas, 1998); Héctor Dada Hirezi, "Los acuerdos de paz y la democratización en El Salvador," mimeographed, San Salvador, February 1995; *De la experiencia salvadoreña a la esperanza guatemalteca* (San Salvador: FLACSO-El Salvador and Instituto Salvadoreña para la Democracia, 1997); David Escobar Galindo, "El primer esfuerzo nacional en la historia," and Salvador Samayoa, "Un cambio político estructural," *Tendencias,* No. 36 (December 1994–January 1995): 26–30, 31–34; FLACSO-El Salvador, "A dos años de la firma de los Acuerdos de Paz," Cuaderno de Trabajo No. 5, November 1, 1994; Fernando Harto de Vera, *El Salvador 1979–1991: La larga marcha hacia la paz* (San Salvador: Fundación Dr. Guillermo Manuel Ungo, 1994); Tommie Sue Montgomery, *Revolution in El Salvador: From Civil Strife to Civil Peace* (Boulder, Colo.: Westview Press, 1995); Jack Spence, et al., *Chapultepec: Five Years Later: El Salvador's Political Reality and Uncertain Future* (Boston: Hemisphere Initiatives, 1997); and William Stanley and David Holiday, "Under the Best of Circumstances: ONUSAL and the Dilemmas of Verification and Institution Building in El Salvador" (paper presented at the conference entitled "Peacemaking and Democratization in the Hemisphere," North-South Center, Miami, Fla., April 11–13, 1996).

2. The U.N. report, however, noted "persistent deficiencies in the judicial system," "a disappointing failure" to adopt recommendations of a U.N.-sponsored truth commission, "disheartening" sluggishness in the land transfer program, and "distortions" in the structure and model of the National Civilian Police. United Nations, "The Situation in Central America: Procedures for the Establishment of a Firm and Lasting Peace and Progress in Fashioning a Region of Peace, Freedom, Democracy and Development: Assessment of the Peace Process in El Salvador," Report of the Secretary-General, A/51/917, July 1, 1997, 16–17, 6, 7, 11, and 3.

The most complete record of U.N. involvement in El Salvador is to be found in United Nations, *The United Nations and El Salvador 1990–1995,* Blue Book Series, vol. 4 (New York: United Nations Department of Public Information, 1995).

3. United Nations, Department of Public Information, Press Release, "Secretary-General Says El Salvador Peace Accord Is 'Crowning Achievement' of Long and Arduous Journey: Urges Support for Reconstruction," SG/SM/4685, CA/61, January 16, 1992, 2.

4. David Escobar Galindo, a member of the Salvadoran government's negotiating commission, has said: "The Salvadoran political system entered into a deep crisis and took us to war. As a result, if we wanted to resolve the war through a negotiated agreement, it had to be of a political nature. . . . it would have been a useless waste to have tried to create a socio-economic model in the agreement."

5. The accords reduced the size of the army and limited its role to external defense. Rapid-reaction counterinsurgency battalions involved in some of the worst massacres of the war were disbanded. The repressive security forces of the past—the National Police, Treasury Police, and National Guard—were abolished and a new National Civilian Police created in their stead.

6. See "Los acuerdos de paz y la transición a la democracia en El Salvador," in FLACSO-Guatemala, *Los retos de la paz, la democracia y el desarrollo sostenible en Guatemala* (Guatemala City: Facultad Latinoamericana de Ciencias Sociales, 1996).

7. The attitudes of members of the private sector and government made getting started difficult, and the forum's activities commenced with little evidence that either side wanted to come to agreement. The most time was taken up with discussions of how to implement agreements signed within the framework of the International Labor Organization (ILO), while issues that the very signers of the peace accords had identified as fundamental causes of the war were practically left off

the agenda. The forum meetings were suspended in late 1993, supposedly so they would not interfere with the beginning of the electoral campaign in November. The forum ultimately was replaced with a Supreme Labor Council (Consejo Superior del Trabajo), which had very little of the scope initially assigned to the forum.

8. Instituto Universitario de Opinión Pública, "La opinión pública sobre las elecciones de 1997," *Revista de Estudios Centroamericanos* (ECA) (March-April 1997), 242.

9. In addition, these shortcomings, and the abstentionism that they cause, may not alter the results on a national level, but they certainly can change the balance of elections in small municipalities, where the margin of victory is decided by very small differences, in some cases by just a dozen votes. See United Nations Development Program, "Resultados estadísticos de las elecciones de 1994 y 1997," Junta de Vigilancia Electoral. "Apoyo al plan de fiscalización y vigilancia del proceso electoral de 1997" UNDP Project Doc. ELS/96/L08 (1997).

10. U.N. Press Release, "Secretary-General Says El Salvador Peace Accord."

11. United Nations Development Program, "Resultados estadísticos de las elecciones de 1994 y 1997," 11. In 1997 approximately 1.1 million persons voted, of a total of 2.6 million qualified to do so. In 1994 a total of 1.4 million people voted. Presidential elections have always attracted greater interest and citizen participation than elections of mayors and legislators.

12. See survey carried out by the Instituto de Opinión Pública of the Central American University (UCA) in the first week of February 1997, in which 66 percent of the population said that they had little or no confidence in the political parties. The judgment was less severe in the case of the Supreme Electoral Tribunal, where the percentage of population with this negative opinion was 50 percent. See "La opinión pública sobre las elecciones de 1997," *ECA*, 248.

13. During the last electoral campaign, the Supreme Electoral Tribunal sponsored its own opinion polls; based on those polls, it celebrated having obtained an evaluation slightly better than that of other state institutions. Most of these institutions, by their very nature, are permanently subjected to claims against them and popular scrutiny. The Supreme Electoral Tribunal, in contrast, is the subject of public attention and scrutiny only during the brief electoral periods.

14. The exit of the group called "los maneques," the circle closest to the party founder in the early the 1980s, was the most visible political expression of this infighting.

15. In late 1996 and 1997 the government admitted there had been an "economic slow-down," a product of the "normal cycles" of the economy.

16. The election of former president Cristiani to head the ARENA party does not appear to have resolved the party's internal disputes. On the contrary, business representatives and idealogues of the right, among them Orlando de Sola and Alfredo Mena Lagos, historically tied to the party, have condemned what they call Cristiani's "oligopolist and mercantilist" intentions.

17. One of the five magistrates of the Supreme Electoral Tribunal, a member of the Partido Demócrata, spoke out publicly against these reforms. Five days before the elections he renounced his membership in the party.

18. The Partido Demócrata Cristiano (PDC) and the Partido Demócrata were the elements most manipulated by ARENA in this strategy. The removal of the Supreme Electoral Tribunal magistrate Eduardo Colindres, designated by the PDC, and his replacement by another obedient to the ARENA strategy came just before the beginning of the electoral campaign. Prior to this, a PDC national convention had elected a directorate presided over by Carlos Claramount, an independent who opposed the subordination of the legislative faction to the directives of the president of the Parliament and of the ARENA party, Gloria Salguero Gross. Moreover, ARENA ignored a decision of the Supreme Electoral Tribunal that ordered the political parties' electoral observers to stop identifying themselves with their colors and emblems, and to wear only tribunal identification. This decision obviously would have eliminated the "psychological" advantage that ARENA's overwhelming and dominant presence at the polling places always gave it.

19. Although this was a less-than-instructive showing of its sense of submission to the rule of law, it is hoped that the new party leadership does not engage in such vices, even at the risk of los-

ing control of the presidency. In January 1997, in response to the series of changes to the electoral rules, the opposition political parties sent the secretary-general of the United Nations a letter of protest over this conduct.

20. A worrisome exception to the relative normalcy with which the elections were conducted on the national level was the case of Ilopango municipality, where disorder and shoving matches among party representatives led to the suspension of voting for several hours and the closure of one polling place before the stipulated hour. Electoral authorities of the municipality and authorities of the department of San Salvador failed to respond.

21. There are no studies on the effects of or the influences on citizens' decisions of this overwhelming presence of a political party's sometimes belligerent contingents at polling places. In any event, it is an improvement over the open coercion of a massive deployment of the army and security forces before and during the conflict.

22. World Bank, World Development Indicator (Washington, D.C.: World Bank, 1997), 50. Ministry of Economy, Information Bureau, "Encuesta de hogares de propósitos múltiples 1996," (San Salvador: Dirección General de Coordinación, Unidad de Investigaciones Muestrales, April 1997), 57.

23. Francisco J. Ibisate "La economía imposible," *Realidad* (July–August (1997): 315, 314, 314–15.

24. Ibid., 318.

25. The battle to have the agrarian and bank debts of the individual and cooperative producers of the sector forgiven, after the last elections, is only the most recent expression of a crisis that has become more aggravated in the 1990s.

26. See "La opinión pública sobre las elecciones de 1997," ECA, 232–233.

27. After the accords were signed, Hugo Barrera was initially named vice minister in charge of public security, under the direction of the Interior Ministry. In 1995, when a separate Ministry of Public Security was created, Barrera continued to direct public security matters, and continues to do so as of this writing.

28. The conduct of the minister caused a breakdown in communications with the president of the judiciary, which led the president of the country to step in to reestablish the damaged relationship.

29. See IUDOP, Estudio ACTIVA, "La violencia en el gran San Salvador," *Boletín de Prensa* 12, No. 5, Universidad Centroamericana José Simeón Cañas, San Salvador (1997). According to the survey data, in the section on "social cleansing," 15.4 percent of those polled accepted the idea of another person killing "undesirable people." Some 46.6 percent would "understand" such an action, while 38 percent would repudiate it.

30. The dismantling of a death squad that called itself the "black shadow" in the eastern zone—a death squad in which agents and officers of the PNC were involved—says much about the loss of trust in legal and institutional procedures to resolve security problems and fight impunity. The process by which the detained agents and officers were cleared left major doubts, given the solid testimony and evidence. Similar events have continued, more sporadically in the western and central areas of the country. Six agents assigned to criminal investigation, quartered in Santa Ana, San Salvador, and Cuscatlán, were arrested in the second half of 1997 for committing crimes.

31. In mid-1996 the Supreme Court of Justice responded publicly through the national press, informing their counterparts in other countries of the circumstances that threatened their investiture and integrity.

32. In the best-known cases, such as the assassinations of the youths Vilanova and Gaytán in separate incidents in September 1995 and January 1996, the judicial process has determined that the Ombudsman was correct, implicitly discarding the influence of political interests in its decisions. In the minister's favor, it should be noted that in the most recent months of this year, he has refrained from renewed public confrontations against other state institutions or their representatives.

33. See IUDOP, Estudio ACTIVA, "La violencia en el gran San Salvador." This coincides with

a study by the Inter-American Development Bank, disseminated in September, that describes El Salvador as the most violent country in Latin America.

34. We have already mentioned that the war to win the hearts and minds of the people required improvements in institutional conduct. The relative modernization of the electoral system during this period was an essential part of that struggle.

35. In a letter directed to the Security Council by the Secretary-General of the United Nations, dated November 3, 1993, (U.N. Doc. S/26689 [1993]), he noted that "the Director of the Human Rights Division indicated . . . that politically motivated human rights violations had become more direct." The director also recalled that the Secretary-General in his report on the recommendations of the truth commission of October 14, 1993, had expressed his concern because illegal armed groups existed "whose methods seem to repeat behavioral patterns prevailing in the past," (*Progress Report on the Implementation of the Recommendations of the Commission on the Truth.* U.N. Doc. S/26581, Annex [1993]; para. 32).

36. The commission determined that "all necessary measures must be taken to ensure that they are disbanded. Given the country's history, prevention is essential in this area. There is always a risk that such groups may become active again." United Nations, New York, and San Salvador, *From Madness to Hope: The 12-Year War in El Salvador, Report of the Commission on the Truth for El Salvador,* transmitted from the Secretary-General to the Security Council, April 1, 1993, S/25500, p. 180.

37. One of the recommendations was to form the Department for the Investigation of Organized Crime (Departamento de Investigación del Crimen Organizado, DICO, as distinct from the Criminal Investigations Division, DIC) within the PNC, which was formed and operated in spite of the tenacious opposition of the then vice-minister of public security, Hugo Barrera, who without any basis accused the entity of being a creation and an instrument of the FMLN. Although the DICO continued to function as of mid-1998, its operative structure was a far cry from what the Joint Group had proposed.

38. Although various kidnappings have been publicized, the most famous of all was that of the son of Saúl Súster, a close advisor to ex-President Cristiani during his administration. Andrés Súster was kidnapped in September 1995 and was released one year later after a ransom payment. In August 1994 a youth, Harold Hill, was also kidnapped and held for a year. In April and May 1996 two dynamite explosions brought back the most difficult moments of the war. The first was the explosion of a vehicle near the residences of the Cristiani and Súster families. The second was at the offices of an insurance business of the Cristiani family. That is why some investigative hypotheses examined a possible political motive behind these acts.

39. This judicial declaration is the first of its kind. Not even the assassinations of late 1993, which were the basis for the investigation by the Joint Group, came to be considered judicially as politically motivated. This is a step forward in the evolution of the judicial system and its greater independence.

40. Quote from the Channel 12 television news, reported in the *Informe del Grupo Conjunto para la Investigación de Grupos Armados Ilegales con Motivación Política en El Salvador,* San Salvador, July 28, 1994, 22 (unofficial translation).

Calderón Sol's statements surprised and scandalized public opinion, because the administration of President Cristiani and the president himself always denied that organized crime and death squads existed.

41. Ibid., 31, 32, 25.

42. It would not be fair to attribute to the police all responsibility for the insufficient eradication of impunity. Although this is not analyzed here, in the judiciary extremely cumbersome procedures are used to remove deficient and dishonest judges and officials, procedures that justify criticisms and lead to its ruinous lack of credibility.

43. See MINUSAL, "Informe de evaluación sobre el sector seguridad pública presentado por ONUSAL el 28 de Septiembre de 1995 a solicitud del presidente de la República," in United Na-

tions, *Ejecución de los acuerdos de paz en El Salvador: Recalendarizaciones, acuerdos complementarios y otros documentos importantes* (San Salvador: Unidad de Apoyo al Enviado del Secretario General, 1997), 93–113.

44. The law on police careers, which among other things establishes the rules for promotion, was not approved until 1996, when the Ministry of Public Security finally sent a bill to the Legislative Assembly.

45. When the new police force was created, there was a need to appoint temporarily a group of commanders, given that the law on police careers had yet to be enacted, and there were no internal norms or procedures governing the selection of whom to promote.

46. The best-known parallel structure with police functions was the Analysis Unit. In an April 1996 report, U.N. Secretary-General Boutros Boutros-Ghali reiterated his concern "over the persistence of some of the most damaging problems referred to by [Mission of the United Nations in El Salvador] MINUSAL. Although I welcome the dissolution of the 'analysis unit' . . . there remain personnel who operate outside the legally established structure of the National Civilian Police. In addition, high-ranking Salvadoran officials continue to interfere in strictly operational aspects of policing, thereby altering the established chain of command of the National Civilian Police and thus not contributing to the strengthening of that institution." United Nations, "The Situation in Central America: Procedures for the Establishment of a Firm and Lasting Peace and Progress in Fashioning a Region of Peace, Freedom, Democracy and Development," U.N. Doc. A/50/935 (1996) 2–3.

47. The previously mentioned Detective Zacarías is currently under investigation in Guatemala for hampering the investigations of delicate kidnapping cases, while being in the service of the Ministerio de Gobernación (Interior Ministry) of Guatemala. (See articles from a Guatemalan magazine reproduced in the morning daily *El Diario de Hoy,* September 1997.)

48. United Nations, *"Informal Report of the Secretary-General on the Status of Implementation of the Peace Accords in El Salvador"* (attachment, letter of the Secretary-General circulated informally to the Security Council), July 31, 1996, 1–2.

49. The frequent public statements since September 1997 by the former presidential commissioner for the modernization of the state, Alfredo Mena Lagos, and by the former superintendent for the privatization of energy and telecommunications, Orlando de Sola, reflect their strong belief in the urgent need to make the economy independent of the groups in power. According to their analysis, such influence, exercised from government positions, is the cause of the enrichment of privileged groups and of the impoverishment of large sectors of the population.

4

Peace and Democratization in Guatemala: Two Parallel Processes

DINORAH AZPURU

Introduction

The signing of the Accord for a Firm and Lasting Peace on December 29, 1996, was one of the most important events in the political history of Guatemala. Not only did it put an end to one of the longest and bloodiest armed conflicts in Latin America, but the entire process of the peace negotiations and the accords derived from it have implications well into the future. In the medium term, they may make it feasible to begin the many reforms urgently needed in the political, economic, social, and cultural life of Guatemala.

However, the peace accords were not the starting point for the construction of a democratic system in Guatemala. Throughout the decade from 1986 to 1996, the process of democratization and the process of making peace mutually influenced and reinforced each other. The process of democratization paved the way for the start of the peace negotiations, and the five years of the negotiations themselves advanced the process of democratization; indeed, the peace accords have as one of their central objectives the further consolidation of democracy in Guatemala.

The issue of whether democracy exists or not in a given country is a long-standing academic debate, and the numerous discussions on this issue go beyond the scope of this chapter. However, few studies of democratization in the hemisphere have included Guatemala. Although in some areas there has been little improvement in the country relative to the situation that prevailed fifteen years ago, in other respects there has been slow but perceptible improvement. Overall, I concur with the view expressed by Roger Plant in Chapter 11 that, compared to the terror experienced in the late 1970s and early 1980s, there has indeed been a sea change in Guatemala.

It is important to define what the process of democratization entails. For the purposes of this chapter, democracy is considered as a gradual process that starts with formal procedures—such as a written and broadly accepted constitution and fair elections—and builds progressively in other areas until it reaches a point of stability in which most of the desirable indices of democracy are met. In regard to these indices, American political scientist Kenneth Bollen proposes that the empirical ranking of democracy should be based on the degree of: (1) press freedom, (2) freedom of group opposition, (3) freedom of group political activity, (4) fairness of elections, (5) elections for executive office, and (6) legislative effectiveness.[1] The "Fitzgibbon-Johnson index" measures democracy on a scale that includes five key measures of democratic performance: (1) free speech, (2) free elections, (3) free party organizations, (4) independence of the judiciary, and (5) civilian supremacy over the military.[2]

In international academic circles, the issue of civil-military relations often has been cited as the central, if not only, variable by which to measure democratic progress in Guatemala. Although an analysis of the democratization process certainly must include civil-military relations as well as the issue of limitations on institutional development, one must take a broader perspective and look also at the maturation of civil society, the gains made in certain basic liberties, and the establishment of respect for the constitution.

It may seem odd to say that there is a degree of democracy in a country whose image abroad has been one of military control and repression. However, in spite of the military's control over "security" issues, the democratization process in Guatemala did permit the functioning of some civilian-run democratic institutions such as Tribunal Supremo Electoral and the Corte de Constitucionalidad (the Electoral Tribunal and the Constitutional Court), while it also allowed for the development of civil society organizations that in turn had an important influence on the peace process. Also, the degree of democratization within Guatemala varied by region: Although the so-called rural conflict areas remained under heavy military

control up until the signing of the peace accords, the capital and other urban areas were experiencing greater levels of democratic freedom. These
areas can perhaps be seen as "poles" in the process of democratization as
it slowly expanded to include other regions of the country.

An interesting point of comparison is the case of El Salvador. According
to Salvadoran analyst Ricardo Córdova Macias, between 1984 and 1987
debate revolved around whether peace negotiations were to precede elections, or whether elections were to be the central vehicle for resolving the
struggle for power.[3] In other words, in El Salvador one of the main issues
under discussion was the Frente Farabundo Martí, (FMLN's) participation
in the elections as a political party. In Guatemala, by contrast, some formal
progress (and even some substantive headway) in the process of democratization already had been made by the time the peace talks began. For that
reason, elections and the democratic and constitutional nature of the
regime were not directly discussed at the negotiating table. The guerrillas'
acknowledgment of certain democratic advances was reflected in the first
content accord signed by the parties (the Querétaro Accord on democratization) in 1991. Subsequent accords focused on the evolution of the democratization process.

Prominent Guatemalan sociologist Edelberto Torres-Rivas has stated
that, in most of the recent armed conflicts in the world, a cease-fire opened
the way for political parties to emerge, free elections to be held, and legitimate governments to be established. But the Guatemalan experience did
not follow this pattern: Rather, "in Guatemala, efforts towards peace
turned out to be a consequence of the process of democratization." Thus
the process in Guatemala is unique in that legal and legitimate governments had begun to exist before peace had been attained formally.[4] Figure
4.1 depicts the basic causal relationships underlying the Guatemalan peace
process.

Figure 4.1
Causal Relationships Underlying the Guatemalan Peace Process.

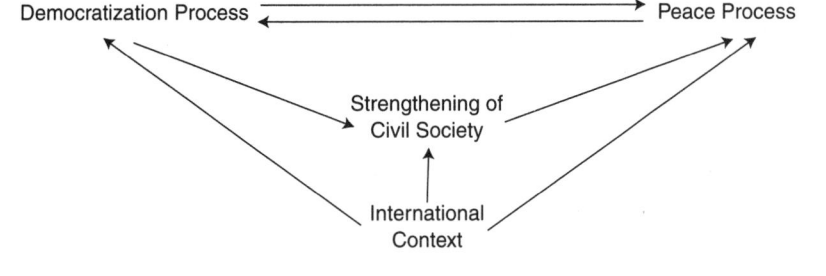

Throughout this chapter I try to show how gradual changes in the democratization process contributed to the end of a bloody and senseless armed conflict that lasted for thirty-six years. The claim is not that procedural democracy was consolidated before the peace process was concluded, but that important advances in democratization—among them the holding of transparent elections, the existence of a certain degree of freedom of press and association, and the leadership of civilian presidents elected beginning in 1986—were made before the peace negotiations were concluded. The argument proposed here is that the process of democratization took on a life of its own after 1984, not necessarily linked to the peace process, and had an impact on the accomplishments made later during the peace negotiations. In other words, the peace process would not have been possible without the parallel progress made in the process of democratization, and the full consolidation of democracy in Guatemala would not have been possible as long as the armed conflict continued.

A Brief Historical Overview: From the Counterinsurgent State to the Democratic Transition

Beginning in the early 1960s,[5] a counterinsurgency policy that was to last for several decades was established in Guatemala in an attempt to neutralize the threat of a revolutionary guerrilla movement. This policy, which fell within the framework of the Cold War and the national security doctrine proclaimed by the United States, was the driving force behind Guatemalan politics for over thirty years. In spite of the fact that Guatemala's political history is full of military governments and even military dictatorships, starting in 1960 and especially after 1963, the military's dominance of the country took on extremely complex dimensions. Pursuant to the counterinsurgent model, the army acquired powers, functions, and privileges that transcended the fight against the guerrillas. At the same time, anticommunist sentiments (which had existed in the country since the 1954 counterrevolution) were exacerbated.

Between 1963 and 1972 the armed conflict essentially took place in the eastern part of Guatemala, a region that ethnically is primarily *ladino* (nonindigenous). By the mid-1970s, after several years of retreat, the guerrillas were redeployed in western Guatemala. In this primarily indigenous region, they reoriented their activity and adopted a strategy based on ethnic and social demands.

In order to counteract this new wave of the revolutionary guerrilla movement, the state imposed what Guatemalan analyst Gabriel Aguilera called a policy of indiscriminate terror, which caused thousands of deaths.[6] Thus by early 1982, under the command of General Romeo Lucas, the country was experiencing one of its worst crises in recent history. Violations of human rights and state and paramilitary violence had decimated the social organization of the country at all levels. Guatemala was isolated from an international community that was shocked by the scope of repression in the country. In spite of this, the Guatemalan guerrillas—who united in 1982 in the Unidad Revolucionaria Nacional Guatemalteca (URNG)—gained ground, particularly in the northwestern part of the country.[7]

During the bloodiest years of the conflict—1979 to 1983—space for political activity was completely closed and moderate options disappeared from the political spectrum. Progressive social forces, which were labeled subversive by the military who were running the counterinsurgent state, were forced either to retreat totally or to ally themselves with those who had taken up arms as the only possible means of political expression. Throughout this period, the counterinsurgency strategy enjoyed the tacit or open support of some conservative elites in the country,[8] in particular the large landholders. Their objective, and that of the army, was to maintain "political stability," understood to mean the status quo—that is, a totally exclusionary economic and political system.

By the end of the Lucas administration, Guatemala had become so isolated from the international community, due to its human rights abuses, that tourism and foreign investment revenues had plummeted. This, as well as rampant corruption among some in the military, directly affected the interests of some business sectors, which led the industrialists and some sectors of the middle class to question the government and to demand a more open political system.[9] During this period the "official" political parties governed the country successively, while the moderate or reformist opposition parties had scant representation in Congress and their leaders were persecuted and repressed. Electoral laws were manipulated to suit the frauds perpetrated by the military governments. American political scientist Kenneth Coleman argues that in Central America, the systematic exclusion of reformists from power fueled the revolutionary insurrections.[10]

In such a context, some sectors viewed the coup d'état of March 1982, led by General Efraín Ríos Montt, as a chance for change in the prevailing political system. However, after Ríos Montt proclaimed himself chief of state in June of that year—displacing the other two members of his government junta—it became apparent that this was simply a readjustment in the military's counterinsurgency strategy. It turned out to be a successful move for the army's purposes: Ríos Montt managed to push the guerrillas back into the mountains through a military campaign that was harshly criticized by international human rights organizations. Nonetheless, the guerrillas were not annihilated.[11]

Although Ríos Montt had agreed to hold democratic elections, he entrenched himself in power until he was replaced through another coup in August 1983. During his rule, however, there was a perceptible change in the level of repression in urban areas, and some moderate civilians participated in his Council of State. American sociologist Timothy Wickham-Crowley states that in 1982, political phenomena began to turn decisively against the possibility of a successful revolution in Guatemala.[12] This might have been due to the fact that moderate opposition groups saw the possibility of reforming the existing political system under Ríos Montt instead of choosing to support the revolutionary movement, as had happened in Nicaragua toward the end of Anastasio Somoza's regime.

The new government of General Oscar Mejía called for elections for a National Constituent Assembly, which were held in July 1984. These elections were run and supervised by an autonomous electoral tribunal and were recognized as valid and transparent nationally and internationally. Three political parties dominated the election: two from the moderate opposition (the Unión del Centro Nacional [National Center Union] and Democracia Cristiana [Christian Democracy]), and one traditional one (the Movimiento de Liberación Nacional [National Liberation Movement]). The Constituent Assembly began a process of consultation with various sectors of society to draft a new constitution; this was novel in Guatemalan political practice, particularly in the climate of counterinsurgency that still prevailed in the country. The drafting of the new constitution was concluded officially in 1985. It contained some important provisions, such as: lifting the ban on parties with a communist ideology (imposed by the 1965 constitution); recognition of the fact that Guatemala is comprised of various ethnic groups (for the first time in the constitutional history of the country); the creation of such new juridical offices as the Human Rights Ombudsman and the Constitutional Court; and the complete autonomy of the Tribunal Supremo Electoral (electoral tribunal).

There is some agreement among Guatemalan analysts that this marked the beginning of the country's democratic opening. This opening, however, was not the result of intense domestic social pressure or of pressure from armed combatants (who had been dealt a serious military blow by

Ríos Montt's counterinsurgency strategy). Rather, it was the result of the wearing down of the military governments, which faced the country's growing economic problems, the erosion of their traditional support from the organized private sector, and the beginning of protests from some social sectors, particularly the middle class.

The external factors that affected this democratic opening also should be borne in mind. These include the wave of democratization that was moving across Latin America, outside pressure exerted on the successive military governments for their violations of human rights (including a shift in United States foreign policy toward Guatemala during the Carter administration),[13] and the events taking place elsewhere in Central America. The 1979 triumph of the Sandinista revolution in Nicaragua and the military and political progress made by the Salvadoran guerrillas led the Guatemalan military to perceive a need to present to the people a democratic alternative and a formal transfer of power to civilians, even if it was still part of a counterinsurgency strategy.[14]

The Beginning of Peace Negotiations

Within the framework of the new constitution, general elections were called for November 1985. The transparency of those elections for all levels (mayors, deputies, and president) was recognized nationally and internationally. Vinicio Cerezo from the Christian Democratic Party was elected president. His party was considered within Guatemala to be progressive or reformist, on the center-left of the national political spectrum. However, when Cerezo took office, direct talks between the government and the URNG were still not feasible. First, a counterinsurgency mentality still prevailed among the Guatemalan military, who seemed willing to transfer the management of many areas of government to the newly elected officials but not in what they called "national security" matters. Second, the URNG had discounted the value of the elections and the meaning of the democratic opening.

In spite of this, during his second year in office, Cerezo instructed a high-ranking leader of the Christian Democratic party, his ambassador to Spain, Danilo Barillas, to make unofficial contact with the URNG. It should be noted that it was Cerezo who promoted the first meetings of the Central American presidents, within the framework of his policy of "active neutrality." The first meeting, called Esquipulas I, took place in Guatemala in 1986; Esquipulas II was held there in August 1987. The latter was of paramount importance for the peace processes in the region: It was the Esquipulas II Accords that set forth the Procedure for Establishing a Firm and Lasting Peace in Central America.

According to Gabriel Aguilera, that accord, along with free elections and the entry into office of democratically elected civilian governments, were the factors that made it possible to begin peace negotiations in Guatemala.[15] Before discussing why that is true, it is important to point out that in the 1985 elections, there was no legal ban on the participation of any political party.[16] In fact, the leftist Partido Socialista Democrático (Social Democratic Party), which included several academics who had returned from exile, participated in those elections.

Stages in the Negotiations and the Democratization Process

Academic assessments conducted at the end of the 1980s seem to agree that the Esquipulas II Accords had a greater impact on Guatemala than on the other countries of the region, particularly with regard to the role and importance of the so-called Comisión Nacional de Reconciliación, National Reconciliation Commissions (CNRs), which in each country were nongovernmental groups formed by prominent citizens to seek political solutions to the armed conflicts in Central America.[17]

Within the framework of Esquipulas II, what is generally labeled the *indirect phase* of peace negotiations began in Guatemala. In September and October 1987 three specific events occurred: (1) a general amnesty was declared for those who had been involved in the armed confrontation; (2) the CNR was formed, chaired by Monsignor Rodolfo Quezada, who was allowed to operate independently of the government; and (3) an official meeting was held in Spain between members of the Cerezo administration and representatives of the URNG. That meeting was not successful, due in large measure to the contrary positions of the parties, particularly the government's requirement that the URNG lay down its weapons as a precondition for dialogue.

An important forum also was bringing together different sectors of society within the country as a result of the Esquipulas II Accords. The CNR convened the Gran Diálogo Nacional (National Dialogue), as it was called, and began its meetings in March 1989. About eighty organizations representing civil society participated, although the private sector, represented by CACIF (the Coordinating Committee of Agricultural, Commercial, Industrial, and Financial Associations), did not.

After the attempt to start a direct dialogue between the Cerezo administration and the URNG virtually failed, the CNR sought alternative mechanisms. To this end, it held a meeting with URNG representatives in 1988; again, little progress was made. Finally, at a meeting held in Oslo, Norway, in March 1990, the first boost was given to the peace process in Guatemala. As the late Guatemalan political scientist Martha Salguero indicates, both the central government and the army gave their blessings to the dialogue undertaken at Oslo; even the internal opposition on the right seemed to favor it.[18]

According to Guatemalan historian Arturo Taracena, the fact that some conservatives in the army were willing to negotiate politically with the guerrillas was due to the failure of an offensive to annihilate the insurgent forces launched by the armed forces in 1988. This failure supposedly convinced military leaders that political bargaining was the only way to prevent a war of attrition that could go on indefinitely.[19] The guerrillas, in turn, were inclined to negotiate both because of the confidence they had gained from the army's failed offensive and because of international events, such as the fall of the Eastern Bloc and the electoral defeat of the Sandinista government in February 1990, which made the success of the revolutionary model increasingly unlikely.

The Basic Agreement on the Quest for Peace through Political Means, signed as a result of the Oslo meeting, established the concept of negotiations and the procedures for holding them. Peace and functional and participatory democracy were set as the goals of the negotiations, and the office of conciliator was created. The agreement also established a mechanism for meetings between the URNG and various sectors of Guatemalan civil society, including political parties, the private business sector, academics, the so-called popular organizations (unions, human right groups, Mayan organizations), cooperatives, and religious groups. These meetings were held throughout 1990. By that time, four years after the process of democratization had begun in the country, its impact was evident in the change in attitude on the part of certain national sectors that previously had been opposed to any peace dialogue whatsoever.

On the internal front, Cerezo had made some changes in the military commanders, putting in leadership positions officers whose strategic orientation was based not on the doctrine of national security but on a doctrine that had emerged from the military itself, called the thesis of national stability.[20] As a result of a perceptible change in the degree of freedom of press and association, especially in the cities, civil society had begun a process of reorganization. The Unidad de Acción Sindical y Popular (Labor and Popular Action Unity) was formed in 1988. It brought together large groups of ladino and indigenous (or Maya) peasants, human rights activists, students, and trade unionists. In other words, during Cerezo's presidency there was a palpable opening of political spaces and a change with regard to respect for certain basic liberties, such as freedom of speech and association.

The discontent among certain conservative groups, both civilian and military, with this readjustment of social forces and the possibility of entering into talks with the guerrillas within the framework of Esquipulas II may have been the cause of several attempts, promoted by conservative leaders, to destabilize the Cerezo administration in 1988 and 1989,[21] under the guise of fighting corruption within his government.

The First Transfer of Power Between Civilians

Pursuant to the country's new electoral laws, the second general elections of the democratic process were called for November 1990. The representative of the political parties to the CNR, Jorge Serrano, ran for president on the promise that he would try to bring peace to the country. Surprisingly, Serrano won in the second-round election in January 1991. His victory has been attributed in large part to the fact that he won the support of the floating vote created by the disqualification of Efraín Ríos Montt as a presidential candidate[22] and to his adept handling of the criticism lodged against the Cerezo administration.

When Cerezo turned over the government to Serrano in January 1991, it was the first transfer of power from one civilian to another in the history of Guatemala. Serrano set up a pluralistic cabinet[23] and made important changes in the military high command. Three months after taking office, he presented his Proposal for a Total Peace and appointed a governmental peace commission (Comisión para la Paz, COPAZ), comprised of civilians and military officers, to negotiate directly with the URNG. Political scientist Susanne Jonas points out that at that point, the army agreed to enter into a direct dialogue with the guerrillas due to numerous domestic and international pressures, including a "broad national consensus in favor of negotiations through political means. Serrano also understood that this would be his best and only chance to legitimize his government."[24]

Thereafter, what is considered to be the *direct phase* of peace negotiations began in Guatemala. For analytical purposes, this phase can be divided into three subphases: January 1991 to May 1993 under the administration of Jorge Serrano; June 1993 to December 1995 under Ramiro de León Carpio; and January 1996 to the present under Alvaro Arzú.

The first meeting between the newly formed COPAZ and the URNG was held in Mexico on April 26, 1991. The meeting, along with subsequent ones during the Serrano administration, were led by the conciliator, Monsignor Quezada. An observer from the United Nations and other members of the CNR also were present as witnesses and guarantors.[25] At the aforementioned meeting, the Procedural Agreement on the Quest for Peace by Political Means (known as the Mexico Accord) and the agenda of the peace negotiations were defined. The Peace Agenda contained several items divided among substantive issues and operational issues relative to the demobilization of the rebels and their reincorporation into civilian life.

Direct negotiations between the government and the URNG without a previous cease-fire (as was initially demanded by the Cerezo government) may seem odd in a context in which it was believed both nationally and internationally that the guerrillas were virtually defeated on the battlefield. However, according to some advisors to the government peace commission, two important forces were at play here: the international context and the domestic process of democratization.[26]

On the one hand, the beginning of a direct dialogue between the parties was partially the result of external pressures stemming from political developments in other Central American countries. Most important, improving Guatemala's image abroad had been a central foreign policy objective of the civilian governments since Cerezo. Civilians were not alone in this concern. A group of army officers was particularly interested in improving the negative image of the Guatemalan armed forces abroad. This was obvious in the diplomatic effort made by the Guatemalan government after 1986 for the United Nations Human Rights Commission, which met in Geneva annually, to remove Guatemala from the list of countries that were violating human rights.[27] Some analysts believe that, in the eyes of the world, the Guatemalan army had won the military war but had lost the political war to the URNG. Obviously, changes in the world scenario, such as the end of the Cold War, were also among the variables that influenced the peace process in Guatemala.

On the other hand, domestically, the determination shown by Cerezo and particularly by Serrano to find a political solution to the armed confrontation can be viewed as evidence of the latitude or margin available to democratically elected civilian presidents. In addition, some analysts believe that the militarization model that had prevailed in Guatemala for decades had been worn out. In light of the dynamic growth of various national social groups, there needed to be a change in the national political system. And the fact that the army probably became convinced that it could not wipe out the guerrillas completely was likely another important factor.

As to the broad scope of the negotiations, several items on the Peace Agenda had been anticipated in the National Dialogue of 1989 and particularly at the meetings between civil society groups and the URNG in 1990. The government and some progressive civil sectors saw the peace talks as the only real opportunity to discuss some extremely complex issues in Guatemala. In the words of one of Serrano's peace advisors, it was the only opportunity and the only forum available in which to seek the democratization of the country.[28]

Discussion of the Substantive Issues

Relatively quickly, an Agreement on Democratization (known as the Querétaro Accord) was signed in Mexico in July 1991. This accord, which laid the framework for subsequent accords, reaffirmed that negotiations had to be carried out within the framework of the existing constitution and established the basic principles for democracy in the country. In contrast to El Salvador, at an early stage in the peace negotiations there was recognition that the ongoing process of democratization was valuable in and of itself.

After the signing of the Querétaro Accord, the parties held several meetings at which they discussed the issue of human rights, which proved to be one of the most complex and important issues in the short term. Putting an end to the human rights violations in the country was obviously urgent; although these violations had diminished somewhat during the democratic administrations, they were still an important cause for concern. Between July 1991 and May 1993, the parties made progress and reached partial agreements or preagreements on several items. However, there continued to be differences of opinion on such issues as when the accord would go into effect.[29]

Meanwhile, Serrano's legitimacy gradually had eroded, largely due to his authoritarian style, which provoked confrontations with the media and other sectors of society. As for the peace negotiations, although they were viewed favorably by most national sectors, there was growing demand that room be made at the negotiating table for civil society to express its opinions on matters of great importance for the country.

On May 9, 1993, midterm elections for mayors were held in several Guatemalan municipalities. The party in power, the Movimiento de Acción Solidaria (MAS), gained a relative victory in those elections, which analysts believe led Serrano to overestimate his political strength and the population's support for his presidency. On May 25 Serrano suspended by decree several articles of the constitution, as well as the Congress, the Supreme Court, the Attorney General, and the Human Rights Ombudsman. He announced that he would call new elections in sixty days.

The Self-Coup and the Installation of a New Government

What Guatemala experienced between May 25 and June 5, 1993, was one of the most intense periods of democratic reorganization in the country. The impact of Serrano's measures was felt primarily in urban areas, especially the capital. But in the end there was an extremely broad consensus regarding the need to maintain democracy as a system of government. This was particularly evident in the Instancia Nacional de Consenso (National Consensus Forum, or INC), which brought together representatives of the private business sector, the main labor and popular organizations, and the political parties, among others, to find a constitutional solution to the crisis provoked by Serrano. As political theorist Rachel McCleary states, "The *Instancia* was thus the first occasion in Guatemalan history when leaders of diverse organizations, among them groups who opposed each other politically and ideologically, voluntarily came together."[30]

The main national groups in the INC were united in their opposition to Serrano's actions; the communications media kept up constant pressure (in spite of the restrictions imposed by the government); and the Constitutional Court, the Supreme Electoral Tribunal, and the Office of the Human Rights Ombudsman firmly opposed Serrano's actions. These factors, along with growing international pressure, led the army finally to decide to follow the instructions of the Constitutional Court to restore law and constitutional order. Jorge Serrano left the country, and on June 5 Congress elected the then Human Rights Ombudsman, Ramiro de León Carpio, as the new president for the remainder of Serrano's term, through January 14, 1995.

The May 1993 crisis and its aftermath had an obvious impact on the peace negotiations. Some analysts believe that Serrano's growing delegitimization during his last months in office had led the URNG to avoid making major commitments to his administration.[31] During the crisis, the

URNG virtually stayed on the sidelines. Its supporters within the country seemed confused and disoriented as to what position to take. It became apparent that the process of democratization in Guatemala had a life of its own and that the URNG was not one of the central players in it, at least not until it was incorporated into the process as a political option for the population.

Ramiro de León's taking over of the presidency greatly changed the balance of power at the peace negotiating table and therefore the dynamics of the process. De León took office with a high level of national and international respect, given his favorable record as Human Rights Ombudsman. However, the conditions surrounding his appointment—he did not belong to any political party and thus had to take over the government without the human resources needed to fill positions left open by the Serrano partisans—caused his administration to get off to a slow start. He did not form a new peace commission to follow up on the negotiations until September. Probably feeling overconfident of de León's positive international image, the new COPAZ presented an initial proposal that was rejected by the rebels and even by other national sectors, since it introduced substantive changes in the negotiating process and weakened the accomplishments that had been made thus far. Intervention by the United Nations during this impasse (which lasted eight months) was crucial and led to the establishment of parameters for resuming negotiations in January 1994.

In Mexico the parties signed the Framework Agreement for the Resumption of the Negotiation Process on January 10, 1994, which introduced some important changes into the dynamic of the peace negotiations.[32] These changes included:

- The national conciliator was replaced by a moderator appointed by the United Nations.
- The Group of Friends of the peace process was formally established, including Colombia, Spain, the United States, Mexico, Norway, and Venezuela.
- The Assembly of Civil Society (Asamblea de la Sociedad Civil) was introduced to enable various sectors of Guatemalan society to unify their points of view and submit proposals to the negotiating table on substantive items on the peace agenda.
- For the first time, the parties agreed to accelerate the negotiation process.

At the negotiating table, the URNG now faced an individual with international credibility; this raised expectations that a political solution could be reached and implied that some pressure would be put on the rebels by countries like Norway and Sweden, which had been the rebels' former supporters. Likewise, according to some analysts, the URNG (whose leaders lived in Mexico) felt pressured by the Mexican government's concerns after the armed uprising in Chiapas in January 1994.[33] De León's government, for its part, needed to maintain its internal legitimacy, which had suffered due to the so-called purging of government agencies. The president also needed to live up to his image abroad in order to maintain the political and economic support of the international community.

On March 29 of that year, under the leadership of U.N. moderator Jean Arnault, the government and the URNG signed the Comprehensive Agreement on Human Rights and a calendar agreement. The human rights agreement included important provisions regarding the rule of law in the country. One of them was the acceptance by the Guatemalan government of immediate on-site verification by the United Nations of the human rights situation in the country. This verification was essential in order to change certain structures held over from the era of counterinsurgency. The Office of the Human Rights Ombudsman had fulfilled an important role in Guatemala, challenging even the army on certain issues. However, the presence of international observers was needed to go beyond the denunciation of violations.

Although the calendar agreement was not kept, in the long run it established time parameters for the discussion of issues, helped accelerate the work of the Assembly of Civil Society, and, in the eyes of the national and international community meant that the parties' decision to put an end to the armed conflict was irreversible. In June 1994 the Agreement for the Resettlement of the Populations Uprooted by the Armed Confrontation was signed, along with the Agreement on the Establishment of the Historical Clarification Commission. Both documents marked significant points of agreement and progress in the peace talks.[34]

Later discussion began on the first of what can be called structural issues: the identity and rights of the indigenous peoples. In a society split into two main ethnic groups (*ladinos* and indigenous or Mayan), in which historically there has been discrimination against indigenous people in all areas, this was quite a complex issue to address. Concluding substantive agreements on indigenous identity took more than nine months. The increasing participation, organization, and consciousness among the Mayan population throughout this period is one of the greatest contributions of the peace process to democratization in Guatemala.[35] The accord on this sub-

ject was signed in Mexico on March 31, 1995. The Mayan organizations
were skeptical of the accord at the beginning, because they were not directly represented at the negotiating table. Nevertheless, after studying its
contents, the main Mayan organizations in the country endorsed and promoted the accord.

It is important to recall that in tandem with the dynamic process of the
negotiations, various social groups were participating indirectly in the
peace process through consensus proposals that were emerging from the
Assembly of Civil Society, which was comprised of representatives of many
social—including Mayan—organizations. The organized private sector
(CACIF) did not participate in the Assembly of Civil Society; however,
some progressive members of the private sector had become interested in
the peace process and formed their own peace commission, called CEPAZ,
in order to analyze and participate in the process. (See Chapter 15 for more
details on this issue.)

Between March and December 1995, the last months of Ramiro de
León's presidency, progress was made and some preliminary points of agreement were reached on the social and economic issues and the agrarian situation, but no final agreement was signed. Like that of the indigenous people,
the agrarian issue can be considered structural, and somewhat complex, because it directly or indirectly affected all sectors of society and was of special
interest to the traditionally conservative organized private sector. The U.N.
moderator had to engage in intense shuttle diplomacy as well as mediation
within Guatemala in order to define some points of agreement on this item.

Call for Another Round of General Elections

In mid-1995 the Supreme Electoral Tribunal issued a call for the third
presidential election since the democratization process had begun in 1985.
As the campaign heated up, it became apparent that the guerrillas had decided not to sign the final peace accord with the de León administration.
According to some analysts, the guerrillas felt it was necessary to continue
the process of implementation of the accords and that it was preferable to
sign a final accord with a government that was going to stay in power for
several years, not with a lame-duck president.

During the second half of 1995 two factors illustrate the linkages between
the process of democratization and the peace negotiations. First, the main
presidential candidates were forced to take a position on the issue of the
peace talks; all of them said that they would continue the talks if elected. This

proved a boon to the negotiations and the accords already signed, since opponents of the peace process (in particular the large landholders) wanted the accords to be viewed as something less than commitments of the state, so that they could be dismissed by Congress or a new president.

Second, the URNG supported the 1995 elections by calling upon citizens to go to the polls. This marked the end of what had been an unyielding position on the part of the Guatemalan guerrillas regarding the democratization process in the country. Throughout thirty-six years of armed conflict[36] the guerrillas had given little credence to democratic progress being made in the country, even to the advances made after democratically elected governments came to power starting in 1986. They had maintained that democracy in Guatemala was a façade. The URNG's new attitude also made it apparent that the guerrillas had decided to end the armed conflict within a certain time frame and to join in the political life of the country.

Another significant change in the democratic system was also in the works: The so-called popular organizations decided to participate in the elections by proposing candidates for president, for Congress, and for municipal offices through the Frente Democrático Nueva Guatemala (the New Guatemala Democratic Front, or FDNG). Generally on the left of the political spectrum, these groups had contended for years that the prevailing political system did not provide the conditions of security and plurality necessary for broad citizen participation. Thus their participation in the 1995 elections reinforced the process of democratization by going beyond formal aspects to become a truly participatory democratic system. Although the Socialist Party had participated in previous elections, its core consisted of academics from the left, and it was never able to work fully in conjunction with the popular organizations.

The results of the November 1995 elections made the Partido de Avanzada Nacional (PAN) the main political force in the country. Not only did it obtain a majority of the seats in Congress (forty-three out of eighty), it also won the mayoral races in many cities (including the capital), and its presidential candidate, Álvaro Arzú, was in position for a run-off election against the FRG candidate, Alfonso Portillo, planned for January 6, 1996.[37] Also noteworthy was the election to Congress of six FDNG members, including well-known human rights and grass-roots activists. This minority representation in Congress led the FDNG to become the third strongest political force in the country. For the first time since the start of the democratization process, a congress was elected that represented the various social forces in Guatemala.

During the interim between the first- and second-round elections, the PAN directly approached the guerrillas, and secret informal meetings were held between their representatives and the URNG. Later these meetings were considered to be very favorable to the peace process.

A Conservative Administration in Office

In spite of its small margin of victory in the elections, Arzú's administration was legitimized by the fact that he included in his government people from various sectors, particularly some considered to be leftist intellectuals and other nonpartisan technical experts.

When Arzú took office, the peace negotiations got the final boost that they needed. Although several complex items remained to be discussed, Arzú made clear his determination to end the armed conflict by visiting the guerrilla commanders in Mexico in February 1996 and by appointing a new peace commission headed by an advisor close to him who had been tied to the URNG for some years. In response, the guerrillas declared a cessation of offensive military operations in March but indicated that they would not suspend their political and propaganda activities. The government accepted this cease-fire. These moves laid the foundations for speeding up the peace negotiations.

In May 1996, after a year of discussion, the Accord on Socioeconomic Aspects and the Agrarian Situation was signed, which was endorsed by both CACIF and the social groups represented in the Assembly of Civil Society. As Edelberto Torres-Rivas states, "this agreement is open testimony to how much the country has advanced in using democratic political language. The objectives repeatedly set forth regarding social participation and concerted political action are as decisive as the institutional reorganization that they imply.[38] However, some analysts believe that the accord did not go far enough on certain issues to help overcome the exclusionary socioeconomic system that still prevails in the country.

An agreement on the last substantive issue of the peace agenda, Strengthening Civilian Power and the Role of the Army in a Democratic Society, was signed in September 1996. Discussion of this issue probably was facilitated by prior actions taken by the government, such as elimination of the military commissioners (during the de León administration), the suspension of the practice of forced military recruitment until a new law was defined to regulate this matter, and the beginning of the demobilization of the so-called Civil Defense Patrols, a process which the army had started after the virtual end to the armed confrontation in March 1996. Beyond matters strictly related to changes in the army's functions and role, particularly putting and end to its involvement in internal security matters, the accord provided for a parallel strengthening of democratic institutions in the country, especially Congress and the judicial branch of government.

Although several operational accords remained to be signed—including ones on such complex and thorny issues as the amnesty and constitutional reforms—once discussion was concluded on the substantive issues, optimism seemed to reign among the parties. They announced that before 1996 was over, they would sign a final peace accord in Guatemala.

However, an unforeseen incident made the peace process falter in the homestretch. In early August, the Organization of People in Arms (ORPA), a faction of the URNG, was involved in the kidnapping of Olga de Novella, an elderly woman from a prominent Guatemalan family. In October, the government captured two guerrilla leaders who participated in the kidnapping and secretly swapped one of them for the elderly victim. (The whereabouts of the other guerrilla leader is still unknown, and the guerrillas claim he was killed by the government.) When news of the swap seeped out, the government was heavily criticized within the country for having illegally exchanged the victim for one of the kidnappers. The furor set off by the kidnapping and the government's response caused the peace talks to be suspended from October 28 until November 7. Before they resumed, ORPA leader Rodrigo Asturias left the negotiating table.

Signing the Final Accords

Once this incident had been resolved, although its repercussions were not, the rest of the accords considered to be operational were signed in December 1996: the Oslo Cease-Fire Accord, the Stockholm Accord on Constitutional Reforms and Electoral Rules, and the Madrid Accord on the Basis for Reincorporation of the URNG into a Legal Framework.

Finally, after almost six years of negotiations, the Timetable for the Implementation, Fulfillment and Verification of the Peace Accords was signed in Guatemala on December 29, 1996, along with the Accord for a Firm and Lasting Peace, which automatically put into force all of the other agreements signed previously (with the exception of the Comprehensive Agreement on Human Rights, which had been enforced immediately). Signing took place at a solemn ceremony attended by prominent national and international figures.

By the end of 1996 Álvaro Arzú was enjoying broad support from the people, as measured by public opinion polls. This popularity was due in large measure to his actions in the peace process and the steps his administration had been taking to fight corruption. The national climate at the time that the peace agreement was signed was one of optimism. However, a more complicated stage lay ahead: implementation of the nearly 200 commitments made in the accords, at the same time that the rule of law and a more participatory democracy were to be established in the country.

Democratization and Peace: A Balance Sheet

The overview offered in the previous section shows that the democratization and peace processes were intertwined and influenced each other for ten years in Guatemala, from 1986 to 1996. In an attempt to summarize this complex interrelationship, it is useful to try to answer two basic questions. First: What made the end of the conflict possible in Guatemala?

The end of the conflict was influenced by what could be considered internal institutional factors: the democratic opening, which in 1986 brought democratically elected civilians into power; the ensuing decision, to one degree or another, by the four democratically elected civilian presidents to begin or continue the process of finding a political solution to the conflict; changes made in the high command of the Guatemalan army by the four civilian presidents, who replaced the traditional army hard-liners with officers more supportive of democratic institutions; the transparency of the seven electoral cycles during this period, which generated credibility for this formal aspect; and the strengthening of certain institutions established in the 1985 Constitution, particularly the Constitutional Court, the Supreme Electoral Tribunal, and the Human Rights Ombudsman.

The second set of internal factors relate to the role played by civil society, particularly the maturation of the social sectors, which became more flexible in their positions with regard to the democratization process and the peace process. This change stemmed in large measure from the fact that throughout the decade of democratization, progress was made on certain basic liberties, such as freedom of speech (with a much more active and critical role played by the media),[39] freedom of association and of organization, and respect for the political rights of the Guatemalan people in general.

Some aspects of this phenomenon are worth underscoring. The private sector organized under CACIF changed the intransigent position it held at the beginning of the ten-year period. Although factions within the organization maintained their conservative outlook, a modernizing trend prevailed, influenced by a desire to partake in the globalization of the economy. The popular organizations, particularly those considered to be on the left, changed from voicing complaints inside and outside the country to making proposals. That is, rather than just criticizing, they accepted the existing democratic political system and even participated in a political party to seek specific positions from which they could have a greater impact on the decision-making process. Although the private and popular sectors were polarized most of the time, the crisis of 1993—Jorge Serrano's self-coup—caused a meeting of the minds between them and showed the URNG that the process of democratization had a dynamic of its own.

Although internal factors were decisive in putting an end to the armed conflict, it is evident that, in the case of Guatemala, certain international components played an important role: The fall of the Eastern Bloc seems to have influenced the change of position on the part of the URNG; it became obvious that the Guatemalan government (including the army) needed to gain greater credibility on the international stage; and the peace process was concluded in El Salvador.

The role of international verification, through the United Nations Mission to Guatemala (MINUGUA) starting in 1994, is also noteworthy, as is the diplomatic pressure exerted by the Group of Friends. And it should be borne in mind that the democratic opening in Guatemala itself was largely influenced by such entities as the Contadora group of countries. On a different level, throughout the years local human rights organizations received considerable economic and moral support from international nongovernmental organizations and even from some Western governments.

The second question is: What changes occurred in the country as a result of the peace negotiations and the process of democratization throughout the ten-year period?

One of the most remarkable positive changes that occurred in Guatemala as a result of the peace negotiations and the process of democratization was that a national debate was held on issues never before discussed in the country, particularly the indigenous question, the socioeconomic structure, human rights, and the role of the army. For the first time, a basic consensus could be formed among the different sectors on these and other issues, particularly through the National Consensus Forum and the Assembly of Civil Society. Largely because of this, the peace accords took shape as a basic intersectoral consensus; and also for the first time in the country's recent history, they were a departure point for a national development plan accepted by all organized sectors in the country.

Along with this basic consensus, it became clear that democracy was to be the preferred political model. Disagreements were handled through legal channels in many cases (which may have prolonged the resolution of certain issues), proving that the political system and its legal channels of expression were acceptable to the main actors in civil society.

Among the other important changes stemming from the negotiation process is that the Mayan groups significantly increased their level of organization and influence, starting an irreversible process in which the Mayan people are demanding to participate in the country's political and social life. Furthermore, the popular organizations and the URNG itself accepted the democratic and constitutional model in place, with the former managing to get representatives elected to Congress.

Some favorable, although minimal, changes can be perceived in the democratic values of the Guatemalan people. In particular, there have been signs of greater tolerance by the *ladino* population and increased support for the political system by the indigenous population.[40] In addition, there has been a readjustment of political forces, particularly among the political parties of the country. The prevailing parties have an image of honesty, which turned out to be a decisive factor for voters. The ideological and partisan spectrum in the country has expanded, and for the first time there is a range of positions that go from the conservative right to the democratic left.

One of the most troublesome aspects of the armed conflict in the country was always human rights violations. As a result of the peace negotiations and democratization, the human rights situation has improved somewhat, largely thanks to international on-site verification.[41] At the very least, and in contrast to the situation some years ago, human rights violations no longer seem to be directly a result of state policy. The April 1998 removal of Guatemala from the list of countries under supervision by the United Nations Commission for Human Rights seems to recognize this fact. Also affecting the human rights situation is the fact that certain structures that were militarizing the country, such as the military commissioners, the Civilian Defense Patrols, and forced military recruitment, have been eliminated.

Finally, as a result of peace and democratization, opportunities were opened for the country in the international community, improving chances for integration into the global economy. Offers for foreign aid to help build the peace process surpassed even the government's own expectations.

Conclusions: The Viability of the Accords and Challenges Ahead

In 1997 Guatemala embarked upon a new historic period: that of building peace. The mere fact of having concluded an armed conflict that had lasted thirty-six years, and having signed along the way several agreements regarding the deep-seated problems in the country, portend a very different outlook for Guatemala than it has known in the past.

Although my previous analysis regarding the democratic progress made in the country may seem optimistic, the truth is that the process of building peace and further consolidating democracy in Guatemala will face *extremely* difficult challenges. During the first few months after the peace accords were signed, there was compliance with most of the commitments in the timetable for that initial period. Compliance with the second part of the timetable has faced some problems, but in general terms the implementation has continued at a slow pace.

However, short-term and structural problems may not only hinder implementation of the peace commitments but may threaten the further development of democracy in the country. Fifteen months after the signing of the final peace accord, the assassination of Bishop Juan Gerardi in April 1998 clouded the hopes that many Guatemalans had built up in regard to the peace-building process. He was murdered shortly after presenting the findings of a church project called the Recovery of Historical Memory, which attributed to the army most of the atrocities that occurred during the harsh years of the conflict. What was so striking about Gerardi's murder was that it made Guatemalans realize that the "ghosts of the past" might not have disappeared as much as had been hoped.[42] By contrast, the generalized revulsion and outcry that the murder provoked also showed that Guatemalans strongly rejected a return to the past. In the words of MINUGUA chief Jean Arnault, the murder generated a perception of the fragility of the peace process and showed that Guatemala was not yet out of danger.[43] Whether this murder ultimately is solved or not relates to another of the substantial challenges that postwar Guatemala faces: the elimination of impunity, which to a great extent is due to the inefficiency of the judicial system.[44]

Another phenomenon at the center of the national debate is the persis-

tence of nonpolitical violence, particularly an alarming increase in kidnapping involving all sectors of the population, vehicle theft and residential
burglaries, assaults on city buses and other common crimes, and several
cases of public lynchings of criminals. Underlying causes of this phenomenon may be the persistence of a culture of violence among the
Guatemalan people; a possible (temporary) vacuum of power on security
matters;[45] and weak institutions—particularly those in charge of public security, such as the national police. The climate of violence may lead many
sectors of the population to support "hard-line" candidates in the belief
that they can restore law and order.[46]

Poverty is prominent among the complex structural problems. Success
in building a peaceful society necessarily implies improving the standards
of living and opportunities for the population. The fact that the masses do
not identify much with the issue of peace is further complicated by a context in which they perceive no personal short-term benefits as a result of
peace. This fact may lead to premature disenchantment with the peace-
building process, or at least to an indifference that delegitimizes the process in the eyes of society and identifies it as an elite project, like so many
others in Guatemala's history. Jean Arnault has asserted that the population measures its relationship with the peace-building process in two main
areas, security and economic well-being: "Since not many advances have
been achieved in those areas, the population has an attitude of indifference
more than discouragement."[47]

The explosive situation of the land tenure system is indicative of the lack
of perceived progress. Although measures are included in the peace accords to handle the problem of land in Guatemala, the issue is complicated
and has led to many illegal takeovers of land by the peasants, which frequently culminate in violence.

The accords have sought to address many temporary and structural
problems. For example, regarding democratization, the accords provide
for improvements in the justice system, the national police, Congress, the
Office of the Public Prosecutor, and other key institutions. They also provide for reform of the electoral system to make it more participatory and
to institutionalize representation of the indigenous population at various
levels. The accords provide for furthering the process of decentralization
and strengthening the system of development councils, and for important
changes in the structure and role of the army. Implementation of these
changes to the political and institutional system may help further consolidate democracy in Guatemala.

One major constraint on the peace-building process is the lack of permanent state economic resources. The reticence of certain factions within the organized private sector to increase direct taxes and the lack of consensus among the major political parties on other taxation issues may hinder the state's ability to implement many of the accords or to have social policies that are oriented toward the alleviation of poverty. The government signed an agreement with the International Monetary Fund on fiscal reform, with the aim of increasing government revenue through taxation. This reform is required to receive funding from other international financial institutions for implementation of the peace accords.

The problem of an unjust tax structure goes against the search for social justice in general and may enhance the chances of future uprisings. As political scientists Edward Muller and Mitchell Seligson maintain, in many places income inequality has proven to be one of the main explanatory variables or causes for revolutionary movements.[48]

The legitimacy of the accords—while still questioned by some conservatives—is based on the endorsement by the Assembly of Civil Society and the organized private sector. But their viability in the medium term depends on certain elements:

1. The government's willingness to have an open dialogue with society, which transcends the work of the committees stemming from the peace accords; in other words, the government's willingness to implement joint decisions rather than party or single-sector decisions.

2. The flexibility of the social sectors that still suffer from weaknesses in democratic practices; this implies greater tolerance, greater openness to different ideas, and minimal sacrifice of sectoral interests.

3. The unification of the still-fragmented democratic left, represented not only by the URNG as a future political movement[49] but by several representative organizations in society, which must seek greater political presence in the decision-making process at all levels; this unification should make itself felt in the presidential elections scheduled for late 1999.

4. The strengthened participation of social entities—such as the Development Councils—from the local through the national level. They may enable those people who now feel excluded to be involved in the decision-making process in the country; not only will this legitimize the peace-building process, but it will strengthen the process of democratization.

5. The emphasis on formal and informal education at all levels. This is geared to raising Guatemalan awareness regarding the importance of

peace in the country and strengthening their democratic culture. This emphasis may help somewhat to overcome the culture of violence and the low level of voter participation.

6. The real dismantling of the structures left over from the era of counterinsurgency, such as the army's Estado Mayor Presidencial (Presidential Joint Staff), ostensibly in charge of the president's security, but often assuming functions beyond its mandate. This will pave the way to true predominance of civilian over military power.

7. The modernization of the state in general, so that it can effectively deliver services and channel demands from the population. This may increase popular support for the political system, in turn enhancing the prospects for a long-lasting democracy.

8. The strengthening of key institutions in charge of public security and justice (the national civilian police, the Office of the Public Prosecutor, and the courts). This is closely related to the elimination of impunity in the country.

In spite of the difficult challenges ahead, the political system in place today is one in which most national priorities are defined through discussions among the different sectors of society. It would appear that the prospects for democracy are better now than at any other point in the history of Guatemala.

Notes

1. Kenneth A. Bollen, "Issues in the Measurement of Political Democracy," *American Sociological Review* 45 (June 1980): 370–90.

2. Mitchell A. Seligson, "Development, Democratization and Decay: Central America at the Crossroads," in James Malloy and Mitchell Seligson, eds., *Authoritarians and Democrats: Regime Transition in Latin America* (Pittsburgh: University of Pittsburgh Press, 1987), 169.

3. Ricardo Córdova Macias, *El Salvador: Las negociaciones de paz y los retos de la postguerra* (San Salvador: Instituto de Estudios Latinoamericanos, 1993).

4. Edelberto Torres Rivas, "Negociando el futuro: La paz en una sociedad violenta," *Debate* No. 36 (Guatemala City: Facultad Latinoamericana de Ciencias Sociales, 1997), 13–16, quote: 24. He includes as examples the cases of Mozambique, Nicaragua, Angola, and others.

5. Guatemalan historians agree that the beginning of the so-called armed confrontation in Guatemala occurred with the uprising of a group of young army officers in November 1960.

6. Gabriel Aguilera, "Preface," in Susanne Jonas, *Guatemala: Plan piloto para el continente* (San José, Costa Rica: EDUCA, 1982), 9.

7. The army never recognized officially the fact that the guerrillas had grown strong, but it is believed that by 1982 there were "liberated" zones in the Department of El Quiché that the army could not penetrate. Colonel Ríos Mejía (army delegate to the Permanent Council for Defense and Cooperation in Central America), speech, Centro ESTNA, a military-dominated center of strategic studies, 1991.

8. See Aguilera, "Preface," and Henry Frundt, "Guatemala in Search of Democracy," *Journal of Inter-American Studies* 32, No. 3 (1990), 8 and 39.

9. See Frundt, "Guatemala in Search of Democracy," 30.

10. Kenneth Coleman, "The Consequences of Excluding Reformists from Power: The View from 1990," in Kenneth Coleman and George Herring, eds., *Understanding the Central American Crisis* (Wilmington, De.: Scholarly Resources, 1991), 51.

11. Arturo Taracena, interview with author, Guatemala City, March 1997. Taracena, a Guatemalan historian, was a member of the URNG political team in Europe for many years. According to him, the Guatemalan guerrillas understood as early as 1982 that they could not take power militarily. They continued fighting, however, believing that they could influence changes in the country through the armed struggle.

12. Timothy Wickham-Crowley, *Guerrillas and Revolution in Latin America* (Princeton, NJ: Princeton University Press, 1992), 290.

13. Although there was a change in United States policy toward Central America during the Reagan administration, the policy toward Guatemala was never again similar to that of the 1960s, when there was open support for the military. There was, in fact, a total cut of military aid over several years, due largely to the involvement of the U.S. Congress, which in turn was pressured by the lobbying of human rights groups.

14. The argument that the democratic opening was originally an extension of the counterinsurgency policy has been offered by Guatemalan sociologist Héctor Rosada in several lectures.

15. Gabriel Aguilera, "Los temas sustantivos de los acuerdos de paz," *Debate No. 24* (Guatemala City: Facultad Latinoamericana de Ciencias Sociales, 1994), 17.

16. The legal constraint on the URNG, or any of the guerrilla movements separately, was that they could not participate until they had relinquished their arms.

17. For example, Martha Salguero, "Perspectivas de la paz en Centroamérica a la luz de Esquipulas," *Debate No. 7* (Guatemala City: Facultad Latinoamericana de Ciencias Sociales, 1990).

18. Ibid., 17.

19. Taracena interview.

20. Héctor Alejandro Gramajo, *Tésis de la Estabilidad Nacional* (Guatemala City: Editorial del Ejército, 1989).

21. David Holiday, "Guatemala's Long Road to Peace," *Current History* 96, No. 607 (Feb. 1997): 68–74.

22. According to Article 186 of the constitution, the following cannot run for the office of president: "Caudillos, nor leaders of a coup d'état, armed revolution, or similar movement that may have altered the Constitutional order, nor those who as a consequence of such acts may have assumed leadership of the government."

23. He included Álvaro Arzú from the National Action Party, (PAN, which is conservative), as minister of foreign affairs and Mario Solórzano from the Social Democratic Party (PSD, which is socialist) as minister of labor.

24. Susanne Jonas, "Guatemala: Encrucijada entre la guerra y la paz," *Espacios,* No. 2 (San José, Costa Rica: Facultad Latinoamericana de Ciencias Sociales, 1994).

25. See Aguilera, "Los temas sustantivos," 40.

26. Amílcar Burgos and Raquel Zelaya, interviews with author, Guatemala City, February 1997. They were members of the government negotiating teams during the Serrano and Arzú administrations, respectively.

27. Asociación de Investigación y Estudios Sociales (ASIES), "Análisis mensual" (Guatemala City, March 1997). Each year beginning in 1986, progressive members of the military were sent to Geneva as part of the government commissions that lobbied in favor of Guatemala.

28. Burgos interview.

29. Other issues were related to the inclusion of a commission to investigate violations of human rights during the conflict and the demobilization of the civil defense committees, known by their Spanish acronym, PAC.

30. Rachel McCleary, "Guatemala's Postwar Prospects," *Journal of Democracy* 8, No. 2 (April 1997): 135.

31. Burgos interview.

32. Ernesto Viteri, in *Memoria de la Conferencia Procesos de Paz Comparados* (Guatemala City: ASIES and Woodrow Wilson Center, 1996).

33. McCleary, "Guatemala's Postwar Prospects," and ASIES, "Análisis Mensuales" (Guatemala City: Jan.–Aug. 1994).

34. Torres-Rivas, "Negociando el futuro," 22. However, some human rights groups viewed the content of the Accord on the Historical Clarification Commission as unsatisfactory. The commission was to produce a report on the major violations of human rights during the armed conflict but would not indicate individual responsibilities or have judicial effect. One probable explanation of the limited scope of the commission as compared to that of El Salvador may be found in the military weakness of the URNG. This was not the case in El Salvador, where a virtual stalemate existed between the FMLN and the government.

35. A change in Guatemala became apparent through the higher profile of organized Mayan groups. This noteworthy transformation came after the granting of the Nobel Peace Prize to Rigoberta Menchú in 1992 and also as a result of the growing unification of indigenous groups in Latin America.

36. With the exception of the 1966 elections, in which Mario Méndez Montenegro was elected president.

37. Some analysts attribute part of Portillo's success to the backing he received from Efraín Ríos Montt after the Electoral Tribunal nullified his own candidacy for president because it went against the Constitution (see note 22, above).

38. Torres-Rivas, "Negociando el futuro," 29.

39. However, there are still frequent clashes between government officials and the media. The latter argue that the government restricts press freedom; the former deny it. In any case, the level of press freedom is definitely superior to that existing during the military governments.

40. *Tercer estudio acerca de la cultura democrática de los guatemaltecos* (Guatemala City: University of Pittsburgh, ASIES, and Development Associates, 1998).

41. Various reports on the human rights situation in Guatemala agree that there were substantial improvements, although they indicate that there are still weaknesses. Among those reports presented in 1997 are the ones from the Guatemalan Ombudsman, the U.S. State Department, and the independent expert appointed by the United Nations Human Rights Commission.

42. Despite the terror of the years of conflict, this represented the first time in the history of Guatemala that a bishop had been murdered. As of this writing (May 1998), an investigation was ongoing. The Guatemalan authorities accepted help from the U.S. Federal Bureau of Investigation to solve the case. Although some hypotheses link the murder to robbery, some sectors suspect political motives.

43. Jean Arnault, interview with the Mexican newspaper *Público de Guadalajara,* reprinted in *Siglo Veintiuno* (Guatemala), May 5, 1998.

44. In recent years, and in contrast to the past, several members of the military have been accused of corruption and some lower-ranking members of the armed forces of crimes (such as in the case of the murder of anthropologist Myrna Mack). However, due to lingering fear and to the inefficiency of the judiciary system in obtaining evidence, few such members actually have been convicted. Judicial inefficiency extends to cases in which civilians are involved.

45. As a result of the accords, the army must cease to perform internal security functions. However, it has been apparent that the National Civilian Police does not yet have the capacity to fight crime adequately. In rural areas, such groups as the Military Commissioners and the PAC also were involved to some degree in aspects of internal security involving the fight against crime.

46. An example is Efraín Ríos Montt, who continues to be a popular presidential candidate in public opinion polls despite the legal ban on his candidacy and despite his administrations record of human rights violations.

47. Arnault interview.

48. Edward Muller and Mitchell Seligson, "Inequality and Insurgency," *American Political Science Review* 81 (June 1987), 427.

49. As of May 1998, the URNG was in the process of forming a political party. As required by the electoral law, after formally registering, the URNG must comply with several requirements in order to achieve the full status of a political party.

Reflections

JULIO BALCONI

I wish to relate part of the untold story of the peace negotiations between the government of Guatemala and the Unidad Revolucionaria Nacional Guatemalteca (URNG).

The negotiations proceeded along two tracks, one formal and the other informal. The formal track took place at the negotiating table, where issues that had been agreed on were discussed and working documents drafted. These drafts subsequently developed into partial agreements. The formal negotiations consisted of small plenary sessions and individual meetings between the parties and the moderator.

I would like to focus on the informal track, something about which we have never before spoken publicly. Those of us in the military who had served on the peace commission since April 1991 knew that there was an atmosphere of deep distrust during the first rounds of negotiations, as was to be expected at the time. For this reason, some of the officers on the peace commission, along with some members of the URNG, looked for a means of rapprochement that would make it possible to replace the distrust with trust. The task of rapprochement between the military and URNG representatives was difficult. It began approximately the time of the first round of negotiations and extended over the course of a year, during which attempts were made to establish somewhat more open lines of communication.

This activity was carried out in secret. Civilian members of the peace commission, moderators, and members of the URNG outside of the general command were not aware that such meetings were taking place.

The intention from the very start was to facilitate progress in the formal negotiations. By no means were we attempting to supplant the negotiating table. We were inclined to maintain secrecy so that if the effort did not

127

work, it simply would have remained an attempt and the formal negotiations at the table would have continued. Fortunately, we were very successful. Both the army and the URNG general command understood that this kind of contact could work in the future, especially after the final signing of the peace accords. Throughout the talks, we were very mindful of what was going on in the peace processes in Nicaragua and in El Salvador. In 1991, for example, when we went to Mexico for the first time to meet with the URNG, we also met with the FMLN and with the Salvadoran Peace Commission, which were still engaged in negotiations.

The private meetings created considerable trust between the general command and the officers on the peace commission. For this reason we decided to bring lower-ranking field commanders from both sides into the meetings. The experience was a very valuable one. For example, in December 1996, when the URNG general command was preparing to arrive in Guatemala to sign the peace accord, the issue arose as to who would provide the necessary protection required for them to attend this event. We spoke with the URNG about the national police, and they said no. We proposed that they select their own people, to whom we could give temporary documents while the final process of demobilization was under way, and they told us with complete candor that their fighters were not prepared for this kind of work. Finally they asked that we provide security. Those who were in Guatemala on December 29, 1996, might have noticed that military personnel from the army were providing security for the URNG. This would not have been possible if it had not been our intention from the very start to achieve a high level of trust. We believe that the negotiations ultimately accelerated because the URNG knew that it would not be running physical risks after the peace accord was signed.

The announcement of the suspension of offensive military operations in March 1996 was also due precisely to the level of trust that we had achieved. The URNG renounced armed confrontation well before the final peace accord was signed. From March 1996 onward, there was not a single incident between military personnel and groups or patrols of URNG combatants who were still in arms throughout the country. There was good coordination and much fluidity in communications.

Although this experience was unique to Guatemala, we are sharing it with other armies that have similar problems. We are making it public now for the first time because it is a story that must be told.

5

The Peace Process in Chiapas: Between Hope and Frustration

NEIL HARVEY

The armed uprising on January 1, 1994, by over 3,000 Mayan Indians in the southern Mexican state of Chiapas took most observers by surprise. The Zapatista Army of National Liberation (EZLN) briefly occupied six towns in the state's central highlands before retreating to bases in the Lacandon forest in the face of a military offensive by the federal army. At least 145 people, mostly Zapatistas, died in the fighting, while many others were injured and over 10,000 displaced from their homes. By the time the government declared a cease-fire on January 12, the EZLN had succeeded in gaining widespread support of Mexican and international civil society for its broad list of social, political, and economic demands.[1]

The significance of this uprising lay not in its military strength but in its radical critique of authoritarianism and social inequalities in Mexico. The Zapatistas called for an end to the political system that has been dominated by the Institutional Revolutionary Party (PRI) since 1929. They also demanded reforms to overcome the continuing marginalization of indigenous peoples. These demands were particularly relevant in Chiapas, where PRI governors and local officials traditionally have relied on the use of violent repression to crush dissident peasant and indigenous movements. Ever since the 1920s the federal government has allowed Chiapanecan elites a certain degree of autonomy over local affairs in exchange for their loyalty to the ruling party, support for the president, and mobilization of the PRI vote. Although opposition parties made significant electoral gains in other states in the 1980s and early 1990s, they remained weak in the mainly rural, indigenous districts of Chiapas, where PRI candidates could count on fraud, intimidation, and violence to guarantee their "victories."

Political power tended to reinforce the economic exclusion of the indigenous peasants and workers who, by the end of the 1980s, constituted one of the poorest and most marginalized groups in Mexico. Although several grass-roots organizations had protested these conditions during that decade, usually they were met with violent repression, with their leaders arrested, imprisoned, tortured, or killed. During the early 1990s political repression continued and was accompanied by the worsening of rural poverty, increasing landlessness, and deteriorating health conditions. It was in this context that indigenous peasants, many of whom had experience in the repressed grass-roots organizations, decided to turn to armed struggle.

The uprising was a wakeup call to the nation, a reminder of the historical debt it owed to its indigenous peoples, as well as a clear attack on the complacency of a distant, Harvard-trained technocratic elite, personified at the time by President Carlos Salinas de Gortari. The rebellion coincided with the first day of the North American Free Trade Agreement (NAFTA), effectively destroying the image of a stable and harmonious Mexico that Salinas had cultivated so carefully among U.S. politicians during the contentious debates leading up to the agreement. Unlike other insurgencies in Latin America, the significance of the EZLN was not to be found in its military strength or political ideology but in the way that it challenged the government to treat indigenous peoples as equal and valued members of the nation. In discussing the prospects for peace in Chiapas, it is essential to understand the nature of this challenge and the obstacles that, by the spring of 1998, continued to hinder a peaceful solution.

What are the prospects for peace in Chiapas? This chapter attempts to answer this question by addressing four main issues. The first concerns the evolution of the EZLN itself and its relationship to the broader struggles of Mexican civil society. By constructing a network of alliances within civil society, the Zapatistas were able to maintain pressure on the government to negotiate, despite their military weakness. This capacity to maintain pressure was evident during the first round of talks in February 1994 and in subsequent months. It was revealed again by the mass demonstrations that followed the decision of President Ernesto Zedillo to launch a new offensive against Zapatista bases in February 1995. Zedillo was forced to call a new cease-fire and establish a body of legislators, the Comisión de Concordia y Pacificación para el Estado de Chiapas (COCOPA), with the goal of reopening the dialogue. The significant involvement of civil society in the peace process is an important feature of the Mexican case.

A second issue concerns the Zapatistas' demand that indigenous peoples have the right to self-determination. In February 1996 a minimal accord was signed between representatives of the EZLN and the Mexican government on indigenous rights and culture. The failure of the government to fulfill these accords was a primary factor in the Zapatistas' decision to suspend the peace talks in September 1996. By the spring of 1998 the lack of a solution to this problem constituted a serious obstacle to the future of the entire peace process in Chiapas.

A third and related issue is the fact that the lack of progress in the peace talks exacerbated tensions within Chiapas. Despite the official cease-fire between the EZLN and government troops, observers referred to "another war" involving paramilitary groups that attack and kill pro-Zapatista community members, particularly in the state's northern, Chol-speaking region. In other words, the struggles that the EZLN sought to direct through peace talks have instead found violent expression through intra-community conflict and politically manipulated factionalism. The massacre of forty-five unarmed Zapatista sympathizers in the village of Acteal in December 1997 was the result of a policy of impunity toward pro-government paramilitary organizations in the region. Peace negotiators will need to give special attention to the problems of paramilitary violence and impunity if and when talks resume.

The EZLN did not wish to seize state power through a prolonged guerrilla war. Government negotiators were faced instead with a far more pragmatic rebel leadership for whom armed struggle constituted a last resort rather than its main tactic. In these conditions, dialogue could indeed start much earlier, with the first round of talks taking place in the Cathedral of San Cristóbal de Las Casas at the end of February 1994, just eight weeks after the New Year's occupation of the same town. Despite this fact, solutions proved elusive. As time wore on, the entire peace process stagnated, culminating in the suspension of talks by the EZLN in September 1996. Moreover, compared to its counterparts in other Latin American countries, the Mexican government lacked the same type of incentives to negotiate and implement the reforms called for by the EZLN. What does this weak level of government commitment mean for the peace process in Chiapas, and what implications does it have for the rest of the country? These questions are taken up in the final section of the chapter.

The Zapatistas and the Incorporation of Civil Society

The government's initial response to the rebellion on January 1, 1994, was to use military force. However, as it soon became apparent that the EZLN was a well-organized insurgency, the political cost of military engagement became untenable. Domestic opposition, combined with international pressure from the U.S. government, obliged President Salinas to accept the need for a political solution. Mass protests against the government's military response helped deepen the Zapatistas' appreciation of civil society as their most effective ally in the struggle for a peaceful solution. Civil society, then, would come to provide the bridge between the local and the national after the first round of peace talks in February and March 1994. As the EZLN delegates returned to their communities to discuss the government's proposals, they sent out a clear message: "Do not leave us alone." This call took on a new urgency after the assassination of PRI's presidential candidate Luis Donaldo Colosio on March 23, an act the Zapatistas interpreted as a sign that hard-liners within the government had taken the upper hand in reaction to the possibility of reforms favorable to the EZLN and the political opposition.

The mobilization of support groups such as the university students' Caravana de Caravanas and the solidarity work of Espacio Civil para la Democracia (ESPAZ), a national coalition of nongovernmental organizations, demonstrated the very clear links to be established between Chiapas and national political reform. This situation became even more apparent when, in mid-June, the EZLN rejected the government's proposals and instead decided to deepen the dialogue with civil society. At the time of the "no" vote, most commentators focused on the possible consequences for finding a peaceful solution in Chiapas and paid less attention to the Zapatistas' call for a National Democratic Convention (CND). Little by little, however, the idea of a citizens' assembly to unite the numerous opposition movements and groups began to catch on. An organizing committee was set up and began to work intensively over the next six weeks to ensure the convention's success.

In Chiapas, the Democratic State Assembly of the Chiapanecan People (AEDPCH) was born as a loose coalition of citizens' groups, peasant organizations, democratic union movements, and nongovernmental organizations. Over sixty groups were represented at its first state convention in early July 1994. The convention supported the EZLN's call for a transitional government, a new constituent assembly, and new federal and state constitutions. The new coalition held a second convention two weeks later to prepare proposals of Chiapas delegates to the first CND meeting. This meeting was scheduled to be held two weeks prior to the national and gubernatorial elections, at a specially constructed site in Zapatista territory named Aguascalientes, after the revolutionary convention of 1914.[2] Democratic conventions were held in several other states during July, and delegates were elected. On August 6 over 6,000 delegates, invited intellectuals, and observers descended on San Cristóbal de las Casas to begin deliberations in five miniconventions on the need for a transitional government, the adoption of peaceful strategies to achieve democracy, an alternative national project, the organization of a new constituent assembly, and the elaboration of a new federal constitution. With this number of people it was impossible to reach more than general agreements in support of the EZLN. The major point of debate concerned the role of electoral participation in bringing about change in Mexico. Some groups on the far left argued that only mass mobilization (possibly including armed insurgency) and not elections could dislodge the PRI from power. However, the debate was constrained by the sheer number of delegates and the desire of the convention organizers to approve a common platform. As the EZLN had itself encouraged participation in the elections and in defense of the vote, the far-left groups were at a clear disadvantage.

The plenary session at Aguascalientes served to demonstrate to the government and other sectors of society that the EZLN was indeed not alone. The EZLN displayed a great deal of political maturity by declaring that it would "step to one side" while it gave the newly constituted CND the opportunity to apply peaceful pressure for political change. In a major speech, the principal EZLN leader who goes by the pseudonym Subcomandante Marcos allayed fears of an imminent armed uprising following the national elections and instead called on the peaceful civic and popular movement "to defeat us," to make armed action unnecessary.[3]

While many observers declared that the election day was relatively free from fraud, it was also clear that the PRI campaign benefited disproportionately from the use of public funds and media time. Hundreds of irregularities also were reported on election day, particularly the lack of sufficient ballot papers at special voting booths, the "shaving" of voters' names from voting lists, and the violation of secrecy of the ballot.[4] In Chiapas, the governorship race on August 21, 1994, was won by the PRI candidate, Eduardo Robledo Rincón, in the midst of widespread protests of fraud and violent clashes in Tuxtla Gutiérrez. The official result gave Robledo 50.4 percent of the vote, compared to 34.9 percent for Amado Avendaño Figueroa, the Party of the Democratic Revolution (PRD) candidate, and

9.2 percent for Cesáreo Hernández of the National Action Party (PAN). The PRD claimed that Avendaño had in fact won and called for civic protests to prevent Robledo from taking office in December. The EZLN issued a strong statement condemning the fraud and called on Robledo not to assume office in order to avoid a potential "bloodbath." In an attempt to avert a renewal of hostilities, the bishop of the Catholic diocese of San Cristóbal de Las Casas, Samuel Ruiz, and several public figures established the National Intermediation Commission (CONAI) in October. However, the government did not give CONAI official recognition until after the crisis provoked by the inauguration of the new state governor in December.

In response to the imposition of Robledo, the AEDPCH and EZLN recognized Avendaño as "rebel governor" and briefly occupied thirty-eight town halls in municipalities outside the declared conflict zone. At the same time, declining investor confidence in the new Zedillo government led to a 40 percent devaluation of the peso as Mexico found itself unable to service short-term debt coming due in January 1995. Faced with bankruptcy, the government agreed to stringent terms of a $50 billion bailout package sponsored by the U.S. government. Then, on February 9, 1995, President Zedillo ordered a new military offensive against the EZLN. Believing that the operation would capture the Zapatista leadership, the attorney general declared the identity of subcomandante Marcos to be Rafael Sebastián Guillén Vicente, a former university professor and leader of one of several regional cells of the EZLN.

As in January 1994, Mexican citizens mobilized quickly to demand the withdrawal of troops from Zapatista communities, holding three mass demonstrations in Mexico City in the space of a week. Unable to capture Marcos, Zedillo called off the offensive, although troops remained stationed close to the communities suspected of supporting the EZLN. Human rights observers also denounced the destruction of domestic items, food and farming implements, by soldiers in villages suspected of supporting the EZLN. Thousands of Zapatistas throughout the Lacandon forest fled their communities in order to avoid arrest. Talks resumed again in April 1995, but it was not until October of that year that substantive issues began to be discussed in San Andrés Larráinzar.[5]

The February offensive clearly revealed the military weakness of the EZLN compared with the Mexican army. The EZLN's future was increasingly linked to the political space it was able to create for its eventual emergence from armed struggle. In this regard, the Zapatistas decided to consult their allies within civil society on their political future. In August 1995 a national and international referendum (*consulta*) was held with the assistance of Alianza Cívica, a nonpartisan organization with experience in monitoring elections. The consulta resulted in the decision to promote a civic, nonpartisan front, the Frente Zapatista de Liberación Nacional (FZLN). The Frente was created officially on January 1, 1996, as a means to articulate a wide range of popular struggles behind the banners of democracy, liberty, and justice. It was also seen as a response to the CND's failure to unify these struggles in the period since August 1994. Internal leadership conflicts within the CND threatened to squander a historic opportunity to reformulate the democratic tasks of the Mexican left and the popular movements. However, the CND worked comparatively better at the grass-roots level. In fact, it was through the local state conventions and Alianza Cívica that the August 1995 consulta was organized. The Zapatistas responded by reaffirming their faith in the nonpartisan associations of civil society, a faith that was clearly articulated in its vision of the FZLN.

The FZLN's political objective was defined not in terms of winning positions of power but in demanding that those who govern do so by obeying collective decisions. This is the principle of *mandar obedeciendo* that the EZLN drew from earlier practices within indigenous communities. During 1996 the FZLN began to build itself from the ground up, through hundreds of civil dialogue committees. The committees' main task was to assist the EZLN in the formulation of proposals for the second round of talks on democracy and justice, scheduled to take place in San Andrés Larráinzar in July 1996. A week prior to the talks, the EZLN organized a special forum entitled "The Reform of the State" in San Cristóbal, which was attended by thousands of delegates from the civil committees as well as from popular movements, opposition parties, and universities. The forum came up with concrete proposals on political and electoral reform in Mexico, including the registration of nonpartisan, independent candidates in elections and the incorporation of referenda and plebiscites in a new constitution. The government was indifferent to this round of talks, and no agreements were reached. The government's lack of interest was due in part to the fact that it and the political parties had agreed upon a more limited electoral reform; the government thus dismissed the EZLN and its proposals.

The Struggle for Indigenous Rights

The Zapatistas' conception of democracy also was shaped by the struggle for indigenous peoples' rights to self-determination. Since the early 1980s, several indigenous leaders in Mexico had been critical of the government's four-decade-long assimilationist policies. During the Salinas administration (1988 to 1994) new movements sought to go beyond the individual rights discourse of liberalism, calling instead for a set of collective rights to be inscribed in a newly reformed section of the constitution pertaining to the civil rights of Mexican people (Article 4). As Mexican social scientist Rodolfo Stavenhagen has argued, collective rights for discriminated groups are a necessary precondition of individual rights.[6] The right to be different is a fundamental democratic right that universal ideals of citizenship have tended to ignore or suppress.[7] Indigenous movements in Mexico sought not only political inclusion of individual citizens but also recognition as different citizens, in which ethnic identities could be asserted in a positive way rather than stigmatized as "traditional" or "premodern." Article 4 was amended in 1991 on Salinas's initiative. It made reference for the first time to the pluricultural character of the Mexican nation, but the enabling legislation that would have specified the collective rights of indigenous peoples was never completed and remained pending at the time of the Zapatista uprising.[8]

The rebellion finally gave the "postindigenista" view of independent movements its chance. Although the early communiqués did not specify the EZLN's ethnic demands, it was not long before the question of autonomy was posed. Of the thirty-four demands presented to the government in February 1994, the following referred specifically to indigenous people: the creation of an independent indigenous radio station; the mandating of compulsory indigenous languages for primary through university education; respect for indigenous culture and tradition; an end to discrimination against indigenous peoples; the granting of indigenous autonomy; the administration of their own courts by indigenous communities; the criminalization of forced expulsion from communities by government-backed caciques; and the establishment of maternity clinics, day-care centers, nutritious food, kitchens, dining facilities, nixtamal (a kind of corn flour) and tortilla mills, and training programs for indigenous women.

The government's attempt to separate local from national reforms led the EZLN to reject the official response and instead turn its attention to building networks of grass-roots support within civil society. It was in this context that the relations with other indigenous leaders and organizations developed. Contesting Salinas's reform to Article 4 provided a point of convergence that indigenous organizations sought to exploit. Traditional demands for land, credit, and fair prices, while necessary to build regional organizations, were increasingly articulated in a cultural-political discourse of indigenous autonomy.

At the same time that the EZLN and indigenous leaders were debating the content of their proposals for the peace talks, landless peasants carried out widespread land invasions throughout Chiapas. Although the government attempted to co-opt the leaders of peasant organizations by making some concessions, the more common practice was the use of public security forces and private armed groups to evict land claimants. The repression of peasant movements culminated in a wave of violent evictions in November 1995, coinciding with the resumption of peace talks between the EZLN and the government in San Andrés Larráinzar. In early October Interior Minister Emilio Chauyffet had met with leaders of the ranchers' associations and promised that land invaders would be evicted following the October 15 municipal elections. The negotiations at San Andrés Larráinzar were, in the words of one commentator, "the eye of the hurricane," as reports of detentions, beatings, and killings came in from around the state.[9] According to the AEDPCH, violent actions against members of popular organizations in 1995 included 860 arrests, 50 evictions, and 40 politically motivated killings.[10]

In what appears to be a recurring pattern, the violent attacks on Zapatista sympathizers coincided with the opening of peace talks between the EZLN and the government. It is clear that local elites in Chiapas are determined to prevent the talks from reaching any accord that would affect their control of land and indigenous labor. Such was the scenario when the two negotiating teams met to present their proposals on indigenous rights and culture in San Andrés Larráinzar in October 1995.

Despite the "hurricane" of land evictions, this moment was marked by a great amount of optimism regarding the possibility of reaching a peaceful solution. The source of optimism was a far-reaching proposal for a framework agreement that was established in the first round of talks in October. This agreement recognized the need for "a thorough reform of the state, to construct a new state that would be decentralized, democratic, inclusive and respectful of pluralism; the establishment of a new constitutional framework that recognizes the right of indigenous peoples to autonomy; and the need for changes in the country's economic, social and cultural model."[11] The accord was promoted by advisors associated with the government's Instituto Nacional Indigenista (INI), which itself was undergoing internal transformation as it sought to defend its own relevance in light of the Zapatista rebellion.

However, the INI advisors suddenly were replaced at the second round of talks in November by representatives of the Chiapas state government. The INI's draft documents, calling for national rather than state-level reforms, were ignored by the new negotiating team, most of whom had not participated in the earlier round and were less knowledgeable regarding indigenous issues.[12] The government team now proposed that indigenous forms of justice be incorporated into existing state-level judicial systems and that indigenous communities be given legal status to elect their own representatives. However, it did not accept the EZLN proposal to allow indigenous communities to choose their own forms of self-government that would act alongside community-level and state government. In short, autonomy was conceived as the ability of each single community to decide on its own affairs within the existing constitutional order. This view of autonomy would allow the government to maintain the current political hierarchy among federation, states, and municipalities simply by adding community-level government. The government's negotiators also omitted any reference to territorially defined rights of indigenous peoples.

The San Andrés talks on indigenous rights and culture reached a minimum accord on January 18, 1996, which was subsequently ratified by EZLN supporters and signed by the two delegations four weeks later. This was the first signed agreement since the January 1994 rebellion and was seen by the Zapatistas as a step toward the redefinition of Mexico as a pluriethnic nation. The accord recommended reforms to several articles of the constitution (including Article 4) that would allow for the redrawing of municipal boundaries and the recognition of the right of indigenous people to compete for public office independent of national political parties. At the state level, similar reforms would be implemented with the goal of increasing political representation of indigenous people in the local congress. In addition, a state-level Law of Justice and Agrarian Development would be drawn up and a special committee would be created to discuss the agrarian problems in Chiapas, with the participation of representatives of the EZLN, other indigenous and peasant organizations, and government ministries. This body also would be responsible for drawing up a census of landholding in the state.[13]

While the EZLN saw these agreements as a step forward, other groups within the indigenous movement saw them as limited by the lack of legal recognition for the regional autonomy of indigenous peoples. Such autonomy would have permitted indigenous people greater control over the use of land and natural resources in their traditional territories by establishing pluriethnic autonomous regions as a "fourth level" of government alongside the current federal, state, and municipal levels. This failure to

recognize a "fourth level" reflected not only the government's unwilling-
ness to meet this demand but also the differences between sectors of the
indigenous movement and Zapatista advisors over the extent to which the
issue of autonomy should be pressed in the adverse political climate of late
1995 and early 1996. The goal of regional autonomy remained a point of
contention within the national indigenous movement during 1996. The
idea of pluriethnic regional autonomy competed with several others such
as community-level or municipal-level autonomy. Some EZLN advisors
also warned against possible state re-regulation of indigenous norms and
traditions under the guise of respect for autonomy.

We also must bear in mind that the political context shifted significantly
between November 1995 and January 1996. During the first round of
talks government negotiators were more open to the idea of regional autonomy for indigenous peoples. This position changed radically when the
team of reformist advisors from the INI was replaced for the second round
by hard-liners from the Chiapas state government. Military maneuvers
close to Zapatista bases in late December were another ominous sign of a
shift in the government's position prior to the final round of talks. During
1996 many observers feared that the continued militarization of Chiapas
and the hardening of the government's position on each of the issues to be
negotiated at San Andrés would lead to a breakdown of the entire peace
process. In September their fears came true. The Zapatistas broke off negotiations, calling on the government to replace its negotiating team and
to comply with its commitment to implement the accord on indigenous
rights and culture. The EZLN also continued to demand the unconditional release of all those detained as suspected Zapatistas during the police and military offensives of February 1995. Another factor in the changing political context was the government's response to the appearance of a
new guerrilla organization, the Ejército Popular Revolucionario (EPR), in
the state of Guerrero in June 1996. The EPR appeared less prepared than
the Zapatistas to negotiate fundamental changes with the government and
carried out several violent attacks on police stations. President Zedillo attempted to portray the EPR as the "bad guerrilla" by speaking more kindly
of the EZLN, a maneuver that the latter rejected as an attempt to justify
indiscriminate repression. The Zapatistas affirmed that they did not have
any links with the EPR but that it was simply another indication of the desperation felt by the majority of Mexicans in the face of a deepening economic crisis.

By December 1996 no progress had been made in reinitiating peace
talks. During that month COCOPA presented the president with a new

proposal for implementing the accords on indigenous rights and culture. This proposal was based on the original text of the February 1996 agreement and was accepted by the leadership of the EZLN. However, President Zedillo chose to reject the document and submit a counterproposal that bore little relation to the existing accords. It was clear that this would be unacceptable to the Zapatistas, who immediately denounced the government for going back on its commitments and for undermining the entire peace process.[14] The distance between the two sides was confirmed in the spring of 1998 when the government presented the Mexican congress with its own initiative on indigenous rights, effectively bypassing both COCOPA and CONAI as well as excluding the other party of the conflict, the EZLN, which refused to give its approval to anything other than the San Andrés accords.

The Other War: Paramilitary Violence in Northern Chiapas

One of the paradoxes of the conflict in Chiapas is that more lives have been lost in often unnoticed acts of violence than in full-scale combat between government troops and the EZLN. In this regard, the "other war" in the northern Chol-speaking municipalities of Tila, Sabanilla, Salto de Agua, and Tumbalá represents a major obstacle in the search for peaceful solutions in Chiapas.

The problems in this region stem from the activities of a paramilitary group supported by the PRI named Paz y Justicia.[15] This group is led by Samuel Sánchez Sánchez, former leader of a faction of the teachers' union in Chiapas and, since October 1995, PRI deputy in the Chiapas state congress. Sánchez Sánchez is accused by human rights organizations of using his political office to obtain arms and other supplies for Paz y Justicia. The group's main objective is to forcibly destroy Zapatista base communities in this mainly Chol-speaking region. In most cases, these communities also have participated in elections by supporting PRD candidates against incumbent PRI authorities.

Zapatista strength in this region is not negligible. Even prior to 1994, support for the rebellion had been organized through an independent peasant organization. The radicalization of Chol Indians between 1989 and 1993 followed a pattern similar to that observed in the Lacandon forest. Prior to 1989, most of the communities participated in a coffee-marketing cooperative. Then, in June 1989, they were hit by the fall in coffee prices and the simultaneous reduction or withdrawal of institutional support by the federal government. Feeling abandoned by the government, many people rejected any link whatsoever with the regime, marking a clear and radical break with the institutionalist strategies adopted by most popular movements in the 1980s. The government response to the coffee crisis led to further polarization. The federal National Solidarity Program (PRONASOL) was the main program that attempted to fill the gaps created by neoliberal restructuring. As in other regions of Chiapas, the state government sought to centralize control over the distribution of Solidarity resources for productive projects. In general, the local CNC and PRI leaders became the key intermediaries in this process. In the Chol region, however, the government sought to co-opt a new organization, the Solidaridad Campesina Magisterial (SOCAMA), an alliance of one faction of the teachers' union and some community leaders. SOCAMA developed strong relations with President Salinas and cooperated in the implementation of Solidarity projects. This relationship created tensions within communal landholdings known as ejidos as PRONASOL funds were channeled only to those members who supported SOCAMA leaders. In the midst of rising debts and depressed coffee prices, many small producers felt excluded and turned to the more radical alternative presented by the EZLN.

Another source of tension resulted from the elections in August 1994. According to investigations carried out by an independent tribunal of electoral observers, irregularities were reported at 57 percent of polling stations in Chiapas. In the Chol region, there was majority support for the PRD's gubernatorial candidate Amado Avendaño. Irregularities—including violations of secrecy of the ballot—were reported at more than 70 percent of polling stations in Tila and over 61 percent in Sabanilla. The failure of the electoral authorities to recognize the occurrence of fraud led dissident groups to abstain from participating in the mayoral and local congressional elections in October 1995. In Tila, abstentionism rose by 24.4 percent between the two elections, from 41.6 percent in August 1994 to 66 percent in October 1995. A similar trend was observed in Salto de Agua, Tumbalá, and Sabanilla. The absence of guarantees for free and fair elections continued to prevent the opposition from competing for office through legal channels. Instead, many abandoned the electoral arena completely, as evidenced by the high rate of abstentionism, but also by the search for greater autonomy in the use of traditional means for selecting community representatives. The goal of indigenous autonomy therefore can be seen as a response to the crisis of the institutional sphere and the continuing absence of democratic guarantees in Chiapas. In these conditions, despite the euphoria of democratic participation in Mexico City, the national congressional elections in July 1997 continued to be seen as a sham in Chiapas. The Zapatistas destroyed polling stations in several districts in an attempt to have the elections nullified. In explaining its position, the EZLN pointed to three factors: the militarization of indigenous areas; the failure of the government to recognize and implement the San Andrés accords on indigenous rights and culture; and the lack of interest shown by all political parties toward the problems of indigenous peoples. Countering those who criticized the EZLN for its abstentionist position, Subcomandante Marcos encouraged people to exercise their right to vote where the conditions allowed, but added: "Who is responsible for the decision of indigenous communities [to participate in the elections]? How is this decision to be made? On what basis can Indians be called on to vote if they are not even able to live under normal conditions? Can they be asked to pretend that they live in a normal civic order for one day, and then return to daily terror the rest of the year?"[16]

The rebellion did not create divisions within Chol and other indigenous communities. They existed prior to January 1, 1994, and were exacerbated by electoral fraud and intimidation of government opponents. What the rebellion did, however, was to bring those divisions into sharper relief as SOCAMA leaders sided with the federal army, the state government, judicial police, the PRI, and the local ranchers' associations in defining a strategy of containment and eventual destruction of the Zapatista movement in the Chol region. Since 1994 the federal government's main objective has been to prevent the spread of the EZLN beyond the area that it successfully occupied on January 1, seeking to restrict it primarily to the Lacandon forest. It has deployed a strategy of low-intensity warfare in which military patrols and constant harassment of Zapatista sympathizers are combined with the provision of food, roofing materials, and health care to factions allied with the government.[17]

In this context, the Chol municipalities are of great strategic importance. To the north, they border the oil fields of Tabasco. To the west lies the Grijalva River with its complex of hydroelectricity dams. To the east is the main line of communication to the Yucatán peninsula. Finally, the *ladino* (non-Indian) ranchers and merchants of Palenque and Salto de Agua have their own interest in limiting the advance of pro-Zapatista organizations. The Chol Indians are separated from the *Cañadas* (Canyons) by only a handful of municipalities that belong to the Tzeltal region. The most important of these is Chilón, where a similar polarization of community factions occurred from 1994 to 1996. In this case, the pro-government group, known as the Chinchulines, attempted to prevent the election in May 1996 of a new president in the municipality's largest ejido, which also happened to be the strongest base of support for the Zapatistas and the PRD. The Chinchulines provoked a violent reaction and their leader was killed, many people were injured, and buildings were destroyed. The state judicial police intervened and arrested supporters of both groups, but the Chinchulines were unable to prevent the PRD from consolidating its control of the municipal government and subsequently saw their influence decline rapidly. This placed SOCAMA leaders in Tila on red alert. In Paz y Justicia they had a significant armed presence that the PRI and local ranchers had supported since the group's formation in March 1995. Attacks were carried out against PRD supporters in the summer of that year, but the events in Chilón increased the stakes even more. In June 1996 several ambushes and assaults took place between *priistas* (supporters of the PRI) and *perredistas* (supporters of the PRD) in Tila and Sabanilla, in which over twenty people were killed and many others injured. Paz y Justicia, with logistical and material support from the police and army, succeeded in terrorizing the opposition and was able to establish control over the principal roads connecting Tila with surrounding municipalities. Group members restricted freedom of movement. In August 1996 a delegation of human rights observers to the region was stopped and threatened, while the state police did nothing to intervene.

The lessons to be drawn from this case are essential for understanding the complexity of intracommunity relations in Chiapas and for finding peaceful solutions to the region's problems. The Zapatista rebellion has led to the formation of new, pan-Indian alliances. However, this process is inevitably limited by the type of divisions created prior to 1994—divisions that are not, therefore, a product of the rebellion but are the product of institutional abandonment and the conscious manipulation by outside elites of internal disputes in the midst of severe economic strain. This point cannot be emphasized enough. Although any form of outside intervention is likely to affect the configuration of power relations within communities, some forms are clearly more destructive than others. Deciding to support candidates registered with an opposition party is one way of involving outside actors. It also happens to be a democratic right. On the other hand, arming paramilitary groups to terrorize local populations certainly disrupts community life, but it has no basis in legality whatsoever. This seems to be an obvious point, but it is striking how official responses to intracommunity violence sidestep issues of power and responsibility. The resulting impunity with which groups such as Paz y Justicia are allowed to operate is probably the major obstacle to achieving peaceful change in the region.

The impunity enjoyed by paramilitary groups led to the massacre of forty-five unarmed people in the village of Acteal, municipality of San Pedro Chenalhó, on December 22, 1997.[18] The victims were members of a local grass-roots cooperative, Las Abejas (The Bees), which supported the goals of the Zapatistas but were not in favor of the armed struggle. They were killed by a group that was found to have been armed and trained by local government authorities, including the PRI mayor and state police officers. Witnesses testified that the attackers acted with brutality, killing defenseless women and children and cutting open the wombs of pregnant women and ripping out their fetuses. Federal police investigators portrayed the attack as an internal community feud between rival families rather than a politically motivated massacre by a well-organized and well-armed paramilitary group. Human rights observers in Chiapas believe that the massacre was part of a counterinsurgency strategy to terrorize local bases of support for the Zapatistas, disrupt communications between pro-Zapatista communities, and allow for further militarization of the region. In response to national and international outrage at the massacre, President Zedillo replaced his interior minister and installed a new PRI governor in Chiapas. However, the government's position toward the EZLN hardened further in early 1998. Dozens of foreign observers were harassed or expelled from Mexico, allegedly for helping the Zapatistas build and operate autonomous rebel municipalities. By May 1998 the government appeared to be committed to a military and political strategy of wearing down local support for the EZLN while attempting to distract national and international attention with its own bill of indigenous rights. The fact that the EZLN, the national indigenous movement, the PRD, COCOPA, CONAI, and many groups in civil society rejected both of these strategies did not seem to deter President Zedillo from pursuing his chosen path.

Mexico in Comparative Perspective

Given the general picture painted in previous sections, it appears that the immediate prospects for peace in Chiapas are slim. Despite the legitimacy of the EZLN within large sectors of Mexican and international civil society, the peace process itself has been frustrated by an apparent indifference on the part of the federal government to its success. Peace also is jeopardized by the federal government's failure to implement the accord on indigenous rights and the persistent use of violence against Zapatista and

PRD supporters in Chiapas. In this context, we must ask how *obstacles* to peace can be turned into *opportunities* for peace.

In approaching this question, it is useful to compare how two main sets of issues affect the outcome of peace processes. These are, first, the creation and maintenance of incentives for governments to negotiate with insurgents and implement peace accords, and, second, the significance of the peace process for broader political reform, generally understood as the democratization of authoritarian structures of government. The main argument here is that if incentives are weak and if the government is able to keep its own political reform project separate from the peace process, the chances for a political solution are lower. On the other hand, if pressure from various sources creates incentives for the negotiation and implementation of accords, and if the accords are seen as inseparable from political reform, the chances for peaceful solutions are greater. Colombia has tended to move back and forth between the two, although by mid-1998 it resembled the first scenario, whereas El Salvador and Guatemala were able to move from the first to the second scenario. Mexico has moved in pendulum fashion, reflecting the shifting national political context since January 1, 1994. (See Table 5.1.)

Table 5.1
The Mexican Pendulum

Peace Process as Part of Democratization	Government Incentives to Negotiate with EZLN		
	Weak	Ambiguous	Strong
Weak	January 1–12, 1994		
			January 12–March 23, 1994
	March 24, 1994–April 1995		
		April–October 1995	
			October 1995–February 1996
		February–July 1996	
	July 1996–May 1998		
Ambiguous	May 1994 (electoral reforms)		
Strong			

If the success of peace processes depends on increasing the incentives for governments to negotiate and on the democratization of national political systems, we need to look more closely at those factors that can help shift the correlation of forces in such a direction and maintain it over time. Here we compare how political rather than military responses have been promoted and/or resisted in El Salvador, Guatemala, Colombia, and Mexico.

In the absence of any revolutionary overthrow of the state, how are incentives created for incumbents to negotiate with insurgents? This is a particularly important question in Guatemala and Mexico, where the military strength of the URNG and EZLN is much weaker than in El Salvador or Colombia. There appear to be three sources of pressure that create such incentives to follow a political rather than a military logic. The first of these is elite pressure. That is, the political and economic elites of a country may see that more may be lost through continuing violence and institutional collapse than may be gained through negotiations and stabilization.

In Colombia, the Barco administration (1986–1990) and the first two years of the Gaviria government were to a large degree encouraged by elite support for peace talks and political reforms that allowed for the reincorporation into political life of the M-19 and EPL. Similarly, in El Salvador, the failure of the armed forces to defeat the FMLN and the crisis of international credibility associated with human rights violations and the murder of Jesuit priests in late 1989 led some sectors of the elite not only to accept but also to favor a political solution. In Guatemala, elite pressure has been less evident. However, elites could feel secure that the military and security threat of the URNG had been effectively defeated and that the government could negotiate from a position of strength. Political stability would be good for business in the new free trade era, and the issue became how long disarmament might take. Finally, Mexico presents a remarkable contrast in that elite pressure has been negligible and may be even opposed to a political solution. Unlike their counterparts in Colombia and El Salvador, Mexican elites have not yet felt that their own project of economic and political hegemony is under threat by the scale of violence and institutional decay. Kidnappings of prominent businesspeople have become more frequent, but the response has not been to pursue political solutions. Instead, pressure is applied to improve public security by increasing police powers, especially in wealthy urban areas and commercial centers. The emergence of the EPR is indeed viewed as a threat, but (at least until now) one that can be competently dealt with militarily. In short, the EZLN has not so radically altered the balance of forces in Mexico that the elites are concerned for the future of their business interests. So, where is the incentive for the Mexican government to negotiate far-reaching reforms with the EZLN?

A second source of pressure in bringing about political solutions in Latin America has been the international community, which includes governments, intergovernmental organizations, and international nongovernmental organizations. This source of pressure was most important in the Salvadoran case, where the military and government were dependent on U.S. aid. In Guatemala, there was less direct pressure from outside the country. However, the parties' acceptance of a role for the United Nations in the process did help move negotiators beyond the impasse in 1994. The role of the U.N. moderator, Jean Arnault, in keeping the political logic on track was an additional, if not the principal, source of pressure on the Guatemalan government. The cases of Colombia and Mexico are far more ambiguous. Both countries are much larger than El Salvador and Guatemala. Their internal conflicts have never been framed in terms of regional security, as occurred in Central America. Nor have they been the site for the same type of Cold War interventionism by the United States. Each government therefore has asserted arguments of national sovereignty in dealing with internal conflicts. Raising the mere question of U.N. involvement is likely to cause a nationalist backlash, especially in Mexico. However, other forms of international pressure also have been lacking. In Colombia, such pressure has come in the form of the ill-fated "war on drugs" that has tended to compound endemic violence and human rights abuses rather than establish the legal authority of the state. In Mexico, while the Zapatistas and Marcos won a large amount of sympathy among the American public, the U.S. government has been reluctant to put pressure on President Zedillo to improve the human rights situation or give greater attention to the peace talks. This can be explained in part by the historical nature of U.S.-Mexican relations, but we also should conclude that for Washington, the main worry is with the fate of NAFTA and neoliberal restructing. The EZLN is an obvious negation of the supposed benefits of NAFTA for Mexican people. Similarly, the Zapatistas' rejection of neoliberalism clearly coincides with the arguments of many opposition groups and social movements on both sides of the border. U.S. policy therefore has sought to bolster President Zedillo's position without pressuring him to negotiate the type of reforms being proposed by the EZLN. Again, there is no incentive to negotiate in the absence of international pressure.

The third source of pressure comes from civil society, which in this analysis includes not only political parties but also social movements, the media, cultural groups, universities, private associations, churches, and unions. It was in Guatemala that the voices of civil society were given greatest formal recognition in the peace process. The creation of the Asamblea de la Sociedad Civil (ASC), in which all but the elite business groups participated, provided a forum to debate the broad scope of issues at stake in Guatemala. Although the ASC's impact on the final accords should not be overstated, its existence at least gave continuing momentum to the talks per se and created a social climate that may have helped keep the balance tipped in favor of the political logic over the military logic. How tragic it was that the nonviolent associations of civil society were not given such a space in 1978–1979. While it is impossible to turn the clock back, we can draw this lesson at least: Political guarantees for the right to free association are essential components of peaceful solutions to violent conflict. However, the high level of electoral abstentionism in the new Guatemala is also a sign of people's disengagement from a political system that appears to offer no solutions to crushing poverty.

Civil society in El Salvador was less formally incorporated and the networks of popular organizations were seen as marginal to the top-level negotiations between the government and the FMLN. This is a serious problem, as evidenced by the crisis of the party system, the high level of abstentionism in elections, and the failure of political reform to address poverty and insecurity. Both Guatemala and El Salvador need to rebuild their "social infrastructure" if democratic rights are not to be lost again to new forms of violence and authoritarianism.

When considering the role of civil society, Mexico again appears to be closer to the Colombian experience, although it is arguably better situated to apply pressure for peaceful negotiations. The pendulum movement between the political and military responses in Colombia has failed to bring an end to a thirty-year-old civil war. The most hopeful moment came with the election of a new constituent assembly and the elaboration of a new constitution in 1991. What was significant about this moment was the fact that the new assembly was not dominated by the two traditional parties, but instead allowed for a broader spectrum of voices to be heard through peaceful deliberation for perhaps the first time in the country's history.[19] The role of civil society in generating novel approaches and pragmatic, nonideological proposals began to be recognized and has taken on growing significance despite an increase in violence (see chapter 6). The best hope for peace in Colombia also may found in civil society.[20]

In Mexico, it appears that civil society offers the main source of pressure that could force the government to have a greater incentive to negotiate. It should not be forgotten that mass civic protests in major Mexican cities thwarted the military logic on two occasions. The first was on January 12, 1994, which led then President Salinas to call a unilateral cease-fire after the initial military offensive had left 145 dead and many wounded. The second occurred in the days following the February 9, 1995, offensive to capture the EZLN leadership. In that case, President Zedillo eventually agreed to negotiations, and over the course of the next sixteen months, most of the suspected Zapatistas were released (again due to pressure from civil society). National and international civil society also has participated actively in numerous forums, consultations, peace camps, cultural activities, local networking, lobbying, and provision of food, medicines, and other aid to Zapatista base communities. The challenge is for civil society to create similar pressures from other actors in the international community and, eventually, force Mexican elites to accept the inevitability of far-reaching reforms.

If the prospects for peace in Mexico are dependent on the capacity of civil society to tip the balance away from the military logic, then the basis for restarting talks and giving them new momentum should be related to a human rights agenda, with immediate application to the Chiapas highlands and Lacandon forest region. In other cases in Latin America, ongoing violence prevented peace processes from continuing. The Zapatistas have insisted that the harassment of indigenous communities sympathetic to their cause inhibits the peace process and have called for demilitarization of the zone of conflict in order for dialogue to resume. It is no coincidence that the turning point in the Guatemalan peace process was the accord on human rights signed in March 1994. Although abuses continued to occur, the accord allowed for greater international verification in the form of the U.N. mission, which in turn increased the political costs of rights violations by the Guatemalan military. The Guatemalan accord explicitly recognized the serious state of human rights abuses, the need for international verification, guarantees for human rights nongovernmental organizations and the strengthening of the government's own human rights institutions. This situation stands in stark contrast with the case of Chiapas, where measures to guarantee protection of human rights remain ineffective or absent, even in the wake of the Acteal massacre. Similarly, international observers in Chiapas lack the type of recognition given in the Guatemalan accord. They therefore have found their status to be ambiguous, precarious, and increasingly dangerous. If the Mexican government wants a peaceful solution in Chiapas, then it should take a lesson from the Guatemalan experience and provide for the legitimate presence of an international verification body that is also acceptable to the EZLN.

Finally, any discussion of the relationship between peace processes and democratization must address the nature of civil-military relations. What role should the armed forces play in Mexico's conflict? However unpopular the armed forces may be, the political fact is that in none of the four countries reviewed here was the military defeated. Just as the military withdrawal in Chile occurred on the terms dictated by General Pinochet, the Guatemalan armed forces emerged strongly from the negotiations with the URNG. This type of transition has been aptly defined as "transition by extrication."[21] Similarly, in El Salvador, the construction of the new civilian government was initially guided by the Cold War security agenda of the U.S. and the Salvadoran military. The neoliberal economic agenda took off from where the Cold War ended in El Salvador, allowing the elites to settle for "democracy by default" rather than continue an unwinnable war.[22] The military emerged politically weaker and less able to protect itself from demands for an overhaul than in Guatemala. In Colombia, by contrast, the military still was able to present itself as a central actor in confronting rising violence. Important sectors of the military have opposed peace talks at crucial moments and have operated more independently of civilian authority.

In Mexico, the military traditionally has been subordinated to the constitution and civilian rule. The official party and the postrevolutionary state were in fact designed to overcome the ambitions of regional military chiefs, or *caudillos,* who dominated political life during the 1920s. The size and budget of the military was deliberately kept small.[23] The military's involvement in Chiapas therefore created some strains in civil-military relations as the army was held responsible for widespread human rights violations.[24] Army commanders countered that the rebellion that they had been called upon to suppress was the result of civilian governments, particularly the corrupt and authoritarian governors whom the indigenous people in Chiapas had endured for over sixty years. However, the abuses do exist and do oblige negotiators to deal with military actions against the civilian population. In short, the military must be given a role that is consistent with its institutional and historical legacy rather than be employed in a counterinsurgency operation of low-intensity warfare. Put simply, that role is nothing else but the defense of the constitution. Low-intensity warfare is not defending the constitution since by nature it entails the repeated violation of the rights of Mexican citizens. The danger for Mexico is that a failure to produce a momentum for political solutions will lead to more violence, more militarization, and less civilian control over the security apparatus, despite the advent of democratic reform elsewhere in the country.

Notes

1. For comprehensive accounts of the Zapatista rebellion in English, see Tom Benjamin, *A Rich Land, a Poor People: Politics and Society in Modern Chiapas* (Albuquerque: University of New Mexico Press, 1996); George A. Collier, and Elizabeth L. Quaratiello, *Basta! Land and the Zapatista Rebellion in Chiapas,* Institute for Food and Development Policy (Oakland, Calif: Food First Books, 1994); Neil Harvey, *The Chiapas Rebellion: The Struggle for Land and Democracy* (Durham, NC: Duke University Press, 1998); and John Ross, *Rebellion from the Roots: Indian Uprising in Chiapas* (Monroe, Maine: Common Courage Press, 1995). In Spanish, see EZLN, *Documentos y Comunicados* (2 vols.) (Mexico City: Era, 1994–1995); Luis Hernández Navarro, *Chiapas: La Guerra y La Paz* (Mexico City: AND Editores, 1995); Carlos Montemayor, *Chiapas: La Rebelión Indígena de México* (Mexico City: Joaquín Mortiz, 1997); and Carlos Tello Díaz, *La Rebelión de Las Cañadas* (Mexico City: Cal y Arena, 1995).

2. Lynn Stephen, "The Zapatista Army of National Liberation and the National Democratic Convention," *Latin American Perspectives* 22, No. 4 (1995): 88–100.

3. Roberto Garduño Espinosa and José Gil Olmos, "No vendrá del EZLN la guerra: Marcos," *La Jornada,* August 10, 1994, 1, 20.

4. Suzanne L. Fiederlein, "The 1994 Elections in Mexico: The Case of Chiapas," *Mexican Studies/Estudios Mexicanos* 12, No. 1 (1996): 107–30; and Jonathan Fox, "National Electoral Choices in Mexico," in Laura Randall, ed., *Reforming Mexico's Agrarian Reform* (New York: M.E. Sharpe, 1996), 185–209.

5. Luis Hernández Navarro, "Los Péndulos del Poder: Negociación y Conflicto en Chiapas," in *Memoria de la Conferencia: Procesos de Paz Comparados* (Guatemala City: Asociación de Investigación y Estudios Sociales and Latin American Program of the Woodrow Wilson International Center for Scholars, 1996), 113–51.

6. Rodolfo Stavenhagen, "Indigenous Rights: Some Conceptual Problems," in Elizabeth Jelin and Eric Hershberg, eds., *Constructing Democracy: Human Rights, Citizenship and Society in Latin America* (Boulder, Colo.: Westview Press, 1996), 141–59.

7. Elizabeth Jelin, "Citizenship Revisited: Solidarity, Responsibility and Rights," in ibid., 101–119; and Iris Marion Young, "Polity and Group Difference: A Critique of the Ideal of Universal Citizenship," in Ronald Beiner, ed., *Theorizing Citizenship* (Albany: State University of New York Press, 1995), 175–207.

8. Héctor Díaz Polanco, "El Estado y los Indígenas," in Jorge Alonso, Alberto Aziz Nassif, Jaime Tamayo, eds., *El Nuevo Estado Mexicano,* vol. 1 (Mexico City: Universidad de Guadalajara/Centro de Investigaciones y Estudios Superiores en Antropología Social/Editorial Planeta, 1992), 145–170; Jane Hindley, "Towards a Pluricultural Nation: The Limits of *Indigenismo* and Article 4," in Rob Aitken, Nikki Craske, Gareth A. Jones, and David E. Stansfield eds., *Dismantling the Mexican State?* (London: Macmillan Press and St. Martin's Press, 1996), 225–43; and Sergio Sarmiento, "Movimiento indio y modernización," *Cuadernos Agrarios* 2 (1991): 90–113.

9. Luis Hernández Navarro, "San Andrés: el ojo del huracán," *La Jornada,* November 21, 1995.

10. Hermann Bellinghausen, "Causaron 'baja' en las pláticas las huestes del Instituto Nacional Indigenista," *La Jornada,* November 15, 1995, 5.

11. Consuelo Sánchez, "Por los caminos de la autonomía," *La Jornada,* November 11, 1995.

12. Julio César López, "El diálogo sobre cultura indígena, casi un monólogo: López y Rivas. Ante la lucidez de los asesores del EZLN, la parte gubernamental se refugia en el rechazo pertinaz," *Proceso* 994 (November 20, 1995): 39–40.

13. "El Diálogo de San Andrés y los Derechos y Cultura Indígena. Punto y Seguido," *La Jornada,* February 15, 1996, 10–11.

14. Luis Hernández Navarro, "Entre la memoria y el olvido: guerrillas, movimiento indígena y reformas legales en la hora del EZLN," *Chiapas* 4 (1997): 69–92.

15. Centro de Derechos Humanos Fray Bartolomé de Las Casas, *Ni Paz ni Justicia, ó Informe general y amplio acerca de la guerra civil que sufren los Choles en la Zona Norte de Chiapas, diciembre de 1994 a octubre de 1996* (San Cristóbal de Las Casas: Centro de Derechos Humanos Fray Bartolomé de Las Casas, 1996).

16. Cited in Jose López Arévalo, "Sobrelineas," *Este Sur,* (July 7, 1997): 16–17.

17. Martha Patricia López Astrain, *La Guerra de Baja Intensidad en México* (Mexico City: Universidad Iberoamericana and Plaza y Valdés Editores, 1996).

18. Centro de Derechos Humanos Fray Bartolomé de Las Casas, *Camino a La Masacre. Informe Especial Sobre Chenalhó* (San Cristóbal de Las Casas: Centro de Derechos Humanos Fray Bartolomé de Las Casas, 1998).

19. Carlos Basombrío Iglesias, *La Paz: Valor y Precio. Una Visión Comparativa para América Latina.* (Lima: Instituto de Defensa Legal, 1996), 82.

20. Ibid., 98.

21. Scott Mainwaring, "Transitions to Democracy and Democratic Consolidation: Theoretical and Comparative Issues," in Scott Mainwaring, Guillermo O'Donnell, and J. Samuel Valenzuela, eds., *Issues in Democratic Consolidation: The New South American Democracies in Comparative Perspective,* (Notre Dame, Ind.: University of Notre Dame Press: 1992), 294–341.

22. Laurence Whitehead, "The Alternatives to 'Liberal Democracy': A Latin American Perspective," in David Held, ed., *Prospects for Democracy: North, South, East, West* (Stanford, Calif.: Stanford University Press, 1993), 312–29.

23. Stephen J. Wager, "The Mexican Military Approaches the Twenty-First Century: Coping with a New World Order," in Donald E. Schulz and Edward J. Williams, eds., *Mexico Faces the Twenty-First Century* (Westport, Conn.: Praeger Publishers, 1995), 59–76.

24. Stephen J. Wager and Donald E. Schulz, "The Zapatista Revolt and its Implications for Civil-Military Relations and the Future of Mexico," in ibid., 165–86.

Reflections

MICHAEL CONROY

If it is true that economic policy affects the consolidation of peace, it is also true that the lack of peace affects the economy. When looking at the Zapatista uprising in Mexico, it is important to keep in mind: its economic underpinnings; the extent to which the EZLN, either dramatically or only temporarily, affected the overall economic picture in Mexico; and qualitative changes in Mexican economic policy that may be linked to the uprising. It is also important to attempt to separate the putative effects of the uprising from the consequences of the financial crash of late 1994 and 1995.

The Zapatista uprising began on January 1, 1994. This was also the start of the North American Free Trade Agreement (NAFTA) with the United States and Canada. If the two years prior to the uprising (1992 and 1993) are compared with the two years after uprising (1994 to 1996), it is apparent that growth in gross domestic product (GDP) more than doubled from 1993 to 1994. In 1995, however, GDP fell by a full 6.6 percent. (See Table 5.2.)

Urban unemployment rose just slightly in 1994, then rose dramatically in 1995. Median real wages in Mexico rose in 1994 by several percentage points and then declined dramatically by year's end; and the 1996 figure illustrates how dramatically the economic crisis affected Mexico; by then real wages fell to below 1990 levels.

In the first year after the uprising, through the end of 1994, exports grew by 17.3 percent. This period corresponds to the first year of NAFTA, and it occurred before the severe devaluation in December 1994.

There is a different story, however, with respect to net resource transfers. Mexico received net transfers of $16.4 billion a year in 1992 and $18.4 billion in 1993; however, transfers were negative in 1994, dropping

153

Table 5.2

Selected Data on the Mexican Economy, 1992–1996

| | Pre-uprising | | | Post-uprising | |
	1992	1993	1994	1995	1996*
GDP growth (%)	3.7	1.9	4.6	—6.6	4.5
Urban unemployment (%)	2.8	3.4	3.7	6.3	5.7
Index of median real wages (1990=100)	114	124	129	114	98.8
Growth in exports of goods and services (%)	N.A.	N.A.	17.3	30.6	20.0
Net resource transfers (billions of $)	16.4	18.4	—1.8	—1.3	—11.4

Source: Economic Commission for Latin America and the Caribbean (ECLAC), *Preliminary Overview of the Economy of Latin America and the Caribbean* (Santiago: United Nations, 1996).
*Preliminary estimates.

by close to $20 billion from the 1993 level. The Zapatista uprising may have scared off a lot of investment, and therein lies another tale.

By December 1994 the EZLN apparently was cornered in a relatively small portion of Chiapas, although it did control some towns and territory. It enjoyed the popular support of Mexican civil society and successfully communicated its message to the international community, and this support served to stay the hand of the Mexican presidency and army.

But during the week the peso collapsed in late December 1994, there occurred a sequence of events that is repeatedly associated, perhaps only indirectly, with the Zapatista movement. That sequence of events is as follows:

On December 17, 1994, Zapatistas and their supporters seized what newspapers reported to be approximately thirty-eight city halls in Chiapas and some in the neighboring states of Oaxaca and Guerrero. A key element of these seizures was that most of them took place outside what the government had previously defined as a *cordon militaire* surrounding and controlling the Zapatistas.

Subsequent analysis suggested that the true number of seizures was closer to twelve or thirteen, but in addition, the Zapatistas downed trees over highways and cut trenches through roads disrupting travel and transport for several days. These were the first major Zapatista action since the tentative cease-fire that had been reached in mid-February 1994.

A persistent rumor in Mexico City suggests that on December 18, a large number of prominent business people in Mexico gathered at the presidential palace of Los Pinos, spent many hours with President Zedillo, and convinced him to unleash the army against the Zapatistas. Members of the private sector argued that guerrilla activities were extremely disruptive, and failure to control them would be dangerous to Mexico's long-term economic prospects.

No one can confirm that that discussion actually took place. What we do know—and what the International Monetary Fund partially confirmed in its 1996 reports—is that there was a massive outflow of foreign exchange from Mexico beginning the following day, December 19. Some observers within Mexico hold that that outflow was caused by Mexican industrialists who had convinced the president to unleash the army and who also knew that such action would lead to a fall in the value of the peso internationally. These businesspeople wanted to get their peso balances into dollars and outside of the country.

Rumor or opinion aside, it is a fact that on December 20, 1994, the government announced that because of currency outflows the previous day, it was going to allow the peso to devalue from 3.3 pesos to 4.0 pesos to the dollar. This represented the first major change in the peso's value in several years. Then, following a second day of massive currency outflows, the government announced on December 21 that it could no longer control the value of the peso.

Over these several days, approximately $4.5 billion of the government's $7 billion in reserves flowed out of its reserve stock. Over subsequent weeks the peso's value plummeted to 5.0, 5.2, and ultimately much less against the dollar.

This period in December 1994 represented the moment of greatest potential Zapatista influence over national economic policy. The group had the ability, had it so chosen, to worsen the peso situation further, a situation beyond the control of the government. International investors were scared. Money was pouring out of the Mexican stock market and government securities so rapidly that the government turned to the United States for help. Not coincidentally, this period of financial crisis represented the only time the Mexican interior minister met with the leadership of the Zapatistas. The meeting took place on January 15, 1995; it aimed at paralyzing further Zapatista actions by making it appear that major breakthroughs were possible.

On January 20, the Mexican government secured confirmation that it would receive what has been called, rather inappropriately, the bailout package. That package was announced on January 24. Two weeks later, on February 9, President Zedillo unleashed the army against the EZLN. The armed forces moved into those territories that had been held by the Zapatistas, forcing the rebels up into the mountains and taking over all the towns previously occupied by the rebels.

U.S. and International Monetary Fund loans helped to restabilize the Mexican economy. At the same time they undercut significantly that moment of leverage that the EZLN possessed.

Several dimensions characterize the linkage between the stalling of the peace talks and the qualitative changes in economic policy in Mexico. First, since 1995, there has been a massive inflow of international resources into Chiapas and Mexico's southern states. The Inter-American Development Bank and the World Bank have provided tens of millions of dollars. During a major trip to Mexico in late 1995, World Bank President James Wolfensohn went to Chiapas instead of to Mexico City and used his time there to emphasize the need for social development and social equity as a precondition for future Mexican growth. It is doubtful that such a visit would have taken place had it not been for the Zapatista uprising. The extent of high-level attention has raised the question in Mexico as to whether insurgent activity or the threat thereof is needed in order to draw resources from the Mexican government and international financial institutions.

Second, the uprising and attempts at a peace process in and around Chiapas have had an impact on the resolution of land questions. The increased rate of invasions of *ladino*-owned lands by indigenous peoples reflects one of the long-term implications of the Zapatista uprising.

The indigenous peoples of Mexico have, as a result of the uprising, acquired an "attitude." In 1996 government commissioners of the land-titling program known as PROCEDE went to the highlands of Puebla, a significant distance from Chiapas, to talk about procedures for giving private title to collectively held lands. They were met by about 3,000 indigenous people who said essentially, "We don't trust you," and "If you want to come and talk to us, send people to us who speak our language." The commissioners were basically run out of town.

In addition, fragmentary information available from El Colegio de la Frontera Sur in Chiapas has suggested that the reconcentration of population within Chiapas has placed more and more of the rural areas and small towns strictly in indigenous hands and that virtually the entire population in many small towns is indigenous. The *ladino* population has been relocating to relatively larger cities, in part because of the tensions and indigenous land takeovers, and in part because of the government's inability to mount a response.

The bottom line is that the insurgency no longer has an important impact on Mexico's overall macroeconomic health, and that is one reason why the Mexican government does not believe that engaging in a serious peace process is important. While there was a time during which the Zapatistas might have had a major effect on the economy, the bailout of the Mexican economy helped the government avoid that moment of greatest Zapatista influence. The international bailout thus also foreclosed a significant opportunity for lasting political reform in Mexico by diluting Zapatista influence at a crucial moment. The lasting impact of the uprising can better be measured in the strengthening of indigenous identity and in the structure of economic development assistance, especially programs with international funding, aimed at the indigenous population of Mexico.

6

Negotiating Peace amid Multiple Forms of Violence: The Protracted Search for a Settlement to the Armed Conflicts in Colombia

MARC CHERNICK

Introduction

Violence has shaped the last five decades of Colombian politics. By the late 1990s, as political assassinations, combat deaths, and massacres of civilians continued to tear apart the warp of civil society and to shatter the reach and legitimacy of the nation's institutions, Colombians from across the political spectrum began to mobilize and demand a renewed effort to reach peace among the nation's violent contenders for power. In October 1997 almost 10 million Colombians voted in favor of a generally worded "mandate for peace." By May 1998 millions heeded the call to stop work for a symbolic hour while tens of thousands more marched in the streets to demand a halt to political violence that had been claiming, on average, 23.4 lives a day and more than 700 a month since 1988.[1] The Colombian government responded by establishing a permanent National Council for Peace composed of key representatives from the state, local government, and civil society and charged with advising the government on ways to reach a negotiated end to the country's armed conflicts.

Civil society organizations also directly seized the initiative, expressly asserting that they did not want to leave the issue of national reconciliation
strictly in the hands of the government or allow it to be reduced to an accord between government and the guerillas. Thus representatives of the
church, labor unions, universities, business associations, civic groups, and
others founded the National Reconciliation Commission to channel the
participation of society in future negotiations.

Similarly, the international community—multilateral development
banks, nongovernmental organizations, other states, and regional and international organizations—began to address the issue of Colombian violence directly and to insist that peace is the key to achieving other policy
goals, from protecting human rights, to promoting development and protecting the environment. Moreover, as the international community became more involved through assisting those displaced by the violence, providing help to local communities torn by the hostilities, denouncing
human rights violations, or contributing to mediation efforts to free captured soldiers or kidnapped victims, many sectors began to call for a more
concerted international involvement in Colombia's peace process. Such a
direct international role would be without precedent in that country. Previous efforts to negotiate peace beginning in the early 1980s were exclusively national efforts.

Peace processes were begun in Colombia well before the successful experiences in El Salvador and elsewhere, when there were scant precedents
for negotiated settlements to civil war or guerrilla insurgency. In 1982 an
unconditional amnesty and pardon were offered to guerrillas and most political prisoners. In 1984 the Colombian government signed cease-fire
agreements with four guerrilla groups and then attempted to engage
them—together with other political sectors—in a grand national dialogue
on the chief political issues of the day, including agrarian reform, education, labor and constitutional issues, and others. A model ahead of its time,
it was echoed over a decade later in Guatemala. But if the model worked
in the late 1990s in Guatemala, it failed in the early 1980s in Colombia.
The government held several rounds of talks with the different guerrilla
movements again, from 1989 to 1994. Surprisingly, these talks led to the
disarmament and reincorporation of several smaller groups, including one
prominent guerrilla movement that had emerged in the 1970s, the April
19th Movement (Movimiento 19 de Abril), or M-19. The accords were
based on a limited negotiating agenda centered on the issues of disarmament, conversion into legal political parties, and proposed special electoral

rules to facilitate representation in Congress. Despite serious attempts to expand the process, the limited-agenda model proved inadequate to lay the foundation for an enduring peace with the larger guerrilla movements, most notably the Fuerzas Armadas Revolucionarias de Colombia (FARC) and the Ejército de Liberación Nacional (ELN).

Colombia has changed significantly since the government's first tentative amnesty and exploratory negotiations with the guerrillas in 1982. The cost of failure has been quite high. Today violence is three times greater, and the political and social arenas more fractured. From 1982 until the present, the geopolitical and global economic contexts were irrevocably transformed, altered by the collapse of the Cold War, the liberalization of the economy, and the impact of a burgeoning global trade in illicit narcotics. International change was mirrored by a radically reconstituted political landscape characterized by a new and democratic constitution that emerged from widespread social discontent and the earlier but limited peace processes, the rise of powerful new social actors tied to the drug trade, the proliferation of paramilitary groups linked to the armed forces and local landowners, militarily stronger guerrilla movements, and a large population of internally displaced people, a population that accelerated the country's already advanced urbanization and large-scale colonization of ecologically sensitive lands. The contradictory realities of the late 1990s made a negotiated settlement between the government and guerrillas more difficult—and more necessary, a fact that perhaps is the key to bringing together a politically atomized and socially fragmented nation in the twenty-first century.

Objectively, this conflict does not appear more intractable than many other armed rebellions around the globe. The conflicts did not arise as a result of ethnic or racial exclusion. To judge from past negotiations and public demands, the ideological distances are not great, nor are the guerrilla demands excessive, comparatively speaking.[2] Yet as time and history pass, the ability to negotiate successfully seems to recede. The guerrillas are more entrenched on a local level and have greater military projection throughout the national territory than at any previous period in the conflict. The state, having expanded its counterinsurgency apparatus and having abetted or acquiesced in the arming of paramilitary forces to confront the guerrillas further, has contributed to the loss of state cohesion and to the privatization and fragmentation of its monopoly on arms. Political violence now revolves around territorial control and competition over small pieces of political geography—a finca, a neighborhood, a municipality, or a region—among these diverse armed actors. Civilian populations are the target of this competition. The old dynamics of a leftist insurgency directed against the state has increasingly given way to a clash of multiple armed actors vying for strategic control of local territory.

This chapter analyzes these different facets of Colombia's insurgency as well as the repeated attempts to reach a negotiated settlement to the armed conflict. The next two sections discuss the guerrilla movements and several conceptual issues and debates concerning the causes of political violence that are critical to understanding the Colombian case and, by extension, other civil conflicts. They focus on evolving perceptions on the causes of guerrilla war, the potential paths to peace, and the relationship between political violence and other forms of violence, including drug trafficking, delinquency, and paramilitary armies tied to landowners and the state.

In analyzing the specific peace strategies of successive Colombian governments, this chapter examines what worked and what did not. It asks which opportunities were seized and which were were missed. The chapter concludes by asking a few fundamental questions concerning future negotiations: What are the key issues in a future peace agenda and who should sit at the table? What role can the international community play?

Armed Rebels in Colombia, 1948–1998

Violence in Colombia has ebbed and flowed for five decades. Over 200,000 Colombians perished in the first phase of violence, known as *la Violencia,* between 1948 and 1958, historically analyzed as a partisan civil war between the liberal and conservative parties (the Partido Liberal and the Partido Conservador). Violence receded following a negotiated power-sharing pact known as the National Front.[3] However, the far-reaching accords, so successful in demobilizing followers of these two parties, did not bring peace. Some groups and communities refused to hand in their arms or recognize the power-sharing arrangement worked out between the traditional party leaders. At the same time new guerrilla movements also took up arms against the elite-dominated coalition governments. Thus the vertical cleavages of a society divided by opposing party affiliations were supplanted by new horizontal cleavages that divided an elite who had direct access to the political arena from those who continued to be excluded politically and socially.

This second phase of the Colombian violence, beginning in 1958 and taking hold in the mid-1960s, remained a relatively low-intensity conflict between guerrillas and the state. Then, in 1982, levels of violence began to surge upward again, eventually surpassing the peaks reached in the 1940s and 1950s. Between 1987 and 1997 over 270,000 homicides were recorded. Most of these were considered social violence and crime, although in Colombia the line between social and political violence is unclear.

In many respects, the more recent phase of the conflict resembles that of 1940s and 1950s. In both periods violence was spawned by a confluence of structural, institutional, and social conditions that inflamed existing social hostilities, accentuated inequalities and fostered bloodletting over compromise or reform. These conditions included:

1. The accelerated concentration of land ownership in the countryside, in the current phase spurred by narco-investments, in the earlier period by the booming coffee trade;

2. The complete absence or, in some regions, the "partial collapse" of the state in large areas of the national territory[4];

3. The massive expulsion of peasants from their lands, creating large numbers of displaced persons, estimated at over 2 million in the 1950s and over 1 million in the 1990s;

4. Large internal migration, both rural to urban, which led to the swelling of the country's urban centers, and rural to rural, which led to the accelerated opening of the country's agricultural frontiers in unsettled areas of the country, beyond state control;

5. The multiplicity of armed actors—disparate guerrilla units adhering to different national leaders, a mosaic of local paramilitary squads, political bosses, landowners—each mostly rooted in local issues, social conflicts, and power struggles.

In the 1940s and 1950s, these local conflicts were concealed only superficially by the larger partisan hostilities between liberals and conservatives;[5] in the 1980s and 1990s, again they are hidden only thinly by the war between guerrillas and the state. Beneath the contours of Colombia's political violence is a social war—played out largely in the nation's rural areas—that has raged throughout much of the twentieth century.[6]

Many of the social and political factors that have fomented violence at the local level have not been addressed for fifty years. This heterogeneous social reality is at the root of the Colombian violence. While shaped by regional and local conflicts, nevertheless it is aided in the fomenting of rebellious and revolutionary projects at the national level. Peace at the national level, as happened in 1957–1958 with the founding of the National

Front, did not bring peace fully to the local level or pacify the myriad of social actors who were at war with each other.

Moreover, the fact that the onset of the National Front coincided with the first years of the Cuban revolution gave new life to the revolutionary option of armed opposition. In Colombia, unlike in other South American nations, guerrillas were able to consolidate their presence in several rural areas during the first decade of the National Front. Despite enormous obstacles and confrontations with the Colombian military, student rebels, dissident Liberal guerrillas, and longtime peasant Communists found some of the most propitious soil for revolutionary activity to be found anywhere in the Americas. The new Colombian guerrilla movements—some consciously organized as Cuban-style *focos* modeled on the revolutionary ideas of Che Guevara,[7] others with roots deep in earlier periods of peasant organizing—were able to insert themselves into remote communities that already had experienced several decades of rebellion and armed social conflict. Guerrillas took hold in communities where the state had little presence and central authority was generally ignored. The barely penetrable and sparsely populated mountains, plains, and jungles only facilitated the growth of these guerrilla projects, particularly within the new human settlements along the expanding agricultural frontier.

By the mid-1960s Colombia's revolutionary landscape had taken shape and the key guerrilla organizations had emerged (see appendix). These were: the Fuerzas Armadas Revolucionarias de Colombia (FARC), built from the communist self-defense groups that had emerged in the coffee-growing regions and along the frontier of agricultural settlement in the 1940s and 1950s; the Maoist Ejército Popular de Liberación (EPL), reflecting the Sino-Soviet rupture of the early 1960s; and the pro-Cuban Ejército de Liberación Nacional (ELN), founded by Colombian students in Havana in the years immediately following the Cuban revolution. Each of these organizations built on the political work and prior organization of armed communist and Liberal groups that were active during *la Violencia*. Moreover, each of these groups, despite its outward expression of international ideologies, built strong relationships moored in the political and economic fissures of Colombian society. Being a communist peasant in the coffee region generally represented a response to the problems facing the Colombian peasantry at midcentury rather than an abstract construct of world communism.[8] Many prominent ELN and EPL militants were drawn from the student movements and the youth and dissident wings of the Liberal Party. The ELN in particular was founded in Havana by middle-class students, several of whom had supported a prominent dissident liberal faction that initially had opposed the National Front. Labor leaders from Colombia's petroleum workers union also helped found the ELN, providing an emphasis on petroleum politics that persists to this day.

A second generation emerged in the 1970s. The most prominent of these groups was the April 19th Movement, founded as a political-military organization with a nationalist agenda designed to confront the hegemony of the traditional parties and prevent the type of suspected fraud that occurred during the presidential elections of April 19, 1970.[9] Other, smaller groups emerged in the narrow institutional space and rebellious greenhouse of Colombian politics. In the absence of direct channels of participation, small parties and regional social movements also began to take up arms. One of these "armed social movements" was the Quintín Lame guerrillas, who emerged in the southern department of Cauca in the early 1980s. The Quintín Lame organized the region's indigenous community into self-defense forces and participated in land invasions and other armed activities on behalf of indigenous rights.

By the 1990s the strong currents of national and international politics led to a shake-out of the nation's guerrilla movements. After several false starts, the Colombian peace process led to final agreements with most of these second-generation movements. The collapse of Eastern European communism, the Sandinista defeat at the polls, the advance of the Salvadoran peace process, the crisis of Cuba, and the political reformism within Colombia itself led the M-19, the EPL, the Quintín Lame, and a few other smaller movements to negotiate their disarmament and political reincorporation into the legal political system.

The government's most attractive offer was the opportunity to participate in a constitutional convention with an open-ended mandate for political and institutional reform. The convention met between January and July 1991. The years between 1989 and 1991 represented an exceptional political moment. It was a time, no doubt influenced by the wider regional and global convulsions, during which many sectors of the Latin American left—including these groups in Colombia—began actively to rethink their historic role and, for the first time, to place a value on democratic and electoral politics as a viable means of reaching power. The new politics meant a renunciation of the armed struggle.[10]

In Colombia, for a brief but exceptional moment lasting approximately three years, the M-19 emerged as the most significant third force in the nation's history outside the two traditional parties. The situation appeared to be a victory not just for the M-19 but for the entire political system and the advocates of reform. The process clearly help relegitimize the traditional parties, especially the ruling Liberal Party. However, the M-19 was unable to sustain the momentum, and by the 1994 elections, the dominant Liberal and Conservative parties once again completely overshadowed the new political movement.[11]

Yet even as the M-19 was enjoying electoral and popular support, the FARC and the ELN refused to lay down their arms. Demanding more than political participation, they continued to propose major social, structural, and economic reforms as part of any peace agreement. They argued that the changes in the Soviet Union did not mitigate the injustices in Colombia.[12] Despite meetings with the government in Caracas, Venezuela, and in Tlaxcala, Mexico, in 1991 and 1992, the two major guerrilla movements could not come to terms with it. Since 1992 both the guerrillas and the government have concentrated their efforts on expanding and strengthening their military capabilities.

Many have asserted that the guerrillas' reluctance to negotiate peace represents their transformation from ideological guerrilla movements into large and successful criminal enterprises. The charge reflects great changes that have occurred in Colombian guerrilla warfare during the last decade, particularly following the momentous international changes from 1989 to 1991. As the Soviet Union imploded and Cuba unilaterally withdrew its support from Latin American guerrilla movements, the guerrillas stepped up their involvement in kidnapping, armed robbery, and extortion of commercial enterprises throughout most of rural Colombia. As a consequence, the policy of imposing "revolutionary taxes," long a financial strategy of the Colombian guerrillas, was widely expanded to cover most productive commercial operations in the countryside. In the coca-producing zones along the agricultural frontier of the northern Amazon Basin where the insurgents' presence is very strong, the FARC and ELN guerrillas charge 15 percent for each transaction between the coca farmers and buyers. By the mid-1990s they were charging tariffs on a wide range of illegal transactions, from imported chemical precursor agents, to the refining of cocaine. They also sustained a strong presence in the newer, higher-elevation opium poppy zones used to produce heroin. At the same time, similar levies were imposed on cattle ranchers, cotton farmers, rice growers, and most other commercial agricultural producers. It is estimated that the FARC annually earns hundreds of millions of dollars from the coca/cocaine boom, kidnapping, and other sources. The ELN reportedly earns similar profits from kidnappings, robberies, and by imposing levies on the petroleum and construction companies that were drawn to the eastern plains (*llanos orientales*) during successive oil booms beginning in the late 1980s and 1990s. Some intelligence sources have placed total guerrilla revenues as high as $800 million in 1996.[13] However, given the size of the Colombian economy and its known difficulties in absorbing illicit monies,[14] this figure is likely to be inflated. The sums, however, have been substantial enough to support a vast expansion in recruitment and territorial action by both guerrilla movements in the 1990s. An official government report based on police and military data declared that in 1985, there was some type of guerrilla activity in 173 municipalities of a total of 1,005 municipalities, or in 17.2 percent of all municipalities. By 1995 the figure had grown exponentially, rising to 622 of a total of 1,071 municipalities, a leap that represents 59.8 percent of all municipalities.[15]

The collapse of the Cold War, then, led to a restructuring of the financing of the Colombia's guerrilla movements. Although Colombian guerrillas long have practiced kidnapping and extortion, only in the late 1980s did large inflows of criminally derived domestic resources, largely based on extorting profits from the drug and petroleum booms, come to replace a functioning although insufficient international support network that flowed through Cuba, Nicaragua, the Soviet Union, Eastern Europe, and at times Libya. Yet although the sources and methods of financing in the post–Cold War world have elevated the role of criminal activities within these organizations, the guerrillas should not be categorized with other forms of organized criminals. For these groups criminal activity is principally a means, not an end. They are fundamentally political organizations that train their fighters and followers and attempt to organize the political and social life of the communities where they maintain influence. In some of the colonization zones they organize basic services, maintain law and order, administer justice, and officiate at weddings and divorces. They operate principally in the pursuit of power—often local power—not riches. They dedicate resources derived from crime primarily to expanding the insurgency.[16]

Colombia's guerrilla movements traditionally have operated separately, reflecting the sharp ideological cleavages over issues of doctrine, strategy, and power that fractured leftist movements across the globe throughout much of the twentieth century: Lenin vs. Trotsky, Mao vs. Stalin, new left Cuban-style *focos* vs. electoral strategies of traditional Communist parties. Despite decades of armed struggle, Colombia's leftist guerrillas were unable to unify their command structures, as eventually occurred in Nicaragua, El Salvador, and Guatemala. However, beginning in 1985, the guerrillas attempted to coordinate both their negotiating and military stances. In 1987 they founded the Coordinadora Guerrillera Simón Bolívar (CGSB). After the separate peace agreements with several groups in 1990 and 1991, the CGSB consisted of the FARC, the ELN, and the dissident faction of the EPL. Then, for the first time, without dismantling individual commands and local units, or *frentes*, the CGSB began to coordinate military activities in certain regions and to negotiate together during the sessions in Caracas and Tlaxcala in 1991 and 1992. Yet even these steps were not sufficient to mask the great differences and continued rivalry among the competing groups. The lack of a fully coherent command structure has continually raised the question: Is it best to negotiate with all the guerrillas movements together, or should negotiations be conducted separately with each movement, as occurred in the peace processes from 1982 to 1986 and the partially successful round from 1989 to 1991? The emerging consensus is that "partial" peace processes with individual groups are highly inadequate and by definition incomplete. Nevertheless, at critical junctures of opportunity, there may be few alternative options.

Why Violence? Competing Explanations of Political Violence in Colombia

There has been an intense debate among scholars and policymakers as to the cause of Colombia's violence during the second half of the twentieth century. This debate has been shaped by changing conditions and political contexts as the country has moved from La Violencia (1948–1958); to the National Front (1958–1986); to the post–National Front, post–Cold War, drug-influenced political and social arenas (1991–).[17] During this period, the country urbanized, modernized, industrialized, went through an oil export boom, extended its agricultural frontier into the northern reaches of the Amazon Basin, and, in the 1980s, became a large illegal export platform for processed cocaine and later heroin. One period of violence gave way to another, almost seamlessly, yet without superseding the original conflict. Violent actors were transformed, issues redefined.

The principal reference for all the subsequent violence has been La Violencia. This period of partisan civil war between the Liberal and Conservative parties nevertheless masked a wide range of class, regional, political, commercial, and community tensions. It wrapped a blanket of partisanship around the combatants but left them to pursue their local and party enemies without national leadership. British historian E. J. Hobsbawm called the Colombian Violencia one of the great mobilizations of peasants in the twentieth century.[18] Yet what differentiated the Colombian Violencia from other mass peasant mobilizations is that it did not lead to revolution, major political upheaval, or social transformation. At the end of the bloodletting, the two multiclass, oligarchical parties were able to set aside their differences and resume control through a constitutionally sanctioned power-sharing arrangement, the National Front.

U.S. political scientist Jonathan Hartlyn has compared the political institutions that resulted from the agreements to certain "consociational regimes" that have attenuated conflict in societies divided by ethnicity, language, or religion such as Belgium or Austria.[19] But if the National Front worked as a successful consociational regime that shared power within a politically divided society and educated populations into tolerance for followers of the other party, it also turned out to be quite exclusive of those members of society who had torn free of the partisan identities and sought to develop alternative forms of political participation. Presidents governed 75 percent of the time using the decree authority of the state of siege and increasingly relied on the armed forces to maintain public order.

A leading early analysis of the violence, then, argued that Colombians took up arms because many were denied channels of participation beyond the patronage politics available through the Liberal and Conservative parties. The National Front was not responsive and thwarted—sometimes through force—the aspirations and social needs of a majority of the nation's citizens.[20] Most citizens took refuge in apathy; some took up arms.

Colombia's leading specialists on violence, or *violentólogos,* also asserted that violence was facilitated by a historically weak state that lacked a continuous presence throughout much of its national territory. These analysts have argued that guerrilla movements, party chieftains, paramilitaries, and later drug traffickers have taken root in those areas where the state has no effective control, both in a territorial sense and in an administrative and legal one. Extralegal armed groups were able to, in essence, substitute for the state and provide basic services, including administering justice, education, and social services. Much of the violence stems from periodic state attempts to assert military authority over these areas,[21] or from clashes over disputed territory between hostile armed groups.

These two ideas—that violence is a consequence of a closed political system and of a state with limited or no presence throughout its national territory—still provide the basis for much thinking about violence and the search for peace in Colombia. Yet as these interpretations became the basis for policymaking, they came under closer scrutiny and have drawn fire from several quarters. Does a moderately closed political system fully explain the recourse to arms? Does the absence of the state necessarily translate into armed, antistatist movements?

Colombian social scientists began to explore more carefully the conditions under which communities take up arms. In the process, there has been something of a paradigm shift from the North American to French schools of revolution and social movement theory. Early analyses, following the work of such theorists of revolution as the North American scholar Charles Tilly, argued that when channels of popular protest are denied, then a logical next step is to take up armed action.[22] For Tilly, the line between peaceful protest and armed insurrection is a continuous one; communities can be expected to choose the path of arms in the absence of other channels of political expression. As such, one would expect that as the National Front increasingly criminalized protests, peasant marches, community strikes, and labor union activities, political activists and entire communities would take up arms as the only viable path.

But as Colombia's violence has persisted without end, and as guerrillas have extended their presence into areas where they were not traditional social actors, the analysis has shifted, moving closer to the French school of social movements, particularly the work of Alaine Touraine.[23] A group of Colombian scholars, many formerly viewed as leftists, have begun to argue that armed movements distort social movements, invite violence, and undermine community leadership. They argue that social movements have had such little success in Colombia not because they were denied channels of participation but because the guerrilla movements subverted their struggles, imposed different logics beyond their immediate social needs, and invited repression from authorities. Instead of there being a fluid line between popular protest and armed struggle, as Tilly would have it, the French-oriented approach would say that popular protest and armed struggle obey separate and contradictory logics. The rise of guerrilla movements has impeded the development of effective social movements. What Colombia needs, therefore, are more social movements free from the logic of armed struggle and guerrilla warfare.[24]

This perspective has contributed greatly to the deromanticization of the guerrilla movement and has led to a rupture between intellectuals and the guerrillas. Particularly by the early 1990s, as guerrillas became more dependent on criminal activities to finance their expanding armies, the revised approach began to be more widely accepted in intellectual, artistic, and nongovernmental organizations and grass-roots activist circles. This fact was starkly demonstrated in a letter from a group of leading intellectuals, including Nobel laureate Gabriel García Márquez, to the nation's guerrilla leaders:

> *Sirs of the Simón Bolívar Coordinating Committee:* As a group of convinced democrats, we oppose violence and authoritarian solutions of all kinds. . . In the current circumstances, we oppose the means you use to carry on your struggle. Armed struggle, instead of leading to greater social justice, has engendered all kinds of extremisms such as the resurgence of reactionary violence, paramilitary forces, merciless crime and excesses committed by the armed forces, which we condemn with equal energy. . . . Today your standard tactics include kidnapping, coercion and forced contributions, all of which are an abominable violation of human rights. . . . Your war, gentlemen, lost its historical significance long ago.[25]

Yet even as the guerrillas lost much of their support among intellectuals, students, grass-roots activists, and the urban middle classes, they continued to draw support in many rural areas affected by the violence. They also began to make major inroads in many of the swollen shantytowns of the major cities, such as Ciudad Bolívar in Santafé de Bogotá, that have absorbed hundreds of thousands of refugees from the rural violence. Even as their political support has declined, the guerrillas have used their regional bases and accumulated wealth to launch a major military buildup, defying early expectations for peace with the end of the Cold War. From strategic zones in the colonization areas east of the Andes, in the oil fields of the eastern plains, and in the traditional highland and coffee regions where they have long held sway, the FARC and the ELN have expanded their territorial presence fourfold and have projected their strength into new regions where they do not have a natural social base or historic presence. This dramatic projection into new areas *has* weakened civil society and thwarted the development of nascent social movements in the target zones. And it has triggered official repression, paramilitary violence, and a large upsurge in social violence and crime.

Underlying the changing positions, strategies, support networks, and alliance structures of key political and social actors in Colombia are the seismic transformations that have occurred throughout the polity and society since 1982, which have further fueled the armed conflicts—and hastened the rejection of armed struggle for others. The principal catalyst for change has been the contradictory effects of the rise of the drug trade, which has altered fundamentally the existing parameters of society and undermined many of the assumptions that were at the foundation of the earlier analyses. The single most disturbing element of the new violence has been the spread of private antiguerrilla armies and the anomic paramilitarization of the war.

Paramilitary violence rose as a by-product of a fifteen-year investment boom in traditional agricultural lands spawned by newly rich drug traffickers seeking to launder money, accumulate assets, and acquire social prestige. Land represented one of the most accessible and penetrable areas of the national economy in which they could invest their profits. These lands were largely cattle ranches concentrated in the northern and Atlantic coast regions and throughout the central Magdalena River valley. They are distinct from the coca-producing colonization zones in the jungles and plains east of the Andes where small and medium-size farmers predominate, many with ties to the guerrillas. In Colombia the drug cartels for the most part buy coca and coca paste from the peasant farmers but do not control the coca-producing lands. Colombia's coffee trade is similarly structured, with small and medium-size farmers selling to a centralized oligarchic—and oligopsonistic—elite.

Throughout the 1980s, just as peace talks with the guerrillas were getting under way, drug traffickers made substantial investments in the traditional areas of the Colombian countryside. One study sponsored by the United Nations Development Program calculated that between 5 to 6 million hectares changed hands, from rural elites to drug traffickers in the 1980s and early 1990s.[26] Rural elites were abandoning their landholdings in record numbers, not only because drug traffickers were offering high prices for choice land. They were abandoning the violence and the extortionary politics of the guerrillas who forcefully imposed "revolutionary taxes" and often kidnapped and killed family members of those who refused to pay.

The drug trade has corrupted many sectors of society. But the corruption manifests in different ways and does not reach all or even most sectors. In the areas where the drug traffickers have purchased large tracts of lands—a process that is effectively a reverse agrarian reform—they have allied themselves firmly with the local political bosses, the traditional landowners, and the armed forces. With deep pockets and extensive political connections, they were able to protect their lands and augment the state security apparatus by investing in private, paramilitary armies. Soon their stated objectives became rolling back the guerrilla inroads, ending the extortionary demands, and ridding their area of guerrilla collaborators and supporters. The Colombian armed forces, with little civilian oversight from the central government, worked directly in supporting and training these groups or acquiesced in their formation; they believed that the expansion of paramilitaries was an effective counter insurgency tactic.[27]

By 1989, when paramilitary forces had become deeply entrenched in the political landscape and periodically had begun to target key government and party officials to pressure against extradition or some other state anti-narcotic policy, top national leaders began to speak out against the paramilitary violence. In a belated attempt to put the genie back in the bottle, in 1989 President Virgilio Barco attempted to reverse course and revoked the law dating to 1965 that permitted the military to arm civilians. By then it was too late. Throughout the 1990s the growth of the paramilitary groups has paralleled the growth of the guerrilla groups.

In contrast to the escalating conflict between guerrillas and paramilitary units in the cattle zones in northern Colombia, in the colonization zones east of the Andes the guerrillas worked closely with the small and medium-size coca farmers who provided the raw material for processing into cocaine. The cocaine export boom turned into a major financial windfall for the guerrillas, although they were benefiting from the least profitable sector of the trade. When the heroin boom erupted in the early 1990s, the guerrillas benefited in a similar way through their presence in the high Andean plateaus and paramos, where the opium poppy crop is cultivated for later processing into heroin.

In terms of conflict and war, the coca and heroin export booms have altered the resources, alliances, and social relations of both the guerrillas and the armed forces. They have transformed a polarized armed conflict between two sides into one in which multiple groups and sectors are armed and, depending on the nexus of social relations in a given region, are allied or in conflict with each other. The drug trade has complicated the original dynamics of leftist-inspired insurgencies and state antisubversive operations. It has proven so lucrative that it has permitted the guerrillas to expand and modernize their weaponry and greatly extend their territorial presence; it also has led to the creation of large paramilitary armies—some with relations to the armed forces, others more independent—that turn their weapons on guerrillas, peasants, leftist politicians, journalists, human right workers, and, increasingly throughout the 1980s and 1990s, judges, state officials, and politicians. By the late 1990s the emergence and rapid expansion of the paramilitary armies had become the principal source of political violence and the main challenge to securing peace.[28]

Since the onset of the drug export boom in the 1980s, officials constantly have asserted that the country is a victim of the illegal drug trade in cocaine and heroin. As the preceding analysis reveals, it is true that the drug trade has contributed to the violence. It has funneled new resources—both financial and military—to old adversaries. It has created new social sectors, particularly the drug entrepreneurial *nouveau riche* who have invested so heavily in the Colombian countryside and in developing the nation's paramilitary infrastructure. But the roots of the contemporary violence are much deeper than the current drug export boom; they tap into long-festering social conflicts, particularly in the countryside, conflicts whose resolutions have been deferred for decades. The drug trade may have heightened and accelerated the violence; it did not cause it.

The Colombian Peace Process: Two Decades of Negotiating Peace in Colombia

For the record, during the past two decades Colombian negotiators have successfully negotiated the cease-fire, demobilization, and reincorporation of five separate guerrilla movements and one urban militia with ties to the guerrillas.[29] These were with: the M-19 (199); the EPL, the PRT and the Quintín Lame (1990–1991); and Renovación Socialista (a dissident faction of the ELN); and an urban militia group in Medellín (1994). At the same time, the Colombian government engaged in regular negotiations with the FARC and the ELN. It signed a cease-fire agreement with the FARC in 1984; the cease-fire collapsed in 1986. Throughout this period, although individuals groups laid down their arms, the number of men and women under arms increased, as did the incidence of political violence and the number of regions affected by it. Moreover, as we have already seen, the number of paramilitary groups increased exponentially.

Despite years of efforts, the armed forces have been unable to defeat the guerrillas militarily. Some have called this a negative stalemate. Neither side is capable of defeating the other. Although the armed forces received large budget increases from 1986 to 1994 while simultaneously restructuring their counterinsurgency capabilities, the negative stalemate has not been altered. One reason is that the guerrillas also have grown in size, have become more professional, and have received greater sums during this period, which have neutralized any advantages the state may have gained. In fact, from 1992 onward, although the guerrillas have not altered the fundamental military equation, they have expanded their range of operations and their military capacity, in many instances outpacing the improved capacity of the armed forces.

Politically, successive governments have struggled with a fundamental quandary: How do you negotiate with insurgent groups that are not internationally recognized without conferring on them an undeserved legitimacy. From the beginning, government negotiators worried whether negotiations conferred a "belligerent status," as understood in international law, and thus elevated the nature of the conflict beyond what the military situation on the ground indicated. This concern has been one of the reasons Colombian governments have demonstrated such reluctance to involve international actors directly. This quandary has severely retarded any potential international role and has undermined most negotiations. Only since 1997, with the clear exhaustion of domestic initiatives and prior models, have the government, the guerrillas, and sectors of civil society directly and openly begun to speak in favor of some form of international assistance. International collaboration will change the dynamics of the earlier models. At this stage, it represents the last frontier of untried policies.

The Colombian peace processes can be classified according to presidential administration: Belisario Betancur (1982–1986), Virgilio Barco (1986–1990), César Gaviria (1990–1994), Ernesto Samper (1994–1998), and now, Andrés Pastrana (1998–2002). Each president has drawn lessons from his predecessor and altered the content and strategy of the peace process.

The Betancur Administration: The Objective and Subjective Conditions of Violence

The first peace process of Belisario Betancur, from 1982 to 1986, focused on three elements derived from the dominant analyses of violence of the early 1980s. Borrowing from Vladimir Lenin, Betancur spoke of the subjective and objective conditions of revolution. A populist-style politician from the Conservative Party, Betancur declared that a peace process would have to address both the needs of individual revolutionaries—the subjective conditions—and the political and structural causes of violence—the objective conditions. His peace process was three-pronged; consisting of: (1) amnesty and assistance to former guerrillas—the subjective aspect; (2) political reform and democratic opening using both guerrilla negotiations, extrainstitutional forums, and the congress to stimulate political reform—the objective aspect, focusing on the consequences of a closed political regime; and (3) a special development program for areas most affected by the violence through a program known as the Plan Nacional de Rehabilitación (PNR, or National Rehabilitation Plan)—the objective and structural aspect, drawing from the idea that insurgency flourishes in areas where the state has little or no presence.

Betancur's vision was ample and still may be the basis of a future peace. However, at the time, the president lacked key political support. The armed forces openly undermined the cease-fire orders, and traditional party leaders were reluctant to back his reform and amnesty programs.[30]

The guerrillas, for their part, overplayed their new role as recognized political actors and assumed they had achieved more than they had. At this early stage, no group seemed to view the peace process as more than a new forum within which to combine political action while preparing and expanding military capability. The M-19 was the most brazen. After a tense ten-month cease-fire signed in August 1984, the M-19 unilaterally broke off further talks and denounced the government for not adhering to the original agreements. Then on November 6, 1985, overestimating its popular support, the M-19 sent a commando unit to seize the Palace of Justice and stage a public trial of President Betancur. The army immediately and without presidential authorization responded to the provocative action; the tragic denouement was twenty-eight hours of combat in the center of Bogotá that left over one hundred dead, including eleven Supreme Court justices and top M-19 leaders.[31] The peace process lay in a heap of rubble in the smoldering remains of the public building that stood for justice. Afterward a visibly aged Betancur went on television to announce that the institutions of democracy were not negotiable. The citizenry seemed shellshocked for days and weeks afterward. How had the peace process gone so awry?

For its part, the FARC actively promoted and expanded its presence in the political arena during the two years its cease-fire agreement with the government held. In 1985 the FARC founded a political party, the Unión Patriótica (UP), which participated in the 1986 congressional and presidential elections with some surprising results: It gained fourteen senators and congressmen and scores of city councilmen. Yet the FARC's experience ultimately ended as bitterly as that of the M-19. The traditional party politicians began to accuse the FARC of "armed proselytism" or of maintaining an electoral advantage in certain zones through a strong and intimidating military presence. The FARC retorted that the old, oligarchic parties have always enjoyed a similar advantage with private armies linked to the armed forces. Hundreds of first-time UP candidates were assassinated, followed by continuing murders of the party's elected officials, including senators, representatives, and two presidential candidates. Shortly after the elections, the cease-fire agreements began to unravel in skirmishes with the armed forces throughout the country. By the end of 1986 the agreements were shattered. The FARC returned to open hostilities while the UP was left an orphan inside the political arena, trying desperately to create an independent identity. Despite the UP's efforts, the dirty war against it was unrelenting. By 1995, ten years after it had been founded, the UP claimed that over 2,000 of its leaders and followers had been exterminated. Still, in 1994 the party managed to elect one senator. He was felled by an assassin's bullet before he could take office.

From 1980 to 1988, a period covering the first attempts to negotiate a settlement to the armed conflict, the number of violent deaths in the country doubled from 10,000 to 20,000 annually. The first peace overture helped spark a dirty war that was facilitated by the convergence of several trends then occurring in Colombia: the rise of the drug export boom, the founding of paramilitary armies by narco-landowners, and the opposition of the armed forces to the peace overtures, leading them to work with the paramilitary forces. Events overtook Betancur's bold and original politics. On his own he did not have the authority to implement or decree change unilaterally, or to negotiate the reincorporation of the nation's guerrilla movements. Domestically he did not have sufficient allies, and the international community was absent from the process. Thus the peace process died a thousand small deaths and ultimately drowned in a rising sea of violence.

The Barco Administation: Unilateral Cease-fire, Disarmament, Reincorporation

On taking office in 1986, Virgilio Barco concluded that Betancur's open-ended and decentralized peace strategy could not work. The president's new negotiating team, which basically stayed in place during two presidential administrations,[32] surveyed the landscape and came up with the following conclusions: First, control of the peace process must be placed in the executive branch. Second, the government must start from the premise that the state is the legitimate political entity and the guerrillas are

operating outside the law. Third, the state could be magnanimous and offer amnesties; however, the government did not need to accept the guerrillas as representatives of civil society. Fourth, the government need not
negotiate political and social reforms with the guerrillas. The appropriate
institutional forums for reform, such as the congress, courts, and departmental assemblies, already existed.

With these conclusions in mind, the new Barco team felt that negotiations should be limited to two fundamental issues: disarmament and reincorporation into society. The state would assist in the process of reincorporation and conversion into a political movement. However, the
insurgent group must first agree that the end result of negotiations would
be disarmament.[33] Where Betancur had decided to avoid the issue of arms,
Barco made it the centerpiece of his negotiations.

Barco also decided to augment Betancur's National Rehabilitation program. He increased the budget and expanded it to include democratic forums called Consejos de Rehabilitación (Rehabilitation Councils), which
were created at both the municipal and regional levels and were designed
to stimulate community participation in development planning. The idea
was to build local support for state initiatives and to "shut the door" on
the guerrillas, as one presidential peace advisor succinctly stated it.[34]

When Barco first announced his negotiating position, few expected any
takers. It seemed like a call for surrender, and, from the guerrillas' perspectives, the narrowing of the negotiating agenda appeared to be a step
backward at the negotiating table.

The Barco administration soon underscored another issue that was
quickly becoming evident throughout society: Social violence and crime
had overtaken political violence as the principal cause of violence in the
country. A special Commission to Study the Violence organized by the
minister of government declared that guerrilla violence represented only
7.51 percent of all violent deaths in 1985. "Much more than the violence
in the mountains and jungles," the report declared, "the violence that is
killing us comes from the street."[35]

Government officials and commentators soon seized on the idea of
downplaying the negotiations with the guerrillas, although this was not
the commission's intention. Yet the report served to remove the guerrillas
from center stage. Moreover, by reorienting the discussion of political violence and peace to the emerging issues of urban violence and crime—
seemingly logical in a society that had become 66 percent urban by then—
it mistakenly diminished the continued centrality of rural violence as a
source of political conflict.

For the first years of the Barco government, the peace process languished. However, in 1989, with only one year left in Barco's single four-year term, the M-19 broke ranks with the other groups within the Coordinadora Guerrillera Simón Bolívar (Simón Bolívar Guerrilla Coordinating Committee, or CGSB) and accepted the president's two preconditions: unilateral cease-fire and agreement that the end result of negotiations would be disarmament and political reincorporation. It was a bold and unexpected move on the part of the M-19, and the Barco government capitalized on the opening, arranging for the fighters to assemble with their weapons in a small demilitarized zone, in northern Cauca, just south of Cali. The two sides agreed that the M-19 would lay down their arms and participate in the upcoming elections. Arms were handed in to an international delegation of the Socialist International.

Two weeks after abandoning their arms, the M-19 participated in parliamentary elections and, two months later, presidential elections. Their first presidential candidate, Carlos Pizarro, was gunned down on an airliner while flying to a campaign rally. It was a provocation, but the M-19 reaffirmed its commitment to the democratic process, chanting at Pizarro's funeral, "The votes for Pizarro will go to Navarro," referring to Pizarro's second-in-command, Antonio Navarro Wolff. Navarro Wolff, an English-trained engineer, went on to receive 12 percent of the votes. Six months later, in special elections for a constitutional assembly, the M-19 slate received almost 30 percent of the vote and Navarro Wolff became one of three copresidents of the assembly charged with rewriting the constitution. It appeared that the decision to abandon arms had paid off.

Barco thus had demonstrated that the government could successfully negotiate a separate peace with one guerrilla group. Yet before the end of his term he was unable to conclude negotiations with the others groups, leaving the early momentum to his successor.

César Gaviria: Constitutional Assembly as a Forum for Peace

César Gaviria was elected in a 1990 campaign that witnessed the assassination of three presidential candidates: Luís Carlos Galán, the leading candidate of the Liberal Party; Carlos Pizarro of the M-19; and Bernardo Ossa Jaramillo of the Unión Patriótica. The 1990 campaign also included a separate ballot, first proposed by a coalition of university students, calling for the reform of the constitution to address the political crisis and violence that was overtaking the country. Upon taking office, one of Gaviria's first aims was to discern how to implement the people's overwhelming desire to reform the constitution as expressed in the informal plebiscite. Gaviria interpreted the mandate broadly and was backed by the Supreme Court. Special elections would be held for the constitutional assembly. The special body would have full authority to write a new constitution.

The Gaviria administration saw this Constituyente as an instrument for peace. It would provide another opportunity for the M-19 to consolidate its transition from armed group to political party. Indeed, Gaviria gave a boost to the new party by appointing its leader, Antonio Navarro Wolff, to his cabinet. He then made participation in the Constituyente, either through elections or by special appointment, a centerpiece of his negotiating strategy with the remaining guerrilla groups. The strategy worked with the EPL, the Quintín Lame, and a small group from the Atlantic coast, the Partido Revolucionario de Trabajadores (PRT).

In negotiating their disarmament and reincorporation, the Barco model was applied: unilateral cease-fire, assembly in a few demilitarized zones, formal surrender of arms. This time, after their disarmament, the amnestied guerrillas would be able to stand for elections to the Constituyente. In addition to the electoral route, the PRT and Quintín Lame were each guaranteed one spokesman at the convention; and the EPL was allotted two representatives with full voting rights. In the elections, the EPL quickly converted their movement into a new political party, Esperanza, Paz y Libertad (Hope, Peace, and Liberty), and established an alliance with the M-19.

The Barco model was successful with these groups, but it failed to win the support of the FARC and the ELN. Both groups declared they were not interested in the limited negotiations and unilateral cease-fire that then defined the peace processes. In the absence of progress, President Gaviria responded by endorsing a military attack on the FARC's principal stronghold, La Uribe, where its leaders had received government delegations since 1984. The attack underscored the government's emerging position that there were two types of guerrillas, those attuned to the changing conditions in Colombia and throughout the world and anachronistic groups, cut off from international currents and increasingly degenerating into criminal vices. The full weight of the military would fall on those groups that did not accept the government's offers.

The government attack on La Uribe unleashed a major offensive by the FARC and the ELN that distracted the work of the Constituyente and underscored yet again the failure of the military solution. Indeed, the guerrillas seemed to be able to strike at will, demonstrating for the first time just how improved their military capabilities had become. The attack and counterattack also thwarted any possible late participation by these guerrilla movements in the constitutional convention.

After the Constituyente finished its work, the Gaviria government once again opened up negotiations with the FARC and the ELN in a final effort to end the insurgencies. This time the government did not insist on a unilateral cease-fire or any preconditions.[36] The government and the guerrillas, united in the Coordinadora Guerrillera Simón Bolívar, met several times in Caracas, Venezuela, and Tlaxcala, Mexico. These were some of the most interesting negotiations and revealed areas of opportunity as well as obstacles. The CGSB expressly rejected the Barco model, asserting that its forces were too large to be assembled in one or two demilitarized zones. Its leaders insisted on a broader negotiating agenda than disarmament and reincorporation.

First on the agenda was cease-fire. The CGSB insisted in maintaining its forces in the areas where it already had major influence. It claimed that it had control in about 600 municipalities (*municipios*) but would be willing to regroup in 200 of them. The government responded with a provocative offer outlining 60 sites where the guerrillas could assemble, in what it claimed to be one location for each guerrilla front. The areas would be "distention zones" and could cover submunicipal areas (*veredas, corregimientos*, or *inspecciones de policía*). The CGSB responded saying it would accept 96 zones, but that each zone had to cover an entire municipality. In these zones, a bilateral cease-fire must be put in place, and each area had to be accompanied by a neutral zone where the armed forces of both sides would be restricted.[37]

The negotiations stalled principally over the issue of how much of the territory within the municipality should be demilitarized. The guerrillas wanted the entire municipality, complete with town center and municipal buildings. The government wanted to recognize only a small camp far from the residential and municipal centers. Although the negotiations broke down, they underscore a central point that is often overlooked: The guerrillas place a strong premium on local politics and power. Concomitantly, major sectors of society and the state resist this recognition of local influence, an issue that echoes back to the 1950s and 1960s when the government denounced local communist control of remote areas as "independent republics."

Without reaching a cease-fire accord, the two sides agreed to meet in Tlaxcala, Mexico, to address further the issues on the agenda that had been developed in the first meetings in Caracas. The government, abandoning the position of the previous administration, once again consented to a broad negotiating strategy and to meetings without prior conditions. The negotiating agenda included:

1. Cease-fire;
2. Relations with the constitutional assembly and other democratic bodies such as the congress;
3. Paramilitary groups, impunity, and the national security doctrine;
4. Democracy and political "favorability" (meaning establishing exceptional conditions to assist the transformation from a guerrilla organization to a political party, such as one-time favorable electoral rules);
5. National sovereignty;
6. Verification of agreements;
7. economic, political, and social democracy.[38]

Yet once the two sides arrived in Mexico, little headway was made on the agenda. The negotiations broke down when the guerrillas kidnapped and killed a former minister of government. As has happened repeatedly, the government suspended the negotiations. They would not resume with the CGSB again during the Gaviria administration.

During that administration's final two years, the government's position reversed itself completely. Having successfully led the Constituyente and the reincorporation of several guerrilla groups, the government now returned to a military strategy against the remaining guerrillas. The minister of defense declared that within eighteen months (by mid-1983), the guerrillas would be forced back to the negotiating table following a major buildup in the capacity of the armed forces.[39] Most analysts interpreted this as a sign that the government would attempt to defeat the guerrillas and, short of that, force them to accept a Barco-style negotiation: a reduced agenda limited to disarmament and reincorporation. The Gaviria government also unleashed a propaganda offensive, stating that the guerrillas had lost their Marxist ideals and were now little more than drug traffickers and criminals.

Complicating the strategy, the M-19 and the EPL–the two groups that had made a major effort to transform themselves into political parties— were not faring well in the political and social arenas. The M-19 witnessed the precipitous drop in its electoral support. In the 1994 elections, for example, its parliamentary delegation was reduced from ten to zero. Its presidential candidate received less than 2 percent of the vote. For the EPL, the situation was worse. Since the group's entrance into political life, its followers had come under attack from their former comrades-in-arms and from paramilitary groups. In places such as Urabá, assassinations and disappearances mounted. Esperanza, Paz y Libertad was never able to consolidate itself as a local political force. With the decline of the M-19, it lost the national presence it had gained through the political alliance that had been forged between the two former guerrilla groups. The plummeting political fortunes of the M-19 and the EPL erected a new barrier to future negotiations. For the FARC and the ELN, the failure of the earlier groups to establish themselves as political forces further discredited the original negotiating model based principally on disarmament and political reincorporation. Any future negotiations had to be based on major structural, economic, and political changes. The outcome of the peace initiatives of the Gaviria administration: partial peace agreements, major constitutional reform, expanded guerrilla activity, higher levels of violence, and dirty war.

Ernesto Samper: Peace Takes a Back Seat to Presidential Crisis

As in earlier elections, the issue of peace was central to the 1994 presidential campaign. Ernesto Samper, in his inaugural address, instructed his newly appointed peace advisor, Carlos Holmes Trujillo, to report back to him in a hundred days on whether the guerrillas and the leading sectors of political and civil society were interested and would be committed to entering into substantive peace negotiations. Through this one stroke Samper restored—if only temporarily—the guerrillas' political legitimacy. They were transformed from bandits, as Gaviria had branded them after the collapse of the Tlaxcala meetings, to potential negotiating partners once again. At the end of the allotted time, Holmes Trujillo confirmed that the guerrillas still represented a political challenge and that a solution to the decades-old armed conflict required a political—that is, negotiated—solution.

This promising beginning was derailed by the political crisis that overwhelmed the Samper administration when audiotapes surfaced linking the newly elected president to the Cali drug cartel. The peace process languished as the government sought to defend itself and Samper practiced the politics of survival. Yet during his first year, the government outlined a general strategy and moved to develop an alternative model of negotiations that substantially departed from the Barco-Gaviria models of assembly-disarmament-reincorporation. For the guerrillas, this was essential. After the political demise of the M-19 and the unrelenting dirty war against the Unión Patriótica and the Esperanza, Paz y Libertad, the remaining groups had few incentives for unilateral disarmament and standing for elections within the quicksand of the Colombian political system.

During the Samper governments first year, it developed a broad framework for negotiations. The government outlined four points to orient its negotiators:

1. Contacts between the government and the guerrillas should be discreet—outside of the glare of the media—but they would not be secret;
2. The government would guarantee the security of guerrilla representatives during the talks;
3. It would talk with all of the CGSB, or with its constituent parts, depending on the guerrillas' preferences;
4. There would be no precondition of a cease-fire, either unilateral or bilateral.

At the same time, the Samper government agreed to change the conduct of the war and commit the state to respect the norms and procedures for internal armed conflicts recognized under international law. Specifically, the president's policy included: (1) the enactment of a general law of disarmament that would incorporate measures to dismantle the paramilitary groups; (2) a unilateral move to "humanizar la guerra" (humanize the war) or apply existing provisions of international law on human rights and the conduct of war; and (3) invitations to respected national and international organizations, such as the International Committee of the Red Cross, to verify compliance by both sides with international norms for domestic war and insurgency.

In 1995 the government and congress went on to ratify the Second Geneva Protocol on internal war. However, the negotiating strategy was never fully implemented as the internal crisis and the crisis with Washington fully occupied Colombian politics and severely debilitated the Samper administration. Three years later, when the Samper government again attempted to move the peace process forward, the FARC responded that it did not recognize the government as a valid interlocutor. At one point the FARC asserted as a condition for negotiating the removal of Samper from office. The politics of survival for Samper meant deepening fragmentation and further spread of the internal war.

Samper, even without the presidential crisis, pursued contradictory policies that offset some of the early positive steps his government had made toward resuming negotiations. In what can only be deemed a profound misreading of Colombian politics and society, the Samper government began a new policy of arming civilians in rural security cooperatives, which later were renamed Convivir (literally, to live together). The Convivir groups quickly became one more armed band, responsible for some killings, although now openly and directly linked to the state. One senior official belatedly admitted that the creation of Convivirs essentially gave a green light to the illegal paramilitary groups.[40] The further rise of paramilitary violence further fueled the already kindled dirty war.

In his final peace initiative during his last months in office, Samper again recognized the need to address the paramilitary question directly. Almost a decade of stated intentions to dismantle the groups had not translated into effective or feasible policy. Samper's advisors posed a new question: If the paramilitary groups cannot be dismantled, should they be invited to the negotiating table? In a public document written by the principal peace advisors, the Samper administration admitted that the paramilitary groups do enjoy some sort of relationship with the state, although they are not fully controlled by the state. The official term used for the groups was "semiautonomous," meaning they have an ill-defined relationship with state actors but are also largely autonomous. They should be viewed neither as insurgents nor simply as criminals; they are the consequences of the internal war. Samper proposed that the government could enter without conditions into negotiations with the guerrillas on political, social, and economic reform. At the same time, it should begin to explore ways to open up a separate dialogue with the paramilitary groups with the idea of pursuing agreements leading to their dismantling in the context of a peace agreement with the guerrillas.[41]

Moreover, in 1997, under great pressure from the United States and with concerted action by key Colombian political figures, the Colombian congress passed laws that would allow the government to seize lands acquired with drug-trafficking profits. If implemented, finally the conditions would be in place for a major land reform in Colombia, returning to the state millions of hectares that then could be made available for redistribution. This alone would be a powerful bargaining chip in a future peace process and would provide an inducement that would be difficult for the guerrillas to reject.[42] Addressing the multiple sources of violence directly may provide greater opportunities than the earlier models based on narrow negotiating agendas.

Peace Is Possible in Colombia: Recommendations

A careful reading of the recent record demonstrates convincingly that there is no military solution to the armed conflicts in Colombia. There are too many actors, state authority is too weak and fragmented, the political and social demands are too great, the historical resentments are too high, and the violence is too rooted in local communities and regional conflicts. Solutions must be found within a broad negotiated settlement that strengthens and legitimizes the state and that facilitates local initiatives for reconciliation and reform.

The violence has degenerated substantially beyond the polar conflict between hegemonic parties and excluded sectors that legitimated political violence at the height of the National Front. Who, then, should sit at the negotiating table? What issues should be on the agenda?

The Samper administration pioneered new territory in proposing some form of talks with the paramilitary groups while refusing to recognize them as political actors. That is to say, according to Samper, for the purposes of negotiating peace, the guerrillas should be recognized as political actors; the paramilitary groups should be recognized as some intermediate category, representing a point between political actor and delinquent. This classification is not broadly accepted, and many, including the guerrillas, refuse to confer any legitimacy or autonomy on the paramilitary groups.

Nevertheless, the idea of two negotiating tables, one with the guerrillas and one with the paramilitary groups, needs to be explored further. Moreover, the armed forces need to participate directly at both tables. Past experience has demonstrated that peace cannot be achieved without the full participation and acceptance of the armed forces. At the "paramilitary table," the government and paramilitary representatives would be the principal participants. At the "guerrilla table," representatives of the government, guerrillas, political society—such as the congress—and civil society—including the church, universities, business, landowners, and others—need to be seated. This more plural and heterogenous table is a key, although still disputed, position of some of the already active groups in civil society. It is also possible that there could be multiple tables formed around specific issues, such as occurred in Guatemala during the years of the Civil Society Assembly beginning in 1994.

What issues should be on the agenda? For the paramilitary table, two items: disarmament and amnesty. Final accords will be reached in the context of a broader agreement with the guerrillas.

The agenda at the principal table should be more open, although not so general as the one established in Caracas. The agenda should address the core issues that have contributed to the growing violence. One of the principal lessons from the Central American peace processes, especially in

Guatemala, is that negotiations can be used as a special forum to address long-standing conflicts and historical grievances. Addressing these issues is not a concession to the guerrillas and does not depend on the combatants' prior military strength.

In Colombia, several basic issues fall within these guidelines and should be part of a future negotiating agenda. These include:

1. Agrarian reform. Land conflicts and rural inequalities continue to be one of the principal motors of political violence in Colombia, both in colonization zones and in traditional agricultural lands. The accelerated process of counteragrarian reform by the drug traffickers has both fueled the rural violence and also created a vast new opportunity. With the new laws permitting the government to expropriate goods and property belonging to the drug traffickers, it may be possible for the government to enter negotiations with several million hectares of land available for distribution and development. This counter- "counteragrarian reform" would prove to be a major weapon—and opportunity—in the government's negotiating arsenal. For the FARC, whose origins date to the peasant conflicts of the 1930s, a substantive proposal of a major agrarian reform would be difficult to refuse.

2. Dismantling the paramilitary groups and ending the dirty war. There can be no peace if the dirty war continues and former guerrillas and new political actors continue to be gunned down and silenced. The UP's experience cannot be repeated. The state, the armed forces, guerrillas, and representative sectors of political and civil society will need to forge commitments to end the dirty war. These commitments need to be backed up with clear institutional guarantees and a strengthened judiciary that can ensure that the reigning impunity will be brought to an end and that violators will be brought to justice.

3. Reorienting the strategic mission of the armed forces and police in the context of internal peace. The missions of the police and armed forces in a postconflict society need to be broadly discussed among military and civilian experts, representatives of the state and civil society, and the guerrillas. Issues to be defined are: the role and structure of police in maintaining order; the demilitarization of society; the relationship of the police to local, regional, and national civilian authorities; civil-military relations and the strategic mission of the armed forces in the defense of sovereignty, national borders, and threats to national security after the war has ended; and demobilization of guerrilla forces and their incorporation into military and police units. The objective is to lay the foundation for the develop-

ment of a postconflict security force and program that will be democratic and responsive to civilian control but that will avoid the vacuums of authority that appeared following other peace processes, particularly in Central America.

4. Incorporating the guerrillas and other community actors into the local structures of state and elective politics. Much of the violence has roots in local social conflicts. Peace will be negotiated at the national level but will be built and consolidated at the local level. One of the major shortcomings of the National Front is that it avoided the issue of local social conflicts. The best guarantor of peace will be the incorporation of guerrillas and previously excluded community leaders into the exercise of power at the local level. The partial peace processes of the early 1990s created favorable conditions for political participation by demobilized guerrilla leaders at the national level. A new accord will need to consider creating similar conditions at the local level. In so doing, the state will in one stroke create the conditions for strengthening, legitimizing, and expanding its presence throughout much of the national territory.

The ELN also would add:

5. Reasserting primary control over the nation's natural resources, particularly petroleum development. The ELN has long identified this as one of its key concerns. It should lead to a national debate on petroleum policy. Although it is not feasible for Colombia to opt out of the global economy, it can seek to maximize and more equitably distribute benefits derived from concessions to multinational oil companies.

A final issue will likely be placed on the agenda: the need for a truth and reconciliation commission. Many are insisting on some form of national accounting; others already are calling for justice; still others insist that all war crimes should be pardoned and forgotten (*perdón y olvido*). As in other countries, from Argentina to South Africa, this issue may prove to be the most controversial of all. After so many decades of violence, few will come to the table with clean hands.

Concessions relating to each of these issues will generate fierce resistance and will require an audacity and vision that no side has demonstrated previously. It is still not certain whether a majority on each side believes that substantive reform is preferable to continued war. One of the key roles of the organized groups in civil society is to lobby continuously and create a growing demand for peace through work stoppages, community strikes, referenda, media, the arts, university teach-ins, and popular forums. Despite the danger from the dirty war, by 1998 civil society had begun to mobilize actively.

The repeated breakdowns and interruptions of the peace process during four presidential administrations convincingly demonstrate that peace is too important to be left to the combatants or the parties in conflict. The public positions of all groups reveal that, in principle, their differences on each of the issues just discussed are not that wide or insurmountable.[43] For these reasons, outside observers/mediators/facilitators need to be brought into the peace process. The government, despite its popular legitimacy and sovereign authority, cannot be judge, mediator, and party to the conflict at the same time. Although that formula worked for the negotiations with the M-19, the EPL, and other smaller groups, it is not likely to work with the constituent parts of the Coordinadora Guerrillera Simón Bolívar.

One of the strongest arguments for internationalizing the peace process is that the Colombian conflict already has become internationalized. Both the drug trade and the U.S. antinarcotics war have placed Colombian political violence at the center of global security concerns. The U.S. military has forged new ties with its Colombian counterparts, and U.S. diplomats have begun to operate as proconsular officials, demanding that Colombia eradicate crops and adjust the political system to better attack organized crime. At the same time, the human rights tragedy brought the European Community into Colombia's domestic politics and has led to the establishment of a United Nations human rights office, one of only two such U.N. field offices in the world.

The peace process will not be an antinarcotics policy. However, its success or failure will have serious consequences for the national and international fight against drug trafficking. Peace will strengthen and extend the state to the large areas of the national territory where the state historically has been absent. Peace will make possible a realistic strategy of alternative development for the coca-growing zones, now dominated by the guerrillas. A successful peace process will lead to a dismantling of the paramilitary groups, many of which are, in essence, the armed wing of the drug cartels. It also will lead to the breaking up of many of their landholdings throughout the country. The peace process will not end drug trafficking, which depends on international economic forces beyond the control of the Colombian state. However, it will place the state in a better position to limit its impact within its national territory and to confront many of the serious social and political challenges that have overwhelmed state institutions during the last two decades.

The choices are stark: Escalate the war in search of a military solution, or escalate the peace attempts in search of a pacific resolution to the multiple conflicts. Of the two approaches, the negotiation strategy is the one with far greater chances for success. The United States is not in the position to assume the role of mediator or peacemaker, but it is in the position to encourage others and support their work. Peace is possible in Colombia. The road to a participatory democracy and a developed economy must pass through a successful set of negotiations that will end the multiple armed conflicts and extend the legitimacy and reach of the state. Failure at this juncture could condemn the leaders of another generation to write their history as their predecessors have: through acts of violence or through political courage that is likely to be rewarded with an assassin's bullet.*

---

*On June 22, 1998, Andrés Pastrana of the Conservative Party was elected to the presidency, declaring peace to be the central objective of his administration. Shortly thereafter, on July 9, the president-elect flew into the jungles and met directly with the longtime leader of the FARC, Manuel Marulanda Vélez, a meeting that was thirty years overdue. The two agreed to begin peace negotiations within three months of Pastrana's taking office on August 7, 1998. Moreover, the new president agreed to the withdrawal of state military forces from five large municipalities in southern Colombia, an area twice the size of El Salvador, to facilitate negotiations. A week after Pastrana's historic meeting with the FARC, a group of civil society leaders flew to Maguncia, Germany to meet with leaders of the ELN, an initiative sponsored by the Colombian and German Catholic churches. At the end of July, another delegation of civil society leaders met with Carlos Castaño, leader of the Autodefensas Unidas de Colombia (United Self-Defense Groups of Colombia, AUC), the nation's largest paramilitary group. A week before the inauguration thousands of people and scores of organizations launched the Asamblea Permanente de la Sociedad Civil por la Paz (Permanent Assembly of Civil Society for Peace) in a multitudinous three-day gathering in Bogotá.

Thus, when President Pastrana took office in August 1998, the stage was set for a renewal of the peace process. In his inaugural address, he supported the creation of a large Fondo de Inversión para la Paz (Peace Investment Fund) to finance the kinds of reforms that will be necessary to construct a lasting peace. He also called for international support to help finance alternative and ecologically sound development assistance to the large expanses of coca cultivation along the agriculture frontier. Pastrana's is the fifth presidential administration to engage in a peace process. It is the beginning of a new stage in that process. No longer are the negotiations confined to the government and the guerrillas. There are now tremendous concern and involvement from civil society—including the church, business, labor, community groups, and universities—and from the international community—including the Inter-American Development Bank, the World Bank, the United Nations, the European Community, other Latin American nations, and the United States. Moreover, the paramilitaries are also demanding a place at the negotiating table, or at least at a separate negotiating table. There is now a consensus in Colombia that peace will require a negotiating agenda that is much more broadly conceived than the narrow agenda of disarmament and reincorporating that worked with the M-19 and other groups in the early 1990s. The outcome will not depend on the battlefield position of the combatants at the time of the negotiations. It will depend on whether a representative group of Colombians with wide national backing will be able to rise to the occasion, seize the opportunity and make the historic reforms and compromises that have so long been deferred in Colombia throughout the twentieth century.

Notes

1. Data Bank of the Comisión Inter-Congregacional de Justicia y Paz, Bogotá. These figures include political assassinations, collective massacres, assassinations presumed to be political, assassinations presumed to be "social cleansing," deaths in combat, disappearances, and deaths under obscure circumstances (which is a general category accounting for over half of the political violence and underscores how inexact and difficult these classifications are). Nevertheless, these numbers, including the latter category, are distinguished in human rights investigations and in this particular data bank from the much higher number of daily and monthly homicides categorized as social violence or crime.

2. See Comité Internacional de la Cruz Roja, Comisión de Conciliación Nacional y Cambio 16 Colombia, "La Paz sobre la Mesa," May 11, 1998. This extraordinary document massively distributed as a separate booklet within the May 11 issue of Colombian magazine *Cambio 16 Colombia* gives the public position on a wide range of issues of the key actors in conflict, including the guerrilla movements, the paramilitary organizations, and the government.

3. In 1957 the two traditional parties negotiated an enduring political pact to end the violent conflict and share power. The political agreements were ratified in a national plebiscite and consisted of a power-sharing pact between the Liberal and Conservative parties requiring the alternation of presidential power every four years for a period of sixteen years, and equal and full representation of both parties (50 percent and 50 percent) in the executive, legislative, and judicial branches of government as well as at the regional and local levels. Other parties were originally excluded from competition. After 1974 the major underpinnings of the National Front were maintained through a constitutional amendment that endured through 1991.

4. The idea of the partial collapse of the state was first put forward by Paul Oquist in his pioneering study of la Violencia. Particularly critical is the collapsing state's inability to maintain order and administer justice. See Paul Oquist, *Violencia, conflicto y política en Colombia* (Bogotá: Instituto de Estudios Colombianos, 1978).

5. For an understanding of the social content of the violence in the 1940s and 1950s, see the seminal work by Germán Guzmán Campos, Orlando Fals Borda, and Eduardo Umaña Luna, *La Violencia en Colombia: Estudio de un proceso social*, vols. 1 & 2, (Bogotá: Carlos Valencia Editores, 1980).

6. For an early discussion of the social content of Colombia's violence, see Marc Chernick and Michael Jiménez, "Popular Liberalism, Radical Democracy and Marxism: Leftist Politics in Contemporary Colombia," in Barry Carr and Steve Ellner, eds., *The Latin American Left* (Boulder, Colo.: Westview and Latin American Bureau, 1993). A recent study conducted between 1990 and 1995 underscores the continued rural basis of Colombian violence. It found that of the most violent municipalities in the country, 93 percent were principally rural in structure, while only 7 percent were urban. See "Mitos del homicidio en Colombia," *Pazpública*, Programa de Estudios sobre Seguridad, Justicia y Violencia, Universidad de los Andes, Carta #1, Santafé de Bogotá, July 1997.

7. See Ernesto "Che" Guevara, *Guerrilla Warfare* (Lincoln: University of Nebraska Press, 1985).

8. See Michael Jiménez, "The Many Deaths of the Colombian Revolution: Region, Class and Agrarian Rebellion in Central Colombia," *Papers on Latin America*, No. 13 (New York: Columbia University Institute of Latin American and Iberian Studies: 1990); also Medófilo Medina, "La resistencia campesina en el sur de Tolima," in Gonzalo Sánchez and Ricardo Peñaranda, eds., *Pasado y presente de la Violencia en Colombia* (Bogotá: Fondo Editorial CEREC, 1986):233–65.

9. On that day, many believe that the former dictator, Gustavo Rojas Pinilla, and his ANAPO party won the election but were then denied victory as a result of fraudulent vote counts by the National Front authorities. The M-19 was founded by members of ANAPO, together with dissident

members of the FARC who wanted to pursue a more urban and more political strategy. The M-19 through its spectacular armed propaganda actions succeeded in highlighting the restrictive and, by the late 1970s and early 1980s, increasingly repressive policies of the National Front. See Patricia Lara, *Siembra vientos y recogerás tempestades: La historia del M-19, sus protagonistas y sus destinos* (Bogotá: Editorial Planeta, 1982).

10. See Darío Villamizar, *Un adios a la guerra* (Santafé de Bogotá: Editorial Planeta, 1997); Joaquín Villalobos, *Una revolución en la izquierda para una revolución democrática* (Quito: CEDEP, 1993); Marc Chernick, "Is Armed Struggle Still Relevant?" *NACLA* (North American Conference on Latin America) 27, No. 4, (Jan.-Feb. 1994):8–14.

11. Darío Villamizar, *Aquel 19 será* (Santafé de Bogotá: Planeta, 1995).

12. Jacobo Arenas, *Paz, Amigos y Enemigos* (Bogotá: Editorial La Abeja Negra, 1990).

13. International Institute for Strategic Studies, "Colombia's Escalating Violence," *Strategic Comments* 3, No. 4 (May 1997).

14. Francisco Thoumi, *Economía política y narcotráfico* (Santafé de Bogotá: TM Editores, 1994), 183–208.

15. See José Noé Ríos and Daniel García-Peña Jaramillo, "Building Tomorrow's Peace: A Strategy for Reconciliation," Report by the Peace Exploration Commission, Santafé de Bogotá, Oficina de Alto Comisionado para la Paz, September 9, 1997. Municipalities are Colombia's core political units. Through 1988, they were governed by appointed mayors. Since then they have been governed by directly elected mayors. After 1991 the number of municipalities increased slightly, mostly reflecting the expansion of settlement and the incorporation of earlier frontier areas.

16. There is a large literature available on the Colombian guerrilla movements. Since the 1980s, several academic and journalistic studies have appeared that have presented the origins, evolution, and perspectives of the major movements. See, for example, Arturo Alape, *Las vidas de Pedro Antonio Marín, Manuel Marulanda Vélez, Tirofijo* (Bogotá: Planeta, 1989); Carlos Arango Z., *FARC veinte años: de la Marquetalia a la Uribe* (Bogotá: Ediciones Aurora, 1984); Jaime Jaramillo et al., *Colonización, coca y guerrilla* (Bogotá: Universidad Nacional de Colombia, 1986); Carlos Medina Gallego, *ELN: una historia contada a dos veces* (Santafé de Bogotá: Rodrigo Quito Editores, 1996); Alfredo Molano, *Selva adentro: Una historia oral de la colonización del Guaviare* (Bogotá: El Ancora Editores, 1987); Eduardo Pizarro, *Las FARC: De la autodefensa a la combinación de todas las formas de lucha* (Bogotá: Tercer Mundo y IEPRI, 1991); and Eduardo Pizarro, "La guerrilla revolucionaria en Colombia," in Gonzalo Sánchez and Ricardo Peñaranda, eds., *Pasado y presente de la Violencia en Colombia* (Bogotá: CEREC, 1986), 391–411. Beginning with the first peace processes, several histories written by amnestied guerrillas or negotiators have appeared. See Jacobo Arenas, *Correspondencia secreta del proceso de paz* (Bogotá: Editorial la Abeja Negra, 1989); Darío Villamizar, *Un adiós a la guerra* (Santafé de Bogotá: Planeta, 1997); and Alvaro Villaraga S. y Nelson Plazas N., *Para reconstruir los sueños: Una historia del EPL* (Santafé de Bogotá: Fundación Progresar y Fundación Cultura Democrática, 1994). Most recently, representing the more complex issues surrounding the overlap of the guerrilla violence with the spread of drug trafficking, a few books associated with the Colombian armed forces have appeared, making the case that the guerrillas have been completely transformed into criminal organizations associated with the drug trade. See Major Luís Alberto Villamarín Pulido, *La cartel de las FARC* (Santafé de Bogotá: Ediciones El Faraón, 1996) and Major Luis Alberto Villamarín Pulido, *El ELN por dentro* (Santafé de Bogotá: Ediciones El Faraón, 1995). The position of these books is echoed as official positions of the Colombian armed forces. See "Statement of Lieutenant Colonel Oscar Enrique González, Commander, Specialized Search Unit of Cali, Military Forces of Colombia National Army, Cali, Colombia," U.S. Congress, House Committee on International Relations, *Overall U.S. Counternarcotics Policy Toward Colombia*, 104th Cong., 2nd ses., September 11, 1996.

17. A note on the periodization: Formally, the National Front was designed to last until 1974; then it was constitutionally extended until 1978 with provisions for continuance of coalition rule after that. In practice, coalition rule endured until 1986, when for the first time since the founding of the National Front, the Conservative party went into the opposition. The underpinnings of the National Front division of power remained in the constitution until 1991.

18. E. J. Hobsbawm, "The Revolutionary Situation in Colombia," *The World Today* 19 (June 1963): 246–258.

19. Jonathan Hartlyn, *The Politics of Coalition Rule in Colombia* (Cambridge: Cambridge University Press, 1988.)

20. See Francisco Leal, *Estado y política en Colombia* (Bogotá: Siglo XXI, 1984); Sánchez and Peñaranda, *Pasado y presente.*

21. The accepted narrative concerning the foundation of the FARC is that when the state, beginning in 1964, began to attack the self-defense communities in Marquetalia, El Pato, Riochiquito, and Guayabero, the communities regrouped and the self-defense forces were converted into mobile guerrillas. See Carlos Arango Z, *FARC veinte años.*

22. Charles Tilly, *From Mobilization to Revolution* (New York: Random House, 1978).

23. See Alaine Touraine, *Production de la societé* (Paris: Seuil, 1974). This idea of armed movements as a blockage to social movements is reflected in the work of French sociologist Daniel Pecaut and has is clearly reflected in the work of several of Colombia's leading analysts of violence, commonly referred to as *violentólogos.* See Eduardo Pizarro, "Elementos para una sociología de la guerrilla colombiana," *Análisis Político,* No. 12 (Jan.–Apr. 1991) 7–22. Gonzalo Sánchez, "Guerra y política en la sociedad colombiana," *Análisis Político,* No. 11 (Sept.–Dec. 1990): 7–27. Daniel Pecaut, *Crónica de dos décadas de política colombiana 1968–1988* (Bogotá: Siglo XXI Editores, 1988); and D. Pecaut, "Colombia: democracia y Violencia," *Análisis Político,* No. 13 (May–Aug. 1991): 35–50.

24. Daniel Pecaut, "Presente, Pasado y futuro de la Violencia en Colombia," *Desarrollo Económico—Revista de Ciencias Sociales* (Buenos Aires), 36, No. 144 (Jan.–May 1997): 891–930.

25. "The Intellectuals' Letter" and "The Guerrillas' Response" in *NACLA* 27, No. 4, (Jan.–Feb. 1994): 10–11.

26. Alejandro Reyes, "Compra de tierras por narcotraficantes," in Francisco Thoumi et. al., eds., *Drogas ilícitas en Colombia* (Santafé de Bogotá: Ariel, Naciones Unidas-PNUD, Ministerio de Justicia, Dirección Nacional de Estupefacentes, 1997), 279–346.

27. Carlos Medina Gallego, *Autodefensas, paramilitares y narcotráfico en Colombia: Orígen, desarrollo y consolidación. El caso "Puerto Boyacá* (Bogotá: Editorial Documentos Periodisticos, 1990); Rodrigo Uprimmy Yepes y Alfredo Vargas Castaño, "La palabra y la sangre: violencia, legalidad y guerra sucia en Colombia," in Germán Palacio, ed., *La Irrupción del Paraestado: Ensayos Sobre la Crisis Colombiana* (Bogotá: CEREC, ILSA, 1990): 105–66; Alejandro Reyes, "Paramilitares en Colombia: contexto, aliados y consecuencias," *Análisis Político,* No. 12 (Jan.–Apr. 1991): 35–41.

28. In 1996 there were 26,664 murders in Colombia, according to the National Police. Such figures make Colombia one of the most violent places on earth, with a per-capita homicide rate surpassed only recently by El Salvador and South Africa. Although it is difficult to separate and classify the different violences, as they all stimulate each other, human rights groups have attempted to separate out political violence. In 1996 the Colombian Commission of Jurists (CCJ), a respected human rights organization, concluded that of the total number of murders in Colombia, 3,086 or 13 percent, were committed for political reasons. These include 1,106 persons killed as a result of combat between government and guerrillas.

When it was possible to attribute authorship, the CCJ concluded: the armed forces were responsible for 7.5 percent of all political deaths; paramilitary groups and rural security cooperatives were responsible for 69 percent; the guerrillas were responsible for 23.5 percent. Source: Colombian Commission of Jurists, cited (without attribution) in U.S. Department of State, Bureau of

Democracy, Human Rights, and Labor, "Colombia Country Report on Human Rights Practices for 1997," January 30, 1998.

29. There is a rich and thriving field of study of political violence in Colombia, popularly referred to as "violentology." Yet curiously only a small body of literature on Colombia's peace processes exists. Most, although not all, are reflections by one or another of the participants, either as governmental or guerrilla negotiator. See Jesús Antonio Bejarano, *Una agenda para la paz: Aproximaciones desde la teoría de la resolución de conflictos* (Santafé de Bogotá: Tercer Mundo Editores, 1995); Mauricio García Durán, *De la Uribe a Tlaxcala: Procesos de paz* (Santafé de Bogotá: CINEP, 1992); Rafael Pardo Rueda, *De primera mano: Colombia 1986–1994: Entre conflictos y esperanzas* (Santafé de Bogotá: CEREC, Grupo Editorial Norma, 1996); and Socorro Ramírez and Luis Alberto Restrepo, *El Proceso de paz durante el gobierno de Belisario Betancur 1982–1986* (Bogotá: Siglo XXI, CINEP, 1989).

30. Marc W. Chernick, "Insurgency and Negotiations: Defining the Boundaries of the Political Regime in Colombia" (Ph.D. diss., Columbia University, 1991).

31. The armed forces moved without cease to retake the embattled building that housed the Supreme Court and the Council of State. The takeover and the subsequent military response led to the deaths of all but one of the guerrillas, half the justices of the Supreme Court and Council of State, and scores of others trapped in the building, on November 6 and 7, 1985. See Ana Carrigan, *The Palace of Justice: A Colombian Tragedy* (New York: Four Walls, Eight Windows, 1993); Olga Behar, *Noches de Humo* (Bogotá: Planeta, 1988); and Ramón Jimeno, *Noches de Lobos* (Bogotá: Siglo XXI, 1989).

32. At the center of this group was Rafael Pardo, who was the principal government negotiator in the talks with the M-19. He later became minister of defense. Pardo attributes the successes during the Barco and Gaviria years to the stability and durability of the core staff of advisors, each succeeding the other as principal negotiator with the guerrillas during the two administrations. See Pardo, *De primera mano*.

33. Presidencia de la República, *El camino de la paz*, vols. 1–2 (Bogotá: Consejería para la Reconciliación, Normalización y Rehabilitación, 1989).

34. Ricardo Santamaría, Asesor Político, Consejería Presidencial para la Reconciliación, Normalización y Rehabilitación, interview with author, Bogotá, October 1987. In practice, another presidential counselor asserted that the Consejos did work with local community actors, including guerrilla representatives, and in some cases did succeed in creating local democratic forums amid the violence. Patricia Cleves, Asesor Asuntos Indígenas during the Barco administration, interview with author, Washington, D.C., April 1998.

35. Comisión de estudios sobre la violencia, *Colombia: violencia y democracia. Informe presentado al Ministerio de Gobierno* (Bogotá: Universidad Nacional de Colombia—Colciencias, 1989), 18.

36. See Pardo Rueda, *De primera mano*; Bejarano, *Una agenda para la paz*.

37. García Durán, *De la Uribe a Tlaxcala*, 226–229; Bejarano, *Una agenda para la paz*, 83–108; Jesús Antonio Bejarano, presidential advisor and chief government negotiator, interview with author, Caracas, August 1994.

38. García Durán, *De la Uribe a Tlaxcala*, 221–222.

39. Marc Chernick, "Colombia: Redefining National Security and Civil-Military Relations in the Fight against Guerrillas and Drug-traffickers," in Louis Goodman, Juan Rial, and Johanna Mendelson, eds., *Civil-Military Relations Toward the Year 2000*.

40. Confidential interview with author, Washington, D.C., May 1998.

41. Noé Ríos and García-Peña Jaramillo, *Building Tomorrow's Peace*, 20–24.

42. On the forfeiture law, see "Question for the Record Submitted to Ambassador-designate Curtis W. Kamman," Subcommittee on the Western Hemisphere and Peace Corps Affairs, Mimeograph, September 10, 1997. Would the traffickers willingly give up such vast extensions of land without mounting resistance, even violent resistance? An argument can be made that they

would be willing to surrender such land peacefully in the context of a defined path that leads to their incorporation into society. This is one of the points where talks with the traffickers and talks with the guerrillas intersect. It is beyond the scope of this chapter, but it should be noted that the government has "talked" with the traffickers on several occasions, including in Panama in 1984, with the Medellín cartel in 1990–1991 regarding their surrender in exchange for reduced punishment, and with the Cali cartel in 1994 and 1995 in the period before members' capture and surrender.

43. See Comité Internacional de la Cruz Roja, "La Paz."

Appendix: Colombia's Major Guerrilla Movements

Founded in the 1960s

FARC-EP. *Fuerzas Armadas Revolucionarias de Colombia-Ejército del Pueblo* (Revolutionary Armed Forces of Colombia-People's Army): the largest of Colombia's guerrilla forces. The FARC's origins can be traced to the communist self-defense organizations of the 1940s and 1950s and Liberal Party guerrilla factions who refused to accept the amnesties offered in 1953 and 1958, when the leadership of the two traditional parties put an end to *la Violencia*. In 1966, following the bombing campaigns by the state against the isolated communist communities known as Independent Republics, the FARC was founded as a mobile guerrilla force with a wider range of action than the early self-defense communities. Since its inception, the FARC maintained ties to the Communist Party of Colombia (*Partido Comunista Colombiano*, PCC), which was traditionally pro-Soviet. The PCC was formally precluded from electoral participation from 1958 to 1970. The FARC negotiated a cease-fire with the Betancur administration in 1984, a cease-fire that endured through 1986. In 1985, the FARC launched a political party, the *Unión Patriótica* (Patriotic Union); its members achieved some electoral successes but became the targets of extreme repression and assassination. After the collapse of the Soviet Union, the FARC became more dependent on such activities as kidnapping, extortion, and so-called revolutionary taxation of productive enterprises—including the coca trade—to finance its expanding insurgency. Yet the movement still operates as an armed political organization with state-like functions in areas where it exerts influence. The FARC participated in formal peace negotiations with the government in La Uribe, Colombia (1984–1986), Caracas, Venezuela (1990), and Tlaxcala, Mexico (1991).

196

ELN. *Ejército de Liberación Nacional* (National Liberation Army): founded as a pro-Cuban guerrilla *foco,* or core insurgent group, with roots in factions of the Colombian student movement of the 1960s. In later years the ELN's ties to Cuba were loosened. After the death in combat in 1966 of one of its early recruits, Father Camilo Torres, the ELN developed an ideology of Christian-Marxism. In the 1980s and 1990s the movement was led by a Spanish priest, Manuel Pérez, and the name was changed to UC-ELN (*Unión Camilista–Ejército de Liberación Nacional*) in honor of Father Torres. The ELN did not participate in the peace negotiations of the 1980s and was the only major group not to sign a cease-fire agreement in 1984. It has oriented much of its armed and propaganda actions against foreign oil concerns operating in Colombia, and regularly blows up the main petroleum pipeline that brings oil from the eastern plains to the Atlantic Coast. At the same time, it has raised tens of millions of dollars by extorting foreign oil and construction firms and through kidnappings. The ELN has repeatedly called for signing agreements to "humanize the war," including Protocol II of the Geneva Conventions, which the Samper government ultimately signed in 1994. The ELN participated in the ill-fated negotiations in Caracas and Tlaxcala in 1990 and 1991.

EPL. *Ejército Popular de Liberación* (Popular Liberation Army): founded as a pro-Maoist guerrilla organization, it later rejected the Chinese strategies of prolonged rural struggle. It adopted instead a combined rural and urban strategy more appropriate to a country such as Colombia, which is almost 70 percent urban. Like the ELN, the EPL also has roots in the university movements of the 1960s. From its inception, the group declared itself the military wing of the Communist Party of Colombia, Marxist-Leninist (*Partido Comunista de Colombia, Marxista-Leninista,* PCML), which broke away from the pro-Soviet Communist Party of Colombia (PCC) in the early 1960s. The EPL signed a cease-fire agreement in 1984 in the city of Medellín, which broke down after the assassination of the EPL's chief negotiator over a year later. In 1990 the EPL again entered into negotiations with the Gaviria government, which led to the demobilization of most of its fighters and to the group's participation in the Constituent Assembly of 1991. One small faction led by the EPL's principal leader refused to sign the agreement and continued to engage in armed struggle in alliance with the FARC and ELN. Those who handed in their arms formed a new political party called *Esperanza, Paz y Libertad* (Hope,

Peace, and Liberty, also known by the acronym EPL). The EPL political
party has witnessed the brutal assassination of many of its followers by both
paramilitaries and still-active EPL guerrillas.

Founded in 1970s and 1980s

M-19. *Movimiento 19 de Abril* (April 19th Movement): founded after the
1970 presidential election, held on April 19 of that year, in which former
dictator-turned-populist Gustavo Rojas Pinilla and his *Alianza Nacional
Popular* (National Popular Alliance, ANAPO) party were alleged to have
been denied victory through electoral fraud. The movement was founded
by ANAPO members along with dissident members of the FARC. The M-
19 was consciously modeled after the *Montoneros* of Argentina and the *Tupamaros* of Uruguay, the first major urban armed movements in Latin
America that sought to combine political action with urban guerrilla warfare. The M-19 combined a strong nationalist rhetoric with a heterodox
brand of Marxism. As an urban guerrilla organization, it sought to adapt
new forms of military and political struggle to the conditions of Colombia.
It became known for publicity-seeking "armed propaganda" actions, such
as the stealing of Simón Bolívar's sword from a museum in downtown Bogotá, and the hijacking of milk trucks in order to distribute the milk to the
poor. It attracted international attention with actions such as the takeover
of the Dominican Embassy in 1980 with fifteen foreign ambassadors inside, and the storming of the Palace of Justice in 1985, which led to the
deaths of eleven supreme court justices, scores of innocent employees, and
all but one guerrilla in an army counterattack. Only one year before the attack on the Palace of Justice, the M-19 had signed a cease-fire agreement
with the Betancur government, but the M-19 unilaterally withdrew eight
months later. In 1990 the M-19 entered into negotiations with the Barco
government, leading to its demobilization and reincorporation into political life. In its first year as a new political party known as *Acción
Democrática M-19* (Democratic Action M-19), it achieved unprecedented
electoral success for a third party in Colombia, culminating in its winning
over 27 percent of the vote for the Constituent Assembly of 1990. In the
years following the Constituent Assembly, the M-19's electoral success
rapidly declined. By 1994 it had been reduced to a party without parliamentary representation and only a few local officials.

Quintín Lame. *Movimiento Armado Quintín Lame* (Quintín Lame Armed Movement, MAQL) was founded in 1984 as an indigenous guerrilla movement that operated in the department of Cauca, a province in south central Colombia that is 40 percent indigenous and characterized by large landholdings, unequal land tenure, and conflict between indigenous reservations and landowners. The Quintín Lame was initially organized as a movement to extend indigenous lands through land invasions and to defend indigenous communities from hostile attacks from landowners, the military, government officials, and other guerrilla movements. The group negotiated with the Gaviria administration from August 1990 to May 1991, leading to its demobilization and simultaneous participation in the Constituent Assembly. Their presence in the Assembly contributed to the fact that indigenous issues were prominently addressed, and major concessions and rights were incorporated into the Constitution of 1991.

CGSB. *Coordinadora Guerrillera Simón Bolívar* (Simón Bolívar Guerrilla Coordinating Committee): After decades of rivalries and independent military actions, including separate negotiations with the government throughout the 1980s, Colombia's guerrilla movements attempted to develop a common political and military front similar to the unified guerrilla forces that waged war and ultimately negotiated peace in Central America. The first attempt was the CNG, *Coordinadora Guerrillera Nacional,* founded in 1985, uniting the M-19, EPL, ELN, Quintín Lame, and the *Partido Revolucionario de los Trabajadores* (Revolutionary Workers' Party, or PRT), a small group operating primarily in the Atlantic Coast region. The FARC, still respecting the cease-fire agreements of 1984, did not participate. In 1987, the CNG was renamed the CGSB, *Coordinadora Guerrillera Simón Bolívar,* this time with the inclusion of the FARC, which had returned to armed actions following the rupture of its cease-fire agreement in 1986. Yet the CGSB never achieved a centralized command structure or common political platform. The M-19 broke ranks in 1989 and began negotiations with the Barco government. The EPL, Quintín Lame, and PRT also subsequently negotiated a separate peace. After 1991 the CGSB consisted of the FARC, the ELN, and a dissident faction of the EPL. Some military actions in some regions were coordinated. Additionally, the CGSB sent a unified negotiating team to Caracas and Tlaxcala in 1990–1991. However, by 1997 the separate groups retained considerable autonomy and the CGSB was barely operating. Source: Based on author's research.

Reflections

JESÚS ANTONIO BEJARANO

Colombia is the country where peace negotiations in Latin America began. Since that time in 1982, a great deal has been learned, and, more important, an intellectual structure for understanding the problematic of peace negotiations has begun to take shape.

The first lesson that has been learned is that successful and wide-ranging negotiations have two central aspects, and when these central aspects are weak or nonexistent, the negotiations are blocked or thrown off course. These two aspects are the objective need for democratization and demilitarization because of the country's past. Obvious cases are El Salvador and Guatemala, where the peace accords became synonymous with the provision of space for redemocratization and demilitarization. This has not been the case for either Mexico or Colombia.

One probably would be hard-pressed to say that Colombia, which has the longest-lasting armed conflict in Latin America, is a country without democracy or is one in which military issues played a dominant role in generating the civil war. For this reason, in Colombia it is hard to find a way out. The situation is different in Mexico, which has had a peace process where there was no war. After a few days the guerrilla threat led to a truce and to negotiations, which provided the space for demanding deep political reforms. But the negotiations in Mexico were not driven by the war itself.

The second lesson learned from the Latin American experience has to do with the scope of the agreements. It is surprising to note the similarity of the negotiating agendas in Colombia, El Salvador, and Guatemala. There was a great similarity between the agenda signed by the Colombian government and guerrillas in Caracas in 1991, the agenda signed in Guatemala afterward, and the agenda developed almost simultaneously in El Salvador, despite the fact that there was no agreement or communication among the negotiators. I was the Colombian government negotiator, and I can assure you that we had no contact with the negotiators in El Salvador.

The negotiating agendas all dealt in greater or lesser degree with military themes, the issue of political reforms, and human rights. The scope of the agenda and the development of specific issues depend on a variety of conditions. First is the intensity of the conflict and the correlation of forces. In the case of El Salvador, the military stalemate was an objective fact, and therefore the military issue was central, as were issues of human rights and political reforms aimed at democratization.

This was not the case in Guatemala, where a military stalemate did not exist. There was, to be sure, a need to democratize and demilitarize. But it is clear that in terms of the balance of forces, the military had resolved the conflict. Military themes played a decidedly secondary role in Guatemala, and the reforms negotiated in this sphere were less far-reaching. As one leader has stated, in Guatemala the guerrillas were not a threat but a nuisance; therefore, at the negotiating table the problem of the war was treated as a nuisance would be. In Guatemala the peace process was the great pretext for talking about democracy. It was the only forum for airing demands not necessarily related to peace in its narrowest sense, understood as an absence of confrontation, but to peace understood as a space for talking about democracy.

Similarly, we cannot speak of a military stalemate in Colombia. But I would argue that the intensity of the conflict and its effects on the entire civilian population are reaching the point that would oblige elite sectors of society to make concessions.

The effects of the war are an obstacle in Colombia. In El Salvador and Guatemala the effect the conflict was having on the behavior of the economy could be examined. This is a variable that is usually not taken into consideration, but it is a decisive one. If the behavior of the Salvadoran economy during the conflict were examined, it would be concluded that anything that could be achieved, any concession, would be small compared to the cost of the war. As everyone knows, the Salvadoran economy was virtually destroyed during the twelve years of war. Peace thus became a strategy of the business community. It was the political plan of the private sector, led, without a doubt, by President Alfredo Cristiani.

The same was not true in Guatemala. The war did not affect the functioning of its economy. During the initial negotiations in Guatemala, leaders of various private-sector organizations, especially the cattle ranchers and farmers, told the ambassadors of the Group of Friends that they were not committing themselves to anything and that reconstruction depended on what could be obtained from the international community. These leaders didn't have to understand the need for sacrifice and commitment in order to build peace.

In the case of Mexico, 99.9 percent of the crisis has to do with factors other than the EZLN (Zapatista Army for National Liberation), which did not disrupt normal activity for the majority of Mexicans. For this reason, there is little prospect of immediate success in the negotiations. No one is in dire need of them.

In the case of Colombia, the economic effect of the war already is being strongly felt. The situation resembles that of El Salvador. The violence is affecting the economy to such a significant extent that, sooner or later, private-sector leaders are going to conclude that any price should be paid—in terms of reforming politics, the economy, or the structure of the armed forces—to avoid the economic costs of confrontation. Introducing the variable of economic costs helps to explain the behavior of many business groups vis-á-vis the commitment to peace.

Finally, the climate out of which the peace accords arise, the antecedents of the negotiations, have much to do with postwar stability. This is particularly true with respect to human rights. When the structures of impunity that have existed throughout the war are destroyed, the stability of the postconflict period is more ensured. One of the great advances of the peace accord in El Salvador was to ensure that this structure of impunity was eliminated. El Salvador is becoming more and more complicated, but not because the core aspects of impunity, the death squads and paramilitary groups, are being re-created. Rather, it is because of inadequate leadership on the part of the ARENA government.

In Guatemala, by contrast, it is not certain that the structures of impunity actually will be dissolved. The truth commission, for example, can talk about the conflict but not identify the guilty. I hope I am wrong, but I am not certain that the peace accords in Guatemala will be stable from the standpoint of preventing a resurgence of paramilitary groups or death squads.

Ultimately, the central issue is whether the negotiations succeed in establishing mechanisms to ensure that the structures of impunity that generated the conflict have been completely dismantled.

Everything else, it would appear, depends on the ability of the international community to oversee the implementation of the accords and to continue promoting the climate of peace that comes out of the negotiations. Unfortunately, however, one lesson that can be drawn from the experiences of El Salvador and Guatemala is that once demobilization has been accomplished, the international community behaves as if peace has been achieved and it no longer has any responsibilities. This is a tremendous mistake. Ultimately, peace is something that is built over the long term. The role of the international community cannot be curtailed as soon as the military conflict has ended. The rest of the peace process may take ten or fifteen years to unfold, and it requires the accompaniment of the international community.

7

Peace in Peru: An Unfinished Task

CARLOS BASOMBRÍO

Introduction

In the early months of 1997, for the first time in several years, violence once again brought Peru to world media headlines with the spectacular and dramatic takeover of the Japanese embassy by the Túpac Amaru Revolutionary Movement (MRTA), the holding of hostages for more than four months, and the impressive military action of the Peruvian armed forces to put an end to the problem.[1] If the international press were to be believed, violence had returned to very high levels, and the MRTA, not the Sendero Luminoso (Shining Path), was the major player. Taking such reports at face value could lead to an erroneous assumption as to what was really happening in Peru in regard to political violence. Interpreting the problem of political violence in Peru and trying to understand the progress of and limits to strategies to deal with it requires viewing the situation in its proper context.

First, the main perpetrators of violence have been, and continue to be, Shining Path. The MRTA "contributed" an average of no more than 3 percent of all such actions of violence. Despite the MRTA's spectacular military action, since the deaths of those who were at the embassy, the organization's numbers have been reduced to those who are still in prison (hence the central importance group members gave to the release of their comrades) and small groups in the central jungle and the province of Jaén, in the northern mountain range. With regard to the problem of violence in Peru, "the MRTA is third-rate, and if it achieved any level of importance, it was in inserting itself into the cracks that the senderistas (Shining Path followers) managed to create. Had Shining Path not existed, the MRTA would probably have been a movement similar to its counterpart in Ecuador, the 'Alfaro Vive Carajo'—in other words, one with virtually no scope."[2]

Second, the true magnitude of the violence must be made clear. Statistically speaking, even with the spectacular military action just mentioned, violence in Peru in 1997 was ten times less than it was before 1992. The embassy takeover aside, the effect of violence on national life, politically and socially, also has decreased dramatically. In the particular case of the MRTA, the takeover of the Japanese embassy was virtually the only relevant military action it had implemented for two years.[3] Since then, the MRTA has not carried out a single military action, and many believe that it will never be able to recover any military or political capability. Compared to five years ago, Shining Path also has weakened, but, unlike the MRTA, it continues to be active in several regions of the country, its "discreet" presence is known in many others, and several analysts agree that it probably is regaining its strength to a significant degree.[4]

In short, to use a medical analogy, political violence in Peru has ceased to be a serious epidemic but has become a persistent and destructive endemic disease; the carrier is not the MRTA but rather has been and continues to be Shining Path. The purpose of this chapter is to discuss the way in which Peru confronted the violence and defeated it. This is not simply an academic exercise; it is of crucial importance to Peru because what is at stake may be the possibility of having a firm and lasting peace, to borrow the Guatemalan phrase.

In the Blink of an Eye: From Catastrophic Balance to Strategic Defeat

Not long ago Peru was on the brink of collapse, largely due to an unmanageable economic crisis and a generalized feeling of chaos, unusual even for Latin America. According to official figures provided by the National Institute of Statistics and Information, inflation was 1,722 percent in 1988, 2,775 percent in 1989, and 7,649 percent in 1990. The gross national product declined 28.9 percent between 1981 and 1991. The real value of wages and salaries declined by 24.6 percent in 1988, 45.4 percent in 1989, and 12.7 percent in 1990.

To that was added the impact of seemingly uncontrollable political violence. By 1989 Shining Path was active at the national level. It had consolidated its presence in the Upper and Mid-Huallaga river valley, where it was building an important social base through its relationship with the coca-growing peasants who were in conflict with the state over the eradication of their crops. At the same time, it was providing itself with an unsuspected source of funds through its link with drug trafficking. Furthermore, consolidated in its original loci of Ayacucho, Huancavelica, and part of Apurímac, it was having a significant impact in Junín, a strategic department for any military and economic attempt to surround the capital. The departments of Cajamarca, Ancash, and Puno, the provinces surrounding Lima, and the capital of the republic itself were already important scenes in the domestic war.

In 1989 the barrier of 3,000 dead per year was broken; figures would be maintained and even grow in the following years. And as had been the case from the beginning, the dead were not military casualties but mainly defenseless civilians. According to the Senate's Special Commission on the Causes of Violence, in 1989, for example, 700 peasants, 260 villagers, 148 laborers, and 144 local authorities died. The economic impact of the violence was also great; in that same year, attacks on electrical transmission towers alone caused the loss of $62 million. The ensuing losses in trade and industry due to power restrictions totaled $600 million. The Special Commission also estimated that violence cost the economy $3.2 billion that year.

In subsequent years—1990, 1991, and 1992—during the administration of President Alberto Fujimori, these conditions intensified, with important cumulative effects. Shining Path announced that it had left the "strategic defensive" and was in the midst of a "strategic balance." On May 17, 1991, on the front page of its semilegal newspaper, *El Diario,* it noted: "the people's war throughout the length and breadth of the country is being expressed at higher and higher levels, and on our eleventh anniversary we are passing through strategic balance on the threshold of the counteroffensive that will produce the class and the people for the conquest of power throughout the country." Shining Path was notorious for exaggerating its strength in order to convince its militants to take bolder steps, which could mean death for them. However, things seemed to have entered at least a catastrophic, if not a strategic, balance. Although Shining Path had no real possibility of advancing much further, by this time it had become a political and military force large enough to jeopardize the country's overall normal development and to make it impossible for Peru to deal with its other problems.

In July 1992, several months after Fujimori's *autogolpe* of April 5, 1992 (we will return to the "self-coup" later), the climax of this "catastrophic balance" would be reached when a brutal senderista offensive, much larger in scope, more highly coordinated, and bloodier than the previous ones, touched the entire country, especially the capital city of Lima. Even after a final peace accord had been signed in El Salvador, the M-19 guerrillas had been reintegrated in Colombia and a new constitution approved, and conversations with the Guatemalan National Revolutionary Unity (URNG) had been going on for some time in Guatemala, Peru seemed trapped in the midst of violence with no real clues about how to get out.

Yet, just a short time later and contrary to all predictions, the situation changed radically. Shining Path was strategically defeated, reduced to a shadow of its former self. Its ability to carry out violent acts decreased statistically from ten to one, and its political impact declined even more. The "catastrophic equilibrium" that had made the country ungovernable was broken.

The September 1992 capture of Sendero's principal leader, Abimael Guzmán Reynoso, changed definitively the course of the internal war in Peru. Understanding the importance, as well as the limits, of that event requires placing it in a broader context.

A Native Version of "Hawks and Doves" or Something Deeper?: A Short History of Two Conflicting Concepts

When violence appeared on the Peruvian political horizon in 1980, a great debate arose over the best way to contend with it. Simply put, on one side were what could be called the militaristic sectors. Among them were many members of the armed forces, prominent political leaders and opinion makers, and, in almost all cases, the authorities in charge of dealing directly with violence. They thought that state counterattacks should be intensified to put an end to the problem "at any cost." Over the years, due to advances made by Shining Path and demonstrations of their extreme cruelty, this militaristic faction gained influence in defining state policies. But, paradoxically, each time its ideas were put into practice, the situation became worse, and the subsequent panic would create a greater demand for those measures.

On the other side were those calling for an "integral strategy." Many such voices have been raised in Peru over the years by human rights organizations, important sectors of the church and the media, some congressmen, many retired soldiers, and most of the "senderologists" (as analysts of the violence process are known in Peru). The key difference and point of departure from the negotiated political solutions attempted in other Latin American countries was that no one in Peru was suggesting a dialogue with the insurgents. That would have been absurd and unworkable in the Peruvian context because of three factors related to Shining Path.

First, Shining Path, which represents an atypical and extreme case of dogmatism even in the political history of the Latin American left, was ideologically fanatical and flatly rejected any possibility of negotiations. It is true that other groups have existed with similar degrees of ideological radicalism, but, unlike Sendero, none ever has managed to escape its absolute marginalization or to put its ideas into practice "successfully."[5]

Second, it had among its enemies not just the armed forces but also much of society. Shining Path was directly responsible for the murder of hundreds of peasant leaders, the indiscriminate massacres of entire communities, and later, in the cities, merciless attacks on all those who stood up to it, especially women popular leaders. (Two from well-known shantytowns in Lima—María Elena Moyano of Villa El Salvador and Pascuala Rosado of Huaycán—were symbols of that resistance; both were brutally murdered.)

Third, although it was never prevented from acting within a legal framework, Shining Path chose not to be part of the country's institutional system. This choice created an unbridgeable gulf between it and the legal left. In Colombia, El Salvador, and Guatemala, because of the countries' different political history and the nature of the armed groups, the dividing line between the insurgents and the leftist political or social movements was more diffuse; in Peru the boundary was always very well defined. The left clearly had opted for legality, and the system allowed it to function without many restrictions; but the sectarian nature of Shining Path kept it absolutely removed from any possibility of establishing alliances with other sectors.

Those who proposed an integral solution were thinking of a combination of political, social, economic, and military measures. The first step would be to isolate the senderistas to prevent their growth among other impoverished sectors of the population and facilitate their repression while respecting the rights of the civilian population and the law. Although those who proposed this approach never had enough power to put their point of view fully into practice, they were able to moderate the worst aspects of the totally militaristic logic.[6]

The argument over ways to view the problem first manifested itself during the administration of Fernando Belaúnde (1980–1985). In retrospect, Shining Path's ability to act in its first two years (1980–1981) was quite limited, consisting of rarely bloody attacks on government offices and centering almost exclusively in the rural zones of some provinces of Ayacucho. The initial reaction of the government and Peruvian society to this unexpected outbreak of violence was, perhaps understandably, confusion. But soon a police response was attempted. Contrary to the idea that later spread quite generally, at first it was reasonably efficient and at the same time respectful of the basic rights of the population.

But all this was happening in an altered political climate in Lima where there was a demand—as passionate as it was ignorant of what was going on in the field—that an iron fist be applied; in other words, that there be repression at any cost. Some government sectors even tried to establish a link between the legal left (by then firmly established in the "system," with broad parliamentary and municipal representation) and the actions of Shining Path. Although this did not come about, Alfonso Barrantes, the leader of the left at that time, was jailed and the minister of justice opened an investigation into the possible links between the two sectors. There was even pressure from the ranks of Belaúnde's own party for the resignation of his first minister of the interior, José María de la Jara, who refused to follow that line of reasoning.[7]

Senderista provocation encouraged the reaction of the "hard-liners." With acts of increasing cruelty and audacity, Shining Path tried to ensure that its prophecy of a revolution in the midst of "rivers of blood" would come true. In response, in 1981 the government approved the first (No. 046) of a long list of emergency decrees aimed at toughening the legal sanctions against those responsible for acts of violence. And in December 1982, a new and definitive turn toward military logic came about when the armed forces were given the task of taking control of and directly confronting Shining Path in Ayacucho.[8] The reasoning was simple: Although the senderistas' strength and capacity for action exceeded that of the police, who were dispersed in small rural posts throughout the country, decisive and energetic action by the armed forces, which were immensely superior to their adversary militarily, should manage to restore order rapidly.

Unfortunately, the result was the opposite. The entry of the armed forces into Ayacucho marked the beginning of what has become known in

Peru as the "dirty war," which escalated the conflict to inconceivable levels. During the first two years that the armed forces were present in Ayacucho, 5,645 deaths occurred in just five of its provinces (Huamanga, Huanta, Cangallo, La Mar, and Víctor Fajardo); that is, 46 percent of all the deaths that would occur in Ayacucho in the fourteen years of violence and—perhaps even more revealing—20.5 percent of those occurring in all of Peru throughout the entire confrontation.[9]

The strategy led not to the defeat of Shining Path (although it came close, as Guzmán himself admits) but—with the breaking of the blockade and fueled by the resentment it generated—rather to its growth throughout the country like an uncontrollable cancer. Thus, in the mid-1980s, Shining Path ceased to be a movement limited to few rural provinces of Ayacucho; it spread forcefully through Huancavelica and Apurímac and tried to enter Puno and the south of Cajamarca. It carried out actions in Lima and attacks in many other places, and it would find, upon its entry into the Upper Huallaga, a new element necessary for its future development.

It is important to recall here the conduct of General Adrián Huamán, military-political chief in Ayacucho in 1984. Although his perspective was not in conflict with the repressive logic of the time, he did understand that success was not possible without sustained social assistance and local development programs. Although his vision was strictly paternalistic and in many senses totally antidemocratic, it basically criticized the idea that indiscriminate military force was the main ingredient for reestablishing peace in the country. Because of his public demands on the government in this vein, Huamán was removed from office.[10]

The administration of Alan García began in 1985 with a critical view of what was taking place. His inaugural address summarized his vision of what it was necessary to do: "We will not combat barbarism with barbarism." He removed the military chiefs responsible for the massacres that had taken place at the beginning of his term in Accomarca and Pucayacu and established a peace commission composed of prominent persons to design alternative peace-related policies.[11] This policy would be short-lived. June 1986 saw "the prison massacre," a simultaneous bloody uprising of mobs in the jails of Lima organized by senderista prisoners. It was met with a disproportionate military response, causing the death of over 200 prisoners, many of them after they had surrendered.[12]

From that time on, all efforts at an alternative policy ended and the approach put into practice by the previous government was stepped up; this

resulted, among other things, in the Cayara massacre (where a military patrol killed about twenty peasants in order to "avenge" a senderista attack
nearby), the appearance of paramilitary groups, the spread of confrontations that "left no wounded," and forced disappearances.[13] As with the
previous government, the result was the same: Shining Path not only was
not defeated but instead extended its range and its capacity for action. By
the end of the term of García's American Popular Revolutionary Alliance
(APRA) in 1990, violence was a national phenomenon and was jeopardizing the country's viability.

Throughout the years of the García administration, many efforts were
also made by others to point out the erroneous and costly nature of those
policies and the need for alternatives.[14] Two are worthy of mention here:
the Senate's Special Commission on the Causes of Violence and Alternatives for National Pacification, chaired by Senator Enrique Bernales, which
played an outstanding role in studying the problem and in drafting and dis-
seminating alternative proposals[15]; and the work of the Congressional Investigative Commission on the events at the prisons, chaired by Senator
Rolando Ames, whose report went beyond the immediate task and made
important contributions by way of analysis and recommendations.[16]

When Alberto Fujimori assumed the presidency in 1990, the situation
was already critical.[17] No great announcement of changes in direction were
made; instead a close relationship between the new president and the
armed forces gradually began to be consolidated. It was based on the president's conviction that by giving the armed forces sufficient support, they
would come up with the ideas and methods needed to end the armed subversion. Perhaps for that reason, Fujimori was against punishing—through
either legislative or judicial means—the perpetrators of the best-known
cases of human rights violations that had occurred in the preceding government term.[18]

Tension about solutions to the problem continued. In this regard, the
unsuccessful experience of the Peace Council should be mentioned. This
institution was created by Law 25237 toward the end of the García administration in 1990. In August 1991, at the initiative of Carlos Torres y
Torres Lara, then head of the cabinet, its regulations were approved and
its implementation was announced. The peace council was established to
involve diverse sectors of civil society in drawing up a national peace plan.
Although late in coming, this was an exceptional opportunity for those
who thought it necessary to alter the course that had been taken in the
country's pacification. Expectations for it were high and its appeal was ex-

tremely broad. The unanimous thinking in the council was that the only authority in the country with sufficient legitimacy to preside over and give strength to its agreements was the Catholic church, in the person of Monsignor Augusto Dammert, the president of the Bishops Conference. It sought to give him a role similar to that filled for many years by Monsignor Quezada Toruño of the National Reconciliation Commission in Guatemala.

In a historic error, apparently by a only narrow majority of votes, the Peruvian bishops decided to abstain "because the Council by its very nature must make decisions of a political and operative nature which have nothing to do with our specific mission as pastors."[19] As a consequence, the council was stillborn; no consensus was reached on any other leader, and many sectors withdrew after former Deputy Francisco Diez Canseco was elected its president. Although the institution formally remains, it has never played a relevant role in the area for which it was created, nor has it influenced executive decisions.

The most notable chapter in this comparison between the proponents of a "militaristic" solution and those seeking an integral strategy occurred shortly afterward in September 1991, following the request made for extraordinary congressional powers to legislate in the area of pacification and the approval of a series of legislative decrees with that goal in November 1991. The "November decrees" strengthened an exclusively military response to the problem of violence: The armed forces' powers were increased, and they were given a broad framework for their intervention; the judiciary's powers were limited; and the National Intelligence Service (SIN) was given great power, not subject to oversight, that turned it into a political arm of the government.[20] Congress rejected the request. An "interchamber conference" was formed, chaired by Deputy Lourdes Flores, and the diverse political camps made a singular (but also late) effort to modify the decrees and design a peace strategy for the country that would combine efficiency with respect for the law and the preservation of the democratic system.

But even as these modifications were being agreed upon with Alfonso de los Heros, president of the Council of Ministers, and although he probably did not know it, the die had been cast: Fujimori already had decided on the *autogolpe*, or self-coup.[21] On April 5, 1992, Fujimori closed Congress, took control of the judiciary, put an end to regional governments, concentrated all government power in his person, and began to govern by decree. There would be no more discussions about different emphases in the peace strategy; the "debate was settled." Beginning then, the most drastic measures that the harshest military sectors always had claimed would be necessary to put an end to subversion were put into practice; they included the end of the democratic regime itself and of its ability to oversee the conduct of the armed forces and the intelligence machinery.

The Long Siege of Peruvian Democracy
(from Within and Without)

The Shining Path insurgency was the most difficult test of the democracy reestablished in Peru in 1980, after two years of constitutional process reflected in the 1978–1979 Constituent Assembly. Throughout those years many recalled that the existence of democracy and knowledge of how to preserve it was the best way to prevent the epidemic of political violence from spreading. Yet some people did not understand that (curiously, almost always among them were the democratically elected authorities themselves), and they began to view democracy as an impediment to countersubversive action. Thus, a terrible perversion came about in Peru as Shining Path and those sectors of society and the government that confronted it both came to view democracy as an obstacle to be removed.

From the very first,[22] Shining Path suggested that it was necessary to put an end to the institutions of the "bourgeois state," beginning in the rural areas and then, when its force grew, spreading to the cities. The group's actions included the systematic assassination of local elected authorities and more and more ambitious attempts to boycott electoral processes through intimidation, the murder of voters and candidates, "armed strikes," and so forth.[23] Paradoxically, voices in the armed forces, the political parties, and the press (all enthusiasts of the logic of war) pointed out that the only way to put an end to Shining Path was to put aside democracy in the country—temporarily. Almost never, at least in public, was there a call for a military coup d'état, but there were demands for the military to be given prerogatives that the constitution and the law did not allow and for suspending the guarantees of the basic rights of citizens.

What came about in practice was a complex situation in which democratic forms—freedom of the press, assembly, association, and so on—remained essentially intact at the national level but not in the zones of intense conflict, where the only real authority was the armed forces, through the military-political commands (predominantly military structures established in emergency zones), and the only "legal framework" was the provision of the constitution allowing for the declaration of an emergency zone (designed for exceptional situations of short duration), which became permanent beginning in 1982.

This tension between the two types of political systems—democratic and constitutional in the capital and in areas not much affected by violence, and armed forces' control in the conflict zones where the law and the constitution were very distant—was maintained for many years, with very negative consequences. The suspension of democracy in the rural areas discredited democratically elected governments and even democracy itself. Because of the prevailing militaristic logic, as Shining Path grew, the request to act with a free hand was more favorably received. Simultaneously, democracy also was losing prestige because it was incapable of punishing those who, in arguing the need to put an end to the violence, were violating the law and the rights of citizens, thus accelerating the process that they believed they were fighting.[24]

This situation also contributed to the discrediting of political parties and social orgnizations in the eyes of the people. Political parties, in spite of the innumerable martyrs each one could point to, were unable to take up the fight against Shining Path at the political level, and early on they abandoned that effort in most rural areas. Shining Path crushed social organizations by force with a great cost in human lives. Populations in the conflict zones thus would often end up with two options: Shining Path or the armed forces.[25] Another important consequence of so many years of violence, combined with the legitimacy crisis of political parties, was that not only politicians but also politics lost ground as the way to solve problems.

Did the Militaristic Strategy Win in Peru? Yes and No

In the months following Fujimori's self-coup of April 5, 1992, in addition to a de facto implementation of all the modifications to the power structure by the "November decrees" that the Congress had opposed, a set of legal modifications came about in the treatment, trials, and sentencing of those accused of the crime of terrorism. Among other things, it was agreed that in exchange for relevant information, benefits would be given to subversives who "repented"; trials were set in military tribunals for cases of "betrayal of the homeland" (aggravated forms of terrorism); new types of crime were defined and punishments were increased for all types, up to life imprisonment; it was decided that trials in civilian and military courts would be secret and carried out by "faceless" judges and prosecutors; the right to defense was restricted and the lengths of trials shortened; bail and all types of jail benefits were eliminated; the age for criminal liability was lowered to fifteen; the charge by a reformed criminal or "repentant one" was in and of itself accepted as sufficient evidence to convict; the police were assigned duties belonging to the prosecutor's office; the prison regimen was made rigid in the extreme; and so on.

Just two years after the *autogolpe* and the implementation of these and other practices, Shining Path was clamoring for a "peace agreement." Is it appropriate therefore to establish a causal relationship between this and the measures adopted as a result of April 5? In other words, were the "militarists" right? Had democracy been the obstacle to ending subversion all along? If we go strictly by the fact that the armed insurgent groups were essentially and strategically defeated in Peru, the response would have to be yes. But if we want to go further, even against the feeling still prevalent in the country, the response is, in essence, no.

Rather than April 5, the key date for understanding the dramatic, surprising, and positive change in the history of Peru is September 12, 1992, the day of Sendero leader Abimael Guzmán's capture, the moment when the balance of the war was changed and Shining Path ended up an "orphan."[26] This event confirmed that

> chance plays an important role in history and—in certain circumstances—can become decisive. It also reminds us that the role of individuals in history is fundamental. In the case of Shining Path, there was a critical linkage between the fundamentalist plan and the figure of Abimael Guzmán Reynoso. Because he was the undisputed ideologist, the political, military, and organizational leader, the only one possessing the truth, the direct organizer of the daily conduct of the party in key zones, the figure above contradiction, the symbol of invulnerability for his thirteen years of impeccable clandestine living, his capture and subsequent capitulation have [had] an effect equal to or greater than all other policies put together. . . .[27]

Guzmán's capture was not the result of the extraordinary measures adopted after the self-coup; it could very well have occurred even if this constitutional violation had not taken place. It was rather the result of specialized police work, led by General Antonio Ketín Vidal, head of DINCOTE (the antiterrorist police), who for some years had been successfully dismantling the Shining Path leadership structure. Guzmán's capture was also important because it created the conditions under which, one year later—in another unexpected and spectacular turn of history—Guzmán himself would reject "armed struggle" and call for peace. This would divide Shining Path and give it the coup de grace.[28]

For many reasons, peasant sectors in the central Andean mountain range ended up linked in one way or another to the senderista plan—because of years of prior political indoctrination by Shining Path, forced recruitment for their ranks, the way that guerrilla *cumpas* (short for compañero), unlike a traditionally corrupt and abusive police department, helped them solve local crime problems[29] and supported certain communities in their conflicts with others, and largely in response to the state's repressive brutality. The senderistas offered hope of a better future that would relieve the peasants of their tremendous suffering and help meet their basic needs. But the peasants' conduct was mainly pragmatic; it allowed them to adapt to circumstances, something that the Andean people have done since the conquest in order to survive so much misery and external aggression.

This pragmatism began to clash with ideology when Shining Path tried to impose difficult war demands on the communities under its influence. Among them was a ban on trading their products in the open market, in order to begin the hunger blockade of the cities, an order that reflected Shining Path's failure to value the importance of that trade for the peasants. From then on, reactions against their domination began to grow and were bloodily repressed (e.g., in the peasant community of Lucanamarca in Ayacucho). Little by little Shining Path ceased to be the "lesser evil" for the peasants, who began to see that it would be better to be "with the other side."

In that way, beginning in 1988, *rondas campesinas,* peasant patrols, or civil defense committees, began to grow in importance. By the early 1990s they had extended to almost all the rural zones with senderista presence.[30] The enormous diversity of the patrols' origins, organizational forms, greater or lesser dependence on or autonomy from the armed forces, type of relationship with the community, presence or not of drug trafficking, use of violence, and so forth make it difficult to describe a single reality, but these patrols do have some important common characteristics. First, although the link with the armed forces is real but varies case by case, the patrols are more autonomous than, for example, what seems to have been the case with civil patrols in Guatemala. Second, as patrol members are averse to committing abuses against other peasants, they have been an important factor in the decline in human rights violations in the rural areas, both because the military has ceased to perceive them as enemies and because their conduct has instead been preventive.[31] Third, they have been effective. These patrols not only remove any possibility for Shining Path to maintain or develop a social base in the rural areas, they also achieve effective military control of their own territories, which prevents the entry of senderista forces. In many cases they also carry out crucial offensive military actions. The armed forces finally has understood the importance of having the peasant population on its side and promoting their organization.[32]

Although it is true that the police work that made Guzmán's capture possible and the rural patrols are the key elements in ending the violence in Peru, the government's "total confidence" in the armed forces and certain measures approved after the *autogolpe* did play a role in accelerating the defeat of the armed insurgent organizations. Setting aside for a moment the unnecessary abuses that accompanied these measures, they include the devastating effects of the denunciations of the "repentant ones" on subversive organizations already on the defensive and demoralized as well as the firmness and celerity of the administration of justice and the firmness of prison control. Once again, however, none of these measures would have been impossible to adopt in a democratic context, especially one in which Congress had been willing to approve extraordinary measures.[33]

Peace in Peru: An Unfinished Task

The end of violence in Peru, or at least of the levels that it had reached in the past, has been accompanied by a weakening of democratic institutions and guarantees of the protection of citizens, a growing and uncontrolled political power of the armed forces, and an increasingly authoritarian government. This situation has not changed with successive elections, nor with Fujimori's reelection to a new term in 1995.

Fearful of a "return to the past," many citizens have been indifferent or even openly supportive of the authoritarian components of the situation[34]: the extreme weakness of Congress and the judiciary compared to the executive; the politicization of the armed forces, their growing power over the civilian population, and the almost total lack of their oversight by civilians; the enormous growth in power of the National Intelligence Service (SIN), governed by questionable figures above any oversight and acting like a clandestine political apparatus at the service of the government; the growing and alarming signs at the highest military levels of corruption by drug trafficking; and the use of military justice both to pressure officers who are critical of the situation and as an instrument of impunity for those who are not.

The situation also includes questionable emergency penal legislation that violates all guarantees of due process, has put thousands of innocent persons in jail, and is a latent threat to citizens; the persistence of important human rights violations, even when the "justification" for this may have virtually disappeared; and the guaranteed and absolute impunity of those responsible for these abuses through legislation that became law in July 1995. It is also evident in the concentration of power and duties in the executive and, more specifically, in the president and those around him, and in the reverses in the regionalization process and the loss of function of local governments, even their economic blockade. All of that, furthermore, is in a political climate in which political parties and social organizations are weakened and discredited, as much by virtue of their own "merits" as by the government's constant and unconcealed effort to undermine them. The weakness of democratic institutions is more acute in rural areas and in towns and villages where the war actually took place. There the military is still the dominant institution, and all manifestations of independent activity in civil society are seen as dangerous and potentially "subversive." Dealing seriously and creatively with these problems, the result of fifteen years of violence and the way in which it was faced, has become the crucial and pending task for consolidating peace in Peru. Doing so requires the direct questioning of the "men of war" in power. This is a political task of exceptional importance, the result of which, to a large extent, will reflect the type of country that Peru will be at the beginning of the new millennium.

Notes

1. An extensive analysis, with background information, of the crisis at the Japanese embassy and its outcome can be found in *Ideele*, Nos. 95, 96, and 97 (March, April, and May 1997, respectively). Also useful for putting the problem in proper context is the article by Carlos Iván Degregori, "El capítulo que falta," *Quehacer*, no. 105 (February 1997):3.

2. Carlos Basombrío I., *La paz valor y precio. Una visión comparativa para América Latina* (Lima: Instituto de Defensa Legal, 1996):167.

3. In December 1995 an MRTA group was arrested as it was preparing to take over the congress of the republic. Among those arrested there were Miguel Rincón, one of its few leaders not yet a prisoner; American Lori Berenson; and Nancy Gilbonio, wife of Néstor Cerpa. Néstor Cerpa managed to escape and subsequently led the takeover of the Japanese embassy.

4. In 1996 Shining Path was responsible for 482 attacks and 174 deaths in Peru. The MRTA, in turn, was responsible for 27 attacks and 2 deaths.

5. "The problem [our] revisionist [friends]," they said contemptuously addressing the legal left, "is not that those governing wear uniforms and boots, or a collar and necktie, or even that they have a beard and tie their pants with a rope [referring to Trotskyist leader Hugo Blanco], since that does not take away their reactionary position or make them revolutionaries. It is not a matter of civilian dictatorships or military dictatorships. It is a matter of class . . . dictatorships. Don't we know that power is won through violence and maintained through dictatorship, that revolution is an act in which a part of the population imposes its will on another with rifles, bayonets and cannons . . . and where the winning party is necessarily obligated to maintain its dominance through the fear that their weapons inspire among reactionaries as taught by Engels?" Quoted by Gustavo Gorriti, *Sendero: Historia de la guerra milenaria en el Perú* (Lima: Editorial Apoyo, 1990):198.

6. Even Colombia has vacillated between the search for negotiated and for military solutions to the problem of violence, clearly seen in the cases of Presidents Betancur, Barco, Gaviria, and Samper. They began by favoring a political solution that, when it stalled or failed for various reasons, was replaced by the application of military logic.

7. Gustavo Gorriti, the most noted historian of the initial years of the Shining Path war, notes: "De la Jara emerged as one of the best Ministers of the Interior that Belaúnde had. And this is not a whimsical statement: few times had Sendero undergone the arrest of so many high-level leaders as then. Ayacucho never again experienced several months of tranquility such as those between October and December 1981. No other minister imposed the jurisdiction of the civilian authority as he did. . . . No other had the concern about affirming democratic legitimacy, the protection of the laws and human rights of those governed, as did De la Jara. Gorriti, *Sendero: Historia de la guerra milenaria*, 240.

8. Some Peruvians might object that it is naive to think that this military response was avoidable. But we could argue that the Mexican government's response to events in Chiapas shows that the option of total war is not necessarily the only one available. In any case, fifteen years after the fact, the debate is academic.

9. Equally illustrative of the level of violence is the fact that "for there to have been a proportionate number of victims in Lima as in Huanta, there would have to have been not 2,014, as there were in reality, but 213,453! And at the national level not 24,117 but 816,540!" See Carlos Basombrío I., "Para la historia de una guerra con nombre! Ayacucho!" *Ideele*, no. 6 (April 1994):28. Shortly before that and with success (at the military level), the Guatemalan armed forces had adopted a similar logic of extermination when confronting the URNG in the mountains of El Quiché and the jungles of Ixcán. It is highly probably that the Peruvian soldiers had that experience in mind when they entered Ayacucho.

10. On the other hand, his predecessor, General Clemente Noel, can be described as a classic and unreconstructed promoter of the "dirty war" logic. One of the worst tragedies of the domestic war in Peru took place during his term—the death, probably instigated by the military but never cleared up reliably, of a delegation of journalists in the area of Uchuraccay in 1983.

11. At the beginning of the García administration, the MRTA called a unilateral truce for a few months in exchange for his governing "in favor of the people." Although a dialogue with the MRTA was never considered as relevant, seen in hindsight and in light of the takeover of the Japanese embassy, perhaps Peruvians should have taken advantage of that opportunity, however marginal the MRTA was and is to the central problem of political violence.

12. Several years later, during Alberto Fujimori's administration, a constitutional accusation was filed against former President García for his responsibility for these acts. Only the votes of Fujimori's followers, García's archenemies in the economic area, prevented this move from prospering—one of the ironies of Peruvian politics.

13. The MRTA's more recent notoriety aside, it should be recalled that on April 28, 1989, in Los Molinos, a column of that organization was intercepted by the army and its sixty-two mem-

bers massacred. There is clear evidence that the soldiers killed the wounded and those who surrendered.

14. Those who tried to get the government to change its policies included many in the media, the church (particularly in the southern Andes), human rights groups, popular leaders and organizations, as well as some local governments. Villa El Salvador is a symbol in Peru of a mass úrban population capable of building a better future with high popular participation. Shining Path did all it could to infiltrate and control their organizations. It must be said that although Shining Path did not succeed, it caused enormous damage in the attempt.

15. The "Bernales commission" published a voluminous report that included a comprehensive analysis of the problem. It noted the inadequacy of the exclusively military and police responses. See Comisión Especial sobre las causes de la violencia y alternativas para la pacificación nacional del Senado, *Violencia y Pacificación* (Lima, DESCO: Comisión Andina de Juristas, 1989).

16. See Congressional Investigative Commission on the Events at the Prisons, Rolando Ames et al., *Informe al Congreso sobre los sucesos de los penales* (Lima: La Comisión Investigadora, 1988).

17. To top it all off, in the final days of the Alan García administration, forty-eight MRTA prisoners, including their leader, Victor Polay, made a spectacular escape. This was demoralizing; some even accused the outgoing government of being an accomplice of the fugitives, some of whom participated six years later in taking over the Japanese embassy.

18. In 1990 and 1991 extrajudicial executions continued, the most notorious case being the murder of sixteen persons attending a *pollada* (popular celebration) in Barrios Altos. There were also forced disappearances, such as that of Ernesto Castillo Páez, a student, and of people from Huancapi. What happened in Huancapi is extremely revealing regarding how erroneous and counterproductive it was to favor blind repression. Huancapi, in the province of Victor Fajardo, in Ayacucho, was one of those isolated places where being a candidate for office became an act of great civic courage and an open challenge to senderista terror. Five professors decided to run in the 1991 municipal elections. On April 19, as they were returning to their homes after having formally registered their candidacies, a military patrol stopped them and took them to the military base. They were never heard from again. Evidently all were murdered. The armed forces, at least in that locality and on that occasion, and although it may seem incredible, were directly collaborating with Shining Path to try to prevent the elections. See Diana Avila P. et al., *Perú 1990: la oportunidad perdida* (Lima: Instituto de Defensa Legal, 1991).

19. The incongruity of that abstention was apparent in 1977 when, at the express request of the government (with which he was extremely close, a fact that his peers in the church synod discreetly questioned), Monsignor Luis Cipriani, one of the most conservative bishops in Peru and a declared enemy of anything that sounded like human rights or a political solution, became one of the guarantors in the completely worldly and, in the end unsuccessful, task of finding a negotiated solution to the hostage crisis at the Japanese embassy.

20. A broad analysis of what happened in the months prior to April 1992 can be found in Diana Avila P. et al., *Perú hoy: en el oscuro sendero de la guerra* (Lima: Instituto de Defensa Legal, 1992).

21. De los Heros would resign from his post as a consequence; none of his colleagues in the cabinet copied this move.

22. The first military action of the senderistas coincided with the elections and consisted of burning ballot boxes in the isolated village of Chuschi in Ayacucho.

23. It should be noted in favor of the Peruvians' democratic compromise, so desired at least in the 1990s, that even though hundreds, perhaps thousands, of candidates and authorities were murdered during those years, each and every elections was able to be held at the national level, and Shining Path managed to obstruct elections only in lightly populated and isolated regions.

24. Innumerable cases illustrate the way in which the response to the violence perverted the possibilities for democracy in Peru. One example is that of Second Lieutenant Telmo Hurtado. In command of a patrol, he ordered sixty-nine peasants killed in cold blood, including women and

children, in Accomarca in 1985, in an exceptionally cruel, but in no way unique, act. The case was extensively documented by the press at the time and Hurtado decided to come clean, explaining that he had acted to help put an end to Shining Path and "in defense of the politicians and democracy." When he was asked how the murder of children could be justified, he explained that they would grow up to be senderistas who could attack and kill his men. Hurtado's fate also reveals the double reality of the time: While his trial was going on, he was promoted to lieutenant; he was then convicted of military crimes, not homicide. In addition, there is information from the press, never refuted, that by 1994 he had been freed, had been promoted again, and was acting as advisor to antisubversive troops in the Huallaga.

25. The best-known exception was in Puno, where a combination of strong social organizations, a church committed to the peasants, and political parties ready not to withdraw became for years the most important barrier to Shining Path in a zone that was crucial for them to control.

26. See Ernesto de la Jara, "Sendero en la orfandad," *Perú 1992: posibilidad y riesgo* (special edition of *Ideele*) (December 1992): 22–35.

27. Carlos Basombrío, "La estrategia del chino" in *Perú hoy: hacia el fin de la violencia sin fin,* special edition of *Ideele* (December 1993): 20–26.

28. Since 1993, and with the open sponsorship of the government, Abimael Guzmán, followed by the majority of the senderista leaders in jail, has been calling for a "peace accord" to put an end to the violence. That a man who had sent people to kill and to die the way he did has not been able to withstand the rigors of prison and has turned his personal defeat into a "political line" deserves further analysis. What is certain is that his change of heart created divisions within the organization. One part, those now following "Feliciano," decided to persevere in the armed option, making a difficult "theoretical" distinction between "Gonzalo thought" (Guzmán's earlier doctrine) and what Guzmán now maintains.

29. As part of its initial penetration strategy, Shining Path punished rustlers and adulterers, divided up properties of small businessmen hated by the peasants, and so on.

30. In 1993, in the Ayacucho provinces of Huanta, La Mar, and Huamanga alone, 100,000 peasants were organized in patrols; in Pasco and Junín there were probably 800 committees, bringing together 48,000 patrolmen. José Coronel, "Comités de Defensa Civil: un proceso social abierto" *Ideele,* no. 59–60 (December 1993):113–15.

31. They differ not just from the PACs (civil defense patrols) but from the entire paramilitarization process in rural Colombia.

32. However, the patrols and the civil defense committees pose crucial problems for the future: What will happen to the hundreds of thousands of armed peasants when Shining Path is no longer the reason for their existence? Are we at the threshold of an enormous process of democratization of the rural area fostered by them or a new militarization that could lead to new forms of violence?

33. With respect to Congress, there is a distorted image that it obstructed all government policies. Nothing could be further from the truth. In addition to the extraordinary powers already alluded to, it should be recalled that both the Chamber of Deputies and the Senate were headed by leaders of the Popular Christian Party (PPC). This political organization so closely identified with the policies then in practice that, a few months before the self-coup, Fujimori himself had attended a meeting at which he was acclaimed an "honorary PPC member."

34. In 1996 and above all in 1997, popular perceptions began to change. What is of interest here is that authoritarianism, which was viewed as necessary in 1992, was seen as the problem in 1997.

8

The Decimation of Peru's Sendero Luminoso

CYNTHIA MCCLINTOCK

Introduction

In contrast to the other national experiences analyzed in this book, in Peru there was no possibility of a peace process between the state and the Shining Path (Sendero Luminoso) movement. The most obvious reason was that Shining Path, intent on pursuing a revolutionary takeover, vehemently rejected dialogue with the Peruvian state. For their part, however, Peru's political leaders—including the political leaders from Peru's other Marxist parties—perceived Shining Path's ideas as wrong and its tactics as illegitimate.

Yet despite the absence of a peace process, the threat to the Peruvian state ended in September 1992 at the time of the capture of Shining Path's leader, Abimael Guzmán Reynoso, and gradually political violence declined.[1] In prison, Guzmán called for peace, and the other imprisoned senderistas heeded his call. Based primarily in coca-producing areas of the country such as the Upper Huallaga Valley, at-large senderistas continued to operate under the leadership of "Feliciano."[2] However, the possibility that the movement could ever again mount a serious threat to the Peruvian state appeared remote.

This chapter addresses the questions: In the absence of a peace process, how did Shining Path's decimation occur in Peru? And what were the implications of the political context of this decimation for democracy and political peace in Peru?

Here I indicate that a peace process, as defined by Cynthia Arnson in Chapter 1, was neither necessary nor desirable in Peru. Rather, in a process of trial and error, successive Peruvian governments gradually developed effective strategies for coping with the Sendero threat; at the same time, the evolving responses of other political actors as well as various inherent characteristics of the Sendero organization represented a confluence of circumstances that facilitated the defeat of Sendero. In other words, numerous actors deserve credit for Sendero's decimation.

Accordingly, this chapter refutes President Alberto Fujimori's appropriation of the defeat as his own personal accomplishment. Fujimori insists that his administration deserves exclusive credit for the defeat. He said in December 1991, for example: "The problem is that there was no intelligence before. In the past ten years Peru lost its intelligence service."[3] The Fujimori government even accused previous administrations of virtual complicity with the insurgency; on the government's video chronicling recent Peruvian history, it is stated: ". . . some political leaders for eleven years tolerated and even stimulated by their inaction terrorism and drug trafficking."[4] The president insists in particular that policies enabled by the *autogolpe* in April 1992 were necessary to the defeat of the guerrillas.[5] The facts, however, are otherwise.

This chapter also seconds the emphasis by Carlos Basombrío in Chapter 7 that some of the strategies Fujimori implemented against Sendero, in particular his judicial reform, were double-edged swords: On one hand, they facilitated the decimation of the group, but on the other hand, they were detrimental to human rights and democratization in Peru. It is suggested that, while it was important to implement a judicial process effective against terrorism, it was not necessary to eschew all considerations of due process.

The chapter begins by indicating the nature of the senderista organization and the reasons for its dramatic expansion during the late 1980s and early 1990s—which are essential to an understanding of why a peace process was not possible in the Peruvian case. This section of the chapter is based on the author's research, which appears in *Revolutionary Movements in Latin America: El Salvador's FMLN and Peru's Shining Path*.[6] The chapter then offers President Fujimori's own version of Sendero's decimation. Next, it documents the actual evolution of the policies that were in fact critical to the defeat: (1) the establishment of a new intelligence strategy by the antiterrorist unit of the Peruvian police; (2) renewed and, in some departments of the country, reformed efforts for the establishment of civil-defense patrols in peasant communities (*rondas*); and (3) judicial reform. It is found that these policies were not dramatic innovations by Fujimori but reinforcements or elaborations of policies initiated by his predecessors, in particular by President Alan García during his final year in office (the last six months of 1989 and the first six months of 1990).

The Sendero Luminoso Insurgency and Paths Toward Peace That Were Not Available in Peru

Until September 12, 1992, Shining Path posed an intense threat to the Peruvian state. More than 25,000 senderistas were prepared to undertake at least elementary military tasks.[7] Sendero was supported by approximately 15 percent of Peruvian citizens and controlled about 25 percent of the country's municipalities.[8] Sendero seemed to advance inexorably, reinforcing its image as "a winner"; starting in the remote southern highlands, it expanded to the coca-producing areas of Peru and into the central highlands, and ultimately to most of the country, including the capital city of Lima. Experts on the threat warned: ". . . the state is on the verge of defeat. The armed forces could tumble down at any moment" and "If they [the Shining Path] continue this way, they will be able to beat the Peruvian state."[9]

However, although in most respects Sendero Luminoso mounted a more intense threat to the state than did any other revolutionary movement discussed in this book with the exception of El Salvador's FMLN, it represented a different kind of threat and required a different kind of response by the state.[10] The key catalyst to most Latin American revolutionary movements, including those discussed in other chapters in this book, was political exclusion: The state sought to repress the political left in order to exclude it from the political arena. Accordingly, the key element of a successful peace process was a political opening by the regime. As a response to an insurgency, the state's political opening may at first be anathema to some officials, but once a decision is made toward this end, it is not inherently difficult to implement, and in the post–Cold War era it enjoys broad international support.

By contrast, political exclusion was not a factor in the emergence of Peru's Shining Path. The sine qua non in Peru's revolutionary equation was the nation's economic crisis. In sample surveys in Lima and in the central highlands in 1990, more than 60 percent of the respondents cited economic crisis, social injustice, or poverty as the principal cause of the guerrilla movement.[11] It is important to note that the economic problems in Peru were not "misery as usual"; rather, poverty between the late 1970s and early 1990s was demonstrably worse.[12]

In particular, poverty was worse among those who were already poor. Between 1971/1972 and 1983, average real household income fell by 29 percent for the poorest 25 percent of households in Peru.[13] Hunger was rampant. In 1988 Peru's daily supply of calories per person was merely 2,269, well below the regional average of 2,728; Peru was one of the few Latin American nations where daily calorie supply declined from the late 1950s or early 1960s to 1988.[14] Hunger was especially severe among the peasants in the rural highlands where Shining Path originated. In 1984, for example, chronic malnutrition was evident in more than 70 percent of the homes of subsistence peasants and day agricultural laborers in Peru.[15] Some Peruvians perceived their economic plight as so severe, and government responsibility for their plight so pronounced, that they would call the government "genocidal." Said one peasant, for example: "Here they've always forgotten us. There's no help. Exactly the opposite—the cost of everything has risen too much, and that's not the way to help. They're killing the poor people."[16] In other words, some peasants believed that the government had cast the first stone.

Not only was poverty severe among peasants, but the middle-class expectations of educated young people were dashed. There was an exceptionally dramatic increase in the number of young people gaining higher education in Peru. Between 1975 and the early 1990s, secondary-school enrollment increased by twenty-six percentage points in Peru, from 46 to 70 percent, versus 16 percentage points in the region as a whole.[17] Between 1980 and 1993 university enrollment skyrocketed by twenty-three percentage points, from 17 percent in 1980 to 40 percent in 1993, versus a scant one percentage point in the region as a whole, from 14 percent to 15 percent.[18]

However, the increase in educational achievement was not matched by an increase in professional employment or in wages. To the contrary. By one estimate, a scant 5 percent of Lima's economically active population was employed in 1990—down from more than 50 percent in the mid-1980s.[19] At the same time, salary trends in Peru were among the most negative in the region; as of 1989, the real minimum wage was only 23 percent of its 1980 value, relative to 75 percent in the region as a whole.[20] By

1991 the percentage was even lower: 16 percent of the 1980 value.[21] Among teachers, a group whom Sendero shrewdly targeted, salaries from 1988 to 1991 were only about $90 a month—less than a third of the levels from 1979 to 1982.[22]

Another important difference between the Peruvian case and others discussed in this book is the nature of the Shining Path movement. Relative to other recent Latin American experiences with guerrilla insurgency, the nature of the senderista organization was probably more important to the development of a strong revolutionary movement in Peru.[23] Sendero's fundamentalist ideology and organizational discipline were attractive to its supporters; Sendero combined the use of force, material benefits, and symbols to create a sense among Peruvians that it was a better, and more powerful, alternative to the Peruvian state. However, while Sendero's organization and strategy were compelling to certain Peruvians, they were repugnant to a much larger number, who deemed Sendero dogmatic, sectarian, and savage.

In any case, the kind of challenge that Sendero mounted against the Peruvian state was new, and accordingly, the identification of an effective response was difficult. To the extent that the appropriate response to an insurgency is to address its root causes, in Peru the appropriate response was to alleviate poverty. But there was a catch-22 to this response for the Peruvian state. In the context of the 1980s Latin American debt crisis, the international financial community would not support Peru financially until the country implemented neoliberal structural adjustment policies; but, of course, at least in the short run, these programs exacerbated poverty.[24]

In his presidential campaign and subsequently as president between 1985 and 1990, Alan García adamantly rejected the implementation of free-market policies and affirmed his commitment to state interventionism.[25] García sought a "developmentalist" response to Sendero: the stimulation of economic development in the remote rural areas of Peru where Sendero had gained strength.[26] The interest rate on Agrarian Bank loans in the southern highlands was reduced to zero, and the number and real value of Agrarian Bank loans more than doubled.[27] Public investment in Ayacucho approximately quadrupled between 1985 and 1986 to about $30 million.[28] In 1987 about 100,000 southern highland residents were provided jobs through a short-term public employment program.[29]

Ultimately, however, the economic aid effort failed to stop Sendero's expansion. There were two major reasons for this. First, to a degree that was unprecedented in Latin America and unanticipated by the García administration, Sendero physically attacked agronomists, engineers, and others who were trying to implement development programs as well as community leaders who worked with government officials.[30] In other words, in areas where Sendero already was entrenched, Peruvian governments could not take the developmentalist alternative because of the nature of the guerrilla organization itself. Second, amid the international financial community's repudiation of García's economic policies as well as mismanagement and corruption within his own administration, by late 1987 the national economy was in desperate straits and scant resources were available for development programs.

President Fujimori's Vision of the Path Toward Sendero's Defeat

This section describes Alberto Fujimori's perception of the route to Sendero's defeat. Here and in subsequent sections, it will be clear that, in significant respects, the envisioned path to Sendero's defeat was not the actual path and the first steps on the actual path were taken under preceding administrations.

For President Fujimori, the most critical component of a successful counterinsurgency strategy was the Servicio de Inteligencia Nacional (National Intelligence Service, the SIN).[31] Responding to a journalist's question "What is your [counterinsurgency] strategy then?" Fujimori answered, "As I have said several times, first you have to strengthen the intelligence service . . ."[32] "The intelligence service," he said, "is the only institution I trust."[33] A key effort was enhanced collaboration and even unification among the seven-odd intelligence services that had operated prior to 1990.[34] The de facto head of the SIN, Vladimiro Montesinos, has been one of Fujimori's closest advisors since 1990; by 1992 he was ranked the fourth most powerful person in Peru in the annual Apoyo poll, and by 1993 the second most powerful, a ranking he retained through 1997.[35]

Ultimately, what was the SIN's contribution to the decimation of Shining Path? As will be discussed, it was not the organization primarily responsible for the capture of Abimael Guzmán, although in certain respects it helped. Nor was it responsible for the development of the *rondas* (civil defense patrols) policy. As Carlos Basombrío mentions in Chapter 7, the SIN's most important role may have been in the psychological campaign that intensified Senderistas' demoralization after the capture and also prompted the imprisoned Guzmán to call for an end to armed struggle. Otherwise, the role of the SIN appears to have been first and foremost what President Fernando Belaúnde feared when he dismantled it: espionage against political opponents.[36]

Fujimori also sought a more collaborative relationship between the executive and the military. Said the president: "I like to get things done, to execute things, and that's why I like working with the military."[37] On another occasion he declared, "When I am with the Armed Forces I feel like a soldier. It is in my nature. . . . If I had not been a mathematician or an engineer, I would have been a soldier."[38] The political power of Fujimori's and Montesinos's military ally, General Nicolás de Bari Hermoza, gradually increased. Although not ranked among the top ten most powerful persons in Peru in 1990 or 1991, Hermoza became army commander in 1992 and rose to the number-seven position that year; in 1993 he reached the number-three position, which he retained through 1995.[39]

Given the situation in Peru in the early 1990s, the obvious route to smooth cooperation between the civilian and military leadership was toleration of the military's human rights abuses. The civilian leadership's efforts to control human rights violations under President García had infuriated many military officers.[40] By contrast, in late 1990 Fujimori signaled his toleration of violations by backing the promotions of various generals who displayed questionable respect for human rights when they had been directing counterinsurgency efforts.[41] In July 1991 a Peruvian television network revealed a secret army intelligence document concluding "The best subversive is a dead subversive; thus, no prisoners will be held."[42] At about the same time, the army commander in the central highlands said, "The State Department is defending the terrorists by talking about human rights."[43] Although the number of forced disappearances decreased, the number of extrajudicial assassinations doubled between 1989 and 1992.[44]

Various extrajudicial assassinations were particularly notorious. These included the November 1991 killings of at least fifteen people at a fundraising barbecue in Barrios Altos, a poor downtown district of Lima; the June 1992 assassination of a professor and nine students from the La Cantuta University in Lima; and the disappearances of more than thirty-six students from the Universidad del Centro in Huancayo within a few months after July 1992. It was widely believed that these killings and others—for a total of more than 100 between 1991 and 1993—were perpetrated by a twenty- to twenty-five man death squad operating under the auspices of the army's intelligence unit and/or the SIN (the Grupo Colina).[45] The fact that most of these assassinations occurred after April 1992 provoked speculation that, with the *autogolpe,* hard-liners had consolidated their power and the new regime's counterinsurgency strategy was to be highly repressive.[46]

Ultimately, what was the military's contribution to the decimation of the insurgency? As will be discussed, the military's played an important role. However, the critical factor was the intensification of the *rondas* policy that had been initiated under President García. In most parts of the country, the *rondas* succeeded not because of repression—the option apparently favored by the hard-liners leading the *autogolpe* effort—but because of civic action programs and a shift in peasant attitudes against Sendero.

The Capture of Abimael Guzmán

The capture of Abimael Guzmán and key Senderista lieutenants in September 1992 was the turning point in the anti-Sendero effort—"a devastating blow" against the movement.[47] Not only was Guzmán captured, but some twelve of Sendero's nineteen Central Committee members were arrested either with Guzmán in his hideout during the raid or a few weeks later as a result of information gained at the hideout.[48] Further, the bonanza of information from computerized files and diskettes at the safe house facilitated the capture of hundreds of mid-level militants, not only in Lima but throughout the country.[49] The police group that initiated the successful intelligence strategy and that carried out the capture was the GEIN (Grupo Especial de Inteligencia), a small, elite squad within Peru's antiterrorist police called the DINCOTE (Dirección Nacional Contra el Terrorismo).[50] Three points about this capture are important to note.

First, the capture was achieved by the DINCOTE and its GEIN—not by Fujimori's favored intelligence unit, the SIN. Of course, in Fujimori's plan, the SIN was to have coordinated the capture. Fujimori and his top security advisors expressed intense resentment that they were not informed of the impending capture and accordingly could not be present at the event to take direct credit and bask in the media glory. They vented their resentment by summarily transferring most of the top officials in DINCOTE and the GEIN to relatively unimportant positions soon after the capture.

Second, the GEIN, the group that masterminded the capture, was established in March 1990—in the final months of the García government.[51]

GEIN leadership and strategy were constant from the group's inception under García through the capture in September 1992.

A third important point to note is that intelligence and the capture of Sendero's leader was not an obvious route to the defeat of the insurgency. Only gradually did the nature of the Sendero organization became evident and did the capture of its number-one leader become clearly important. Rarely has the capture of a revolutionary leader been a critical event in Latin America.[52] In most Latin American revolutionary movements, the organization was less hierarchical and leaders were replaceable; by contrast, Guzmán was a "philosopher-king," a virtual deity revered by his disciples—and a deity whose claims to the truth and to invincibility would be shattered by his capture.

Capturing a revolutionary leader was not only usually less important than in Peru but also more difficult. Many key revolutionary leaders lived outside their home country for considerable periods of time; when they returned, they resided in rural areas where their organizations enjoyed widespread support and where their comings and goings could be well protected. By contrast, when Guzmán moved to Lima in the late 1980s, none of these conditions applied. But the intelligence apparatus that captured Guzmán has been unable to snare his successor, "Feliciano," who probably resides in rural areas in the remote Upper Huallaga Valley where the movement remains strong.

It also should be noted that, given numerous historical precedents, democratic governments such as Peru's during the 1980s have good reason to fear that military intelligence units will not operate according to democratic principles; thus their reluctance to strengthen these units is understandable. During the 1960s Peru's military intelligence units had acted against civilian political leaders—and this precedent was probably uppermost in President Belaúnde's mind when he dismantled those units shortly after becoming president in 1980. In any case, in July 1985, at the end of the Belaúnde administration, Peru's antiterrorist intelligence capability was minimal.[53] The antiterrorist police recorded intelligence by memory or at best handwritten in notebooks.[54]

By contrast, the need for intelligence was keenly apparent to Alan García. During his electoral campaign in 1985 and also during his presidency, García repeated that enhanced intelligence against Sendero and the capture of Guzmán in particular were key priorities.[55] As president, García was quickly at odds with the Peruvian military; however, working with his close friend Agustín Mantilla at the Interior Ministry, García established a cooperative relationship with the police. Gradually the antiterrorist police unit's resources and staff were augmented.[56]

The development of appropriate tactics for the antiterrorist police was difficult. Approaches such as the infiltration of Sendero were considered but did not prove viable; Shining Path's mechanisms for spotting infiltrators and spies were well developed, and new members were required to submit to a long period of probation, during which they had to commit crimes. Also, one of Guzmán's key tactics was to limit the information that each member had about his superiors in the organization; accordingly, even if a senderista succumbed to torture, there was little that the militant could reveal.

The antiterrorist police unit's first widely acclaimed achievement was the June 1988 capture of Osmán Morote, the number-two senderista leader at the time. Morote, four colleagues, and forty notebooks including details about Sendero's organization and debates were seized at a hideout in Lima. In February 1989, primarily in a stroke of good luck, police also arrested Víctor Polay Campos, the head of MRTA at the time, at the Hotel de Turistas in Huancayo.

In March 1990 Interior Minister Mantilla authorized the formation of the twenty-seven-person GEIN and charged it with the mission of capturing Guzmán and other top senderista leaders. A key impetus to the formation of the GEIN came from the man who was to be its leader, Benedicto Jiménez Baca, who had worked within the antiterrorist police unit for many years but had become dissatisfied with DINCOTE. Jiménez apparently considered DINCOTE insufficiently professional; by 1990 it employed hundreds of police, and many analysts perceived it as unwieldy and perhaps even infiltrated by Sendero and vulnerable to leaks.[57] Jiménez was a police officer from humble origins who rose within the force through diligent study and hard work.[58]

The key principle guiding the GEIN was the concentration of its effort against the apex of the senderista hierarchy. The conventional norm for the Peruvian antiterrorist police was to seize senderista suspects as quickly as possible and interrogate them, hoping to gain information from them about their leaders' whereabouts. This strategy was flawed not only for ethical reasons, but, as noted earlier, because Guzmán's hideouts were known to only a few other top leaders. The GEIN's strategy was not to seize suspects immediately but rather to track them, believing that eventually their trails would lead to Guzmán. At times this strategy was at odds with the political goals of higher-level officials, who wanted demonstrable results that their counterinsurgency strategy was succeeding—demonstrable results in the form of captured militants. GEIN police were taunted as "followers of phantoms."[59] It was true, however, that a key challenge for the GEIN was to determine when it had gained as much information as was possible from surveillance and accordingly arrest was appropriate.

The GEIN's first major intelligence breakthrough was the seizure of a safe house in the wealthy suburb of Monterrico on June 1, 1990. By tracking various senderista suspects, the GEIN had identified a network of numerous likely safe houses. Supported by other DINCOTE agents, the GEIN broke into them; one turned out to be a senderista headquarters. The GEIN gained many valuable documents: numerous identity cards, reports of meetings, and letters written to Guzmán by new senderista recruits that included their real names as well as their pseudonyms and their addresses. This information facilitated various important arrests, including that of a Central Committee member in September.[60] Numerous personal belongings of Guzmán were found as well: a pair of his glasses, medicines, and writings. The GEIN had missed Guzmán himself by less than a week.[61]

However, the success at the Monterrico safe house did not boost the GEIN's stature. Of course, Guzmán himself was still at large. Many DINCOTE officials disparaged the GEIN as "Mantilla's guys."[62] In the first year and a half of the Fujimori government, there were several changes in DINCOTE's leadership; as noted, the government sought to centralize intelligence information in the SIN, and the ensuing turf battles between DINCOTE heads and de facto head of the SIN Vladimiro Montesinos and/or army commander General Nicolás Hermoza led to turnover at the apex of DINCOTE.[63] When General Ketín Vidal (DINCOTE's head at the time of the capture) was appointed in November 1991, it was—ironically, as things turned out—in part because he enjoyed a good working relationship with Montesinos.[64] However, none of these turf battles significantly affected the GEIN, which maintained the same personnel and strategies as under the García government.

The GEIN's second breakthrough was the discovery of a safe house at 265 Buenavista Street in another wealthy suburb, Chacarilla del Estanque, on January 31, 1991. Following in particular the trail of a senderista whom they called "Sotil" ("The Subtle One," whose real name was Luis Alberto Arana Franco and who appeared to manage legitimate academies, which were actually institutions for guerrilla training), the GEIN had identified the house as a likely senderista hideout by mid-November. The GEIN observed preparations for a celebration there in late November but unfortunately decided to wait to break into the house, and Guzmán celebrated his birthday there on December 3. When they did finally enter, they found a treasure: videotapes of the funeral of Guzmán's wife, Augusta La Torre, that showed a drunken Guzmán dancing with other key Central Committee members. Not only did the videotapes facilitate further captures, but they tarnished Guzmán's image as a philosopher-king.

Still, it was to be more than eighteen months until Guzmán himself finally was captured. Apparently DINCOTE chief Vidal, a man widely described as cautious and prudent, feared that another raid that failed to capture the senderista leader would reinforce Guzmán's image as invincible.[65]

In any case, the key GEIN decision was the arrest of "Sotil" in June 1992. The GEIN had been following "Sotil" for more than two years but had not arrested him because his tracks had led to so many other senderistas. By June 1992 the GEIN had assembled enormous quantities of taped telephone conversations and videotapes that proved his militancy in Sendero. Apparently after "Sotil's" capture, Jiménez promised that, if he provided valuable information, he would be helped under the terms of the "repentance law" (see below) that was being implemented at about this time.[66] "Sotil" revealed that he had been taken to a meeting with Guzmán the previous month; although he had been blindfolded and did not know the precise location of the safe house, he pointed the GEIN to its general area. "Sotil" also may have denounced as a senderista Maritza Garrido-Lecca, the ballet teacher at whose home in the Los Sauces neighborhood Guzmán was hiding at the time of his arrest.[67]

As of approximately July, the GEIN began to watch Maritza's house. Numerous anomalies were apparent; but the house seemed too small for both Maritza and her husband as well as Guzmán and his colleagues. Finally, however, Winston Light cigarettes—the same brand as had been discovered at the Buenavista house—in the rubbish bin convinced Jiménez otherwise. On September 12, 1992, after informing Vidal, Jiménez directed the successful raid on the Los Sauces house. No blood was spilled, and Guzmán was taken to DINCOTE headquarters.

Vidal did not inform Fujimori that the capture was likely to be imminent, and the president was out of Lima fishing.[68] At the time, credit for the capture was taken almost exclusively by Vidal and DINCOTE; neither Vidal nor the GEIN acknowledged any role for the SIN or for the United States. Not surprisingly, Fujimori was furious that he was not present and could not make his claim to be directing the counterinsurgency struggle and building new, effective counterinsurgency institutions.

The truth of the matter appears to be that the SIN did indeed play a role in the capture. Ironically, however, this role is not on the public record, and the SIN does not want to acknowledge it publicly in any case: It consisted of the securing of substantial support for the GEIN from the United States government, in particular from the Central Intelligence Agency (CIA). A relationship between Peru's antidrug police and the CIA had begun as early as 1986; it seems probable that the CIA provided support for the GEIN from its very inception.[69] However, when Montesinos emerged at the apex of the SIN, he was able to secure considerably more resources for the GEIN as well as some training.[70] The resources included funds as well as equipment, in particular sophisticated cameras, video recorders, and listening devices. Also, the SIN might have been the architect of a deception strategy that aimed to reinforce Guzmán's overconfidence about his invulnerability and induce him to lower his guard; the false rumor was spread to the Peruvian media that the police thought Guzmán was in Bolivia.[71] At the same time, however, some Peruvian analysts believe that the SIN's role was more negative than positive—constantly prodding DINCOTE for more "results," more quickly, and seeking to bring DINCOTE's activities under the SIN's own control.[72]

The Establishment of *Rondas Campesinas*

In the Peruvian countryside, the most important measure in the decimation of Sendero was the establishment of *rondas*.[73] However, just as the other measures discussed in this chapter were not new Fujimori initiatives in the wake of the *autogolpe*, *rondas* were a strategy analyzed and implemented by both Presidents Belaúnde and García. Although there were some important innovative dimensions to the *rondas* policy under Fujimori, the key difference in the relative success of the policy under different presidents appears to be not the policy itself but the degree to which peasants accepted it. More precisely, by the early 1990s more peasants in highland communities were turning against the guerrilla movements and accordingly were more inclined to collaborate in the *rondas*.[74] The shift toward repudiation of Sendero among many peasant communities in Peru contrasts with the continuation of support for revolutionary movements among peasant communities in Guatemala and El Salvador, and this difference is the most important factor explaining the relative success of *rondas* in Peru vs. their relative failure in the Central American countries.[75]

When the Belaúnde government first sought to establish *rondas* in the early 1980s, the policy was largely disastrous. In many communities, there was considerable peasant support for Sendero; soldiers were unable to distinguish pro-senderista peasants from anti-senderista peasants, and often indiscriminately abused community members. In 1983 and 1984 more "forced disappearances" were recorded than in any other years except 1989.[76] The prevailing result in these communities was intense resentment against the security forces and stronger support for Sendero.[77] However, it is important to note that in some communities where support for Sendero was scant, or where peasants had already turned against the guerrilla organization, Belaúnde's *rondas* policy was in fact effective.[78]

As would be expected, the overall failure of this *rondas* policy gave subsequent policymakers pause. Concerns about the policy arose virtually across the political spectrum. Many analysts feared that peasants might use their weapons against rival communities and that Sendero would immediately target the *rondas,* reducing the *ronderos* to cannon fodder.[79] Among leftist political leaders in particular, the precedents in Guatemala and El Salvador were not encouraging; they feared what was called "militarization"—in particular, peasant communities' subordination to military authority.[80] For their part, many military officers feared that peasants did not oppose Sendero and might use their weapons for rather than against revolutionary groups.[81]

Accordingly, when García began to promote *rondas* vigorously in approximately 1989, he did so despite considerable military opposition.[82] Just like other advocates of *rondas,* García argued that peasants had a right to defend themselves in what was a war first and foremost against them.[83] The president's first major public demonstration of his support for the *rondas* was his giving of his pistol to "Comandante Huayhuaco," who had organized *rondas,* in Ayacucho in December 1989.[84]

Gradually, given that García's *rondas* policy seemed to be working, Fujimori promoted it more vigorously. Initiated in the southern highlands departments of Ayacucho and Apurímac, the policy was extended to the central highlands and other parts of Peru. As of mid-1993 there were more than 4,000 *rondas* including approximately 300,000 members, to whom roughly 10,000 rifles had been given.[85] Whereas in the late 1980s the military had provided peasants only shotguns, in the early 1990s better firearms, such as old Winchester and Mauser rifles, were distributed. Perhaps Fujimori's most important innovation with respect to the policy was soldiers' provision of much more resources—food, medicine, and civic action projects—which in many communities facilitated the development of collaboration between the peasants and the soldiers.[86]

However, although the scholarly consensus has been that the large-scale establishment of *rondas* in the late 1980s and early 1990s was critical to the decimation of Sendero, in some areas more than in others, analysts' original concerns about the *rondas* were proven valid. In many communities, the military did compel peasants' participation; peasants who refused to serve as *ronderos* were considered subversives and often executed (at times by other *ronderos*).[87] Military imposition seemed to be more common in the central highlands near Huancayo than in the southern highlands.[88]

Moreover, as of 1996, military bases remained in many parts of the Peruvian highlands. The Peruvian military continued its surveillance of *rondas*. It seems unlikely that the military's role does not compromise the democratic autonomy of highlands peasant communities.

Judicial Reform

Judicial reform was a third change that was important to the decimation of Sendero.[89] In contrast to the establishment of the GEIN and of the *rondas*, implementation of changes in Peru's antiterrorist laws did not occur until Fujimori's administration. In the late 1980s President García had authorized significant changes, but these were not implemented. Unfortunately for Peru's democratic process, however, the legal changes Fujimori initiated facilitated the conviction not only of several thousand suspects who were senderistas but also more than 1,000 innocent persons.

In other Latin American countries, there was not a clear pattern of judicial failure to convict persons who were guilty of terrorism. In Peru, however, new challenges to the judicial process were raised by the nature of the senderista organization. In particular, the senderistas worked hard to maintain their identities clandestine, and most of their military actions were hit-and-run terrorist attacks rather than conventional combat. Also, to a greater degree than in other Latin American nations, Sendero delegated the actual carrying out of attacks to new recruits, forced recruits, or even innocent children who did not know that what they had been asked to carry was a bomb. Accordingly, whereas for conviction of a guerrilla suspect Peruvian law required—logically enough—evidence that the suspect had himself or herself committed a crime, such evidence often was dif-

ficult to impossible to gather against senderista leaders.[90] The vast majority of terrorist cases did not even come to trial because judges ruled that
there was "insufficient evidence to proceed."[91]

The senderista guerrillas posed new challenges to Peru's judicial process
for other reasons as well. In contrast to most Latin American guerrilla
groups, Sendero had no compunctions about the intimidation and assassination of unarmed civilian judges. Also, as a result of its activities in the
coca-producing regions of Peru, Sendero enjoyed an unusually large war
chest, which it used to bribe judges.

For these various reasons, of 4,158 terrorist suspects brought before the
Peruvian courts between 1981 and 1990, only 985 were tried; of these,
635 were absolved and a scant 350 were convicted.[92] In other words, only
12 percent of the total number of suspects were convicted. In a report for
1988, merely 5 to 10 percent of suspected terrorists were convicted.[93] Presumably many—perhaps most—of the released suspects were in fact guilty.

Not only did the obstacles to conviction embolden Sendero, but they
often were a factor prompting human rights violations by military officers.
Explained one human rights activist:

> Human rights violations often stem from a combination of frustra-
> tion and fear. Say I'm an officer and I have a battle with Shining Path
> and I arrest 15 guerrillas . . . I know that if I take them to the judge,
> they're going to go in one door and out the other, because the jus-
> tice system doesn't work. Then, I know that while they're in custody
> they're going to start claiming "human rights" and they might say
> something that would screw up my career. And finally, I know that
> Shining Path believes in revenge, and if I send these people to jail
> they might come after my children, my wife, or me. So I kill every-
> body. No witnesses.[94]

Often President Fujimori suggested that his administration was the first
to be concerned about Peru's judicial process.[95] This suggestion is false. As
early as 1981, the Belaúnde government established a new antiterrorist law
(Legislative Decree No. 046), that established a framework for terrorist
cases and penalties against convicted terrorists—none of which existed in
Peru's 1924 penal code.[96] Especially given that Peru had only just
emerged from twelve years of military government and that the nature of
the Sendero organization was not yet widely understood, there was serious
concern at the time that even Legislative Decree No. 046 restricted civil
liberties.[97]

President García also was concerned about the effectiveness of Peru's judicial process for terrorist cases.[98] In June 1987, in Law 24,700, he authorized sweeping judicial changes.[99] While maintaining key elements of due process, the law enabled the establishment of special tribunals for cases of terrorism, in which greater protection would be provided for judges.[100] But these were not implemented. Apparently the reforms were opposed by Peru's Supreme Court and by the National Association of Magistrates, which doubted that the protection for the special tribunal judges would be sufficient and accordingly feared that they would become easy targets for the terrorists. Further, both Law 24,700 and its 1989 successor, Law 25,103, included provisions for repentance; a "repentant" terrorist could receive clemency in return for information leading to the arrest of other terrorists. Again, however, the repentance provisions were not implemented. García also may have tried, but failed, to make membership in a guerrilla movement a crime.[101]

Why did so little come of García's initiatives?[102] Probably blame should be shouldered in part by García, who did not push hard enough for them; by leftist opposition political parties and human rights groups who backed the reforms but again did not push very hard for them; and most of all the judges themselves, who should have developed a deeper dialogue with the executive about their concerns—for example, indicating that without an easier burden of proof in terrorism cases, judges in special tribunals would be too vulnerable to senderista reprisals. Further, many military officers doggedly sought military jurisdiction for cases of terrorism as well as the death penalty and rejected García's compromise measures.[103]

Without judicial reform, large numbers of probable guerrillas continued to be released, and gradually debate about new antiterrorist legislation increased.[104] During the 1990 presidential campaign, the FREDEMO (Frente Democrático, a coalition of parties that supported Mario Vargas Llosa's candidacy) prepared a judicial reform proposal that included harsher sentences, repentance provisions, broader definitions of terrorist crime (especially to enable the conviction of the "intellectual authors" of terrorist crimes), and a vague "special process for the investigation and judging of terrorist acts."[105] Accordingly, the FREDEMO coalition, which enjoyed a plurality in the post-1990 Congress, favored judicial changes. In January 1991 the president of the Supreme Court prepared a bill that sought to provide greater protection for the judges of cases of terrorism, including in particular a provision to keep their identities secret.[106] In April 1991 the directors of Peru's most influential print media, including the heads of *El Comercio, Expreso,* and *La República* newspapers, and *Caretas* magazine, proposed harsher sentences, lower age thresholds for prosecutions, and the "simplification" of judicial processes.[107]

Astoundingly, however, President Fujimori ignored these apparently logical responses to the problems posed for Peru's judicial process by Sendero. Until November 1991 (more than a year into his first term), no legislation was introduced despite the fact that provisions in the 1979 constitution allowed the executive to issue decrees in any policy area if authority were so delegated to it by the legislature; this authority had been so delegated to Fujimori.[108] Perhaps Fujimori did not propose legislation because, to justify his *autogolpe,* he wanted to be able to charge the legislature with do-nothingism as well as obstructionism.[109]

Only as Fujimori's authority was about to expire in November 1991 did he issue an avalanche of some 126 decree laws. In a special session two months later, the legislature approved 78 percent of these laws but repealed 22 percent of them. Most of the repealed laws concerned counterinsurgency. However, many severely restricted civil liberties; one, for example, would have banned the publication of any information deemed secret by the government, imposing sentences of five to ten years in prison for offenders.[110] Still, the impasse was overcome; in March 1992 negotiations between the executive and the legislature continued, and agreements between Fujimori's prime minister and legislative leaders were to be submitted for congressional approval on approximately April 7. The *autogolpe* occurred on April 5.

Between April 5 and August 1992, Fujimori introduced draconian new antiterrorist legislation.[111] Whereas under the previous antiterrorist legislation, the problem was the release of many actual guerrillas, under Fujimori's decrees the problem was the reverse: the conviction of many innocent persons. By December 1996, when an estimated 5,000 persons had been jailed for crimes of terrorism since 1992, Peru's national coordinator of human rights estimated that 1,504, or about 30 percent, were probably innocent.[112] In 1996 Human Rights Watch/Americas called for the review of more than 5,000 cases of convictions for terrorism.[113]

Under the new legislation, there has essentially been a presumption of guilt.[114] DINCOTE was granted extraordinarily broad powers in investigating and charging suspects. Trials were secret and procedures summary. The rights of the defense were drastically reduced: Access to the evidence presented against defendants was prohibited; cross-examination of prosecution witnesses also was prohibited; and at times defense counsel were notified of the time of a trial only hours before it was to occur. Judges were "faceless": Their faces were covered by large masks and their voices distorted. Minimum sentences of not less than twenty years' imprisonment were mandated.

Perhaps the most widely repudiated change was the decree that crimes of "treason against the mother country" (*traición a la patria*) be tried in military courts. The crime of treason was not precisely defined; even distributing Shining Path propaganda could be classified as "treason."[115] The responsibility for distinguishing between the lesser crime of terrorism (tried under the provisions indicated above but in civilian courts) and the crime of "treason" was given to DINCOTE rather than to the judiciary. An overwhelming 97 percent of suspects tried in military courts were convicted.[116]

Another extremely controversial change was the new repentance law. By June 1994 more than 4,100 former guerrillas apparently had "repented": provided information about the guerrilla organization, usually information that would lead to the arrest of other guerrillas, in exchange for shorter sentences or even pardons.[117] Many senderistas who believed both that the organization's opportunity to win power ended with the capture of Guzmán and that a former comrade might betray them to the authorities repented. However, many of the persons denounced by repentants were in fact innocent—denounced only because of a personal vendetta with the repentant or even, in some cases, because they had been especially hostile to Sendero.[118]

Conclusion

As Carlos Basombrió analyzes more fully in chapter 7, the decimation of Sendero Luminoso occurred amid the personalization and centralization of power in Peru. President Fujimori often cited his administration's achievements against the insurgency as evidence of the need and efficacy of "strong" government in Peru.

However, the actual facts of the defeat do not support Fujimori's interpretation. The pivotal event in the government's counterinsurgency effort, the capture of Guzmán, was carried out by the GEIN, a small, specialized unit within DINCOTE that had been established in March 1990 under the García administration. The institution that Fujimori touted as most significant to the counterinsurgency effort—the SIN—played a role in the capture and in the demoralization of the guerrilla organization in the aftermath of the capture—but only a secondary role. Similarly, President

García made the decision to promote the establishment of *rondas* in the countryside over considerable military opposition. A government that was only seeking support from the Peruvian military might not have tried to implement *rondas*. The *rondas* policy was successful in 1989 and thereafter—as it had not been during the Belaúnde government—for a confluence of reasons: In many areas of the country, soldiers exhibited greater respect for human rights; more emphasis was placed on civic action programs; and among Peru's peasants, there was more widespread rejection of Shining Path. Finally, although Fujimori was clearly the first president to implement judicial reform, proposals for changes in antiterrorist legislation were made by previous presidents as well as by various political actors during the first twenty months of Fujimori's presidency—proposals that might have enabled not only more effective but also fair trials. Of the various policies that the Fujimori government implemented against terrorism, the draconian judicial reform was particularly antithetical to democratic principles.

The decimation of Sendero Luminoso was an achievement that could have been celebrated as the culmination of the efforts of many diverse actors. It could have been cause for national pride and national reconciliation—similar in some respects to a peace process in other nations. Amid the celebration and reconciliation, a valid analysis of the reasons behind Sendero's original expansion might have been thrashed out among Peruvian intellectuals as well as citizens; and, of course, when history is understood, it is less likely to be repeated.[119] Unfortunately, none of this was to be. The achievement was appropriated for the partisan objectives of President Fujimori. By this action, Fujimori reinforced authoritarian and personalist tendencies—in particular, Peruvians' tendency to pin all their hopes on one person or one party as Peru's "savior."[120]

Moreover, although Shining Path and the MRTA were decimated in Peru, the root causes provoking the rage that these movements channeled were not fully addressed. Coincidentally, the decimation of the insurgencies coincided with Peru's reinsertion into the international financial community; as new international loans and investment were forthcoming, the Peruvian economy rebounded. However, severe poverty and inequality endured. At the threshold of the twenty-first century, there is no clearer consensus about the path toward the resolution of these economic problems than there was during the 1980s. Until these economic problems are ameliorated, however, the breeding ground of Peruvians' anger remains fertile.[121]

Notes

1. Whereas the number of deaths attributed to Shining Path averaged more than 2,250 per year between 1989 and 1992, the number was about 300 in 1996, according to data in Isaías Rojas Pérez, "Sendero y el MRTA después de la crisis," *Ideele* 98(1997):53.

2. The real name of "Feliciano" is Oscar Alberto Ramírez Durand. The son of an Arequipa-based army general, he joined Shining Path during the 1970s. One of the five members of Sendero's "political bureau" at the time of Guzmán's capture, he is one of the few original Shining Path leaders still at large.

3. Jonathan Cavanagh, "Political Interview," *The Peru Report*, 5(December 1991):3.

4. Comments by the narrator of the video *Tres Años Que Cambiaron La Historia* (Lima: Edimovie S.A., 1993). The video is a political history of Peru according to the Fujimori government.

5. Among many statements by Fujimori to this effect, see his affirmation to Panamericana television that "There was a political system that had led the country to poverty and to stagnation by various means, be they economic problems, corruption in the judicial branch, or terrorism. I believe . . . that the drastic measures that were adopted were necessary. "Reported in *Foreign Broadcast Information Service*, Latin America, 92–211, October 30, 1992, 35.

6. Cynthia McClintock, *Revolutionary Movements in Latin America: El Salvador's FMLN and Peru's Shining Path* (Washington, D.C.: U.S. Institute of Peace Press, 1998). The research includes thirty-three interviews with senderistas, various formal and informal surveys among citizens, and the analysis of political-violence data (collected primarily by the U.S. Department of State and human rights organizations in Peru and the United States) and economic data (published primarily by the World Bank and the Inter-American Development Bank).

7. Carlos Tapia, *Las Fuerzas Armadas y Sendero Luminoso* (Lima: Instituto de Estudios Peruanos, 1997), 111–112. As Tapia suggests, the lines between senderista militant, combatant, and well-armed and well-trained combatant are difficult to draw.

8. Data for Lima in Carmen Rosa Balbi, "A Disturbing Opinion Poll," *QueHacer* 72(1991):40–45; for cities nationwide, *F.A.S. Public Interest Report* 45(1992):9; for towns and rural areas, Simon Strong, *Terror and Revolution in Peru* (New York: Random House, 1992), 109, and "The Political Report," *The Peru Report* 6(1992):3. For comprehensive discussion of this controversial point, see McClintock, *Revolutionary Movements*, chap. 2.

9. Charles Lane et al., "Peru: Into the Cross Fire," *Newsweek*, August 19, 1991, 29. James Brooke, "Marxist Revolt Grows Strong in the Shantytowns of Peru," *New York Times*, November 11, 1991, A1.

10. This theme is elaborated in McClintock, *Revolutionary Movements*. The point was also made by Alberto Bolívar Ocampo, presentation to the Inter-American Council, Washington, D.C., April 30, 1997.

11. McClintock, *Revolutionary Movements*, chap. 6, table 6.2. The second most-cited reason was "bad government," mentioned by 20 percent of the respondents in Lima and 8 percent in the central highlands. By contrast, only about 35 percent of Salvadoran respondents cited economic problems as the principal cause of the guerrilla movement.

12. Some scholars, such as Theda Skocpol, underestimate the possible role of economic factors in revolutionary movements by considering poverty a constant. See Theda Skocpol, *States and Social Revolutions* (New York: Cambridge University Press, 1979), 115.

13. World Bank, "Peru: Country Economic Memorandum 1985," *The Andean Report*, special suppl. (Washington, D.C.: World Bank, 1985): 169.

14. McClintock, *Revolutionary Movements*, chap. 4, table 4.6. These data are from the World Bank, *Social Indicators of Development 1990* (Baltimore: Johns Hopkins University Press, 1991), 89, 93, and 245. Further data on this point are provided in McClintock, *Revolutionary Movements*, chap. 4.

15. William P. Mitchell, *Peasants on the Edge: Crop, Cult, and Crisis in the Andes* (Austin: University of Texas Press, 1991), 128.

16. Interview with a peasant by the author's research team, near Virú, Peru, August 1983.

17. For figures for Peru, see World Bank, *Social Indicators of Development 1993* (Baltimore: Johns Hopkins University Press, 1993), 263; regional average calculated for the twenty nations for which information was available in this volume and also in World Bank, *Social Indicators of Development 1998* (Baltimore: Johns Hopkins University Press, 1988).

18. World Bank, *World Development Report* (New York: Oxford University Press, 1994 and 1996 eds.), 216–17 and 200–1 respectively.

19. Instituto Cuánto, *Ajuste y Economía Familiar 1985–1990* (Lima: Cuánto, 1991), 30.

20. Inter-American Development Bank, *Economic and Social Progress in Latin America* (Washington, D.C.: Johns Hopkins University Press, 1990), 28.

21. Richard Webb and Graciela Fernández Baca, *Perú en Números 1992* (Lima: Cuánto, 1992), 524.

22. Figures on the absolute salary are in Hernando Burgos, "Adiós a las Aulas: Del Ajuste Económico al "Shock" Educativo," *QueHacer* 73(1991):42, among other sources; figures on the decline are provided in Juan Ansión, Daniel Del Castillo, Manuel Piqueras, and Isaura Zegarra, *La Escuela en Tiempos de Guerra* (Lima: Centro de Estudios y Acción para la Paz, 1992), 44.

23. For a particularly strong statement of this view, see Gustavo Gorriti, *Sendero: Historia de la guerra milenaria en el Perú* (Lima: Apoyo, 1990), 172. Moderate emphasis is put on Sendero's "political will" ("voluntarism") by Carlos Iván Degregori, "The Origins and Logic of Shining Path: Two Views," in David Scott Palmer, ed., *The Shining Path of Peru* (New York: St. Martin's Press, 1992), 51–62, and David Scott Palmer, "The Revolutionary Terrorism of Peru's Shining Path," in Martha Crenshaw, ed., *Terrorism in Context* (University Park: Pennsylvania State University Press, 1995), 253.

24. An excellent overview of the Peruvian economy in the context of the international economy in the 1980s and early 1990s is Efraín Gonzales de Olarte, ed., *The Peruvian Economy and Structural Adjustment: Past, Present, and Future* (Miami, Fla.: North-South Center Press, University of Miami, 1996).

25. Among other analyses, see Philip Mauceri, *Militares: insurgencia y democratización en el Perú, 1980–1988* (Lima: Instituto de Estudios Peruanos, 1989), 50–56, and John Crabtree, *Peru under García: An Opportunity Lost* (Pittsburgh: Pittsburgh University Press, 1992), 45–58 and 108–112.

26. Ibid.

27. Webb and Fernández, *Perú en Números,* 436.

28. Central Reserve Bank, *Ayuda Memoria* (Lima: Central Reserve Bank, 1986).

29. Central Reserve Bank, *Programa de Apoyo al Ingreso Temporal (PAIT)* (Lima: Central Reserve Bank, 1987).

30. Mauceri, *Militares,* 55–56; Crabtree, *Peru under García,* 55; Carlos Bendezu (director of CORFA), interview with author, Ayacucho, Peru, November 22, 1987.

31. The SIN includes the intelligence services of the various military services as well as of the police and the foreign ministry; it was under the jurisdiction of the presidency.

32. Jonathan Cavanagh, "Political Interview," *The Peru Report* 5(December 1991):2.

33. James Brooke, "Peru's Leader Clears a Path with Sharp Elbows," *New York Times,* February 22, 1993, A3.

34. Mariella Balbi, interview with Enrique Obando, "El campo dió la espalda a Sendero," *La República,* February 16, 1992, 11.

35. Augusto Alvarez Rodrich, "VII Encuesta Anual del Poder en el Perú," *Debate* 19, No. 95 (1997):10.

36. Philip Mauceri, "State Reform, Coalitions, and the Neoliberal *Autogolpe* in Peru," *Latin American Research Review* 30(1995):24.

37. Christina Lamb, "My People Trust and Love Me," *The Spectator* 273, No. 8666, August 13, 1994:14.

38. President Alberto Fujimori, interview on Lima Radio Programas del Perú, "Fujimori Interviewed on Military, Economy," *Foreign Broadcast Information Service,* Latin America, 93-089, May 11, 1993, 37–52.

39. Annual issues of *Debate* (Lima, Peru). Hermoza also became chairman of the joint chiefs of staff in 1994.

40. Carlos Iván Degregori and Carlos Rivera, "FFAA, Subversión y Democracia: 1980–1993," Instituto de Estudios Peruanos Documento de Trabajo No. 53 (Lima: Instituto de Estudios Peruanos), 11–12; Enrique Obando, "The Power of Peru's Armed Forces," in Joseph S. Tulchin and Gary Bland, eds., *Peru in Crisis: Dictatorship or Democracy* (Boulder, Colo.: Lynne Rienner, 1994), 111–112.

41. The generals in question were José Valdivia, who was widely considered responsible for a notorious massacre in a peasant community in Ayacucho, and Jorge Rabanal, who had directed the Republican Guard unit that executed prisoners in the guerrilla cellblocks at the Lurigancho prison after they had mutinied but then surrendered.

42. Lane et al., "Peru," 31.

43. Ibid., 32.

44. "Forced disappearances" usually occurred during military sweeps of rural villages, in which young men in particular were seized indiscriminately, killed, and their bodies hidden. The number of "forced disappearances" in 1991 and 1992 was about 300, approximately 70 percent of the figure in 1989, according to "Desaparecidos," *PerúPaz* 13, No. 18 (January 1994):20. However, the decline may merely reflect a greater inclination by the military to engage Shining Path guerrillas in combat or even merely to report dead guerrilla suspects as killed in combat rather than to "disappear" them. This possibility is suggested by Sally Bowen, "Political Report: Human Rights Roundup," *The Peru Report* 6, No. 6 (1992):4. In any case, "extrajudicial assassinations" (in general, targeted assassinations by death squads in cities) doubled between 1989 and 1992; figures were compiled by the Coordinadora Nacional de Derechos Humanos. The 1989 and 1990 figures are reported in Carlos Chipoco, *En Defensa de la Vida* (Lima: Centro de Estudios Peruanos, 1992), 220; the same figure for 1990 and the figures for 1991 and 1992 are reported in "Ejecusiones extrajudiciales," *Ideele* 48(1993):28.

45. U.S. Department of Justice, *Peru: Human Rights and Political Developments through 1994* (Washington, D.C.: Immigration and Naturalization Service, Resource Information Center, June 29, 1995), 28–30.

46. Among the numerous sources, see Degregori and Rivera, "FFAA, Subversión y Democracia," 14.

47. Carlos Iván Degregori, "Shining Path and Counterinsurgency Strategy Since the Arrest of Abimael Guzmán" in Tulchin and Bland, eds., *Peru in Crisis: Dictatorship or Democracy?* 93. Among the many similar assessments, see Carlos Basombrío, *La Paz: Valor y Precio: Una visión comparativa para América Latina* (Lima: Instituto de Defensa Legal, 1996), 205; and Fernando Rospigliosi and Jorge Santistevan, comments as panelists in *The Transition from War to Peace in Peru: A Conference Report* (Washington, D.C.: Woodrow Wilson Center, 1997), 5–6 and 10–11.

48. James Brooke, "Snaring the Top Guerrilla, 'Bingo! We Got Him,' " *New York Times,* September 15, 1992, A14; James Brooke, "Peru Waiting to See if Rebels Open Offensive," *New York Times,* October 18, 1992, 19.

49. Among the many sources, see Brooke, "Peru Waiting," and Russell Watson and Brook Larmer, "It's Your Turn to Lose," *Newsweek,* September 28, 1992, 28.

50. The most authoritative sources are Carlos Reyna, "Cómo fue realmente la capture de Abimael Guzmán," *Debate* 17, No. 82 (1995):46–50; Gustavo Gorriti, "El Día que cayó Sendero Luminoso," *Selecciones del Reader's Digest* (December 1996):117–42; Benedicto Jiménez Baca, "Asi Fue la Captura del Siglo," *La República*, September 12–14, 1996, 1–6; and Richard Clutterbuck,

"Peru: Cocaine, Terrorism, and Corruption," *International Relations* 12, No. 5 (1995):77–92. My analysis in this section is also based on my interviews in Lima, Peru, with Enrique Bernales, July 23, 1996; Fernando Rospigliosi, July 23, 1996; Enrique Obando, July 21, 1996; Carlos Chipoco, July 27, 1996; Agustín Mantilla, June 16, 1997; Carlos Tapia, June 20, 1997; and other off-the-record interviews.

51. Gorriti, "El Día que cayó Sendero Luminoso," 119–20, and Reyna, "Cómo fue realmente la captura de Abimael Guzmán," 46–50.

52. The exception is Che Guevara.

53. Alberto Bolívar Ocampo, "Intelligence and Subversion in Peru, "*Low Intensity Conflict and Law Enforcement* 3, No. 3 (1994):418–20; and Gorriti, *Sendero*.

54. Journal of the Federation of American Scientists. "Peru: Desperately Ill and Confronting a Maoist Mafia," *F.A.S. Public Report* 45, No. 4 (1992):8.

55. Marcial Rubio, interview with author, Lima, Peru, August 8, 1991. Instituto de Defensa Legal, "La actuación del Estado" and "La creación de fondo de defensa nacional," *Informe Mensual* 1, No. 9 (December 1989):22–23.

56. José Bailetti, interview with author, Lima, Peru, August 14, 1991; Tom Marks, "Shining Path to Oblivion?" *Soldier of Fortune* 21, No. 7 (1996):68.

57. Enrique Obando, interview with author, Lima, Peru, August 14, 1991.

58. Gorriti, "El Día que cayó Sendero Luminoso," 119–20.

59. Reyna, "Cómo fue realmente la captura," 46–50.

60. Ibid., 48; Gorriti, "El Día que cayó Sendero Luminoso," 125.

61. Mantilla interview.

62. Reyna, "Cómo fue realmente la captura," 49.

63. Mantilla interview.

64. General Edgardo Mercado Jarrín, interview with author, Washington D.C., July 11, 1997.

65. Clutterbuck, "Peru," 84; Mantilla interview.

66. "Fujimori Discloses Details about the Capture of Guzmán," *Andean Newsletter,* No. 91, June 27, 1994, 5. The chronology and specifics are somewhat vague. In general, repentance provisions were to persuade militants to surrender, not to gain information from those who already had been captured. Although the DINCOTE's operation often is praised as "clean" and "professional," the possibility that "Sotil" was interrogated severely or even tortured exists. As Mantilla said in our interview, "torture has always been used and some speak more easily than others."

67. "Fujimori Discloses Details," 5; Clutterbuck, "Peru," 84–85.

68. Exactly why Vidal did not inform his superiors is not clear. Vidal has made the point that, on other occasions when superiors were informed, raids were delayed to enable the superiors' presence, and the suspects escaped. For its part, however, the Fujimori government apparently felt that Vidal was trying to maximize his own personal political position.

69. Mantilla interview; author's off-the-record interviews with knowledgeable U.S. Department of State officials.

70. For published statements, see Christopher Simpson, *National Security Directives of the Reagan and Bush Administrations: The Declassified History of U.S. Political and Military Policy, 1981–1991* (Boulder, Colo.: Westview Press, 1995), 641; Reyna, "Cómo fue realmente la captura," 50; Clifford P. Krauss, "The U.S. Reaction is Mixed," *Houston Chronicle,* September 14, 1992:5; Sally Bowen, "Political Indicators," *The Peru Report* 5, No. 2 (1991):44; and Jonathan Cavanagh, "Political Interview," in *The Peru Report* 6, No. 8 (1992):3. Among the author's numerous interviews on this issue, the most knowledgeable on-the-record confirmation of the CIA's role was by Agustín Mantilla.

71. Bolívar, "Intelligence and Subversion," 426.

72. Fernando Rospigliosi, interview with author, Lima, Peru July 23, 1996.

73. Carlos Iván Degregori, José Coronel, Ponciano Del Pino, and Orin Starn, *Las Rondas campesinas y la Derrota de Sendero Luminoso* (Lima: Instituto de Estudios Peruanos, 1996); Car-

los Tapia, *Autodefensa Armada del Campesinado* (Lima: CEDEP, 1995); and Carlos Basombrío, *La Paz: Valor y Precio: Una visión comparativa para América Latina* (Lima: Instituto de Defensa Legal, 1996), 206.

74. This is not the place for a comprehensive discussion of the complex and controversial question of peasant support for Sendero. However, on the substantial initial support for Sendero in Ayacucho communities, see Billie Jean Isbell, "Shining Path and Peasant Responses in Rural Ayacucho," in Palmer, ed., *The Shining Path of Peru*, 79–82; Orin Starn, "Missing the Revolution: Anthropologists and the War in Peru," *Cultural Anthropology* 6, No. 1 (1991):212–26; Mitchell, *Peasants on the Edge*, 196; Raymond Bonner, "Peru's War," *The New Yorker*, January 4, 1988, 44–45. However, for various reasons, in particular Sendero's increasingly numerous assassinations of community members and its efforts to enforce its ideology upon communities after successful initial inroads, more peasants rejected Sendero; see Tapia, *Autodefensa*, 17–19; Degregori et al., *Las Rondas Campesinas*, 62–67; Isbell, "Shining Path and Peasant Responses," 89–92; and Bonner, "Peru's War," 44–45.

75. On the Guatemalan experience, see for example, Americas Watch, *Civil Patrols in Guatemala* (New York: Americas Watch, 1986):33; on the Salvadoran, see A. J. Bacevich, James D. Hallums, Richard H. White, and Thomas F. Young, *American Military Policy in Small Wars: The Case of El Salvador* (Washington, D.C.: Pergamon-Brassey's, 1988), 40–42. Also, the historical role of the military in Peruvian rural areas was less repressive than the historical role of the military in Central American areas, implying that there would be less peasant mistrust in Peru than in the Central American countries; see McClintock, *Revolutionary Movements*, chap. 2, and Hugh Byrne, *El Salvador's Civil War: A Study of Revolution* (Boulder, Colo.: Lynne Rienner, 1996), 148–49.

76. "Desaparecidos" 20.

77. Ronald H. Berg, "Peasant Responses to Shining Path in Andahuaylas," in Palmer, ed., *The Shining Path of Peru*, 116.

78. Such was the case in the Andean community of Huancasancos. In an informal 1996 survey of sixty-five respondents by my research team, 100 percent said that there was a time when Sendero was strong in the community, but that it was not any longer; 83 percent attributed the decline of Sendero to the formation of *rondas*, which occurred in 1984. The case of Huancascancos is mentioned in Bonner, "Peru's War," 45.

79. Among the many discussions, see "Rondas Campesinas: Armas para la paz?" *Ideele*, No. 27 (July 1991): 8.

80. Among the many discussions, see "La opinión de los dirigentes campesinos," *Ideele*, No. 28 (August 1991): 15–16; and the various comments in *Foreign Broadcast Information Service*, Latin America, 91-003, May 14, 1991, 43.

81. For the interview with General Howard Rodríguez (former military commander in the Ayacucho emergency zone) see "Armar a los Comuneros sería fatal," *La República*, June 11, 1989, 10–12. (Rodríguez repeated this view in an interview with the author in Lima, Peru, November 12, 1990; and "Who is Winning the International War?" *Latin American Weekly Report*, August 8, 1991, 3.

82. See the comments by General Sinesio Jarama in *Foreign Broadcast Information Service*, Latin America, 91–093, May 14, 1991, 43, and Carla Anne Robbins, "Cocaine, Communism and Crisis in Peru," *U.S. News and World Report*, September 18, 1989, 45–49. In the author's research team's survey of mid-level security force personnel in mid-1990, only 37 percent of the respondents favored the establishment of armed *rondas*. Even in late 1990, Defense Minister General Jorge Torres Aciego did not positively assess the *rondas*; see "Defense Minister Views Armed Forces Situation," *La República*, September 9, 1990, 10–13.

83. Philip Mauceri, *State Under Siege: Development and Policy Making in Peru* (Boulder, Colo.: Westview, 1996), 144.

84. "El pueblo se arma contra terrorismo, Alan García entregó escopeta a legendario Comandante Huayhuaco," *La República*, December 9, 1989, 2–3.

85. Carlos Iván Degregori, "Shining Path and Counterinsurgency Strategy Since the Arrest of Abimael Guzmán," in Tulchin and Bland, eds., *Peru in Crisis,* 89. Degregori's source is the head of the joint command of the armed forces.

86. Bolívar, "Intelligence and Subversion in Peru," 424; Basombrío, *La Paz,* 206, among many other sources. This was the case in Acopalca, an ex-hacienda near Huancayo that I visited in July 1996.

87. Mauceri, "State Reform," 25; Lane, "Peru," 32; Don Podesta, "Joint Patrols Challenge Peru's Rural Rebels," *Washington Post,* September 8, 1992, A14; and Holly Burkhalter, "Human Rights and U.S. Foreign Policy in Peru," Testimony before the House Foreign Affairs, Subcommittees on Western Hemisphere Affairs, Human Rights and International Organizations and International Organizations and International Narcotics Task Force, mimeograph, 1991, 9.

88. The key studies that are highly positive about the implementation of the *rondas*—Tapia, *Autodefensa,* and Degegori et al., *Las Rondas Campesinas*—focus almost exclusively on the southern highlands. On coercion as a more important factor in the central highlands, see Simon Strong, "Political Report: Ronderos in the Mantaro Valley," *Peru Report* 6, No. 1 (February 1992):1–4, and Francisco Reyes, "519 detenidos . . . y desaparecidos," *La República,* August 22, 1993, 21. The egregious number of abuses by the military in the Huancayo area during the introduction of the *rondas* in the early 1990s was reported to me in numerous interviews in the area in July 1996; it was also indicated by Diana Avila of the Instituto de Defensa Legal, interview with author, Lima, Peru, August 14, 1991.

89. Among other sources, see Tapia, *Las Fuerzas Armadas,* 80–81, and Marks, "'Shining Path' to Oblivion?" 68.

90. On the actual antiterrorist law during this period, see Comisión Especial del Senado sobre las causas de la violencia y alternativas de pacificación en el Perú, *Violencia y Pacificación* (Lima: DESCO and the Comisión Andina de Juristas, 1989), 317–18. For further discussion and analysis, see Clutterbuck, "Peru," 87; James Brooke, "Peru Convicts Maoist Leader and Sentences Him to Life," *New York Times,* October 8, 1992, A3. Sendero's number-two man, Osmán Morote, was initially found innocent of terrorism, and in a mock trial in January 1992, Guzmán himself was found innocent.

91. Clutterbuck, "Peru," 87.

92. "Apoyo a organizaciones de autodefensa," *Andean Newsletter,* No. 51, February 11, 1991, 5. The newsletter is discussing a report by the government's attorney general.

93. Douglas Waller and Michael Smith, "Dueling Death Squads," *Newsweek,* December 26, 1988, 37; James Brooke, "Human Rights Abuses Raising Little Alarm in Peru," *New York Times,* March 25, 1990, 23.

94. Eugene Robinson, "Peru's Human Rights Record in Question," *Washington Post,* August 12, 1991, A12.

95. Fujimori government's video, *El Infierno quedó atrás* (Edimovie S.A.: Lima, 1993).

96. Comisión Especial del Senado, *Violencia y Pacificación,* 317.

97. Ibid., 318–19.

98. See García's own statements in, for example, Alan Riding, "Peru Offers Laws to Combat Terror," *New York Times,* August 21, 1988, 9.

99. Americas Watch, *Una Guerra Desesperada: Los Derechos Humanos en el Perú después de una década de democracia y violencia* (Lima: Comisión Andina de Juristas, 1990); Raúl Ferrero Costa, interview in *Washington Report on the Hemisphere* 7, No. 23 (1987):2; Comisión Especial del Senado, *Violencia y Pacificación,* 321–29; Rospigliosi interview.

100. Apparently protection was envisioned primarily in the form of bodyguards, but other mechanisms such as secret identities do not appear to have been ruled out.

101. Congress Approves Terrorism Law; IU Snubs Session," *Foreign Broadcast Information Service,* Latin America, 87–040 (March 2, 1987), J3; and "State of Emergency Extended for Sixty More Days," *Foreign Broadcast Information Service,* Latin America, 87-059, May 27, 1987, J1.

102. This interpretation is based on my interviews in Lima, Peru, with: Lourdes Flores, July 22, 1996; Rolando Ames, July 23, 1996; and Rospigliosi, July 23, 1996. With respect to the judges, the interpretation also is based on Henry Pease García, presentation at George Washington University Seminar, "Andean Culture and Politics," Washington, D.C., March 17, 1992, and Luis Pásara, "Jueces: Se Necesita," *Caretas,* October 7, 1991, 33.

103. The Peru Report [Michael Reid] interviewed retired army general and former minister of the interior Luis Cisneros on 14 September 1987," *The Peru Report* 1, No. 10 (October 1987):3C–1.

104. On continued releases, see James Brooke, "Peru Convicts Maoist Leader and Sentences Him to Life," *New York Times,* October 8, 1992, A3.

105. Jerfe Asociados, "Estudio de Legislación Represora del Terrorismo y Opciones de Reforma: Informe Final, 1990." The report was given to me by one of the antiterrorist experts on the FREDEMO team.

106. "Apoyo," *Andean Newsletter,* 6.

107. "Encarando la Subversión: Medios escritos elaboran un planteamiento," *Caretas,* April 22, 1991, 28–29.

108. By contrast, after the bombing in Oklahoma City on April 16, 1995, U.S. President Bill Clinton introduced new antiterrorist legislation within two weeks; see John F. Harris, "President Widens Proposal for Countering Terrorism," *Washington Post,* April 27, 1995, 1.

109. For an example of President Fujimori's criticisms of the Peruvian legislature, see his comments in *Foreign Broadcast Information Service,* Latin America, 92–111, October 30, 1992, 38.

110. Henry Pease García, *Los Años de la Langosta: la escena política del Fujimorismo* (Lima: IPADEL, 1994), 120–30.

111. For an excellent analysis of this legislation, see Comisión de Juristas Internacionales, *Informe* (Lima: Instituto de Defensa Legal, 1994).

112. Douglas Farah, "Peru's Jails Find Few Defenders," *Washington Post,* January 5, 1997, A20.

113. Gabriel Escobar, "Rights Group Assails Peru's Anti-Terror Laws," *Washington Post,* August 7, 1996, A23.

114. Among the various sources, see Coletta Youngers, *After the Autogolpe: Human Rights in Peru and the U.S. Response,* (Washington, D.C.: Washington Office on Latin America, 1994), 18.

115. Ibid.

116. Ibid.

117. "Key 'Red Sendero' Leader Captured," *Latin America Weekly Report,* June 9, 1994, 244.

118. Human Rights Watch/Americas, *Human Rights Watch World Report 1995* (New York: Human Rights Watch, 1995), 40.

119. This point is made by many analysts in the Woodrow Wilson Center Latin American Program and the Instituto de Defensa Legal, *The Transition from War to Peace in Peru.*

120. Of course, inevitably these hopes are dashed, and meanwhile more years have passed without the construction of political institutions. For a discussion of the history of this pattern in Peru, see Cynthia McClintock, "Presidents and Constitutional Breakdowns in Peru," in Juan J. Linz and Arturo Valenzuela, eds., *The Failure of Presidential Democracy* (Baltimore: Johns Hopkins University Press, 1994), 360–95.

121. In Peru, the common reference is to the continuing *caldo de cultivo.*

Reflections

CARLOS IVÁN DEGREGORI

How were Shining Path and MRTA defeated strategically, without the negotiations and peace accords that existed in other Latin American countries? Why is there nothing like a truth commission in Peru? Why has there
been no punishment for the human rights violations committed by state
entities, nor any significant public pressure to this end? Why does the administration's strategy and that of the armed forces generally receive majority support in the court of public opinion?

Here are some of the reasons.

The first concerns the arbitrary nature of the insurgency. Armed insurgents frequently exhibit a certain amount of arbitrary behavior, but in the
case of Peru it was much greater. Shining Path was politically arbitrary, and
the MRTA was both politically and socially arbitrary.[1]

While the armed struggle in Central America began during an era of repressive dictatorship, in Peru it began with the culmination of the transition to democracy, which was attained with the broad participation of
grass-roots movements. Shining Path began its armed struggle in May of
1980, on the very eve of the first presidential elections in seventeen years,
by burning ballot boxes. This constituted an explicit attack on representative democracy. Three years after Shining Path began its armed struggle,
the MRTA was formed.

One must bear in mind that the 1979 Peruvian constitution, which established the framework for the transition to democracy, while not as advanced as the Colombian constitution of 1991, was broad and politically
inclusive. It gave illiterates the right to vote and granted extensive freedom
of speech and of political activity. *Izquierda Unida* (United Left) became
the largest leftist socialist party in South America during that period, and

251

Shining Path itself was allowed to sell its newspaper on street corners until 1988.

This was, therefore, what Colombian political scientist Eduardo Pizarro calls political violence in a nonrevolutionary situation.[2] The beginning of the armed struggle was essentially a political decision in which structural and institutional factors did not play a decisive role but, rather, came to be felt over the course of time. What was therefore surprising was how much Shining Path advanced. Perhaps this can be explained by the fact that, while it was politically arbitrary, it was not socially arbitrary. The hard-line senderistas were young people, teachers, people from the provinces, and more educated mestizos. With these as its hard core, Shining Path built up a certain social base in rural areas and made headway until 1989. Then it decided to step up the "prolonged popular war" to a new level, that of strategic equilibrium.[3]

The second reason that there have been no peace talks in Peru has to do with the self-delegitimization of Shining Path. One does not have to dispute the legitimacy of violence in legal or philosophical terms to recognize that for most Peruvians, Shining Path's violence was always illegitimate. But Shining Path also delegitimized itself in the eyes of its own peasant ranks and in the eyes of those social sectors that potentially could have supported it in the cities, and those who for ideological, political, and humanitarian reasons (or out of sheer fear) would have been susceptible to supporting peace talks or a peace accord between the government and Shining Path. When Shining Path tried to enter the phase of strategic equilibrium in the countryside, it had to increase its demands on the peasantry—for more food and recruits, among other things—and this was met with peasant resistance. At the same time, peasants found that the armed forces had switched from a strategy of indiscriminate repression to one of more selective repression and paternalistic treatment. While this may seem insignificant, it was all that sizable segments of the peasantry needed to turn about and ally themselves with the armed forces.

Shining Path also delegitimized itself in the cities. Peruvian sociologist Carmen Rosa Balbi conducted a fascinating poll in 1991 in which she found that 13 percent of the population of Lima felt that the problems of the country could be solved only through violence.[4] In other words, 13 percent of the population was radicalized and disillusioned with democratic methods. These people could have become a social base for Shining Path. However, while 13 percent felt that the country's problems could be solved only through violence, they did not necessarily agree with the form or intensity of the violence Shining Path was waging in the cities: target-

ing grass-roots leaders and local authorities, and employing blatant terrorism, such as planting car bombs in public places and even in private buildings.

The third reason there were no peace talks is that there was no incentive
to hold them. It takes more than one side to negotiate, and Shining Path
had no interest in talks. (One month before Abimael Guzmán's capture,
the spokesperson for the Shining Path in Europe told *Der Spiegel:* "There
is nothing to negotiate with the reactionary armed forces; they should just
surrender unconditionally.") Of all the armed movements in Latin America, Peru's is the most puzzling in ideological terms. The notion of representing an ideology and a vanguard translated into an intransigent and self-
righteous refusal to participate in any negotiations. The hard core of
senderista identity was formed around violence, not just as midwife, but as
mother to history.

Shining Path thus got into polemics with other left groups. It accused
the legal left in Peru of pandering to electoral politics and accused the
Colombian and Central American armed groups that engaged in peace
talks of being reformists and traitors. There is information in documents
that have now become public that lead one to believe that when Guzmán
proposed that Sendero attempt to achieve strategic equilibrium, he knew
that he did not have enough military strength. What led him to this strategy was a desire to "retreat by going forward," and the combination of
massacres in the countryside and provocations in the cities was intended to
bring about this self-fulfilling prophesy.

Guzmán began to say that in order for the revolution to triumph, a million people had to die. Presumably Shining Path was looking for an over-
reaction by the armed forces, similar to that which occurred in Ayacucho
in 1983 and 1984. Then Shining Path would seem like the lesser of two
evils, this time on a national scale. Shining Path also thought it could provoke a U.S. intervention.

It is interesting to note in this regard that while there were Drug Enforcement Administration advisors in Peru, there were virtually no U.S.
counterinsurgency military advisors. However, Shining Path's graffiti
throughout Peru read "Yankee Go Home," when the Yankees had not
even left home! It seems that Guzmán wanted to provoke an intervention
and, copying the Chinese model, get the patriotic sectors of the middle
class to rally in opposition.

There is a fourth reason there were no peace talks. Negotiations do not
occur because the various actors suddenly become peaceful, but because
they are forced to negotiate. These are incentives viewed from another an-

gle, that of the need to negotiate. The swift collapse of Shining Path took
away any incentive to negotiate. Shining Path was built on a cult of personality centered on Guzmán, unique among guerrilla movements in Latin
America. This aspect gave the movement an ideological cohesion that prevented a split between the military and political wings, as had occurred often in other Latin American guerrilla movements. But once Guzmán was
captured, what had been a strength became a weakness. Twice the FMLN
in El Salvador lost a significant part of its national leadership but rebuilt its
leadership and attained strategic equilibrium. But in Peru, the fall of Abimael Guzmán was a devastating blow. Even more devastating was when
letters of his began to circulate on October 1, 1993, asking for peace talks.
Then there was his appearance on television, asking for negotiations. Overtures toward peace were within the realm of possibility of almost any armed
group in Latin America, but they were totally unheard of for Shining Path;
its identity was based on nonnegotiation. As Shining Path dissidents of the
so-called Red Path rejected Guzmán proposal, they became even more entrenched in their position of no negotiations. Guzmán's letters led to the
first split in the Shining Path in thirteen years and to an even more drastic
reduction in the violence that had already diminished since his capture. As
a result, the government had even less incentive to negotiate.

Finally, the swift collapse of Shining Path prevented violence from becoming a way of life. Unlike in Colombia, violence did not become a
means of economic livelihood for the masses in the city or countryside.
Also, the outbreak of armed struggle in Peru in 1980 did not occur within
a context of decades of intense political violence, as was true for Guatemala
and Colombia. Our dictatorships of the 1950s were relatively mild compared with those of other Latin American countries. Between 1958 and
1964 there was a very large peasant movement that recovered or took over
hundreds of thousands of hectares of land, but in six years there were only
170 deaths, which is fewer than the number of casualties that occurred
weekly in 1992. Later, at the end of the 1970s, the most important urban
movements in the history of modern Peru emerged, and again the death
toll was no more than a dozen.

There was not enough time for violent behavior to settle in by inertia,
such as contributed to the problem of the *recompas* and *recontras* in
Nicaragua, and which allowed armed groups to proliferate in Colombia.

Furthermore, and although it might sound morally repugnant, the level
of political violence in Peru has been, by comparison, relatively low, despite the ferocity of Shining Path. Fewer than 30,000 people died, between
4,000 and 5,000 people were disappeared, and approximately 500,000

people were displaced. These figures do not compare with those of El Salvador, Guatemala, and Colombia. While in 1983 and 1984 the violence was much more intense and even genocidal in Ayacucho, since that happened in rural areas, in indigenous areas and places removed from the government's vital centers, its impact on the political class was not important.

Rural violence had limited political impact because during the first few years of the war, Peruvian society's racist tendencies resurged with a vengeance. As long as Indians were dying, there was no real problem. That was when the government practiced indiscriminate violence. By the end of the war, when the violence had spread through the entire country, the main perpetrator was Shining Path. By then the population was willing to accept violations of human rights committed by the government, because that seemed a lesser price to pay in order to regain peace of mind, law, and order. Thus Shining Path's violence fostered a trend by which the population turned a deaf ear to talk of peace negotiations and, in general, human rights.

Why was there nothing like a truth commission? This has to do with the virtual disappearance of the legal left and the triumph of a kind of pragmatic common sense associated with neoliberal hegemony, which makes people want to be more forward than backward looking.

This spirit, shall we say, of declaring amnesty extended even into the areas hardest hit by the violence, such as Ayacucho. In the communities of Ayacucho, the rural social structure favored the reabsorption of the *rondas campesinas* (peasant civil patrols). In this regard, Peru differs from Guatemala and Colombia in two ways. First, compared to the civil patrols in Guatemala, in the Peruvian *rondas* there was a lesser degree of imposition by the state. In many places peasants showed a willingness to participate in an alliance subordinated to the armed forces. Within this subordinated status, the peasants were able to establish their own relative independence or autonomy. Second, in Colombia, the state's loss of a monopoly on weapons had consequences not found in Peru. With the exception of the coca-producing areas, once the violence decreased in Peru, the *rondas campesinas* did not become hired killers for the drug traffickers or members of paramilitary squads. Rather, they were reincorporated into the fabric of society. All they wanted was to build up their households. The former *rondas* members did not find a market for their newly acquired military skills, given the social structure in the countryside of the Peruvian Andes where no large landholders exist; land reform and the peasant movements themselves had put an end to them. Instead there are traditional communities with hierarchical structures and a system of authority that allows *rondas* members to be reabsorbed.

The areas of coca growing and narcotrafficking are the exceptions to this rule, but to a lesser extent than in Colombia. Peruvian drug traffickers have not been willing to invest money in buying rather unproductive land in the Andes. Thus there are no large landholders willing to finance private armies. To be sure, some abuses were committed by the *rondas;* but to a far lesser extent than those carried out by the civil patrols in Guatemala.

What would have happened if Abimael Guzmán had not been captured? The government strategy that finally had been put in place, which I call authoritarian but not genocidal, had not been consolidated. True, the armed forces had gone from indiscriminate repression to selective repression, but selective repression still can be quite dirty.

Guzmán's capture strengthened intelligence work as well as tactics that did not violate human rights. It consolidated what can be called the Peruvian model, with all the corresponding political costs: institutional weakness, excessive prerogatives of the armed forces, and impunity. And when structures of impunity are not dismantled, the postconflict period is unstable.

Notes

1. In general, an arbitrary act is one that is not appropriate or proportional to a specific stimulus. For example, if someone is pushed in the street and responds by machine-gunning the person who did it, the response would be arbitrary. Politically speaking, an arbitrary act is one that is not correlated more or less directly with other political or social realities. If striking workers stage a peaceful march, for example, and the police open fire, that response would be arbitrary. Further, the less articulated a movement's social base is, the more arbitrary it is for that movement to claim that it acts in the name of a social base.

2. See Eduardo Pizarro Leongómez, *La Guerrilla en Colombia en una Perspectiva Comparada* (Bogotá: Tercer Mundo Editores e Instituto de Estudios Políticos y Relaciones Internacionales, 1996).

3. "Strategic equilibrium" is a Maoist term implying that forces in any war are approximately equal. In a nonconventional war, the equilibrium need not be strictly military; it also can be political. For the senderista leadership, strategic equilibrium meant making the country ungovernable.

4. See Carmen Rosa Balbi, "Una inquietante encuesta de opinión," *Quehacer,* No. 72 (July–Aug. 1991): 40–45.

9

The Role of the United Nations in El Salvador and Guatemala: A Preliminary Comparison

TERESA WHITFIELD

Introduction

The peace processes in El Salvador and Guatemala have had two distinct phases: the negotiation, under the auspices of the United Nations, of a complex package of accords that allowed for the conflicts themselves to be brought to an end and the implementation of those accords under U.N. verification. A number of factors contribute to the similarity of the two processes: The two countries are neighbors; they share a common history of authoritarian rule, economic hardship reinforced by widespread repression of the poor, and armed revolutionary movements that arose to protest these conditions; the civil conflicts in each country developed in circumstances that were profoundly affected by the politics of the Cold War; they

The views contained within this chapter are those of the author, who works as an official within the United Nations Department of Political Affairs, and do not necessarily reflect those of the United Nations. The author would like to thank Jean Arnault, Marrack Goulding and Álvaro de Soto for the insights they provided her with during the writing of the chapter and Cynthia Arnson, David Holiday, and Elisabeth Wood for their comments on earlier drafts. The author is entirely responsible for any errors that may remain.

257

concluded in consecutive negotiating processes (El Salvador, from 1990 to 1992; Guatemala from 1991 to 1996); and the far-reaching accords that emerged from the negotiations attempt to address the root causes of the conflicts in order to prevent their resurgence, through an initial emphasis on respect for human rights. While Guatemalans of all political hues insisted the experience of El Salvador could "never" be repeated in their nation,[1] the Salvadoran peace process was bound to be a point of reference for that in Guatemala. In both cases the United Nations' impartiality, political leverage, and ability to mobilize resources have played an irreplaceable role in their successful outcomes.

However, a number of important differences between the two processes have been reflected in the role played in each by the United Nations. Above all, the two countries themselves differ profoundly in their geography, history, and ethnic composition, and in the length and nature of their civil conflicts and in the forces and rationale that brought the parties to the negotiating table. Circumstances in El Salvador gave rise to negotiations that were conducted, in the (retrospective) words of the U.N. mediator Álvaro de Soto "almost in laboratory conditions."[2] Those on Guatemala were considerably more complex—spanning three governments, for example, in an obvious contrast to the single government that took part in negotiations in El Salvador—and conformed much less readily to a textbook model. The two processes also differ greatly in their relation to developments beyond their countries' border: While the negotiating process in El Salvador intersected neatly with—and was directly influenced by—the collapse of the Soviet bloc and the heady days of the supposed "new world order," the lengthier process in Guatemala was conducted against a background in which the complexities of the post–Cold War world were only too evident. The United Nations was by no means immune to this change.

The United Nations of the Salvadoran process was riding the crest of a wave. As it emerged from decades of Cold War paralysis, the organization appeared ideally placed to take on the role of world troubleshooter. Successes in Afghanistan and Namibia before its involvement in El Salvador took shape, the observation of elections in Nicaragua in February 1990 (which represented not only the organization's first political operation in Latin America but also the first time it had observed elections in a sovereign state), the comprehensive mandate assigned to it in Cambodia by the agreements concluded at the Paris Conference in October 1991, the preparations under way for a more complex U.N. involvement in Angola, and the signing of the Salvadoran peace accords in the final moments of Javier Pérez de Cuéllar's term as secretary-general on December 31, 1991, all contributed to raise the confidence of and in the United Nations to unprecedented levels. In *An Agenda for Peace,* which was published in June 1992, it was with the "new departures in peace-keeping"—such as El Salvador—in mind, that Pérez de Cuéllar's successor, Boutros Boutros-Ghali, introduced the concept of postconflict peace-building.[3] A few months later, in his first report on the work of the organization, Boutros-Ghali would cite El Salvador as one of five conflicts that epitomized the organization's role in peacekeeping in the broader sense in which it was coming to be understood: "each is unique, requiring a specific response, yet all require a comprehensive approach that takes into account the wide range of substantive issues and calls for a coordinated and multidimensional international effort."[4]

By a curious twist of history, Boutros-Ghali's final public appearance as U.N. secretary-general was at the signing ceremony of the agreement on a firm and lasting peace in Guatemala City on December 29, 1996. Circumstances could not have been more different. Although he had come to the office of secretary-general buoyed by the same wave as that upon which his predecessor had departed, Boutros-Ghali's five-year term had seen U.N. standing plummet to an all-time low, as the organization took the blame for the failures of the international community at large in Somalia, Rwanda, and Bosnia and struggled to implement long-overdue reform while in the midst of the worst financial crisis in its history. Moreover, public attention during Boutros-Ghali's final six months—which also happened to be the final six months of the Guatemalan negotiations—was fixed firmly on his doomed attempt to resist U.S. efforts to force his departure. This unfortunate episode had surprisingly little effect on the Guatemalan process. While Pérez de Cuéllar's personal interest in the Salvadoran process had been vital to its success, the Guatemalan process had been, by contrast, something of an orphan within the U.N. hierarchy. Although it was ably moderated by Jean Arnault and supervised by the under-secretary-general for political affairs, Marrack Goulding, it was of little interest to the secretary-general and those around him, for whom it seemed to represent a somewhat anachronistic remnant of the Cold War, of little geopolitical import.

In the years since the Salvadoran peace accords were signed, many lessons have been learned, not only by the United Nations but also by the other actors involved in the taxing business of postconflict reconstruction.

A number of these lessons have been applied directly to Guatemala, even as the experience of El Salvador—which has been widely judged to have been successful—has demonstrated just how difficult it is for countries to make the profound kind of transformation put forward in blueprint form by an ambitious package of peace accords. This chapter can offer only a preliminary comparison of the experiences of the United Nations in El Salvador and Guatemala for an obvious reason: Implementation of the complex package of accords negotiated for Guatemala, for which a four-year process is envisaged, was in its early stages as of this time of writing. The full account of the role played by the United Nations in assisting national actors to resolve the conflicts El Salvador and Guatemala and to establish the basis for lasting peace will have to wait until at least 2001.

Entry: A Foot in the Door

In the early 1980s, when conflicts raged in the countries of Central America, the United Nations had no history of involvement in the region. On the contrary. The United States had consistently let it be known that the United Nations had no business in its backyard; unrest in Central America had been stirred by Cuba and the Soviet bloc and would be addressed by the United States within the bipolar context of the Cold War. While the appointment of the first Latin American secretary-general, the Peruvian Javier Pérez de Cuéllar, in 1981 had helped bring the region to the organization's attention, it is notable that the Security Council managed to make not a single reference to Central America until 1983. Even then, the resolution (530) adopted in May 1983 was a mild one: The members of the Security Council (which included Nicaragua at that time) "commended" the efforts of the Contadora countries (Colombia, Mexico, Panama, and Venezuela) to bring peace to the region.

A weak gesture though this resolution may now appear, it opened an all-important avenue for the further engagement of the United Nations by asking the secretary-general to keep the Security Council informed of further developments. Officials in the Secretariat eager for a more active role for the United Nations in Central America took note. Foremost among them was Álvaro de Soto, executive assistant to his compatriot, Pérez de Cuéllar.

In retrospect, Contadora's efforts appear both too ambitious in trying to address the problems of Central America as a whole and not ambitious enough in failing to recognize that a solution to the region's conflicts would have to involve the various insurgent forces.[5] Contadora, however, filled the vacuum that had been created by resistance to action by either the United Nations or the Organization of American States (OAS). The Central American governments' dependence on U.S. support led them to be suspicious of U.N. involvement, while the Frente Farabundo Martí para la Liberación Nacional (FMLN) in El Salvador and the Unidad Revolucionaria Nacional Guatemalteca (URNG) in Guatemala, like the Frente Sandinista para la Liberación Nacional (FSLN) in Nicaragua, saw no virtue in appealing to the OAS, which they believed to be wholly obeisant to the United States.

For the United Nations, the most effective way around these Cold War vetoes was to work directly with the OAS. Accordingly, in late 1986 Pérez de Cuéllar invited João Baena Soares, the OAS secretary-general, to New York; together they summoned first the ambassadors of the five Central American countries and then those of the Contadora countries and the Contadora Support Group established in 1985 (Argentina, Brazil, Peru, and Uruguay) and presented them with a "menu" of options for action. This initiative was followed by a January 1987 tour of the region by the eight Contadora foreign ministers and the two secretaries-general. At the end of the trip, on which the visitors had met exclusively with government representatives, Pérez de Cuéllar was asked if he believed the necessary political will existed in the region to achieve negotiated settlements to the conflicts. He gave a one-word answer: "No."[6]

One of the more interesting meetings of the trip was that with the then president of Costa Rica, Oscar Arias. De Soto remembers that "he gave the impression that he had something up his sleeve." That something matured into Esquipulas II, the agreement on "Procedures for the Establishment of a Firm and Lasting Peace in Central America" reached by the Central American presidents on August 7, 1987, by which they undertook to initiate processes of democratization and national dialogue in their countries, to bring about cease-fires and promote free and fair elections. The presidents set up an international verification mechanism (Comisión Internacional de Verificación y Seguimiento) consisting of the foreign ministers of the Contadora and support group countries as well as of the five Central American countries and the secretaries-general of the United Nations and OAS. This unwieldy mechanism was not exactly a recipe for success.

Its lack of success led the five Central American presidents, gathered in a summit meeting on the coast of El Salvador in February 1989, to call upon the United Nations to become involved in the verification of the Esquipulas agreements. This was to be facilitated by a landmark resolution (637) of July 1989, in which the Security Council commended the efforts of the Central American countries and expressed its firm support for Esquipulas II. Most important, for those seeking a greater U.N. involvement in the peace process, it gave "its full support to the Secretary-General to continue his mission of good offices" in support of the Central American governments in their efforts to achieve the goals set out in Esquipulas II.[7] Under the broad umbrella of these "good offices," the United Nations would be able to do what others engaged in diplomatic efforts to resolve the Central American conflicts had so far refused to contemplate: work toward including the insurgencies within a process of dialogue and negotiation. In November 1989 the Security Council again acted to establish the United Nations Observer Group in Central America (ONUCA) to verify compliance by the Central American countries with the security aspects of Esquipulas II. Meanwhile, Nicaragua's request for U.N. supervision of the elections it had announced for February 1990 had led to the establishment of the United Nations Observer Mission for the Verification of Elections in Nicaragua (ONUVEN) in August 1989.

A "Ripe Moment"

The timing of resolution 637 was particularly apposite for El Salvador, where international and national conditions combined to make 1989 a turning point in the war. The end of the Reagan era and the rise of perestroika had helped to create a climate favorable to the settlement of the Cold War conflicts. Changes within the Soviet bloc also were contributing to an evolution in the thinking of the FMLN. A series of consultations undertaken by the FMLN General Command in the second half of 1988 within Latin America and the socialist bloc had indicated solid support for a negotiated solution to the conflict. Throughout 1989 the FMLN would pursue a bold double strategy that combined increased pressure for a political solution to the conflict with preparations for the largest military offensive of the war. The victory of the Nationalist Republican Alliance (ARENA) in the presidential elections of March 1989 was another factor that contributed positively toward what Ignacio Ellacuría, the Jesuit rector of the Central American University, would call a "new phase" in the Salvadoran process: This ultraconservative party represented the real forces within Salvadoran society more closely than the Christian Democratic government of José Napoleón Duarte had ever done; the incoming president,

Alfredo Cristiani, had committed himself to dialogue with the FMLN and was under pressure from an opposition strengthened in its unity to the left of the government.[8]

Two unsuccessful rounds of negotiations were held in September and October 1989, to the second of which the United Nations and OAS were invited as observers. However, it would take the dramatic events of November 1989, in which the FMLN launched its largest offensive of the war, to bring both sides to face military stalemate and prepare the way for substantive negotiations. While the FMLN proved itself stronger militarily than the governments of El Salvador and the United States had imagined, the offensive also revealed the impossibility of a popular insurrection; at the same time the possibility of military success for the long-term counterinsurgency strategy backed by the United States was also severely diminished. Rather, the offensive had revealed the Salvadoran conflict to be "ripe" for negotiation, in accordance with the concept of ripeness developed by I. William Zartman. "Ripeness," Zartman has written, "is associated with conditions where parties realize that their attempt to solve the problem and pursue their goals alone are unlikely to succeed at an acceptable price. . . . A ripe moment may therefore be characterized as a mutually hurting stalemate for specific parties with a way out."[9]

Neither the "ripeness" of the moment in El Salvador nor the fact that the negotiations already tentatively under way represented a "way out" had been lost on those following developments from the U.N. Secretariat. In the meantime, the fact that OAS credibility had been undermined by an ill-fated visit of its secretary-general to El Salvador at the height of the offensive meant that the regional organization was effectively out of the picture.[10] Requests for the U.N. secretary-general to play a mediating role to bring the conflict to an end came soon both from the FMLN, which met with de Soto in Montreal in early December, and President Cristiani, whose position was put forward in a statement issued by the Central American presidents later in the month requesting Pérez de Cuéllar "to take the necessary steps to ensure the resumption of the dialogue between the government of El Salvador and the FMLN."[11] Cristiani followed up the request with a visit to New York in late January 1990 that launched de Soto on an intensive period of shuttle diplomacy, eventually to bear fruit in the form of an agreement signed in Geneva on April 4, 1990.

The Geneva agreement established: a fourfold purpose to the process (to end the armed conflict through political means, promote democratization, guarantee unrestricted respect for human rights, and reunify Salvadoran society) leading to political agreements to be verified by the

United Nations; that the process should be carried out under the auspices
of the secretary-general and in a continuous manner; and for it to consist
of face-to-face negotiations as well as shuttle diplomacy by the secretary-
general's representative. It also provided for the secretary-general to consult at his discretion with other governments, as well as Salvadoran individuals and groups, that might be useful to the process. As such, it
represented a carefully articulated framework that would determine the
form of the Salvadoran negotiations over the months to come.[12]

Negotiating El Salvador

De Soto's description of the "laboratory conditions" within which the negotiations on El Salvador were conducted referred to the political dynamics that had brought the parties to the negotiating table as well as to the
international context within which the negotiations were set and to the
United Nations' clear leadership of the process. However, it should not be
taken to mean that the process was, for these reasons, easy. The agenda
agreed on at a meeting held in Caracas in May 1990 established that the
negotiating process would address a series of political agreements—on the
armed forces, human rights, the judicial system, the electoral system, constitutional reform, economic and social issues, and verification by the
United Nations—before addressing a cease-fire.[13] In the end it would require twenty months of intense negotiations, during which the process
weathered a number of crises, before agreement on a comprehensive package of accords could be reached.[14]

Inside the United Nations itself, the team working on El Salvador was
fortunate to count on the total support of and access to the secretary-general. De Soto was rightly considered to be something of a protégé of Pérez
de Cuéllar, whom he had known for many years; while authority for the
conduct of the negotiations was delegated to de Soto, the secretary-general remained available for those moments when the process required the
weight that only his office could bring to bear. In the meanwhile, the
United Nations' position within the negotiations was reinforced by an
agreement between the parties, in the face of stalemated talks on the military in October 1990, to strengthen the role of the secretary-general's representative to that of a more active mediator, able to put forward written
proposals to either side.

A further feature of the Salvadoran negotiations was the fact that they
took place in isolation from other actors within the country. While the

Geneva agreement stated that "the political parties and other existing representative social organizations. . . . have an important role to play in achieving peace" and had provided the United Nations with the means by which to consult with groups and individuals within El Salvador, the negotiations were conducted within the logic of the war and almost exclusively between the two parties to the ongoing conflict. The FMLN's identity as an insurgent force was translated by the negotiating table to that of reformer, putting forward concrete proposals for how to address what was wrong with the country. These proposals were supported by the pressure maintained on the negotiations by the FMLN's intense military activity throughout 1990 and 1991. Within this dynamic, the government team was hampered not only by the abilities of its negotiators, some of whom had less political experience than some of those representing the FMLN, but also by the fact that, in its defense of the status quo, it had no option but to reject and parry the FMLN initiatives.

The United Nations was called upon to break the deadlocks that inevitably ensued. A well-known example of this was the human rights accord "pulled out of a hat" by the United Nations in June 1990 at a moment when the talks appeared impossibly mired in discussions on the armed forces.[15] The agreement, which described a number of basic rights the parties were to respect, provided for the establishment of a U.N. human rights verification mission and gave a much-needed impetus to the negotiations as a whole, followed a confidential meeting of international human rights experts gathered in Geneva earlier that month to advise the U.N. negotiators. The first draft had been written overnight by Pedro Nikken, a Venezuelan jurist who had become consultant to de Soto's negotiating team and its principal scribe. Human rights groups in El Salvador were not consulted in its preparation, in part because wartime polarization of society was so extreme that they, like other representatives of civil society in opposition to the government, were perceived to be aligned with the FMLN.

The next major breakthrough in the negotiations came in April 1991, after a marathon negotiating session, with the signing of the Mexico Accords on constitutional reform. The cliff-hanging conclusion of the round was determined by the need to have any proposed reforms approved by the legislative assembly before it was disbanded at the end of the month. Specific amendments to the 1983 constitution paved the way for a package of reforms that included "a clearer definition of the subordination of the armed forces to the civil authorities" and amendments, which had been endorsed by El Salvador's opposition political parties, that changed the selection process for the Supreme Court of Justice and introduced some elements of electoral reform. While the judicial reforms the accords contemplated were considerably weaker than those regarding the military—in part because of the FMLN's lack of expertise in this area (and even, it appeared to some negotiators, a failure to understand its importance)—agreement was reached to form a Commission on the Truth to investigate the most serious acts of violence and human rights violations that had occurred since 1980.[16]

A critical factor in reaching these agreements and pushing them through the legislative assembly before the April 30 deadline had been pressure from the external actors in the negotiating process. Most important, for the influence it wielded over the Salvadoran government and within the region as a whole, was the United States. While the U.S. government had publicly indicated its support of a negotiated settlement to the conflict after the FMLN offensive of 1989,[17] the messages from Washington had been mixed with respect to support of the United Nations' role in the process. The murder of six Jesuit priests (including Ignacio Ellacuría) by the Salvadoran military during the November 1989 offensive, which was the subject of ongoing monitoring by a U.S. congressional task force, had served to maintain congressional pressure on the Salvadoran army to an unprecedented extent. Credible threats to impose large cuts in military aid (which totaled more than $4 billion during the course of the war) were a key factor in the felicitous advance of negotiations on military reform. In the meantime, however, some individuals within the State Department maintained a war of attrition against de Soto in particular and the United Nations in general that made for some extremely uncomfortable private meetings. De Soto and Marrack Goulding, who was mediating the negotiations of the military aspects of the conflict, were under constant pressure to give priority to negotiation of a cease-fire—a pressure they resisted stalwartly because it was clear that leaving the cease-fire to the end, as the Caracas agenda had specified, underpinned the FMLN's entire negotiating position.[18]

The Mexico Accords, however, were key to Washington's perception that the FMLN was willing to end the war through negotiations. A new-found engagement on the part of the United States was evident in the next few months, while confidence in the progress of the negotiating process was lifted by the Security Council's decision to deploy the United Nations Observer Mission in El Salvador (ONUSAL) in July 1991 to verify the provisions of the human rights agreement. A most notable development was the letter sent to the secretary-general in August 1991 by the U.S. Secretary of State, James Baker, and the Soviet Foreign Minister, Aleksandr Bessmertnykh. The letter came in response to a list of ideas Pérez de Cuéllar had given to the governments of both countries, suggesting how they might revitalize talks that were, once again, stalled. The two countries' response both distanced them from their Cold War positions in Central America and provided the impetus for the secretary-general to convene an extraordinary session of talks in New York in September. That session, to which the secretary-general invited President Cristiani to attend in person, would lead to the next breakthrough in the negotiating process and agreements on a new National Civilian Police (PNC), a new National Commission for the Consolidation of Peace (COPAZ), an ad hoc commission to oversee the "purging" of the armed forces, as well as measures providing for the subordination of the army to the constitutional authorities and a series of preliminary resolutions on the key issue of land.[19]

While the United Nations consulted regularly with a number of other countries regarding the negotiating process in El Salvador—some, such as Cuba, with an obvious political interest in the region, and others, such as the Nordic countries, precisely because they had none—an innovative feature of the Salvadoran process was the creation of the group of Friends of the Secretary-General for El Salvador, consisting of Colombia, Mexico, Venezuela, and Spain. This group was formed in response to a desire on the part of the Secretariat not only to form alliances with interested countries in the region—and, in the case of Spain, a member of the European Union deeply involved in Latin America—that could be relied on to provide a useful counterweight to members of the Security Council (such as the United States and Soviet Union) with clearly defined bilateral positions on El Salvador; another purpose of the group was to try to harness rival would-be mediators to ensure that their efforts would support, rather than be at cross-purposes to, the work of the secretary-general. De Soto regularly, and usually individually, briefed ambassadors of the four countries, whether in New York, El Salvador, or the country in which negotiations were taking place, on the status of the negotiations from early 1990 on. It was understood that representatives of these countries were at the disposal of the secretary-general; on a number of occasions they, or their countries' foreign ministers or presidents, provided useful services to the negotiation process at the secretary general's request.

The Friends were publicly described as such only after July 1991; by this stage in the process they also began to meet as a group. Like other actors engaged in the Salvadoran negotiations, they were aware that the clock was ticking: Pérez de Cuéllar was due to leave the United Nations at the end of the year. No one knew who his successor might be, but he or she could not be Latin American, and it was generally agreed that the last few months of 1991 offered the best chance to reach a final peace agreement. Throughout December of that year pressure on the negotiations mounted: the United States and the former Soviet Union issued a joint statement calling for a cease-fire before the end of the year; on December 6—and after meeting with the ambassadors of the four Friends—Pérez de Cuéllar suggested that the negotiations, which were stalled in Mexico at the time, should move to New York. A phone call on December 26 would summon President Cristiani himself. Five frenzied days later, and with the benefit of intense persuasion and cajoling on the part of U.N. officials, a high-level U.S. delegation and the ambassadors of the four Friends, as well as a last-minute rush to negotiate the quite complicated military aspects of the agreement (a sine qua non for the Salvadoran government's acceptance of the package, of course), a hastily prepared New York Act, committing the parties to the signing of a final peace agreement on January 16, 1992, at Chapultepec Castle in Mexico City, was signed in the last few moments of Pérez de Cuéllar's term in office.[20]

Reaching a Framework for Guatemala

In early 1990, when the Salvadoran parties signed the Geneva agreement, the prospect of a peaceful solution to the thirty-year-old conflict in Guatemala was still distant. The "scorched-earth" counterinsurgency tactics of the military government in the early 1980s, which had led to the massacre and displacement of tens of thousands civilians, primarily from the indigenous population of the country's highlands, had abated in the latter half of the decade, having achieved a strategic military defeat of the URNG that stopped short of eliminating their forces entirely. The guerrillas had continued to offer a low-intensity resistance to the government (even after it returned to civilian power in 1986) but had few illusions about their ability to take power by military force; gradually they began to explore pursuing a political settlement. While it is widely believed that this resistance provided the justification for the military to retain and abuse its power in Guatemalan life, in its official discourse the army maintained that the URNG had been defeated militarily and refused to countenance any proposal for dialogue.[21] Meanwhile, U.S. influence over the Guatemalan government and military was a less important factor than in El Salvador, in part because Guatemala's rejection of military assistance following U.S. criticism of its human rights record in the Carter years meant that U.S. support of counterinsurgency activities by subsequent administrations was largely of an indirect, and even covert, nature.

The URNG's evident inability to force upon the Guatemalan elites the kind of "mutually hurting stalemate" seen in El Salvador led many observers, including some within the United Nations, to doubt that the Guatemalan process would ever be "ripe" for negotiation. In retrospect what can be seen is a slow process toward maturity, during which a consensus among a fragile coalition of interest groups gradually was built around the idea that peace, in Guatemala as in El Salvador, did not mean solely the end of hostilities but could be achieved only by addressing the major problems in the country that had given rise to the armed conflict in the first place. As an initial step, in 1989 the Commission for National Reconciliation (CNR) that had emerged from the Esquipulas II process convened a National Dialogue to discuss the problems facing Guatemala.[22]

The talks held in Oslo in March 1990 between the CNR and URNG (organized by the Norwegian government and Lutheran World Federation) followed directly from this process. They led to an accord that committed the participants to a "search for peace by political means" and provided for a series of meetings between the URNG and Guatemalan political parties and popular, religious, and business sectors to be held. The secretary-general of the United Nations, represented in Oslo by Francesc Vendrell, who had followed the Central American process with de Soto throughout the 1980s, was asked formally to observe these meetings and to act as "guarantor of compliance" with the commitments entered into in the agreement.[23]

The first round of direct talks between the URNG and Peace Commission (Comisión de la Paz, COPAZ) of the new government of Jorge Serrano Elías were held in Mexico in April 1991. The agreements reached during this meeting committed the parties to a procedure for negotiations toward political agreements on a broad agenda of issues,[24] but in the years to come progress was to be painfully slow. Persistent stumbling blocks were the government's attempts to force the URNG to agree—contrary to the Mexico accord of April 1991—to a cease-fire before negotiating the substantive issues on the agenda and the question of U.N. verification of any resulting agreement. The experience of El Salvador contributed to Guatemalans' fears regarding a U.N. mission in the country; in El Salvador, the signing of the final peace accords in January 1992 had led to the deployment of a major U.N. presence. The white jeeps and blue berets rapidly dispersed throughout the neighboring country appeared to Guatemala an infringement on national sovereignty that it could never accept.

Sensitivity about the role of the United Nations led also to the demise of Vendrell when it was revealed that he was assisting in arranging a meeting between Serrano and the URNG *comandancia* (General Command) in the offices of the Lutheran World Federation in Geneva. A somewhat embarrassed government insisted that he was dismissed for having exceeded the terms of his mandate as "observer." He was succeeded by Jean Arnault, who was considered sufficiently junior within the U.N. hierarchy to play the role of a "real" observer of a process that most within the United Nations had little faith in. Prolonged disagreement on the issue of human rights contributed to the process's deterioration into crisis before the *autogolpe* of President Serrano in May 1993.

Under the government of President Ramiro de León Carpio, things began to change. The advantages of U.N. mediation of negotiations, rather than just their observation, gradually became evident as both parties came to realize that a purely bilateral process had its limitations and to suspect that the international prestige, impartiality, and resources that the United Nations brings would work to each of their advantages. Key for the URNG was a visit to New York during which its representatives had an extended meeting with Marrack Goulding, who explained to them the possible range of U.N. involvement in a peace process. In January 1994, shortly after this meeting, negotiations resumed. This time the parties asked the secretary-general to provide the negotiations with a moderator, with the capacity to "make proposals to facilitate the signing of a firm and lasting peace," and the United Nations to verify the implementation of all agreements reached between them.[25] Jean Arnault was appointed to the position of moderator that same month.

Moderating Guatemala

The Framework Agreement signed in January 1994 already prefigured Guatemalan negotiations of a more diffuse nature than those on El Salvador. In addition to enhancing the status of the United Nations, the agreement recognized the role played in the process initiated by the Oslo Accords by the various sectors of organized civil society and gave them a legitimate place within the negotiating process in an Assembly of Civil Society (ASC). This assembly, the agreement stipulated, would have three distinct functions: the formulation of consensus positions on the substantive issues of the negotiating agenda; the transmittal of its nonbinding recommendations to the parties and the United Nations; and the possibility to consider, and ultimately endorse as a "national commitment," the bilateral agreements reached by the parties.

This innovative arrangement arose directly out of the somewhat unorthodox dynamics of the Guatemalan process as a whole. Without the necessary military weight behind it to exert strong pressure on the government, the URNG sought to bolster its strength through alliances with national and international actors. Meanwhile, the increasingly active popular and indigenous organizations that had proliferated during the process of limited democratic opening that had begun in the late 1980s had found that the negotiations provided an avenue for their concerns otherwise denied them in Guatemalan society; therefore, they insisted on being given a clearly defined role within the negotiations. By May 1994, when the ASC was formally established under the chairmanship of Monsignor Rodolfo Quezada, it included not only these grass-roots organizations but also a wide range of political parties, universities, and small and medium-size business associations (but not the most powerful representative of the private sector, CACIF, which refused to participate).

That the Framework Agreement also institutionalized a group of Friends of the Guatemalan Peace Process established from the outset important differences between this group, which was made up of Colombia, Mexico, Norway, Spain, the United States, and Venezuela, and the more flexible Salvadoran antecedent.[26]

Although the United States had been added to the Salvadoran Friends after the signing of the Chapultepec Accords as a strange kind of numerical appendage (the Friends would be referred to most commonly as the "Four plus one"), its status and comportment as a Guatemalan Friend reflected both the change in administration in Washington and a wider change in the international political climate.[27] Officials of the Clinton administration joined those of the other Friends in supporting both the negotiations and the U.N. role within them with a consistency that had been absent in the case of El Salvador. Even as past U.S. policy was increasingly battered by revelations of Central Intelligency Agency involvement in Guatemalan's dirty war,[28] the regional domination of the United States and its unquestioned superpower status made it an influential factor in the process and an important instrument of pressure on the Guatemalan elites.

Newly invigorated by the Framework Agreement, the parties moved rapidly ahead in the months that followed. In March 1994 they reached an agreement on human rights that asked for the immediate deployment of a U.N. mission to verify its provisions and assist in the strengthening of national institutions it had identified[29] and an ambitious timetable that provided for a final peace agreement to be reached before the end of 1994. In June agreements were reached both on the resettlement of populations displaced by the war and on the establishment of a commission "to clarify past human rights abuses and acts of violence that have caused the Guatemalan population to suffer."[30]

The latter agreement marked a critical moment of the process. Military resistance to the formation of a commission to investigate the truth about past violence had been intense. The publication of the report of El Salvador's Truth Commission in March 1993 had not helped. That commission had far exceeded expectations, not only in the extent to which it attributed blame in 85 percent of the cases for which it received denunciations to state agents, paramilitary groups, or death squads aligned with them, but also for the fact that in cases where it had incontrovertible proof of responsibility it named names, and among them were senior members of the Salvadoran military.[31] Under pressure from the international community, the Guatemalan parties eventually agreed to create a Historical Clarification Commission; with a mandate considerably weaker than that of the Salvadoran commission, it specifically ruled out the naming of names and reflected the imbalance of forces at the negotiating table.

The URNG, the United Nations, and the process as a whole were criticized intensely for this watered-down truth commission, particularly by human rights organizations and representatives of the popular movement within the ASC. This criticism was reinforced by government delays in implementing its commitments based on the human rights agreement and an extended delay, until November 1994, in the deployment of the U.N. verification mission, MINUGUA. The United Nations itself recognized the valuable contribution that the early deployment of such a mission could make to the peace process. However, there was a deliberate policy of Under-Secretary-General Goulding to go slow in the deployment of MINUGUA in order to put pressure on the parties as negotiations bogged down over discussion of indigenous rights and prolonged differences over the timetable for implementation. While the URNG held out against pressure to agree to a new deadline for the negotiations, the United Nations sought to break the deadlock. A letter from the secretary-general to both parties asked them to indicate what they would do to get the peace process back on track. The replies he received only deepened the impasse[32]; Goulding was dispatched to the region to present the parties with a revised set of proposals. The URNG's rejection of this package prompted the United Nations to issue an ultimatum: The parties either returned to the original negotiating format, by which substantive items would be considered before operative items (and all of them before a target date of August 1995), or the secretary-general would inform the General Assembly and the Security Council "that the modalities for the participation of the United Nations in the peace process would have to be reconsidered."[33]

Acceptance of this ultimatum allowed for negotiations to move forward and a far-ranging agreement on indigenous rights, which drew heavily on International Labor Organization (ILO) Convention 169 and characterized Guatemala as a multiethnic, pluricultural, and multilingual nation, to be signed on March 31, 1995.[34] Discussion of the next item on the agenda, "socio-economic aspects and the agrarian situation," began the same day with somewhat deceptive dispatch. More than a year would pass before agreement on the item would be reached, but the resulting accord can be considered as among the most distinctive in the Guatemalan process.

Within the context of the Central American peace process as a whole, it was remarkable that socioeconomic issues even were the subject of a substantive agreement. In El Salvador, the FMLN conducted negotiations with an ARENA government that was clearly committed to an economic policy of macroeconomic stabilization and structural adjustment before, during, and after the negotiating process. The terms of this policy, it was evident to both the FMLN and United Nations, would not be subject to negotiation. In the end the FMLN left consideration of any social and economic issues to the last moment and limited it to questions related to the reintegration of its combatants and civilian base, for the most part through a land transfer program (Programa de Transferencia de Tierras, PTT), whose implementation would prove one of the most complex aspects of the entire process.[35] For the URNG as well as many of the groups represented in the ASC, this weakness of the Salvadoran accords was a deficiency they would not accept in Guatemala. In their pursuit of social and economic reform through negotiation they were assisted by the electoral calendar, which provided for presidential elections in late 1995, as it was becoming increasingly clear that the government of Ramiro de León Carpio lacked the necessary authority with the private sector to make much more headway.[36] Meanwhile, a growing constituency recognized that the social and economic defects of Guatemalan society were at the root of its problems. Although there would remain significant differences between the kind of structural problems identified by the different actors inside the country and out, this constituency eventually would include those within and outside the government as well as some elements of the army. It found support within the World Bank and Inter-American Development Bank (IDB), the two international financial institutions most deeply engaged in the country, and the donor community at large, and held that economic, social, and ethnic inequality, low taxation, and low social investment were obstacles to Guatemala's long-term prospects for development.

This emerging consensus helped overcome one of the weaknesses of the Salvadoran process, as perceived by the United Nations—namely, the lack of communication between the Secretariat and concerned international financial institutions during the negotiations—which had had important consequences when it came to implementation of the peace accords. Writing with Graciana del Castillo in the March 1994 issue of *Foreign Policy,* de Soto had described the lack of transparency and coordination between the Bretton Woods institutions regarding the economic program of the ARENA government they sponsored and the U.N. Secretariat regarding the accords it brokered. "It was," the authors stated in a much-quoted phrase, "as if a patient lay on the operating table with the left and right sides of his body separated by a curtain and unrelated surgery being performed on each side."[37] The consequences of this dislocation in El Salvador—a dislocation compounded of course, by the lack of adequate mobilization of domestic resources—had been difficulties in financing some of the most costly and important elements of the peace agreements, such as the formation of the National Civil Police and the land transfer program. In Guatemala the need for coordination was even greater, not only because there was a socioeconomic accord on the agenda but also because the international financial climate was such that donors were likely to be less forthcoming in their support of the peace process.

An informal donor meeting convened by the World Bank in June 1994 had revealed that donors were acutely aware of the need for early coordination of their support for implementation of future peace accords, taking into account the lessons of the Salvadoran experience. In his briefing to this group, Arnault had explained that there was "an awareness in Guatemala that a structured negotiation with international involvement and verification may offer a viable framework to carry out overdue adjustments."[38] In the following months the World Bank paid consistent attention to the requirements of a sustainable peace process, while both the bank and the IDB indicated a willingness to provide Arnault with such assistance as he might require to facilitate negotiation of the socioeconomic accord. As discussion of this item was beginning, a further informal donor meeting was held in June 1995, this time in the presence of the Guatemalan government and CACIF. The messages to the Guatemalans were clear: Not only should every effort be made to reach an early conclusion of the final peace agreement, but tax reform was a necessity and external assistance could only supplement the mobilization of domestic resources for peace and social development.[39]

During the election campaign and in his first weeks in office, incoming President Álvaro Arzú Irigoyen of the National Vanguard Party (PAN), a scion of the private sector, had regarded the draft economic and social agreement with skepticism. His subsequent turnaround and acceptance of the position that eventually would be reflected in the "agreement on socio-economic aspects and the agrarian situation" that was signed in Mexico on May 6, 1996, marked one of the most significant shifts in the peace process. Although the agreement, which combined broad economic and social targets with more precise recommendations in a number of key areas, inevitably fell short of the expectations of sectors that had pushed for a more profound land reform and increased socialization of the economy and frustrated the entrenched views of the private sector's right wing, it represented a carefully constructed compromise, pieced together by the United Nations in its role as moderator, that had the virtue of representing something that "might just work," as Arnault put it in early 1997.[40] Eventually endorsed by the ASC, the accord was adopted by Arzú's government as the basis for its economic and social policy.[41] This decision would have far-reaching implications for Guatemala and its peace process: While it placed the peace accords at the center of a national agenda for development, democratization, and the modernization of the Guatemala state to which the government would, it was envisaged, be held accountable by the international community, it also would expose the peace process to a certain vulnerability through its reliance on the highly charged issue of fiscal reform for the raising of revenue necessary to pay for commitments contained within the accords as a whole.[42] That it represented a new challenge for the United Nations in the area of verification was clear; its signing prompted Goulding to call an unusual meeting of representatives of U.N. agencies and programs in June 1996 to address the need for the U.N. system to work as one to implement the agreements reached within Guatemalan peace process and would lead to the inclusion within MINUGUA of a dedicated team of socioeconomic experts.[43]

President Arzú took power in January 1996, committed by an agreement between all political parties brokered by the Central American Parliament on the island of Contadora in August 1995 to respect peace agreements already reached as "accords of state." Arzú was supported by his party's majority in a congress more representative than any yet seen in Guatemala. Following an unprecedented appeal from the URNG to the Guatemalan population to vote, a center-left front of popular and indigenous organizations (Frente Democrático Nueva Guatemala, FDNG) had been formed and won six (out of a total of eighty) seats in the assembly. However, Arzú's pursuit of the progressive agenda represented by the peace process would not be straightforward. He owed his slim majority over the conservative Frente Republicano Guatemalteco (FRG) party of former dictator General Efraín Ríos Montt in the second round of the presidential elections (51.2 percent to 48.8 percent) to strong support in the capital city; in contrast, his party, PAN, lost eighteen out of twenty-two of the country's departments to the FRG.[44]

The president-elect soon demonstrated his support for the peace process. He held two confidential meetings with the URNG before his inauguration, under the aegis of the Catholic Sant' Egidio community based in Rome, and, on assuming power, acted quickly to promote change by purging both the military and the police force of some of their most reactionary and abusive elements. He appointed a progressive foreign minister, Eduardo Stein, and also decided that the newly configured COPAZ would be headed by Gustavo Porras, who was not only his private secretary but also a former URNG militant.

Confidence-building measures, such as the March decision by both parties to the negotiation to introduce an informal cease-fire and the URNG's announcement, following the signing of the socioeconomic agreement, to abolish their practice of extracting war tax from landowners, helped promote the sense in Guatemala that 1996 would be the year to achieve peace. During the course of the year Arzú pressed very hard for this, even to the extent, in the closing stages of the negotiations, of going faster than the United Nations—having lived with the consequences of eleventh-hour haste in El Salvador—would have wanted. Arzú's defense minister, General Julio Balconi Turcios, who was a long-standing proponent of reform within the armed forces and had been a military representative at the negotiating table since April 1991, was a key figure in this acceleration of the process. During 1995, together with a few trusted senior officers, Balconi had held a series of secret meetings with the URNG General Command outside the formal framework of the negotiations and unbeknownst to the civilian members of COPAZ or other members of the URNG.[45] These meetings contributed significantly to the rapid formal negotiation of the "strengthening of civilian power and the role of the armed forces within a democratic society," which was begun immediately after the conclusion of the socioeconomic agreement. Agreement on this key accord, which addressed the once-taboo issue of the demilitarization of Guatemalan society, was reached in a matter of weeks.

The agreement signed on September 19, 1996, contained a comprehensive package of provisions stipulating that, under a reformed constitution, the police would be restructured, strengthened, and consolidated into a new National Civil Police and that the army would limit its role to external defense, adjusting its doctrine, training, deployment, size, budget, and role in intelligence functions accordingly.[46] However, in explicit recognition that the army had already accepted disciplinary measures imposed by Arzú and tacit acknowledgment of the importance of the military's more progressive wing as a necessary partner within the peace process—that also could be read as an indication of the military's strength in setting limits for the peace process—the agreement contained no provision for a military purge such as that conducted by the ad hoc commission in El Salvador and no language that impugned the honor of the Guatemalan army, as Guatemalans considered occurred in El Salvador. Moreover, provisions for the restructuring of the Guatemalan police force fell far short of the detail and profundity of the arrangements stipulated in El Salvador for the creation of that country's PNC.

A major break in the process was caused in late October by the involvement of a senior field commander of one URNG faction in the kidnapping of an elderly woman in Guatemala City. This was a flagrant violation of the human rights accord and the spirit of increased confidence within which negotiations were being conducted. The secretary-general deplored the incident, and, as negotiations were suspended, Arnault shuttled between the parties in an attempt to put the process back on track. Eventually the URNG accepted political responsibility for the kidnapping and offered to suspend all armed propaganda activities and to resume negotiations—in the absence of the leader of the URNG faction involved—with priority attention being given to agreement on the terms of a definitive cease-fire. However, the incident weakened the URNG substantially and ensured that it would present no serious obstacles in the concluding phase of the negotiations. Direct talks began again on November 9, and December 29, 1996, was named as the date for the signing of a final peace agreement.[47]

Most complex of the remaining items on the agenda was the agreement on "the basis for the legal integration of the URNG." In contrast to what had occurred in El Salvador, where the issue was left to the Legislative Assembly, here the parties at the negotiating table had to address the controversial issue of a legal mechanism to allow for the return of the URNG to Guatemalan life, presumably involving some kind of limited amnesty, and then turn the matter over to the assembly for its passage of a Law of National Reconciliation.[48] The agreement therefore presented negotiators with a particularly delicate challenge: the combination of the requirements of national reconciliation with the need to counteract impunity[49] and ensure reparation to victims of major human rights abuses. For the United Nations the difficulties involved the inevitable tension between the nonnegotiable principles of human rights and international law upon which the organization had been founded and the pragmatic requirements and limitations of a particular political process. In Guatemala, as in many other countries emerging from conflict, this tension was complicated by the fact that some members of both parties bore direct responsibility for acts that, under a strict application of the law, would land them behind bars.

In the end the agreement, which was signed on December 12, 1996, in Madrid, defined the central elements involved in the reintegration of the URNG into Guatemalan society and provided the basis for the passage of a Law of National Reconciliation on December 19 that included provisions extinguishing legal responsibility for political crimes and connected common crimes committed in the internal armed conflict, with the exception of crimes that are inviolable, or *imprescriptible* (without statute of limitation), by the terms of either national law or the international treaties to which Guatemala is party.[50] Among these latter were included torture, enforced disappearance, and genocide. That the law was unceremoniously rushed through the legislature by the governing party, without consultation with representatives of civil society who were advocating that, at the least, the crime of "extrajudicial execution" also be exempt from amnesty, contributed to a growing controversy among national and international human rights groups.

The two parties were accused of favoring a law that was concerned primarily with the preservation of their own interests, while the United Nations was criticized for having brokered an agreement that paved the way for an amnesty law that did not live up to the principles it espoused. The criticisms, while understandable, initially obscured attention from the avenues for future legal action that the law left open through its nonapplicability to civil and administrative responsibility.[51] As MINUGUA would point out in a statement it issued in early January, application of the law also would depend to a considerable extent on the judicial authorities' interpretation of the phrase "in the armed conflict," which in the mission's view could be interpreted as excluding from amnesty violations of human rights that occurred outside the strict context of the armed conflict itself and that clearly constituted excesses.[52] To the surprise of many of the law's critics, in the early weeks of 1997 petitions for amnesty filed with the lower courts by defense lawyers in some of the most notorious human rights cases were rejected on these grounds.[53]

Implementation and "Active" Verification

The final peace agreement in Guatemala was signed on December 29, 1996, in Guatemala City, less than three weeks before the fifth anniversary of the signing of the Salvadoran agreements in Mexico City on January 16, 1992. Verification of those peace accords had been a difficult process, subject to innumerable setbacks and delays. While the parties consistently expressed their will to implement the accords fully, they nevertheless benefited from the active presence of the United Nations on the ground and, on repeated occasions, from the impartial authority of the secretary-general, whether expressed through letters addressed to the parties or via the dispatch of high-level envoys from New York. Unsurprisingly, the timetable for the implementation of the Guatemalan accords had been prepared with the experience of El Salvador in mind, where five years after the signing of the accords the organization still had a residual field office in the country to oversee outstanding aspects of the peace agreements.[54] The timetable agreement (which also had been signed on December 29, a few hours before the final ceremony) therefore envisaged a four-year period of implementation, in a rare recognition of the long haul represented by a realistic postconflict peace-building operation.

The agreements in El Salvador had provided for the creation of a number of bodies to oversee their implementation, draft legislation deriving from them, negotiate broad social issues, resolve land disputes, put reconstruction funds to use, and review past abuses. These commissions, fora, and other structures envisaged a broader political participation than had existed during the negotiating process through the assignment of important roles to various government entities, the opposition political parties, the Legislative Assembly, nongovernmental organizations, trade unions, and even business groups. However, as implementation progressed, it became clear that, while some of these mechanisms allowed for lacunae within the accords themselves to be filled by the process of implementation (the mandatory recommendations for constitutional reform issued by the Commission on the Truth are an obvious example of this), for the most part, the dynamic that prevailed was that of the negotiating table in which the key actors had been the two parties and the United Nations. The most salient example of this was the failure of COPAZ, the National Commission for the Consolidation of Peace, to live up to expectations. It had been created as a mechanism for a variety of political forces to monitor and participate in the implementation of the agreements in parallel to ONUSAL itself.[55] However, with the passage of time the dominance of the two parties—which was compounded by the disintegration of the political parties in the center of the Salvadoran political spectrum and the disarticulation of the popular movement, in part as a result of an eventual split within the FMLN—increasingly isolated the other actors represented within it.

The accords had contained a complex timetable for the reintegration of the FMLN into civilian life that was carefully articulated with a number of important steps to be taken by the government, such as the dissolution of the old security forces. Gradually a pattern developed whereby problems would be resolved by tripartite deliberation arbitrated by ONUSAL; when this failed and crisis threatened, the parties resorted to meetings at the highest level with representatives of the secretary-general sent on flying missions from New York. During 1992, for example, Boutros-Ghali dispatched Under-Secretary-General Goulding, and at times de Soto as well, to El Salvador on a number of occasions when the peace process appeared imperiled: in March to address problems arising from land seizures by *campesino* organizations, evictions by government forces, and prosecutions by landowners; in August to resolve persistent delays in the timetable by overseeing one of its re-calendarizations; in September-October to renegotiate the question of land transfer, which had emerged as a major impediment to the further demobilization of the FMLN; and again in

November, when the initial deadline for a formal end to the armed conflict had passed and tensions were rising over the government's compliance with the recommendations of the Ad Hoc Commission, which, calling as they did for the dismissal of more than a hundred army officers, including the minister of defense and most of the High Command, far exceeded expectations and stood little chance of being implemented without heavy pressure from the United Nations.

Over the following years this kind of direct reinforcement of the verification conducted by ONUSAL on the ground would become more infrequent and be reserved for moments of particular concern—such as the spate of politically motivated killings in the run-up to the elections of 1994, which led the United Nations to press for belated compliance with a Truth Commission recommendation that alleged activities of death squads should be further investigated.[56] However, throughout their time in El Salvador, ONUSAL and its smaller successor missions undertook a judicious use of the organization's good offices mandate to maintain a leading role within the sometimes ungainly vehicle that was the peace process—certainly not in the driver's seat, as that position was rightly held by Salvadorans, but never beyond getting out for a push, or even redirection, when the process threatened to slow or be diverted from the proper course established in the peace accords.

At the time of this writing, it is probably still too soon to assess the long-term impact of the peace accords whose negotiation and implementation the United Nations has overseen. Initial assessments of the peace process as, to cite de Soto's much-quoted phrase, a "negotiated revolution" could not have foreseen the attrition that the dramatic escalation in violent crime inflicted on the population's sense of well-being, crime that is a bleak companion to persistently high levels of poverty. However, the positive legacies of the peace process are undeniable: The armed conflict itself was brought to an end and does not appear likely to recur; gross abuses of human rights are a thing of the past; the military was reduced in size and its role in Salvadoran national life redefined; the hated security forces were dissolved and a civilian police force deployed throughout the country; commissions were created to purge the military and uncover the truth of the violence of the past; the FMLN was legalized as a political party and has established itself as the second political force in the country, most emphatically through the substantial gains it made in the legislative and municipal elections of March 1997[57]; a series of constitutional and legislative reforms have been adopted, revising the selection process for the Supreme

Court and introducing other reforms in the area of public security and the judicial system; a government-funded human rights ombudsman has been established and is widely respected by the population; the acquisition of lands by former combatants from both sides was facilitated; and large amounts of international assistance flooded into the country in support of national efforts at reconstruction.

In early 1997 the United Nations no longer had the resources available to deploy a multifunctional mission of the scale and size proportional to Guatemala that ONUSAL was to El Salvador in 1992, even if, in its estimation, verification of the peace accords had required it. That it did not can be attributed to a number of factors: the difference in the nature of the military conflict, and indeed size of the guerrilla presence in the country with respect to the scale of the country itself; the difference in the accords themselves, which, while of a generally wider scope in Guatemala, also tended to be less detailed with regard to timetabled provisions requiring U.N. verification; and, not least, the kind of presence deemed appropriate to the prevailing political conditions in Guatemala. However, in some respects the United Nations was considerably better prepared for the task in hand that it had been in El Salvador. In Guatemala, after all, the verification mission, MINUGUA, had not only been active throughout the country for more than two years but was established after a conscious, and by and large successful, effort to build the lessons of El Salvador into its structures and activities right from the start. In addition to organizational measures, such as the establishment of interdisciplinary teams made up of civilian, police, and military observers, the application of lessons from the experience of ONUSAL included making institution-building a focus of the mission's work from the start; the maintaining of close, constructive, and frank relations with nongovernmental organizations; and the development of a close working relationship with other U.N. programs and agencies active in the country. In its two years of existence, the mission had been able to contribute significantly to the profound changes under way in Guatemala. This fact was reflected not only in the decline in human rights abuses it documented but also in the increased political tolerance that allowed the peace process to advance.[58]

The timetable agreement made clear that implementation of the peace accords in Guatemala would follow a very different path from that of El Salvador, not least because the government was in charge of most of the burden of executing the accords, while the URNG could not be expected to wield the same leverage as the FMLN had. The timetable divided implementation into three distinct phases—the first, to April 15, 1997, allowed largely for the establishment of the many different sectoral commissions that would provide for the broad participation of different representatives of Guatemalan society in the implementation in the second (the remainder of 1997) and third (through the end of 2000) phases.[59] Between the sectoral commissions and the government's lead body in the process, the Peace Secretariat, a Follow-up Commission was to play a crucial role of analysis and oversight, ensuring that the commitments made in the accords were properly fulfilled.

In its composition the Follow-up Commission aimed to represent a microcosm of the fragile coalition of different sectors of Guatemalan society whose support had contributed to the achievement of negotiated agreements in the first place and that would be needed to keep the peace process on track in the years ahead. In addition to two representatives each of the two parties, the commission was made up of "four citizens from different sectors of the population"—a representative of the private sector; a leader of the *cooperativista* (agrarian cooperative) sector; an indigenous leader; and Gert Rosenthal, a widely respected Guatemalan who had served as head of the United Nations' Economic Commission on Latin America and the Caribbean (ECLAC)—as well as the president of Congress and the head of the United Nations' verification mission, who had the right to speak, but not to vote, within the commission.[60] As Jean Arnault has pointed out, the composition of the commission could provide no guarantee, but at least it represented "an indication that Guatemala might implement the accords through the same mechanism of social consensus that made it possible to achieve the accords in the first place."[61] As implementation of the Guatemalan accords got under way in 1997, it soon emerged that, in the absence of the kind of predominance of the two parties that had negotiated the accords in national life that had been seen— and in some respects was to be regretted—in El Salvador, the question of "ownership" of the process by broad sectors of Guatemalan society would be key to the effectiveness of the participatory mechanisms upon which implementation of many of the accords would depend.[62]

Partly in recognition of the fact that the United Nations' role as moderator of the Guatemalan peace process would not cease with the signing of the peace agreements, the secretary-general departed from established U.N. practice—by which the tasks of negotiator and verifier are assigned to different individuals—and appointed Arnault to head the expanded U.N. mission to verify all aspects of the peace accords. Under the terms of

the timetable agreement, the expanded MINUGUA had a fourfold function stretching across all areas of the accords: verification, good offices, advisory services, and public information. Given the complexity of the accords themselves, the fulfillment of these functions would necessarily
involve extensive coordination with and even delegation to other members
of the U.N. system, the international financial institutions, and bilateral
donors active in Guatemala and all sectors of the nation's society. Success
would depend on the extent to which all these actors, whose consensual
support of the peace agreements was demonstrated most vividly (and lu-
cratively) by the Consulative Group meeting held in late January 1997 in
Brussels, at which $1.9 billion was pledged in support of the Guatemalan
peace process, would be able to work together in the years ahead in support of national actors committed to the pursuit of the peace accords as a
pillar of a new national agenda for Guatemala.

For the United Nations, as for the wider international community engaged in the transformation of Guatemala held out as a promise in the
peace accords, Guatemala represents an important testing ground. The restructuring of MINUGUA to address the challenges ahead was conducted
as the United Nations, under the leadership of a new secretary-general,
embarked on a complex process of reform that will have long-lasting consequences for the efficacy with which it is able to carry out those responsibilities it is charged with by its charter. One of the fundamental aspects addressed by this exercise is the extent to which improved coordination
within the U.N. system and among other actors of the international community can be brought to bear in peace-making, peacekeeping, and postconflict activities. While many within the United Nations view El Salvador
simply as a "success story" safely shelved in the past and Guatemala as an
anomalous and somewhat confusing operation in a part of the world, Latin
America, that is unlikely to require extensive U.N. involvement in the future, taken together the two processes represent a resource for United Nations efforts for peace that is too important to be overlooked.

Despite the many differences in how U.N. involvement in the negotiation of peace agreements unfolded in El Salvador and Guatemala—differences that stem from the "ripeness" of the moment for engagement in El
Salvador and the slow coming to maturity of the Guatemalan process; the
extent to which the military conflict impinged on the national conscience
and, indeed, on the negotiations themselves in each case; and the strength
of the parties at the negotiating table with respect to the wider pressures
for peace being exercised by society at large—the two processes have ele-

ments in common that will, in time, be of greater importance to their sustainability. Throughout the negotiation and implementation of the agreements in El Salvador and Guatemala, the United Nations has recognized the need for lasting peace to be crafted from measures that address the root causes of the conflicts. As a result, the agreements provided for the relatively long-term engagement of the organization in the building of peace in the postconflict phase. In Guatemala in particular, and as a direct consequence of experience in El Salvador, the United Nations learned the importance of working in close coordination with other members of the international community and of encouraging the development of the host country's capacity to provide for the financing of the commitments contained within the peace accords. These basic but hardwon lessons will be of value, however, only if they come with the humble recognition that success does not mean that "progress in fashioning a region of peace, freedom, democracy and development," as the annual resolution on "the situation in Central America" of the U.N. General Assembly is titled, will be easy in this or any other region of the world whose history has been sadly lacking in all four commodities.

Notes

1. See Susanne Jonas, "Between Two Worlds: The U.N. in Guatemala," paper presented at the North-South Center Conference on Multilateral Peacekeeping, Miami, April 1996, for a discussion of the Never-in-Guatemala phenomenon.

2. Alvaro de Soto, luncheon address, in Nicole Ball and Tammy Halevy, eds. *Making Peace Work: The Role of the International Development Community,* report of the Overseas Development Council Conference May 9, 1996, Washington, D.C. (Washington, D.C.: Overseas Development Council, 1996), p. 12.

3. Postconflict peace building was defined as "action to identify and support structures which will tend to strengthen and solidify peace in order to avoid a relapse into conflict". Boutros Boutros-Ghali *An Agenda for Peace: Preventive Diplomacy, Peacemaking and Peace-Keeping, report of the Secretary-General pursuant to the statement adopted by the summit meeting of the Security Council on 31 January 1992* (New York: United Nations, 1992), A/47/277-S/24111, para. 21.

4. The other conflicts were Cambodia, the former Yugoslavia, Somalia, and Angola. Boutros Boutros-Ghali, *Report on the Work of the Organization from the Forty-sixth to the Forty-seventh Session of the General Assembly* (New York: United Nations, September 1992), paras. 132, 155.

5. From 1983 to 1987 the Contadora group presented a series of proposals for regional peace through mutual demilitarization and reduction of the numbers of foreign advisors as well as agreements to cease supporting insurgent forces in other states. The proposals reflected an exclusively intragovernmental approach to the Central American conflicts.

6. Alvaro de Soto accompanied the secretary-general on the trip and was the source of this account.

7. Resolution 637 of July 27, 1989, in United Nations, *The United Nations and El Salvador: 1990–1995* (New York: United Nations, 1995), 91–92.

8. Ignacio Ellacuría, "Una nueva fase en el proceso salvadoreño," *Estudios Centroamericanos* (ECA), No. 485 (March 1989): 167–97.

9. I. William Zartman, "Ripening Conflict, Ripe Moment, Formula and Mediation," in Diane B. Bendahmane and John W. McDonald, Jr., eds. *Perspectives on Negotiation: Four Case Studies and Interpretations* (Washington, D.C.: Foreign Service Institute, U.S. Department of State, 1986), 205–27.

10. Baena Soares's attempt at mediation was manipulated by the Salvadoran government, which announced that he was in the country at its express invitation (rather than as an independent mediator who would have access to both parties) and thus lost him any hope of gaining the confidence of the FMLN. He was subsequently trapped inside the Hotel El Salvador when the hotel was occupied by a unit of the FMLN fleeing from the Salvadoran army.

11. "Declaration of San Isidro de Coronado," annex to Oscar Arias Sánchez et al. *Letter dated 12 December 1989, from the permanent Representative of El Salvador to the United Nations, Addressed to the Secretary-General,* A/44/872-S/21019, in U.N., *The United Nations and El Salvador,* 100–2.

12. "The Geneva Agreement," 4 April 1991, annex to Oscar Santamaría et al. *Letter dated 8 October 1991 from the Permanent Representative of El Salvador, Addressed to the Secretary-General,* A/46/551-S/23128, U.N., *The United Nations and El Salvador,* 164–65.

13. "General Agenda and Schedule for the Comprehensive Negotiation Process, Issued at Caracas on 21 May 1990" annex II to *Report of the Secretary-General,* A/45/706-S/21931, ibid., 117.

14. Terry Lynn Karl's article, "El Salvador's Negotiated Revolution," still provides the best overview of the negotiating process, *Foreign Affairs,* 71, No. 2 (Spring 1992): 147–64.

15. The phrase was de Soto's, as cited in ibid., 156.

16. "The Mexico Agreements," annex to *Letter dated 8 October 1991 from the Permanent Representative of El Salvador to the United Nations, Addressed to the Secretary-General* A/46/553-S/23130, U.N., *The United Nations and El Salvador,* 167–74.

17. On February 8, 1990, Secretary of State James Baker told the Senate Committee on Appropriations, "this is the year to end the war through a negotiated settlement." FY 91 Hearings (Washington, D.C.: U.S. Government Printing Office, 1990), p. 10.

18. In February 1991 this pressure had taken the form of an apparently planned leak in the *New York Times.* An unnamed source charged that de Soto was "less than energetic pursuing the peace process" and that he "accedes to the guerrillas' delaying tactics," seriously undercutting the efforts of the United Nations at a crucial point in the negotiations. Clifford Krauss, "UN Aide Assailed in Salvadoran Talks," *New York Times,* February 1, 1991 A3.

19. "The New York Agreement" annex to *Letter dated 26 September 1991 from the Permanent Representative of El Salvador to the United Nations, Addressed to the Secretary-General* A/46/502-S/23082 in U.N., *The United Nations and El Salvador,* 159–63.

20. While the deadline imposed by the impending departure of Pérez de Cuéllar certainly was effective in bringing the negotiations to a successful conclusion—not least because Pérez de Cuéllar's successor, Boutros Boutros-Ghali, had contributed to the pressure on the Salvadorans by indicating to President Cristiani that, should the negotiations remain under way when he assumed office, he would have little time to dedicate to them and it would therefore be in El Salvador's best interest to conclude the process earlier—it was not without its costs. Most notable was the weakness of the aspects of the accords dealing with the reintegration of former combatants, and particularly the provisions relating to land transfer, a key structural issue underlying the war. The sketchy terms of the Chapultepec agreement, which were in part attributable to the failure of the FMLN's negotiating team to address the issues earlier, would require substantial renegotiation by the United Nation in October 1992, when lack of progress on land transfer led the FMLN to suspend demobilization of its combatants. See U.N., *The United Nations and El Salvador,* 28–29.

21. See David Holiday, "Guatemala's Long Road to Peace," *Current History* (February 1997): 68–74 for a comprehensive overview of Guatemala's peace process.

22. A first meeting between the Guatemalan government and the URNG, which was convened by the Spanish government and held in Madrid in October 1987, had achieved little except to reveal how distant was the prospect of substantive dialogue in Guatemala. Forty-seven organizations and eighty-four delegates, including representatives of the government, popular organizations, other representatives of civil society, and some business sectors took part in the national dialogue (organizations representing the private and agrarian sectors refused to participate). See Tania Palencia Prado, *Peace in the Making: Civil Groups in Guatemala* (London: Catholic Institute for International Relations Briefing, 1996), 11.

23. The Oslo Agreement, annex III to *Report of the Secretary-General*, A/45/706-S/21931, in U.N., *The United Nations and El Salvador*, 118–19.

24. The agenda included: democratization and human rights; strengthening of civilian authority and the role of the army in a democratic society; the identity and rights of indigenous people; constitutional reforms and the electoral system; socioeconomic aspects; the agrarian situation; resettlement of populations uprooted by the armed conflict; the basis for bringing the URNG into the country's political life; arrangements for a final cease-fire; and a timetable. "Agreement on the Procedure for the Search for Peace by Political Means. Signed at Mexico City on 26 April 1991," annex to *Letter dated 2 May 1991 from the Permanent Representative of Guatemala to the United Nations, Addressed to the Secretary-General*, A/45/1007-S/22563. "Agreement on a General Agenda, Signed at Mexico City on 26 April 1991," annex to *Letter dated 7 May 1991 from the Permanent Representative of Guatemala to the United Nations, Francisco Villagrán de León. Addressed to the Secretary-General*, A/45/1009-S/22573.

25. "The Framework Agreement for the Resumption of the Negotiating Process between the Government of Guatemala and the Unidad Revolucionario Nacional Guatemalteca" annex to *letter dated 17 January 1994 from the Secretary-General to the President of the General Assembly and to the President of the Security Council*, A/49/61-S/1994/53.

26. The formal incarnation of the Friends as a group was a distinct improvement on a previous initiative by which the three Latin American Friends and Spain were requested by President Serrano to constitute themselves as Friends of the Guatemalan President. Considerable diplomatic footwork was necessary to redirect the proffered "friendship" toward the peace process itself.

27. Norway was included in recognition of its long-standing involvement in Guatemala's negotiating effort.

28. See Susanne Jonas, "Dangerous Liaisons: The U.S. in Guatemala," *Foreign Policy*, No. 103 (Summer 1996): 144–60, for an account of this complex relationship. Pressure on the administration intensified after revelations, in March 1995, that a Guatemalan officer on the payroll of the Central Intelligence Agency had been involved in the murders of a guerrilla commander, Efraín Bámaca, who had been married to a U.S. lawyer Jennifer Harbury, and Michael De Vine, a U.S. citizen.

29. "The Comprehensive Agreement [on] Human Rights," annex I to *Letter dated 8 April 1994 from the Secretary-General to the President of the General Assembly and to the President of the Security Council*, A/48/928-S/1994/448.

30. "Agreement on Resettlement of the Population Groups Uprooted by the Armed Conflict," and "Agreement on the Establishment of the Commission to Clarify Past Human Rights Violations and Acts of Violence that Have Caused the Guatemalan Population to Suffer," annexes I and II to A/48/954-S/1994/751.

31. Particularly damaging had been the Jesuit case: the Truth Commission found that the actual minister of defense, General René Emilio Ponce, in the presence of other members of the army high command, had given the order to kill the Jesuits and leave no witnesses. *From Madness to Hope: The 12-year War in El Salvador*, Report of the Commission on the Truth for El Salvador, annex to Letter dated 29 March 1993 from the Secretary-General Addressed to the President of the Security Council, S/25500, in U.N., *The United Nations and El Salvador*, 290–414.

32. For a discussion of this episode see "Identical Letters Dated 17 February 1995 from the Under-Secretary-General for Political Affairs to the President of Guatemala and to the Members of the Comandancia of the Unidad Revolucionaria Nacional Guatemalteca," annex I to A/49/857-S/1995/168, paras. 1–6.

33. Ibid.

34. "The Agreement on Identity and Rights of Indigenous Peoples," annex to *Letter dated 5 April 1995 from the Secretary-General to the President of the General Assembly and to the President of the Security Council* A/49/882-S/1995/256, 1995.

35. See note 20 above. In the early months of 1998 some residual aspects of the land transfer program still remained to be implemented.

36. In late 1995 the private sector business organization CACIF (El Comité Coordinador de Asociaciones Agrícolas, Comerciales, Industriales y Financieras) threatened to prosecute Héctor Rosada, the leader of COPAZ, the governmental negotiating team, for conducting "illegal" negotiations with the URNG.

37. Alvaro de Soto and Graciana del Castillo, "Obstacles to Peacebuilding," *Foreign Policy* No. 94 (Spring 1994): 74. Elisabeth J. Wood is among those who have criticized this metaphor, arguing that El Salvador is "far from a passive and unitary patient undergoing twin surgeries . . ." and instead "made up of divergent groups whose conflicting interests not only fueled the war but continued actively to shape the peace." Elisabeth J. Wood, "The Peace Accords and Postwar Reconstruction," in James K. Boyce, ed., *Economic Policy for Building Peace: The Lessons of El Salvador* (Boulder, Colo: Lynne Rienner, 1996), 73–106.

38. World Bank, aide-mémoire of informal donors meeting held in Paris on June 15, 1994.

39. Jean Arnault, interview with author, New York, Feb. 2, 1997.

40. Ibid.

41. See, for example, the Message of President Arzú, in the introduction to "Peace Program: The Opportunity for Guatemala," report submitted by the Government of Guatemala to the Consultative Group Meeting, Brussels, January 21–22, 1997.

42. This vulnerability would be revealed by events of February 1998, when protests against a property tax law approved by the Legislative Assembly in December 1997 in compliance with the peace agreements, fanned and manipulated by right-wing sectors opposed to tax reform, led President Arzú to request the assembly to repeal the law, creating serious concern about the financial sustainability of the peace process in the years ahead.

43. Marrack Goulding, Under-Secretary-General for Political Affairs, "Statement to the Meeting of the United Nations System on Guatemala," June 14, 1996.

44. See *The Situation in Central America: Procedures for the Establishment of a Firm and lasting Peace and Progress in Fashioning a Region of Peace, Freedom, Democracy and Development,* A/50/878, 1996, para. 17.

45. Balconi described these meetings in his presentation at the Woodrow Wilson Center on March 14, 1997 (See his "Reflections" to Chapter 4 in this volume.) A member of the URNG General Command confirmed his account of them to the author.

46. "The Agreement on the Strengthening of Civilian Power and on the Role of the Armed Forces in a Democratic Society," annex to *Identical letters Dated 30 September 1996 from the Secretary-General Addressed to the President of the Security Council,* A/51/410-S/1996/853, 1996.

47. See The United Nations Mission for the Verification of Human Rights and of Compliance with the Commitments of the Comprehensive Agreement on Human Rights in Guatemala, *Report of the Secretary-General,* A/51/695-S/1996/998 for an account of these events. Agreements on a definitive cease-fire, on constitutional reforms and the electoral regime, and on the basis for the legal integration of the URNG were to be signed in Oslo, Stockholm, and Madrid respectively in early December.

48. The National Reconciliation Law approved by the assembly in El Salvador on January 23, 1992, granted amnesties in some cases but left the door open for the investigations to be conducted by the Truth Commission. In this respect Salvadorans were assisted by the fact that it had not been

specified in the peace agreements whether the Truth Commission would assign responsibility in the cases it investigated or not.

49. The human rights accord had stated: "The Parties agree on the need for firm action against impunity. The Government shall not sponsor the adoption of legislative or any other type of measures designed to prevent the prosecution and punishment of persons responsible for human rights violations." "Joint Statement by the Government of Guatemala and the Unidad Revolucionaria Nacional Guatemalteca" annex III to *Letter dated 8 April 1994 from the Secretary-General to the President of the General Assembly and to the President of the Security Council*, A/48/928-S/1994/448, 1994 para. 1.

50. "The Agreement on the Basis for the Legal Integration of the URNG," annex II of *Identical letters dated 16 January 1997 from the Secretary-General Addressed to the President of the General Assembly and to the President of the Security Council*, A/51/776-S/1997/51, 1997.

51. Among other features of the law that went largely unreported was the contents of Article 10, which significantly strengthened the Clarification Commission, by endorsing its mandate and making cooperation with the commission a legal obligation for all branches of the government. See Memorandum of Margaret Popkin, program director of the Robert F. Kennedy Memorial Center for Human Rights, Washington, D.C., to Interested Colleagues, "Update on the Guatemalan Amnesty," March 17, 1997. The residual ill-feeling against the United Nations was perhaps partly responsible for the harsh response of some human rights organizations to allegations that surfaced in April and May 1997 that Arnault (in his capacity as moderator) and MINUGUA had covered up information regarding the alleged disappearance of "Mincho" (Juan José Cabrera Rodas), a URNG combatant, during the government's interception of the October 1996 kidnapping of the elderly woman in Guatemala City. (The URNG had consistently maintained that the midlevel field commander had acted on his own; therefore, it did not denounce the loss of "Mincho.") As a result of these allegations, on May 28, a few days after MINUGUA issued a public report on the findings of its investigation so far, the secretary-general dispatched a fact-finding mission to Guatemala to review the United Nations' handling of this delicate case. The mission subsequently provided the secretary-general with a confidential report; after reading it, the secretary-general declared his "complete confidence" in both Arnault and MINUGUA. However, the episode already had caused considerable damage to the mission's credibility at a delicate stage of the peace process.

52. MINUGUA Statement to the Press on the National Reconciliation Law, January 8, 1997.

53. Such cases include the murders of Jorge Carpio and Myrna Mack, and the Xamán massacre of 1985.

54. The United Nations Observer Mission in El Salvador was in the country under a mandate of the Security Council until April 31, 1995. It was followed by the much reduced Mission of the United Nations in El Salvador (MINUSAL, May 1, 1995–April 30, 1996) and still smaller Office of the United Nations for Verification in El Salvador (ONUV, May 1, 1996–December 31, 1996) and Support Unit in El Salvador (January 1, 1997–June 30, 1997) under mandates of the General Assembly.

55. It was composed of two representatives of the government, including a member of the armed forces, two representatives of the FMLN, and one of each of the parties or coalitions represented within the Legislative Assembly, while the archbishop of San Salvador and a delegate of ONUSAL were to have access as observers to the commission's work and deliberations.

56. In an arrangement that was brokered by the United Nations, a Joint Group for the Investigation of Politically Motivated Illegal Armed Groups was formed. See "Report of the Joint Group for the Investigation of Politically Motivated Illegal Armed Groups in El Salvador," annex to *Letter dated 11 August 1994 from the Secretary-General Addressed to the President of the Security Council*, S/1994/989, 1994.

57. The FMLN won twenty-seven seats in the Legislative Assembly, to ARENA's twenty-eight; the remaining twenty-nine were divided between smaller parties. The FMLN also improved its standing at the municipal level dramatically, winning a total of fifty-three mayoralties, including, in

a coalition with two other parties, San Salvador; six of the fourteen departmental capitals; and ten of nineteen municipalities in the department of San Salvador.

58. See Stephen Baranyi, *The Challenge in Guatemala: Verifying Human Rights, Strengthening National Institutions and Enhancing an Integrated UN Approach to Peace* (London: The Centre for the Study of Global Governance, London School of Economics, 1995), for a useful analysis of MINUGUA's first year in the field.

59. "The Agreement on the Implementation, Compliance and Verification Timetable for the Peace Agreements," annex I of *Identical letters Dated 5 February 1997 from the Secretary-General Addressed to the President of the General Assembly and to the President of the Security Council*, A/51/796-S/1997/114, 1997.

60. See ibid., section V, p. 32.

61. See Arnault's "Reflections" to this chapter.

62. See A/51/936, para. 72, and A/52/757, para. 90.

Reflections

JEAN ARNAULT

What is interesting about the Guatemalan peace process is above all the context in which it has unfolded. Unlike that which occurred in El Salvador, what has characterized Guatemala is the existence of a gradual process of democratization beginning in 1985. Also significant is that the Guatemalan conflict was of very low military intensity—it was not the kind of all-out confrontation that took place in El Salvador.

The Guatemalan process also has been characterized by a prolonged political crisis not unlike the political crises of other countries in Latin America and the world. The crisis is not so much rooted in military issues as it is in socioeconomic and public safety issues, the issue of multiculturalism, and the coexistence of indigenous and Spanish-speaking peoples.

What has distinguished the peace process in Guatemala is that the armed confrontation is not the fundamental factor setting the national agenda; rather, it is a peripheral element.

Given this context, it was not possible for the United Nations or the international community to play a role similar to the one it had played in El Salvador or to one it would play in any country where the military confrontation constituted the core of the national agenda. Other political and social factors have predominated. Even into 1997, when Guatemalans were asked how important the military conflict was in the life of the country, people ranked the war in ninth or tenth place. Ranked higher were issues of security, poverty, the cost of living, and so on. In other words, not only did the military issue not dominate national life, the issue of the negotiations themselves did not have the legitimacy or urgency of many other problems. This phenomenon is also evident in other countries; thus, it is useful to extract from the Guatemalan experience lessons about the extent to which the international community can play a role.

In El Salvador, the role of the international community was focused primarily on the issue of mediation, carried out virtually autonomously and independently of other national factors. It is true that the Group of Friends played an important role, but overall one has the impression that in El Salvador the peace process was relatively isolated from other social factors. The weakness of the Salvadoran process stems precisely from the fact that the negotiations were conducted largely in isolation from international or internal factors and therefore did not create a sense of "ownership" of the peace process by other elements of Salvadoran society.

One of the problems that arose during the implementation phase of the Salvadoran process was that no social sectors had come to "own" the reforms or had committed themselves to them; now that the war is over and the international presence also has come to an end, many reforms cannot be implemented with only the state or the FMLN participating.

In Guatemala, what characterized the process from the beginning, from the very first contacts between the government and the URNG, was a kind of vicious circle. Given that the military conflict was of very low intensity, it did not generate in either the URNG or the government the political will required to end the armed confrontation and achieve peace.

To a large extent—and I believe that the URNG now recognizes this— between 1987 and 1994 there were not many prospects for real change in Guatemala through negotiations. The URNG viewed the negotiations rather as a battleground, an arena for tactical confrontation over the government's international prestige and over domestic political issues. At the same time, and precisely because the negotiations were being conducted absent significant political will, the peace process was competing as a social process with many others simultaneously under way in the country. These included struggles over issues of public security, the agenda of cultural transformation promoted by indigenous organizations, and issues of social transformation promoted by popular sectors and the union movement.

Hence, running parallel to the effort to find a negotiated settlement to the war were a number of independent political agendas pushed by a very active civil society, with the aim of renewing the economic development of Guatemala.

There thus developed a contradiction of sorts. On one hand, the negotiations process could gain legitimacy only if it incorporated the other agendas of social transformation; on the other hand, however, the negotiations could not in exchange manufacture the sufficient political will to make these reforms a reality.

Between 1991 and 1994, what characterized the vicious circle of ambition and weakness in the peace process was the inability to gain internal legitimacy within a context of low-intensity conflict.

The role that the international community played at that time (1993–1994) was precisely to bring to the peace process what it was unable to generate from inside, despite the valient efforts of individuals such as Monseñor Rodolfo Quezada Turuño, who served as moderator in the name of the Catholic church. The United Nations provided legitimacy, authority, and credibility, without which there can be no political solution to a peace process of such low intensity.

There is, however, an important difference between the role of the United Nations in El Salvador and in Guatemala. In the case of El Salvador, the United Nations came out of the period from 1990 to 1993 with the moral power and international legitimacy to play a legitimizing role in the peace process.

By contrast, the United Nations came to Guatemala in 1994 after failures in Somalia, Rwanda, and Burundi, and with a fairly fragile image given its handling of verification in El Salvador. In other words, if it had just been a question of the role of the United Nations as an institution, I do not believe that the Guatemalan process would have been able to develop these fundamental elements of credibility and legitimacy. What allowed the process to develop national credibility was a combination of factors: the international dimension, represented by both the United Nations and by the Group of Friends, and internal factors such as the Assembly of Civil Society, which grouped together many actors who, even if they were not powerful, were highly visible on the national scene.

The roots of the success of the peace process lie in the Framework Agreement of January 1994.* The agreement gave the peace process what it had heretofore lacked: the legitimacy, credibility, and authority to impose itself not as a marginal process alongside many other processes competing to define the Guatemalan agenda. The agreement transformed the peace negotiations from a discussion between a group of 1,200 guerrillas and the Guatemalan state into a catalyst for a national agenda to renew the social contract, one that would generate new institutions and establish a

---

*The Acuerdo Marco para la Reanudación del Proceso de Negociación elevated the role of the United Nations from observer to moderator; established the Asamblea de la Sociedad Civil (Assembly of Civil Society) to provide substantive input into the peace talks from civic organizations; and created a Group of Friends of the Guatemalan Peace Process consisting of Colombia, Mexico, Norway, Spain, the United States, and Venezuela [ed.].

new modality for relations between various social sectors, between the army and the civilians, and between indigenous peoples and ladinos. The main lesson to be learned from the Guatemalan peace process is that in order for the negotiation process to succeed, it has to be strengthened, consolidated, and progressively converted into the core of the national agenda.

Another fundamental element relates to partial successes. As anyone who was in Guatemala in 1995 can attest, the immediate implementation of the March 1994 Accord on Human Rights and the reduction in violations of human rights starting in 1996 played a critical role in the success of the Guatemalan peace process. Had it not been for partial successes, which included the informal cessation of hostilities and the purging of the security forces in 1996, I believe that the fate of the peace process would still be in question.

A final point concerns implementation. The case of El Salvador highlighted several weaknesses: in national verification mechanisms, in the organizational capacity of social sectors that would benefit from the accords, in state institutions, and finally, in the coordination of foreign aid.

The peace process in Guatemala is facing exactly the same problems in implementation. The accords raised high expectations with respect to socioeconomic and indigenous and other issues, and the obstacles to fulfilling those expectations are basically the same as in El Salvador. In fact, the weakness of the state in Guatemala is even worse than in El Salvador.

Nevertheless, precisely because the Guatemalan process was one in which a national consensus played a much larger role, there is reason to be more optimistic regarding other aspects of implementation. A national verification entity has been established that does not include just the parties but also representatives of indigenous peoples, the private sector, and the popular sector. Although this is no guarantee, there is at least an indication that Guatemala might implement the accords through the same mechanism of social consensus that made it possible to achieve the accords in the first place.

One of the great strengths of the peace process in Guatemala is that, even though it took a great deal of time to conclude the accords, the process involved organizations of refugees, the internally displaced, the indigenous sectors, and the popular movement. Major problems notwithstanding, there exists in Guatemala a level of "ownership" by beneficiaries of the accords that is much greater than that which existed in El Salvador.

Furthermore, in El Salvador, the lack of coordination in the area of foreign aid and the absence of coordination of the international community as a whole created major difficulties in the implementation of the accords. Partly as a result of the mistakes that were made in El Salvador, the international community has exhibited a surprisingly high degree of political will in regard to Guatemala.

Our hope is that the same avenues that made it possible to overcome the weakness of the state and civil society in order to conclude the peace accords can be used to implement them; in other words, that, above all, a very broad social consensus regarding the objectives of peace will be consolidated.

10

Between Memory and Forgetting: Guerrillas, the Indigenous Movement, and Legal Reform in the Time of the EZLN

LUIS HERNÁNDEZ NAVARRO

An unjust and criminal economic system, the Mexican political system, forced a group of citizens, for the most part indigenous peoples, to take up arms to make themselves heard and to call attention to the serious problems of the indigenous peoples in Mexico. The political route for dialogue and the solution of the main demands of the Mexican people will not come from the supreme government, but rather from civil society, independent social and political organizations. The new peace, the one we Mexicans need, the one we deserve, will come from ourselves, from our effort, from our hope . . .
—Comité Clandestino Revolucionario Indígena-Ejército Zapatista de Liberación Nacional (CCRI-EZLN)

Dangerous Relations

On February 16, 1996, two years after the Zapatista uprising of January 1994 had begun, the Zapatista Army of National Liberation—EZLN—

This work owes great debts to many people. Among others, I wish to express gratitude for the teachings and comments of: Laura Carlsen, Adelfo Regino, Aristarco Aquino, Fidel Morales, Lorenzo Gómez, Antonio García de León, Ramón Vera, Herman Bellinhausen, Eugenio Bermejillo, Miguel Tejero, Josefina Aranda, Victor Pérez Grovas, Carlos Monsivais, Julio Miguel, Gustavo Esteva and Gilberto López y Rivas, Ricardo Robles, Cindy Arnson, Jerónimo Hernández, and Magda Gómez. The final responsibility for what is said is mine.

297

and the Mexican government signed the San Andrés Accords on Indigenous Rights and Culture. These agreements were the result of the first of five rounds of talks planned between the two parties to resolve the issues leading to the insurrection.

The signing of the accords was a significant achievement for Mexico, a country with the largest indigenous population in Latin America. According to the 1990 census, 8.7 million persons, over 10 percent of Mexico's total population, speak an indigenous language.[1] The real number actually could be larger: Experts allege that official data underestimate the indigenous population, and the population growth rate in indigenous areas exceeds the national rate.[2] In the southern states of the republic, which are areas of extreme poverty, with high rates of illiteracy, malnutrition, and mortality, many municipalities have an indigenous population of over 70 percent.

These indigenous peoples have an awareness of their own identities.[3] They preserve, to a greater or lesser degree, their institutions, culture, and language and want them to continue, but with legal recognition. Their demand for autonomy has been aggravated by the lack of specific constitutional guarantees as well as the failure of policies aimed at this sector, policies that are included in different versions of what has been called *indigenismo*.[4]

This work explains briefly the background of the San Andrés Accords, the formation of the new indigenous movement that has adopted those agreements as part of its struggle, and the events that followed after the accords were signed.

The Background of the Peace Negotiations

The legal framework within which negotiations between the EZLN and the federal government took place is the Law for Dialogue, Conciliation and a Worthy Peace in Chiapas, which was promulgated and went into effect on March 11, 1995, immediately after the military offensive against the EZLN on February 9 of that year. The law's objective was to establish juridical bases for promoting dialogue and conciliation in order to solve the armed conflict in a just and lasting way. Reaching this goal would entail attending to the issues that gave rise to the conflict, including the EZLN in the political process, reconciling the demands and interests of the Chiapanecan peoples, promoting social well-being, and proposing the outlines for an amnesty.

Under the law, in addition to the federal government and the EZLN, three other participants were recognized: the Commission for Conciliation and Peace (Comisión de Concordia y Pacificación, COCOPA), the National Intermediation Commission (Comisión Nacional de Intermediación, CONAI), and the Commission on Follow-up and Verification (Comisión de Seguimiento y Verificación, COSEVER). COCOPA is comprised of members of the national congress, one representative of the local congress, and one from the executive branch of the state of Chiapas. Its principal functions are to set out the bases for the dialogue and negotiation, and to facilitate the process. CONAI is made up of leading members of civil society and is chaired by the bishop of San Cristóbal, Samuel Ruiz. Its role is to mediate among the parties. COSEVER is comprised of three representatives of the EZLN and three of the federal government, five permanent invitees from each side, two alternates, two temporary invitees, one representative from COCOPA, one from CONAI, one from the state government, and another from the local congress. It is responsible for providing follow-up and verification of compliance with the accords.

Between April and September 1995 the parties held six meetings in the municipality of San Andrés at which they discussed, without success, the bases for military détente and, with consensus, procedures for the negotiations. Finally, on September 11, 1995, the document entitled "Agenda, Format, and Rules of Procedure of the Protocol of Bases for Dialogue and Negotiation of an Agreement of Concord and Pacification with Justice and Dignity" was signed. With the procedural aspects resolved, the negotiation was open to substantive topics. On October 1 the first round of talks began on indigenous rights and culture.

The Zapatistas called for the negotiations to include a gamut of leaders, academics, and intellectuals, Indians and non-Indians, with backgrounds in and knowledge of the topic, representing a rich diversity of thought on the issue. The federal government, on the other hand, preferred to bring to the table only indigenous leaders linked to the National Solidarity Program, low-profile lawyers, government officials from Chiapas and from the Interior and Agrarian Reform ministries, and a few specialists.

An intense mobilization of Indian peoples was generated around the negotiations. Fora and debates took place throughout the country to reflect on and systematize the indigenous question. They brought out the deplorable living conditions of the indigenous peoples, attempted to articulate their historic demands, and proposed projects based on the new relationship between the state and the Indian peoples. Such a mobilization, unprecedented in the recent history of the country, culminated in the National Indigenous

Forum called by the EZLN from January 3 to 8, 1996. This forum showed the deep support and authority that the Zapatistas had earned within the country's indigenous population: 500 delegates participated from 178 indigenous organizations, including members of 32 Indian peoples.

Between November 28 and December 1, 1995, the federal government organized National Consultation Forums on Indigenous Rights and Participation in twenty-one states. Even though over a quarter of those attending came from government institutions and many of the delegates belonged to official organizations, positions were established at these forums that came very close to those put forth by the Zapatista camp in San Andrés.

The San Andrés Accords and the Constitution: Importance and Limitations

Even though the Mexican nation since its founding has been pluriethnic and pluricultural, its constitutions have not reflected this reality. To assimilate the Indians, to force them to abandon what makes them Indian, has been an obsession of the ruling classes since the 1824 constitution. To be rid of the colonial heritage, to resist foreign intervention, and to combat ecclesiastical and military forces, modernization had led to prioritizing a vision of national unity that excluded cultural differences.

The 1917 constitution did not include Indian peoples in its recognition of the existence of collective and social rights of Mexico's citizens. However, even this lack of legal recognition and the thorough integrationist policies followed by revolutionary governments did not put an end to the indigenous peoples who found, in the spaces created by agrarian reform and in the work of specialized institutions aimed at caring for them, some toeholds for resistance. Although they had managed to preserve their identity and some of their institutions and culture, the homogenizing ideal had led to their exclusion, discrimination, marginalization, oppression, and exploitation by the rest of national society. Indians were condemned either to disappear as such or to live lives of pretense and deception.

Although the 1992 reform of Article 4 of the constitution made reference to the existence of Indian peoples and recognized their cultural rights, it did not specify the principles, relations, and institutions within which those rights would materialize, and it relegated their application to secondary laws (nonexistent in many cases, contradictory in others).[5] Nor did the revision of Article 4 include any substantive demands, such as those for autonomy or for the exercise of self-determination.

The San Andrés Accords on Indigenous Rights and Culture signed on February 16, 1996, sought to rectify this omission. The accords are comprised of four different documents. The first is a joint pronouncement on the need to establish a new pact between the Indian peoples and the state and the characteristics that it should have. The second contains a series of joint proposals of national scope that the federal government and EZLN should send to the national congress. The third establishes a set of special reforms for Chiapas. The fourth is a text signed by the parties, to which were added some positions that were not incorporated into the first three documents.

The points negotiated with the government do not resolve all the indigenous demands, but they do promise to solve some of the most important, among which are:

1. Recognition in the constitution of the indigenous peoples and their right to self-determination in a constitutional framework of autonomy;[6]
2. Expansion of their participation and political representation and recognition of their economic, political, social, and cultural rights as well as collective rights;
3. Guarantee of full access to the system of justice, access to state jurisdiction, recognition of their governing systems, respect for difference;
4. Promotion of the cultural manifestations of Indian peoples;
5. Promotion of their education and training, respecting and making use of their traditional knowledge;
6. Fostering of production and employment, and protection of migrant indigenous groups.

The accords state that "National legislation should recognize the indigenous peoples as those subject to the rights to self-determination and autonomy." The joint proposals define autonomy as "the concrete expression of the exercise of the right to self-determination, expressed as a framework shaped as part of the National State. . . . Indigenous peoples shall, as a consequence, be able to decide their form of internal government and their ways of political, social, economic, and cultural organization."[7] Recognizing Indians as social and historical peoples means modifying the bases of Mexican society to include indigenous peoples in the concept of citizens.

The exercise of autonomy by Indian peoples implies the real transfer to them of powers, duties, and jurisdictions that currently are the responsibility of government agencies. Internal political representation would allow them to name authorities at the community and municipal levels through mechanisms such as the *sistema de cargos* (a form of representation based on cultural traditions and political-religious hierarchy) and community assembly, which are different from the electoral democracy practiced in the rest of the country. Autonomy in the justice system would be established by applying indigenous normative systems to regulate and solve internal conflicts. These systems, although oral, are issued and validated at general assemblies, are relatively flexible, and are applied in a collegial manner. (The municipal president never judges alone.) They are cohesive regulatory systems derived from their historic and cultural experience, which not only resolve problems between one indigenous individual and another but rule community and municipal life.

Among the points that could not be agreed upon was the call for the creation of pluriethnic autonomous regions to form a so-called fourth level of government (added to the federal, state, and municipal levels). The federal government wanted each individual community to handle its affairs, but within, not alongside, the existing order. The government also wanted indigenous forms of justice to be incorporated into the state-level judicial systems.

The Outcomes

The armed indigenous insurrection in Chiapas, as well as the rise in the peaceful and civil struggle for rights in practically all the Indian regions of the country and the military mobilization that accompanied it, showed that profound changes in the old relationship between the state and the Indian peoples were required.[8] The Chiapas insurrection questioned the effectiveness of government policy toward the Indian peoples, and the Zapatistas had won sufficient legitimacy for themselves for that point to become part of the negotiation agenda.

The negotiations at San Andrés began in the midst of the most drastic economic crisis in recent years. The "error of December" 1994, which had precipitated a drastic devaluation of currency and a massive flight of capital, was the starting point that led to the fall in the 1995 gross domestic product (GDP) of 6.9 percent (the worst since 1932 when, as a result of the Great Depression, the GDP fell by 14.9 percent) and the loss of over 1 million jobs (plus another million that were not created in order to allow the entry of youths into the labor market); there was 52 percent inflation, and the foreign debt grew by over 20 percent. The financial weakness of the Mexican economy and the enormous accumulated social malaise due to the adjustment policies forced the government to try to prevent unorganized popular discontent from finding common purpose with the EZLN.

In the political field, according to the government's logic, agreeing to indigenous reform was a way to prevent a possible coalition between the Zapatistas and the opposition political parties; granting the EZLN a small amount of legitimacy would give the government time to negotiate with party leaders on electoral reform without "interference" from other sectors.

On the one hand, the San Andrés Accords were a response to international issues. Immediately after their approval, government negotiators left for Europe to explain the scope of the minimum accord signed with the EZLN to the members of the European Union (EU). Meanwhile, Mexican embassies on the continent began an information offensive to play up their government's "will to negotiate." This diplomatic campaign on the Chiapas question had three objectives. The first and most important was to "clean up" the image of an administration discredited by its continuous and documented violations of human rights (an image aggravated by the deportation of three priests who worked with the diocese of San Cristóbal) and by its injustices toward the Indian peoples. The majority of EU countries had indicated that they would sign a trade agreement with Mexico on the condition that it pass the test of the "democratic clause."[9] The second objective was to try to counter what had been pointed out at the meeting of the ILO's Commission on the Application of Norms (held in Geneva on June 16, 1995): that serious acts were committed in Mexico against rural and indigenous workers and calling for the Mexican government to rectify its native policy.[10] The third was to try to counter the Zapatistas' growing influence in various European circles.

On the other hand, the accords also were the result of an alternative plan drawn up by indigenous leaders and intellectuals. The conceptual center around which their demands were articulated is the right to self-determination and autonomy. To Indian peoples, gaining full equality before the law will in fact result from winning the right to be different. They see in winning this specific right—not a privilege—the way to change from permanent minorities into majorities, to put an end to the deception and the unequal relationship they have with national political institutions, and to be in a stronger position to face the main task of reestablishing themselves as peoples.[11]

Between the Signing and Reality

The government delegation really proposed to the EZLN just a mechanism for it to construct its political program and to forge links with other social sectors; the government did not enter into negotiations on substantive questions. San Andrés was the route to reintegrating the rebels into civil society without granting them any significant political gains. From this perspective, the Accords on Indigenous Rights and Culture were the bait to keep the Zapatistas from trying to derail the reintegration process. Moreover, the Mexican government has a long history of making commitments that are later broken. In this vein, the government delegation held that its only responsibility was to forward the accords signed in San Andrés to the national debate and decision bodies, not to implement the accords themselves.[12]

For the EZLN, the accords were an obvious victory. The government, by promising to meet part of the EZLN demands, was granting legitimacy to the movement. The accords also provided a programmatic instrument to support and sustain the rising national struggle of indigenous peoples and facilitate their integration into the country's political life. However, the Zapatistas did not have many illusions about the government's commitments. In the public evaluation they made together with their advisors, they noted: "The Zapatistas understand clearly the enormous limitations that a regime such as the current one has, the limited capacity that prevents the government from taking into its hands the solution of problems that now escape their possibilities of management and control."[13] Their skepticism was made clear when the EZLN command refused to sign the documents in public.

The Impasse

For the first the two months after signing the accords, things seemed to be proceeding normally. On March 18, 1996, the minister of interior met in private with the members of the government delegation and COCOPA, and pointed out to them that in April, once they had the results of the National Consultation on Indigenous Rights, a corresponding bill could be drafted. The next day Senator Pablo Salazar introduced the accords to the full Senate. On March 20 the Ministry of Interior (Secretaría de Gobernación) reported that it had set up an office to provide compliance with the accords; meanwhile COCOPA delivered the accords to the chief of the

State Executive Office and to the local congress; almost a month later, on April 16, it did the same to President Zedillo.

However, as of that moment, the process of drafting the initiative came to a halt. The then vice-minister of interior, Natividad González Parás, was commissioned to prepare a proposal for constitutional reforms on the topic but never did. In fact, the intergovernmental commission that worked on the topic was rife with internal conflict; its members' positions ranged from maintaining that constitutional reforms were not needed, just a regulatory law for Article 4 of the constitution was, to those who saw in the San Andrés Accords an upper limit for drafting the proposal, not a starting point.

Meanwhile, the second round of talks on democracy and justice went into crisis. The government's refusal to include guests and advisors in the first round had turned it into a discussion among the EZLN guests and advisors, not an exchange of views between them and the government participants; this showed a lack of seriousness on the part of the government. There then followed a series of violent evictions of peasants who had occupied lands in Chiapas, which led to several dead, and the announcement of the end of land distribution in the state, acts that coincided with the dates of the negotiations. Finally in May a local judge convicted Javier Elorriaga and Sebastián Entzin, alleged Zapatistas, of terrorism. The Zapatistas interpreted this as a direct provocation, left the negotiating table, and declared a red alert.[14]

Although the official government position was that the verdict was an independent decision of the judiciary, the importance of the action and the traditional dependency of that branch on the executive made the judge's action difficult to view as an autonomous action. There was an additional implication: If the Zapatistas were terrorists, why was the government negotiating with them? Did this not imply that the Mexican state was recognizing the existence of terrorism in its realm?

The crisis was resolved, after the government lost the public opinion battle, with the release on June 7, 1996, of those who had been arrested and charged with terrorism in May. More important, the resolution apparently exceeded the limits of the dispute calling for renegotiations of the format of the talks. The new rules established that COCOPA was the only body that could declare that the dialogue was broken off and that the accords would be politically binding. During this period deep disagreement was evident within the federal government on how to handle the conflict, as various officials publicly voiced different positions. Finally the minister of interior, in a dispute with those in charge of the government commission for negotiations in Chiapas, assumed a greater role in the talks, based on the growing interlocution of COCOPA with the EZLN.

As of that moment, behind the scenes, an alternative "route" was hatched outside the formal framework of the negotiations. The main participants would be the EZLN, COCOPA as mediator, and the Ministry of Interior, apart from the government delegation. This new fast track consisted, essentially, of the EZLN signing the peace and withdrawing the declaration of war, after the approval in congress of the constitutional reforms on indigenous rights and culture—in short, a variation of the Palestinian model.

The release of Elorriaga and Entzin and the redefinition of the negotiation procedures allowed the dialogue to resume. In that context, the EZLN, with the assistance of COCOPA and the participation of CONAI, called for a Forum on Reform of the State between June 30 and July 6, 1996.[15] Fifteen hundred representatives participated, among them some of the most important persons in the fight to democratize the country. Although formally there was no special working group for the indigenous movement, the event gave special attention to promoting the organization process and elevating its participation in national political life.

At that same time, a new political-military organization appeared in the state of Guerrero, the Popular Revolutionary Army (Ejército Popular Revolucionario, EPR), which explicitly rejected the route of dialogue with the government. Although concerned by the emergence of another armed group, the government used it to downplay EZLN presence in the media while it increased its militarization in the indigenous zones. Days later, between July 27 and August 3, 1996, the First Intercontinental Gathering for Humanity and Against Neoliberalism was held in Chiapas. There the native struggle was emphasized, now on the international level.

However, the resumption of the dialogue between the EZLN and the federal government lasted only a short time. During the final phase of the negotiations on democracy and justice, the government gradually began to restrict its offers to smaller and smaller subjects and areas, in part not to coincide with the electoral negotiation process that the Ministry of Interior was carrying out with the political parties. The rebels saw the government as willing to talk but not to negotiate and even less to comply. They decided, after consultation with their bases, to suspend the dialogue on September 2, 1996; one day afterward, in his annual presidential address, Ernesto Zedillo would make no mention about the accords signed by his government on February 16.

The Indigenous National Congress and the Withdrawal of the EZLN

The National Indigenous Congress decided to hold its meeting in Mexico City between October 8 and 12, 1996, and to invite a delegation from the EZLN. Just the announcement that a Zapatista delegation might leave Chiapas precipitated an intense national debate. On the one hand, the Ministry of Interior indicated that the Zapatistas could not leave the state of Chiapas; if they did, they would be arrested. Some government spokespersons even suggested at the most prickly moment in the discussion that an offensive military action was imminent. On the other hand, a broad coalition of forces held that the Law for Dialogue protected all the rights of the Zapatistas, including the right to travel to the federal district of Mexico City.

The debate on the departure of the Zapatistas for the federal district intensified the relationship between the rebels and the government and once more put the indigenous question at the forefront of the national agenda. The EZLN held that its trip was to ratify the way chosen to solve their problems: that of peaceful dialogue. It would call not for taking up arms but rather for engaging in politics, for creating the conditions that would allow the establishment of a true dialogue.[16]

The conflict was resolved on the basis of negotiations in which CO-COPA played a key role, and the government accepted the transfer of a Zapatista delegation to Mexico City. The EZLN then decided to give the government a slap on the wrist by sending as its delegate Commandant Ramona, a tzotzil leader who had a serious kidney disease. This move sought to make evident the foolishness of government strategy that was trying not to resolve the conflict but rather to defeat the EZLN, by devising a political solution with moral overtones—would the government arrest a seriously ill woman?[17]

Tens of thousands of people took to the streets of Mexico City to greet Ramona. Her departure (in the middle of the news about the discovery of a skeleton in the garden of a house of the brother of ex-President Salinas de Gortari, who was accused of masterminding the murder of his ex–brother-in-law) gave the Zapatistas indisputable political capital, especially in contrast to the circus of national politics. It gave the national indigenous movement greater prominence, gave COCOPA greater negotiating potential, and gave the Ministry of Interior the means to displace the special commission responsible for the negotiations. The fast track began to gain ground.

The Tripartite Model

The Zapatistas' breakthrough allowed the construction of a negotiations model different from that of San Andrés, called "tripartite" after its style of informal talks among the EZLN, mediators, and government agencies—developed in meetings separately among the EZLN, COCOPA, and CONAI; and in meetings among COCOPA, the Ministry of Interior, and, sporadically, the president of the republic. In the midst of bargaining and recriminations, the plan made room for agreement and the formal establishment of COSEVER in November 1996.

It was on the basis of this model that the bargaining began over ways to translate the Accords on Indigenous Rights and Culture into constitutional reforms. The Ministry of Interior promised not to submit any initiative that was not endorsed by the Zapatistas. Both the EZLN and the federal government drew up a first-draft proposal. According to the opinion of the legislative commission, the Zapatistas were aiming very high and the government very low. On November 19 COCOPA met with the rebel command in the jungle and there set out its strategy: It would not reopen negotiations on San Andrés; it would draw up a single text based on a final document prepared and submitted by each of the parties. The only valid document would be the one prepared by COCOPA. The parties agreed to approve or reject that document, without modifications, to avoid the unending process of editorial changes or the reopening of dialogue via the back door.

On November 29 the legislative commission gave the EZLN and the Ministry of Interior the final text. The next day the Zapatistas pointed out that important points remained to be incorporated but that they accepted it. The Ministry of Interior accepted the document but asked for time to make a statement while awaiting the president's return from a trip to Asia. On December 2 the Ministry of Interior met with CO-COPA, said that the government did not agree with the document, and offered several suggested changes. The Zapatistas rejected the proposed changes and made it clear to COCOPA that they would withdraw to mountain positions if the initial agreement was not respected. On December 6 and 7, 1996, new meetings took place with the minister of interior and the president at which COCOPA was accused of favoritism toward the EZLN. President Zedillo then asked for two weeks to consult constitutional law specialists. The Zapatistas agreed but leaked information about the negotiations to the media. This marked the end of "discreet negotiations, public results."

When the president sent his remarks, the Zapatistas asked for twenty days to analyze them. On January 11, 1997, they made public their position: The president's remarks were in fact a new proposal, as different from the COCOPA proposal as from the San Andrés Accords; as such they were unacceptable. This marked the end of the tripartite negotiation model; the parties would not sit down together again soon.

The Crisis of the Crisis

Few times in the history of the 321 modifications that have been made to the 1917 Mexican constitution has such debate been generated. Many factors combined to give the discussion of constitutional reforms on the subject of indigenous rights and culture the tone and the intensity that it had reached: The nature of the proposed changes would affect the structure of the Mexican state; the reform initiative was a result of negotiations with a guerrilla group and the deployment of a broad national indigenous movement demanding rights and not assistance; the climate of political decay was created by an exhausted regime; international agreements were signed by the Mexican government; and there was for all intents and purposes an absence of constitutional jurisprudence on the topic. And few constitutional reform initiatives have had to face so much resistance. Racism, always present in indigenous regions but latent until then in the rest of the country, became manifest and precipitated an avalanche of opinions that were a mixture of ignorance about and intolerance of the Indian peoples. With the stagnation of the dialogue at the end of 1996, President Zedillo undertook a personal campaign against the reforms, saying that they sought to establish rights and privileges that would lead the country to Balkanization and disintegration.[18]

Zedillo's rejection of the constitutional reform initiatives that COCOPA drew up to finalize the San Andrés Accords had no technical or legal basis. The government's denial of the legislative commission's document was simply part of an old tradition in national politics: Erect a smoke screen to legitimize the breach of an agreement and seek, if not to convince public opinion, at least to confuse it.

The reasons for this attitude were basically political. Before the July 6, 1997, elections, President Zedillo sought to remove the EZLN from national politics, to push it into the mountains and keep it from influencing the electoral process. The government, confident that military force would support its noncompliance with the agreement, decided to assert a golden rule of governmental political tradition: An agreement is to be respected only as long as the conditions that made it possible do not change. Judging from the presidential attitude, those conditions had changed.

On the eve of the elections, the government party was in serious danger of losing its absolute majority in congress. The PRI was going to give it everything it had and, with the campaign of opposition leader Cuauhtémoc Cárdenas for mayor of Mexico City and the growing strength of the opposition in other areas, the PRI did not want to lose even a single vote or allow the political climate to stand in the way of its "triumph." Respecting the San Andrés Accords and reforming the constitution accordingly would give the Zapatistas sufficient strength, legality, and legitimacy to change the political environment in a real way. The PRI sought to exclude from the scene a participant that it did not control and that could build bridges to the opposition—the EZLN.

But within the presidential cabinet resistance to compliance with the San Andrés Accords was not limited to electoral considerations. Certain officials believed the accords were dangerous, not because they truly thought they would Balkanize the country or create privileges (as they had stated), but rather because they saw in the accords the creation of a space for the organization and development of the Indian peoples on the fringes of traditional government control and a legal instrument that would give communities greater power to resist the government project embodied in Salinist reforms to Article 27 of the constitution, which sought to seize for the nation natural resources that were still under indigenous control.

As elections neared, the government increased military presence in EZLN zones and insisted that elections take place as usual. The EZLN called for abstention from voting in occupied zones that lacked minimum conditions for honest elections and for voting where conditions allowed. Nevertheless, although the Federal Electoral Institute confirmed the lack of adequate conditions for carrying out free elections in some districts in Chiapas, the polls were installed. The PRI was risking its own survival as a dominant force even at the cost of the nation's political decay. For its part, the EZLN gambled, in the short term, on international pressure and national indigenous response to win public opinion. It was relatively successful. The growth of the indigenous struggle was notable; international pressure, especially European, was significant.[19] The publicity campaign launched by the Mexican government in Europe turned out to be a boomerang.

Summary

Beyond the destiny that constitutional reforms on indigenous rights and culture may have, peace talks in Chiapas are in crisis. There are no immediate prospects that the parties will again sit down to negotiate.

The issue is that the government does not have a peace policy for the Chiapanecan conflict, only a negotiation plan. A peace policy would seek to resolve in depth the causes of the rebellion and seek to continue negotiation as a part of a state policy to transcend the immediate interests of the government and the parties. A negotiation plan is merely the application of measures to "contain" the enemy and to try to defeat it, using the conflict according to national political expediency.

In this way, certain decisions made during the negotiation process, such as sustaining the military truce, incorporating the army directly into the dialogue, involving the political parties as contributors, and allowing some participation of civil society, yielded fewer results than expected. Pouring economic resources into the region has served to muffle social discontent and reincorporate some political clienteles, but doing this does not develop the state, create institutions, or resolve the causes that started the conflict.

Central themes of the government's negotiation plan include cutting the participants down to size, "Chiapanizing" the conflict, and offering the Zapatistas a plan for civil reinsertion without real negotiation of their demands. But three basic obstacles have interfered with implementing this plan:

1. The lack of unified leadership on the part of the government participants involved in the process has translated into the lack of a single, explicit, and coherent policy. This lack of unity has led to the increasing intervention of a special commission headed by Bernal del Valle, of the Ministry of Interior, and of the president of the republic, all with different positions. Also, it has made it easy for the governor of the state or persons, such as the minister of agrarian reform or special commissioner for Chiapas Dante Delgado, to influence the process with their own agenda and use provocation and political co-optation as instruments of intervention, at the same time as they announce the end of agrarian distribution and violently evict groups of peasants.

2. The government has tried to "administer" the conflict instead of resolving it; for instance, the San Andrés talks were put on hold to gain time while the government was negotiating with the parties about elec-

toral reform, and the signing of the Accords on Indigenous Rights and Culture was made to coincide with President Zedillo's tour through the European Union.

3. The government's decision to dismantle the negotiations because they were not unconditional first caused containment and weakening of CONAI and then the decline of COCOPA, the only special legislative commission that has had positive results; this removed the possibility of resolving the conflict in the short term and increased the possibility of having to resort to international mediations.

The Difficult Road to Peace

None of what is happening militarily or politically in Chiapas is accidental. A war is going on, and nothing could be more planned than that. The formation of autonomous municipalities by the EZLN, the expansion of paramilitary activity in Chenalhó and the massacre in Acteal, and the attack by the paramilitary group Paz y Justicia (Peace and Justice) against the bishops of the San Cristóbal diocese were not spontaneous acts. They were part of the combatants' strategy and the expression of a new phase of the war.

The outlines of this new stage became apparent in December 1996 when the federal government canceled, at least temporarily, political negotiations as a way to resolve the conflict. Its refusal to accept the constitutional reform proposal drawn up by COCOPA, which it "justified" on the pretext of technical legal objections, was intended both to keep the EZLN out of the electoral process of July 1997 and to avoid compliance with the San Andrés Accords.

This decision was based on the assumption that the Zapatistas were isolated socially and contained militarily and that the federal elections would remove them from the national political spotlight. By this reasoning, the presence of the army and aid programs would be sufficient to stop the EZLN. But the government's strategy did not take into account the rebels' ability to concentrate their efforts in parts of the region, to move ahead in setting up de facto autonomous areas, to develop new regions, to encourage the formation of new political actors on the national stage such as the National Indigenous Congress, and to strengthen their international ties.

The march of 1,111 Zapatistas to Mexico City in September 1997 demonstrated that the Chiapas war had entered a new phase. It showed that, despite the presence of the army, the EZLN had grown, had established an autonomous power base in several parts of the state, and had solidified a significant current of opinion favoring its cause. It also showed that the government was unable to solve the conflict within the new electoral context that began on July 6. The march made clear that the balance of forces that existed before December 1996 had been broken. The government's response to this expansion was to spread the "paramilitarization" of the war.

The paramilitary groups operating in Chiapas are different from the *guardias blancas* and the death squads. The *guardias blancas* are groups of gunmen who work for landowners and follow their orders. The death squads are clandestine groups acting primarily in urban areas, threatening and attacking activists and defenders of human rights. They usually are held together by anticommunist ideologies and made up of members of law enforcement agencies. The paramilitary groups, on the other hand, are a network of small irregular armies whose leaders are Indians, poor peasants, and teachers recruited from groups that benefit from the PRI's traditional patronage system. They are trained and financed as a type of "joint venture" by the public security forces and local ruling groups whose main objective is to try to stop the expansion of independent organizations.

Beyond internal factors, the appearance of paramilitary groups stems from a strategic decision by the power structure. Unlike the army and the police, the paramilitary forces do not have to answer to anyone; they escape public scrutiny. They can act with total impunity and even present themselves as "victims." They are the army's instruments to conduct a war to stop the expansion of the insurgency that the army cannot conduct directly. It is no accident that they have arisen in key areas of Chiapas. The theater of operations of Paz y Justicia, in the Tila lowlands, is intended to block the Zapatistas' natural corridor for expansion or escape. The Chinchulines action in Bachajón was an attempt to establish an area of containment in the southern front of the northern zone. And now the group Primera Fuerza (First Force) in Chenalhó is attempting to break the back of autonomous Zapatista expansion in Los Altos.

The experience of peace efforts in other countries shows that negotiating impasses are tied to two basic factors: power and commitment (legitimacy). The parties tend to negotiate in situations of dynamic equality, when the weak side is growing and the strong side is weakening. To break an impasse it is necessary to have a policy of recognition, dialogue, compliance with agreements, and unified leadership in the negotiations. The insurgency must be recognized as a legitimate actor, and the government must reaffirm dialogue as a solution to the conflict and comply with commitments that have been agreed to. Its negotiators must maintain a unified position and be able to demand respect for it within the government.

In the case of Chiapas, only two of these four conditions to break the impasse have been met. The EZLN was recognized as a legitimate actor in the first negotiations in the San Cristóbal Cathedral in 1994 and later in the Law of Concord and Pacification of March 11, 1995. From that time on it has been agreed that dialogue is the way to resolve the conflict, although the federal government broke this commitment on February 9, 1995, and—although the government has not admitted it—immediately after the Acteal massacre of December 22, 1997. The government did not comply with what was agreed on about indigenous rights and culture, and, practically speaking, it boycotted the negotiations on democracy and justice. Neither mediation nor collaboration, both of which are the guarantees of any negotiations, was strong enough to force compliance with what had been agreed to. This situation has been aggravated by the periodic disarray in the federal government. Over and over again officials contradict each other and the official strategy.

The executive branch's attempt to create a new correlation of forces to compel an unfavorable outcome for the Zapatistas ended in failure. The increase in the number of troops and their redeployment in Chiapas seriously damaged the government's international image and evoked public repudiation. Rather than giving in, rebel communities responded to the military escalation with peaceful resistance by women and children. The xenophobic campaign to discredit international observation efforts was not received well in European governmental circles.

At the center of this new interruption of the peace process is a basic issue: The government is not seeking peace but a way to regain the political-military initiative. A peace policy would attempt to resolve in depth the causes of the rebellion and continue the negotiations as part of a state policy transcending the immediate interests of the government and political parties. A negotiating plan is merely the application of measures to "contain" the enemy and try to defeat it, using the conflict in different ways depending on the political moment.

The central themes of the government's negotiating strategy have been to diminish the importance of the actors, to restrict the conflict to Chiapas, and to offer the Zapatistas a way to return to civilian life without really negotiating over their demands. In its most recent phase the government has attempted to regain the initiative by presenting a proposal for constitutional reforms concerning indigenous rights and culture that differs markedly from the San Andrés Accords and to discredit mediation. It has tried to refocus the ideological battle to end the insurrection without addressing its causes and without recognizing its principal actor as a negotiating partner. The government is trying to destroy the legal framework and institutional fabric built up during more than four years of dialogue and negotiations. It criticizes intellectuals for their lenient attitude toward EZLN's strategies and procedures, it controls the media, and it organizes a xenophobic campaign against international observers.

In this way the undeniable achievements of the negotiation process—the military truce, incorporation of the army into the dialogue, including the political parties as collaborators, and allowing some participation of civil society—have been abandoned. Also, pouring economic resources into the region has eased social discontent and reincorporated some political constituencies. But this has not developed the state, created institutions, or resolved the causes of the conflict.

Around 40,000 troops are distributed over 136 points in 63 municipalities of Chiapas. Social life has been militarized: The profound imposition of the army in the state is evidenced by the wasteful expenditure represented by so many troops and by the number of social programs that fall under the military's responsibility. In the same way, the presence of paramilitary groups tied to the official party, which receive advice and instruction from the army, is notable; in the northern part of the state, they are responsible for murders, expulsions, rapes, and robberies, all with official complicity.[20] The government strategy of not living up to its agreements (the presidential initiative on indigenous rights and culture recognizes rights only as long as they cannot be exercised) broke with a basic principle of any negotiation: creating certainty and confidence.

The Indian peoples have been placed, by their own right, in the center of the political arena. They have created a broad consensus that the nation has an enormous historical debt to them that it must settle. Their mobilization has a long-term vitality that nourishes the Zapatista insurrection. In Mexico, the nineteenth and twentieth centuries began with indigenous insurrections of great vigor. This century may end with another. Troublesome and inconvenient actors, the indigenous peoples, demand their rights. The country's political stability depends on the solution to their demands and on how these demands mesh with the calls for political democracy and alternative development models made by the indigenous and by other sectors of the population.

Notes

1. See Arnulfo Embriz, ed., *Indicadores socio-económicos de los pueblos indígenas de México, 1990* (Mexico City: Instituto Nacional Indigenista, Dirección de Investigación y Promoción Cultural, Subdirección de Investigación, 1993).

2. See Miguel A. Bartolomé, "De mayoría a minoría," *Crónica Legislativa*, No. 7, Organo de Información de la LVI Legislatura (Feb.-Mar. 1996).

3. By "indigenous," I refer to the definition given by the International Labor Organization (ILO) in Agreement 169, Convention Concerning Indigenous and Tribal Peoples in Independent Countries. According to Article 1, section b, persons "are considered indigenous through the fact of descending from populations that inhabited the country or a geographic region to which the country belongs at the time of the conquest or the colonization or of the establishment of the current state frontiers and that, whatever their legal situation, preserve all their own social, economic, cultural, and political institutions, or part of them." Article 2 notes: "The awareness of their indigenous or tribal identity shall be considered a fundamental criterion for determining the groups to which the provisions of this Agreement are applied."

4. The institutional policy aimed at tending to the indigenous population is called *indigenismo*. It is simultaneously an anthropological theory, a state ideology, and a government practice. Its main objective is to protect the indigenous communities in respect to their integration with the rest of national society. Among the vast bibliography on the topic, see Guillermo Bonfli Batalla, *Etnodesarrollo y entocidio* (San José de Costa Rica: FLACSO, 1982).

5. Article 4 of the constitution establishes: "The Mexican Nation has a pluricultural composition originally upheld in its indigenous peoples. The law shall protect and promote the development of their languages, cultures, uses, customs, resources and specific forms of social organization, and shall guarantee their members effective access to the jurisdiction of the State. In agrarian lawsuits and procedures in which they are a party, their juridical customs and practices in the terms established by law shall be taken into account."

6. For an in-depth study of the meaning and scope of these terms, see Adelfo Regino, "La autonomía: una forma concreta de ejercicio del derecho a la libre determinación y sus alcances," *Chiapas*, No. 2 (1996).

7. *Nunca más sin nosotros. Acuerdos de la Mesa de Derechos y Cultura Indígenas entre el Ejército Zapatista de Liberación Nacional y el Gobierno Federal* (Mexico City: Juan Pablos Editor, 1996).

8. This fact was recognized by Jorge del Valle, one of those responsible for the negotiations: "Negotiation is not a function of the correlation of forces, but of the case to be resolved. If we had negotiated according to the correlation of forces, our offer would have been a different one." Blanche Petrich, "El tiempo 'nos favorece a nosotros, no al EZLN': Del Valle," *La Jornada*, January 29, 1996: 11–12.

9. Unlike the United States, the countries of the European Union, and others on the European continent try to establish trade agreements with countries that respect human rights and are democratic.

10. Kyra Nuñez, "Sugiere la Comisión de Aplicación de Normas de la OIT: Debe México rectificar su política indigenista," *La Jornada*, June 25, 1995:21.

11. In addition to their existence as peoples, the indigenous argue their claims to the right to difference in light of international agreements signed by the Mexican government and new tendencies in law toward the formal recognition of collective rights. No juridical consideration of the San Andrés Accords in general, or the COCOPA bill in particular, can overlook the fact that Agreement 169 of the ILO was approved by the Mexican Government in September 1990 and included as law in its publication in the *Diario Oficial de la Federación* on January 24, 1991.

12. It could not be otherwise: The executive branch does not have the authority to approve constitutional reforms; the president cannot assume functions that belong to the legislative branch.

13. The Dialogue of San Andrés and Indigenous Rights and Culture. Punto y seguido. *Nunca Más Sin Nosotros,* 86.

14. Among the points that the Zapatistas made as a condition for resuming the talks were the end of the violence in the northern region of the state, a government delegation with the capability to provide solutions, the installation of COSEVER, and the release of the alleged Zapatistas who were imprisoned in various jails around the country.

15. According to the "General rules of the agenda, format and procedure of the dialogue and the negotiation of the agreement of concord and pacification with justice and dignity" approved in San Andrés, Chiapas, on July 11, 1996, it is established that:

I. The forums are part of the National Dialogue for the Reform of the State and their development shall have as its purpose to contribute elements and proposals within its framework, and to strengthen the peace process to allow for the signing of the "Agreement of Concord and Pacification with Justice and Dignity" between the Federal Government and the EZLN . . .

III. The forums do not constitute a body of decision or resolution on the topics contained in the dialogue that is developed between the Federal Government and the EZLN.

IV. The results and the proposals of the forums shall be transferred to the bodies of national dialogue and to the Congress of the Union by the Commission on Concord and Pacification : . . .

16. The EZLN also indicated that its members would go by making use of their rights. The legal framework for the negotiations between the EZLN and the federal government is the Ley para el Diálogo, la Conciliación y la Paz Digna en Chiapas. In its first article, the law recognizes the EZLN as "a group of persons who are identified as an organization of Mexican citizens, in their majority indigenous persons, who are in disagreement for a variety of reasons and got involved in the armed conflict that began January 1, 1994 in the state of Chiapas." This implies that its members are citizens fully exercising their civil and political rights.

This same law establishes, in Article 2, section 3, that among the objectives of the agreement is "To foster the participation of the members of the EZLN in the exercise of politics within the peaceful channels that the State of Law offers, with absolute respect for their dignity and the guarantees of Mexican citizens." In other words, the law recognizes as its objective what the Zapatistas planned to do in Mexico City. Article 4 suspends apprehension orders and procedures against members of the EZLN while negotiations continue. Published in *Diario Oficial,* March 11, 1995.

17. Commandant Ramona is, on her own merits, one of the EZLN's most relevant and beloved figures. Ramona is, along with the older Ana María (the soldier responsible for the Zapatista forces in Los Altos) and Commandant David, the initiator of conspiratorial work in that region of Chiapas.

18. Both in San Pablo Totoltepec on February 12 and in Xilitla on March 26, President Zedillo stated that he was very much opposed to the reform initiative presented by COCOPA.

19. First Danish deputies (Soren Sondergaard, et al., "Piden diputados daneses que se respete la propuesta de la Cocopa," *La Jornada,* January 27, 1997:2) and later 120 Italian members of parliament from all political parties demanded publicly that the president lift the veto on reforms on indigenous issues. That was followed by appeals by Spanish and French deputies, among others. Behind them is the pressure of thousands of citizens and organized forces that are demanding a peace with justice and dignity and that have demonstrated in front of Mexican consuls in dozens of cities and in the United States. The PRI deputy, Juan José Osorio protested ("Opiniones in-

jerencistas de diputados daneses sobre propuesta de la Cocopa: Osorio Palacios," *La Jornada,* February 1, 1997:2) what he characterized as the interfering opinions of the Danish deputies.

20. Centro de Derechos Humanos Fray Bartolomé de las Casas, *Ni Paz, Ni Justicia: Informe general y amplio acerca de la guerra civil que sufren los Choles en la Zona Norte de Chiapas, diciembre de 1994 a octubre de 1996* (San Cristóbal de las Casas: Centro de Derechos Humanos Fray Bartolomé de las Casas, 1996).

11

Indigenous Identity and Rights in the Guatemalan Peace Process

ROGER PLANT

Introduction

In March 1995, as part of the peace negotiations in Guatemala, the parties to the conflict signed an Agreement on the Identity and Rights of Indigenous Peoples. It is a remarkable document, providing a blueprint for the creation of a new multiethnic and multicultural society and establishing unique mechanisms for indigenous participation in the manifold legal and administrative reforms that will be necessary to end centuries of discrimination, to provide for meaningful indigenous participation at all levels, and to promote and recognize the role of indigenous institutions in a new multiethnic society.

Guatemala's indigenous agreement, it goes without saying, is a highly sensitive document in a country where indigenous peoples of Mayan extraction comprise over half of the national population but have until now been excluded from equal participation in the country's civil, political, economic, social, and cultural life. It is also of vital importance, as an ambitious exercise in nation-building without which the peace process in this ethnically diverse country can never be truly consolidated. To tackle deep-rooted discrimination and to create a new institutional framework in the legal, political, and also economic areas, the reform process must be seen

319

as a long-term endeavor. In a November 1996 speech, Guatemala's foreign minister, Eduardo Stein Barillas, referred to this agreement as one to be implemented in full over three or four generations, although a start could and should be made in the immediate future.

Not much more than a decade ago, the indigenous highlands of western Guatemala were the principal war zone in this country's conflict, indigenous peoples bearing the brunt of the violence and providing the bulk of the dead, the disappeared, the refugees, and the internally displaced. Compared with these times there has been a sea change in Guatemala, and the peace process in its entirety is of particular importance for the country's indigenous peoples.

Moreover, the relevance of Guatemala's indigenous agreement goes way beyond this country alone. It deals with complex issues of ethnicity, cultural identity, and political representation that now confront other Latin American countries where indigenous peoples comprise a significant proportion of the national population and continue to suffer from severe de facto discrimination. In Mexico, Bolivia, Ecuador, and Peru (in each of which indigenous peoples have to some extent been regulated by a special legal status, while at the same time they have been integrated within national society mainly as cheap labor on agricultural enterprises), the indigenous revival is now provoking some major rethinking of national identity. In several of these countries, recent constitutional reforms have recognized the multiethnic, multicultural, and plurilingual nature of their national societies, pledging in general terms to build new and cohesive national societies on the basis of respect for indigenous institutions, values, and customary norms.

Yet in all of these countries, including Guatemala, a basic dilemma faces the indigenous movement itself. On one hand it is pressing for the right to participate on an equal footing in national society, albeit through representative indigenous institutions. On the other hand it is striving for a special and sometimes separate status for the social, cultural, and even economic and political institutions of indigenous peoples. It is the degree and meaning of indigenous autonomy and self-management—and also the relative importance to be attached to demands for the various kinds of autonomy, rather than improved participation and inclusion within the existing state and its institutions—that may well become a controversial issue as the peace process develops further in Guatemala.

This chapter aims first to describe the means by which the peace process in Guatemala became a vehicle for the expression of the cultural, economic, political, and social demands of the country's indigenous majority.

It examines how diverse indigenous organizations first emerged from clandestinity in the late 1980s, how they began to orchestrate demands vis-à-vis the state even before the peace process got firmly under way, how the indigenous issue was placed on the negotiating table, and how the members of the indigenous movement became actively involved in placing demands before the negotiating parties.

It then provides a brief overview of the content of the indigenous agreement itself, aiming to place the agreement within the perspective of recent Latin American trends both to promote indigenous rights and to establish the parameters of multiethnic and multicultural societies.

After brief examination of the experience to date, a final section provides some reflections on future challenges in implementing Guatemala's indigenous agreement. Once again, the aim is also to place the Guatemalan indigenous experience in the broader Latin American perspective.

Indigenous Peoples and the Guatemalan Social Structure

Until the late 1980s, the issue of specific rights for Guatemala's indigenous peoples of mainly Mayan extraction was a decidedly taboo issue. In the mid-1970s there was a short-lived attempt to create an indigenous political party. In the meantime issues of ethnic identity had been keenly debated since the 1960s mainly by leftist intellectuals, divided between those who belittled many elements of Mayan culture and traditional institutions (some, even to the point of arguing that many elements of "traditional" Mayan culture were in fact a colonial creation) and those who argued that ethnic and racial discrimination were the fundamental issues to be tackled in the search for a more equitable society.[1] This nationalism vs. ethnicity debate was later to be a source of contention within the guerrilla Unidad Revolucionaria Nacional Guatemalteca (URNG) itself, with dissident groups apparently pressing for a higher degree of autonomy than the revolutionary leadership was willing to contemplate.[2]

To comprehend the nature of these debates, one has to understand the rather unique nature of Guatemala's indigenous population, compared with that of other Latin American countries. In most countries indigenous peoples are a relatively small minority of the national population, usually living outside the mainstream of the country's economic and social life. In only one other country—Bolivia—are indigenous peoples a majority. In both Bolivia and Guatemala, indigenous peoples have been integrated for centuries within the country's economic life, in a situation of severe disadvantage as

the providers of servile or low-paid labor on agricultural estates. Nevertheless, in Bolivia, indigenous communities benefited both economically and
politically from the country's 1952 revolution and agrarian reform.

In Guatemala Mayan Indians comprise an estimated 60 percent of the
national population.[3] They are divided into twenty-one separate linguistic
groups (Cakchiquel, Mam, Kekchi, and Quiché having by far the largest
numbers). In addition to the Mayan peoples, small ethnic groups include
the Garifunas on the Caribbean coast and Xinca indigenous peoples near
the Salvadoran border.

Social indicators for Mayan communities are the lowest in the hemisphere, in large part because indigenous peoples historically have been exploited as cheap agricultural labor by the landowning elite. A key feature
of Guatemala's economic and social development has been the need for
cheap indigenous labor for its agro-exports, first coffee after the nineteenth-century liberal revolution, then sugar, cotton, cardamom, and rub-
ber in the 1950s and 1960s. All of this has led to an increase in the demand
for indigenous labor over time and also a change in the pattern of labor demand. The expansion of the coffee economy required forced labor systems
right up to the 1940s. Many indigenous communities lived in fairly feudal
conditions within the large plantations. Additional seasonal harvest labor
was provided through coercive recruitment systems for the few months of
the harvest season. The latest stage of the agro-export economy after the
1950s not only brought renewed pressure on indigenous lands but also
(because of the nature of the new export crops, cotton and sugar) led to a
huge increase in the demand for seasonal labor.

In this context, it is important also to comment on aspects of
Guatemala's geographic, demographic, political, and military structures.
Coffee has been grown mainly in piedmont areas, dominated by large plantations since the late nineteenth century. After the 1950s the new export
crops took over the Pacific coast. Indigenous peoples live for the most part
in the western highlands, supplementing their small farm income with migrant labor earnings. Others have been regular farm workers, referred to in
Guatemala as the *mozos colonos.*[4] And there has been steady migration,
mainly by Kekchi Indians, to lowland areas of eastern Guatemala and the
Petén rain forest.

While there are areas in which indigenous peoples predominate, reaching as high as 90 percent or above in some departments, there are no exclusively indigenous areas. Typically, nonindigenous *ladinos* have monopolized political offices and the main bureaucratic positions in all
municipalities.

While the incidence of poverty is generally high in Guatemala, there is evidence that indigenous peoples suffer disproportionately from both poverty and extreme poverty. World Bank estimates in 1994 were that 87 percent of all indigenous households are below the poverty line (as opposed to 66 percent of all households) and that 61 percent of all indigenous households are below the extreme poverty line (as opposed to 38 percent of all Guatemalan households).[5] Moreover, income inequality increased during the 1980s overall and for indigenous people in particular.

The 1980s also saw massive movement and displacement of indigenous peoples, mainly as a result of the military's counterinsurgency policies in the first part of that decade. The Catholic church has estimated that approximately 1 million people from the largely indigenous highlands (representing about one-quarter of its total population) were forcibly displaced at the height of the civil war.[6] Tens of thousands fled over the border to neighboring Mexico. Others took to isolated mountain regions or sought anonymity in Guatemala's ever-growing capital city and other smaller towns.

Thus one legacy of the war is the growing indigenous presence in Guatemala City itself. No reliable figures can be given of the numbers involved, as many family members move to the city for only short periods, perhaps seeking work in construction, perhaps selling agricultural and artisan products in urban markets. But as many as 1 million of the population of Guatemala City itself and its periurban areas may now be of Mayan extraction.

For decades the military has been the only significant state presence in outlying departments. Built up under a series of military dictatorships since the nineteenth-century liberal reforms, the national army was greatly strengthened under the dictatorship of General Jorge Ubico (1930–1944), who deployed *jefes políticos* (political bosses) throughout the country. Beyond its well-known counterinsurgency role in the decades of civil conflict, the military and military police had played an important role in providing security to large landowners.

Given the weak state presence outside the military and the *jefes políticos,* traditional authorities (councils of elders, *cofradías* (confraternities), Mayan priests, and the like) have been able to manage many aspects of community affairs without external intervention. Obviously the situation has varied from region to region, with traditional structures being most heavily eroded in the parts of the country where indigenous peoples are predominantly farm laborers. Altogether, spiritual and religious institutions were the most likely to be subject to repression. And as the violence escalated in indigenous areas in the late 1970s, there are indications that the leaders of institutions such as the councils of elders were forced to go underground when they became prime targets for military reprisals.[7]

Indigenous Organizations and Demands Under the Civil Conflict

It is customary to refer to some thirty-five years of armed conflict in Guatemala, beginning with the short-lived guerilla groups of the 1960s (active mainly in Guatemala City and in the nonindigenous eastern regions of the country) and ending with the groups that have comprised the URNG until its current demobilization.

In fact, however, armed conflict in Guatemala has been sporadic, virtually disappearing in the late 1960s and early 1970s, first reappearing in the mid-1970s, escalating in the late 1970s to mid-1980s, and barely affecting most parts of the country over the past decade until the 1996 final peace agreement.

Indigenous peoples, as we have observed, have borne the brunt of this conflict since the late 1970s. They have provided the vast majority of the combatants on both sides (although not at the top commander level on either side). The war has been fought almost exclusively on their lands. In consequence, they have provided the vast majority of both external refugees and the internally displaced. In the worst years of conflict, 1980 to 1982, entire indigenous villages disappeared.[8]

Concerning indigenous attitudes to this conflict, there is a growing and controversial bibliography. There is much consensus that two factors behind a growing indigenous participation in guerrilla ranks after the 1970s were the military and paramilitary violence linked to a spate of land evictions and the repression of new forms of cooperative and labor organization among highland small-farming communities and rural plantations alike. As the violence grew, and any indigenous organizer became a target for military violence, the leadership of the more militant indigenous peasant organizations began to side more openly with the guerrillas.

Before the height of the conflict in the 1970s and 1980s, the only organized indigenous voice was that of the mass peasant organizations, such as the Comité de Unidad Campesina, Committee for Peasant Unity (CUC). CUC, whose public demands were for land and better labor conditions, developed close links with the Ejército Guerrillero de los Pobres, Guerrilla Army of the Poor (EGP). Out of the conflict new indigenous or pro-indigenous organizations emerged, linked to the political opposition and the so-called popular movement, such as the widows' group, Coordinadora Nacional de Viudas de Guatemala, CONAVIGUA.[9] Their platform was basically one of human rights, antimilitarization, and the abolition of the civil patrols that had underpinned the counterinsurgency operations in the indigenous highlands.

By the late 1980s a new form of indigenous movement began to emerge. Unlike the Mayan popular organizations, which placed their emphasis on social and economic demands, the new movement gave priority to the cultural rights and political status of indigenous peoples within the Guatemalan state. Before the 1986 democratic transition, which brought Christian Democrat leader Vinicio Cerezo to the presidency, Guatemala's 1985 constitution had for the first time recognized certain specific rights for indigenous communities. Following the general Latin American trend of the time, the constitution affirmed that the state should recognize, respect, and promote the "ways of life, customs, traditions, forms of social organization, dress, languages, and dialects" of the country's indigenous communities. Other articles of the new constitution dealt with the special status of indigenous lands and indigenous forms of labor, and required that these matters should be governed by a special law of indigenous communities.

In part, the emergence of these more specifically Mayan organizations can be attributed to the efforts of indigenous professionals to take advantage of the new space offered by the constitutional reforms and to try to give more concrete form to the somewhat vague guarantees thereby provided. In part, however, their emergence also represents a rejection of the guerrilla opposition and its support groups. Many articulate indigenous leaders insisted that Mayan communities had been betrayed by the guerrilla groups that launched a strong offensive in the western highlands in the early 1980s and then retreated, leaving indigenous peoples to bear the brunt of the army's retaliation. Equal rejection of both the army and the URNG has since been a constant theme of this group of Mayan intellectuals.

First during the Cerezo period (January 1986 to January 1991), then more noticeably in the 1990s, the "culturalist" indigenous groups began to orchestrate demands in both the specifically cultural and the more broadly political areas. In the linguistic area, a landmark was the creation of the Academy of Mayan Languages of Guatemala (ALMG), initially founded in 1986 and later recognized in 1990 as an official body with guaranteed state funding. In the political area, the international movement for the recognition of specific rights of indigenous peoples also made its mark in Guatemala during the 1980s. Indigenous delegations attended the United Nations Working Group on Indigenous Populations, created in 1982 with a view to drafting new international standards on indigenous rights. And in 1989 the adoption by the International Labor Organization (ILO) of its new Indigenous and Tribal Peoples Convention (Convention No. 169, 1989) quickly sparked off a movement for the ratification of this instrument in Guatemala.

A typology of the indigenous movement and its diverse organizations can be only approximate. First in the late 1980s, then more manifestly in the first half of the 1990s, a vast array of new indigenous organizations began to emerge at national, regional, and local levels. Indigenous peasant organizations such as CUC, driven underground during the height of the political violence, resurfaced. CUC, CONAVIGUA, and a host of others linked to the popular movement merged into an umbrella group, the Instancia de Unidad y Consenso Maya (Civil Movement for Mayan Unity and Consensus, IUCM). Grass-roots and service nongovernmental organizations, concerned with local community development and sometimes enjoying substantial financial assistance from abroad, began to articulate a more specifically indigenous identity.

For the emergence of a nationwide movement with a specifically indigenous consciousness, the first years of the 1990s were of critical importance. The growth of the movement was perhaps stimulated by the 1991 decision by the parties to the peace process to include indigenous identity and rights on their negotiating agenda. In this same year the Council of Mayan Organizations of Guatemala (COMG)—an umbrella grouping that coordinated a mixture of cultural, linguistic, academic, and development organizations—published a booklet on the specific demands of the Mayan people, for the first time placing issues of political and regional autonomy on the Mayan agenda.[10]

The year 1992 marked the five hundredth anniversary of the colonization of the Americas; in addition, the Guatemalan indigenous personality Rigoberta Menchú Tum was awarded the Nobel Peace Prize. An event held in the country's second largest city, Quetzaltenango, to mark the anniversary by declaring 500 Years of Indigenous and Popular Resistance brought to a head some of the differences between the two strands of the indigenous movement. Mayan "culturalist" groups expressed their distrust of the influence of international leftist ideologies on parts of Guatemala's indigenous movement. Conversely, the "popular" movement criticized its adversaries for placing an exclusive emphasis on the cultural demands of indigenous peoples.

An essential part of these controversies has been attitudes of indigenous organizations and personalities toward the state and the government. The distinction often drawn in the literature between the so-called popular and Mayanist groups does little to explain the complexities of indigenous demands and internal discussions within their organizations. While some of the more cultural demands can be seen as moderate, such as those for educational reform or greater respect for indigenous forms of spirituality, others had far-reaching implications for relations between indigenous peoples and the state. But in the aftermath of the conflict, most of the "popular" movement rejected any form of cooperation with the government and official institutions. Others were keen to take advantage of the political space offered by democratization, seeking tenuous alliances with traditional political parties and a gradual expansion of indigenous participation in diverse official institutions.

Negotiating the Indigenous Agreement: The Role of Indigenous Organizations

To what extent were indigenous peoples themselves involved in negotiating the 1995 indigenous agreement? Directly, the answer is barely at all. The agreement was negotiated between the government's Peace Commission and the URNG commanders and advisors. The government's deputy minister of education, an indigenous Cakchiquel, was the only member of the Mayan community actually to sign the agreement.

Indirectly however, Guatemala's indigenous organizations had substantial influence on the document. When the peace negotiations were resumed in early 1994 under U.N. moderation, the parties had agreed to create an Assembly of Civil Society organized on the basis of eleven different sectoral groups, including the Mayan sectors. Several months later, in May 1994, several of the Mayan organizations (including the IUCM, COMG, and the Academy of Mayan Languages) agreed to create a new umbrella group, the Coordination of Organizations of the Mayan People of Guatemala (COPMAGUA), to be their representative on the Assembly of Civil Society.

Drawing quite heavily on the earlier work of COMG and others, COPMAGUA quickly produced a set of proposals for the assembly. A subsequent document of the assembly itself, which provided the framework for the negotiations between the parties, was based largely if not exclusively on the initial COPMAGUA proposals. Some contentious issues relating to political autonomy were excluded.

The final text of the indigenous agreement then was negotiated over several months in Mexico in late 1994 and early 1995. While some of the assembly's proposals relating to land rights, labor concerns, militarization, and the civil patrols do not figure in the final text (essentially because these issues were to be dealth with in later agreements, notably those on socioeconomic aspects and the agrarian situation, and on the strengthening of civil society and the role of the army), their influence remains unquestionable.

The Indigenous Agreement: An Analysis of Content

Apart from the assembly and COPMAGUA proposals, at least two main sources of influence on the indigenous agreement can be detected. The first is the ILO's 1989 Indigenous and Tribal People's Convention referred to earlier. The second is the intellectual conviction of some of the negotiators and their advisors, in particular on the government side, that the concept of the Guatemalan nation has up to now been fictitious and that henceforth national unity can be built only on a radically new approach to interethnic relations with full respect for the identity, values, traditions, and customs of Guatemala's indigenous peoples.

These rather different underpinnings merit some reflection before we analyze the specific commitments of the agreement in more detail.

The ILO's Convention No. 169 of 1989 is in fact *not* a new international instrument. Rather, it represents a partial revision of an outdated 1957 convention on the integration and protection of indigenous, tribal, and "semitribal" populations. The older instrument, while pioneering in its time, had been subject to widespread criticism by indigenous peoples for its paternalist and overtly integrationist spirit. At a time when the United Nations as whole was moving toward new standards in the indigenous area, addressing the issues of autonomy and self-management, the ILO had been under pressure to adopt a new instrument more in line with the aspirations of the more vocal indigenous groups internationally. The outcome of the ILO's revision process was an interesting hybrid, a convention that retains some highly protectionist clauses (applicable to the more vulnerable of the world's indigenous peoples), that continues to call for special measures of protection, that at the same time recognizes the importance of equality of rights, that stresses the need for consultative and participatory mechanisms, and that also emphasizes the right of indigenous peoples to exercise the maximum possible degree of control over their development, lives, and institutions.

An issue that does *not* figure expressly in the ILO Convention, but which has figured increasingly in Latin American constitutions in recent years, is the concept of multiethnicity and multiculturalism. In states where indigenous peoples have been subject to severe de facto discrimination at all levels but have nevertheless been integrated within the economy, the concept of multiethnicity is a challenging one the legal and political implications of which have yet to be articulated. An undercurrent of Guatemala's indigenous agreement, clearly reflected in the preamble, is that the Guatemalan nation has never really existed because a historical reality of ethnic and racial discrimination "has affected and continues to affect these peoples profoundly, denying them the full exercise of their rights and political participation, and hampering the configuration of a national unity which should adequately reflect the rich and diversified physiognomy of Guatemala with its wealth of values"; "until this problem affecting Guatemalan society is resolved, its economic, political, social and cultural potential will never be able to develop fully and neither will it be able to take its place in the community of nations due to it by virtue of its ancient history and the spiritual grandeur of its peoples."

The third basic source, as noted, is the range of demands relating to the specific rights of indigenous peoples (to spirituality, language, dress, their own education, customary law, respect for their own institutions and authorities, their land rights, etc.).

As regards substantive issues and commitments, the agreement is structured into separate chapters relating to, respectively: the identity of indigenous peoples; the fight against discrimination; cultural rights; and civil, political, social, and economic rights.

The first chapter deals with identity of indigenous peoples, recognizing that their identity is fundamental to the construction of national unity, and identifying the various linguistic Mayan, Xinca, and Garifuna groups who make up the Guatemalan nation.

The second chapter deals with the struggle against discrimination. It contains a series of commitments to, inter alia, classify ethnic discrimination as a criminal offense; review all laws that could have discriminatory implications for indigenous peoples; promote legal office for the defense of indigenous rights and the provision of free legal assistance to indigenous communities; promote the rights of indigenous women; and promote the ratification of international instruments relating to the elimination of discrimination and the protection of indigenous rights.

The third chapter deals with a wide range of cultural rights. Subsections relate to language, names and place-names, spirituality, temples and ceremonial centers, use of indigenous dress, science and technology, educational reform, and communications and the mass media. The section requires limited constitutional reforms and a significant number of legal reforms to give effect to these rights, each of them to be enacted after detailed consultation with indigenous peoples and their representative organizations.

The fourth chapter deals broadly with the civil, political, social, and economic rights of indigenous peoples. It proved the most difficult section of the agreement to negotiate, precisely because it attempts to strike the delicate balance between *indigenous participation within the state and its institutions,* on one hand, and *respect for the autonomy of indigenous institutions,* on the other hand. This section is divided into six separate subsections: the constitutional framework, local indigenous communities and authorities, regionalization, participation at all levels, customary law, and rights relating to the land of indigenous peoples.

The land rights provisions are limited to the communal and collective nature of the relationship between indigenous peoples and their lands. (It was agreed that other aspects would be dealt with in the next item on the negotiating agenda, the Agreement on Socio-Economic Aspects and the Agrarian Situation, eventually signed in May 1996.)[11] There is emphasis on land tenure regularization, on natural resource management, and on improved legal protection of the rights of indigenous communities. Perhaps the most sensitive issues here are the commitments relating to restitution of communal lands and compensation for rights. However, while the restitution issue might open a veritable Pandora's box depending on the admissibility of historical land claims, the government's specific commitments are not particularly far-reaching or controversial. The government basically commits itself to suspend the awarding of any supplementary titles to lands over which indigenous peoples have an outstanding claim, to avert land evictions when there are overlapping claims, and to provide compensation for land loss in select cases.

Arguably the most unique feature of the indigenous agreement is the mechanisms to provide for indigenous participation in the reform process. Unlike some of the other peace agreements (in particular those since 1996 negotiated under the government of President Alvaro Arzú), there is no time frame for meeting any of the manifold commitments, nor does the agreement specify which governmental agency should have responsibility for coordinating its commitments. Yet what does permeate the agreement throughout, in both its substantive and operational aspects, is the principle spelled out in the preamble: "That all matters of direct interest to indigenous peoples need to be dealt with by and with them, and that the present Agreement seeks to create, expand and strengthen the structures, conditions, opportunities and guarantees regarding indigenous people's participation, with full respect for their identity and the exercise of their rights."

To this effect the agreement provides for a series of commissions with indigenous participation, to prepare the ground together with the government for the innumerable constitutional, legal, and administrative reforms required. Three of these commissions (educational reform, institutional reform and participation, and indigenous land rights) are to be comprised of equal numbers of government and indigenous delegates. Additional commissions are to work on the identification of sacred indigenous sites and the officialization of indigenous languages.

Implementing the Agreement: The Experience to Date and Future Challenges

Like all the partial peace agreements with the exception of the 1994 Comprehensive Human Rights Agreement, the indigenous agreement entered fully into force only upon the signing of the final peace on December 29, 1996. There was one exception. The parties concurred that the aspects relating to nationally recognized human rights (including those contained in international instruments ratified by Guatemala) should have immediate force and application. The United Nations Mission for the Verification of Human Rights, MINUGUA, was requested to verify these aspects.[12]

In practice, at first the government did very little to disseminate the agreement or to prepare for its eventual implementation. Throughout 1995, its only real initiative was to collaborate with the United Nations Development Program in the preparation of a project for the agreement's dissemination throughout the country. At the same time, unlike the other peace agreements, the text of the indigenous agreement was not reproduced in the national press. Indigenous organizations, in particular COPMAGUA, embarked on their own dissemination programs. Of the technical issues covered by the agreement, only educational reform and proposals for bilingual education received significant attention from indigenous groups in the first year. Notably, however, after some initial hesitation, the major indigenous organizations endorsed the agreement as an important tool for advancing their interests, even if it did not meet all their aspirations. In many ways MINUGUA took the lead in giving visibility to the agreement and in building technical cooperation programs around its key human rights provisions. Field projects were undertaken in the areas of free legal interpretation and free legal assistance, aiming to devise appropriate models for enabling state institutions to meet these commitments on a national basis. At the same time, the mission recognized the importance of addressing the issue of customary law, as technical preparation for the complex process of law reform expected to get under way after the signing of the final peace agreement.

In the course of 1996, there were important changes. In the presidential campaign in late 1995, Partido de Avanzada Nacional (PAN) candidate Alvaro Arzú and principal advisors included ethnic issues on their electoral platform, pledging a major campaign against discrimination and raising the issue of a separate agency to deal with indigenous affairs. Nobel Peace Prize winner Rigoberta Menchú launched a major campaign for electoral participation. At the municipal level, a significant number of indigenous mayors were elected through civic committees, challenging the dominance of the traditional political parties in rural areas. And it was a sign of growing indigenous participation in political life that Mayan organizations were able to host pre-election workshops in which the major candidates had to put forward their views on indigenous identity and rights and the eventual implementation of the agreement.

Upon entering office, the government first pushed and then dropped its idea for a ministry or secretariat of indigenous affairs. The idea was almost universally opposed by the major indigenous organizations and political figures, who roundly rejected any initiative that could box or segment indigenous affairs into any one government agency. Instead, they argued, there should be an agency for interethnic affairs, to give real weight to the concepts of multiethnicity and multiculturalism. And during 1996 the most significant initiative by the government was the tardy implementation (and partial revamping) of the project to disseminate the indigenous agreement among indigenous and nonindigenous communities. The project aimed not only to divulge the contents of the agreement itself, but also to solicit proposals at municipal, regional, and ultimately national levels regarding the law reform proposals envisaged by the agreement. It was, in other words, an initial government-backed exercise in bottom-up participation for the eventual reform process.

In the meantime, the national indigenous organizations themselves made major headway in 1996, in particular preparing the ground for indigenous participation in the joint commissions. COPMAGUA took the initiative of creating eight working commissions on the substantive areas covered by the agreement (educational reform, reform and participation, indigenous land rights, officialization of indigenous languages, sacred sites, rights of indigenous women, constitutional reforms, and customary law). By early 1997 this preparatory process had paid dividends. While rivalries continued between diverse indigenous organizations and tendencies (inevitably so, in a country where indigenous peoples comprise the majority of the national population), indigenous peoples were ready to meet the challenge of the initial stages of implementation. Under the important timetable agreement (Acuerdo Cronograma) that divides the implementation of the peace agreements into three separate stages between 1997 and 2000, there were three important commitments for the indigenous agreement in the first ninety days between January and April 1997: the establishment of the commissions on educational reform, officialization of indigenous languages, and sacred places. The other commissions had to be established in the remaining months of 1997.

The various joint commissions were in fact created on schedule in the first half of 1997. The stage thus was set for an unprecedented dialogue between the government and indigenous organizations. In the months and years ahead, indigenous and other actors were to face some major conceptual and political challenges. These final comments aim to identify the more difficult issues at stake.

A major challenge is how to reconcile the role of traditional indigenous institutions and national democratically elected institutions. After many decades of conflict and effective militarization, Guatemala is trying to strengthen its civil society through democratic and representative institutions. The view is sometimes voiced that democracy must be consolidated first, before the government can give attention to the specific rights, values, and institutions of indigenous peoples. The counterview, clearly expressed in the indigenous agreement, is that national unity can be constructed only on the basis of respect for and consolidation of indigenous institutions.

But what should be the status and powers of indigenous authorities? In public administration or conflict resolution, how do they interact with elected authorities, in particular in those municipalities where indigenous and nonindigenous peoples live side by side? And in this context, what should be the scope and limitations of customary law? At its maximum, the issue of customary law can be invoked to demand autonomy and self-regulation, a separate jurisdiction over criminal and civil affairs that is largely independent from the state's positive legal system. A more minimalist approach to customary law would delineate only certain issues (e.g., minor thefts, family matters, inheritance, etc.) that should be dealt with through traditional forms of conflict resolution, while more serious offenses should be dealt with through the national legal system.

Predictably, it is the concept of parallel structures, with rights and status determined on the basis of ethnicity, that is causing strong opposition to the agreement from nonindigenous sectors. Much of the muted press coverage of the agreement has been hostile. Both the agreement and the ILO's Convention No. 169 have been criticized as instruments suitable only to minorities; otherwise they promote separatism and fragmentation of the state, and threaten to turn the small Republic of Guatemala into a new Yugoslavia.

It remains unclear how the Guatemalan actors will deal with these concerns. The Chiapas peace negotiations in neighboring Mexico eventually foundered over the issues of indigenous autonomy, customary law, and institutions. Although initial agreements were reached, it later became apparent that the government was reluctant to cede any of the central state's authority. The Guatemalan agreement tries to strike the delicate balance, improving indigenous participation in the state, empowering local institutions to manage their own affairs at the community level, all within the framework of territorial unity. Calls for an indigenous parliament, for example, are likely to exacerbate interethnic tensions. But there is broad scope to remodel the institutions of local government in rural areas, ensuring that traditional indigenous institutions are amply reflected within their organizational structure.

Yet many of these issues are left open in the text of the indigenous agreement itself. The document has been seen both as a force for national integration and as an instrument promoting indigenous separatism in some walks of society, precisely because these key issues were not—and arguably could not be—resolved at the negotiating table. And it is here that the different sources and influences behind the agreement are most strongly felt. One source is emerging international law on indigenous rights, in which there are differences between approaches that stress indigenous autonomy, self-government, and self-determination (most evident in the United Nations draft declaration on indigenous rights),[13] and those that seem to place more emphasis on the manner in which an integrated multicultural society can be achieved through the incorporation of indigenous values and cultures in all national institutions (evident in a 1997 draft American declaration of indigenous rights prepared by the Organization of American States).[14] On top of this are the intellectual premises underlying the agreement that only the promotion and full incorporation of indigenous cultures can create a real sense of national identity.

In this sense, the concepts of multiethnicity, multiculturalism, and indigenous rights and autonomy are not moving in different directions. Rather, each can be understood and applied in a different way. A "multiethnic" and multicultural nation must always be contrasted with an "exclusive" and elitist nation whose political, judicial, and economic institutions represent the interests of one ethnic group. But such a nation-state can be formed or re-formed in different ways. One way is to reexamine all of the state's existing institutions, adapting them in so far as possible to the values of the different sectors that make up a national society. Another approach is to see the nation as comprised of different ethnic groups, each with its own values and institutions. An extreme version of this latter approach would be an ethnically determined federal structure. But in a country like Guatemala, where indigenous and nonindigenous peoples live alongside each other and share participation in almost all sectors of the economy, it is difficult to see any future in that kind of approach.

The land rights issue also will be contentious. In a country where indigenous peoples have lost much of their land base, where only a small proportion of indigenous lands apart from forests are held on a communal basis, the provisions of the indigenous agreement relating to communal and collective lands have only limited practical relevance. In some regions land titling may improve indigenous land security; in others it may only facilitate further land sales. As yet, no indigenous organization has formulated a consensus position on the land question. The views of these organizations inevitably vary, among those representing farm workers; seasonal laborers; landless small farmers; medium farmers with a stake in the export economy; the communities that still retain a communal structure; and people who are pursuing claims to specific land areas from which they or their ancestors have been dispossessed.

Of the remaining issues, none will be easy to negotiate. Seeking official status for some or all of twenty-three indigenous languages poses a formidable challenge for a small developing country. The joint commission on educational reform will be carrying out its work parallel to a major state effort to modernize the educational system, with extensive funding from international financial institutions. Even the identification of sacred indigenous sites, apparently a relatively straightforward task, has to take into account the fact that many such sites are located on large private estates.

In the short term, the major contribution of the indigenous agreement and its implementation mechanisms will be to inspire confidence among indigenous peoples and their representative organizations that they are now participating in national life. On the modalities for participation, or on the future legal status and capacities of indigenous people's own institutions, the agreement provides for broad principles rather than determined outcomes. Indigenous peoples themselves have to decide whether, how, and on what terms they wish to participate in the present state apparatus.

On a more practical level, indigenous organizations so far have made little headway in the technical aspects of reform proposals. This is no surprise, when recently formed indigenous organizations enjoying few resources, more used to denouncing than to formulating creative proposals, find themselves with a challenge of this nature. But if the Mayans are to avail themselves of the opportunities opened up by the indigenous agreement, their professionals, technicians, and grass-roots activists will have to work together. They also will have to learn from experience in other Latin American countries, notably Bolivia and those Andean countries with economic, social, and demographic characteristics similar to those in Guatemala.

This being said, there is really no model. While several Latin American states now have embraced the concepts of multiethnicity and multiculturalism, the parameters and the legal and political implications of these concepts have yet to be determined. Do they imply a legal, political and institutional pluralism, in the sense of separate if interconnected legal and political systems that make up the unity and integrity of the nation? Or do they rather imply some rethinking and reform of the civil law institutions, imported mainly from Europe in the early independence period, that underpin the modern democratic state in these Latin American countries?

Notes

1. See, for example, Severo Martínez Pelaez, *La patria del criollo* (Mexico City: Ediciones en Marcha, 1994) for the class-based approach; and Carlos Guzmán-Bockler and Jean-Loup Herbert, *Guatemala: una interpretacion histórico-social* (Mexico City: Siglo Veintiuno, 1970) for the ethnicity-based viewpoint.

2. A fascinating insight into some of the dissident URNG thinking on the autonomy issue is contained in Mario Payeras, *Los pueblos indígenas y la revolución guatemalteca* (Guatemala City: Magna Tierra editores, 1997). This is a posthumous publication of a series of essays written between 1982 and 1992 by a Guatemala writer and intellectual who spent many years with one of the URNG groups before breaking away in the 1980s.

3. As throughout Latin America, there are widely varying estimates concerning the indigenous proportion of Guatemala's overall population. A recent World Bank study, drawing on the findings of a 1989 National Socio-demographic Survey, has given a figure as low as 36 percent for the indigenous population. This figure is based on self-definition as indigenous, rather than on such external characteristics as the observance of historical cultural traditions, speaking a native language, or wearing traditional clothing. Most recent estimates, however, taking into account a combination of external characteristics and self-definition, give a figure ranging between 55 and 65 percent. Diana Steele, "Guatemala," in George Psacharopoulos and Harry Patrinos, eds., *Indigenous People and Poverty in Latin America: An Empirical Analysis* (Washington, D.C.: The World Bank, 1994): 97–126.

4. *Mozo colono* is the term used for the workers who reside on a permanent basis on agricultural estates. Traditionally, they have been given the right to cultivate a subsistence plot within the estate in exchange for low paid or even unremunerated labor for the landowner, in particular during the harvest season.

5. Steele, "Guatemala."

6. Cited in Philip Wearne, *The Maya of Guatemala* (London: Minority Rights Group 1994).

7. For a good survey of the changing role of traditional institutions, see: Rachel Sieder, *Customary Law and Democratic Transition in Guatemala*, Research Paper No. 48, (London: Institute of Latin American Studies, 1997).

8. A comprehensive account of the gross human rights abuses of the early 1980s is contained in Robert M. Carmack, ed., *Harvest of Violence: The Maya Indians and the Guatemalan Crisis* (Norman, Okla.: University of Oklahoma Press, 1988). See also, Shelton H. Davis and Julie Hodson, *Witnesses to Political Violence in Guatemala: The Suppression of a Rural Development Movement* (Boston: Oxfam America, 1982), and the several reports produced by such international human rights organizations as Amnesty International and Human Rights Watch/Americas.

9. Most analysts of the Guatemalan indigenous movement tend to draw a distinction between Mayan "popular organizations" linked to grass-roots, human rights, peasant, or political movements; and the more strictly Mayan or indigenous movements whose demands relate exclusively to ethnic concerns. The former include nonindigenous as well as indigenous members, although the vast majority tend in practice to be indigenous. They have not, at least until recently, campaigned on a platform of indigenous rights. See, for example, Víctor Gálvez Borrell et al. *Qué sociedad queremos? Una mirada desde el movimiento y las organizaciones mayas* (Guatemala City: FLACSO-Guatemala, 1997); Demetrio Cojti Cuxil, *El Movimiento Maya* (Guatemala City: Editorial Cholsamaj, 1997); and Santiago Bastos and Manuela Camus, *Abriendo Caminos: Las Organizaciones Mayas desde el Nobel hasta el Acuerdo de Derechos Indígenas* (Guatemala City: FLACSO-Guatemala, 1995). While there are continuing tensions between the two strands of the indigenous movement, there has been some fusion of their demands and approaches since about 1993.

10. For accounts of the growth of diverse Mayan organizations since the democratic transition, see: Demetrio Cojti Cuxil, *El Movimiento Maya*, and Santiago Bastos and Manuela Camus, *Abriendo Caminos.*

11. Contrary to some expectations, the socioeconomic agreement did not enter into detail into the land tenure and land claims aspects that are of most relevance to indigenous peoples. The latter agreement placed most of its emphasis on market-based approaches to land policy, reflecting current international orthodoxies on the issue. However, there is reference to indigenous peoples and their communal lands, including a commitment to reinstate communities or individuals when their land has been usurped or has been allocated in an irregular or unjustified manner involving abuse of authority. An important commitment in the socioeconomic agreement is to create by 1997 a presidential office for legal assistance and conflict resolution in relation to land, with powers to intervene in land disputes at the request of a party. This office was in fact created in mid-1997, and since its inception it appears to have given particular attention to conflicts between indigenous communities.

12. MINUGUA was created officially in September 1994 and commenced its operations in Guatemala in November of that year. Apart from its human rights verification mandate, it also was given the task of strengthening key national institutions, both governmental and nongovernmental, involved in the protection of human rights. By early 1995 it had created thirteen regional and subregional offices throughout the country, several of them in areas where indigenous peoples formed the vast majority of the population (e.g., Cobán, Huehuetenango, Quetzaltenango, Quiché, and Sololá). Since its inception, provision had been made for an advisor on indigenous peoples in MINUGUA's central office in Guatemala City. After the signing of the indigenous agreement in March 1995, measures were taken to increase the indigenous component of the mission's work. Additional experts on indigenous issues were recruited at headquarters, and U.N. volunteers with specific responsibility for indigenous issues were assigned to each of the regional offices.

13. Since the mid-1980s the United Nations has been preparing a draft Declaration on Indigenous Rights. The latest version dates from 1994 and places much of its emphasis on indigenous rights to exercise control over their internal affairs, land, and resources. The philosophical emphasis thus tends toward the recognition of separate institutions for indigenous peoples, under their own control.

14. The draft was approved by the Inter-American Commission on Human Rights at its 1333d session in February 1997 (OAS Doc. Ser/L/V/II.95, Doc. 6, February 26, 1997).

Part II

Consolidating Peace and Reform

12

Truth, Justice, and Reconciliation: Lessons for the International Community

JOSÉ ZALAQUETT

Over the last fourteen years the issue of how to deal with past human rights violations during a transition to democracy has grown into a distinctive field of political and human rights practice and of the attending academic disciplines of political theory, ethics, and human rights. The body of international theory has been built by accretion, as fresh insights are gained from new political transitions or from the benefit of hindsight regarding older political processes.

In previous publications I have proposed elements for a framework to analyze the policies on truth, justice, and reconciliation adopted in different transitional processes.[1] Here I shall first add to those earlier reflections about a proper framework to deal with this topic. I shall then discuss the way in which the transitions in Argentina, Uruguay, Chile, and El Salvador have affected the nature of the truth-telling process and the search for justice. The case of South Africa will be brought in for comparison.

In Search of a Framework to Try to Understand, Compare, and Judge Different Transitional Processes

With the election of President Raúl Alfonsín, in 1983, Argentina returned to civilian government, marking the beginning of a stream of closely watched political transitions. The Argentine case attracted considerable international attention for a number of reasons: First, it occurred at a time of heightened international awareness and sensitivity about human rights issues. Second, the downfall of the Argentine military government, which ruled from 1976 to 1983, represented the first demise of a regime notorious for resorting systematically to "disappearances," a practice that the international community came to label a crime against humanity. Third, at the outset of his government, President Alfonsín, who had been an ardent opponent of the military regime, showed considerable resolve to disclose the truth about the past and bring to trial the culprits. The latter was facilitated legally after the incoming Argentine congress annulled an amnesty law passed by the military regime before relinquishing power.

At the time of the Argentine transition, the paramount precedent on how to deal with a legacy of egregious crimes was still that of the Nüremberg and Tokyo trials. They were a key component in the Allies' efforts to build a new order in Germany and Japan, and indeed a new international order, after World War II. The traumatic experience of that war was also the chief reason for the proliferation of treaties on human rights and on humanitarian law in the late 1940s and thereafter.

Such focus on justice and on the need for humanitarian standards subsequently subsided as the Cold War set on in earnest. In the environment of the Cold War, contending ideologies monopolized the discourse about political values. The ideologies on the radical left implied a political ethics of ultimate ends rather than of means. Their mirror image were ideologies on the far right, which emphasized the ultimate end of eradicating the leftist threat at any cost.

It was in that climate that in the early 1960s an international human rights movement began to emerge. It gained momentum in the beginning of 1970s and subsequently spread to most parts of the world. Its development was in good measure a response to the need for a political ethics of means that could be universally agreed upon. Rather than attempting to provide value-related answers to a wide range of political, economic, or social questions, the human rights movement focused on certain minimum standards of humane behavior to hold every government accountable, independent of its nature or ideology. These standards stemmed from norms established in the postwar human rights treaties, but now they were being acted on by an international movement.

By the early 1980s, the values of human rights and democracy had gained unprecedented international legitimacy. So when the first major transition to democracy of this period took place, in Argentina, human rights standards were, understandably, a preeminent ethical reference.

However, the experience of the human rights movement had been to emphasize an ethics of means, demanding respect for certain rights. The *duty to respect* means that states must comply, at core, with the negative duty to refrain from killing, torturing, arbitrarily arresting people, and the like. By and large it is in the power of governments to comply with such negative obligations.

Yet, when what is expected is truth and justice, governments must fulfill, at core, positive rather than negative duties. Often it is not in the power of governments to comply fully with such obligations. Moreover, the positive duty of seeking truth and justice is part of a larger endeavor—to pursue the ultimate objective of building or rebuilding a stable, fair political system (and the intermediary objective of securing governability during the process of doing so). Often such duties and objectives are at least partially in conflict with each other.

The Argentine case was the leading precedent in the stream of recent transitions. It was also, to some extent, a confusing precedent. The downfall of the country's military regime was precipitated largely by a defeat at the hands of a foreign power, outside Argentina's continental territory. Following the fiasco of the Falklands war, the Argentine military was in disarray. This situation facilitated the efforts of the new civilian government to disclose the truth about past human rights violations and to bring to trial the leaders of previous military juntas. However, these initial developments obscured the fact that the military still retained the monopoly of armed force within the country; they used this power to apply great political pressure once they managed to regain a measure of cohesiveness and unity.

After the Argentine case, many countries have set about addressing, in one way or another, the legacy of repression of the recent past. Several of these transitions (including the ones in Uruguay and Chile, countries that underwent a process of democratic breakdown and human rights violations comparable to that of Argentina) further stressed the difficulties faced by new governments. It became, then, evident that dealing with a legacy of past repression is as much a question of political feasibility as it is one of moral desirability.

What considerations must be taken into account when fashioning a conceptual framework to study and judge the search for truth, justice, and reconciliation during a transitional process? I propose the following:

- The search for truth, justice, and reconciliation during a transition to democracy must be recognized and treated as a dilemma of political ethics.

- As to the ethical component of the problem, there is a logical abyss—often referred to as Hume's axiom[2]—between the realms of what is and what ought to be. The fact that rules often are not observed in practice does not deny their ethical value; the fact that they are endowed with such value does not mean that they necessarily will be observed in practice. It is in that tension between reality and duties that societies search for ultimate meaning. Such tension is found at the core of all political discourse.

- We also know that it cannot be predicated of ethical propositions that they are true or false, but only that they are right or wrong, fair or unfair, convenient or inconvenient, and so on. It may, however, be argued that a particular normative system should guide us in transitional processes—for instance, the normative system of international human rights law. In such cases, while none of the specific rules contained in human rights law can be pronounced in itself true or false, it may be said that it is true or false that a particular rule (say, a rule mandating always to punish grave human rights violations) is part of existing international human rights law. These last points are by no means purely academic. Opposite camps exist among human rights practitioners as well as among legal scholars who concern themselves with political transitions. What divides them, often sharply, is chiefly their respective positions regarding which normative systems ought to be applied to transitional processes and what such systems specifically contain.

- Transitions to democracy have been the subject of abundant political theory literature. Seen from the angle of ethics, some of the most critical political factors that affect transitions are: the nature and intensity of the political crisis and moral breakdown that is being left behind; whether the country has a previous history of rule of law and democratic institutions; the particular mode of the transition and the correlation of forces and/or legitimacy among key actors, particularly the present ruling groups and the sectors representing the previous regime; the stature, prestige, and ability of the new leadership.

- As to the particular mode of the transition, I have drawn an initial typology of situations (taken from contemporary examples of that time) based on the character and degree of the restrictions faced by the new governments in their efforts to deal with past abuses: (1) absence of significant political constraints due to the fact that the dictatorial regime suffered a complete military defeat; (2) the armed forces representing the previous government have lost legitimacy and cohesiveness but retain control of armed power; (3) military rulers allow for a civilian government to come to power, following a negotiation or under terms imposed by them; (4) after a gradual process of political opening, the worst violations become part of the relatively distant past and there is a measure of popular forgiveness; (5) following the fall of a dictatorship, a new civilian government must face continued armed struggle against its former allies and must rely, in order to fight them, on the strength of the military that supported the previous dictatorship; (6) ethnic, national, or religious divisions stand in the way of pacification, and the new government may find it difficult to investigate past human rights violations without exacerbating divisions that may threaten national unity.[3] The developments of recent years have added new examples. Among them: (1) the downfall of the communist regimes made patent a whole set of new problems, including where to draw the line in the pursuit of justice for past abuses, when they were committed by agents of an omnipotent state involving, at different levels, countless perpetrators? (Moreover, the military and civil servants of the past regimes may have to be counted on for the continued operation of basic state functions); (2) peace accords are reached after protracted internal armed conflict without a victor (El Salvador and Guatemala); (3) the case of South Africa, which, due to the regime of apartheid imposed on it for decades, is in a category of its own and does not fit well in the situation described above in (6).

- Needless to say, political transitions are evolving processes during which the above factors shift in relevance and new ones emerge. This is why attention must be paid, when analyzing transitions, to the importance of the *sequence* of different policies, because the implementation of some (say, revealing the truth) may increase the possibilities of others (say, accomplishing justice). It is also crucial to bear in mind that transitions are often fragile; the new leaders must, therefore, pay due attention to the *sustainability* of the process, including their very ability to complete their term of office and to carry to fruition their key policies on matters of truth, justice, and reconciliation.
- As to the relationship between ethical and political considerations, we have learned that the easy assumption that ethics and politics have nothing to do with each other must be rejected.[4] But the belief that the same set of ethical rules should be applicable to all human realms, including family relationships, commercial transactions, or the exercise of political power, is equally untenable.

- From an ethical perspective, a number of factors makes the political realm distinct: (1) political power ideally rests on legitimacy, but ultimately it is underwritten by the legitimate or illegitimate control of force; (2) the success or failure of given policies depends not only on the will or power of the policymakers but also on factors they do not control, such as an upsurge of unforeseen opposition or other unexpected turns of events; (3) the effects of the most critical political decisions fall on the whole nation; (4) democratic governments are elected and sustained by the vote of confidence not of heroes but of the average citizen.

- The political realm is not the only thing that is distinct. There are also diverse *political times* that pose different political objectives and ethical dilemmas. Special sets of ethical rules, such as the laws of armed conflict and the legal standards about emergency rule, apply to certain political times, in addition to the norms that may be deemed of general validity for all times. After a deep crisis, such as an international or internal armed conflict, a period of political chaos, prolonged dictatorship, or other situations of moral breakdown, countries often face what may be termed a *foundational time*. This is a period when societies (or, as happened after World War II, the international community) set about addressing the most essential questions concerning the very basis of the political system they are about to build, rebuild, or transform. At such times the framers of the new order feel compelled to visit again or reformulate basic notions of political and moral philosophy. These notions include questions such as the ultimate purpose of organized societies and their basic institutions; the meaning of justice and fairness; which paramount values must guide the process of political change that is being promoted; and how, in light of such values, political compromises can be justified.

- The ultimate purpose of this "foundational time" is to construct or reconstruct a moral order, that is to say, a just political system. The way a nation deals with questions of values during a foundational time is of seminal importance because it may mark the particular nation's culture and its institutions for years to come. The new government and indeed the whole nation must face the past because it impinges on the present and on the future. Of course, governments also must be concerned about the present—transitions can be fragile and the possibility of major backlashes is often a distinct one. Finally, they must aim at securing a future of peace and national unity where there was conflict and political polarization. Many of the specific measures and policies adopted during a transition, such as reports from truth commissions or trials, have a bearing simultaneously on the legacy of the past, on the present, and on the future.

- The ultimate purpose of building a just political system comprises a series of specific principles. Some of them are absolute. Others admit exceptions and relativizations. But even principles that are stated in absolute terms are subject to the condition of feasibility. Yet, although political leaders may be absolved morally for not having been able to comply with absolute duties, due to insurmountable factual restrictions, the state still can bear responsibility under international law for such failings.
- As to the specific principles:

1. Concerning past human rights violations, it is important to repair as much as possible the damage caused and to erect a system that helps prevent such violations from recurring. Doing so calls for measures of truth and justice. Prevention also calls for policies that promote national unity and reconciliation. The two are not necessarily in contradiction but, more often than not, they cannot be harmonized completely.

2. The policies designed to address the past must be based on as full and public as possible a disclosure of the truth about repressive practices and about specific instances of the gravest forms of victimization.[5] The truth must be established in an official, impartial manner, so it may be generally accepted and incorporated as part of the nation's historical memory. When human rights violations have been committed on a massive scale, the truth must reveal both the overall working of the repressive machinery and the fate of individual victims of the worst crimes. Different methods may be called for to account for these distinct but related aspects of the truth.

3. It is important for the truth to be not only known but also acknowledged by all institutions and individuals concerned and by society at large. Acknowledging the truth implies both admitting the veracity of the facts accounted for and recognizing that they amounted to wrongdoing. Doing so contributes to affirming the value of the norms that were violated, which, as stated earlier, is particularly important during a foundational period.

4. Justice with regard to the crimes of the past has several dimensions. One of them is the vindication of the memory and good name of the victims. A second dimension is the need to compensate the victims' fami-

lies. Third, there is the prosecution and punishment of the perpetrators or other sanctions, such as disqualification from public office.

5. The truth, particularly about concealed crimes, must be deemed an absolute value, but criminal justice ought to be balanced against the possibility of forgiveness and the necessity of reconciliation.[6] The actual and expected capacity of the judicial system to deal with large-scale prosecutions fairly and in a timely way also must be taken into account. Extensive amnesties or pardons may be legitimate, but only if they are adopted when the truth is known, through legitimate means, and they do not include those crimes that always must be prosecuted according to international law.

6. For forgiveness really to serve the function of promoting reconciliation and contributing to advance values that will be part of the political order that is meant to be built, ideally it must meet several conditions. The truth must not only be known but acknowledged, as stated earlier. This reaffirms the validity of the principles transgressed and expresses a resolve not to let such transgressions happen again. In practice such acknowledgment seldom occurs when the main protagonists of the recent past still wield a measure of power. Nevertheless, this fact does not deny the validity of this criteria as part of the guidelines for the process of transition.

7. The goals of truth seeking and justice may be quantified to some extent. The goal of achieving national unity or reconciliation is much more elusive. Indeed, it cannot properly be considered a goal but rather "a general direction, a kind of guiding star."[7]

Certainly different frameworks for the analysis of transitions may be proposed, but whichever is adopted, it must be clear that the study of such political processes can hardly aim at scientific conclusions. In effect, while on one hand ethical statements cannot be said to be true or false, on the other hand, rarely can hypotheses about political processes be fully tested. This is so not only because of the inherent limitations of social sciences. It is also because many of the most interesting hypotheses in this field are about supposed different outcomes had alternative courses of action been followed. A characteristic example is to postulate that if a given civilian leader had chosen to confront the military instead of appeasing them, at a certain crisis point during a transition, by calling for popular expressions of support, he could have defused the crisis. Regarding such hypotheses, only educated guesses are possible.

How the Transition in Four Latin American Countries Affected the Nature of the Truth-telling Process and the Search for Justice

Here I apply the "elements for a framework" laid out in the last section to analyze and compare some key aspects of the main Latin American transitions of recent years—Argentina, Uruguay, Chile, and El Salvador. In these countries most of the relevant policies applied to the legacy of past human rights violations have largely run their course (although certainly many problems still remain). Three of them established truth commissions whose work and reports have been the subject of much study.

The case of South Africa will be brought in for comparison, with all due caveats. The South African case is illustrative because the government studied with great deliberation the Latin American examples before setting up its own Truth and Reconciliation Commission. This commission already has greatly added to the pool of international experiences on this matter.

The Crisis that Preceded the Transition

The political developments of the last decades in Argentina, Chile, and Uruguay present some relevant similarities.

First, starting in the late 1960s, parties and movements that advocated a socialist revolution were increasingly active in all three countries. Their main ideological inspiration was the Cuba of Fidel Castro. A process of increased political polarization ensued. As a response to the ascendancy of revolutionary politics, political strategies and counterinsurgency methods of "dirty war" were developed by the respective military establishments and ideologues on the right.

Second, in all three countries (although more markedly in Uruguay and Chile) there was a political system that, it could be argued, allowed for the interplay of a wide range of political options rather than a tyrannical oppression that might justify rebellion and insurgency.

Third, in all three countries the military leaders who eventually took power (in 1973 in Uruguay and in Chile, and in 1976 in Argentina) and the political sectors that actively supported them saw the previous polarizations as local and regional expressions of the East-West political struggle. This vision was certainly shared and encouraged by the U.S. government and military establishment.

Fourth, the military governments in Argentina, Chile, and Uruguay therefore felt that theirs was a supreme mission: The very life of their nations was in danger, and their duty was to step in, stamp out the communist threat, and build a system that would prevent such danger from recurring. Thus they saw their taking over power as a *foundational* time in politics. Political repression was their perverse version of retributive justice and preventive measures.

Fifth, in all three countries the military government was institutional in character, representing all branches of the armed forces (in Chile the police participated too) rather than the personal rule of a dictator or a small group supported by armed forces that play the role of a praetorian guard, as often had been the case in Latin America.

All these factors greatly contributed to harden the resolve of the military in Uruguay and Chile, during the time they prepared to hand over power to the newly elected leaders and, in the first years of the civilian governments, to oppose widespread prosecutions for past crimes or any other measures they deemed as vengeful. In Argentina, the same factors were the basis on which the military eventually rebuilt a sense of institutional cohesion, after their defeat in the Falklands war and the trial and conviction of the junta leaders, and managed to exert great pressure against President Alfonsín's human rights policies.

It is important to stress that, at present, public opinion in these countries widely believes that while the above-mentioned political polarization may or may not have justified the respective military takeover (a point on which there is still much disagreement in all three countries), it could never justify crimes such as political assassinations, "disappearances," or torture. Yet the military establishment in Uruguay and Chile has refused to acknowledge such a distinction and admit to the wrongness of their human rights abuses. In Argentina such an admission was made publicly in 1995 by General Martín Balza, the head of the Argentine army.[8]

Despite the similarities just mentioned, there were some important differences in the political processes of all three countries. The leftist "enemy" to be fought had reached political power in Chile. In Uruguay it had not, but it represented a significant sector of the population even without counting the Tupamaros guerrillas. In Argentina the military considered as its main enemy thousands of mostly urban young militants of movements or factions of parties that advocated armed revolution. Once it took over power, the military in Chile and Argentina resorted to disappearances on a massive scale. Uruguay avoided this repressive method, at least within its territory, concentrating on prolonged imprisonment and severe torture. In Argentina and Uruguay the respective guerrilla movements had committed acts of terrorism or other humanitarian abuses, particularly just prior to the military takeover. Following the 1973 military takeover in Chile, there was barely any resistance against the military dictatorship, but some guerrilla activity started in 1979. All military governments meted out extensive punishment, including military trials and convictions for these acts of armed struggle or resistance. During the subsequent transitions, the need to determine what to do with remaining political prisoners who had opposed the previous governments became a major consideration, particularly in Uruguay and Chile. Further, in Chile the Commission for Truth and Reconciliation included in its report an account of the humanitarian abuses committed by armed opposition groups.

In both Uruguay and Chile the transition was initiated after the de facto regimes were defeated at the ballot box. However, in both countries the military was able to keep united and to present its acceptance of the electoral defeat as evidence of the seriousness of its plans to gradually restore its countries to democratic rule. In Argentina, as already stated, the 1982 defeat of the military in the Falklands war precipitated its downfall.

In Argentina, Chile, and Uruguay the new civilian governments faced the task of reconstructing and perfecting the political system. They had, particularly the latter two nations, a political culture and past democratic institutions to build on.

The political transition in El Salvador was much different. The country did not have a history of functioning democratic institutions and practices. Its political system had failed to incorporate vast sectors of the population. Indeed, control of the land, of economic and political power, and of military force traditionally had been in the hands of an oligarchy. It could reasonably be argued that it was hardly possible to attempt major political change in El Salvador working within the political system.

During the internal armed conflict that started in 1980, tens of thousands are estimated to have been killed, the vast majority of them by government forces. Eventually, in 1992, the parties to the internal conflict agreed on peace, mediated by U.N. representatives.

The political process that began in El Salvador in the early 1990s around the peace process and after the peace accords is foundational in the stricter sense, namely, it is about attempting to build genuine democratic institutions in a country where they have not taken root before.

Common Factors and Some Key Differences Influencing the Political Transitions Under Study

Concerning all the just-described transitions, the importance of the world-wide changes that cultimated with the end of the Cold War, and led to a revaluation of the idea of democracy and rule of law cannot be underestimated. However, these changes had a more tangible impact in the Chilean and Salvadoran transitions, both of which date from the early 1990s, than in the Argentine and Uruguayan ones, initiated respectively in 1983 and 1984. Most of the "enemies" on the left, fought by the military regimes in all four countries, evolved ideologically during the years of their political or armed struggle against dictatorship. Their declared ultimate goal, which at one point was to accomplish a socialist revolution, came, with the passing of time, to be further redefined as the establishment of a democratic system and the attainment of social justice. By the late 1980s those politicians on the left who were still living under a dictatorship or continued to engage in armed struggle were even more ready to accept a peaceful transition to democracy and were resigned to the necessary compromises to achieving it.

South Africa was certainly not immune to these world changes. For decades the apartheid regime had resisted strong international pressure. One of the factors that helped it to harden its stance was the fact that the opposition African National Congress (ANC) not only embraced the strategy of armed struggle but was seen as including in its midst political factions aligned with the Soviet Union.

Another important factor that distinguishes different transitions is the extent to which activities for the protection of human rights could take place in the countries in question during the height of the respective human rights crisis. In some of the countries considered in this chapter, there were local human rights organizations gathering evidence, providing legal and moral assistance to the victims or their families and denouncing the violations committed. They were particularly strong in Chile, where they developed and operated under the umbrella of the Catholic church and enjoyed the active support of a number of other religious denominations. By the time of the transition to democracy, these organizations had amassed substantial evidence on all but a small percentage of the gravest violations committed under military rule. El Salvador also had well-organized church-sponsored human rights organizations. Such support from the church's hierarchy was lacking in Argentina and Uruguay. In Argentina humanitarian activism was performed largely by victims' relatives. While they gathered much information, they did not have the resources or institutional support to conduct the kind of thorough documentation carried out by the Chilean organizations. In Uruguay there was even less ability to document systematically human rights violations during the years of dictatorship. Yet the enormity of the human rights violations, the fact that most were committed in the countryside, and the very character of the internal armed conflict imposed serious restrictions on the process of documenting human rights violations.

In South Africa a broad range of church-sponsored, social, and political organizations gathered information on the crimes committed by the apartheid regime.

Another critical factor in all transitions is the correlation of political and military force between the new regime and the sectors responsible for past human rights violations. The four Latin American countries discussed represent three types of correlation of forces during transitions. South Africa is in a category of its own.

Chile and Uruguay may be said to fall roughly within the same type. As stated earlier, in both cases the transition was marked by the defeat of the military regime at the ballot box. Yet the process of transfer of power to a civilian government triggered by such defeat did not cause the armed forces to lose their sense of unity and control. However, Chile and Uruguay differ in at least four important respects, besides the fact that the sectors the military considered to be the "enemy" had attained political power in Chile and not in Uruguay:

First, serious human rights violations were committed in Uruguay—prolonged imprisonment without trial and severe torture—which affected probably a higher percentage of the population than in most other countries. Yet the fact that those in power did not resort to a systematic practice of "disappearances" made for a relevant difference. Some 164 Uruguayans were victims of political assassinations or disappearances during the military regime, about 80 percent of them while in exile in Argentina; the deaths of the remaining 20 percent are widely assumed to have been caused by severe torture. Needless to say, such atrocities cannot be belittled. However, the systematic and massive practice of "disappearances" poses particularly grave problems. It leaves a trail of unrelenting anguish, unburied dead, and the stigma upon the state of having set up a concealed machinery for the premeditated extermination of certain categories of people. The clamor for truth, acknowledgment, and justice concerning such grievous crimes cannot be overstated.

Second, as already mentioned, in Chile well-endowed programs were established for the defense of human rights. Nothing of the sort happened in Uruguay.

Third, the Chilean transition followed an itinerary fixed by the military in the 1980 constitution and was designed to secure its rule until 1997, had it won a yes-no vote that was scheduled to take place in 1988 and that was meant to ratify the rule of General Augusto Pinochet for another eight years. After Pinochet lost the 1988 plebiscite, competitive presidential elections were scheduled for 1989, as specified in the 1980 constitution. Any candidate backed by the military faced certain defeat. This fact facilitated negotiations between the military government and the political forces opposing it. Many constitutional amendments were agreed upon. However, no other compromises are known or may be reasonably suspected to have been made. In Uruguay it is widely assumed that the Colorado Party led by Julio Sanguinetti agreed with the military to a policy of impunity, prior to the 1984 elections that brought him in power.

Fourth, the military in Uruguay did not attempt to pass an amnesty law for its own benefit before the transition, on the grounds that it had nothing to be forgiven for.[9] An amnesty was indeed approved for the opposition guerrillas. In Chile the military government had promulgated an amnesty in 1978, forgiving all the political crimes committed since the 1973 coup d'état. These included the systematic "disappearances" conducted by DINA, the secret police active in that period. One major crime was exempted, due to strong pressure by the U.S. government—the 1976 assassination in Washington, D.C., of Orlando Letelier, a former cabinet minister of the Allende government, and an American colleague of Letelier. The practice of disappearances was discontinued after 1978, although many other crimes continued. The different branches of the armed forces could not agree on the need for a second amnesty before leaving power. The Chilean navy and air force, which had withdrawn from active participation in the political repression by the time of the 1978 amnesty, felt that the slate had been wiped clean once and there was no justification for a second amnesty. These facts allowed for the successful prosecution of the 1976 Letelier case and some of the most egregious cases of human rights violations committed by the military regime after 1978.

The type of transition Argentina went through is, with the sole exception of cases of the complete military defeat of the previous regime, the one that, in principle, gives the incoming government the broadest powers to deal with the past. After the defeat in the Falklands war, the Argentine military did not have the time or muscle to compromise with the opposition, and its hastily arranged dispositions for leaving power and securing impunity soon crumbled down. The incoming elected parliament declared the military's self-amnesty to be null. The critical question in Argentina was the sustainability of the process of dealing with the past, as will be discussed.

In El Salvador agreement about pacification and political and institutional reforms was achieved by negotiation between the warring parties. Both sides had a record of violations of basic principles of humane behavior, albeit the violations were far more numerous on the side of the government forces. Peace was possible because of an actual military stalemate and because the forces representing both sides had evolved to the point where they could acquiesce to political arrangements that neither would have accepted ten years earlier. The main restriction on the possibility of seeking truth and justice concerning abuses by both sides was precisely the fact that both had an interest in impunity for their ranks.

The bases for the South African transition also were agreed to by compromise, providing for a definite dismantling of the apartheid system and for a series of steps contemplated in an interim constitution, culminating in free competitive elections in 1994. During the period leading to such election, the ruling National Party, the party of apartheid, passed successive amnesties. Further, the interim constitution agreed upon by the ANC and the National Party contained a final clause that provided for a future amnesty for political crimes of the past.[10]

As mentioned earlier, South Africa falls in a category of its own. The transition is meant as the beginning of a process aimed at building a just political system where none existed before. Under apartheid, South Africa had a functioning democracy but only for the ruling white minority. The long-term objective of building a united country above racial or ethnic distinctions imposes a need for national unity and for peaceful overcoming of the past, while acknowledging it fully.

In South Africa there were two distinct sets of major grievances concerning the crimes of the past regime. One was the systemic daily abuses consisting of the very enforcement of a regime of segregation and denial of basic rights to all but a white minority. The second was the secret or denied crimes, illegal even under the laws of apartheid, committed by agents of the apartheid regime against its opponents. These secret crimes included acts of state terrorism abroad, killings in custody, and political assassinations and torture. On the other hand, and notwithstanding the justice of its cause, the ANC also was known to have committed abuses against some of its members or against alleged collaborators of the regime.

Analysis of the Actual Content and Outcome of Main Policies Concerning Truth, Justice, and Reconciliation

In all the countries discussed there was no question of attempting to mete out justice for all political crimes. Even if in theory any of the new governments had had the power to do so, the sheer magnitude of the problem would have made the task of fair prosecution and trial of every case impossible. But in all those countries there certainly were expectations for the revelation of the truth and for trial and punishment regarding the gravest crimes. This expectation was greater where such crimes involved the loss of life and all the more intense in the case of disappearances.

It became evident, starting with the Argentine case, that although trials could shed light on the details of individual crimes and the whereabouts of the victims, the case-by-case approach characteristic of judicial proceedings was not suited to achieve an overall account of the repressive machinery, its methods, the enormity of the damage caused, and the overall moral breakdown of the nation. Thus the Argentine solution of a truth commission, which later was emulated by Chile, El Salvador, and South Africa, among several other countries. Uruguay did not institute a proper truth commission, unless we count the rather unsatisfactory work conducted in 1985 by a parliamentary commission that reported on 164 disappearances (mostly of Uruguayans living in Argentina) during the years of military rule.

Truth commissions are meant to function as moral panels, not legal courts. A relative exception is that of the South African Truth and Reconciliation Commission, as will be discussed.

The Argentine commission produced an impressive report about the repressive system, its operational methods, and its victims. It could not, however, investigate and come to a considered conclusion on the nearly 9,000 cases of disappeared brought to its attention. It merely listed the names in a second volume. This failure was due largely to the great numbers involved and to the fact that no strong human rights institution centralized and systematized information during the height of the political repression.

The report of the Argentine commission and its dissemination certainly facilitated the 1985 trial and conviction of former members of three successive ruling juntas, after a military investigation had ended clearing the military leaders. Subsequent judicial investigations and trials encountered great difficulties. Eventually, under military pressure, the government had a law passed, in December 1986, establishing a deadline for starting new prosecutions (*Punto Final*) and later, in June of 1987, a second law establishing the excuse of superior orders (*Obediencia debida*) for all but the highest military ranks.

President Alfonsín enjoyed undoubted prestige as an honest person and a convinced democrat when he was inaugurated as president of Argentina. But he was unable to sustain the policies he adopted and ended up by signing impunity bills. Arguably, the effects of such backlash are more damaging for the transition than the fact that a president resigns himself to not being able to change an inherited self-amnesty, but refuses to accept its legitimacy and to pass laws that may convalidate it, as President Patricio Aylwin did in Chile. In Argentina the laws that secured impunity created great frustration and a sense of betrayal in broad sectors of the population and embittered the human rights debate for years to come. President Menem's subsequent pardon to the convicted military leaders, after they served only a few years in prison, further fueled such sentiments. That frustration has been a main factor why relatives of the disappeared have refused to accept any compensation. A major positive step, however, took place in 1995, when the head of the Argentine army acknowledged the institution's past wrongdoing.

Where did President Alfonsín go wrong? Was it mainly a lack of realism or a lack of consistency and resolve? It has been argued that the latter is more the case as there was demonstrated capacity in Argentina to resist military pressure.[11] I would not dispute that assertion, but I have argued[12] that the annulment of the self-amnesty passed by the military, while a legitimate measure, left a very great number of military personnel liable to prosecution. The military then closed ranks and refused to provide information about individual cases of disappearances. Securing collaboration of some members of the military, through some sort of plea bargaining or partial amnesty for lesser crimes in exchange for information, likely would have broken their implicit pact of silence. The experience of South Africa, where at the time of this writing several thousand petitions for amnesty in exchange for information have been filed, suggests that the culprits' cost-benefit calculus may in some cases be the only effective means of loosening the bonds created by shared liability and peer pressure.

The quality of President Aylwin's leadership is acknowledged by most Chileans, supporters and former opponents alike. Right after his inauguration he made it clear that he would personally direct the policy concerning the past.

The Chilean Commission on Truth and Reconciliation could produce a report detailing every one of the nearly 3,000 cases of killings and disappearances it examined, reaching a firm conclusion in over 70 percent of them. It was left to a successor commission (Corporación de Reparación y Reconciliación) to complete investigation of the rest, as well as of cases not submitted to the truth commission in time. This second commission finalized its work in 1996.

The report of the Chilean commission, solemnly announced by the president to the nation and widely disseminated, produced a salutary shock in the country. Yet public debate on the report abruptly subsided when, less than a month after its publication, Senator Jaime Guzmán, the leading political figure on the right, was assassinated by order of an extreme left group.

In the years that followed, reparations were instituted by law and accepted by the victims' relatives. Prosecution of some salient cases not covered by the 1978 amnesty law resulted in a score of convictions. Judicial investigations of cases covered by the amnesty continued at the behest of the president and were facilitated by the findings of the truth commission. However, little progress was made due to lack of cooperation from the military, whose members enjoyed the immunity granted by the 1978 amnesty. Different political sectors have acknowledged the truth contained in the commission's report, but the army has failed to admit to any wrongdoing.

There has been some fair criticism of the policies of the Aylwin administration—that dissemination of the commission's report, though wide, could have been encouraged to a far greater extent. Criticism of the apparent inclination of the successor government of President Eduardo Frei to downplay human rights issues is also well grounded. However, the view that President Aylwin bears responsibility for not having attempted to repeal the 1978 amnesty law is less tenable. While this amnesty law must be deemed utterly illegitimate, the president stood no chance of passing a repeal law through Parliament. He could not have mustered a majority vote, due to the fact that the constitution he inherited included nine appointed senators who tipped the balance to the right. To start his government with a sure political defeat would have weakened his ability to institute the truth commission and to press for prosecutions of the crimes that could legally be prosecuted.

In my view, this is an example of a policy (by no means perfect) adopted with a view of enlarging future scope for action while being able to sustain the course followed.

In the case of Uruguay, it seems clear that President Julio Sanguinetti privately assured the military that there would be no trials. I believe he honestly but wrongly concluded that this was the best possible course of action.

The main point of criticism is that the impunity measures were adopted without a process of revelation of the truth and without acknowledgment of wrongdoing on the part of the military. Such failings elicited a strong reaction on the part of Uruguayan citizens. Acting according to a constitutional right to initiative, more than 25 percent of all registered voters signed a petition for a plebiscite on the repeal of the impunity law passed by Congress. After the plebiscite was lost, the matter was pretty much settled. Yet the country exhausted itself in such battles in the very first years of the transition, an experience that badly scarred the nation.

As in any country where sharp internal conflict exists, in El Salvador an agreed-on solution depended on the leadership on both sides. In this case the facilitating role of the United Nations was instrumental.

The establishment of a United Nations Commission on the Truth for El Salvador, composed of three distinguished non-Salvadorans, signified a new precedent. Probably it would not have been feasible to set up a commission of Salvadorans acceptable to both parties. Yet although the commission's report is no doubt a powerful document that produced considerable impact in El Salvador, it also could be criticized on some accounts.

Working within a tight deadline to investigate crimes that by most accounts amounted to tens of thousands, the commission ended up by providing detailed information on a limited number of cases of human rights violations, in the process naming the names of perpetrators of such deeds.

The Salvadoran case raises two separate questions that deserve analysis: The first one is whether it is appropriate for a truth commission publicly to attribute individual guilt for the crimes committed. For some, this information is an essential part of the truth and is, in itself, a form of moral sanction. Not to reveal the names of the culprits is to contribute to secrecy and impunity. Yet although the conclusions of truth commissions do not apply legal sanctions, the naming of individual culprits by an official, highly visible report, without them having been heard, is the moral equivalent of conviction without due process. It violates if not the letter, at least the spirit, of the rule of law, and it establishes a dangerous precedent. Neither the Argentine nor the Chilean truth commission passed judgment on individual culprits, but on the responsibility of the state and its organs. The information both commissions gathered on individual involvement in the crimes ended up in the courts and thus could be made public. The case of the South African commission is different. It was given, by law, the power to grant amnesty in exchange for full disclosure. Those who are investigated by the commission have the right to a judiciallike hearing.

The second question has to do with the fact that the Salvadoran commission's report revealed the truth, including the names of perpetrators, only in some cases. Although the cases were indeed significant, some people ended up being named and some were not, on both sides. Further, the abuses committed by the military were related with much greater level of detail.

This created obvious political problems for President Alfredo Cristiani. Only days after the report was published, he rushed an amnesty law through parliament. This precipitous move has been rightly criticized. The president may have had spurious motives for passing the amnesty law, but the report handed him the seemingly plausible political argument that otherwise the peace process could have been thrown off course.

In South Africa the decision to dismantle apartheid and agree on a peaceful transition was due both to the leadership of then leader of the National Party and president, F. W. de Klerk, and the leader of the ANC, Nelson Mandela. The subsequent policies to deal with the past met, however, with the objections of the National Party, which joined the new Mandela administration in a national coalition for some time. There can be little doubt regarding President Mandela's singular moral and political stature in contemporary politics. He is widely regarded in South Africa and abroad as the driving force and guarantor of a successful transition.

In South Africa true popular participation in political decisions has been absent for too long. Therefore, the process of revealing the truth has been deemed as important as the content. The procedure to set up the Truth and Reconciliation Commission in South Africa involved widespread national participation. The commission itself had a broader mandate, greater powers, and by far more human and financial resources than any of the Latin American ones had. Its hearings were public. Undoubtedly the lessons from this exercise will greatly influence future political transitions worldwide.

Notes

1. The more relevant of these publications, for the purposes of this chapter are: José Zalaquett, "Confronting Human Rights Violations Committed by Former Governments: Principles Applicable and Political Constraints," *State Crimes: Punishment or Pardon*, papers and report of the conference, November 4–6, 1988, Wye Center, Maryland. (Queenstown, Md.: Justice and Society Program of The Aspen Institute, 1989): 23–69; introduction, *Report of the Chilean National Commission on Truth and Reconciliation* (Notre Dame, Ind.: Notre Dame University Press, 1993): xxiii-xxxiii; chap 4, Alex Boraine and Janet Levy, eds., *The Healing of a Nation?* (Cape Town: Justice in Transition, 1995): 44–55; "Balancing Ethical Imperatives and Political Constraints: The Dilemma of New Democracies Confronting Past Human Rights Violations," *Hastings Law Journal* 43, No. 6 (August 1992): 1425–1438; interview, Carla Hesse and Robert Post, eds., *Human Rights and Political Transitions: From Gettysburg to Bosnia* (New York: Zone Books, forthcoming);

and opinions published in Henry J. Steiner, ed., *Truth Commissions: A Comparative Assessment*, transcript of an international meeting organized by the World Peace Foundation and the Harvard Law School Human Rights Program, May 1996, Cambridge, Mass., (Cambridge, Mass.: World Peace Foundation, 1997).

Other important works include: Neil J. Kritz, ed., *Transitional Justice: How Emerging Democracies Reckon with Former Regimes*, vols. 1 to 3 (Washington, D.C.: United States Institute of Peace Press, 1995); A. James McAdams, ed., *Transitional Justice and the Rule of Law in New Democracies* (Notre Dame, Ind.: University of Notre Dame Press, 1997); Naomi Roht-Arriaza, ed., *Impunity and Human Rights in International Law and Practice* (New York: Oxford University Press, 1995); M. Cherif Bassiouni and Medeline H. Morris, eds., *Accountability for International Crimes of Serious Violations of Fundamental Human Rights*, special symposium publication of *Law and Contemporary Problems* 59, No. 4 (Autumn 1996). See also, *Set of Principles for the Protection and Promotion of Human Rights Through Action to Combat Impunity*, U.N. Doc. E/CN.4/Sub.2/1997/10/Rev.1, Annex II (1997): 13.

2. David Hume, *A Treatise of Human Nature* (London: Penguin Books, 1969), Book III, Part I, Sect. I.

3. Zalaquett, "Confronting Human Rights Violations," 45–47.

4. Max Weber, "Politics as a Vocation," in H. H. Gerth and C. Wright Mills, eds., *From Max Weber: Essays in Sociology* (New York: Oxford University Press, 1946): 77–120.

5. I have argued that the truth is an absolute value (Introduction to the Report of the Chilean National Commission on Truth and Reconciliation, 1993:xxxi). National unity cannot be built on a divided memory about basic facts of the common history. Without knowledge of the truth, any policy would be blind. If it leans towards severity, it may be tantamount to sheer revenge. If it favors clemency, it may amount to mere impunity. The truth is particularly essential with regard to secret crimes which continue to be denied.

6. We refer here to formal societal forgiveness, like amnesties or pardons; the forgiveness from the victims or their relatives is an intimate, personal matter which can hardly be the subject of state policies, although such policies may indeed impinge on the probability of forgiveness taking place.

7. These words from Professor Agustín Squella, from the Universidad de Valparaíso were pronounced at a round table convened by the Corporación Nacional de Reparación y Reconciliación and held in Santiago de Chile, on October 19, 1996. To my knowledge they have not been published.

8. In a televised statement of April 25, 1995, General Balza admitted that the Argentine army had committed killings and other crimes and reaffirmed "old military regulations" providing that it is a criminal offense to violate the constitution, to impart and to obey immoral orders and to resort to unjust, immoral means to achieve an end one deems just. "Argentina despertó ayer conmocionada," *Diario La Epoca*, April 27, 1997, 2.

9. The Uruguayan military are said to have privately justified their systematic torture on the grounds that torture allowed the military to avoid the disappearances and killings committed in Chile and Argentina.

10. The relevant paragraph of the final clause of the interim constitution of 1983 reads: "In order to advance such reconciliation and reconstruction, amnesty shall be granted in respect of acts, omissions and offenses associated with political objectives and committed in the course of the conflicts of the past. To this end, Parliament under this Constitution shall adopt a law determining a firm cut-off date, which shall be a date after 8 October 1990 and before 6 December 1993, and providing for the mechanisms, criteria and procedures, including tribunals, if any, through which such amnesty shall be dealth with at any time after the law has been passed."

11. Juan E. Méndez, "Accountability for Past Abuses," Working Paper #223, The Helen Kellogg Institute for International Studies, University of Notre Dame, September 1996.

12. José Zalaquett, "From Dictatorship to Democracy," *The New Republic*, December 16, 1985, 17–21.

13

In Pursuit of Justice and Reconciliation: Contributions of Truth Telling

PRISCILLA B. HAYNER

Despite the benefit of watching past transitions to peace in Latin America and elsewhere, the relationship among justice, truth, and reconciliation, and the means by which these ends might be reached, is still unclear. There are certainly basic assumptions that are widely shared: that ending impunity requires justice in the courts, that establishing the truth about past abuses helps a society put the past behind it, that reconciliation—either individual or societal—is dependent on a full knowledge of atrocities committed on both sides. Some of these assumptions have not been, and perhaps cannot be, fully tested, as the factors influencing each transition are different and because the psychology of healing and reconciliation is imprecise. But the assumption continues that truth, justice, and reconciliation are by definition positive entities and positive ends toward which a peaceful transition should aim.

Official truth-seeking, meanwhile, is fast becoming a staple in the diet of transitional peacemaking, while justice for human rights crimes remains illusive, or at least rare, especially in Latin America. There remain many unanswered questions about these three parallel but overlapping processes,

The research for this chapter was made possible by research and writing grants from the John D. and Catherine T. MacArthur Foundation and from the United States Institute of Peace. The opinions, findings, and conclusions or recommendations expressed in this chapter are those of the author and do not necessarily reflect the views of the MacArthur Foundation or the Institute of Peace.

truth, justice, and reconciliation: how they impact on each other, what might be expected from them, and what factors influence whether they actually are obtained and how. For example, open questions exist about the relationship between truth and justice. How can truth-seeking enhance justice in the courts, and to what degree do trials reveal a picture of the truth? And what is the impact of truth or justice on a desired process of reconciliation?

This chapter will address three distinct questions. First, it evaluates the impact truth commissions have on justice, either directly by forwarding information to prosecuting authorities for action or in longer-term contributions to judicial reform, with particular attention to those commissions in Chile, Argentina, and El Salvador. Because the Truth and Reconciliation Commission in South Africa has received considerable international attention for its power to grant individual amnesty in exchange for the truth, this chapter looks at whether that model could be extended to Latin America. Second, the chapter offers a framework for evaluating reconciliation, including what basic ingredients may be necessary to advance its progress. Third, it suggests an approach to evaluate the feasibility or usefulness of an official truth-seeking process in a transitional country and the factors that determine the likely effectiveness of such a process. The chapter concludes by suggesting distinctions between truth commissions arising out of different transitional contexts.

"Truth commissions," the acquired name of official truth-seeking bodies that document a pattern of past human rights abuses, have attracted considerable attention in recent years. Although there have been some twenty such bodies in the past twenty-three–odd years, many have received very little international attention (such as those in Chad, Sri Lanka, and the Philippines), despite the fact that they often have been quite contentious and garnered considerable interest from the press and public at the national level. Truth commissions have been multiplying rapidly around the world in recent years, each new commission different from the others, but each growing out of similar transitional dynamics and with the same general ends in mind.[1] Differences between commissions are to be expected: Each country must shape a process out of its own historical, political, and cultural context and respond to the needs and constraints of its own national circumstances.

Truth commissions should be distinguished from international tribunals, such as the International Criminal Tribunal for the former Yugoslavia and the International Criminal Tribunal for Rwanda, both created by the United Nations, or the permanent International Criminal Court, which was agreed to in 1998 and will be set up in the coming years. Such international tribunals also are established in response to massive state violence, but they function with the purpose and powers of a court, very different from a commission of investigation, which typically has fewer powers but a much broader scope of inquiry.

Latin America has had some of the better-known truth commissions. The National Commission on the Disappeared in Argentina was the first to attract significant national and international attention. It was set up by the Argentine president, Raúl Alfonsín, in 1983 as one of the first acts of the postmilitary government. In nine months the commission compiled information documenting nearly 9,000 cases of disappearances that took place under military rule from 1976 to 1983. The commission's report, *Nunca Más,* quickly became a best-seller in Argentina: Over 150,000 copies were sold in the first two months after its release, and about 5,000 copies continue to sell each year, nearly fifteen years after its release. It is now one of the most-sold books ever in Argentina.[2]

The Chilean truth body, the National Commission on Truth and Reconciliation, also was started almost immediately after that country's return to civilian rule in 1990. Unlike most truth commissions, it was able to investigate all cases reported to it that fit within its mandate (disappearances, political killings, politically motivated kidnappings, and deaths due to torture). It concluded its report in nine months, and President Patricio Aylwin released it to the public with an emotional appeal, broadcast on national television, begging pardon and forgiveness from the families of the victims.[3] Unfortunately, a few high-profile political killings in the weeks and months following the report's release derailed a planned process of national discussion and public recognition of the commission's findings.[4]

The Commission on the Truth for El Salvador was created through a U.N.-negotiated peace accord between the government and the armed opposition, the Farabundo Martí National Liberation Front (FMLN), in 1991. Initially given six months, the commission worked for a total of eight or nine months, including preparation time and an extension of two months, and covered a much broader mandate than the commissions of the Southern Cone. Directed to investigate "serious acts of violence . . . [whose] impact on society urgently demands that the public should know the truth," the commission's report outlined massacres, political killings, disappearances, and the blatant obstruction of justice by members of the judiciary and the military during twelve years of civil war, 1980 to 1991. In contrast to the presidentially appointed and government-funded commissions in Argentina and Chile, the commission in El Salvador was spon-

sored by the United Nations, funded by voluntary contributions from
U.N. member states, and staffed only by non-Salvadorans, led by three
high-level, internationally respected commissioners from Colombia,
Venezuela, and the United States. Its report, released to the public in
March 1993, included the names of over forty persons responsible for
abuses or for covering up evidence and blocking investigations, including
senior members of the armed forces and FMLN and the president of the
Supreme Court.[5]

Justice from Truth?

As issues around truth and justice take center stage in negotiations out of
civil war or an end to authoritarian rule, an important but not well-articu-
lated question has arisen regarding the relationship between these two
ends. As truth-seeking has been seen in some countries to replace or displace justice, there is worry that justice sometimes may be replaced solely
with formal investigations of the truth, with the duty to prosecute ignored.

Such concern is justified. In El Salvador the release of the truth commission report was followed by the immediate passage of a sweeping
amnesty. In Guatemala the truth commission was prohibited explicitly
from having any "judicial effect," although the intended meaning of this
phrase was not precisely clear. In Chile the president announced the formation of the truth commission as the Aylwin administration ended its initial efforts to override the 1978 amnesty law. In South Africa the truth
commission was given the power to grant amnesty to those who confessed
their past crimes and proved them to be politically motivated. Given this
collection of experiences, the picture looks bleak. Do truth commissions in
fact make amnesties easier and prosecutions less likely, effectively providing governments with a lower-cost and lower-risk way of "dealing with the
past"?

Not necessarily. Important examples on the other side of the equation
show that truth commissions can contribute to trials, if political or other
dynamics allow it. Typically, truth commissions are directed to hand over
information to the courts where there is evidence of criminal wrongdoing.
In Argentina this model worked well. Perhaps because the commission was
a number of years ago, or perhaps because of the pardons since, Argentina
has been underappreciated for the example that it offers of a truth commission directly contributing to successful high-level trials. When the commission finished its work, it handed its information directly to the prose-

cutors, allowing them to build a case quickly with a large number of primary witnesses. According to then-deputy prosecutor Luis Moreno Ocampo, the timing and nature of the trial would have been impossible without the information from the commission.[6] In just over five months the prosecution reviewed the commission's nearly 9,000 case files to choose over 800 witnesses to be presented in the trial, covering some 700 individual cases. The trial itself began just eighteen months after the military had left power, when the momentum for accountability and public interest was still strong. Five of the nine junta leaders on trial were convicted of a range of charges, including homicide, torture, unlawful arrest, and robbery.[7]

Elsewhere, such as in Haiti, Uganda, and Chile, a similar approach was used, although with less success. In Chile, despite an amnesty that prevents punishment for most acts prior to 1978, information from the commission has helped to establish individual culpability in the courts in a number of cases before the amnesty has been applied. In Haiti and Uganda a lack of concrete evidence, badly functioning judicial systems, and pervasive fear have prevented many trials from moving forward, despite extensive documentation from truth commissions.

Whether a truth commission results in fortifying trials or easing an amnesty will be determined by the political dynamics at hand and the limitations imposed by other forces. In Latin America the lack of justice in the courts has been most influenced by resistance to prosecution from the armed forces, which have been responsible for past abuses and often maintain considerable power during and after a transition. If other ingredients are in place—a functioning judicial system, fair and impartial judges, and a military sufficiently democratized or weakened that trials are allowed to take place—there is no reason why a truth commission cannot directly contribute to trials, as was seen in Argentina.

If truth commissions have not always resulted in direct justice in the courts, they can contribute in a variety of ways to making justice more likely in the long term. Many commission reports have outlined the role of the courts in the system of repression, where judges often either turned a blind eye or were in full support of the authorities' policies and practices, ignoring or covering up evidence or simply refusing to move on cases involving abuses by the state.[8] By providing a clear description of the courts' record, which usually no other official body is in a position to do, a commission can help to prompt changes. In addition, most commissions leave behind recommendations for reform that point to structural or other problems that keep the judiciary from functioning fairly, efficiently, and free of political bias.

It is often argued that trials are preferable to truth commissions not only because they impart justice but because trials themselves reveal the truth. But given the nature of trials, the truth that is revealed is often very narrow. Trials can reveal or confirm details about specific cases but generally cannot outline a broader pattern of events over time, and they certainly cannot enter into an analysis of institutional responsibility, general practices of the state or the guerrillas, or root causes of the conflict, all of which usually are the focus of a truth commission. In addition, the adversarial nature of a trial, especially in common-law systems, only reinforces mechanisms of denial, especially when some cases result in acquittals. Justice in the courts is important for a host of reasons—ending impunity, reinforcing the rule of law, providing solace to victims—but trials are limited in their ability to establish a global record of the truth and honor or acknowledge victims' experiences.

South Africa: A Model for Latin America?

The South African Truth and Reconciliation Commission crafted a new model in the burgeoning world of truth-seeking and linked together more explicitly truth and amnesty in a way never done before: The commission itself had the power to grant individual amnesty to those who come forward to tell all they know about their past political crimes. Because the South African commission created a new model for the field, and because of the considerable attention it received both within the country and abroad, it deserves close attention before considering any future truth-seeking in Latin America. Is the South African model applicable to Latin America, or does it contain elements that should be imported for future truth-seeking in the region?

The commission was the center of attention in South Africa for its full two and a half years of work, beginning in December 1995, in part because its hearings of victims and most hearings of those applying for amnesty were public. It was covered in detail by the press, with the hearings broadcast live on the radio for several hours a day and clips shown on television in the evening.

The aspect of the South African commission that attracted the most attention around the world is its power to grant amnesty to individual perpetrators. This amnesty comes with conditions: It is granted only to those who tell all they know about their past crimes and show that the crimes were politically motivated and in proportion to the political objective pursued. The amnesty hearings produced extraordinary scenes of public admission to brutal acts of terror, including on prominent cases such as the killing of Steven Biko. In one case, for example, former police captain Dirk Coetzee testified to "barbecuing" African National Congress activists over a fire, while he and his security force colleagues drank beer and enjoyed themselves nearby. This is certainly the first time anywhere in the world that so many perpetrators on both sides of a conflict, and at senior levels, have publicly admitted to gruesome details of their past atrocities. Coupled with the hearings of victims, this constant wave of revelation, pain, and occasional apology had a tremendous impact on society and helped to change the way the country understands its history.

The offer of amnesty was designed to work as an enticement for perpetrators to speak, as the "carrot," while the threat of prosecution would act as the stick. High-profile trials in the first years after the democratic election in South Africa involved former military and civilian leaders at the highest levels. Meanwhile, as the truth commission's public hearings were taking place almost daily, and as victims or amnesty applicants were implicating offenders, pressure increased for perpetrators to come forward. (The fact that the deadline to apply for amnesty was in September 1997, long before the truth commission was to conclude its report in October 1998, made these dynamics more difficult for those deciding whether to apply: Each perpetrator had to wager whether his or her name might surface in later hearings or commission investigations.)[9] Unfortunately, acquittals in some major cases in 1996, particularly in the trial against Magnus Malan, the former minister of defense, and nineteen codefendants, eased the threat of prosecution, resulting in fewer people applying for amnesty than had been hoped, especially from the former regime's civilian and military leadership. This problem was exacerbated by the fact that some of the attorneys general—all of whom remained in their posts after the end of the apartheid regime—resisted prosecuting former senior members of government or their accomplices.

Although the South African judiciary still is composed of many civil servants from the apartheid years (including attorneys general and judges), the justice system as a whole functions better than those in many other posttransition countries.[10] For high-level trials to take place so early after a transition is rare; it requires a functioning judiciary, which is lacking in so many transitional countries emerging from civil war or dictatorship. Much of transitional Latin America (and especially Central America) would have had difficulty staging trials at the level and with the sophistication (in investigation and prosecution strategy, for example) that has been seen in South Africa.

Additionally, from the perspective of Latin America, the very public nature of the hearings in South Africa is quite astonishing. Only a small percentage of victims (about 5 percent) who gave statements to the South African commission also appeared in a public hearing; those with security or other concerns could provide their information confidentially. But the public hearings were central to capturing public attention and helped to prompt perpetrators to apply for amnesty. No Latin American truth commission has held public hearings nor seriously considered doing so, in large part due to security concerns and to victims' continued widespread fear. It should not be expected that these fundamental dynamics will change any time soon. Thus, the interplay seen in South Africa between the testimony of victims and the admission of perpetrators could not be replicated and would not provoke the domino effect of perpetrators applying for amnesty after their names were named in public testimony.

But not just the amnesty provision makes the South African truth commission stand out. It is notable as well for its sheer size, the resources at its disposal, and its sophistication. The depth and breadth of it staff, the number and kind of hearings it was able to hold, and the level of investigation it undertook not only determine the impact it would have on society but also allowed its amnesty-granting provision to work. Individualized amnesty was possible only with extensive investigations, including into each application for amnesty—numbering close to 7,000. The commission was larger and better financed than any truth commission to date, with a staff of 300, four offices around the country, and a budget of approximately $18 million a year for each of two and a half years. The commission's extensive investigative staff had to investigate and make a decision on each case brought to it from victims (which has been done previously only by the Chilean commission, working with fewer than 3,000 cases). The commission also set up a sophisticated witness protection program, with a network of safe houses established around the country, to shelter those persons who put themselves in danger by providing information.

The South African commission also stood apart from others in the level of transparency with which it undertook its work, an area in which many truth commissions in Latin America have not been strong. The process by which the South African commissioners were selected, for example, was an impressive show of democracy in commission making: Over 300 nominations were taken from the public, a selection committee with strong representation of nongovernmental organizations vetted the list and held public hearings of finalists, and President Nelson Mandela himself selected the seventeen commissioners from a list of finalists. The commission maintained regular contact with the public and press through press conferences and frequent public statements. In brief, the South African commission clearly recognized that its process, and not just its product, would determine its mark on history.

While some elements of the South African commission may not be possible to institute in Latin America, the experience of that commission does suggest some helpful working guidelines. Most clearly, it shows how powerful a truth-seeking process can be, if done well, appropriately empowered, and given strong political backing. It also points to the need for significant resources in order to carry out such an effort. Widespread denial of the facts of the past, and the abuses on which apartheid was based, would now be very difficult in South Africa. Perhaps making such denial difficult should also be the aim when options are considered for Latin America.

Thoughts on Reconciliation

What Does Reconciliation Look Like?

Despite frequently being cited as a goal in national peace processes and a gauge to measure the likely return of future conflict, it is not always clear exactly what reconciliation is and how its progress might be measured. Reconciliation together with forgiveness and healing are ends seen as necessary and good, even while it is not always clear exactly how to get them or when they have been reached successfully. It goes without saying that prescribing the means is difficult if the ends are hard to define or measure, impossible to guarantee, and depend in part on circumstances beyond one's control. But the slipperyness of reconciliation should not deter efforts at understanding it and contributing to its development.

Perhaps the most basic question is: What does reconciliation look like? If there is a process of reconciling under way, or if a society has achieved a degree of reconciliation, what would be the signs of such a process or end? Perhaps the answer could be found in the following three questions:

1. *How is the past dealt with in the public sphere?*

Is there a lack of bitterness over the past in political and other public relationships? Have past conflicts and past abuses been processed or absorbed in such a way that people can talk about these events—if not easily, then at least civilly—even with former opponents?

2. *What are the relationships between former opponents? Specifically, are relationships based on the present rather than on the past?*

Newly formed relationships between former opponents may depend on new interests or challenges that result in benefits for all. These binding forces or elements might include economic development or reconstruction projects, family or community ties, or even another war against an outside enemy (such as the Malvinas/Falklands war, which temporarily rallied Argentines in support of the armed forces despite the previous half-dozen years of brutal military rule, or the impact of World War I in psychologically joining the U.S. North and South fifty years after the end of the Civil War).

3. *Is there one version of the past, not many?*

Reconciliation means not only reestablishing friendly relations but reconciling contradictory facts or stories, bringing facts or statements into harmony or compatibility when they appear in conflict. As one set of South African writers has noted, reconciliation "is the facing of unwelcome truths in order to harmonize incommensurable world views so that inevitable and continuing conflicts and differences stand at least within a single universe of comprehensibility."[11] These writers continue:

> Reconciliation, in this its rich and meaningful sense, is thus a real closing of the ledger book of the past. A crucial element in that closing is an ending of the divisive cycle of accusation, denial and counter-accusation; not a forgetting of these accusations and counter-accusations, but more a settling of them through a process of evaluation—like the accountant's job of reconciling conflicting claims before closing a ledger book.[12]

In countries where simmering conflict and violence have returned in cycles over many years or generations, a root problem often has been in fundamental differences in perceptions of the past. The Palestinian-Israeli conflict and the depth of hatred that has arisen between Serbs and their neighbors are examples. In Latin America fundamental differences in perception of the cause or justifiability of a recent civil war or military coup can prevent true reconciliation. In Chile unease still exists—although it rarely is discussed directly—between different sectors of society about the roots of the 1973 coup: The armed forces and their supporters hold a different version from those on the left about what caused the brutalities of the 1973 coup, whether a "state of war" existed, and whether the abuses therefore were somehow justified. No member of the Chilean military has ever publicly accepted the conclusions of the National Commission on Truth and Reconciliation nor apologized for his acts. In El Salvador senior military officers still deny well-documented events, insisting, for example, that the massacre at El Mozote[13]—proven through an extensive exhumation of bones—was not a massacre at all but instead a simple battle be-

tween the guerrillas and the army.[14] Where fundamentally different versions or continued denials about such important and painful events still exist, reconciliation may be only superficial.

What Factors Encourage Reconciliation?

If those three questions may help identify where reconciliation exists or is
under way, then what might contribute to its progress? This question
should be considered from the perspective of the victim; perpetrators are
more likely to assume that reconciliation has been achieved before victims
feel the same. The following four elements might contribute to reconciliation taking root:

1. *An end to the violence or threat of political violence.*

This point is seemingly obvious but in fact often is overlooked. A transition to peace implies that the war or overt conflict has ended, but this
does not mean that all political violence or the threat of violence has
ceased. Often it has not. Whether in the form of unrestrained paramilitary
groups that continue to roam Haiti; the threats to Rwanda that continued
after its 1994 genocide from Hutus based in Zaire (now Congo); or unre-
pentant military or paramilitary members who continue to threaten activists in parts of Latin America, threats of political violence and intimidation sometimes continue long after a formal cease-fire or signed peace. To
the degree that such a threat continues, reconciliation may not take root.

2. *Acknowledgment and reparation.*

Second, official recognition of the facts of the past, either by perpetrators themselves or by civilian representatives of the bodies under question (such as a statement by the president upon receipt of a truth commission's report), is crucial to the process of societal healing. Victims
often say that they cannot forgive their perpetrators and have no desire
or ability to reconcile until those who caused them pain acknowledge
their acts and, ideally, ask for forgiveness and provide some form of symbolic reparation.

To be effective, such acknowledgment should go beyond generalities or
implied justifications; a statement from authorities that "errors were
made" is not sufficient and indeed could hurtful, given the nature and extent of the abuses referred to.

It is rare that perpetrators themselves admit to their acts, but the case of
Argentina shows how powerful such admission can be. In 1996 a retired
navy officer in Argentina, Francisco Scilingo, gave a long interview to a
journalist in which he admitted, among other things, that he had taken

part in throwing live, drugged political prisoners out of an airplane into the sea, a practice that he described as a common tactic of "disappearing" people by the armed forces.[15] Although this practice had been mentioned in the truth commission report twelve years before, Scilingo's admission and vivid descriptions sparked public outrage, reawakening the subject of the disappeared and leading to further demands for a full truth-telling.[16]

Reparations to victims, in addition to providing some monetary relief or other benefits, also serve as a formal acknowledgment of wrongs done. In Chile families of those killed or disappeared who receive checks from the government refer to the checks as a monthly reminder and acknowledgment of the government's responsibility.[17] Where there have been so many rights violations that individual reparations are unlikely, as is true for many countries, symbolic or community wide reparations should be considered.

3. *Binding forces.*

In some circumstances it may be helpful to encourage projects that bring opposing parties together for joint gain, such as development or reconstruction programs. The degree to which there is contact between former opponents will, in part, determine whether reconciliation between parties takes root. In some Latin American countries there may not be natural links between former opponents, if the conflict was played out along sharp political or class lines. In order to encourage reconciliation, the question of how to create such links should be addressed.

4. *Time.*

Reconciliation rarely takes place quickly. For many reasons, some countries do not begin to grapple seriously with the weight of their past until many decades have elapsed. Elsewhere, initial efforts of a truth commission, reparations, or trials may begin a process of healing, but the legacy of the past might continue to haunt future generations and demand continued attention. Some healing may depend on factors and dynamics that cannot be predicted or controlled.

Clearly, a truth commission can contribute to reconciliation in a number of ways. The mere creation of a commission can serve as a form of acknowledgment by the state and may prompt acknowledgment by individual perpetrators. A commission can help to unsilence the past and begin a public process of accounting so that the past can be discussed more openly without sparking conflict. It can recommend a reparations program for victims. And ideally, a truth commission will help to establish one accepted version of the past, ending a practice of widespread lies.

But an important distinction should be made between individual, personal reconciliation and national or political reconciliation, a distinction that carries important implications.[18] The strength of a truth commission process is in advancing reconciliation on a national level. By speaking openly and publicly about past silenced or highly conflictive events, and by establishing the facts behind high-profile cases, a commission can ease strains that otherwise may be present in national legislative or other political bodies. An official accounting and conclusion of the facts can allow opposing parties to debate and govern together without latent conflicts and bitterness over past lies. This is not to suggest that the knowledge or memory of past practices should not influence current politics, but if basic points of fact continue to be a source of bitterness, political relationships may be strained. In a negotiated transition out of civil war these latent tensions may be of special concern, as opponents may move quickly from the battlefield to the floor of congress. In addition to easing individual political relationships, a truth commission may be able to relegitimize national institutions that have lost the trust of the public, by holding institutions accountable and outlining needed reforms.

On an individual level, however, reconciliation is much more complex and much more difficult to achieve, especially by means of a national commission. There certainly are examples of a truth commission process leading directly to individual healing and forgiveness for some individuals, but knowing the global truth, or even knowing the specific truth about one's own case, will not necessarily lead to a victim reconciling with his or her perpetrators. Forgiveness, healing, and reconciliation are deeply personal processes, and each person's needs and reactions to peacemaking and truth-telling may be different.

Prescribing the Suitability and Forecasting the Effectiveness of a Truth Commission

In What Circumstances Is a Truth Commission Appropriate?

Some countries may emerge from a horrid civil war with no interest in investigating the details of recent events. Where this reflects a broad consensus, a policy of reconciliation through forgetting should be acceptable and accepted by the international community. In the great majority of cases, however, some groups or sectors of society do very much want the full truth revealed, while other groups have interests that are better served either by silence or by allowing only a narrow portion of the truth to be revealed. It is in these circumstances where continued denial is likely to lead to continued conflict and to hinder attempts to promote societal healing.

In both Cambodia and Mozambique, for example, two countries that have seen wars and massive atrocities, the internationally negotiated peace accords included no focus on the past; indeed, there was an understanding in both countries that dwelling on past crimes was not an option either for the negotiations or for the government that was to follow. In both countries political factors loomed large, as an investigation would have directly implicated those in power on both sides of the two conflicts. But other powerful factors caused the wider public, among them the victims themselves, to have little desire to dig up the past, including an exhaustion with war and a fear that talking about the past could respark violence; a struggle for basic needs in extremely poor societies, which placed victims' immediate priorities elsewhere; a lack of structural mechanisms to provide the security and support for truth-seeking; and perhaps cultural factors that discouraged confrontation or, at least in one case, provided alternative, local mechanisms for working through past crimes.[19]

What might point to the usefulness or importance of such a truth-seeking body, if it is not a universal good for all countries at the immediate point of transition? Neither the quantity or type of human rights abuses nor whether those abuses already have been documented will determine the suitability of official truth-seeking. Instead, two simple factors might be considered.

First, is there a denied past, or was there a policy and practice of deniability in the abuses that took place? A practice of disappearance is the clearest example: By its very nature, the practice of disappearances is intended to obscure facts and hide evidence, allowing official denial more easily. But a firm practice of denial has extended far beyond disappearances, as in El Salvador, where the Salvadoran and U.S. governments insisted for years that the army was innocent of widespread abuses or massacres, or in the massive killings in Guatemala in the early 1980s, where restricted press access and military control over parts of the country prevented word of the massacres to spread. This is not the same question as "Is the truth known?" because often the truth is known, especially by victim communities, and sometimes it is thoroughly documented, but still it is denied by authorities. Chile provides a classic example: The active and organized community of human rights organizations brought most cases of disappearance to court at the time each person was first seized, but the courts refused to act on the evidence, thus reinforcing the Pinochet government's denials that there were ongoing rights abuses.

→ There must be a desire

The second factor determining the suitability of a truth commission is whether there is a desire for a truth-seeking process. Is there a demand from victims or former combatants to clarify and unsilence the past? This factor is hard to pin down, as often it is difficult to measure in concrete terms, but the desire for truth or for silence often makes itself known. In those countries where there is a wide disinterest in digging into the past, observers describe this sentiment reflected at all political and social levels: a preferred letting-go, an uncomfortableness in talking of the past, an exhaustion with the violence, and a passion for peace and rebuilding. Elsewhere, the demand for truth and accountability is made clear through public demonstrations and lobbying from human rights or victims' organizations or in the negotiating position of the parties to peace talks. The nature of the violence in Latin America suggests a likely demand for a full truth-telling in most if not all countries emerging from conflict.

Forecasting the Effectiveness of a Truth Commission

The list of basic ingredients necessary for a strong and effective truth commission is relatively straightforward: sufficient funds, appropriate staff,[20] strong political support and operational independence, a flexible but powerful mandate, and a government willing to implement recommendations and give credence to its findings. But what will determine how close to this best-case model any given commission will be? The idea of a truth commission is in fact quite pliable, and one can be created in almost any shape or size and to fit any number of agendas, depending on the circumstances and who holds the most influence over its design and operation. In addition, forces external to the commission will help to determine its impact. But in those countries that may soon embark on a truth commission process, what factors or dynamics might determine what kind of process it will turn out to be? Five areas might be considered: ˙

basic ingredient

1. A truth commission's mandate and powers will be determined by the balance of power and authority of those playing a role in its creation. Whose interests are being served by such a process (and whose may feel threatened), and how much influence do those persons hold? The actors may include the government, armed or unarmed opposition, the military, victims and survivors, nongovernmental organizations, and others. In a negotiated agreement, the mandate will come from those sitting at the negotiating table, but it also may be strongly influenced by those on the outside. In Guatemala, for example, the restrictions written into the

accord for the Historical Clarification Commission were met with strong objections by the popular organizations and others watching the process; by some accounts, the strength of these objections almost derailed the peace talks.[21]

2. Once the commission is established, the strength of its political backing may determine its reach. Clear government support can provide increased security, give the commission a higher public profile and a firmer funding base, and allow access to classified or restricted government documents. The level of political interest also will determine how the commission's report is received and whether its recommendations are implemented. But political support should coincide with full operational independence, which is necessary for impartial investigation into sensitive topics.

3. The strength and sophistication of civil society. Input from civil society can help shape the mandate and provide information to back up the commission's investigations. Past commissions have benefited from the archives of human rights organizations (as in Chile, Argentina, and El Salvador), or from nongovernmental organizations receiving statements from victims to be submitted directly to the commission (in South Africa).

4. Level of fear or security. Truth commissions usually are set up in countries where fear of talking about abuses has been intense. Where military, paramilitary, or guerrilla presence has been strong, and perhaps continues, there will be a logical resistance from witnesses and victims to come forward with their stories. It is impossible to guarantee the security of those who give testimony; there are many past examples of threats against those who cooperate with a truth commission as well as against members of the commission itself. Victims' fears may be sparked by unexpected circumstances: In El Salvador some who came to give testimony were fearful merely of entering the wealthy neighborhood where the commission's offices were located, afraid that rightists would see them and retaliate.

5. Finally, the role of the international community can be important in providing political backing to the process, perhaps helping to subdue those who resist or threaten the commission, as well as in providing funds, where needed. Some foreign governments, particularly the United States, hold extensive information in their files about past abuses and the responsibility of specific individuals in many countries. If these governments choose to make such information available to a truth commission, and do so early enough in the process so that it can be of use in the investigations, the commission's research may be sig-

nificantly enhanced. The U.S. government's record in this area is not strong: In El Salvador only slowly did it allow the commission access to classified documents on a somewhat limited basis, although it proceeded to fully declassify 12,000 related documents eight months after the commission finished its work; in Haiti the United States released no information to the truth commission, despite its extensive documentation of the facts under study, and it refused to return the many documents it had taken from the offices of the Haitian armed forces and a major paramilitary group when U.S. troops arrived in 1994.

The international community can play an important role in pushing for the implementation of a commission's recommendations, including necessary reforms. Because of the United Nations' role in El Salvador's postwar transition, and because of a prior agreement that all recommendations from the truth commission would be obligatory, the United Nations paid close attention to the implementation of that commission's recommendations, evaluating progress in the regular oversight meetings held between the parties to the accords.

Transitional Peacemaking and the Origins of Truth-Seeking: Postdictatorship or Ending Civil War?

One might expect that a truth body created out of politically negotiated agreements would be weaker than those unilaterally created by postdictatorship civilian governments, which perhaps could dictate terms more freely. But this turns out not to be true. There are examples of very strong commissions growing out of negotiations, such as in South Africa,[22] and examples of commissions unilaterally imposed by a new government that are weakened by a limited mandate, lack of funds, or lack of strong political support or popular enthusiasm for its work, such as in Haiti or Uganda. El Salvador's commission mandate was quite strong; Guatemala's included some limitations demanded by parties at the negotiating table.[23] The strength and impact of a truth commission will be determined by a host of variables, but the fact that its mandate might be "negotiated" should not necessarily limit its reach.

Not all political transitions that follow a period of abusive government fit the neat mold of either negotiated peace process after civil war or transition to civilian democracy after a military dictatorship. (A number of recent transitions in Africa, for example, would be less easy to categorize.)

But these two transition types have been common in Latin America, and a number of countries there have produced truth commissions in the process. So a comparison may be useful: How do the different transitional origins affect the structure, strength, or impact of a truth commission?

After a swift transition from military rule to civilian democratic government, as in Chile and Argentina, a truth commission typically would be created through presidential decree. This allows it to be established quickly and does not require either the support or authorization from the legislature or armed forces. But this founding approach carries inherent limitations, particularly in the implications for what parties may be committed or interested in collaborating with the investigations and in the powers given to the commission. A presidentially appointed commission usually cannot subpoena witnesses to give testimony or turn over evidence, powers requiring an act of parliament; instead, it can only invite cooperation and request documents, hoping for voluntary compliance. The commissions in Argentina and Chile both had minimal cooperation from the armed forces: In Chile a few retired officers did offer testimony, confidentially, although no active members of the armed service came forward. In both Chile and Argentina the commissions sent letters to the military requesting information on the disappeared, usually asking for details on specific cases, but received no cooperation in response, only letters claiming such information was not available.

In El Salvador and Guatemala, in contrast, the armed forces helped to shape the peace accords, and thus the mandate of the truth commission, through their influence on the government at the negotiating table. When the Guatemalan commission was agreed to, for example, the armed forces officially supported it (and had helped put in place some of the limitations in its mandate, such as disallowing it from naming perpetrators). The military in El Salvador cooperated with the truth commission in some areas (in part through submitting its own list of FMLN abuses that it wanted the commission to investigate as well as meeting with the commissioners in response to specific requests), but its cooperation with investigations into abuses by its own members was minimal. If a commission's source of authority lies in a peace accord, it can be given powers that are not possible in a presidentially appointed commission and that might be difficult to impose even by a parliamentary-created commission. The Salvadoran commission was given the power to show up unannounced at any state facility to request information; it used this power on at least one occasion to interview prisoners.

Although the presidential commissions in the Southern Cone (and elsewhere, such as in Haiti, Uganda, and Sri Lanka) were created without input or explicit restraint from the armed forces (or former military or paramilitary), all of these commissions imposed constraints on themselves, at least in part as a response to the de facto pressures they felt in a fragile political environment. Both the Chilean and Argentine commissions chose not to name names of perpetrators, for example, although they had clear evidence of some persons' culpability. (The explanations for the decision to omit names differ among participants: Some commissioners expressed concerns for due process, while others describe the pressures and de facto constraints on a commission coming so soon after a powerful military regime.)

Another likely difference between commissions rooted in these two transition types is in the role of the international community in their work. Truth commissions growing out of peace accords negotiated by international actors are more likely to be funded and closely monitored by the international community (perhaps through the United Nations, for example, as in El Salvador and Guatemala), and also may be staffed by nonnationals. National commissions might turn to nonnational staff or seek international funding (as was done by the National Commission on Truth and Justice in Haiti, for example, and, to a lesser degree, by the truth commission in South Africa), but they are less likely to do so, and will begin with no general commitment of international support that is likely to follow an internationally negotiated arrangement. The commissions in Argentina and Chile were entirely national bodies, funded out of the national treasury and staffed only by nationals. The Guatemala commission is also partly funded by the Guatemalan government and has both national and nonnational staff.

Many questions remain open in the difficult search for truth, justice, and reconciliation and in understanding the relationship or interplay among these three processes or ends. These questions are especially challenging when they are addressed in the midst of a fragile peace process, where a mediator's first priority is to end the fighting. But examples worldwide make clear that if longer-term problems and sources of future conflict are not addressed, peace may be short-lived. The demands for justice, the desire for truth, and the need for initiatives to promote reconciliation warrant continued attention toward understanding how best to reach these ends.

Notes

1. For further information on past truth commissions, see Priscilla B. Hayner, "Fifteen Truth Commissions—1974 to 1994: A Comparative Study," *Human Rights Quarterly* 16 (1994): 597–655, and Priscilla B. Hayner, "Commissioning the Truth: Further Research Questions," *Third World Quarterly* 17, No. 1 (1996): 19–29.

2. National Commission on the Disappeared, *Nunca Más: Informe de la Comisión Nacional Sobre la Desaparición de Personas* (Buenos Aires: Editorial Universitaria de Buenos Aires, 1984), or, in English, *Nunca Más: The Report of the Argentine National Commission on the Disappeared* (New York: Farrar Straus Giroux, 1986). Sales figures from Editorial Universitaria de Buenos Aires.

3. "Statement by President Aylwin on the Report of the National Commission on Truth and Reconciliation (March 4, 1991)" in Neil J. Kritz, ed., *Transitional Justice: How Emerging Democracies Reckon with Former Regimes,* vol. III (Washington, D.C.: United States Institute of Peace, 1995): 169–173.

4. Phillip Berryman, translator, *Report of the Chilean National Commission on Truth and Reconciliation* (Notre Dame, Ind.: University of Notre Dame Press, 1993).

5. United Nations, Report of the Commission on the Truth for El Salvador, *From Madness to Hope: The 12-Year War in El Salvador,* U.N. Doc. S/25500, Annex (1993).

6. Luis Moreno Ocampo, interview with author, Buenos Aires, Argentina, December 11, 1996.

7. All were later pardoned by President Carlos Saúl Menem in 1989 or 1990.

8. The weakness or complicity of the judiciary and the politically biased actions of the judges can allow repression to continue unchecked. The El Salvador truth commission report, for example, describes how the judiciary's "ineffectiveness steadily increased until it became, through its inaction or its appalling submissiveness, a factor which contributed to the tragedy suffered by the country" United Nations, *From Madness to Hope,* 172–73. The commission in Chile noted that "legal oversight was glaringly insufficient" and that the "posture taken by the judicial branch during military rule was largely, if unintentionally, responsible for aggravating the process of systematic human rights violations," offering "the agents of repression a growing assurance they would enjoy impunity for their criminal actions, no matter what outrages they might commit" *Report of the Chilean National Commission,* vol. 1, 117–19. Similar statements were made by the commissions in Argentina, Uganda, and elsewhere.

9. The initial application deadline was extended to May 1997; then, due to parliamentary delays in passing the extension, it was further extended to September 30, 1997. The closing date of the commission was also extended from March 1998 to October 30, 1998.

10. The negotiated transition in South Africa included an agreement that civil servants of the old regime would not lose their jobs when the new democratic government took power.

11. Kader Asmal, Louise Asmal, and Ronald Suresh Roberts, *Reconciliation Through Truth: A Reckoning of Apartheid's Criminal Governance* (Cape Town: David Philip Publishers, 1996), 46.

12. Ibid., 47

13. In 1981 some 700 unarmed civilians who had taken refuge in El Mozote and surrounding villages were killed by the Atlacatl Battalion of the Salvadoran armed forces. Although long denied by the government and their international backers, exhumations in 1992 provided scientific proof of the massacres. See United Nations, *From Madness to Hope,* 114–21.

14. General Mauricio Vargas (Ret.), interview with author, San Salvador, El Salvador, April 12, 1996. Vargas, who in 1996 was the government's representative on the commission for the implementation of the peace accords, argued that the killings at El Mozote were not the result of a massacre.

15. This extensive interview with Francisco Scilingo has been published as a book. Horacio Verbitsky, *The Flight: Confessions of an Argentine Dirty Warrior* (New York: The New Press, 1996).

16. The 1983–84 Commission on the Disappeared did not have access to military archives, for example. Family members continued to demand a new investigation with wider access to official records.

17. Interviews with author, Santiago, Chile, November, 1996.

18. Credit for this point must go to the Reverend Danny Chetty of Practical Ministries, interview with author, Port Shepstone, South Africa, September 3, 1996. The reverend first articulated this distinction to me, describing how differently people in his region perceived reconciliation on

the national level, which was accepted, vs. personal or local reconciliation, which was seen as nearly impossible.

19. The cases of Mozambique and Cambodia, and the broader question of why certain societies show little interest in truth-seeking, are explored at greater depth in a forthcoming book by the author: 1999.

20. While circumstances and needs differ between countries, staff may include lawyers, human rights experts, computer specialists, criminal investigators, researchers, therapists and social workers, forensic specialists, historians, data entry staff, and security personnel. Staffing should be designed to meet the needs of each situation.

21. The accord for the Commission to Clarify Past Human Rights Violations and Acts of Violence that have Caused the Guatemalan People to Suffer, as it is formally called, was agreed to early in the negotiations, in spring 1994. The accord explicitly states that the commission could not "individualize responsibility" and would have not "judicial effect," although it was not clear exactly how these restrictions would be interpreted. See "Agreement on the Establishment of the Commission to Clarify Past Human Rights Violations and Acts of Violence That Have Caused the Guatemalan Population to Suffer," U.N. Doc. A/48/954/(1994)/S/1994/751, Annex II. The commission did not start until July 1997, months after the final peace accord was signed. From 1994 to 1997 at least two independent truth-seeking efforts were started by Guatemalan non-governmental organizations. These include a project through the Human Rights Office of the Archbishop of Guatemala (Recuperación de la Memoria Histórica, or REMHI) and another that reached out to popular organizations (the Center for the Investigation of International Human Rights). As the commission was set to begin, many organizations collaborated in compiling cases to present to it.

22. The South African commission was created via national legislation, going through a number of drafts and inviting input from many parties, including the opposition and nongovernmental organizations, before being finalized in 1995.

23. The mandate of the commission in El Salvador left many decisions to the commissioners, such as whether to name names of perpetrators. The implementation of the commission's recommendations were also agreed in advance to be mandatory. In contrast, the mandate for the Guatemalan commission states a number of explicit limitations. (See note 21.)

Reflections

ÁLVARO DE SOTO

I would like address the questions of truth and reconciliation from the perspective of what I would call the peacemaker's dilemma. The peacemaker faces enormous pressure to try to bring about just that—peace, and peace understood in its most narrow sense, which is cessation of combat, the end of the conflict.

The peacemaker, however, should, if he or she is worth his salt, also face another conundrum, which I would call the peace builder's conundrum. What a true peacemaker must try to achieve is more than simply the end of combat but also a durable peace, one that is sufficiently deeply rooted to ensure that conflict will not recur, that there will not be a relapse into fighting. And doing so includes addressing the causes of the war that is being brought to an end, whether, as in most cases, they are exclusionary policies, the lack of a judiciary, or simply outright repression. The peacemaker's role also includes creating avenues for the resolution of conflict that probably were not available at the time that the conflict broke out and that explain why it broke out in the first place.

One could argue that a peace builder, one who is seeking the much more ambitious goal of ensuring durable peace rather than simply separating combatants, must address questions of justice as part of his or her mission. But a peace builder sometimes faces great difficulty in resisting the strong pressures to achieve short-term goals. Under the pressures a peacemaker or a peace builder face, reconciling that goal of achieving peace with ensuring justice becomes extremely difficult.

In countries where a proper criminal justice system exists, this should not be a dilemma. But normally conflicts have broken out precisely because there exist no such avenues for solution of problems as a proper criminal justice system.

In an ideal situation, one would bring crimes—crimes out of the ordinary, beyond the acceptable or desirable rate—to justice through trials. In Chapter 13 Priscilla Hayner has pointed out the failings and the insufficiency of trials to solve that greater trauma to society created by the overarching, overwhelming, and all-pervading violence that has occurred in society.

From the viewpoint of a peace broker, the problem is more dramatic where no proper judiciary or judicial systems exist. In El Salvador there was a proposal at the negotiating table to send a signal that the impunity of the past had come to an end through exemplary trials and exemplary punishment.

That raised insurmountable problems. Special trials and special tribunals, under what law?

Five years after the peace accord in El Salvador, one might argue that the international community has found a proposed solution that has yet to materialize in a satisfactory way: international tribunals, as have been created for the former Yugoslavia and for Rwanda. But the circumstances that give rise to the creation of international tribunals on that scale are exceptional and not likely to be repeated frequently. The tribunals for the former Yugoslavia and Rwanda arose, by and large, from overwhelming international outcry and the pressure of public opinion on governments that were either unwilling or unable to take the enforcement action necessary to stop the horrendous acts that took place in those countries.

Clean solutions are not always available. As José Zalaquett has stated in Chapter 12, one has to balance the ethical desirability of coupling justice and peace with the political feasibility of actually being able to get there, get to justice, without jeopardizing the goal of ending combat. Thus trade-offs are inevitable at the negotiating table.

In an environment in which justice is out of reach, however, bringing out the truth can operate as a salutary, cathartic compensation, at least at the societal level. Granted, it does not solve the problems or the pain of the victims, or of the loved ones that they leave behind in case of death or disappearance. Therefore, bringing the truth to light about a conflict, "unsilencing" the past, can be accomplished through the creation of what are now fashionably and generically known as truth commissions. They can take many different shapes to achieve the goals that are fundamental to putting the past where it belongs, that is, in the past.

The approach to dealing with the past taken by South Africa has not been uncontroversial or unquestioned. But I turn green with envy seeing the resources available to the South African commission, because there appears to be the genuine possibility of achieving some measure of individual justice, retribution, and compensation, while at the same time carrying out a cathartic process at the national level so that society as a whole can put the past behind it.

What is the main difference difference between what is taking place in South Africa and the compromise solutions that have been evident in Latin America and elsewhere? I would summarize it in one word: leadership. That is the key. And that leader has a name: Nelson Mandela. What is key is the capacity of a leader to assume the responsibility of the state for violence carried out against its own citizens, for the state's own violation of the pact between it and society during certain years.

This leadership capacity is not necessarily absent in Latin America. Many people will recall—and the entire country of Chile recalls vividly—the appearance of President Patricio Aylwin on national television and radio to apologize to the victims of violence on behalf of the state, to assume the responsibility of the state for such acts, something that constitutes a monumental step toward turning the page.

The exercise of leadership during the follow-up to the work of a truth commission is far more important than details of procedures such as whether a commission can name names or not. Possible failings in a commission's mandate can be overcome if the commission carries out its work properly and if the leaders who are responsible for following up on its recommendations do just that.

Indeed, I would venture that how the recommendations of a truth commission are handled by a government in transition from war to peace is probably the single most important test of whether leadership exists, whether it is possible to grapple with the past not by burying it but by making clear what happened. In El Salvador, the government itself bears a heavy responsibility for not having followed up on the recommendations of the Commission on the Truth, but repair work is still possible. One way it can be done is to make sure that the truth commission report and all that it revealed has an imprint on the "software" of the future, that it has a place in the history books, and that its conclusions are debated.

As for reconciliation, it is not something that occurs just between people or between sectors of society. It is also a phenomenon that occurs at the cognitive level between members of society and the society as a whole. There is a need for at least the broad outlines of a consensus regarding what actually happened—if not an official history, an official version of what occurred.

Whether truth commissions of the sort that have arisen in Latin American over the last ten or fifteen years will be successful in achieving reconciliation is something that can be measured only over the long term.

14

Renegotiating Internal Security: The Lessons of Central America

GEORGE R. VICKERS

After decades of dictatorship and civil conflict, all but one of the countries in Central America and the Caribbean now have democratically elected governments. That is not the same thing, however, as saying that they are now democratic societies. The legacy of authoritarianism remains manifest in corrupt and inefficient judicial systems, abusive law enforcement institutions with little capacity to investigate and solve crimes, continued impunity for the powerful, and the residue of authoritarian political culture that acts as a drag on efforts to consolidate democratic electoral transitions by making accountable the key institutions responsible for protecting and promoting democratic values and practices. Rampant crime and enduring economic hardship pose a serious threat to the long-term sustainability of faith in the democratic option.

The international community has a significant stake in the outcome of the struggle to consolidate democracy in Central America and the Caribbean. The United Nations and the inter-American system have played key roles in designing and brokering the democratic transition as well as in verifying and helping to implement democratic reforms. The United States, Canada, and the countries of Europe and Scandinavia are heavily invested in supplying the moral, political, and financial support essential if democratic forces are to prevail over the legacy of authoritarianism. The models and lessons of Central America are being applied to other postconflict and postauthoritarian situations elsewhere in the world, and a

389

failure to consolidate democratic reforms in the Western Hemisphere will have profound ramifications.

Nowhere are the stakes higher or the challenges more formidable than in efforts to establish effective judicial systems and to demilitarize and professionalize mechanisms for maintaining internal security and public order. Prior to and during the civil conflicts that engulfed Central America in the 1970s and 1980s, responsibility for maintenance of public order and internal security was usually part of the role and mission of the armed forces. Militarized internal security forces, together with paramilitary "death squads" organized by and linked to these forces, were responsible for many of the most notorious and brutal practices of torture and assassination. Somewhere in the neighborhood of 300,000 Central Americans died violently during these conflicts, the majority of them noncombatants.[1]

Despite international outrage and pressure, few of even the most notorious cases were investigated seriously by law enforcement authorities. In those few cases where charges were brought against low-level military or police personnel, poorly trained judges were intimidated or corrupted into letting them off or at least ensuring that investigations did not pursue the involvement of higher-ups.

Given the central role played by internal security forces in repressing civil unrest, it is not surprising that a principal topic of negotiations aimed at ending the conflicts was how to restructure and "demilitarize" responsibility for internal security. In the context of negotiations, the focus was on separating responsibility for public order from the role and mission of the armed forces and establishing civilian control. While there were important differences in the circumstances under which internal security reforms were undertaken in different countries, there were also important similarities in the nature of reforms undertaken to prevent a recurrence of past abuses. These similarities included:

- Reducing the size of the military and subordinating it to civilian control.
- Redefining the role and mission of the armed forces to focus on protection from external threats.
- Separating the police from the military and giving police the sole responsibility for maintaining internal security and public order.
- Professionalizing the military and police by reforming doctrines, codifying procedures, improving training and standards, and raising salaries.

These negotiated reforms, as well as similar reforms undertaken in Panama and Haiti where the United States used force or the threat of force to remove repressive military regimes, were designed to correct the perceived flaws of existing military-controlled public security forces in order to prevent a recurrence of massive abuses. The reforms did not anticipate the dramatic increases in both common and organized crime that confronted public order forces in the postconflict situation.

Peace negotiations also addressed judicial reform, but in a far more limited way. A basic problem that confronted negotiators was that Central American judicial systems are extremely hierarchical, with the highest court typically controlling appointments and access to all lower levels. While in theory this meant that reforms at the top could lead to rapid transformations below, in practice it meant asking those at the top to give up much of their control. And the existing judicial authorities were in a position to block or slow the implementation of peace accords by challenging the constitutionality of the agreements. As a result, reforms to the judicial system have been much slower to be adopted and implemented than reforms to the military and police.

This chapter examines the impact of peace processes on mechanisms for maintaining internal security in Central America, the challenges posed by postconflict security conditions to those mechanisms, the principal obstacles to reform, and the role of domestic actors and the international community in overcoming those obstacles.

Nicaragua: Reforming Internal Security Without a Peace Accord

Following the defeat of the Somoza government in 1979, the victorious Sandinista National Liberation Front (FSLN) set about creating a new security apparatus linked to the party. A new Popular Sandinista Army (Ejército Popular Sandinista, EPS) replaced the defeated National Guard, and a new National Police force was established under control of the Ministry of Interior. The EPS was headed by Humberto Ortega, brother of President Daniel Ortega, while the minister of interior was Tomás Borge, a founder of the FSLN and one of its more "hard-line" leaders. The Ministry of Interior had primary responsibility for internal security functions, although in practice the distinction was blurred by shared responsibility for "state security." Both the EPS and the National Police were highly politicized and included as central elements of their mission the "defense of the

Sandinista Revolution." This new security structure was formalized in the political constitution that came into force in January 1987.

Within a year of the Sandinista triumph, former members of Somoza's National Guard, funded and equipped by the United States, began to organize an armed opposition to the new government and staged cross-border raids from bases in Honduras. Gradually this opposition spread to become a full-fledged civil war. While Sandinista leaders continued to portray the "contras" as an army of ex–National Guard members, disaffected peasants and Indians from the Atlantic Coast came to make up the bulk of the guerrilla movement.[2] Failure of the Sandinista government to make good on pledges to give land to peasants was a major factor in spreading discontent, but harsh security measures taken against suspected contra sympathizers and a widely unpopular draft law also led to growing support for the insurgents.

Although there were a series of international efforts to negotiate an end to Nicaragua's civil war as part of a larger peace process in Central America, there were no direct negotiations between the Sandinista government and the Nicaraguan Resistance (Resistencia Nicaragüense or RN, as the contras came to call themselves) until 1988.[3] In the meantime, and despite an economic collapse that wiped out the gains of the early years of Sandinista rule, the Sandinista army and security forces prevented the contras from becoming free of reliance on logistical support and supplies from bases in Honduras.

As Rose Spalding describes in Chapter 2, when negotiations did finally take place between the Sandinista government and the RN, the agenda was focused narrowly on security issues, with a promise of political dialogue during a cease-fire and elections following demobilization of the contras. The dialogue quickly broke down, and a later Central American accord to link demobilization of the contras to political concessions by the Sandinistas prior to elections was rejected by the United States and RN leaders.

Thus it was that the surprise defeat of the FSLN by an ideologically diverse coalition of fourteen political parties (Unión Nacional Opositora, National Opposition Union, or UNO) in national elections held in February 1990 brought to power a new government with FSLN leaders still in control of the army, police, and intelligence services and the RN forces still mobilized. In a transition agreement negotiated between Humberto Ortega and Antonio Lacayo (son-in-law of the president-elect, Violeta Chamorro), the new government agreed to leave Ortega as head of the army in exchange for his resignation from the National Directorate of the FSLN and a pledge to depoliticize the armed forces. The agreement permitted the new government to name a new minister of interior but also kept Sandinista René Vivas in command of the National Police.[4]

The transition agreement outraged many in the UNO coalition as well as the contras and their supporters in the United States. This complicated efforts by the Chamorro government to negotiate the demobilization of contra forces who demanded an end to the Sandinista presence in the military. A series of ad hoc reforms were adopted in response to repeated incidents of renewed armed conflict, among the most important of which were arrangements to permit demobilized contras to serve as police in areas that supported the insurgents.

The terms of the transition agreement were a cause of continuing political conflict in Nicaragua in the ensuing years, as the size of the armed forces declined and the political indoctrination of soldiers ended.[5] In an effort to formalize the delicate understandings of the transition accord, a new military code was approved in September 1994. It gave the president the authority to elect or reject the head of the military from candidates proposed by the Military Council. The term of office was for five years. The president could dismiss only for specified reasons, among them being violation of the military's nonpartisan status. The accord set the terms for Ortega's retirement with pension benefits, also established by the code. The new head of the military, Joaquín Cuadra, came into office in February 1995. The name of the army was changed through the constitutional reform process to the Nicaraguan National Army.

The retirement of Humberto Ortega and the earlier replacement of René Vivas by Fernando Caldera did little to satisfy the harshest critics of the transition process, since both Cuadra and Caldera were also Sandinistas. Public perception of the police as an instrument of Sandinista influence gradually declined, however, as the police repeatedly carried out government orders to break up violent Sandinista-organized street demonstrations against the economic austerity policies of the Chamorro government. But the continuing extreme political polarization of the country and the anti-Sandinista stance of U.S. Senator Jesse Helms (R-NC) prevented the mobilization of sufficient political will and resources to undertake a fundamental restructuring and modernization of the National Police.

The failure to negotiate internal security reforms as part of an overall peace settlement in Nicaragua and the lack of international verification of such reforms contributed to the country's continuing instability during the 1990s.[6] As international observers witnessed the continuing polarization of Nicaraguan society and the resulting paralysis of democratic institutions following what should have been a celebration of the promise of democratic elections, there was a growing consensus about the importance of formal pacts and the need for prolonged international verification and assistance. This consensus helped shape a very different peace process in El Salvador.

El Salvador: Military Stalemate Permits Negotiated Reform

The Salvadoran military effectively ruled the country directly between 1932 and 1979, and an important role of the security forces was political repression and exclusion. Three branches of the armed forces carried out internal security functions: the National Police and the Treasury Police, which operated primarily in urban areas, and the National Guard, which operated in rural areas. The 1983 constitution gave the Salvadoran armed forces responsibility for both external and internal security. A separate National Intelligence Directorate gathered intelligence information and targeted suspected guerrilla sympathizers. Police officers were trained in the military academy with a doctrinal emphasis on anticommunism and counterinsurgency. Officers moved freely between security forces and regular army assignments.

Besides being politicized, the old security forces were not very good at policing. The essence of the old system was maintaining order through vigilance and intimidation. The security forces had extremely poor investigative skills and lacked the most basic skills for protecting, recording, and using evidence. They depended heavily on extrajudicial confessions extracted by torture and abuse to obtain convictions of suspects.[7] Their reputation for brutality and arbitrariness created very poor community relations, and they seldom obtained information about criminal activity from cooperative citizens, which further hampered their ability to investigate crimes.[8] The ineffectiveness of the old security forces as police units is suggested by the fact that El Salvador has historically suffered from one of the highest national homicide rates in the world—roughly five times the homicide rate in the average large city in the United States.[9]

At the outset of negotiations the Farabundo Martí National Liberation Front (FMLN) insurgents demanded the dissolution of the armed forces and later proposed the creation of a merged force that would combine the government and guerrilla armies. The government side rejected both proposals. What eventually emerged was an agreement with the following key provisions:

First, the accords called for the restructuring and reducing the size of the armed forces to 31,000 troops over a two-year period.

Second, under the terms of the accords, the military's educational system was to be revamped, incorporating its new constitutional mission and doctrine into training programs. A new academic council for the military academy, made up of civilians and military, was to be responsible for overseeing curriculum, admissions procedures, and designating faculty.

Third, a central issue in the negotiations was how to "cleanse" the armed forces, so that Salvadoran military officers known to be responsible for human rights violations would be discharged or transferred. The accords stipulated that all Salvadoran armed forces officers would be evaluated by an ad hoc commission composed of three prominent Salvadorans. Two military officers were to participate in a limited way in the commission.[10] Respect for human rights was to be a primary criterion for evaluating each officer's record, and the commission was authorized to establish command responsibility, especially in cases of serious or systematic failure to correct and sanction troops under the officer's command. Professional competence and ability to adapt to working in a democratic society were also criteria. A serious deficiency in any of these categories could be sufficient basis for recommending the officer's transfer or discharge.[11]

The accords empowered the commission to recommend the discharge or transfer of officers reviewed. The commission was not required to use a particular standard of evidence and was authorized to use information from any source it considered reliable. It was required to interview officers before including them on the list for administrative action. Its decisions were to be independent of and have no impact on possible recommendations of a separate truth commission, including judicial actions.[12] No review or appeal process was established for the commission's decisions, nor was there any requirement that the commission explain or justify its conclusions.

Fourth, the peace accords also called for the dissolution of the security forces and the military's intelligence apparatus (National Intelligence Directorate or Dirección Nacional de Inteligencia, DNI), creating in their place a new national civilian police force and an intelligence agency under direct executive control. The new National Civilian Police force (Policía Nacional Civil, PNC) was to be made up of individuals who had no history of direct involvement in the armed struggle, with two specific exceptions: Equal numbers of former National Police and former FMLN would be allowed to join the force, on the condition that they jointly constitute less than half of the force. All entrants would have to pass rigorous admission requirements and participate in a training program at a new civilian National Academy for Public Security established to train cadets and officers for the new Civilian Police.

Finally, the accords called for the creation of a Human Rights Ombudsman's office with broad powers to investigate rights violations, to inspect police and military installations without advance notice, and to refer cases to the courts. The judicial system also was to be reformed, with measures to require broader political consensus for the appointment of Supreme Court judges and minimal standards of professional qualification. Compared with the detailed agreements dealing with military and police reform, however, the accords dealt with judicial reform only in fairly general terms.

The negotiators recognized that there would be a *transitional period* during which existing security forces were being dissolved and new police recruits were being trained and deployed. The accords provided that during this period the old National Police would be responsible for public order. To avoid the presence of the National Police in conflict zones, the accords permitted the deployment of Auxiliary Transitory Police (Policía Auxiliario Transitorio, or PAT) units made up of PNC cadets under U.N. supervision and leadership.

The extensive and detailed Salvadoran agreements on internal security reform reflect the fact that the negotiations took place in the context of battlefield stalemate. To induce the FMLN to lay down arms and demobilize, Salvadoran government negotiators had to agree to dramatic reforms, with international verification and guarantors, that would assure demobilized guerrillas of their personal security and ability to continue to compete peacefully for political power. Peace negotiations in El Salvador began in April 1990 and ended on December 31, 1991. Attesting to the centrality of security reform issues on the agenda of the FMLN, the entire year and a half of negotiations focused on security-related issues with the exception of a July 1990 agreement on human rights verification, a session in April 1991 focusing on constitutional reforms, and a brief period at the very end of the process that debated social and economic reforms.

Guatemala: An Unequal Balance Makes for Limited Reform

The peace negotiations in Guatemala reflected both the very different correlation of forces from El Salvador and the fact that the mediator and parties to the negotiations had an opportunity to observe the process of reform in El Salvador and to analyze its strengths and weaknesses. (See

Chapter 9 for a detailed description of the Guatemala negotiations.) In El Salvador the negotiations took place in the context of a dynamic stalemate on the battlefield, while in Guatemala the armed forces had achieved strategic dominance through a scorched-earth campaign in the early 1980s and the insurgents were reduced to a few small and remote pockets of territorial control.

Internal security functions in Guatemala were traditionally the province of the armed forces, although under the 1985 constitution the Public Ministry was given responsibility for a civilian police force. In practice, however, the police remained entirely dependent on the military for investigation of crimes and were poorly trained and paid. Special military units and an extensive paramilitary structure under military control had de facto responsibility for maintaining internal security.

The internal security reforms of the Guatemalan agreement were modeled on those in El Salvador, but with important differences that reflected the very unequal battlefield strengths of the parties to the negotiation:

- The new peace accord specified that the role of the armed forces is limited to external defense and called for revised doctrinal and training programs to reflect the military's new role in a democratic society. The accord set a target of reducing the army by one-third during 1997. The army reduced its size from 35,000 troops to 31,000, technically missing the one-third goal.

- During the peace negotiations, the Guatemalan army refused to consider any kind of equivalent of the Salvadoran ad hoc commission that reviewed officers' records. It did agree to the creation of a "commission to clarify the past" that could investigate past human rights abuses, but the commission had a limited time frame in which to operate and was prohibited from naming individuals responsible for abuses.

- The accord also specified that members of the military charged with common crimes must be tried by civilian courts and that military tribunals may not judge civilians.

- The Guatemalan agreement also called for the dissolution of military units carrying out police functions and the civil defense patrols (patrullas de autodefensa civil, or PACs) that were established during the 1980s as the principal instrument for the counterinsurgency strategy of the army. The PACs were implicated in widespread abuses, including the assassination of a former presidential candidate.

- With regard to reforming the police, the Guatemalan accord, like the one in El Salvador, called for the creation of a public security academy to provide a minimum of six months' training to all members of a new National Civilian Police (PNC).

- The new PNC is to have sole responsibility for maintaining public order and internal security. The accord did not provide for any vetting of current members of the police, nor did it prevent military officers "downsized" from the army from joining the police.

- Local communities are to be involved in the recruitment process, and the new force is supposed to reflect the multiethnic character of the country.

- The Guatemalan peace agreement addressed reforms of the intelligence apparatus in more detail than the Salvadoran accord. It limited military intelligence operations to external defense functions, required the dissolution of the notorious *Estado Mayor Presidencial* (presidential general staff)—a military intelligence operation that controlled the president's schedule and allegedly targeted and carried out assassinations of civilians suspected of being dissidents—and authorized the establishment of a criminal intelligence unit within the Public Ministry. It also authorized the creation of a secretariat of strategic analysis under the president to gather information and carry out analysis of policy issues. This secretariat is prohibited from carrying out its own investigations.

- The Guatemalan accord did not establish firm deadlines for implementing many of the security reforms, although it did set very ambitious timelines for increasing the size of the new police force from 12,000 to 20,000 by the end of 1999. (See Chapter 4 for a more detailed discussion of the Guatemalan peace accords.)

In mid-1996, before the Guatemalan government and the URNG began negotiations on civil-military issues, the minister of the interior announced that Guatemala would be adopting the "Spanish Civil Guard model" of policing and negotiated a major cooperation package with Spain. During subsequent negotiations the Guatemalan government sought to write its agreement with the Spanish Civil Guard into the peace accords as the center of its police reform efforts. Under pressure from the United Nations and other bilateral donors, however, the government agreed to revise current public security legislation and structures. Such revisions, as stipulated in the September 1996 accord on Strengthening Civilian Power and the Role of the Army in a Democratic Society, were to be "based on the present accord, and for which [process] it will request international cooperation and that of [the United Nations verification mission] MINUGUA, taking into account international standards in this area."

The peace negotiations in Guatemala were more drawn out and in some respects far more complex than those in El Salvador. Negotiations over internal security reforms occupied a relatively small amount of time (about two months), while negotiations over a social/economic accord dragged on for more than a year. There were also significant accords dealing with the return of refugees and with rights of the indigenous population. The decreased emphasis on internal security reflected the URNG's limited ability to insist on reforms the army was unwilling to grant, given the dramatic imbalance of forces, as well as a tacit understanding by the negotiators that the framework for negotiations on this theme would be the Salvador accords.

Postconflict Security Conditions and Obstacles to Reform

The ad hoc reforms in Nicaragua and the negotiated reforms to internal security structures in El Salvador and Guatemala were oriented to the past—to correcting the flaws in the existing system and trying to prevent a recurrence of the massive abuses under that system. The reforms did not (and to some extent could not) address the security conditions that prevailed in the postconflict period. In all three countries those conditions pose great challenges to the reformed system. Among the central features of the postconflict security situation are the following four:

First, there was an economic crisis with high unemployment at the end of the conflict.

Second, large military and internal security forces remain in place and are a significant political force. In Central America there were no effective civilian public order forces independent of the military.

Third, members of insurgent forces awaiting demobilization feared for their personal safety and their economic prospects.

Fourth, with bad economic conditions and a plentiful supply of guns and people who know how to use them, crime has increased dramatically.

These conditions pose immense challenges to successful reforms of internal security mechanisms. Rampant and rising crime threatens to overwhelm the capacity of nascent civilian police forces and generates public support for hard-line elements resisting the reform process.

The Impact of Crime on Support for Reform

El Salvador has been overwhelmed by crime. It has the highest murder rate in the Western Hemisphere, well above that of Colombia, usually considered the hemisphere's most violent country. Everyone talks about crime and has personal stories to relate, in addition to the more spectacular crimes luridly portrayed in the media. In an October 1995 Instituto Universitario de Opinión Pública (IUDOP) poll, 37 percent of respondents said crime was the principal problem (twenty points ahead of the second-ranked problem); a June 1996 IUDOP poll listed combating crime as the most important task for the government. A January 1997 CID-Gallup poll had 95 percent rank crime as "very serious," ahead of economic problems.

Emboldened by polls showing citizen concern about crime, hard-line forces successfully forced the government to pass tough anticrime laws in 1996. The new laws reduced the rights of defendants by permitting extrajudicial confession in some circumstances and forms of preventive detention. The already stuffed jails quickly filled to overflowing. In late 1996, deputies of the ruling Alianza Republicana Nacionalista (ARENA) party narrowly pushed through the first round approval of a constitutional amendment to reinstate the death penalty.[13]

In Nicaragua reported crimes increased 112 percent from 1990 to 1995, and a fifth of the respondents in an August 1996 CID-Gallup poll claimed that they or someone in their household had been the victim of a robbery within the prior four months. Police are drastically underpaid and routinely extort bribes to overlook traffic violations and other minor crimes. There are only 16 police officers for every 10,000 inhabitants, and they are poorly trained and equipped.

Guatemala faces a similar epidemic of crime. Car theft and kidnapping are everyday occurrences, with some ransom demands as low as $1,000. Private security squads have multiplied as the wealthy seek an alternative to the police, but in one recent incident the members of a private security squad were arrested in the act of kidnapping members of a family they were hired to protect. There are increasing incidents of vigilante justice against petty criminals, and there has been widespread support for a new law that reinstated the death penalty.

In both El Salvador and Guatemala organized crime is a particular threat to institutional reform through infiltration and corruption of police units. In October 1996 Guatemalan authorities broke up an organized crime ring that included the vice minister of defense and other high-ranking military officers, top police officials, customs officers, and private businessmen. According to officials the ring was stealing 30 percent of all customs duties. Other military and police officials have been implicated in smuggling activities. In El Salvador police investigative units have been accused of covering up criminal activity by organized crime.

In these circumstances a crack, veteran police force would be challenged. The National Police in Nicaragua and the National Civilian Police in El Salvador and Guatemala are neither. Massive crime is only one of the major challenges to successful reform of internal security, however.

Resistance to Reform

The peace accords in El Salvador and Guatemala envisioned a professional, apolitical, and rights-based police force, using a community-grounded presence to prevent crime and employing modern investigative techniques to solve them. The United Nations and international police training groups, from the United States and Spain in particular, have pushed this conception.

Yet this vision is not universally shared by all key actors in the two countries. Other conceptions have been competing for influence. Some in the business community wanted a force whose leadership would address crimes they wanted solved while avoiding white-collar crime. Some involved in wartime death squads or corruption wanted to assure their continuing influence in a new police force. Still others retain a belief in using the police as a repressive force to advance personal or partisan political agendas.

While it is too soon to assess the final outcome of this struggle among competing visions, the experiences to date highlight a number of serious problems,[14] including resistance by those who would be adversely affected by the accord, infiltration of the police, the creation of parallel police forces, and the failure of internal discipline.

Resistance by the Military and by Officers Who Would Be Adversely Affected by Terms of the Accord

The Salvadoran government tried to avoid dissolving the old security forces by relabeling them as new military units. Although the United Nations mediated an agreement whereby the security forces definitively would be dissolved and the Legislative Assembly repealed laws creating two security forces, many National Guard and Treasury Police members continued to serve in public security roles when the National Police incorporated over 1,000 of them along with entire units from one of the demobilized attack battalions.[15] In addition, the government steadily postponed or rescheduled planned demobilizations of the old National Police on the grounds that crime was out of control. The official demobilization took place more than two years later than the date set in the accords.

In Guatemala the accords called for the dissolution of the Mobile Military Police (Policía Militar Ambulante, PMA). While the accords permitted ex-military members to join the new PNC, they were required to go through the same selection and training process as new recruits. To get around this requirement, the Guatemalan government transferred the PMA into the Treasury Guards and interpreted the six-month training requirement to apply only to new recruits. For members of the old police force and the Treasury Guards, it set a shorter training course of three months.

Infiltration of the New Police by Criminal and Corrupt Elements

In El Salvador two special law enforcement units composed of military personnel, the Comisión de Investigación de Hechos Delictivos (the Commission for the Investigation of Criminal Acts, better known to U.S. officials as the Special Investigative Unit, or SIU) and the Unidad Ejecutiva Anti-Narcotráfico (UEA, the Executive Anti-Narcotics Unit) were transferred wholesale into the PNC.

The transfer of these units represented a major violation of the peace accords and of the Ley Orgánica (Organic Law) of the PNC. The United States previously had invested millions of dollars in training these units and argued that they would provide an investigative capacity for the PNC right at the beginning. Under terms of a special agreement, detectives from the SIU and UEA were to be transferred as individuals, pending a screening process to be verified by the United Nations and retraining at the Academia Nacional de Seguridad Pública, ANSP. In practice, the training never took place, hundreds of additional security forces and military personnel were transferred into these units *after* the agreement was signed, and public security officials resisted, until late 1994, fulfilling their obligation to send UEA and SIU members to the civilian academy.

Preserving these units proved to be false economy. They brought with them a culture of impunity and brutality that was completely at odds with the spirit and doctrine of the PNC. After considerable vacillation, in late 1994 the government finally decided that it would rotate them through a normal course at the academy. This triggered strikes by both units. By March 1995 most members of these units were gone, leaving the government to start from scratch to develop new investigative units, but relieved of the potentially cancerous presence of representatives of the old order.

The Creation of Parallel Police Forces

One of the most serious problems confronting the PNC in El Salvador was the formation of "parallel" police units not contemplated in the accords (or the Ley Orgánica of the PNC) and comprised largely of nonacademy graduates. The public security minister formed several special units directly under his control that bypassed the director of the PNC and carried out operations independent of other units.

In addition, a few years ago private-sector individuals concerned about kidnappings formed their own antikidnapping unit headed by a Venezuelan named Víctor Rivera. This unit operated outside of the PNC with private funding. The minister of public security treated this unit as de facto members of the PNC operating under the authority of the ministry, even though none of its members is an ANSP graduate. This unit duplicated the official kidnapping unit of the Criminal Investigations Division.

In Guatemala, MINUGUA has reported the existence of an illegal antikidnapping unit operating out of the Estado Mayor Presidencial, a military-staffed intelligence unit based in the office of the President of the Republic that has been accused of many major human rights abuses in the past.

The Failure of Internal Discipline

The design of the PNC in El Salvador included several mechanisms for internal regulation: a control unit responsible for evaluating police procedures, organization, and general discipline; a disciplinary unit responsible for investigating violations of regulations and laws by PNC personnel; a disciplinary tribunal that adjudicates cases; and an inspector general's office empowered to investigate any aspect of the functioning and regulation of the PNC.

Effective functioning of all of these institutions is essential to ensuring that the PNC develops an organizational culture of probity and accountability. Unfortunately, these institutions were established months after the PNC began to function and have not lived up to their mandates.

The PNC functioned without an inspector general until October 1994.

The first inspector general was dismissed for failing to perform his job effectively and, according to some reports, a drunken shooting spree. The minister nominated as a replacement an attorney with whom he had long-standing personal and professional ties. Human rights ombudswoman Victoria de Avilés rejected that appointment on the grounds that the nominee was too close to the minister and would not show sufficient independence. A stalemate ensued until a new inspector general was named in October 1995.

Although the Guatemalan accords have been signed only recently, many of the same issues that arose in El Salvador seem likely to arise in that country. After the accords were signed, for example, the Guatemalan government proposed and the congress approved a new Ley Orgánica for the police. The new law does not incorporate key provisions of the accords, including the creation of a new police academy, and makes no mention of internal discipline units. There is already talk of transferring military officers into the police to help instill "discipline" in the new force.

The Role of International and Domestic Actors

In Nicaragua the absence of international involvement in negotiating or implementing internal security reforms contributed to continuing political instability. Yet the principal vulnerability of internal security reforms in both El Salvador and Guatemala is that they are in essence an international import rather than an indigenous product.

In El Salvador the idea of the PNC and the public security academy grew out of the FMLN's need to have some assurance that its members would be safe as they rejoined public life and participated in the politics of the country. Police reform thus can be viewed as something demanded, and won, by the FMLN rebels, even though it was not their original priority in seeking to demilitarize Salvadoran society. Yet to a large extent, El Salvador's police reform bears a foreign stamp. The government, though amenable to the idea of a police force that was separate from the Ministry of Defense, wanted simply to transfer the existing police forces from Ministry of Defense control to civilian control, rather than replace them with something completely new. The FMLN favored a new force but was primarily interested in assuring that its own personnel be assigned to police FMLN zones of influence. The vision for a truly national, apolitical, professional force came largely from U.N. advisors rather than from the Salvadoran parties themselves.[16]

During the peace negotiations, the United Nations embraced the idea of a new civilian police force and proposed a set of specific parameters for the new police institutions that would ensure not only the protection of the FMLN but a broader guarantee to all Salvadorans that the police would no longer be an instrument of political repression. U.N. advisors drafted proposals for the police reform sections of the accords as well as initial drafts of enabling legislation. The United States briefed negotiators on the types of training and assistance it was prepared to offer following an accord. The Salvadoran parties each made minor modifications to these proposals and eventually agreed to them. The doctrine of the new police emphasized the defense of individual rights. A core goal of the new institutions was therefore to provide a style of policing that placed greater emphasis on skill rather than force, investigation rather than coerced confessions, and public service rather than intimidation.

In a sense, the PNC and the new ANSP were an experiment in whether the international community could transfer the norms and institutions of civilian policing to a society that had never had a genuine police force. Because of the radical nature of the reforms, and because they were to be implemented in a highly polarized, uncertain post–civil war context, all parties understood from the beginning that the United Nations and bilateral donors would play a crucial role in implementation. A technical team of U.S. and Spanish police advisors designed the curriculum of the new police academy, and foreign instructors provided much of the teaching during its first two years. At the urging of the United States, the U.N. mission and the Salvadoran government reached an agreement under which U.N. police officials gave advice and practical training to the new force as it began to deploy.[17] The U.N. missions (ONUSAL, then the smaller MINUSAL after April 1995) have closely monitored the development of the new institutions and used their political leverage to influence public safety policies and the selection of top officials.[18] Several countries, including the United States, Spain, Chile, Norway, France, Sweden, and Germany, as well as the European Union, have provided material and technical assistance and added their voice to international pressures for faithful implementation of the project as outlined in the peace accords and annexes.

From the outset, serious resistance to the police reforms was predictable. The history of "nation building" efforts by world powers is rife with examples of the resistance of domestic political and institutional orders to changes promoted by outsiders, even where the international actors have substantial material resources to offer.[19] Domestic political actors, especially those who occupy official positions within the state, have tremendous capacity to resist pressures to give up prerogatives in the interest of democratization or state reform. Even where a majority of state officials strongly embrace reform, those who are opposed can put up effective resistance, especially if they are well placed within the bureaucracy. The fact that the lead international protagonist of change in El Salvador would be the United Nations rather than a bilateral actor did not necessarily improve the odds of success. The reforms provided for in the peace accords were to be implemented by a governing party (the Nationalist Republican Alliance, ARENA) with a history of involvement in political violence, close ties to the armed forces, and defense of impunity.[20]

Despite the potential for resistance to or distortion of the new institutions, international actors did have some important political resources for seeing the projects through. The peace accords provided a detailed road map for the creation of the ANSP and PNC; they specified a timetable, who could join the new force, who was empowered to make and confirm key appointments, how the new PNC and ANSP would be structured, how the PNC would be internally regulated, and what doctrines the police and the academy would uphold. Since all these elements were included in the text of the peace accords, and since the United Nations was given broad powers to verify those accords, the United Nations had license to involve itself in verifying the government's implementation of the ANSP and PNC. These were extraordinary powers, well beyond those usually enjoyed by international agencies attempting nation building. International clout was supplemented by the fact that the Salvadoran government faced enormous financial burdens associated with postwar reconstruction, demobilization and "reinsertion" of former combatants, and institutional reforms mandated by the peace accords. The government was highly dependent on receiving a clean bill of health from the United Nations; major criticisms of its implementation of the peace accords could translate into reduced financial support from abroad and a potentially disastrous inability to carry out essential postwar policies.

The presence of the U.N. observer mission with its extraordinary powers and the relative enthusiasm of bilateral donors to contribute during the initial cease-fire and reconstruction phase were inherently short-lived. From the start it was clear that the international community's role would decline over time and that, in the long run, the democratic and apolitical nature of the PNC and ANSP would depend on the choices made by Salvadorans. When donors failed to respond as generously as hoped to U.N. requests for aid for the new police project, it became clear that the international community's contribution would be more qualitative than quantitative. Only 9 percent of project costs were financed by international donors in 1993 and 1994 (mostly by the United States), with the balance falling on the Salvadoran government. With a relatively brief window of political influence, and with few resources to work with, international agencies could only hope that during the first few years of the project, they could inculcate enough democratic policing doctrine, institutionalize healthy enough procedures and methods, teach enough technique, and raise high enough public expectations that the new force would remain genuinely civilian-controlled, professional, apolitical, and accountable to the public.[21]

The United Nations belatedly tried to create a domestic actor with a stake in internal security reform by recommending the creation of a National Council of Public Security composed of prominent individuals to oversee the PNC and to design solutions to ongoing problems. The council was established in early 1996 but has yet to develop a unified vision of its role and mandate. One problem has been the limited time commitment of the high-profile members.

In Guatemala the basic framework is the same as in El Salvador, but the United Nations has tried to begin much earlier to focus on strengthening the involvement of domestic actors. The domestic verification mechanism includes representatives of civil society as well as the parties to the negotiations. MINUGUA, the U.N. verification mission in Guatemala, began in-country verification of the human rights accord a year and a half before a comprehensive settlement was reached (compared with four months before the settlement in El Salvador) and included institutional strengthening as a primary task from its inception. The Guatemalan accords also called for the establishment of technical commissions with membership drawn from affected sectors to work out detailed plans for implementing each of the agreements.

The lack of tight coordination and coherence between the URNG and many civil society organizations also led a few human rights organizations and think tanks to develop some focus on and expertise in internal security issues while negotiations were taking place. They developed proposals that were submitted to negotiators and have been quite active in monitoring implementation and pressuring for full compliance.

Although the U.S. Department of Justice's International Criminal Investigative Training Assistance Program (ICITAP) and MINUGUA continue to provide cooperation to police reform efforts in Guatemala, the current division of labor puts the Spanish Civil Guard contingent in charge of overall restructuring, particularly in the operations of the new training academy. ICITAP is concentrating its own $3 million assistance program on training and restructuring a criminal investigations unit and the crime laboratory, courses for command levels, support for an internal investigations unit, and training for investigators from the human rights ombudsman's office.

Although MINUGUA is offering technical support for police reform, the Guatemalan Ministry of the Interior has not made that mission a full partner in planning and implementing the overall program. The accord limits the United Nations' verification role to only a few aspects of reform, and to date the mission has been hesitant to comment publicly on progress in implementing police reforms.[22]

Lessons Learned

The very different historical contexts in which internal security reforms were attempted in Nicaragua, El Salvador, and Guatemala make facile generalizations dangerous. The domestic and international dynamics of peace processes in each country also differed in critical ways, so no simple formula can be derived for application in other settings. Nevertheless, the similarity of certain problems encountered in each case does suggest some common themes that are likely to arise in other contexts.

The first and most important observation is that *political will* by the national government to carry out agreed-upon reforms is essential to success. Among the benchmarks of political will are the following:

- Has the government named reform-minded officials to key posts?
- Do these officials have sufficient power and commitment to confront sectors opposed to reforms of internal security?
- Are government officials able and willing to discipline cases of abuse by the postaccord security forces?
- What is the track record of postaccord security forces in investigating cases of political violence and organized crime?
- Are military and public security budgets transparent and subject to effective oversight?

A second observation is that the *time span* needed to accomplish fundamental reforms of internal security mechanisms is substantially longer than the one- to three-year period typically provided for in peace accords. What is involved is not simply the creation or strengthening of institutions but the transformation of political culture. Systems with no legal tradition of oral trials in which public security forces traditionally have been instruments of state repression, lacking basic training in criminal investigation and forensic science, cannot overnight be transformed into systems boasting professional, rights-based police forces. The task is made more difficult by the continuing deep polarization that makes the historical victims of police repression suspicious and/or dismissive of even the possibility of reform.

A third observation, which follows from the last, is that greater attention must be paid to ensuring that *domestic organizations have the capacity to monitor* and oversee internal security reforms. International assistance and verification necessarily will be of limited duration and cannot succeed without the active support and involvement of quasi-governmental and nongovernmental actors who can continue to press for reform after the international presence is gone.

The *quality of police leadership* plays a crucial role in success or failure of the reform effort. Given the strong legacy of authoritarianism, the attitude and example of top and midlevel officials sets the tone for the behavior of rank-and-file police officers. The recruitment and training of officials committed to, and capable of, building and supervising a demilitarized and professional police force must be a top priority of the reform process.

Vetting and retraining of officers who served in the military or in the old security forces is essential. The record suggests that officers with a history of abusive behavior will repeat that history in the new force, and their behavior will poison efforts to create a different institutional culture. Even when officers do not have such a history, it is essential that they be retrained in the new doctrine and procedures of the reformed institution. It is also a mistake to transfer intact into the new force units from the military or old security forces. They invariably become centers of resistance to the reform process.

Internal discipline mechanisms must be established and staffed at the very beginning of the reform process. This is important symbolically as a statement of seriousness about reform and practically as an essential step to prevent the spread and consolidation of corruption and abuse within the new force. Internal disciplinary mechanisms must have sufficient independence and authority to carry out their responsibilities.

Judicial reform must accompany police reform. A corrupt and inefficient judicial system is an obstacle to building a competent police force because it undermines both the morale and the performance of civilian police. Failure to prosecute and convict those arrested for common crimes encourages extrajudicial punishment by the police, while continued judicial impunity for political crimes and crimes by the elite fosters cynicism and corruption at all levels.

There are other important priorities, of course. Raising standards and salaries to attract better-qualified personnel is essential, as is an ongoing program of advanced training to supplement the basic course. But in the absence of attention to the issues just cited, such measures are unlikely to lead to a more professional public security force.

The last, but by no means the least, observation concerns the process of *transition* from the old force to the new. In a context of rampant and rising crime, with a potential security vacuum created by the withdrawal of the military from internal security functions, the experience of Central American countries suggests that there is no satisfactory way to provide interim security free from the risks of abuse and involvement of elements of the old security forces. The best that can be achieved is to make this involvement as transparent as possible and to build a firewall between the interim mechanisms and the creation of a new force. In El Salvador (and in Haiti), this was done by providing international police monitors to accompany the interim force, but this is an expensive option that is not available in Guatemala.

In El Salvador and Guatemala interim security measures also have included assigning military units to police duties under the command of civilian police officials, but there are reasons to doubt the effectiveness of civilian control in these situations. Nevertheless, the alternatives to such "messy" arrangements are even worse. Failure to reduce crime leads both to vigilante actions by outraged citizens and to calls for a return of repressive measures. Speeding up the training and deployment of new police forces is ineffective in reducing crime and tends to generate disillusionment with the reform process before it can be consolidated. While far from satisfactory, it seems better to accept the need for "impure" mechanisms of interim security while the new force is adequately trained and gradually deployed to maximize the chances of success in the long term.

The experiments with police reform in Central American and the Caribbean demonstrate the limits of and obstacles to internal security reform, but they also demonstrate the possibility of building a national consensus to create civilian institutions capable of respecting rights and providing citizen security. It is still a bit early to judge how successful these new public security forces will be at restoring public confidence in the ability of democratic governments in the region to provide basic security while at the same time avoiding the corruption and repressive excesses of their predecessors. The obstacles to success are formidable, and the temptations to revert to more familiar patterns are substantial. The international community's challenge in trying to increase chances for success must be to remain engaged for the long haul with technical assistance and support, to help countries learn from their own and others' experiences, and to respectfully insist that basic values and principles are at the root of law enforcement in a democratic society.

Notes

1. Although there is no definitive tally of deaths, the best estimates are that approximately 140,000 people died during Guatemala's civil war, 50,000 during the civil war against Somoza in Nicaragua and another 30,000 in the "contra war" against the Sandinistas, and 75,000 in the conflict in El Salvador.

2. See, for example, Alejandro Bendaña, editor, *Una Tragedia Campesina: Testimonios de la Resistencia* (Managua: Editora de Arte, S.A. y Centro de Estudios Internacionales, 1991), and Orlando Núñez, ed., *La Guerra en Nicaragua* (Managua: Centro para la Investigación, la Promoción y el Desarrollo Rural y Social, 1991).

3. For a description of these efforts, see Jack Child, *The Central American Peace Process, 1983–1991: Sheathing Swords, Building Confidence* (Boulder, Colo.: Lynne Rienner Publishers, 1992).

4. Although a brief written version of the transition agreement was published, there were continuing rumors of additional secret agreements. For one account of the transition, see Nuñez, ed., *La Guerra en Nicaragua.*

5. Despite the lack of agreement, the budget and size of the Nicaraguan armed forces have declined drastically. Troop levels fell from 96,600 at the time of the 1990 elections to 28,500 in 1991, 21,000 in 1992 and 15,250 in 1993. The budget declined from $177 million in 1990 to $70.5 million in 1991, $43 million in 1992, and $36.5 million in 1993. See United Nations Development Program, *El Ejército de Nicaragua* (Managua: UNDP, January 1994).

6. For a more detailed overview of the political dynamics during the 1990s, see David R. Dye, Judy Butler, Deena Abu-Lughod, and Jack Spence with George Vickers, *Contesting Everything, Winning Nothing: The Search for Consensus in Nicaragua, 1990–1995* (Cambridge, Mass.: Hemisphere Initiatives, 1995). Also see Judy Butler, David R. Dye, and Jack Spence with George Vickers, *Democracy and Its Discontents: Nicaraguans Face the Election* (Cambridge, Mass.: Hemisphere Initiatives, 1996).

7. National Police, Treasury Police, and National Guard intelligence units were highly effective at counterinsurgency work during the war but relied more on terror and indiscriminate killings, particularly early in the war, than on legal investigation. Their dominant mode of operation later in the war was to arrest suspects and extract extrajudicial confessions often written by the police themselves. For an illustrative case of the later pattern, see Margaret Popkin, *El Salvador's Negotiated Revolution: Prospects for Legal Reform* (New York: Lawyers Committee for Human Rights, 1993), 90.

8. According to a January 1992 national opinion survey conducted by the University of Central America, 50.1 percent of respondents had "little" or "no" confidence in the existing security forces and 64 percent favored dissolution of the Civil Defense structure. See "Los Salvadoreños ante los acuerdos finales de paz," Instituto Universitario de Opinión Publica (IUDOP), April 30, 1992, San Salvador. In a February 1993 survey of the urban population, IUDOP found that 76.4 percent of crime victims did not report incidents to the police. See Instituto Universitario de Opinión Pública (IUDOP) "La delincuencia urbana: Encuesta exploratoria, *Estudios Centroamericanos* 534–535 (April/May 1993): 471–9.

9. See Bernard Cohen, "Political Death and Homicide in El Salvador," Queens College and the Graduate Center of the City University of New York, Sept. 1, 1984.

10. The members of the commission were Abraham Rodríguez, a prominent businessman and former personal advisor to ex-President Duarte; Eduardo Molina, a founding member of the Christian Democratic Party; and Reynaldo Galindo Pohl, legal counsel to the Osorio (military) government and one of the authors of the 1950 Salvadoran constitution. President Cristiani named two former defense ministers, Generals Eugenio Vides Casanova and Rafael Humberto Larios, to represent the military on the commission.

11. The criteria listed in the accords were: "the evaluation will take into account the record of each officer, including especially: (1) his history in terms of observing the legal order, with particular emphasis on respect for human rights, both in his personal conduct and the rigor with which he has corrected and sanctioned irregular acts, excesses or violations of human rights carried out under his command, especially if serious or systematic omissions are observed in this respect; (2) his professional competence; (3) his ability to adapt himself to the new reality of peace, within the context of a democratic society, and to promote democracy in the country, guarantee unrestricted respect for human rights and reunify Salvadoran society, which is the common purpose agreed to by the parties in the Geneva Accord." "Acuerdo de paz," *ECA: Estudios Centroamericanos* (Jan./Feb. 1992): 105.

12. The Truth Commission was authorized to have an observer on the ad hoc commission.

13. Constitutional reforms must be ratified by two consecutive Legislative Assemblies to take effect.

14. For a comprehensive account of progress and problems in the implementation of the internal security components of the Salvadoran peace accords, see the following reports of Boston's Hemisphere Initiatives: George Vickers and Jack Spence with David Holiday, Margaret Popkin, and Philip Williams *Endgame: A Progress Report on Implementation of the Salvadoran Peace Accords* (December 3, 1992); Margaret Popkin with George Vickers and Jack Spence, *Justice Impugned: The Salvadoran Peace Accords and the Problem of Impunity* (June 1993); William Stanley with George Vickers and Jack Spence, *Risking Failure: The Problems and Promise of the New Civilian Police in El Salvador* (September 1993); Jack Spence and George Vickers with Margaret Popkin, Philip Williams, and Kevin Murray, *A Negotiated Revolution? A Two Year Progress Report on the Salvadoran Peace Accords* (March 1994); Margaret Popkin with Jack Spence and George Vickers *Justice Delayed: The Slow Pace of Judicial Reform in El Salvador* (December 1994); Jack Spence, George Vickers, and David Dye, *The Salvadoran Peace Accords and Democratization: A Three-Year Progress Report and Recommendations* (March 1995); Jack Spence, David Dye, Mike Lanchin, Geoff Thale with George Vickers, *Chapultepec: Five Years Later: El Salvador's Political Reality and Uncertain Future* (January 1997). See also William Stanley with George Vickers and Jack Spence, *Protectors or Perpetrators? The Institutional Crisis of the Salvadoran Civilian Police* (Washington, D.C.: Washington Office on Latin America, January 1996).

15. United Nations, *Report of the Secretary-General on the United Nations Observer Mission in El Salvador,* U.N.Doc. S/23999, May 26, 1992, p. 10. Also see Stanley with Vickers and Spence, *Risking Failure,* p. 17.

16. Author interviews with U.N. officials, December 1991, New York; and June 1993 and November 1994, San Salvador. One U.N. official who participated in the negotiations said that the FMLN envisioned its forces being "sheriffs" in areas where it had large numbers of supporters. U.N. advisors convinced FMLN members to consider a more institutionalized, national force. The accords were fairly specific regarding the doctrine, mechanisms of civilian control, and initial makeup of the PNC. A draft of the PNC's Ley Orgánica was annexed to the accords. The police experts who designed the reform represented Canada, Spain, France, Sweden, and Venezuela. The mission was headed by Jesús Rodes, director of the Escuela de Policía de Cataluña, who also served as a U.N. advisor on police issues during the peace negotiations. For a more complete discussion, see Gino Costa, "Las Dificultades de Desmilitarizar la Seguridad Pública; Las Naciones Unidas y la creación de la Policía Nacional Civil en El Salvador 1990–1996," July 1997. The United States also briefed the negotiators on the types of training and equipment it was prepared to offer if a settlement was reached.

17. The Police Division of the United Nations Observer Mission in El Salvador (ONUSAL) was deployed originally to accompany the old National Police (PN) during the transition phase and to ensure that the PN did not commit abuses. As the new civilian force began to deploy, ONUSAL police provided practical training and advice, until that relationship was suspended by the government in September 1993. By the time the training relationship was restored in mid-1994, ONUSAL's police division was scaling back, making it impossible to return to the close, daily support that the mission provided at the outset.

18. The original United Nations Observer Mission in El Salvador was replaced in April 1995 by a smaller mission called the United Nations Mission in El Salvador (MINUSAL), which was to verify government compliance with the remaining elements of the peace accords, including land transfers, judicial reform, and public security. In May, 1996, MINUSAL was replaced by an even smaller mission, the United Nations Office of Verification in El Salvador (ONUV). In January 1997 remaining U.N. personnel involved with verification were attached to the United Nations Development Program office in El Salvador.

19. Michael D. Shafer, *Deadly Paradigms: The Failure of U.S. Counterinsurgency Policy* (Princeton, N.J.: Princeton University Press, 1988); Douglas J. MacDonald, *Adventures in Chaos: American Intervention for Reform in the Third World,* (Cambridge, Mass.: Harvard University Press, 1992); Mark Peceny, "The Promotion of Democracy in U.S. Policy During Interventions" (Ph.D. diss., Stanford University, 1992); and Mark Peceny, "Two Paths to the Promotion of Democracy During U.S. Military Interventions," *International Studies Quarterly* 39, No. 3 (September 1995): 371–401.

20. See Craig Pyes's Pulitzer Prize–winning series of articles in the *Albuquerque Journal,* December 18–22, 1983 and William Stanley, *The Protection Racket State* (Philadelphia: Temple University Press, 1996). See also declassified documents of the Central Intelligence Agency Directorate of Intelligence, "El Salvador: Dealing with Death Squads," January 20, 1984; "El Salvador: D'Aubuisson's Terrorist Activities," March 2, 1984; "Members and Collaborators of the Nationalist Republican Alliance (ARENA) Paramilitary Unit Headed by Hector Regalado" and "El Salvador: Controlling Rightwing Terrorism," February 1985.

21. The most important international actors were ONUSAL, the United States Justice Department's International Criminal Investigations Training and Assistance Program (ICITAP), and the Spanish government's police training program.

22. For a more complete analysis of initial progress in Guatemalan police reforms, see Rachel Garst, *The New Guatemalan National Civilian Police: A Problematic Beginning* (Washington, D.C.: Washington Office on Latin America, 1997).

Reflections

FRANCISCO THOUMI

There are five basic categories of violence associated with drug trafficking. First there is violence within drug mafias. Second is violence between the mafias, which usually brings a smile to the faces of those in society who are not part of the mafia. Third is violence between the drug "industry" and the state, characterized by the kinds of assassinations of political leaders carried out by Medellín cartel leader Pablo Escobar. Fourth is the violence of the drug industry against specific social targets. This kind is puzzling because often it can generate popular support, as in the "social cleansing" murders in the city of Cali of *desechables* (literally, the disposable ones), or street people.

Fifth is the industry's random violence, exemplified by the bombs placed by Pablo Escobar in public areas in Bogotá, Medellín, and other cities. One great irony, however, is that these bombs often reduced the number of violent deaths in the country. The context of violence in Colombia is such that, when a bomb went off, no one would go out at night, and this would reduce the number of killings in places such as bars. Victims of the bombings died, but other lives were spared.

The most ominous consequence of all of the violence related to drugs has been its snowballing effect, reflected not only in levels of criminality but also in all other illegal and violent activity in the country. Drug trafficking has made it increasingly difficult to draw a line between criminal violence and political violence. It has greatly increased the violence being waged in Colombia by various guerrilla groups, some of which are at least partially involved in drug trafficking, and by paramilitary groups, some—if not a majority—of which are related to drug trafficking. However, there is evidence that some of these paramilitary groups are becoming independent and are getting into the business of abduction and extortion. Then there also is the violence of the army, the police, and common criminals.

415

The situation of violence is so complex that some Colombians believe that it is impossible to negotiate a comprehensive peace and that the best that can be hoped for is to negotiate to make the war more humane.

Colombia resembles a Central America that did not break up into separate countries. And this failure to break apart is perhaps that greatest obstacle to a negotiated peace in it. That is, if Colombia were a collection of such imaginary countries as Farquiña, Elenia, Petrolea, and Macondo, it would be feasible to begin peace negotiations on a local level, as was done in Central America. However, the situation in Colombia is so complex that trying to launch comprehensive peace negotiations seems an almost impossible task.

One fundamental problem for the Colombian state arises from the fact that wherever the army goes, it is the outsider, whereas the guerrillas and the mafias are local organizations. In Central America I do not believe that it has gotten to the point that the army is viewed as foreign.

It is unclear whether Colombia is going through a process of transition, or rather whether it is an evolutionary process that is leading to an explosion. The Colombian experience is worth studying because, contrary to appearances, it is not an aberration but a precursor and a warning. There are many places in the world approaching the situation in Colombia.

15

Postconflict Political Economy of Central America

RACHEL M. MCCLEARY

Two events define the past and future of Central America: the signing of a Guatemalan peace agreement in December 1996, which brought to a culmination the Esquipulas II Agreement, and the economic integration of Central America in preparation for a Free Trade Area of the Americas agreement by the year 2005. In a postconflict setting, economic recovery and reconstruction are critical priorities. They constitute key aspects of an overall regional strategy to accelerate and consolidate peace by addressing fundamental social and development issues that, in the medium to long term, will contribute directly to the productivity and well-being of the Central American people.

The peace accords in El Salvador (1992) and Guatemala (1996), to varying degrees, seek to redress fundamental social inequalities in those societies and to create opportunities for democratic participation. Yet the Central American presidents recognize that to consolidate peace effectively and attain adequate standards of human development, rapid and sustained economic growth will have to occur on a regionwide basis. Beginning with the Tegucigalpa Protocol (1991), integration in Central America has been based on mutual cooperation to achieve, through various means, "a region of peace, liberty, democracy, and development. . . ."[1] The first significant step taken was the signing of the Alliance for Sustainable Development (1994) in which the promotion of trade is central to the implementation of sustainable development policies, practices, and regulations.[2] Other steps taken were the revitalization of the Central American Common Market (CACM), the reform and modernization of the Central American Integration System (SICA), and the creation of the Central American Union.[3]

Liberalization of markets is key to the creation of rapid and sustained economic growth. With the success of the East Asian countries in shifting from import substitution to export liberalization, the export-led growth of Chile's economy under the guidance of the Chicago Boys (the economic liberalism of Milton Friedman at the University of Chicago), followed by that of Mexico, established the dominance of the liberal orthodoxy in international economic thinking.[4] But will the liberalization of markets bring with it a narrowing in social disparities? Recent studies are showing a correlation between the liberalization of markets and an increase in incomes among the lower levels of the population coupled with a drop in real incomes for the wealthiest. However, this only helps offset further erosion in income distribution, but it does not address the issue of further developing human and social capital so as to eliminate existing inequalities. Government policies and resources need to be directed specifically to critical aspects of social inequalities, such as universal primary education and preventive health care, which contribute to higher growth rates and the establishment of a virtuous cycle of economic growth.[5]

In this chapter I examine the new focus in Central America on export-led growth and the use of regional integration as the primary mechanism for promoting that strategy. I look at how the emphasis on the liberalization of trade requires implementing policies that specifically target reduction in poverty and income inequality. Finally, the strong empirical correlation between a country's level of development and the degree of education of its labor force means that, if economic objectives are to be attained, the state will have to increase quickly the efficiency of its social services delivery. Otherwise political instability and uncertainty during difficult transitions from the end of armed conflicts to the consolidating of democratic rule may well undermine the terms of peace.

Regional Integration and Trade Issues

The first experience the Central American countries had with economic integration was the establishment of the Central American Common Market in 1960. The CACM was created as a customs union whose primary purpose was to harmonize the tariff structures so as to promote trade diversion. The objectives were to reduce Central American dependence on tertiary markets for imported goods, improve trading terms within Central America, and promote industrialization in the region.

For various reasons, the CACM did not succeed; however, it is important to note that the benefits gained from trade diversion were concentrated in the relatively more industrialized countries to the detriment of Honduras and Nicaragua.[6] Part of the difficulty attributed to the failure of the integration scheme of Central America was the small size of the market and low levels of socioeconomic development. The region simply could not provide the level of demand required to sustain the process of industrialization and to attract new investment in the region.

In addition, political instability, armed insurrections, and migratory flows contributed to the restriction of supply of goods within the region.[7] Infrastructure was not developed, and, in Guatemala, Nicaragua, and particularly El Salvador, the armed insurgencies intentionally targeted infrastructure for destruction. Finally the sale of exports to markets outside Central America was negatively affected by the 1981 world recession; in response, the Central American governments adopted (in varying degrees) secondary import substituting industrialization policies and undertook the long-delayed stabilization and adjustment programs. By 1985 the CACM was experiencing a severe decline in overall trade. With the armed conflicts continuing to hamper economic growth in the region, both in terms of supply and demand, regional integration efforts were abandoned for the moment.

The revitalization of the Central American Common Market has taken place within a post–Cold War global environment, the liberalizing of markets, and within Central America an environment of peace and the fostering of democratic governments. From 1986 to 1992 the average annual increase in intraregional trade as a percentage of total exports has been faster (19 percent) than that for extraregional trade (3.5 percent). That percentage rose to 24 percent in 1994 and dropped to 20 percent in 1995.[8] In spite of this drop, the CACM is very close in percentage of regional trade of total exports to Mercosur (21 percent) with the Andean Pact lagging behind at 11 percent.

Central America's intraregional trade is more diversified and distributed among several sectors than its trade to other markets. It consists of 25 percent in agricultural products, 20 percent in chemicals and pharmaceuticals, and 10 percent in textiles. By contrast, trade to tertiary markets is concentrated in agricultural and food products (79 percent of total exports to tertiary markets). However, the issue for the Central American countries is how to achieve rapid and sustained economic growth. The market there consists of 32 million consumers, with a significant percentage (estimated at 60) living in rural areas and in poverty. To attain rapid and sustained growth, the Central American countries will have to reduce poverty levels while simultaneously creating new opportunities for employment through exports for external markets. But, in order to be more competitive in the global market, social indicators must be raised and sectors that currently do not generate optimal economic growth will have to be reconstructed so as to do so.

Initially, as intraregional and international trade expanded (1990–1994), Costa Rica, El Salvador, and Guatemala saw an increase in their levels of economic growth. By contrast, the growth rate in Nicaragua and Honduras remained low. Honduras is in the weakest position in terms of industrialization but exports agricultural and raw materials. The bulk of the value of intraregional trade is concentrated in Costa Rica, El Salvador, and Guatemala. These trends are not surprising given that Nicaragua and Honduras, the two countries in the region with the least industry and the weakest capacity to compete, export the least to other Central American countries. The large differences in economic development among the five countries, with Honduras and Nicaragua consistently at the lower end, raise serious questions about the viability of regional economic integration. (See Table 15.1.)

Further perpetuating the low levels of development in Nicaragua and Honduras are high external and intraregional debts, which leave these countries seriously overexposed in terms of debt-servicing obligations vis-à-vis their payment capacity. During the Sandinista government,

Table 15.1

Percentage of Each Country's Total Exports/Imports That Went to Partners in the Central American Common Market, 1994

Intraregional Exports (%)		Intraregional Imports (%)	
El Salvador	43	Nicaragua	35
Guatemala	31	El Salvador	18
Costa Rica	19	Honduras	14
Nicaragua	16	Guatemala	10
Honduras	8	Costa Rica	9

Source: Inter-American Development Bank, *Centroamérica: Documento de Programación Regional*, Rp-Ca (Washington, D.C.: IDB, September 1995) Annex 4, Page 3, Cuadro: Centroamérica Exportaciones Intrarregionales.

Nicaragua's debt reached nearly $11 billion. With one of the highest per-capita debts in the world, interest payments currently account for 20 percent of exports.[9] Honduras, with an external debt of $4.3 billion and interest payments consuming 35 percent of its current exports, like Nicaragua, cannot develop without a major reduction in its external debt.

Given that a large percentage of Nicaragua's and Honduras's exports to tertiary markets are in agricultural products, the liberalization of the agricultural and livestock sector in these countries could provide them with a competitive advantage they currently lack. However, to do so would mean placing at risk the most vulnerable groups in their societies or, for that matter, in Central America—the small producer who has managed to survive on low productivity due to government protectionist measures and pricing policies.[10]

The high levels of external and intraregional debt carried by Nicaragua and Honduras also translate into low investment in infrastructure; infrastructure improvements have been shown to be essential to the growth of intraregional and foreign trade. An estimated 95 percent of intraregional trade takes place by land transportation. Improving land infrastructure throughout Central America would increase trade by reducing costs and improving delivery time. Furthermore, demand for adequate land infrastructure will only increase as the countries continue to liberalize their economies.

Recognizing the critical linkage among roads, exports, and increasing incomes at the lower levels of the population, particularly in the rural areas where the incidence of extreme poverty is highest, the Guatemalan government, through its *carreteras de la oportunidad* (roads of opportunity) program is constructing tributary roads in the interior of the country so as to provide small to medium-size agricultural producers access to markets. The development of land infrastructure is linked directly to increasing productivity, particularly with regard to nontraditional exports in rural areas affected by the armed conflict.

The CACM is being revitalized so as to strengthen further intraregional free trade and to continue to develop consistent regional economic policies.[11] These objectives, coupled with the modernization of regional institutions, are seen as stepping-stones to converging with hemispheric agreements such as the Free Trade Agreement of the Americas and implementing World Trade Organization regulations. This collective process of "readiness" is, for better or worse, a gradual one. Yet, given the disparity in economic and social development among the countries of Central America, it is unclear that revitalizing the CACM and using it as a springboard into hemispheric trade agreements will bring about the requisite domestic reforms, concentration of resources on education and health, development of infrastructure, and changes in trade policy so as to be able to compete internationally. The CACM certainly has not served as such a springboard in the past. And the pace at which the CACM reforms are taking place may preclude its usefulness as a mechanism for entry into the North American market.

To complicate the scenario, the distinct national security issues of the Central American countries as well as their individual political development often have worked against regional cohesiveness that must be higher in a customs union than in a free trade area. In a free trade agreement, members eliminate all tariffs and quotas on goods from member states. With respect to tertiary markets, each member of a free trade agreement maintains its own arrangements and restrictions. The attraction of a free trade agreement is that each member country benefits from the opening of trade with the other. This arrangement has optimal benefits if each country's primary trading partner is one or more members in the trade arrangement (which is not the case with the Central American countries). Ideally, in a common market arrangement, such as the CACM, tariffs with tertiary markets are set uniformly for all members as well as among members.

However, the tendency of the Central American countries to pursue national interests frequently hampers regional cooperation and contravenes agreements made on regional integration. The Central American Common External Tariff set in 1993 with the signing of the Protocol of Guatemala has been difficult to achieve for several reasons. First, each country, from a fiscal point of view, is heavily dependent on customs income. Second, macroeconomic crises, such as the one that occurred in Costa Rica in March 1996, pressure a government into unilaterally raising tariffs.[12] Third, a country's perceived need to protect its local industry takes precedence over regional interests. Fourth, macroeconomic fragility combined with being a small economy translates into limited access to tertiary markets. This, in turn, drives each government to enter into bilateral agreements that contravene the terms of regional agreements. For example, the terms of Costa Rica's 1994 free trade agreement with Mexico (which went into effect on January 1, 1995) violates the Central American Common External Tariff agreement (1993), and each Central American country has a bilateral trade agreement with Panama. Currently El Salvador, Guatemala, and Honduras (known as the "northern triangle") are negotiating a free trade agreement with Mexico as is Nicaragua on its own.

Thus the trend is contradictory; as they seek markets outside of Central America, the countries pursue their own interests and establish tariffs vis-à-vis these tertiary markets.

The agreement on the regional implementation of tariff reductions (Nicaragua is the exception) by the year 2001 already has translated into cheaper imported goods to the detriment of local industry.[13] Furthermore, the countries have not uniformly adopted the implementation of the tariff reductions. El Salvador unilaterally lowered its rate on capital goods to 1 percent in 1996; this caused the manufacturing industries of neighboring countries to object. Because industry in the region survives in a protected environment, its main market is domestic followed by those of other countries in the region.

Finally, U.S. foreign policy toward the region served to exacerbate differences among the Central American countries. With the Soviet Union's ties to Cuba, Cold War ideology drove the United States to intervene, drawing the Central American countries into the East-West superpower conflict. There remains a grave danger for the Central American countries that the United States will neglect the region as it pursues its own economic interests with larger and strategically important markets such as China. Central American exports to the United States account for 59.86 percent of that region's total foreign trade. Yet protectionist views and domestic politics in the United States exclude Central America from enjoying privileges of the North American Free Trade Agreement (NAFTA), which gives preferential trading terms to Mexico and Canada. Providing favorable Central American access to the U.S. market on a par with Mexico would be beneficial in that it would alter the way in which the two parties historically have related to one another.

After the Wars: El Salvador, Nicaragua, and Guatemala

Regional integration is the dominating paradigm for the Central American governments to overcome consequences of decades of war and to promote democracy in the region. The presidents of Central America reaffirmed their commitment to regional political stability, democratic regimes, and sustainable development through the creation of the Central America Union.[14] These objectives are to be achieved by: (1) creating dynamic and healthy economies via economic integration and free trade, (2) strengthening democracy and good governance, and (3) promoting environmental protection as part of sustainable development. The establishment of a

Central America Union crystallizes in an important way what the region's presidents agreed to in the Central American Democratic Security Treaty (San José, Costa Rica, December 15, 1995) and the Declaration of San José signed with President Bill Clinton (May 8, 1997).

The notion of a Central America Union will take time to become a reality, given the social and economic disparities not only among countries but within them as well. Furthermore, the ending of the wars has underscored endemic and often structural social problems confronting the countries. The years of armed conflicts in the region exacerbated the already unequal distribution of resources through large migration flows and a surge in urban populations, low to negative investment in social services and large military budgets, weak public institutions and ideologically polarized societies, lack of investment in infrastructure and its maintenance, and the devastation of the environment (particularly in El Salvador).

During the 1980s, when wars were being fought in El Salvador, Guatemala, and Nicaragua, the percentage of the population living in poverty in Central America increased from 60 percent in 1980 to 68 percent in 1990, with the most extensive and entrenched poverty in rural areas, where the highest incidences of poverty, illiteracy, and infant mortality rates are found. Yet, compared with South America, where an estimated 80 percent of its population lives in urban areas, Central American countries are less urbanized (40 percent) and more agrarian.

Guatemala has the additional issue of a predominantly indigenous rural population characterized by twenty-two linguistically distinct groups; among these people are found the highest rates of poverty and illiteracy rates in Latin America. In its peace accords, the government of Guatemala committed itself to targeting the indigenous populations in terms of providing access to social services including bilingual education, the promotion of a multicultural society, and the protection of indigenous communal and sacred lands. Literary programs begun in 1993 currently are offered in fourteen indigenous languages and reach an estimated 30,673 people. The government's goal is to attain 70 percent literacy rate among the indigenous populations by the year 2000.[15]

Central America has 32 million inhabitants, making its population similar to that of California. Its population is relatively young with high fertility rates (2.8 percent as compared to Latin America's 1.8 percent).[16] Due to decades of armed conflict and migration within the region as well as to the United States, female participation in the labor force increased as high as 51 percent in El Salvador in 1990. During the 1980s poverty in urban areas grew more rapidly, by 73 percent, as compared to rural poverty, which increased by 43 percent. This increase was due in large part to populations uprooted by decades of armed conflicts in Nicaragua, El Salvador, and Guatemala. By the beginning of the 1990s, approximately one-third of all Central Americans could be considered the "new urban poor." Yet even with populations migrating to urban areas, the majority of the poor and extremely poor populations of the three countries that experienced wars live in rural areas.

Poverty and education attainment is highly correlated. A recent World Bank study based on ten countries found that education level is the single most important determinant of poverty and economic inequality.[17] In El Salvador 31 percent of the population is illiterate. In Guatemala 70 percent of the rural population is illiterate; among indigenous populations, the rate reaches 71.9 percent. In Nicaragua the illiteracy rate is 50 percent. However, overall, Nicaragua's adult illiteracy rate is low (13.9 percent) in comparison with El Salvador's (27 percent) and Guatemala's (44.9 percent); Guatemala has the second highest adult illiteracy rate in Latin America.[18] Although there exists near-universal access to primary education in Nicaragua with a net primary enrollment rate of 90 percent, as compared with 68 percent in Guatemala and 81 percent in El Salvador, in all three countries rural illiteracy rates remain high due to a variety of factors.

First, government investment in education dropped significantly during the years of armed conflict; this directly translated into low-quality education (e.g., teacher training, curriculum development, infrastructure) and the failure to promote the value of education among the general population as a way out of poverty. (Nicaragua seems to be the exception, as dropout rates among poor children ages eight to twelve are relatively low.)[19]

Second, the wars disrupted the social and economic patterns of rural areas. This translated into high-dropout as well as repetition rates. Third, the administration of education is highly centralized, inefficient, and costly given the rate of return for the investment per child. In Guatemala the fact that state-financed bilingual education is virtually nonexistent contributes to high illiteracy rates among indigenous populations, particularly women. Fourth, distance and lack of funds among the poor act as disincentives that also contribute to high dropout and repetition rates. And as children reach adolescence, they are more likely to drop out to work.

The rural poor primarily derive their income from agriculture, either as self-employed farmers or as wage laborers. As trade liberalization begins taking place in the agricultural sector, programs to address the consequent displacement of workers will be needed to deal with adjustment and adaptation difficulties. Migration flows in the region during the 1980s were primarily in response to the armed conflicts in El Salvador, Guatemala, and Nicaragua. Costa Rica and Mexico absorbed a significant number of refugees. Migration to urban areas also occurred as a result of the armed conflicts, and it continues as people seek employment. Most of the population of Nicaragua and El Salvador already reside in urban areas. Guatemala is experiencing an annual migration rate of 5 percent to its capital city (in contrast with its annual population growth rate of 2.9 percent). Immediate health concerns for Guatemala City and Managua are proper waste collection and disposal, the protection of sources of potable water, and increasing overall access to the sanitation system.

As the governments of the region anticipate trends such as the urbanization of their populations, current policies seeking to alleviate poverty and reduce income inequality will continue to target rural populations. In order to integrate the rural areas into the overall focus on export-led growth, governments are developing infrastructure so that small to medium-size producers have access to markets. Attempts are being made to lower the costs of transportation and of information technology, as well as to streamline and eliminate complicated, discretionary and costly export procedures and requirements.

Economic growth that favors labor-intensive sectors tends to reduce poverty faster than growth that concentrates on imports and diminishes the importance of the domestic labor force. Growth that increases employment tends likewise to improve wages, with the poorest segments of society receiving the benefits.[20] As trade liberalization takes place and generates new employment, the Central American countries will have to develop exports in advanced goods and services. In order to do so they will have to raise the level of education of their populations.

But as studies indicate, faster growth by itself is not sufficient if the poor are to benefit and not fall behind. Governments, through the social investment funds of international financial institutions, now are creating supplemental social services programs to aid the poorest of the poor.[21] However, for two reasons—first, insufficient funds and resources and, second, poor public sector administration and organization—such funds are only a small and immediate solution to addressing social inequalities.

An assumption of liberal orthodoxy is that the market itself will bring a reallocation of resources across society.[22] This reallocation includes addressing social inequalities. El Salvador, Guatemala, and Nicaragua recently made the transition from authoritarianism to procedural democracy during their wars. By imposing liberal orthodoxy on these countries before democratic culture has developed sufficiently, conceptions of what are public goods will not be integral to democracy. Rather, public goods will be viewed as artifacts of the market. From the perspective of liberal orthodoxy, addressing social inequalities is relevant only insofar as doing so supports the productivity and competitiveness of the private sector.

Thus the governments of El Salvador, Guatemala, and Nicaragua intentionally will have to identify a process of addressing public goods in society. However, this does not imply that the state is the agent to continue to deliver social services. The tenets of liberal orthodoxy call for the "renovation" of the public sector, defining a minimal state that regulates rather than directly intervenes in economic activities. Complementing a minimal state is a robust and active private sector that functions as the "engine" of a relatively unfettered market. Organizations in civil society will serve to mediate state–private sector relations. How much input these organizations have in the policy formulation process will determine, to a large extent, what are public goods and how they are best addressed.

The implementation of liberal orthodox tenets requires countries to adopt a two-pronged approach. The first prong is targeting the extreme rural poor and rapidly integrating them into the national system. Rural productivity is at crisis proportions in Nicaragua, El Salvador, and Guatemala as former combatants, refugees, and displaced populations are resettling in former war-afflicted areas and resuming farming.[23] Land disputes in all three countries are politically sensitive and bureaucratically complicated for the governments. In El Salvador, which has the second highest population density in the hemisphere (263.5 people per 100,000 square hectares), an annual population growth rate of 2.3 percent, and severe environmental degradation, land reform may ameliorate political differences and fulfill terms of the peace accords, but agrarian-based labor will not address the medium to long-term economic needs of the country.

By contrast, Nicaragua, with the lowest population density in the region and an annual population growth rate of 3.3 percent combined with rich soils, could become the "breadbasket" of Central America. Agriculture is essential, over the medium term, to Nicaragua's rapid and sustained economic growth, accounting for over 34.9 percent of the Gross Domestic Product in 1996.[24] The production of basic grains for domestic consumption has been rising and is expected to continue to rise.[25] (By contrast, El Salvador's production of basic grains is decreasing and domestic demand is being met by imports from the United States.) However, this increase in production is due primarily to an increase in the number of producers who were former combatants.

The overarching dilemma for Central American small farmers as producers of basic grains is that they cannot compete with subsidized grain imports from the United States. Either protectionist policies will have to be implemented on a regional basis to ensure a market for Nicaraguan grains or market niches overseas for nontraditional exports will have to be developed, such as has taken place in Guatemala with vegetables, nuts, and spices.[26]

High levels of unemployment/underemployment contribute to crime in the form of car theft rings, drug trafficking, contraband, and kidnappings. Physical security is currently a major issue for Central American countries as they attempt to reconstruct their societies and encourage investment in the region. Without significant economic growth, organized crime, corruption, and violence will continue to undermine the strengthening of democratic institutions in these societies in transition.

In El Salvador, Guatemala, and Nicaragua, former combatants, unskilled and lacking employment, are turning to crime. In Nicaragua former combatants organize armed bands and recruit others to participate in their criminal activities. The more troubling problem in that country has been the remobilizing of combatants. Between 1992 and 1993 an estimated 23,000 former contrast and Sandinistas rearmed. From 1991 to 1992 forty-two separate accords were signed between the government and what became known as *recontras* to end the violence and reincorporate them into civilian life. (See Chapter 2.)

In Guatemala the military and former combatants of the Unidad Revolucionaria Nacional Guatemalteca (URNG) are involved in bank robbery gangs using arms originating from El Salvador and Nicaragua.[27] Military personnel have been implicated in car theft rings, contraband, and kidnappings. In September 1996 the discovery of a large criminal network involving high-level military officers, police, and customs personnel demonstrated how endemic corruption is in the security forces. The Arzú administration suspended two brigadier generals as well as other military personnel implicated in the criminal network. The dismantling of the military security system in the countryside called for in the peace accords compounded the security problem by leaving a vacuum without implementing a short-term alternative system until the National Civilian Police force was trained and could take over.

With the highest homicide rate in the Western Hemisphere, El Salvador is faced with a network of gangs interconnecting its urban areas with cities on the western coast of the United States. The availability of armaments contributes to the ease of organized criminal activity. An estimated 200,000 firearms are in circulation, and the type of weaponry available overpowers that available to the National Police.

Thus the second prong during the transition after ending the wars is to strengthen democratic institutions and to define clearly the rules of the democratic game. Governments need to establish open and transparent mechanisms of conflict resolution. Judicial systems need to be strengthened so as to guarantee the rights and liberties of citizens as well as foreigners. Legal stability and constitutional guarantees are essential for the fostering of civil society and the promoting of private initiative in a country.

Reforms currently under way in El Salvador, Guatemala, and Nicaragua to privatize state enterprises will be compatible with democracy only if that process is not perceived to further enrich those who already are well off. To better ensure growth with equity, governments need to move away from their customary tendency to engage in income transfers (e.g., subsidies) and create asset transfers (skills and ownership of property).[28] Government emphasis on wealth-sharing mechanisms, such as universal primary education, preventive health care, affordable public transportation, and access to infrastructure, as state reforms are taking place, will distribute benefits across society and not be seen as going to certain sectors alone.[29]

To begin to strengthen democracy in the region, the Central American countries are cooperating on a regional level to establish a juridical framework that will uniformly protect the rights and physical security of their citizens. Through regional agreements, the countries are cooperating to establish an Institute of Police Advanced Studies as well as a regional military force. In cooperation with the United States, these countries are addressing the trade in illegal arms, narcotrafficking, and corruption, environmental issues through the Alliance for Sustainable Development, stolen vehicles, and transnational migratory flows. The governments are keenly aware of the need to address these foreign policy concerns of the United States as they seek access to northern markets.

NAFTA, Central America, and Western Hemispheric Free Trade

In March 1997 the trade ministers of the Central American countries proposed negotiating a free trade agreement with the United States, their largest tertiary market.[30] After three years of unsuccessfully attempting to gain accession to the North American Free Trade Agreement, the Central American countries, like Chile, decided it was time to reevaluate their strategy and opted to pursue a bilateral free trade agreement with the United States. Achieving a bilateral free trade agreement will depend, in part, on the "readiness" of the Central American countries to participate in a reciprocal trade relationship with the United States.

This readiness includes macroeconomic stability and the consolidating of democratic forms of governance in the region. It also depends on the political will of the United States to open up its market to a cheaper workforce geographically near and in competition with Mexico.

The United States is the largest and fastest-growing tertiary market for Central America absorbing 50 percent of the region's total exports in 1995. This is primarily the result of burgeoning nontraditional exports representing 45 percent of total exports from the region to the United States. From 1994 to 1995, Nicaraguan exports to the United States rose nearly 50 percent; Honduras, 31.4 percent; El Salvador, 30 percent; Guatemala, 19 percent; and Costa Rica, 12.1 percent.[31] In 1990 approximately 80 percent of the nonpetroleum exports from Central America to the United States were tariff free; the remainder of products entered the U.S. market with low tariffs (4.2 percent).[32]

Since the inception of NAFTA, the Central American countries have been experiencing a decrease in exports in textiles, sugar, and manufactured apparel, areas in which Mexico has preferential status. Central America also experienced market erosion with regard to agricultural products when the United States signed an agreement with the Andean Pact in November 1989. Until the implementation of NAFTA, the Central American countries experienced strong export growths with the United States. After NAFTA overall exports decreased.[33]

Currently U.S. relations with the region tend to be on a case-by-case basis and defined by unilateral concessions on the part of the United States to the countries of Central America. The lack of a free trade agreement means that Central America's relations with the United States are derived from U.S. goodwill offered through the Caribbean Basin Initiative (CBI) and the Generalized System of Preferences (GSP). The unilateral granting and defining of concessionary terms under CBI, but particularly the GSP, create a degree of uncertainty for the Central American countries in terms of access to the U.S. market. And the temporary nature of the GSP often has been a disincentive to foreign investment in the region.

A free trade agreement would allow Central American exports currently excluded by the CBI and the GSP to be competitive with those products for which Mexico and the Andean Pact have preferential access. Access to the U.S. market for products currently excluded by CBI would contribute to job creation in the Central American region, an essential element to rapid and sustained economic growth.

As trade liberalization has been occurring, the Central American countries with the highest economic growth rates (Costa Rica, El Salvador, and Guatemala) have seen a dramatic increase in imports from outside the region.[34] This increase has been primarily the result of lower import tariffs coupled with favorable economic growth and not an increase in exports from Central America. Central American exports to destinations outside the region have not increased rapidly during trade liberalization.

Access to the U.S. market through the creation of a free trade agreement would correct this trend, stimulating commerce through the establishment of new trade currents between the United States and Central America that in turn would displace costly national production of goods. Furthermore, freer access to the U.S. market would directly affect trade flows among the Central American Common Market. A free trade agreement with the United States would continue to deviate trade from the members of the Central American Common Market to the United States by substituting expensive imports from member nations for cheap imports from tertiary markets (United States) and vice versa. Overall, the net effect of a free trade agreement between the United States and Central America would be to convert the Central American Common Market into a free trade area through increased trade with the United States.

To date, the United States has demonstrated little political will to enter into free trade agreements with Central America or Chile. The argument against doing so is the loss of jobs and the compromising of job creation in the United States, despite evidence that shows that the United States has seen a record job-creating environment since NAFTA went into effect.[35] The other argument against liberalizing markets is that, without government intervention, economic disparities are not redressed. Yet evidence shows that trade liberalization is progressive, increasing the real incomes of the poorest 20 percent of the population.[36]

By entering into a free trade agreement with the United States, the Central American countries gain greater access to northern markets, clarity with respect to concessions, and established rules regarding the nature of trade and investment. In exchange for these benefits, the Central American countries will provide the United States with greater access to their labor force, legal stability, and constitutional guarantees for investment and intellectual property. And, given that Central America has 1 percent of the earth's landmass with 12 percent of earth's biodiversity, U.S. companies will have greater access to the region's natural resources.

Conclusion

As was demonstrated during the height of the Central American Common Market, Central America, by itself, cannot provide the level of demand required to attain adequate levels of rapid and sustained economic growth. The countries of Central America need to capture international market niches to allow small to medium-size producers to compete, diversify exports, and penetrate a variety of export markets, not just the United States.

Since 1990 the countries of Central America have, generally speaking, seen their economies progress substantially. They have experienced real growth, trade liberalization, and success in attracting new productive activities to the region such as ecotourism and export processing. Since 1992 the region has been experiencing a sluggish upward trend in foreign direct investment with the lion's share (approximately 50 percent) going to Costa Rica. During the same period Central American exports grew by 11 percent per annum, with nontraditional exports increasing 15 percent between 1990 and 1992. All of these are positive indicators for future growth potential and job creation in the region.

However, economic regional integration faces several obstacles, chief among them being the disparity in development among the five Central American countries in terms of debt, infrastructure, human capital, and national interest. Given these wide disparities in political, social, and economic development, the countries will continue to prefer to "go it alone" to attract investment and to meet their national interests. Any attempt at creating a level playing field through the reform and modernization of the common market is simply illusory.

The more beneficial, and realistic, way to understand regional integration in Central America is as a political arrangement, one established to ensure that armed conflict does not occur again in the region. If we correctly view the Central America Union as primarily an arrangement to fulfill political objectives, then, with time and like the European customs union, which they sought to emulate with the creation of the CACM, the countries will be prepared to accept losses derived from entering into a preferential trade arrangement so as to achieve wider political objectives: peace and prosperity.

Notes

1. *Tegucigalpa Protocol to the charter of the Organization of Central American States (ODECA)*, U.N. Doc. A/46/829-S/23310, Annex III (1991).

2. See *CONCAUSA Declaration and Action Plan*, U.S. Department of State dispatch supplement 6, No. 2 (Washington, D.C.: G.P.O., Supt. of Docs. 1995).

3. See the *Declaración de Nicaragua*, September 2, 1997, http://www.sicanet.org.sv/documentos/index.html.

4. For a discussion of this model and its limitations, see Frederick Jaspersen, "Growth of the Latin American and East Asian Economies," in Nancy Birdsall and Frederick Jaspersen, eds., *Pathways to Growth: Comparing East Asia and Latin America* (Washington, D.C.: Inter-American Development Bank, 1997), chap. 3.

5. A cogent argument for this position is put forward in the introduction by Luis Carlos Bresser Pereira, José María Maravall, and Adam Przeworski, eds., *Economic Reforms in New Democracies: A Social-Democratic Approach* (Cambridge: Cambridge University Press, 1993), 1–15.

6. See Victor Bulmer-Thomas, "The Central American Common Market: From Closed to Open Regionalism," *World Development*, 26, No. 2 (February 1998):313–22.

7. Ibid.

8. United Nations Economic Commission for Latin America and the Caribbean, *CEPAL News* 17, No. 5 (May 1997):3.

9. United States Agency for International Development, *Nicaragua 2000: Challenges for Developing a Stable, Democratic, Prospering Society* (Managua: United States Agency for International Development, 1995).

10. According to the prevailing view at the Inter-American Development Bank, the liberalization of the agricultural sector will take some time, due not only to the reluctance to eliminate tariffs and nontariff barriers but because of bureaucratic inefficiency, which causes delays and complications at border posts.

11. The ministers of commerce of the Central American nations have reiterated their commitment to negotiating as a regional trading bloc particularly as they seek to enter the North American Free Trade Agreement. Interview with Juan Mauricio Wurmser, Guatemalan minister of economy, in "Guatemala Continúa en el Triángulo Norte," *Prensa Libre*, economic section, March 21, 1998.

12. Costa Rica invoked the safeguard clause in the Central American Tariff Agreement to temporarily raise its tariff by 8 percentage points for all products imported from outside the CACM until the legislature could approve a tax package aimed at ameliorating the fiscal situation. The safeguard remained in effect until December 31, 1996.

13. United Nations Economic Commission, *CEPAL News*, gives the 1996 figures on exports in dollars as compared to imports for the five historic countries of Central America.

14. *Declaración de Nicaragua.*

15. Government of Guatemala, "Peace Program: The Opportunity for Guatemala," inventory of projects (Report prepared for the Consultative Group Meeting, Brussels, Belgium, Jan. 21–22, 1997).

16. Nicaragua's fertility rate is 4.9 children per woman of childbearing age. (Its annual population growth rate is 3.8 percent.) El Salvador's fertility rate is 3.9 children per woman of childbearing age in the urban areas and 4.8 in rural areas. (Its annual population growth rate is 2.2 percent.) Guatemala's fertility rate is 5.2 with an annual population growth of 2.9 percent, reaching 13 percent in the northern region of the country. For the fertility rates, see United Nation's Children Fund (UNICEF), *The State of the World's Children 1996* Table 5: Demographic Indicators, (Oxford: Oxford University Press, 1997), 88. For annual population growth rates, see *The World Bank, Trends in Developing Economies 1995* (Washington, D.C.: The World Bank, 1995), "El Salvador," 166–69, "Guatemala," 211–14, "Nicaragua," 378–81.

17. Juan Luis Londoño, *Poverty, Inequality and Human Capital Development in Latin America, 1950–2025* (Washington, D.C.: World Bank, 1996).

18. The national average for number of school years completed are: Nicaragua, 4.5 percent in 1995, with extremely poor urban dwellers averaging 3 years and extremely poor rural dwellers averaging 1.6 year; El Salvador, 4.5 percent in 1994, with urban dwellers completing 7 years and rural dwellers completing 2.8 years; Guatemala's extremely poor average 1.6 years of schooling while nonpoor average 5.8 years. These statistics were drawn from the World Bank, *Staff Appraisal Report: Nicaragua Basic Education Project* (Feb. 22, 1995); *El Salvador: Recent Developments, Major Reforms and Prospects* (Prepared by the Inter-American Development Bank for the Consultative Group Meeting, Paris, France, June 22, 1995); World Bank, *Guatemala: An Assessment of Poverty* (June 28, 1994).

19. World Bank, *Republic of Nicaragua: Poverty Assessment* (Washington, D.C.: World Bank, June 1, 1995), vol. 7.

20. For a broader discussion of these issues, see Sebastian Edwards, *Crisis and Reform in Latin America: From Despair to Hope* (Oxford: Oxford University Press and the World Bank, 1995), chap. 8.

21. For a description of the social investment funds, see Center for Democratic Education, *A Guide to the Inter-American Development Bank and World Bank: Strategies for Guatemala* (Silver Spring, MD: Center for Democratic Action, 1997).

22. See, for example, David Lipton and Jeffrey Sachs, "Creating a Market Economy in Eastern Europe: The Case of Poland," *Brookings Papers on Economic Activity* (1990): 75–145.

23. Nicaragua's 72,000 member Ejército Popular Sandinista was downsized in 1990 and an estimated 23,000 contras were demobilized; El Salvador's 7,500 combatants of the Frente Farabundo Martí para la Liberación Nacional (FMLN) were demobilized in 1992–1993; and the estimated 3,000 Guatemalan Unidad Revolucionaria Nacional Guatemalteca (URNG) combatants were demobilized by November 1997.

24. Statistics provided by the Central American Department, The World Bank.

25. United States Agency for International Development, *USAID/Nicaragua: Results Review and Resource Request (R4)* (Managua: USAID, March 29, 1996), 17–18.

26. Guatemala has had considerable success developing markets for its nontraditional exports, which accounted for 41 percent of its total exports in 1996 and $1.2 billion worth compared to traditional exports, which lag slightly behind in U.S. dollars.

27. Carlos Ajanel Soberanis, "Lo que no se ha dicho de los robos de bancos," *Siglo Veintiuno*, National News section, December 4, 1997.

28. For a discussion of these concepts, see José Edgardo Campos and Hilton L. Root, *The Key to the Asian Miracle: Making Shared Growth Credible* (Washington, D.C.: The Brookings Institution, 1996), 44–49.

29. One of the wealth-sharing mechanisms implemented by the East Asian Tigers and one that will not occur in a major way in Guatemala is land reform. As a consequence, other wealth-sharing mechanisms unique to the Central American context will need to be established to ensure greater income distribution.

30. Meeting of Central American Trade Ministers in their joint declaration to United States' government representatives, March 12–13, 1997, Guatemala City, Guatemala.

31. Figures compiled from official statistics of The United States Department of Commerce. U.S. Trade Data Flow: General Imports. Type: Customs Value, Partner: Nicaragua, Honduras, Guatemala, Costa Rica, and El Salvador. U.S. Department of Commerce, U.S. Bureau of the Census Computer Data base, 1997.

32. Naciones Unidas, Comisión Económica para América Latina y el Caribe, *Centroamérica y el TLC: Efectos Inmediatos e Implicaciones Futuras,* Cuadernos de CEPAL (Mexico: CEPAL, May 1996), 85–86.

33. Naciones Unidas, Comisión Económica para América Latina y el Caribe, *El Impacto del Tratado de Libre Comercio de América del Norte de las economías pequeñas de la región: Una evaluación empírica preliminar,* U.N. Doc LC/MEX/R.0506, (Mexico, D.F.: CEPAL, 1995).

34. Costa Rica: 42 percent in 1990, 52 percent in 1994; El Salvador: 32 percent in 1990, 43 percent in 1994; Guatemala: 22 percent in 1990, 31 percent in 1994. Percentage were calculated based on statistics from International Monetary Fund, *Direction of Trade Statistics 1996* (Washington, D.C.: International Monetary Fund, 1996).

35. U.S. House of Representatives, Committee on Ways and Means, Subcommittee on Trade, Testimony of Sidney Weintraub, "U.S. Trade Policy in the Western Hemisphere," March 18, 1997.

36. Juan Luis Londoño and Miguel Székely, "Distributional Surprises After a Decade of Reforms: Latin America in the Nineties," in Inter-American Development Bank, *Latin America After a Decade of Reforms: Economic and Social Progress: 1997.* (Washington, D.C.: Inter-American Development Bank, 1997), 17. The study of thirteen countries demonstrated this correlation. According to Sidney Weintraub, at the inception of implementing liberal economic reforms, there is a period of higher unemployment, but eventually it is lowered through sustained economic growth. See his article, "The Achilles' Heal of Liberalism," *Hemisfile* 8, No. 4 (July/August 1997): 1, 2 and 12.

Reflections

JAMES K. BOYCE

After the signing of the Chapultepec Accords in January 1992, serious tensions emerged in El Salvador between economic policy on one hand and the peace process on the other. Similar tensions have arisen in other countries in postconflict transitions and are likely to arise as the Guatemalan peace accords are implemented.

The tensions were graphically portrayed in the essay that Alvaro de Soto and his colleague, Graciana del Castillo, published in March 1994 in the journal *Foreign Policy,* where they depicted El Salvador as a patient on an operating table with a curtain drawn the length of his body, on either side of which two doctors were performing surgery, neither of them cognizant of what the other was doing. On one side was the United Nations, trying to ensure implementation of the peace accords, and on the other side were the Bretton Woods institutions—the World Bank and the International Monetary Fund (IMF)—pursuing their usual economic stabilization and structural adjustment policies. De Soto and del Castillo wrote that each doctor needed to take account of what the other was doing, arguing that neither operation would succeed if the other failed.[1] Given the identity of the authors, however, the essay was widely seen as a pointed critique of the Bretton Woods institutions.

Partly in response to these tensions, the United Nations Development Program in San Salvador asked me to design and to coordinate a study that would analyze economic issues in El Salvador in greater detail. The study became known as the Adjustment Toward Peace project; one outcome was a book, *Economic Policy for Building Peace: The Lessons of El Salvador.*[2]

During the transition from war to peace, two sets of critical economic issues arise. For the most part, neither has been addressed adequately by economists. In the short run, the critical issue is how to reconcile economic stabilization and political stabilization. In the long run, the central problem is how to achieve what is sometimes called "growth with equity," although a more appropriate formulation might be equity with growth: that is, how to ensure that the economic development process addresses the underlying economic sources of conflict.

The short-run problem is of most immediate relevance to the unfolding peace process in Guatemala. But we should not neglect the long run. Long-run issues are not those that can be deferred until later. The seeds of solutions to these problems have to be sown at the outset, not at some point in the future.

One long-term problem in both El Salvador and Guatemala, for example, is the viability of small-scale agriculture. It is not possible for small farmers in the region to compete successfully with U.S. maize producers in the market as currently structured. U.S. producers reap substantial subsidies, including government purchases of surplus grain for free or concessional distribution as food aid in Central America and elsewhere. At the same time, the campesinos of Central America and Mexico provide important environmental services, managing watersheds and conserving genetic diversity in maize, the ultimate foundation for stability and growth in maize production worldwide. The campesinos receive no compensation whatsoever for these valuable services: While U.S. maize farmers receive subsidies, Central American and Mexican maize farmers, in effect, provide them. The dramatic deterioration in the terms of trade for maize growers in the region is a problem that ought to be corrected, not a fact of life that should be accepted.

The conventional short-run focus of macroeconomists is on economic stabilization—on fiscal and monetary policies to correct imbalances, such as government budget deficits, current account deficits, and so on.

But in the postconflict setting, political stabilization is equally, and sometimes more, important. This poses two key questions for the international donor community. The first is how to finance peace-related needs, many of which are spelled out in the peace accords. The second is how to ensure that external assistance serves to maintain a balance among the internal actors who are crucial to the continuation of the peace process.

Governments have four main options for financing peace programs. One option is to draw on external assistance. A second option is to use deficit financing, that is, to print or borrow money to meet spending needs. A third option is to raise taxes to generate new government revenues internally. And a fourth option is to shift expenditures so as to restructure government spending.

When the peace accords in El Salvador were signed, it was estimated that $1.8 billion in external and domestic resources would be needed for their implementation. This included $1.1 billion for "high-priority" needs, such as the formation of the new National Civilian Police force (PNC), the land-transfer program for ex-combatants, the building of new democratic and judicial institutions, and the demobilization of ex-combatants. The remaining $700 million was for lower-priority needs, mainly infrastructure projects for energy, roads, bridges, and so on.

As of January 1994, two years after the signing of the accords, the government of El Salvador and the international donors each had committed about $300 million to high-priority peace programs, leaving a $500 million funding gap. At the same time, the government had committed a little less than $100 million and the donors over $400 million to the lower-priority needs, leaving a gap of less than $200 million.

A notable feature in the pattern of external finance is the discrepancy, particularly for donors other than the U.S. government, between the priorities set forward by the peace process and the funding priorities of the donors. While the governments of El Salvador and the United States allocated more than three-quarters of their peace-related funding to high-priority programs, other donors allocated more than three-quarters of their resources to lower-priority programs.

Several factors help to explain the reluctance of many donors to commit more to high-priority programs. These include constraints on the aggregate volume of aid; legislative impediments on certain types of aid, such as aid to the police; preferences for what is euphemistically called "trade-related" assistance, that is, aid tied to imports from the donor country; a traditional conception of infrastructure exclusively in terms of physical assets rather than institution building; and the belief that the government of El Salvador ought to have done more to finance these programs and that its failure to do so arose from a lack of political will rather than a lack of resources.

Given the shortfalls in external resources, a second option was to run a larger government deficit, relaxing the targets set in the government's IMF agreement. While fiscal discipline usually is to be applauded, there is a substantial intermediate terrain between rigid adherence to tight macroeconomic targets on the one hand and profligate deficit spending on the other. This middle ground is particularly important if the deficit is related to the building of peace.

In some cases governments may face unavoidable trade-offs between social tensions arising from budget deficits and social tensions arising from inadequate peace expenditures. Beyond some point, too large a budget deficit can have negative effects on the peace process by triggering hyper-inflation and economic disruption. Short of this point, however, easing up on budget targets so as to finance peace programs could ameliorate social tensions.

International financial institutions tend to assume that the relaxation of budget deficit targets would have grave effects on the economy, and hence on the peace process, whereas some U.N. agencies are more inclined to see scope for trade-offs between the two. Both sides can presumably agree, however, on the desirability of reducing social tensions as much as possible within any given level of the deficit. This shifts attention from the size of the overall deficit to the composition of government revenue and expenditure.

Raising revenue through taxation is an attractive way to finance peace accords in that it minimizes dependence on external donors. But raising tax revenues must be consistent with the long-term objective of promoting equity. That is, the increased taxes must be expected to come primarily from the wealthier strata of society, who can best bear the cost.

In El Salvador, the tax coefficient was very low: From a prewar peak of about 16 percent of gross domestic product, it had fallen to less than 8 percent in 1989. By 1995 it was raised to about 12 percent, but regrettably this has been achieved primarily by relying on regressive value-added taxes, rather than by more progressive taxes.

In the Adjustment Toward Peace study, we recommend raising the tax coefficient to 15 percent, primarily through improved income-tax collections from high-income individuals, sales taxes on purchases of luxury goods, tariffs on luxury imports, and taxes on high-value property transfers. But all of these are easier said than done and would take time to implement.

Expenditure shifting offers more immediate possibilities for mobilizing domestic resources to finance the accords. The most obvious candidate for budget cuts to free resources for peace programs is military expenditure.

As of 1992, according to IMF figures, El Salvador had the highest share of government expenditure devoted to the military in all of Latin America and the smallest share devoted to social security and welfare expenditures. Military expenditure has been reduced considerably since the end of the war, but to this day it remains far above the prewar level, which was less than 1 percent of gross domestic product (GDP). Nevertheless, the international financial institutions have resolutely avoided raising the issue of military spending with the Salvadoran government.

This is ironic. For at the very time the Salvadoran peace accords were being negotiated, top officials at both the IMF and the World Bank had begun to raise the issue of military expenditure or, in the standard diplomatic phrase, "unproductive expenditure." In October 1991 IMF Managing Director Michel Camdessus declared military expenditure to be "a proper subject for our attention." In December 1991 the outgoing World Bank president, Barber Conable, wrote, in an op-ed piece in the *Washington Post*, that the bank should press borrowers to reduce excessive military spending. While weak civilian governments might publicly protest this as an invasion of their sovereignty, Conable wrote, he knew from experience that "such pressure may be privately welcomed by the new democracies."[3]

Yet while political space for addressing this issue was opening up, that space was not exploited in El Salvador. This may reflect the heterogeneity of opinion within the international financial institutions as well as the slow pace of institutional change. An August 1996 World Bank study, titled *El Salvador: Meeting the Challenge of Globalization*, stresses the need for fiscal austerity and for increased investment in infrastructure and human capital.[4] Still ignored, however, is the potential to address these conflicting objectives by compressing military expenditure.

In Guatemala the scope for financing peace-related expenditures by budgetary reallocations is more limited since military spending has been a smaller proportion of GDP. Raising the country's tax coefficient—now the lowest in Latin America—is critical for financing both new democratic institutions and long-term human development. The Guatemalan peace accord mandates increases in the tax coefficient from 8 percent of GDP in 1996 to 12 percent by the year 2000; at the same time it requires the tax system to be "globally progressive." Indirect taxes (such as the value-added tax) are administratively the easiest way to raise revenues quickly; yet the goal of distributional equity would be better served by direct taxes on incomes and property. The tension between these two policy objectives can be eased by selectively raising taxes on luxury goods, such as automobiles and electronic appliances, so as to combine ease of collection with a progressive tax incidence.

With respect to the two-doctors metaphor, we conclude in the Adjustment Toward Peace study that the key problem arising from the disjuncture between the policies of the international financial institutions and the Salvadoran peace process was not so much that their macroeconomic conditionalities prevented the government from doing what it wanted to do but rather that they failed to deploy their leverage to encourage the government to take difficult but necessary steps to advance the peace process. In this specific sense, the conditionalities of the international financial institutions were not too tight but rather too loose. The vigorous exercise of "peace conditionality" by external assistance actors could do much to advance peace processes unfolding in Central America and elsewhere.

Notes

1. Álvaro de Soto and Graciana del Castillo, "Obstacles to Peacebuilding," *Foreign Policy* 94 (Spring 1994): 69–83.

2. James K. Boyce, ed., *Economic Policy for Building Peace: The Lessons of El Salvador* (Boulder, Colo.: Lynne Reinner, 1996).

3. Barber B. Conable, Jr., "Growth—Not Guns," *Washington Post*, December 24, 1991, A13.

4. Gloria M. Grandolini, et al., *El Salvador: Meeting the Challenge of Globalization* (Washington, D.C.: World Bank, 1996).

Reflections

GERHARD HENZE

The conflicts in Central America had a number of notable aspects for the European Union or, as it was called at the time, the European Community.[1] First were the different perceptions of the meaning of that conflict in Europe, on one hand, and the United States or, to be more precise, the Reagan administration, on the other. Second, for the first time a number of players cooperated in the attempts to find a solution to that conflict. And, third, the search for a solution to the conflict started in the region.

The first attempts to find a solution were made by the neighboring countries—Mexico, Panama, Colombia, and Venezuela—which were concerned about the possibility that the conflict could spread beyond the region. Their efforts, which were named after Contadora, a small island in Panama where the leaders met for the first time, failed because there was strong resistance from the United States and from El Salvador and Honduras. The Contadora proposals were unacceptable to Washington in particular because they were seen as a guarantee of the continued existence of the Sandinista regime in Nicaragua.

Three years later, in 1987, President Oscar Arias of Costa Rica proposed a peace plan, which later won him the Nobel Prize. That peace plan led to an initial agreement signed in Esquipulas, Guatemala—Esquipulas I—it was called by the presidents of the five Central American countries, including Daniel Ortega of Nicaragua. The agreement contained a cease-fire and a commitment to dialogue with the opposition, to democratization, to non-interference, and to the cessation of aid to the so-called irregular forces or the armed opposition from neighboring countries, which, of course, mainly referred to Nicaragua and El Salvador. The agreement also set up a commission to work out a peace plan.

In the preamble of the Esquipulas document, the European Community's contribution to the solution of the conflict was expansively mentioned, and

443

not by accident. Esquipulas I represented the first time that the European Community had played a major role in the search for a solution to the conflict in Central America.

The Community had been particularly concerned about the implications of this conflict because in Washington it was viewed in the context of the Cold War as part of the struggle between East and West and as an effort to destabilize the situation in the U.S. hinterland. That mind-set prompted the Reagan administration to devote a great deal of attention to Central America, especially when compared to that paid to Mexico at the outbreak of the first major debt crisis.

The Europeans were also afraid that the United States could become entangled militarily in the conflict. Such an occurrence could not only have weakened U.S. involvement in Europe; it also could have had negative implications for relations between the United States and the Soviet Union and, thus, on wider East-West relations, a particular source of concern for a country then at the border between East and West, namely, Germany.

The European Community viewed the roots of the conflict as the inability to reform an economic and social structure dominated by a very conservative oligarchy, in countries where blatant inequalities in wealth and income existed. This was particularly true for El Salvador and Guatemala, but also for Nicaragua during the Somoza years. Another source of the conflict, in the European view, was the lack of democracy and the disregard for human rights.

On the basis of these concerns, Germany's well-known foreign minister, Hans Dietrich Genscher, developed together with President Luis Monge of Costa Rica the idea of an interregional dialogue between the Central American countries and the European Community.

The first such meeting took place in 1984, at the level of foreign ministers, in San José, Costa Rica, a place that gave its name to the entire dialogue process. At the next meeting in Luxembourg the following year, the Europeans and Central Americans agreed to have regular annual meetings at the foreign minister level, and the European Community and countries of Central America concluded their first agreement on economic cooperation. This dialogue began even before the Esquipulas process.

Based on the 1995 agreement, Central America became a priority area for economic cooperation from the European Community. From 1984 to 1994, for example, the total amount of economic assistance from the European Community and its member countries to Central America rose to $4.1 billion, the bulk of which went to El Salvador ($608 million) and to Nicaragua ($1.8 billion). Germany always has been the biggest bilateral donor country, in addition to providing 30 percent of Community assistance.

The European Union is still the biggest donor community in Central America, although as an individual country Japan now holds first place. As a reflection of the importance of Central America to the European Union, the region continues to receive the highest per-capita assistance of anywhere in the world.

In addition, the Europeans pledged in Luxembourg to open their markets, a commitment that soon became a reality. From 1985 to 1994 community exports to Central America increased by 43 percent; more important, the imports from Central America into the European Community increased by 74 percent. Germany took more than 30 percent of these imports. In the late 1990s Europe still receives about 18 percent of the Central American exports.

In 1992 a special trade preference system was established similar to the one established for drug-producing countries in South America. That system was extended in 1994.

Throughout all these years, the political dialogue within the San José process gained in importance. At the outset, the major issue was the conflict. Today the dialogue is much broader and covers issues beyond Central American affairs. But democracy and human rights, which Europeans saw as the major causes for the conflict, have remained central issues in this dialogue.

The European Community also was very much involved in creating the necessary conditions for democracy and human rights in Central America, along with the Organization of American States and the United Nations; many players cooperated in this regard.

The European Community monitored the first elections after the end of the civil war in Nicaragua in 1990 and in El Salvador 1994. In addition, German political foundations participated in fostering the conditions for democracy, helping, for example, in reorganizing party structures and turning the Sandinistas into a real political party. In El Salvador, Germany's Konrad Adenauer Foundation and the Friedrich Ebert Foundation were instrumental in creating the necessary political conditions for the process of democratization. I still remember from my days as Minister Counsellor at the German embassy in Washington how suddenly the White House's and State Department's perception of the work of the political foundations began to change; often we were asked whether our foundations could do certain things to promote democracy and respect for human rights that would have proved difficult for governments, since it could be seen as interference in international affairs.

In 1992 the European Community Commission also started a multiyear program with an annual contribution of approximately $2 million to foster respect for human rights, which, among other things, supported the work of the Central American Human Rights Institute in Costa Rica. The European

Community also provided essential assistance to the demobilization in Nicaragua and in El Salvador, in particular by training demobilized soldiers and guerrillas and by providing the first seed money to create work and employment for them. Today such efforts would be called "postconflict peace building," an area that has become important in the peacekeeping operations of the United Nations. The lessons we learned in Central America under very difficult circumstances and not always with entirely satisfactory results have been very useful in our efforts to contribute to the development of a concept for the work of the United Nations. In addition, the Community supported the United Nations Observer Group in Central America (ONUCA), the 1989 United Nations peacekeeping operation that helped stabilize the situation in Central America. It was one of the first U.N. peacekeeping operations in which Germany participated.

In 1993 the European Community and countries of Central America concluded a second cooperation agreement, a so-called third-generation agreement, which includes the promotion of democracy and respect for human rights. Whereas in the early days of contact between the Community and Central America, the Central American countries had great difficulty even talking about democracy and human rights, nowadays they regard these areas as essential for political stability and for economic and social development.

Gradually, the efforts of the European Community led to a change in Washington's perceptions, from suspicion over community "interference," to recognition and even gratitude for our efforts to stabilize the situation in a neighboring region.

One lesson we have learned in Central America is that commitment has to be maintained for quite a long time in order to ensure that peace will last and finds a solid basis in economic and social development. The European Community has tried to do that, whereas the United States—under the pressure of events in other regions of the world—turned its attention elsewhere once the conflict was over and a political solution was found.

Note

1. With the entry into force of the Maastricht Treaty on European Union in November 1993, terminology regarding the European Community and some of its institutions changed. The European Union became the new umbrella term, but the European Community continued to exist as a legal entity within the broader framework of the Union. Because some of the policy decisions regarding Central America discussed by Ambassador Henze continued to be made by the Community rather than the Union, the term European Community is predominantly used throughout this commentary. See Office of Press and Public Affairs, European Commission Delegation, European Union News, "Post-Maastricht: EC Now Named European Union," Washington, D.C., December 13, 1993: 1. [ed.]

16

Conclusion: Lessons Learned in Comparative Perspective

CYNTHIA J. ARNSON

To attempt to summarize the rich and complex contributions in this volume is a humbling exercise. Nonetheless, some effort at recapitulation is in order, to contribute to the understanding of ending insurgent conflict through political negotiations.

Peace Processes and Democratization

The six case studies of individual Latin American countries demonstrate that there is a positive correlation between democratic transitions and the end of guerrilla war. Even if war initially serves as a pretext for the destruction of democratic space and the suppression of normal politics,[1] war itself can generate pressures to devise or expand mechanisms of participation and inclusion. "From above," these mechanisms may be designed to provide a political alternative to the guerrillas in the context of counterinsurgency. "From below," however, they represent the expression of civil society's disenchantment with the fighting and an insistence on an alternative to a military solution.

If, as several have argued in this book, prior democratization is essential to the opening of a peace process, the act of negotiation itself furthers democratic transitions by providing the opportunity to establish blueprints for structural and institutional reforms that cannot be carried out within existing political institutions and processes. (See Chapters 3, 4, and 5.) These institutional changes—in the public security apparatus, judicial system, and electoral regime, to name a few—are necessary if a democratic system defined procedurally by free elections is to *function* democratically, by allowing all across the political spectrum to participate, by holding public officials accountable, by subordinating the armed forces to civilian authority, and by providing a stable institutional framework for the expression and mediation of interests and conflict. These substantive or qualitative elements of democracy are by no means guaranteed by a peace process, but the record is clear that they are impossible to attain in a situation of war.

The correlation between peace and the transition to more democratic regimes manifests itself in several ways. In Guatemala and El Salvador, for example, political "space" expanded prior to the signing of a formal accord. But opportunities for participation continued to be circumscribed in a highly militarized environment, in which the notions of opposition and subversion often were conflated. The political system's representativity expanded after an accord was reached and armed opponents were incorporated into the political system. Guatemala stands out, moreover, for the degree to which the peace process established blueprints and mechanisms for the participation of the country's indigenous majority, although tension persists regarding the precise meaning of inclusion vs. autonomy. (See Chapter 11.) The peace process in both Guatemala and El Salvador yielded agreement on needed institutional reform, even if the process of implementation remains highly problematic in both countries.

In Colombia negotiations with and demobilizations of five guerrilla groups or factions since the 1980s coincided with—and in certain respects contributed to—major constitutional reform. Yet the proliferation of armed actors, narcotrafficking, dirty war, and guerrilla attacks on elected officials and the electoral process have undermined the state's legitimacy as well as democratic governance. As Chapter 6 argues, further efforts to negotiate the social and economic dimensions of the conflict are needed.

In Mexico, the only country examined in this book in which there are guerrillas but little actual troop engagement, part of the significance of the Zapatista uprising lay in its critique of Mexico's authoritarian political system and economic and social inequality. (See Chapter 5.) The government has responded with preemptive reform, especially in the electoral arena, as a way of separating the guerrillas from allies in civil society and forestalling the need for a peace process with the Ejército Zapatista de Liberación

Nacional (EZLN). Such reforms have weakened the guerrillas politically (and strengthened the electoral opposition), even if they might not have been attempted in the absence of the Zapatista uprising. Meanwhile, the roots of the conflict—hunger for land, paramilitarism, and ethnic discrimination—have not been addressed.

In Nicaragua, as Chapter 2 has shown, negotiations over a cease-fire to end the war became entangled with an electoral transition following the Sandinistas' defeat at the polls, precluding a wider national dialogue to overcome sources of polarization. Procedural democracy manifested minimally in the rotation of leaders via regular elections has advanced since the end of the war, but few mechanisms exist to mediate conflict in civil society or resolve disputes without violence. The ongoing lack of political capacity on the part of ex-combatants remains an additional source of instability.

Only in Peru is the relationship between insurgency and democratic transition the reverse of what it has been elsewhere. Chapters 7 and 8 have emphasized how the Fujimori government set about to destroy democratic space as an explicit strategy of counterinsurgency, in contrast to other countries where a limited opening was pursued to provide a political alternative to the guerrillas. That the guerrillas themselves emerged when the political system was open and sectors of the left amply represented in government further distinguishes the Peruvian case from others in Latin America. Elements of the authoritarian state created by the Fujimori government have not been dismantled since the "strategic defeat" of the guerrillas, and the solution achieved through military/police action and repression has not been coupled with political or socioeconomic measures that would transform a momentary advantage into more permanent democratic consolidation.

In discussing the relationship between peace processes and democracy, it is important to underscore what may seem a self-evident point: that by aiding in a country's democratic transition, peace processes do not presuppose the *consolidation* of that system, and the question of "transition toward what?" becomes more relevant than ever. Timelines and calendars negotiated as part of a peace accord provide a detailed schedule as well as mechanisms for implementing agreed-on changes, but the process of change and institution building extends beyond a period of formal compliance with a peace agreement and may never be complete.[2]

Although the significance of attaining or strengthening procedural democracy should not be underestimated, effective governance and the rule of law remain a distant dream in all of the postwar societies examined in this study.[3] As Chapters 3, 4, the Reflections to Chapters 12 and 13, and Chapter 14 have argued, widespread impunity reflects the ongoing incapacity of judicial systems, whose ineffectiveness in serving as a means of peaceful conflict resolution led to the outbreak of war. Meanwhile, the explosion of criminal violence in postwar societies reflects multiple failures: to absorb adequately and retrain ex-combatants, to provide productive employment to ever greater numbers of young people, to combat gender discrimination, and to create independent, professional police forces with the resources, personnel, and capacity to investigate and resolve cases without recourse to extraconstitutional means. The expansion of criminal activity coupled with deficiencies in the police and justice systems invite vigilantism and the privatization of justice, further weakening the state and its legitimacy.

Indeed, it is an open question whether the process of institutional transformation set in motion by peace processes—something that might take decades or even generations to consolidate—can keep pace with a countervailing process of social disintegration and the propensity of organized crime to take advantage of institutional weaknesses. The rise in social and criminal violence and the number of actors involved in it has detracted from public faith in peace processes. An overall disenchantment with politics itself, reflected in low voter turnouts in El Salvador and Guatemala, a lack of faith in the capacity of traditional politicians in Nicaragua and Colombia, and, it seems, a widening gulf between the system of political parties and the social realities of several countries, complicates the horizon.[4] As Guatemala has yet to hold general elections subsequent to the signing of the peace accord, it remains to be seen whether the broadening of political space will have offset widespread disaffection with the political process in general.

That citizens' enjoyment and exercise of rights is not synonymous with the formal expansion of rights indicates that peace processes are not panaceas for the ills of a nation or even guarantors of constitutionally mandated liberties but rather factors in the political evolution of a country. By addressing underlying structural causes of conflict and reordering the "rules of the game" by which future conflicts are processed, they may not "solve" all of society's problems at the bargaining table but may rather create new, more democratic and participatory forms in which debates can unfold in the postwar order.

Managing expectations about what a peace process will yield is thus a key task. As Felipe González, former prime minister of Spain, is said to have warned, what may be gained at the bargaining table is not the resolution of all issues but rather an opening of the door, an opportunity to participate in the struggle over future outcomes.[5]

In practice, the desire for rapid transformation may run headlong into the legacy of a weak state with a limited capacity for administration and service delivery or for prevailing over more powerful and better-organized sectors, such as the armed forces or business community. Managing expectations thus requires leadership in a delicate balancing act, involving generating enthusiasm for the peace talks and the long-term process of transformation they launch, while at the same time minimizing the frustration that inevitably results when the direction of change is imperceptible or, at times, backward.

Why Negotiate?

The discussion of peace processes in this book has underscored the preeminent role of political choices made by leaders of both contending parties in the achievement of peace settlements. So-called objective conditions—the existence or not of a military stalemate, for example—may be less important than the *perceptions of interest* of key actors as to the costs of continuing the war and as to their future with or without a negotiated settlement. The "need" and incentive to negotiate thus does not derive simply from the insurgents' military strength and the level of pain it has inflicted on society but is also a product of political will, a *voluntad de paz*,[6] on the part of leaders of both sides, and the scope of their agendas that can or cannot be satisfied in the absence of peace. The centrality of perceptions over some hard-to-define "objective condition" leaves open the possibility that "ripe moments" can be created and orchestrated, and need not depend entirely on battlefield conditions.[7]

How, then, can perceptions be measured, to identify when they actually have changed and when talks are put forward simply to gain time or tactical advantage? Herein lies the importance of gestures and intermediate accords, not only as catalysts and confidence-building mechanisms but also as barometers of good faith. As Chapter 9 has demonstrated, in both El Salvador and Guatemala human rights accords that opened each country to international verification of human rights practices were concluded months and even years before a comprehensive peace was signed. In both cases abuses diminished. This concrete change, as well as the presence of international observers, lent credibility to the peace process in a charged and polarized environment.[8]

Similarly, in Guatemala an informal cease-fire declared first by the Unidad Revolucionaria Nacional Guatemalteca (URNG) and then by the government nine months before the end of formal hostilities held without incident; later the URNG suspended its so-called war tax following the signing of an accord on socioeconomic issues. These intermediate steps contributed to the climate of trust that made an agreement possible.

However, if small steps and respect for intermediate accords demonstrate political will, the reverse is also true. As Chapter 10 has pointed out, the Mexican government's failure to take the necessary steps to implement a 1996 accord on indigenous issues, and even to demand the renegotiation of several points after the accord was signed, detracted from the credibility of its stated desire for peace.

If the number of issues placed on the bargaining table—or the very existence of that table—is not defined entirely by the correlation of military forces, it would be naive to assume that the level of battlefield stalemate plays no role in the outcome of negotiations. The very different outcomes in El Salvador and Guatemala with respect to the armed forces—the extent of military and police restructuring and purging and of the reach and prerogatives of truth commissions—are rooted in the insurgents' military strength, the level of the armed forces' disrepute nationally and internationally and their degree of dependence on or autonomy from outside powers, and the ability of civilians to capitalize on weaknesses and/or disunity to promote greater oversight and control.

The strength—moral and otherwise—of the armed forces going into a negotiation affects the degree to which they are able to protect their interests during the negotiation and behave as an "authoritarian enclave" in the postsettlement period. In countries in which civilian control of military establishments is weak to begin with, it may be that peace processes are unlikely to encroach on reserve domains in the absence of military as well as political challenges to the power of the armed forces. Furthermore, even when peace accords have on paper prescribed sweeping changes in military structures, the role of the international community, particularly the United Nations, in ensuring compliance cannot be overestimated.[9]

However, the Salvadoran and Guatemalan cases also reveal that peace processes provide an opportunity for the armed forces to downsize, modernize, and professionalize in accordance with their own reassessment of their role and mission in a democratic society.[10] The benefits of such restructuring—in exchange for not having to fight a war, shucking off unsuitable and highly politicized missions such as internal security, and regaining public confidence—should not be underestimated.

If theories of conflict resolution and theories of democratic transition coincide on the central role ascribed to elite contingent choice, it is also clear from this book that elites alone cannot generate sufficient momentum to conclude a peace process. A key determinant of "ripeness" for a negotiated settlement is the degree to which civil society, including social movements in general, has tired of the conflict and make its preferences known in a politically significant way. The indifference of civil society to peace can pose a serious obstacle to progress in peace talks, while active involvement, through reconciliation commissions, referenda, and other formal and informal mechanisms, can greatly enhance a propitious climate for negotiations.

Guatemala represents the most extensive and novel role for civil society before and during the peace talks, which in many ways compensated for the military weakness of the guerrillas and their lack of political representativity. As Chapter 4 has demonstrated, prior contacts between the guerrillas and sectors of civil society in Guatemala opened the way to formal talks between the insurgents and the government. As the Reflections to Chapter 9 have argued, public indifference to the peace talks and what they could produce in the way of real reform gradually ceded to the use of the negotiating table to articulate a variety of grievances and demands. Through the Assembly of Civil Society, whose stature was acknowledged in the 1994 framework accord, civil society provided substantive input into the talks. Although some mechanisms were established in the postconflict period to integrate the coalition behind the peace process into the process of oversight and verification of the accords, civil society's role has greatly diminished.[11]

As in Guatemala, calls to *desgobernizar* ("degovernmentize") the peace process in Colombia reflect not only a lack of faith in the capacity of both sides to come to an agreement by themselves but also the conviction that neither side fully represents the interests of broader society. Mexico, however, illustrates the limits of civil society's involvement. The mediating role of the party-based Comisión de Concordia y Pacificación (COCOPA) and church-based Comisión Nacional de Intermediación (CONAI) could not survive the crisis of confidence generated by escalating violence and lack of progress in implementing existing agreements. (See Chapters 5 and 10.)

Conceptualizing the role of civil society in a peace process thus has several aspects. First, the incorporation of civil society can create an expanded constituency for the peace process, at the same time that the process strengthens and legitimizes such organizations, whose role is critical to the subsequent functioning and consolidation of democracy. Second, formalizing that role in the postwar period, overcoming, in essence, the crisis of representation reflected in war, is an important task. Finally, civil society involvement is a necessary but insufficient condition for concluding an agreement. It can provide substantive input as to the content of the accords and strengthen the will of the parties to reach an agreement, but it cannot substitute for such will.

The Role of the International Community

Thus far this discussion of ingredients of successful peace processes has focused on factors internal to each country. El Salvador and Guatemala also stand out for the extensive role of the United Nations in mediating the negotiations and in establishing a substantial verification apparatus to oversee their implementation. Some have argued that the extent of international involvement, not only as mediators and verifiers but as assumers of quasi-governmental functions in the peace-building phase, distinguishes advancement from failure in peace processes.[12] International involvement can lend legitimacy and impartiality to a process and, depending on the skill of the individual mediator, forge agreement where compromise and consensus appear elusive.

The involvement of the international community is not, as some have mistakenly presumed, equivalent to the granting of belligerent status to the insurgents, that is, recognition of a status of de facto statehood in which insurgent hostilities are legalized.[13] Indeed, the whole notion of belligerent status in internal armed conflicts has passed largely into disuse in international jurisprudence, supplanted by Common Article III of and Protocol II additional to the Geneva Conventions of 1949. These provisions of international law obligate parties to an internal armed conflict to adhere to humanitarian norms of conduct designed essentially to protect victims of armed conflict, while taking no sides on the question of the legal status of dissidents.[14]

As a practical matter, sitting down to negotiate does confer a degree of political legitimacy on the guerrillas, just as agreeing to international mediation and allowing peacekeepers or human rights observers on one's soil represent a relinquishing of sovereignty to some degree. It is still true, however—and the record in Latin America has demonstrated—that the

benefits to a peace process of international participation appear to out-
weigh the costs. It is also true, as with civil society, that the involvement of
the international community cannot substitute for the will and commitment of the parties to reach and implement an accord.

Needs of the Postconflict Phase

The role of elites in designing and implementing an accord, of civil society
in establishing its credibility and representativity, and of the international
community in fostering and guaranteeing what is put on paper must keep
as a central reference point the satisfaction not only of former combatants
who must be reintegrated politically and economically but also of the majority of those affected by the war. As several contributors to this volume
have suggested, the needs of postwar reintegration of combatants, reconstruction of the economy and infrastructure, and social attention to the affected areas necessitate combining a capitalist imperative to create wealth
with a socialist imperative to distribute it. (See Chapters 2, 3, and the Reflections to Chapter 15.) Particular care must be taken to reconcile stabilization and adjustment policies with postwar goals for reinsertion and recovery,[15] and, as Chapter 15 points out, to consolidate peace by
addressing fundamental social and development issues.

In an age of globalization, however, the postwar dilemma of reconstruction may no longer pit proponents of structural adjustment and fiscal
discipline against advocates of increased government spending to ameliorate poverty. Rather, the question might better be formulated as: how to
liberalize markets *at the same time* that governments direct resources into
public goods such as education in order to create the human and social
capital that in the long run will increase incomes among the poorest sectors of the population.[16]

Efforts by the international donor community—both financial institutions and individual governments—to coordinate their efforts during, not
after, peace talks and to reconcile them with the social goals of an accord
represent a positive learning curve from El Salvador, where such coordination did not take place. Meanwhile, the need for progressive tax reform
and for private sectors to pay taxes in order to generate internal, not just
international, resources for such efforts remains critical.

Finally, if, as Alejandro Bendaña has argued in the Reflections to Chapter 2, the terms "postwar" and "postconflict" are not equivalent, efforts at
reconciliation within societies must accompany efforts at material recon-

struction and institutional reform. Decades of bitter armed conflict leave emotional and spiritual wounds more difficult to repair than damaged infrastructure. Who will account for horrible crimes committed during the war? Who will compensate victims, punish perpetrators, and reveal the truth about what took place?

As Chapter 12 has emphasized, transitions such as those from war to peace or from authoritarianism to democracy are foundational times, periods that provide societies a fresh opportunity to establish norms and behaviors that distinguish the new period from the old. The reconstruction of a moral order has implications beyond ethics, touching on the nature of institutions and political culture for years to come.

How then to grapple with the legacy of the past? Chapters 12 and 13 argue that the ability to prosecute and punish through trials varies widely from case to case, depending on such factors as the existence of a functioning judiciary, political leadership, and the ability of those accused of crimes to threaten the transition itself.

But the establishment of individual accountability through prosecutions is only part of the effort to repair the damage of massive brutality and prevent its recurrence. Truth commissions that "unsilence" the past, outlining broader patterns of abuse and institutional responsibility, are essential to establishing a shared version of history and separating the past from the present or future. They also can make recommendations for future reforms, propose reparations for individual victims or their survivors, and contribute to the evidentiary base for trials, as Chapter 13 points out. National reconciliation and personal reconciliation are complementary, not identical, tasks, but both are helped by acknowledging the truth in a situation where continued denial likely would lead to renewed conflict.

The Remaining Challenges

How might some of the experience of peace processes in Central America apply to other Latin American cases where guerrillas still fight to take power? The external dimension of the Central American crisis—the imposition of superpower competition on local conflicts and the importance of external actors—is simply not repeated in the Andes or in Mexico. Many have argued, in fact, that the degree of international penetration of Central America's wars accounts in important measure for the ability to end them when the logic of the Cold War dissipated. (See Chapters 1, 2, 3, 4, and 9.)[16]

While not contesting the relative autonomy and independence of the Colombian, Peruvian, and Mexican insurgencies vis-à-vis international factors, it still can be argued that internal, not external, factors were the central determinant of the outcome of peace processes in Central America and that the collapse of the Soviet Union and end of the Cold War did not signal the "end of ideology" among guerrilla movements but only the degree to which internal conflicts could be viewed as proxy wars.

As Cynthia McClintock has argued in Chapter 8 and elsewhere, however, post–Cold War insurgencies obey a different logic than their Cold War predecessors, in that they are less rooted in the exclusionary political practices of an authoritarian regime than in economic crises that interact with organizational, political, and international variables (especially the posture adopted by the United States).[17] This does not mean that peace processes that have solved crises of political inclusion will be irrelevant but rather that future strategies for peace must include as central the socioeconomic agenda that has proven so difficult to negotiate and implement elsewhere.

The belief sustained in this book that insurgencies arise when conflict can no longer be mediated in the political sphere suggests that there are indeed commonalities between Central America and the continent's remaining conflicts. Whether they are "ripe for resolution," however, is an entirely different question.

Mexico

In Mexico the administrations of Carlos Salinas de Gortari and Ernesto Zedillo sought to maintain a dialogue with the EZLN, to project an international image of stability and restore the confidence of foreign investors, and because there are no political conditions in Mexico to undertake an exclusively military strategy against the Zapatistas. But the parties were and are divided over what the negotiations are supposed to achieve. The government consistently has sought to limit the talks to issues specific to the region of Chiapas; it has been intent on denying the Zapatistas the authority to negotiate on behalf of a nation—that is, to cede at the bargaining table any advances not reflected on the battlefield.[18]

That the government negotiated at all with the EZLN, however, was testimony to its initial success in galvanizing a broad range of center-left forces opposing the regime, for whom an end to political corruption, democratization of governing structures and of the ruling Institutional Revolutionary Party (PRI), and social reform were long-standing demands.[19] Thus a peasant uprising that lasted two weeks served as a catalyst for reformers throughout Mexican society.[20] The very weakness of the guerrillas militarily—the fact that they represented a fresh, nontraditional, and noncorrupt political force—helped facilitate an initial, and unprecedented, urban-rural alliance between those with shared grievances engendered by repeated electoral fraud and the depth of Mexico's ongoing economic crisis. The tenuousness of this alliance, however, was reflected in the results of an August 1995 referendum sponsored by the Civic Alliance (Alianza Cívica), in which a majority endorsed the EZLN's reform agenda but called for the group's conversion into a political party.

The clash of agendas that divided the EZLN and the Mexican government showed little sign of diminishing in mid-1998. The government's failure to carry through on commitments acquired in the February 1996 accord on indigenous rights and culture—and the EZLN's insistence that those commitments be upheld—created an impasse deepened by the resignation of mediator Bishop Samuel Ruiz and the dissolution of the mediation commission, CONAI. With no viable formula for the talks, the crisis of confidence gathered steam.

While heightened repression and growing paramilitarism in Chiapas have enhanced costs for both sides (for the EZLN in terms of its social base and for the government in terms of lost prestige and condemnation following the Acteal massacre of December 1997), the costs did not appear to be sufficient to create incentives leading to renewed talks. This situation could be expected to change if burgeoning instability throughout southern Mexico—reflected in the existence of the Ejército Popular Revolucionario (Popular Revolutionary Army, or EPR) or uncontrolled factional violence in Chiapas—further undermines the government's image at home or abroad, or if peace talks with the EZLN appear to government officials as a way to enhance the government's legitimacy in the face of multiple crises besetting the country at the end of the twentieth century. Nonetheless, the root causes of the Chiapas peasant uprising—competition for land, army and police repression, ethnic discrimination, and political corruption—will not go away, and local elements of the crisis will continue to find resonance elsewhere in Mexican society. One hopeful scenario would repeat a pattern found in peace negotiations in El Salvador and Guatemala: that reformers within the governing party use the peace talks with the EZLN as a way of reestablishing legitimacy, pursuing long-overdue reforms, and marginalizing recalcitrant elites. The politics of alliance, not military strength, serve as a useful precedent.

Colombia

The drug-trafficking scandal that engulfed the administration of President Ernesto Samper precluded any serious advance in peace talks between the Colombian government and the guerrilla insurgency. Yet several developments augured well for the continuation of a peace process under the successor government of President Andrés Pastrana. First, increased military activity on the part of the guerrillas and important setbacks for the armed forces had the perverse effect of thrusting issues of war and peace to the center of the national agenda. The burgeoning involvement of civil society in demands for peace, and the unprecedented intersection of the war with economic performance, potentially created new incentives to end the conflict. Second, and in contrast to previous administrations, a peace coalition that first emerged within the Samper government accepted that dealing successfully with remaining guerrilla groups meant going beyond previous schemes of disarmament and reincorporation by "negotiating the conflict" and its root causes.[21] This perspective continues to inform the peace strategy of the Pastrana administration. Third, by the end of Samper's term, the possible role of the international community was debated not as anathema but as advantage in an eventual negotiation.[22]

Numerous factors complicate the search for a negotiated settlement in Colombia, however, and few of them resulted from the Samper government's crisis of legitimacy. The multiple and overlapping sources of violence in Colombia—guerrillas, agents of the state, paramilitary groups, drug traffickers, and criminals—make peace with one such agent difficult to achieve in isolation. Apart from the fact that political violence is a small proportion of overall violence in Colombia, negotiations to address simultaneously several of these various actors and the overlapping relationships among them is a complex task.

The relative autonomy of paramilitary groups—originally created and fomented by the government, backed by narcotraffickers, and ultimately strengthened by elements of the Samper government in the guise of rural defense cooperatives—poses another major challenge. The year 1998 witnessed heightened military activity by paramilitary groups, much of it involving massacres of the civilian population in rural areas where guerrillas were active. Proposals at the end of Samper's term for a parallel but lesser "table" of negotiations with the paramilitary groups might be a realistic, if unsavory, option,[23] but it is unclear whether the government, the guerrillas, and the paramilitary groups share a vision of the scope of such negotiations.

Another difficulty is that the political alliances that characterized guerrilla movements in Guatemala, El Salvador, and Mexico are absent in Colombia. While 1997 and 1998 witnessed an increasing clamor in civil society for an end to the war, the political isolation of the guerrillas, and the divisions among groups joined under the banner of the Coordinadora Guerrillera Simón Bolívar (CGSB), remained deep. Moreover, the experience of guerrillas demobilized in earlier peace talks has been sobering. Former guerrillas saw electoral fortunes rise and fall, or were murdered in a dirty war at times involving their former colleagues in arms. Formulas for political inclusion must go beyond old recipes for disarmament and incorporation into the current system.

Unlike in Mexico, where actual fighting is minimal, the costs of ongoing stalemate in Colombia are substantial, measured in the lives of combatants and noncombatants alike, violations of human rights and international humanitarian law, and destruction of infrastructure and the environment. Translating these costs into modifications in the political visions of the contending parties, however, is a necessary precondition of successful negotiations. It remains to be seen how greater calls for international involvement—in ameliorating the human costs of the tragedy, monitoring human rights, and providing informal "good offices" through a Group of Friends—might affect the parties' relative autonomy from external influences.

Finally, a peace process may be unable to address, let alone resolve, the full spectrum of social ills that give rise to violence in Colombia. Drug trafficking and common crime have a dynamic that intersects with the war but for the most part is separate from it. Loading such issues onto a peace process may pose an unfair burden and detract from the opportunity to address the armed conflict, the paramilitarism and dirty war associated with it, and the specific constellation of socioeconomic deficiencies that sustain the insurgency. If it is true that the war does not explain all violence in Colombia, taking away the pretexts for violence created by war is a necessary step in the consolidation of Colombian democracy.

Peru

In Peru the fifteen-year war waged by Sendero Luminoso and, to a lesser extent, the Túpac Amaru Revolutionary Movement is over. But it would be overblown to mistake superficial calm for a stable peace. The profound ethnic, class, and geographical divisions in which the insurgency flourished remain. And the "strategic defeat" of the guerrillas via the death or capture of most of their leaders may prove illusory in the absence of attention to the root causes of conflict, primarily economic in origin. (See Chapter 7.)[24]

There has been no peace process in Peru, and the absence of calls for one from any organized sector of Peruvian society, including the left, is testimony to the guerrillas' isolation and fanaticism. Nonetheless, the war to defeat Sendero occasioned the most severe restrictions on democratic practices of any of the six countries under study, exemplified most dramatically by the *autogolpe* of President Alberto Fujimori in 1992 in which he dissolved the legislature and the judiciary. (See Chapter 8.) That this was done with the support of broad sectors of the population is further testimony to the horror with which Peruvians reacted to the prospect of a victory by Sendero Luminoso.[25]

The question, then, is twofold: (1) Can democratic forms be reconstructed out of the ashes of guerrilla defeat? Can, in Basombrío's words, democracy be seen as the vaccine against future insurgency rather than as an impediment to fighting it? and (2) can social policy advance quickly enough to address the marginalization and core of economic grievances that gave the guerrilla movement its recruiting ground? Part of the answer, as in other conflict situations, lies with demands organized and articulated from civil society. Another part, however, lies almost wholly with the government, whose interest in self-preservation may conflict directly with an interest in pluralistic democratic forms.

If the preceding assessments of chances for durable peace in Mexico, Colombia, and Peru are sobering, it is also true that there are no exclusively military solutions to the remaining armed insurgencies on the continent. Coming to grips with that central truth may and probably will exact a terrible toll in human lives and well-being. But the promise of peace processes is that they represent an alternative path to social and political change, one with trade-offs and pitfalls, to be sure, but one whose value is increasingly recognized by protagonists on all sides of the remaining military, political, and ideological divides.

Notes

1. There is no assumption that political space existed prior to the outbreak of revolutionary violence. Theorists of social movements would argue that in cases such as Nicaragua, Guatemala, and El Salvador, armed struggle had as a root cause an exclusionary political regime that offered few alternatives to peaceful change.

2. Juan J. Linz and Alfred Stepan, *Problems of Democratic Transition and Consolidation: Southern Europe, South America, and Post-Communist Europe* (Baltimore, Md.: The Johns Hopkins University Press, 1996), 5–6.

Guillermo O'Donnell, discussing the transition from authoritarianism to democracy, has argued that a "second transition" from a "democratically elected *government* to an institutionalized, consolidated democratic *regime*" may never occur. Guillermo O'Donnell, "Delegative Democracy," *Journal of Democracy* 5, No. 1 (Jan. 1994): 56.

3. Jorge I. Domínguez and Abraham F. Lowenthal, *Constructing Democratic Governance: Mexico, Central America, and the Caribbean in the 1990s* (Baltimore, Md: The Johns Hopkins University Press, 1996), 6–7.

4. On the Salvadoran case, see Rubén Zamora, "Los Partidos Políticos: Transformaciones en el Proceso de Transición " in Facultad Latinoamericana de Ciencias Sociales, El Salvador and Woodrow Wilson Center, *De los Acuerdos de Chapultepec a la Construcción de la Democracia*, No. 5 (San Salvador: FLACSO-El Salvador, 1998), 8–14.

5. According to FMLN negotiator Ana Guadalupe Martínez, González was contrasting the FMLN's more guarded expectations of the peace process with the expansive ones of the URNG. Interview with the author, San Salvador, February 23, 1995.

6. General (ret.) Mauricio Vargas, interview with the author, San Salvador, February 1995.

7. Fen Osler Hampson has argued that "ripeness is a cultivated, not inherited, condition" and that "outside third parties must help former combatants in the conflict in their own efforts to nurture and sustain the ripe moment." See Fen Osler Hampson, *Nurturing Peace: Why Peace Settlements Succeed or Fail* (Washington, D.C.: United States Institute of Peace, 1996), 210.

8. While it is possible in retrospect to see human rights accords in El Salvador and Guatemala as stepping-stones on the path to a wider agreement, they must be viewed as contributing to, but in no way guaranteeing, a final agreement, which depends ultimately on many other factors.

9. See Teresa Whitfield's Chapter 9 for an indication of the number of occasions in which senior U.N. diplomats or the secretary-general himself intervened in El Salvador to overcome a crisis caused by noncompliance.

10. See General Nelson Iván Saldaña, "Las Fuerzas Armadas: Su Papel en la Transición a la Democracia" (paper presented at the conference "De los Acuerdos de Chapultepec a la Construcción de la Democracia," sponsored by Facultad Latinoamericano de Ciencias Sociales-El Salvador and Woodrow Wilson Center, San Salvador, August 26), 1997, 1–18.

11. This can be explained in part by the absence of a unifying goal—to reach an accord—in the postnegotiation phase, when tasks and their complexity proliferate.

The departure of leadership, lack of human resources, and historical denial of opportunities to participate also undoubtedly play a role. Presentation by David Holiday, Creative Associates, (seminar entitled "Civil Society and Guatemala" sponsored by the Washington Office on Latin America, Washington, D.C., April 8, 1998); and presentation by Denise Cook, United Nations desk officer for Guatemala, "The Role of Civil Society in the Guatemalan Peace Process" (Woodrow Wilson Center, Washington, D.C., May 13, 1998).

12. Hampson, *Nurturing Peace*, 221–33.

13. This fear has been voiced frequently in Colombia, particularly by the armed forces.

14. Protocol II explicitly states that "Nothing in this Protocol shall be invoked for the purpose of affecting the sovereignty of a State or the responsibility of the government, by all legitimate means, to maintain or reestablish law and order in the State or to defend the national unity and territorial integrity of the State."

See Protocol Additional to the Geneva Conventions of 12 August 1949, and Relating to the Protection of Victims of Non-International Armed Conflicts (Protocol II), Article 3 (1).

The author is grateful to Robert Goldman, Inter-American Commission on Human Rights, and Jemera Rone, Human Rights Watch, for their assistance in clarifying this matter.

15. Patricia Weiss Fagen, former United Nations High Commissioner for Refugees director for El Salvador, has identified major tasks for postwar reconstruction, including reintegrating displaced populations, building communities by providing emergency aid as well as aid for long-term development, and assisting vulnerable populations such as women and children. Quoted in Hampson, *Nurturing Peace*, 10, *n.* 15.

16. See, also Jorge I. Domínguez, "Democratic Transitions in Central America and Panama," in Domínguez and Marc Lindenberg, eds., *Democratic Transitions in Central America* (Gainesville: University Press of Florida, 1997), 4–10.

17. See Cynthia McClintock, *Revolutionary Movements in Latin America: El Salvador's FMLN and Peru's Sendero Luminoso* (Washington, D.C.: United States Institute of Peace Press, 1998), 11–19 and 299–312.

18. See Luis Hernández, "Los Péndulos del Poder: Negociación y Conflicto en Chiapas," in Asociación de Investigaciones Económicos y Sociales (ASIES) and Woodrow Wilson Center, *Memoria de la Conferencia Procesos de Paz Comparados* (Guatemala City: ASIES, 1996) pp. 113–51.

19. Presentation by Sergio Aguayo, Mexican Academy for Human Rights (seminar organized by the Washington Office on Latin America, January 24, 1995).

20. See Jonathan Fox, "The Challenge of Democracy: Rebellion as Catalyst," *Akwe:kon* (special edition on Chiapas) (Summer 1994): 13–19.

21. This concept has been developed extensively by former peace advisor Jesús Antonio Bejarano. See ASIES and Woodrow Wilson Center, *Memoria de la Conferencia*, 91–100; and Jesús Antonio Bejarano, *Una Agenda para la Paz* (Bogotá: Tercer Mundo, 1995), 151–256.

22. Presentations by Daniel García-Peña before National Defense University/Woodrow Wilson Center panel entitled "Peace and Human Rights in Comparative Perspective" (National Defense University Conference on Security Issues in Colombia, Washington, D.C., May 18, 1998); and at a Woodrow Wilson Center roundtable discussion, May 20, 1998.

23. José Noé Ríos Muñoz and Daniel García-Peña Jaramillo, "Building Tomorrow's Peace: A Strategy for Reconciliation" (Report by the Peace Exploration Commission to the President of the Republic, Bogotá, September 9, 1997), 19–23.

24. See also Instituto de Defensa Legal and Woodrow Wilson Center, *De la Guerra a la Paz* (Lima: Instituto de Defensa Legal, 1996).

25. See Carlos Iván Degregori, "The Origins and Logic of Shining Path: Return to the Past," and Gustavo Gorriti, "Shining Path's Stalin and Trotsky," in David Scott Palmer, ed., *Shining Path of Peru* (New York: St. Martin's Press, 1992), 33–44 and 149–70, respectively.

Contributors

Jean Arnault is the special representative of the Secretary-General and director of the United Nations Verification Mission in Guatemala (MINUGUA). He was appointed U.N. observer to the peace negotiations in June 1992 and become moderator when the negotiations resumed under U.N. auspices in January 1994. He has held numerous other posts within the United Nations, including official responsible for registration and electoral operations in northern Namibia; officer-in-charge of the Kabul headquarters of the Secretary-General's office in Afghanistan and Pakistan; political advisor to the special representative of the Secretary-General for the Western Sahara; and desk officer for Central America in the Department of Political Affairs. He holds a degree from the Sorbonne in linguistics and philosophy.

Cynthia J. Arnson is assistant director of the Woodrow Wilson Center's Latin American Program, where she directs the project on Comparative Peace Processes in Latin America. Previously, she was associate director of Human Rights Watch/Americas. She has taught at the American University's School of International Service and served as a senior foreign policy aide in the House of Representatives during the Carter and Reagan administrations. She is author of *Crossroads: Congress, the President, and Central America, 1976–1993* (Penn State Press, 1993) as well as numerous other articles on Central America, human rights, and U.S. policy in Latin America. She has a Ph.D. from the Johns Hopkins University School of Advanced International Studies.

Dinorah Azpuru is on leave as director of the Political Research Department of the Asociación de Investigación y Estudios Sociales (ASIES) in Guatemala, to pursue doctoral studies at the University of Pittsburgh. She has previously been professor, vice-dean of the College of Political and Social Sciences, and director of the Department of Political Science at the Rafael Landívar University in Guatemala. Her publications include *El Sistema Político Guatemalteco* (1991) and *Estudio de la Realidad Política de Guatemala* (1994). She received graduate training at the University Institute of Development Studies in Geneva and at Uppsala University, Sweden. In February 1997, following the signing of the peace accord in

465

Guatemala, she was appointed executive secretary of the Electoral Reform Commission.

Julio Balconi was minister of defense of Guatemala from January 1996 until July 1997. Previously, he served as deputy chief of staff and also as general inspector of the armed forces. During his tenure in these latter two posts, he served as the armed forces' representative to the government Peace Commission (COPAZ) and participated in the peace negotiations with the URNG. At other times in his military career, he has served as director of the Center of Military Studies, director of the Military Academy "Escuela Politécnica," and commander of several military bases in Guatemala City and in the countryside. He received his military training in Guatemala and the United States, and holds a master's degree in administration of resources and technology from the Francisco Marroquín University.

Carlos Basombrío is deputy director of the Instituto de Defensa Legal in Lima, Peru, a former fellow of the Woodrow Wilson International Center for Scholars, and co-founder of the project on Comparative Peace Processes in Latin America. A sociologist by training, he has written widely on Latin American politics and on human rights, democracy, and citizenship issues. He is an editor of the Peruvian magazine, *Ideele*. His books include *Educación y ciudadanía: La educación en derechos humanos en América Latina* (Consejo de Educación de Adultos de América Latina, 1992), and *La Paz, Valor y Precio: Una Visión Comparativa para América Latina* (Instituto de Defensa Legal, 1996). He recently edited *"?Y ahora qué? Nuevos desafíos para los derechos humanos en América Latina"* (Diakonía, 1996).

Jesús Antonio Bejarano is professor at the Universidad Externado de Colombia and also teaches at the Universidad Nacional de Colombia. He was advisor to the Consejería Presidencial para la Reconciliación from 1986 to 1990. As presidential advisor for peace from 1991–1992, he served as the Colombian government's principal negotiator with the FARC and ELN guerrillas. He served as Colombia's ambassador to El Salvador 1992–1993, and to Guatemala 1993–1994. He is the author of *Una Agenda Para la Paz: Aproximaciones desde la teoría de la resolución de conflictos* (Tercer Mundo, 1995), a comparative study of peace processes in Colombia, El Salvador, and Guatemala, as well as other books on economics and economic history.

Alejandro Bendaña is director of the Centro de Estudios Internacionales in Nicaragua, a center devoted to popular education programs in peace building and social reconstruction. He has served previously as secretary general of the Nicaraguan Foreign Ministry and as Nicaragua's ambassador to the United Nations. He holds a Ph.D. in history from Harvard University and has been a visiting professor at the University of Chicago. He is currently a consultant for the UNESCO Culture of Peace Program. His most recent book is *Power Lines* (Olive Branch Press/Inter Link, 1996).

James K. Boyce is professor of economics at the University of Massachusetts, Amherst. He is the editor of *Economic Policy for Building Peace: The Lessons of El Salvador* (Lynne Rienner, 1996). He is also the author of *The Philippines: The Political Economy of Growth and Impoverishment in the Marcos Era* (Macmillan, 1993), and *Agrarian Impasse in Bengal: Institutional Constraints to Technological Change* (Oxford University Press, 1987), among other publications. He is currently engaged in a study of the role of international financial institutions in post-conflict transitions.

Antonio Cañas heads the media and publications unit of the United Nations Verification Mission in Guatemala (MINUGUA), and from 1995–1998 served as a consultant to the United Nations Mission in El Salvador (MINUSAL). Between 1986 and 1992, he directed the Centro de Información, Documentación, y Apoyo a la Investigación Sociopolítica at the Universidad Centroamericana José Simeón Cañas (UCA) in San Salvador. He has served on the editorial board of the journal *Estudios Centroamericanos,* and taught philosophy of science at the UCA. He received his degree in philosophy and anthropology from the UCA, and a degree in mechanical engineering in Brazil.

Marc Chernick teaches in the Department of Government and the Center for Latin American Studies at Georgetown University. Previously, he was the acting director of the Latin American Studies Program at the Johns Hopkins University School of Advanced International Studies, and assistant director of the Institute of Latin American and Iberian Studies at Columbia University. While on a Harry Frank Guggenheim Foundation fellowship from 1992–1994, he was a visiting professor at the National University of Colombia, as well as a visiting scholar at FLACSO-Ecuador and at the Institute of Peruvian Studies in Lima. He currently works as a consultant to the World Bank on issues of peace and rural development in Colombia. He holds a Ph.D. from Columbia University and is completing a book on the peace process in Colombia.

Michael Conroy is a program officer of the Ford Foundation in New York and from 1994–1998 was a program officer in its Mexico City office. Previously he served as associate chairman of the Department of Economics and director of the Latin American Economic Studies Program at the University of Texas at Austin, where he taught for over 20 years. He has published widely on privatization and deregulation in Latin America, as well as on issues of sustainable development in Central America. His work at the Ford Foundation office in Mexico focused on environmental issues and natural resource management in Mexico, peace and sustainable development in Central America, and local responses to processes of globalization.

Héctor Dada is the director of FLACSO-El Salvador, a position he has held since 1992. From 1985–1991, he served as an economic affairs officer in the Mexico City office of the Economic Commission for Latin America (CEPAL), and previously as a consultant for the Institute for Latin American Integration and at the research group CEESTEM. In 1979, he served as El Salvador's Foreign Minister and joined the Revolutionary Junta of Government in 1980. Prior to that, he chaired the Economics Department of the Universidad Centroamericana José Simeón Cañas (UCA), and served as a deputy in the Legislative Assembly. He is the author of *La Economía de El Salvador y la Integración Centroamericana, 1945–1960* (UCA Editores, 1978), among other publications.

Carlos Iván Degregori is a principal researcher and former director of the Instituto de Estudios Peruanos in Lima, Peru. An anthropologist by training, he has taught at a number of universities in Peru and abroad, including the Universidad Nacional Mayor de San Marcos, Columbia University, and the École des Hautes Études en Sciences Sociales in Paris. He is a former Guggenheim fellow and former senior fellow at the Inter-American Dialogue in Washington, D.C. He is the author of numerous publications about Peru, including *El Surgimiento de Sendero Luminoso* (Instituto de Estudios Peruanos, 1992), and co-editor of *Las Rondas Campesinas y la Derrota de Sendero Luminoso* (Instituto de Estudios Peruanos, 1996) and *The Peru Reader* (Duke University Press, 1995).

Priscilla B. Hayner is an independent writer finishing a book comparing truth commissions worldwide. She is also a program consultant to the Ford Foundation and was previously a program officer covering international human rights at the Joyce Mertz-Gilmore Foundation. Her articles on accountability for past human rights abuses have appeared in *Human Rights Quarterly, Third World Quarterly,* and Duke University's *Law and Contemporary Problems.*

Neil Harvey is assistant professor in the Department of Government at New Mexico State University. He is the author of several articles, book chapters, and research papers on peasant movements in Chiapas, including *The New Agrarian Movement in Mexico, 1979–1990* (Institute of Latin American Studies, 1990) and "Rebellion in Chiapas: Rural Reforms, Campesino Radicalism, and the Limits of Salinismo" (Center for U.S.-

Mexican Studies, University of California, San Diego, 1994). He is editor of *Mexico: Dilemmas of Transition* (Institute of Latin American Studies and British Academic Press, 1993) and author of *The Chiapas Rebellion: The Struggle for Land and Democracy* (Duke University Press, 1998).

Luis Hernández Navarro is a social anthropologist and an advisor to the Coordinadora Nacional de Organizaciones Cafetaleras in Mexico. He is also a researcher with the Centro de Estudios para el Cambio en el Campo Mexicano and journalist with *La Jornada* newspaper in Mexico City. In November 1996 he was appointed secretary of the Follow-up and Verification Commission for Chiapas. He has written extensively for Mexican periodicals on the conflict in Chiapas, and is the author of numerous articles on conditions in rural Mexico. He is author most recently of *Chiapas: La Guerra y La Paz* (ADN Editores, 1995).

Gerhard Henze is ambassador and deputy permanent representative of Germany to the United Nations, a position he has held since July 1993. He has held a number of senior government positions, including director general for Latin American Affairs in the German Foreign Office, director of Foreign Trade, Export Financing, Arms Export, and International Debt in the Foreign Office, and minister counselor of the German Embassy in Washington, D.C. In the late 1970s he served as spokesperson of the western industrialized countries in the United Nations Conference on Trade and Development, and was a member of the German delegation to the Conference on Security and Cooperation in Europe, where he was in charge of negotiations on the Helsinki Final Acts' provisions on freedom of movement and information.

Rachel M. McCleary is a Washington, D.C.–based consultant on political and economic issues in Central America and an adjunct professor at the Johns Hopkins University School of Advanced International Studies. She has taught at Georgetown University, Princeton University, and the Rafael Landívar University in Guatemala City. In 1994 she was a Fulbright research fellow in Guatemala, where she conducted research on contemporary politics. Her articles on Guatemala, international environmental issues, and political theory have been published in numerous journals. She is editor of the book *Seeking Justice: Ethics and International Affairs* (Westview Press, 1992) and author of the forthcoming *Dictating Democracy: Elites, the State, and the Guatemalan Transitions 1982–1993*. She holds a Ph.D. from the University of Chicago.

Cynthia McClintock is professor of political science and international affairs at George Washington University. During 1994–1995, she was president of the Latin American Studies Association, an international scholarly association. She is the author of several books on Peru, including *Peasant Cooperatives and Political Change in Peru* (Princeton, 1981) and the co-editor of *The Peruvian Experiment Reconsidered* (Princeton, 1983; Spanish version, Instituto de Estudios Peruanos, 1985). She is most recently the author of *Revolutionary Movements in Latin America: El Salvador's FMLN and Peru's Sendero Luminoso* (United States Institute of Peace, 1998). She holds a Ph.D. in political science from the Massachusetts Institute of Technology.

Roger Plant is an independent writer and consultant specializing in land and resource rights issues. He has served as a technical advisor for the International Labor Organization's Convention on Indigenous and Tribal Peoples. Beginning in March 1995, he was indigenous issues advisor for the United Nations Verification Mission in Guatemala (MINUGUA), and in July 1997 became head of its socioeconomic area. In 1997 he also served as consultant coordinator for the Inter-American Development Bank's project on indigenous peoples and poverty. He holds undergraduate and graduate degrees from Oxford University, and has published several books on human rights and development issues. He is currently finishing a book on *Land Rights and Human Rights.*

Álvaro de Soto is the United Nations assistant secretary-general for political affairs, with responsibility for the Americas, Europe, East Asia, and the Pacific. Prior to assuming that post in 1995, he was senior political advisor to United Nations Secretary-General Boutros Boutros-Ghali from 1992 to 1994. He joined the United Nations in 1982 as special assistant to Secretary-General Javier Pérez de Cuéllar. As the Secretary-General's representative, he conducted the two-year negotiations between the government of El Salvador and the FMLN that culminated in the 1992 peace accord. He is on special leave from the Peruvian diplomatic service, where he holds the rank of career ambassador.

Rose J. Spalding is professor of political science at DePaul University. Her work includes two books on Nicaragua, *Capitalists and Revolution in Nicaragua: Opposition and Accommodation, 1979–1993* (University of North Carolina Press, 1994) and an edited collection, *The Political Economy of Revolutionary Nicaragua* (Allen & Unwin, 1987). She chaired the Latin American Studies Association Task Force on Nicaragua/Central America in 1989–1991 and co-directed LASA's delegation to observe the Nicaraguan election in 1990.

Francisco Thoumi was a 1996–1997 fellow at the Woodrow Wilson International Center for Scholars. Prior to that, he was director and professor at the Center for International Studies of the Universidad de Los

Andes, Bogotá. His previous positions include regional coordinator of the UNDP Research Program on the Economic Impact of Illegal Drugs in Bolivia, Colombia, and Peru, and research associate at the U.N. Research Institute for Social Development in Geneva. He holds a Ph.D. in economics from the University of Minnesota and has taught at California State University and George Washington University. He has been a consultant to the World Bank and the Inter-American Development Bank. His most recent book is *Political Economy and Illegal Drugs in Colombia* (Lynne Rienner, 1995, and Tercer Mundo Editores, 1994).

George R. Vickers is executive director of the Washington Office on Latin America (WOLA). Previously, he was professor of sociology at Brooklyn College and the Graduate Center of the City University of New York, as well as director of the Institute for Central American Studies in New York. He is a member of the board of directors of Hemisphere Initiatives and served as co-leader of its election monitoring missions in Nicaragua and El Salvador. He received his Ph.D. from Washington University, and has written extensively about Central America and the dynamics of the peace process in the region.

Teresa Whitfield is special assistant to the United Nations assistant secretary-general for political affairs. Prior to joining the United Nations in 1995, she worked as a freelance writer and television producer based in London. She spent several years in Central America, principally in El Salvador, where, from 1990–1992, she conducted research for her book, *Paying the Price: Ignacio Ellacuría and the Murdered Jesuits of El Salvador* (Temple University Press, 1994). She received her undergraduate degree from Cambridge University and her M.A. in Latin American Studies from London University.

José Zalaquett is a lawyer and professor of human rights at the Law School of the University of Chile, where he also teaches ethics and government. Following the 1973 coup in Chile, he headed the human rights department of the Committee for Peace, later known as the Vicaría de la Solidaridad. He was imprisoned and expelled in 1976. During his exile, he served as the chair of the international executive committee of Amnesty International and is currently a member of the mandate committee of Amnesty International, the International Commission of Jurists, and the advisory board of Human Rights Watch/Americas. In April 1990 he was appointed by the President of Chile to serve on the National Commission for Truth and Reconciliation (the Rettig Commission). He has received several honorary doctorates, including from the University of Notre Dame and the City University of New York.

Index